THE VALUATION
OF REAL ESTATE

Third Edition

Alfred A. Ring, *Ph.D., M.A.I., S.R.P.A.*
Professor Emeritus
of Real Estate
and Urban Land Studies
University of Florida

James H. Boykin, *Ph.D., M.A.I., S.R.E.A.*
The Alfred L. Blake Chair Professor
of Real Estate
and
Director, Virginia Real Estate Research Center
Virginia Commonwealth University

Prentice-Hall, Englewood Cliffs, New Jersey 07632

Library of Congress Cataloging-in-Publication Data

RING, ALFRED A.
 The valuation of real estate.

 1. Real property—Valuation. I. Boykin,
James H. II. Title.
HD1387.R5 1986   333.33'2   86-3190
ISBN 0-13-939935-6

Editorial/production supervision
 and interior design: Dee Amir Josephson
Cover design: Ben Santora
Manufacturing buyer: Ed O'Dougherty

Prentice-Hall International (UK) Limited, *London*
Prentice-Hall of Australia Pty. Limited, *Sydney*
Prentice-Hall Canada Inc., *Toronto*
Prentice-Hall Hispanoamericana, S.A., *Mexico*
Prentice-Hall of India Private Limited, *New Delhi*
Prentice-Hall of Japan, Inc., *Tokyo*
Prentice-Hall of Southeast Asia Pte. Ltd., *Singapore*
Editora Prentice-Hall do Brasil, Ltda., *Rio de Janeiro*
Whitehall Books Limited, *Wellington, New Zealand*

This book is dedicated to the multitude of real estate valuation instructors and practitioners who have added to and refined the body of knowledge central to informed real estate value decisions.

CONTENTS

PREFACE

Since the first edition of *The Valuation of Real Estate* was published in 1963, great strides have been made in perfecting the art of property valuation and in elevating the status of appraising as a field of specialization. The role of the appraiser, too, as a professional practitioner in the broad area of real estate economics is increasing in importance. The bulk of national wealth, both public and private, is invested in realty consisting of land and its fixed improvements, and no significant transfer of ownership of real property is likely to take place without professional assistance from experts in the field of valuation.

The current edition of this book is a distillation of the authors' many years of experience in teaching, research, and appraising. This popular book has been updated substantially, reorganized and expanded to strengthen time-honored appraisal methodology by integrating contemporary valuation thinking and procedures. Each chapter contains review questions and selected readings so the student can test his comprehension and expand his understanding of chapter material by reading other works. Completed form and narrative appraisals allow the reader to see how professional appraisal reports are prepared. An actual professionally prepared income property appraisal report is included (Appendix II). This illustrative report is enhanced with annotations and references to related sections of the book, and many questions are raised that should provoke valuable insights and classroom discussion. Other attractions of this book are its logical grouping of chapters, use of step-by-step problem solutions, standardized symbols used by the leading appraisal societies, and the explanation of valuation problems by use of financial tables and calculators.

The ever-increasing importance of ownership of real property as an estate-building asset, as a hedge against inflation, as a tax shelter device, and as a permanent and secure investment has caused ownership of realty to become popular and widespread. This is evident from the increasing number of realty transactions that are presented annually for public recording. To assure "arms-length" bargaining in these transactions at prices reflecting market supply and demand, an expert opinion concerning value is deemed essential.

This book is written essentially as a teaching guide for candidates who seek membership in the principal appraising societies. It has been revised specifically to serve as a text for classroom use and study in schools of business and commerce and in case study and extension course work sponsored by professional appraisal societies. Every effort was made to keep this writing and the applied theory and practice of property valuation technically current yet "down to earth." There is, however, no easy road to learning. A book, no matter how masterly written, can by self-study alone contribute little to an expansion of human wisdom or to the perfection of human judgment. These human attributes can best be obtained through the broad school of field experience and professional involvement. A well written book, nevertheless, can stimulate experience, challenge the reader to reach for perfection, and encourage him through interesting arrangements of facts and explanatory statements to seek mastery of the art of a chosen profession.

It is important to remember that *value* is the heart of economics. More important still is the indisputable fact that only *people* can make value. A sound theory of value, thus, must keep the human factor in focus and be attuned to practices that are the outgrowth of socio-political forces that operate within a capitalistic economy where dollar democracy expresses itself in free and open market operations.

The book is an outgrowth of nearly six decades of teaching appraising principles and practices at the college level and for real estate appraisal and other related professional groups throughout the United States. Added to this background is the over-60-year consulting and appraising background of the authors. Although the topical presentation of subject matter is traditional and follows procedure recommended for use by leading appraisal societies, new concepts of valuation theory and practice are introduced to stimulate classroom study and discussions and to aid in the modification of field practices where tested results warrant their application.

The authors want to acknowledge the special contributions made to this writing by their many students at the professional, graduate and undergraduate level, whose questioning of valuation concepts and teaching methods have contributed greatly to this latest edition. Grateful acknowledgement is made for valuable assistance and continued encouragement and support over the years from a long time friend and colleague Herbert B. Dorau (deceased), Professor of Economics Emeritus and formerly Chairman of the Department of Real Estate at New York University. For valuable suggestions offered during the manuscript stages of earlier versions and for constructive editorial comments, our thanks are expressed to Richard U. Ratcliff (deceased), MAI, University of Wisconsin; W. D. Davis, MAI; William N. Kinnard, Jr., MAI, SREA, University of Connecticut; H. Grady Stebbins, Jr., MAI, SREA; and Ronald O. Boatright, Ph.D., a former doctoral candidate and instructor in real estate and urban land studies at the University of Florida. We also recognize the valuable assistance from colleagues on the faculty of the College of Business Administration at the University of Florida.

Several people provided us with valuable suggestions in the writing of the present edition. These include: Terry V. Grissom, MAI, University of Texas-Austin; Joseph M. Davis, MAI, SRPA, Arizona State University; James D. Vernor, SRPA, Georgia State University; Wallace F. Smith, University of California-Berkeley; Kenneth M. Lusht, SRPA, Pennsylvania State University; Anthony B. Sanders, Ohio State University; and Scruggs Love, Jr., MAI, SREA, San Antonio, Texas. Andrew S. McBride and R. Jackson Smith, III, graduate students at Virginia Commonwealth University, reviewed the manuscript. Two ladies who were invaluable in the typing of the manuscript were Brenda W. Sullivan, the Real Estate and Urban Land Development Program secretary at Virginia Commonwealth University, and Debra C. Isley.

Not only are the authors grateful for the many ideas offered by contributors to the earlier and the current edition, but welcome your suggestions for improving this book.

Alfred A. Ring
James H. Boykin

SECTION I   *Fundamentals of Value*

1

NATURE AND IMPORTANCE OF VALUE

Learning Objectives

After reading this chapter, you should be able to:

Understand the difference in value of a property to an individual and the value of the same property to the general public

Appreciate how prices generally occur when the forces of supply and demand are in equilibrium

Explain why there is more than one type of value

Discuss the meaning of market value and the requisites for its existence

Comprehend the characteristics required for a good or service to have value

Real estate valuation may rightfully be designated as the heart of all real estate activity. In fact, valuation is the heart of all *economic* activity. Everything we do as individuals or as groups of individuals in business or as members of society is influenced by the concept of value. A sound working knowledge of the principles and procedures of valuation is essential in all sorts of decisions relating to real estate buying, selling, financing, developing, managing, owning, leasing, trading, and in the ever-more-important matters involving income tax considerations. Sound valuation is basic to zoning, ad valorem taxation, city planning, and to effective management of urban affairs in order to put land and its improvements to the highest, best, and hence most profitable use.

Although the importance of value as an economic measure is generally recognized, there exists a wide variance of understanding as to the character, nature, and meaning of value, especially among the general public who comprise

broad market for real property. This wide variance, and the lack of under-
nding of the available uniform means of measuring the magnitude of value,
may be explained by the failure of most persons to recognize fully the difference
between the value of a property to a particular individual and the value of that
same property to the public in general.

INDIVIDUAL VERSUS GENERAL MARKET VALUE

In the final analysis all value, no matter how defined, has its origin in individual
measures of worth. Everyone has a scale of preference for given goods or services. This preference, or *desire-pull relationship* between an individual and the
object or service wanted, is influenced continuously and in varying degrees by
personal traits and by cultural, religious, and governmental forces which influence each person as a member of society. This subjective value can readily be
demonstrated by a scatter diagram, wherein each circle represents the worth (or
sacrifice a person would willingly make for it) of a given quantity of a good or
service as measured in units of dollars. Each circle may stand for one or more
individuals, or it may represent a second or third measure of worth by one or
more individuals for additional units of the same good or service.

Thus someone may be willing to pay $60,000 for a home, offer no more
than $50,000 (as an investment in a like residence), and express no desire (de-
mand) for ownership of a third property. Another person may offer no more
than $55,000 for the same property and express no interest in another even as
a recommended investment on a reduced or discount basis. Each person thus
expresses his or her preference (or estimate of subjective worth) for one or more
units of a commodity or service by bidding along a scale as shown in Figure 1.1.
The fitted curve may then appropriately be labeled as a composite diagram that
projects the relationship of offering prices for given goods or services to quantities of such goods, or services offered for sale at a given time and place in an
open, free, and generally normal market.

Demand for goods or units of service arises from necessity or from
human desires which are backed by purchasing power, cash, or credit. As individual or group desires are modified or molded by environmental influences,
human behavior reacts accordingly and expresses itself in a changed pattern for
the kinds of goods or services sought after in the marketplace. To gain a better
understanding of the ever-changing socioeconomic forces which underlie the
concept of objective value, a study of the basic law of market supply and demand
is therefore deemed essential.

An offer to exchange a quantity of dollars for a quantity of goods or
services does not, by itself, create a market or an opportunity to barter. There
must be owners who supply these goods and services and who are ready, willing,
and able to meet the demand at the prices offered. Each unit of an economic
good or service must be *produced* or supplied at a certain sacrifice of the various

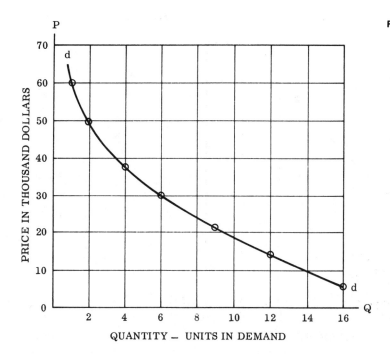

Figure 1.1

QUANTITY — UNITS IN DEMAND

factors of production involving land, labor, capital, and entrepreneurial effort. Some suppliers are more efficient than others; and as a result of volume of production, increased mechanization, or other factors which lower construction or manufacturing costs, they are able to market their products at lower prices.

In market areas where producers' earnings are relatively high, and where market demand is considered expandable, other suppliers of goods and services are competitively attracted. Ignoring for the moment customers' ability or willingness to pay even the warranted cost of an efficient producer, a scale of increasing individual producer costs can be plotted as a scatter diagram, as illustrated in Figure 1.2. The most efficient producers are able to supply the wanted product at the lowest possible cost; they are followed along the scale by producers of lower quantities and generally lower efficiency and higher per unit costs.

By superimposing the demand curve in Figure 1.1 on the cost of production curve in Figure 1.2, it is possible to measure the interaction of market supply and demand for given quantities of goods or services. As shown in Figure 1.3, where the supply and demand lines intersect at this point, the individual value forces of users and producers merge into a market-determined measure of value. The demand below the point of merger is classified as submarginal, or inadequate to meet the marginal costs of production. The supplier's costs above the point of merger are likewise submarginal—that is, above the highest bids offered at the time and place for the good or service in demand.

Figure 1.2

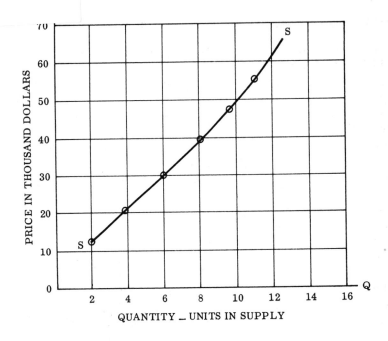

QUANTITY — UNITS IN SUPPLY

Figure 1.3

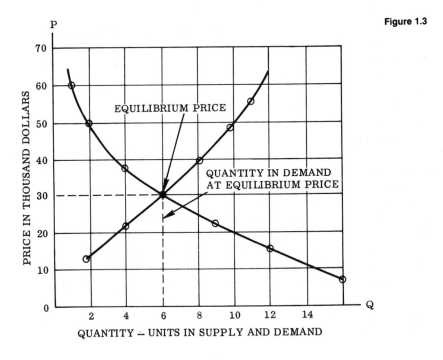

QUANTITY — UNITS IN SUPPLY AND DEMAND

MARKET CONDITIONS AND TERMS
OF SALE INFLUENCING VALUE

Where analysis of market data permits accurate presentation of the interacting economic forces which influence the shape of the supply and demand curves shown in Figure 1.3, the resulting findings offer conclusive evidence in support of the equilibrium price or market value as verified by actions in the open market. The market price thus obtained is in effect a synthesis or equilibrium of the interacting subjective values or forces which comprise a *market*. No informed person who buys with due care is warranted to pay more than the prevailing market price, and no equally informed seller will accept less. Attention is called to the fact that in all value discussions here it is assumed that the forces of supply and demand are in equilibrium and that no artificial or temporary barriers impede either supply or demand. Scarcity in supply as well as over- or under-consumption will temporarily influence the price of the product and cause payments of either premiums or discounts, depending on the nature of market conditions. Therefore, in solving a value problem it is essential to stipulate either whether or not market conditions are normal; or, if they are not, the dollar extent to which value adjustments must be made to reflect peculiarities of the market that favor either buyers or sellers.

To illustrate: After World War II the scarcity of residential properties due to a moratorium on construction was so great that market prices of homes available for sale reflected a premium for occupancy ranging from 15 to 20 percent above replacement cost. To reflect this abnormal market condition, a home that sold for $23,500 in 1947 might have represented a composite of market value as follows:

Replacement cost	$20,000
Premium paid due to excessive demand in relation to available supply	3,500
Market value—as of date of sale	$23,500

Another condition requisite in a determination of market value is that the exchange of dollars for quantities of goods or services is in *present* dollars on a cash or cash equivalent basis. Promises of future dollars create interest costs and hazards of collection which must be compensated for over and above the value imputed to a good or service on a *cash* or cash equivalent basis.[1] Just as favorable terms of sale increase the price at which realty is exchanged in the open market, conversely restrictive terms, such as high mortgage interest rates, can decrease the price below the amount a property would command if available

[1]"Cash equivalent" as used here and in subsequent chapters refes to typical financial terms: equity down payment plus mortgage loan amounts which are currently available to a typical purchaser.

for transfer on typical—that is, conventional—terms of sale. Further consideration will be given in Chapters 3 and 4 to the impact of *terms* of sale on *prices* of real estate.

WHAT MAKES VALUE?

The question most frequently posed is: What makes value? Is a property or a commodity valuable because it possesses *intrinsic* qualities such as are attributed, for instance, to gold or silver, or is value entirely *extrinsic* to the object and being created wholly in the minds of people who seek to possess that object? Theoretically, support can be given to a contention that, to be valuable, a product must possess certain qualities which attract the buyer and user and thus create a desire for ownership. Such qualities, if indeed assignable to an inanimate object, are then classified as intrinsic and thus inherent in the product per se. Those subscribing to a humanistic philosophy of value hold that value is a product of the mind, and that in the final analysis *people* create value—not wood, steel, brick, or mortar. Adherents to this school of thought hold that value is extrinsic in character, and that logically an object or service cannot possess intrinsic value. This contention they illustrate as follows. If gold or silver, for instance, should suddenly rain like manna from the heavens, its so-called intrinsic value would disappear; in fact its superabundance might create a nuisance that would give it a negative rather than a positive value under the circumstances. Changes in modes and fashions, too, it is pointed out, cause an object (through no fault or diminution of its intrinsic qualities) to be classed as obsolete or relatively useless.

Progress in the arts and sciences, development of new and rapid modes of transportation, and changes due to computerized technology all give weight to the concept that to a large degree it is people who make value and that value, therefore, must be considered as basically being extrinsic in character. Nevertheless, at a given place and moment of time, the object under value study must possess certain economic and legal characteristics in order to be wanted and thereby claim attributes of value.

VALUE CHARACTERISTICS

For a good or service to have value it must possess certain economic and legal characteristics, specifically the following: (1) utility, (2) scarcity, (3) demand, and (4) transferability.

Utility may be defined as the power of a good to render a service or fill a need. Utility must be present for a good or service to be of value. Utility, however, is only one of the characteristics that make up value. Thus where utility is present but demand or scarcity is absent, market value will not exist. For instance, water and air possess utility—yes, total utility, for both are essential to life itself. The value of neither air nor water, however, is measurable in terms of dollars for each is abundant and free to all. To have market value, therefore, a useful good or service must be scarce. The influence of utility on value, too, must be considered in relation to the size, shape, or form of the property, its geographic or spatial location, and its mobility and availability at given times. Variations in utility characteristics influence value; value differences, therefore, are caused by form, space, or time utility, as the case may be.

Scarcity is a relative term, and must be considered in relation to demand and supply and the alternate uses—present or prospective—to which the good or service may be put. Thus Christmas trees may be scarce the day before Christmas, and most abundant the week after. Value, too, will fluctuate accordingly. Gold and silver are relatively scarce, but their degree of scarcity, and hence value, can be affected by discovery of new sources of supply or the introduction of a new metal offering equal or even greater utility. Everything else remaining equal, value differences will result with changes in the relative scarcity among market goods and services. Generally, the greater the scarcity, the more spirited becomes the competitive bidding for goods or services and the higher, as a rule, the transaction price or market value.

Demand is an economic concept that implies not only the presence of a "need" but also the existence of monetary power to fill that need. Wishful-buyer thinking or necessity alone, no matter how strong, does not constitute demand; to bring about the latter, purchasing power must be available to satisfy the perceived need. Builders, developers, and investors in particular should keep the purchasing-power aspects of demand in mind. For example, large-scale housing developments are often planned and carried out to fill a long-felt "need," only to end in financial grief because of failure to consider accurately the effective buying power of the prospective tenants. Hotels, amusement enterprises, and large commercial projects have also experienced a high rate of financial mortality chiefly because of failure to distinguish between need and demand, and because of inability to measure accurately the effective purchasing power of their customers.

Transferability is a legal concept that must be considered in the determination of property value. Even though the characteristics of utility, scarcity, and demand are present, if the good or thing cannot be transferred in whole or in part, market value cannot exist. The moon, for instance, has utility; it is scarce (there is only one); and there might possibly be a demand for it if ownership and use of it could be controlled. The lack of transferability, however, keeps the moon a free good marketwise. Transferability does not necessarily mean physical mobility—it means rather the possession and control of all the rights which constitute ownership of property.

Assuming that other things remain relatively equal, a change in any one of the characteristics of a property—be it utility, scarcity, demand, or transferability—will inevitably be reflected in its value. Consequently, an increase in utility as evidenced by greater soil fertility will increase the net income productivity of farmland and thus enhance its value. An increase in relative scarcity resulting from an increase in population, all other things being equal, will also be reflected in higher values for marketable properties. An increase in demand caused by a rising standard of living will increase competitive bidding for more and better home sites, increasing the values of the properties so affected. Transferability, too, has an important influence on value. Generally, the greater the liquidity of a commodity, the greater its value because of the greater opportunity and flexibility present to exchange one property for another or its price equivalent. The appraiser must therefore consider with great care possible changes in value characteristics, especially where forecasts need to be made for the economic life of properties extending over 30, 40, or more years into the future. The same concern pertains to nonresidential property where the holding period may be for 10 years or less. The nature, type, and impact of forces which influence value characteristics of real properties will be more fully discussed in Chapters 4 through 8.

TYPES OF VALUE

Although logic would dictate that only *one* type of value could possibly measure the economic significance that individuals attach to a good or service in a given market, common usage has put in vogue many types of value, a few of which are listed below:

Appraised value	Liquidation value
Book value	Mortgate loan value
Capital value	Nuisance value
Cash value	Potential value
Depreciated value	Real value
Economic value	Rental value
Exchange value	Reproduction value
Extrinsic value	Sales value
Face value	Salvage value
Fair value	Sound value
Improved value	Speculative value
Insurance value	Stable value
Intrinsic value	Tax value
Investment value	Use value
Leasehold value	Warranted value

This listing by no means exhausts the many uses to which the term *value* is being put today. A complete enumeration would take many pages, especially if the variations of value related to political, social, and religious matters were added to those used to define the importance of business and economic operations. Is it any wonder that a learned U.S. Supreme Court Justice once said that "value is a word of many meanings"? Undoubtedly, the late Justice Brandeis had in mind the many uses of the term that prove puzzling to business managers even to this day.

The question may now be asked: Can there really be that many types of value? Is there one value for the buyer, another for the seller, a third for the lender, and so on? The answer is "yes" where the estimate of value is to serve a special or limited purpose. To illustrate, value for fire insurance purposes would differ in amount from value for mortgate loan purposes. In the former case, emphasis is placed on the replacement cost of improvements which are subject to fire hazards regardless of the marketabilty or income-producing capacity of the subject property. Where the value estimate is to serve as a basis for mortgage loan determination, principal reliance must be placed on the earnings capacity of the property and on its marketability in case of default in mortgage payment. This illustration points up the fact that a property can have different values for different persons where investment, commercial, or special-use purposes must be considered and given due weight in the value estimate.

To prevent misinterpretation and error in acting on the basis of a value estimate it is most important that the purpose of the valuation assignment be clearly stated in the letter of transmittal as well as in the body of the appraisal report, and that a definition of value be fully expressed as a guide to action by the reader or client to whom the report is submitted.

Where the estimate of value is to establish the most probable price that a property can command if exposed for sale in a relatively free, open, and competitive market, and at a given time, place, and under specified market conditions, there can be only *one* value. This kind of value, which most frequently is the object of economic search and analysis, is created by the multitude of buyers and sellers who cause a synthesis or interaction of the forces of supply and demand for specific goods or things which are traded in an open market.

THE MEANING OF MARKET VALUE

Although by the exclusion of subjective and special purpose property uses we have narrowed the economic realm in which the forces that forge market value operate, we still find divergence in professional judgment as how best to define the concept of market value. Therefore, to pinpoint the problem, it is necessary that a single clear-cut definition be formulated. The meaning of value can best be expressed in two closely related ways:

1. "The power of a good or thing (service) to command other goods or things in exchange."
2. "The present worth of *future* rights to income."

The first concept of value, generally known as the "barter" or purchasing power definition of value, is useful in measuring the worth or power of exchange of one commodity directly for another: in short, how much fish for how much game, or how much wheat for how much corn. Under this definition of value no money as a medium of exchange is necessary to measure the value-power of one good compared with another. If a standard dwelling of a given size and quality is worth the equivalent of five automobiles of a given kind and make in a given year, and ten years later the relationship of these commodities remains the same, then no change in value has taken place so far as autos and houses are concerned—no matter what happened to the value of money or to the level of prices. In a broader sense, we measure to a large extent the welfare of a group or a nation by the hours of labor (value) necessary to achieve a given standard of living or quantity of goods and services.

The second definition of value is more helpful and more readily applicable as a measure of value where *money* serves as a medium of exchange. Most goods and services are sold for specific purposes—generally to render buyer satisfaction (utility) for one or more years into the future. Thus a home is purchased for a sum of X thousand dollars to provide, throughout the economic life of the dwelling, rental savings as well as psychic income (amenities) derived from the pleasure and prestige of home ownership. Where the direct and/or indirect income from goods and services over future years through study of market behavior of buyers and sellers can be translated into money or money's worth, the present worth or value of such goods and services can be determined by *discounting* these future rights to income into a present sum or *present value*. This process of discounting, better known as *capitalization*, will be explained more fully and demonstrated in Chapters 16 through 18.

With the introduction of money as a medium of exchange the barter relationship of one commodity to another became more complex. In a dollar economy, prices essentially serve as a measure of the exchange power of goods for dollars and dollars for goods. This price relationship in a free market has caused acceptance of the meaning of value as being synonymous with the term *exchange* (or *market*) value. As used by real estate appraisers, and as sanctioned by court decisions, market value is currently defined under the "willing buyer, willing seller" concept as follows:

> Market value is the highest price estimated in terms of money which a property will bring if exposed for sale in the open market allowing a reasonable time to find a purchaser who buys with knowledge of all the uses to which the property is adapted and for which it is capable of being used.[2]
> Market value is the most probable price in terms of money which a property should bring in a competitive and open market under all conditions requisite to a fair sale, the buyer and a seller, each acting prudently, knowledgeably, and assuming that the price is not affected by undue stimulus.[3]

[2]V. Viliborghi, Prescott School, District 55, Arizona 230, 100 Pac. (2nd ed., 1940), p. 178.
[3]See Byrl N. Boyce, *Real Estate Appraisal Terminology* (Cambridge, Mass.: Ballinger Publishing Co., 1981), p. 160.

These definitions, like most others that concern value, were judicially enunciated and currently are widely used by practicing appraisers everywhere. Nevertheless, the concept that market value is the *highest* price that a property will bring suggests to the lay reader of a valuation report that there also must be a *lowest* or at least a lower price which a purchaser should initially offer. Under the equilibrium market value theory, the price that a property commands in the open market is in fact neither the highest nor the lowest—as measured by individual worth—but rather one balanced or equated by all the prevailing forces of market supply and consumer demand. Thus it may be said that market value is that price that a property ordinarily would bring under usual market conditions.

Market value, as usually defined, seems to suppose that ordinary buyers and sellers are bestowed with the patience, resources, and mental prowess to be fully cognizant of all conditions influencing the present and future uses of a property. These conditions seldom exist, however. Also, it is questionable whether an appraiser can actually ascertain whether a party to a sales transaction possesses such knowledge. Additionally, these definitions are unclear with regard to "reasonable time," "fair sale," and "undue stimulus."[4]

While market value continues to be the basis for most appraisals, the definition itself is cumbersome and smacks of artificiality. It is like describing "economic man" rather than those persons generally dealing in the real estate market. Stated differently, it depicts what ought to be in an ideal sense rather than actual conditions that face market participants. It is questionable whether these buyers and sellers are ever fully informed of all the present and future uses of a property. One key group of participants, real estate brokers and sales agents, when listing a property, are concerned about the price that it will probably bring within a reasonable period, which is usually the 60- to 90-day listing period. Therefore, it is suggested that greater emphasis be placed by appraisers on the price a property is likely to bring ("probable sales price") within a given time frame and the economic environment in which the sale is expected to occur than on such matters as expressed in an idealized market value definition. The give and takes of prospective buyers and sellers is depicted in Figure 1.4.

To reinforce the understanding that an estimate of value is a studied and considered approximation of the most probable amount for which a property can be exchanged under cash or cash-equivalent terms of sale, a more precise definition of market value for use in appraisal reporting is offered as follows:

> Market value is the price expressed in terms of money which a property is estimated to bring, at a given time and place where buyers and sellers act without compulsion and with knowledge of the uses to which the property is capable of

[4]For more on this topic, see, for example, "The Probable Price versus Market Value Controversy," in *Contemporary Real Estate: Theory and Practice*, Gaylon E. Greer and Michael D. Farrell, eds. (Hinsdale, Ill.: The Dryden Press, 1983), pp. 326–329.

Figure 1.4 Price Range Refined Through Negotiation to Reflect Market Value

being put. The estimated price is further contingent on the sellers' ability to convey title with all rights inherent in the property and allowing sufficient time for the transaction to mature normally under cash or cash-equivalent terms of sale.

As this definition suggests, the time of sale, the terms of sale, the relationship of the parties, knowledge concerning rights to be conveyed, present and possible potential uses to which the property may be put, time for the transaction to mature and close normally, and the immediate transferability of good and marketable title all influence the estimate of a warranted price. More detailed consideration to the impact of conditions and terms of sale will be given in succeeding chapters.

REVIEW QUESTIONS

1. Explain how a property can have one value for an individual but a different value for the public in general.
2. What does the term "equilibrium price" mean in the context of market-determined value?
3. Why is it necessary for the appraiser to understand fully and state clearly the specific value sought in an appraisal report?
4. List the key components of the market value concept.
5. Discuss how a knowledge of value characteristics is useful in appraising real property.
6. Critique the market value concept, setting forth both its strengths and weaknesses.

READING AND STUDY REFERENCES

COLWELL, PETER F. "A Statistically Oriented Definition of Market Value," *The Appraisal Journal* 47, no. 1 (January 1979), pp. 53–58.

ENTREKEN, HENRY C. "Are We Really Seeking Market Value?" *The Appraisal Journal* 48, no. 3 (July 1980), pp. 428–431.

PENNELL, CARROLL E., II. "The Role of the Professional Appraiser in the 1980's," *The Appraisal Journal* 49, no. 2 (April 1981), pp. 205–213.

RATCLIFF, RICHARD U. Chapters 3 and 4, "The Physical Foundations of Real Estate Value," and "The Locational Basis of Real Estate Value," *Real Estate Analysis*. New York: McGraw-Hill Book Company, 1961.

TREADWELL, DONALD H. "Value in Use in Perspective," *The Appraisal Journal* 46, no. 2 (April 1978), pp. 223–229.

VAN MANEN, FRANCIS J. "Real Estate Value As It Relates to Business Value," *The Appraisal Journal* 46, no. 4 (October 1978), pp. 592–597.

WENDT, PAUL F. Chapter 1, "What Is Value" *Real Estate Appraisal: Review and Outlook*. Athens: University of Georgia Press, 1974.

2

HISTORY AND IMPORTANCE OF VALUE THOUGHT

Learning Objectives
After reading this chapter, you should be able to:

Trace the key contributions to value theory made by early thinkers

Relate the early theories of value to contemporary appraisal practice

Appreciate the evolution of valuation theory and techniques advocated since the early part of this century

Better appreciate the relative merits of present valuation procedures in view of the support and criticism each has received over the years

Development and progress in any art or science depends heavily on the knowledge which accumulates throughout history. In a way, we must stand on the shoulders of those leaders in a given field who have gone before us in order that we may raise our sights beyond the horizon of present-day knowledge and perfect the application of established principles and practices.

The field of valuation has a rich history. Much of the value thought that has developed over the past centuries is of significance today, and an understanding of the history of this thought is essential for those who seek professional status as real estate appraisers. It is the purpose of this chapter to trace the landmarks of value thought and to demonstrate their impact on prevailing methods and theories in the field of property valuation.

The concept of value as a ratio measuring the significance of goods or services demanded in exchange for other goods or services dates back to the Middle Ages. Religious beliefs, moral customs and philosophical reasoning influenced the measures and standards by which men judged the fairness of servitude, trade or barter as practiced among people. St. Thomas Aquinas, in his greatest work, *Summa Theologica* (1266–1273), as translated from Latin, speaks of true value and just price. To sell a thing for more than its worth he regarded as immoral. Economic motives were thus subjected to ethical appraisal. To this day we find social, political, and other nonmarket measures influencing the thoughts of men, judges and jurors who are called on to rule what constitutes fair, true, real, sound, or just value, especially where the taking of property is compulsory as in "eminent domain" proceedings or in instances where there is absence of unimpeded trade and exchange.

MERCANTILISM

The first organized theory of value is ascribed to a group of thinkers and writers known as *mercantilists*. Under the theory of *mercantilism*—which held sway for nearly three centuries before the American Revolution in 1775—the power and well-being of a nation depended on ever-increasing stocks of gold and silver or bullion and the maintenance of a favorable balance of export-import trade. Manufacturing and employment of productive labor (for exportable goods) were encouraged in order to increase national wealth through international barter. The goal of mercantilists in guiding and shaping economic policy was to strengthen and increase the status of national and military power. Economic planning, generally, was directed to further national productive capacity. By edict or decree, export was encouraged and imports discouraged in order that a greater share of the world's stock of precious metals might be secured by the individual nation as a measure of national power and security.

During the sixteenth, seventeenth, and part of the eighteenth centuries (the mercantilistic period in the history of trade), a transition took place from religious, moral, and philosophical concepts of value to pseudo-economic concepts based on intrinsic and extrinsic values. The latter constituted objective value as molded by the forces of market supply and demand, whereas intrinsic value was a measure of the objects' inherent utility to render service or satisfaction in use. Development, too, of the natural sciences gave rise to a "natural" value based on competitive forces in place of "just" value that primarily rested on philosophical and moral supports. The mercantilists also emphasized production rather than distribution of wealth, and counted merchants among the best and most profitable members of the commonwealth.

Although mercantilism as an economic policy is long outdated, the theory underlying this nationalistic value and power concept is still very much relevant. The relative international power status of a nation continues to be basic not only to the welfare of its individuals but also to the value of the goods and services it trades in the open market. Appraisers as well as economists should pay careful heed to data which measure national well-being and prestige in terms of balance of international trade and value of domestic currency. These and other economic measures such as employment, fiscal policy, and inflation should be carefully observed in order to be alert to changes that influence property value.

THE PHYSIOCRATS

A revolt against mercantilism, with its emphasis on balance of trade, wealth, power, and frequent national wars took place in France. François Quesnay, a brilliant court physician to Louis XV, undertook at the monarch's request a study of the production and distribution of the national wealth. As a by-product of this study—and to support his findings—Quesnay conceived his famous *Tableau economique,* in which the production, distribution, and circulation comprising the economic activity in France was diagrammatically demonstrated. Quesnay is recognized as the founder of the physiocratic school, which is credited with laying the groundwork for the study of economics as a science as well as for the related field of political economy.

The physiocrats effectively demonstrated that production rather than trade constituted the life of a nation and that trade in fact was a "sterile," derived, and secondary economic activity depending wholly on that nation's vigor, strength, and volume of production. In the eighteenth century this production was principally agricultural in character and later writers, beginning with Adam Smith, labeled the physiocratic theory as the "Agricultural System."

It is interesting to note that the physiocrats did not regard value as intrinsic or inherent in things. Further the concepts of price and value were accepted as interchangeable terms, both reflecting a market ratio of exchange that could far exceed the cost of production. Generally, the physiocratic theory may be viewed as a revolt against trade and the role attributed to nonproductive (money) wealth.

Study of physiocratic economic doctrine is rewarding to a student of appraising, since it reveals historical support for the productivity theory of value and the application of the net income or earnings approach as a measure of value.

CLASSICAL ECONOMICS

No attempt will be made here to discuss the writings of all those individuals in many nations who contributed to the science of economics as it developed after the publication of Adam Smith's *Wealth of Nations* in 1776. Emphasis will be placed rather on the individuals and the important theories which brought about the evolution of the concept of value specifically.

Classical economics and the development of early value theory were chiefly founded on the lectures and writings of Adam Smith, Thomas Malthus, and David Ricardo. In fact, Adam Smith is often called the founder of economics as a science. Although this is not strictly true, he was nevertheless the first to bring together in one comprehensive volume a logical and well-written treatise on the operation of those economic forces which create value and control the well-being of a nation. Smith effectively reasoned that labor constituted the foundation of national wealth, and that the *value* of any good or service is equal to the quantity of labor which it allows its owner to purchase or command. Even though the importance of land and capital as factors of production were minimized by Smith, his *barter* definition of value ("the power of a good to command other goods or labor services in exchange") remains valid to this day.

Two other significant contributions to modern value theory were made by Adam Smith. First, he stressed the important distinction between "value in use" and "value in exchange." He logically demonstrated that it was only when the utility of a service or good was accompanied by conditions of scarcity and demand that exchange or market value could arise. His second important contribution to value thought was the noteworthy distinction between the concepts of "market value" and "market price." Market (or "natural") value undoubtedly referred to "normal" prices that covered long-term costs of wages, rent, and profit. Market prices—to the extent that such differed from natural prices—reflected short-run influences exerted by temporary forces of scarcity or monopoly. To Smith, value was basically a cost-of-production theory. Since technological changes were slow in developing during the eighteenth century, it was left to later thinkers to stress the importance of *replacement cost* rather than *reproduction cost* as a better and more reliable measure of value.

Smith's greatest contribution to economics as a science was his analytical study of the impact of the division of labor and his logical development of the price system in which exchange value was the center of economic life. In retrospect, Smith's economic philosophy—in which he viewed national progress as best secured by freedom of private initiative within the bounds of justice—is judged overindividualistic and unrealistically motivated by "unreal" economic men.

The optimistic outlook of Adam Smith—that the uncontrolled economic interests of the individual (the laissez-faire economy) will best tend to increase the wealth of nations—was given a pessimistic twist by his classical-theory successors. Malthus, for example, was to gain prominence with a startling theory— that the world's natural population growth would eventually outstrip the possible and effective growth of its food supply, The tendency for man to increase in number geometrically, as compared with the arithmetic increase in agricultural production capacity, forecast a dire economic state at low subsistence levels for society at large unless artificial measures could be taken to check the birthrate. Although technological developments in the century following Malthus' writing appear to have disproved his population theory, modern economists—in pointing to present-day population growth problems in China, India, and even in much of the western world—find Malthus' scholarly analysis of population-growth tendencies essential to a better understanding of current economic theory and practice.

In the development of value thought, Malthus was the first to work out a theory of underconsumption. He warned that production does not create its own demand (as held by Adam Smith and Ricardo) and that overproduction or underconsumption may in fact create market gluts. The economic experience during the deep business depressions of later years proved not only the validity of Malthus' early theory but also his deep understanding of economic phenomena. Malthus, too, made a noteworthy contribution to a better understanding of the role of *rent* as a price-determined (surplus) return to the landowner and not, as held by Adam Smith, a price-determining cost of production. This rent theory was enlarged upon and refined by his contemporary and friend David Ricardo.

The residual theory of land value as taught today has its documentary beginning in David Ricardo's work, *Principles of Political Economy and Taxation.* Although Malthus in prior writings stressed the importance of soil quality as a rent-producing source of income, it was Ricardo who developed the theory that long-term prices (value) equaled the cost of production at the marginal point where the last and poorest land was brought into cultivation. On this marginal soil (no-rent land) the price of the product exactly equaled the cost of labor and cost of capital. Thus the greater productivity possible where more fertile land was employed yielded a surplus, or land residual return—*rent*—which accrued to the landlord and not to the employing capitalist. With an ever-expanding population and the need to bring poorer and less desirable land into production increased costs of production would cause prices to rise, thus yielding an ever higher return to the better and relatively more fertile lands.

Rent as defined by Ricardo was the excess payment over the amount necessary to bring land into production and consisted of that portion of total income paid to the landlord for the original and indestructible powers of the soil. In analyzing this residual earning capacity of land, Ricardo developed the theory of the interacting margins of intensive and extensive development of land that is valid and important in land utilization studies to this day. Where (after "apparently" full capacity of land use) it was possible to make the land more productive by an expenditure of additional units of labor or capital, and by doing so produce an excess of income above that derived where like amounts of labor or capital were expended on adjacent land of like or inferior quality, then the more intensive or vertical use of land would produce a higher residual rent than could be realized by extensive or horizontal land utilization.

This theory of the interactions of margins in the intensive and extensive utilization of land is of vital importance presently whenever appraisers are charged with the responsibility to ascertain the highest and best use of land, as will be more fully developed in the following chapter. For a continuity of value thought, Ricardo's concept that land has no claim on income and the residual economic rent has no influence on price, which is established on "no-rent land," should be kept firmly in mind.

The rather cold and dismal picture of an "economic man" struggling for bare subsistence was disputed by later writers and critics of the classical school of economics. Two writers who took exception to the pessimism of Malthus and Ricardo were the French economist Frédéric Bastiat (1801–1850) and the American writer Henry Carey. Both were optimists who saw a great future, with mankind enjoying the wonders of bountiful nature. To Bastiat, value was measured not by the labor expended but rather by the labor *saved* through effective use of investment capital. The harmony he saw in the economic system was later attacked by socialistic writers such as Karl Marx as a theory of exploitation of the labor class and a means to perpetuate the class struggle.

Carey's optimism sprang from the seemingly limitless economic opportunities which were open to all in the new and virgin territory of America. He is best known for taking exception to Ricardo's theory of rent, which was based on the extensive utilization of successively poorer (marginal) land. Carey, on the contrary, held that the poorest land was generally cultivated first and that better and more fertile land was reached as population growth made clearing of forest lands and draining of river-bottom land a necessity. Carey's theory, overinfluenced by the special and short-run conditions peculiar to virgin territory, had no lasting impact or influence on the development of value thought.

An attempt to restate the classical school of economic thought and to humanize the theory of political economy was made by a brilliant and clear-thinking writer, John Stuart Mill. Mill's greatest service was to clarify the classical economic doctrine and to inject his social philosophy in order to help formulate a concept of welfare economics. As far as the theory of value is concerned, Mill agreed with Adam Smith to the "truck and barter" concept of the power of a good to command other goods in exchange.

In his book *Principles of Political Economy,* published in 1848, Mill differentiates between *normal* value and market price. The former concept of value, he reasoned, is set and determined at the lowest point of profitable production cost; whereas market price may be higher because of temporary or disturbed market situations. Since a rise in price above normal value will increase the supply of goods, an equilibrium of price and value is bound to be established over the long run of economic activity.

Mill was also the first economist to use the term "unearned increment" as applied to rising land values. Ascribing this increment in value to social (increased population) causes rather than landlord's capital improvements, he favored the taxing of such excess and unearned windfalls of value. This at the time, appealing mechanism to establish a more equitable distribution of wealth was readily supported by other welfare economists, and sparked a political campaign for a single (land) tax and the ultimate public ownership of land. The implementation of such a tax was espoused dramatically as the true remedy for economic injustice by Henry George in his well-known book *Progress and Poverty—The Remedy,* published in 1879. The fallacy of a single tax as well as the error of the classical school to take a minimum market demand for granted was belabored by a later school of economists, as will be noted below.

A further significant contribution to the development of value thought was made by the German estate owner and economist Johann Heinrich von Thünen. In his book, published in 1826, entitled *Der Isolierte Staat* (The Isolated State), von Thünen improved on Ricardo's rent theory by introducing the effect of economic location. Although largely hypothetical, von Thünen's writings offered a valuable study of how the economy of a region is affected by distance from the imaginary city and with changes in prices and taxes. Von Thünen was the first economist to treat clearly and systematically the influence of distance from the marketplace on cost and production of agricultural economics. Stress was laid in his writings on the interacting forces of intensive and extensive land utilization. Von Thünen pointed out that an intensive utilization of land near villages caused the cost of production to rise, extensive utilization of land at more distant places became profitable. Cost of transportation served as a balancing factor between the extensive and intensive margins of land use. Thus even at equal fertility, rent as a measure of land value was ascribable to location in reference to marketability for the products in demand. Von Thünen laid some of the groundwork on which the marginal utility economists in later years built their theory of value. He is also recognized as the founder of the economic theory of agriculture, which is based on land location and the market theory of supply and demand.

THE AUSTRIAN SCHOOL OF ECONOMICS

The classical economists conceived value to be influenced and determined by cost of production. The nature of the economy prevailing at the close of the eighteenth century caused classical writers to take the demand for a product largely for granted. Evolution in production and increasing importance of product utility gave rise to a new theory, and school, of economic psychology, founded in Austria by a trio of writers: Karl Menger (1840–1921), Friedrich von Wieser (1851–1926), and Eugene von Böhm-Bawerk (1851–1914). These writers developed the Austrian or *marginal utility* theory of economics which greatly influenced economic thought for nearly half a century.

The shortcomings of the classical school in overemphasizing one extreme of economic analysis—production—were overcompensated for by the Austrian-school adherents to the other extreme of economic analysis—demand. Menger, in fact, held that the value of any good or product was determined by the marginal utility of the last unit essential to meet demand irrespective of the cost necessary in its production. The principal weakness of the utility theory, when judged with hindsight, rested on its failure to distinguish the effects on value of both short-run and long-run economic tendencies and market forces as influenced by supply and demand. Considering short-run market conditions alone, however, the dominant role of utility as a concept of value unquestionably must be acknowledged.

Another important contribution to economic analysis made by the Austrian school was the theory of *imputation*. As logically presented by von Wieser, the value of the whole (product) in essence is derived or inferred from the value of the respective component parts. The theory of imputation served to explain the distribution of the value product—income—over the factors of production as measured by rent, wages, and profits. Von Böhm-Bawerk further refined the utility theory by developing a *market-merger* measurement (a market synthesis) of the individual scales of consumer preferences for market goods. Market price was held to be a compromise of marginal preferences supported by the subjective valuation of buyers and sellers. Von Böhm-Bawerk was also the first to develop a logical and practical theory of interest. He conceived interest to be a measure of time preference for the immediate use or consumption of capital, and present value as a discounted sum of future rights to capital income. This Austrian-school theory thus became the cornerstone of the present utility or income concept as a measure of economic value.

Since value from the individual point of view is largely subjective in character, it follows that utility in a sense "sanctions" sacrifice and thus the cost of production of a good or service. The weakness of this applied theory as espoused by the Austrian school rests chiefly in the concept that costs have no price-determining importance. The pendulum of economic theory marking the actions of the classical school had by the beginning of the twentieth century reached the extreme reaction where causation of value was explained by a search for the greatest utility at the least possible sacrifice.

THE HISTORICAL AND INSTITUTIONAL SCHOOL

This school made no direct contribution to the theory of value, but aided greatly in the growth and development of economics as a mature social science. It had its origin in Germany, where the philosophy of Hegel stressed the importance of the *state* as an institution. Under this philosophy, importance was placed on the value of historical study as an aid to better understanding of human relations. In essence this school rejected the rugged individualism of the classical school, epitomized by the "economic man" and the "iron law of wages" in a laissez-faire society, and emphasized instead the evolutionary and historical importance of economic doctrine in an ever-changing society. Representatives of this school included the German writers Werner Sombart, Max Weber, and Richard Ehrenberg. In this country, Thorstein Veblen is best known as an outstanding economic institutionalist. His famous writings included *The Theory of the Leisure Class* and *The Theory of Business Enterprise*. Other American members of the institutional and historical school included Wesley C. Mitchell, best known for his study, *Business Cycles*, and John R. Commons, best known for his *History of Labor in the United States*.

Historical economics as a *school of thought* did importantly contribute to a better understanding of the interaction of "noneconomic" motives on economic activity. Adherents to this school of thought appropriately emphasized the fallacies of extreme individualism and the doctrine of unbridled laissez-faire. The foundation was thus laid for historical and institutional adherents to broaden the scope of economics as a social science.

THE NEOCLASSICAL AND EQUILIBRIUM SCHOOL OF ECONOMICS

The important and lasting impact on value theory made by the Austrian or utility school of economics was principally because of the importance placed on the *human* or *demand* concept of value. People, it was argued, in the final analysis determine value—not objects or things. Since the wishes and economic needs of people are given expression on the demand side of the economic equation, the pendulum of value reasoning swung to the opposite extreme of that held by the adherents of the classical school of value thought.

The need for a reappraisal of economic principles grew steadily greater in a world becoming increasingly mechanistic and industrial in character. Alfred Marshall (1842–1924), a brilliant, scholarly individual, trained for the ministry in his youth. Drawn into economic studies by the widespread existence of poverty and exploitation nurtured by monopolistic competition, he dedicated his life to economic teaching and writing and brought his influential concepts to the world's attention in his world-famous book *Principles of Economics,* first published in 1890. Alfred Marshall is best described as the father of modern economic thought and modern economic analysis.

Recognizing the importance and validity of the utilitarian concepts of value, Marshall reintroduced with diagrammatic skill the importance that prodution costs exert in affecting an equilibrium of market value in the interplay of the forces of supply and demand. Marshall expertly likened the underlying causes and value influences of cost versus marginal utility (or demand) to the functions served by the blades of a pair of scissors. Each blade, he reasoned, is important, but both are needed to effect smooth and efficient cutting. This balance or interplay of economic forces in the determination of value as seen by Marshall caused his teachings to be called the *equilibrium school.*

Another noteworthy contribution to economic analysis made by Marshall was the development of a *dynamic* as opposed to a *static* theory of value. He effectively demonstrated that the separation and study of any given economic force or cause under the doctrine "everything else remaining equal" was fraught with pitfalls and errors of logic. This he made clear by referring to the position and gravity force interplay of billiard balls in a glass bowl. The removal of any one of the balls in a bowl would bring about a realignment and repositioning of the remaining balls. Modern textbooks on appraising stress the Marshallian theory of value by emphasizing the importance of correlating the social, political, and commercial activities of individuals and society in the final determination of value. The impact of changes in the purchasing power of money, in economic potential and social prosperity, in population growth and composition, and finally, in fashions, taste, and habits of society all influence forces of supply and demand and the relative prices or values at which goods and services can be exchanged.

After its publication in 1890, Marshall's *Principles of Economics* served as the bible of economic theory in all the leading universities for nearly a generation. It was left to later economists—identified with the neoclassical school—not to supplant but rather to build on the equilibrium theory in areas which during the fading years of the nineteenth century did not pose current problems in applied economics as it then served business, industry, and commerce. Development of economic thought as deduced from the study and operation of the business cycle theory and the imperfect, or monopolistic competition theory was a task left to later writers such as Joan Robinson, A. C. Pigou, Edward Chamberlain, Dennis H. Robertson, and John Maynard Keynes.

EARLY TWENTIETH CENTURY VALUE THEORY

The periodic impact on employment, consumption, capital flow, interest, prices, and value caused by variations in the business cycle as measured by economic booms, recessions, and depressions logically led to a restudy of "traditional" economic theory in the light of social welfare and public policy. Paving the way for current value theory and practice was the scholarly contribution made by Wesley Clair Mitchell in the field of business cycles.[1] Based on extensive and analytical research into the causes and effects of cyclical business behavior, Mitchell drew the substantiated conclusion that cyclical business behavior was not due to accident or acts of God but rather to the inevitable results of unrestricted workings of the economic system within the framework of capitalistic society. Mitchell's studies exploded the theory of an economic norm, or equilibrium, and strengthened the acceptance of an ever-changing norm in accordance with the economic principle of change and the resultant integration and disintegration of economic components—in time. To Mitchell, an equilibrium as conceived by the classical and Austrian schools of economics was nonexistent. He saw instead a continual cumulative change from one phase of a business cycle to another. Thus a boom contains seeds of recession that lead to a depression, and the latter contains seeds of prosperity that bring recovery and a recurring boom.

Another shock to traditional classical and neoclassical economics was administered by the influential writings and teachings of John Maynard Keynes.

---

[1]Mitchell's pioneer works were *Business Cycles* (Berkeley: University of California Press, 1913) and *Business Cycles, The Problem and Its Setting* (New York: National Bureau of Economic Research, Inc., 1927).

His unorthodox theories, born in depression years, were at first rejected. Today, however, Keynesian economics is taken seriously not only as a theory but also as a basis for influencing, if not guiding, public economic and fiscal policies.

It is generally recognized that Keynes has made far-reaching contributions to the theories of consumption, employment, savings, interest, and investment. Specifically, Keynes rejected the equilibrium concept as conceived by the classical and neoclassical schools even where applied to dynamic economic society. Keynes demonstrated that in a rising economy, the propensity to consume diminishes as individual incomes climb to higher brackets. Conversely, the propensity to save increases proportionately. Thus Keynes held that underconsumption rather than overproduction was the basic cause of lasting depressions. To prevent money hoarding by saving, he advocated a fiscal policy that would encourage investment and plant expansion to increase employment and consumption in times of economic stress. Conversely, at "full employment" the reverse fiscal policy is called for; savings are encouraged by rising interest rates (tight-money policy) to avoid or at least mitigate inflation. The Keynesian theory of full employment and deficit financing where necessary to maintain maximum productive capacity had significant influence on economic and political policies throughout the world.

After almost four decades of experimentation with fiscal and economic policies on a national level, Keynesian economic theory, designed to adjust the forces of supply and demand, became a firm and nationally accepted policy.

The operations of the national economy, at least as far as total investment, employment, and money-spending power are concerned, can no longer be left to an uncontrolled laissez-faire system. In fact, the latter system lacked a stabilizer or an economic thermostat designed to adjust planned savings and planned investment at a level to maintain "full employment." To achieve a feasible equilibrium level of income and production and to safeguard the purchasing power of the dollar, government fiscal and political policy until the early 1980s attempted to stabilize the national economy by:

1. Changing tax rates with a rise or fall in national income.
2. Increasing or decreasing public expenditures to "heat" or "cool" the economy.
3. Priming the economic pump in times of recession through payments of unemployment compensation and increased welfare (social security) transfer.
4. Providing subsidies through farm-aid programs.
5. Establishing financial aids or interest rate controls to encourage or discourage corporate and family savings.

A new generation of economists in the 1970s began to question the accuracy of Keynesian doctrine with regard to unemployment, fear of saving, and its unjustified faith in government intervention. Much of this doctrine has been replaced by what has come to be known as "supply-side" economics. These economists hold that Keynesian thinking has increased unemployment and depressed savings in part by relying too much on central government. Savings have been depressed to the lowest level among industrialized nations in recent years because of:

1. Tax rules that penalize savings.
2. A social security program that makes saving virtually unnecessary for the majority of the population.
3. Credit market rules that encourage large mortgages and extensive consumer credit while limiting the rate of return available to the small saver.
4. Perennial government deficits that absorb private saving and thereby shrink the resources available for investment.[2]

Since a stabilized economy also promotes a stabilized value for real and personal property, the appraiser must know and study government socioeconomic activity, which now serves as the fifth and "steering" wheel that controls and directs the wheels of production—land, labor, capital, and entrepreneurial management—on which the capitalistic value system is dependent.

CONTRIBUTIONS OF VALUATORS AND VALUATION THEORISTS

The term "theory" means "a belief," "an unproven assumption that nevertheless is plausible." Further, theories concerned with real estate value may be thought of as plausible and generally accepted principles that explain phenomena affecting the value of real estate. Although complex at times, the means used to derive or predict value are better classified as procedures and processes—and not as valuation theories.

The time span for the development of real estate value theory is divided into three eras. The first period extends roughly from 1906 through 1944. The second period is the post–World War II era extending to the early-1960s. The final era extends to the present.

1906–1944

Pioneering work on the related topics of capital value and income capitalization was done by Irving Fisher shortly after the turn of the century. He clearly enunciated several key concepts in his book in 1906. He wrote "The rate of interest acts as a link between income-value and capital-value." He also stated that "value is simply the present worth of the future income from the specified capital."[3] He correctly observed that it made no difference whether the income was level, variable, or accrued continuously or intermittently.

[2]Martin Feldstein, "The Retreat from Keynesian Economics," *The Public Interest* (Summer 1981); reprinted in *Annual Editions Economics 82/83*, Glen Besson and Reuben S. Slesinger, eds. (Guilford, Conn.: The Dushkin Publishing Group, Inc., 1982), p. 125.

[3]Irving Fisher, *The Nature of Capital and Income* (New York: The Macmillan Company, 1906), p. 202.

Fisher also presented an early expression of highest and best use theory, which over the years has been a conceptual cornerstone of appraising. His early version made use of an agricultural model wherein the highest capitalized value was viewed as the optimum land use.

Frederick Babcock's initial book, *The Appraisal of Real Estate,* was published at this time (1927). Some of the key observations set forth by Babcock in his first book were that (1) there is no absolute iron-clad method of computing real estate values.[4] Later with the founding of real estate appraisal societies, the admirable effort to elevate appraisal standards often froze both appraisal thinking and technique. The aversion to depart from accepted dogma also has stunted experimentation and the advance of individualized value problem solutions. Even in the 1920s Babcock advocated different processes for different classes of property; seldom were all three of the traditional approaches to value thought to be necessary.

During the 1920s and 1930s there was a propensity to refer to appraising as a science. Depth and corner reference tables and curves were devised for assessment of lots. It was considered "another important fundamental principle of scientific appraising to separate land and building values."[5] State law required this separation in most states and it was held that common sense should require it elsewhere. Land values and building values were judged to be subject to entirely different conditions and any composite appraisal method would be both illogical and inequitable. Not all appraisers agreed with this notion.

Despite having devoted considerable effort to present value theory, Frederick Babcock saluted the market comparison approach in at least two important ways:

1. Value is a market phenomenon and the market approach cannot be avoided; and it is necessary to translate future productivity into present value, by discovering how the typical and informed market translates such factors into present value.[6]
2. The presence of a quantity of conveyances does not necessarily connote fair market value. Thus Babcock held that the warranted price should dictate market value, not mere sales.[7]

Later in the 1960s we would hear much about probable value, the avoidance of point value estimates, and the strong logic to expressing estimated value within a specified range. Babcock in his landmark book on measuring the ac-

---

[4]Frederick M. Babcock, *The Appraisal of Real Estate* (New York: The Macmillan Company, 1927), p. 2.

[5]W. L. Prouty, Clem W. Collins, and Frank H. Prouty, *Appraisers and Assessors Manual* (New York, 1930), p. 13.

[6]F. M. Babcock, "Common Errors in Appraisal Method—An Analysis," *National Real Estate Journal* (November 24, 1930), p. 17.

[7]*Ibid.*, p. 15. An excellent source of information related to changes in the income approach used in this paper and recommended to the reader is James H. Burton, *Evolution of the Income Approach* (Chicago: American Institute of Real Estate Appraisers, 1982).

curacy of an appraisal held that the mathematics of probability should be used and the estimated value would be given along with upper and lower brackets within which the value was situated.[8]

Babcock, in estimating accrued depreciation, relied chiefly on accounting methods such as sum-of-years' digits, sinking fund, and Hoskold's formula.

The depreciated cost approach would be under continued attack to the present. Babcock, in his 1932 book, quoted the "Standards of Appraisal Practice" of the National Association of Real Estate Boards as follows: "It is unethical for an appraiser to issue an appraisal report on a property in which the total reported value is derived by adding together the market value of the land (or leasehold) as if unimproved, or the value of the land (or leasehold) as if improved to its highest and best use, and the reproduction cost of the improvements less accrued structural depreciation."[9] Two principal merits of a knowledge of the actual cost of a new or proposed structure are to ascertain if (1) the required yield is achievable, and (2) if the investment exceeds the value as revealed by income and transfer data.

Later, Babcock voiced renewed criticism of the cost approach by saying that it was suspect. He further chastised appraisers for falling back on it when there was an alleged lack of market data. He wrote: "If we find difficulty in applying a correct process, we cannot improve the valuation by using an incorrect one." He also was critical of the correlation phase of the appraisal process. Babcock went so far as to state that this practice was "dishonest and disgracefully misleading."[10]

Babcock stated that cost and value were distinct. Replacement cost was not, in itself, valuation and was considered an incorrect approach to value. Unlike later writers, who argued against the validity of depreciated cost as a measure of market value, he was against equating cost and value, but later would oppose the cost approach as well. During the early 1930s, many appraisers favored the cost approach due to the ease of estimating reproduction costs and the difficulty of making an accurate earnings forecast.

A fairly common practice during the late 1920s and 1930s was where one appraiser found the value of the site and another derived the value of the improvements, with the site value being estimated without any consideration of the improvements, and vice versa. This summation approach violates the principle of consistency as we know it today. During this era a distinction was made between normative or market price and "justified price." The latter price differed from the price that people in general were paying and was that price that was justified under the present conditions. Two of Philip W. Kniskern's observations in 1933 still have not been resolved over a half century later. He argued against

[8]F. M. Babcock, *Valuation of Real Estate* (New York: McGraw-Hill Book Company, 1932), p. 532.

[9]*Ibid.*, pp. 178–79.

[10]F. M. Babcock, "The Three Approaches," *The Real Estate Appraiser* (July–August 1970), pp. 5–6.

the division of either income or value between land and building. Any division between land and building was thought to be arbitrary. He also refuted the practice of valuing the fee estate by valuing the equity and adding that value to the unpaid face amount of the mortgage.[11]

An early contribution to appraisal education and theory was made by Thurston H. Ross who developed the band-of-investment theory. Ross first developed this procedure in 1925. Then in 1927, he applied this procedure in an empirical study of properties sold two to five years prior to a consulting study he performed for a Los Angeles bond house. He discovered the expected mortgage terms and equity yields of recently conveyed real property. Significantly, he may have been the first to consider the effect of mortgage terms as well as equity return on capitalization rates. His formula made no provision for equity or debt recapture. Later, these two items would be included. Not until 1936 did this theory have a name. Harry Grant Atkinson, with Ross's consent, labeled it the "band-of-investment theory."[12] Following Ross's 1937 article in *The Appraisal Journal*,[13] appraisers made widespread use of his procedure.

S. Edwin Kazdin in 1944 refined Thurston Ross's band-of-investment theory for deriving capitalization rates. Instead of just using the weighted average of mortgage interest rate times the loan-to-value ratio, he recommended use of the mortgage constant, which provided for loan amortization.[14] Presumably the equity yield rate provided for a similar return of capital. Thus a full accounting was made for return on and of capital in the capitalization rate so derived.

An improvement suggested in value theory at this time failed to have a great impact for a number of years. Arthur A. May criticized George L. Schmutz et al.'s built-up capitalization rate method.[15] This rate commenced with a "safe rate" and was adjusted by allegedly recognizing influences on rates caused by management, risk, and illiquidity. This discredited method continued in the appraisal literature up until 1978.[16]

POST WORLD WAR II–1962

This period was a fertile era in refining value theory. The term "most probable market price" was introduced during this period. This term was introduced in a 1953 book by the Italian economist Giuseppe Medici. He seemed to be con-

[11]Philip W. Kniskern, *Real Estate Appraisal and Valuation* (New York: The Ronald Press Company, 1933), p. 476.

[12]Thurston H. Ross, correspondence with James H. Boykin, April 2, 1984.

[13]Thurston H. Ross, "Rate of Capitalization," *The Appraisal Journal* (July 1937), pp. 216–17.

[14]S. Edwin Kazdin, "Capitalization under Present Market Conditions," *The Appraisal Journal* (October 1944), p. 314.

[15]Arthur A. May, *The Valuation of Residential Real Estate* (New York: Prentice-Hall, Inc., 1942), p. 190.

[16]See American Institute of Real Estate Appraisers, *The Appraisal of Real Estate*, 7th ed. (Chicago: American Institute of Real Estate Appraisers, 1978), pp. 367–368.

centrating on the most probable net income which would be capitalized into value.[17]

Three names were especially prominent in this period, even though their contributions to value theory would continue for nearly two more decades. These persons were Paul F. Wendt, Leon W. Ellwood, and Richard U. Ratcliff.

Paul Wendt, in addition to offering new ideas on real estate appraising, questioned much of what already had been written. Wendt expressed concern over contemporary capitalization theory being "replete with highly technical mathematical symbolism which in many ways lacks a supporting body of theoretical rationalization." Wendt was a proponent of the gross income multiplier over the capitalized income method. The perceived advantages were: (1) data are usually available in the market; (2) for comparable properties, it removes some of the guess work implicit in the capitalized income method; and (3) the GIM method is simpler and more easily understood than some variations of the capitalized income approach.[18]

Both he and Babcock agreed that it was an invalid notion that value indications produced by the market comparison, capitalized income, and depreciated cost approaches should be equivalent. In a later book Wendt held that such equivalence was ignored in security analysis.[19]

As early as 1950, Richard U. Ratcliff criticized use of the split capitalization rate. He argued that whatever the sources of income, the rate is undifferentiated. Consequently, it is improper to divide the income stream. Any risk affects equally each dollar in the net income prediction. Hence different rates, as applied to land and land improvements, are inappropriate.[20]

In his 1965 book, Ratcliff argued for using the concept of "most probable selling price"[21] (introduced by Giuseppe Medici over a decade earlier). He also suggested that the appraisal process should be a predictive model rather than a measurement process. The only two acceptable devices for predicting value were said to be statistical inference and simulation. He recognized that ordinarily, insufficient data are available to use the former. Simulation, however, was important in that the appraiser should use the same assumptions and formulas as the investor.[22] The failure to do this caused him to criticize the cost approach, Inwood, Hoskold, and to a lesser degree, Ellwood's technique.

Several times in his writings, he derides the depreciated cost approach,

[17]Giuseppe Medici, *Principles of Appraisal* (Ames: The Iowa State College Press, 1953), pp. 29–30.

[18]Paul F. Wendt, *Real Estate Appraisal: A Critical Analysis of Theory and Practice* (New York: Henry Holt and Company, 1956), pp. 145–46.

[19]Paul F. Wendt, *Real Estate Appraisal: Review and Outlook* (Athens: University of Georgia Press, 1974), p. 23.

[20]Richard U. Ratcliff, "Net Income Can't Be Split," *The Appraisal Journal* (April 1950), p. 172.

[21]Ratcliff, *Modern Real Estate Valuation: Theory and Application* (Madison, Wis.: Democrat Press, 1965), p. 5.

[22]*Ibid.*, p. 65. See also Ratcliff, "A Neoteric View of the Appraisal Function," *The Appraisal Journal* (April 1965), p. 174.

especially its inability to predict value. Additionally, he saw no merit in either the land or the building residual techniques since they had little relation to investor practices and offered no improvement over the property residual method. On the other hand, investors are strongly inclined to the price/earnings ratio method (GIM).

Ratcliff, in 1964, pointed out that there had been few significant advances in appraisal theory and practice for over 40 years. He was apprehensive of the future professionalization of the real estate appraisal field in large part because due to his own efforts the appraiser is recognized as a journeyman capable of only having a single skill—the determination of value. Professionalization will not arrive until the appraiser is more knowledgeable and capable of solving a variety of complex problems on the basis of professional knowledge.[23]

Leon W. Ellwood's widely recognized tables for appraising and financing were first published in 1959. His mathematical procedure for deriving a capitalization rate abruptly departed from prevailing theory. It refuted such accepted techniques as direct capitalization with straight-line recapture, declining annuities, split rates, and much of the accepted thinking on the various forms of accrued depreciation. A principal contribution by Ellwood was to substitute the forecast holding period of a property usually used by investors in place of the much longer and uncertain remaining economic life of the building since there was no need for the latter even if it could be computed.[24] Another break from the past was set forth in Ellwood's contention that property appreciated as well as depreciated. Such future increases in value could be accompanied in a capitalization rate. He also held that property seldom sold for all cash; therefore, the mortgage terms should be considered as well as the probable resale proceeds available to the buyer. This premise built on the earlier mentioned work of Ross and Kazdin.

One of the most articulate practitioner-theorists has been James E. Gibbons. At least since 1962, he has stressed the interrelationship between money market behavior and capitalization rates for real estate. His logic has been sound, especially in view of the competition between the money and real estate markets for institutional investment funds. Additionally, Gibbons stressed the importance of appraisers comprehending after-tax equity yields. The validity of after-tax income analysis has been supported from counseling, appraising, and investment analysis perspectives. Later, in 1980, Gibbons developed a methodology for deriving real estate investment equity yields from stock market data. He concluded that bond yields were excellent predictors of mortgage interest rates.[25]

[23]Ratcliff, "A Restatement of Appraisal Theory," *The Appraisal Journal* (January 1964), p. 53. See also Ratcliff, "The Price and Rewards of Professionalization," *The Real Estate Appraiser* (August 1967), p. 4.

[24]Leon W. Ellwood, "Analysis and Reconstruction of Operating Statement of Walk-Up Apartments," *The Appraisal Journal* (October 1957), pp. 524–25.

[25]James H. Burton, *Evolution of the Income Approach* (Chicago: American Institute of Real Estate Appraisers, 1982), p. 191, citing James E. Gibbons, "Equity Yield," *The Appraisal Journal* (January 1980), p. 35.

1963–PRESENT

The Wisconsin Colloquium on Appraisal Research convened in March 1963 for the purpose of providing an opportunity to raise fundamental questions, identify weaknesses, and point the way toward the refinement of appraisal theory and practice.

Some key observations brought out in this colloquium were as follows:

1. Human reactions and behavior in response to the value characteristics of real estate are the fundamental bases for the judgment of the appraiser.
2. In arguing for more widespread use of simulation models and multiple correlation analysis, it was stated that the fact should be substituted for the fallible judgment of appraisers whenever possible.
3. To properly appraise investment real estate, the appraiser must first understand investor behavior and influences on their behavior, such as financing, tax considerations, and their own investment objectives.
4. Educators at universities had begun to redirect appraisal education to reflect the fact that appraisal is a form of research and thus an analytical function. This education should convey an understanding of the business world and land economics.[26]

William Kinnard offered a companion theory to Medici's and Ratcliff's "most probable selling price." This was the "most probable use." Kinnard's most probable use was defined as the use to which the land and building would most likely be put. It was a market-oriented notion rather than an idealized value maximization model or "abstracted set of conditions unlikely and probably impossible to be achieved."[27]

In his 1972 book, *Valuation for Real Estate Decisions*, Ratcliff contended that appraisal is a behavioral science and that "people establish prices."[28] He quarreled with use of the income approach as currently structured as a valid simulation model in part because:

1. The predictions of productivity represent the judgment of expert appraisers and do not necessarily equate with the predictions in actual use by investors in the market.
2. Most of the conventional capitalization models are not actually in general use by investors for many types of income property.[29]

Beginning in the 1970s, greater emphasis was placed on the development of quantitative valuation techniques such as regression analysis. The lack of

[26]Richard U. Ratcliff, ed., *The Wisconsin Colloquium on Appraisal Research: Papers and Proceedings.* Madison: Bureau of Business Research and Service, University of Wisconsin, August 1963, pp. 67, 68, 70, and 71.

[27]William N. Kinnard, Jr., "New Thinking in Appraisal Theory," *The Real Estate Appraiser* (August 1966), p. 8.

[28]Richard U. Ratcliff, *Valuation for Real Estate Decisions* (Santa Cruz, Calif.: Democrat Press, 1972), p. 66.

[29]*Ibid.*, pp. 246–47.

observations (rentals and sales) has caused some lack of acceptance of this method for nonresidential appraising. Even for residential appraising, other than mass assessment work, there is some question of absolute reliance on this technique. For example, in 1975 an empirical study of four residential neighborhoods using multiple regression analysis led W. Porcher Miles to conclude that "the accuracy of this method is less than could be expected from a competent appraiser using conventional methods."[30]

With the introduction of sophisticated quantitative and statistical models came the question raised earlier by Ratcliff: Is the appraiser's role to measure or predict value? In either case, it seems necessary that the theorist have a clear grasp of the intricate interworkings of the real estate markets, land economics, investor motivation, and primary criteria used in real estate decision making.

A topic that received particular attention during the mid-1970s (and up to the present) was equity yields. Different approaches were used in considering this subject. One of the initial equations used excluded consideration of equity yields. This was the capitalization equation offered by Ronald E. Gettel: $R = M(f)/\text{DCR}$, where M is the loan-to-value ratio, f is the annual mortgage constant, and DCR is the debt coverage ratio.[31] Nevertheless, this model produced results reasonably close to computed overall capitalization rates. One article reported a difference of only 0.2 percent.[32] Critics quickly faulted this theory because it failed to recognize equity yield. Kenneth M. Lusht and Robert H. Zerbst modified this equation to provide for the present worth of the equity return (based on the long-established property residual method) by taking into account the present worth of the cash flow instead of net operating income, plus the present worth of the equity reversion.[33] During this period, it became popular to extract equity rates from the market and to use the cash flow band of investment method to synthesize an overall rate for an appraised property.

Recent contributions have been made in the area of real estate investment analysis by refining discounted cash flow analysis, risk analysis, and by presenting a clearer understanding of internal rate of return. However, missing from much of the theoretical modeling of recent years has been the lack of empirical studies, especially regarding investor practices, priorities, and methods used to reach investment decisions. For example, two empirical studies found that investors preferred cash flow as the key financial criterion in analyzing real estate in-

---

[30]W. Porcher Miles, "Applied Multiple Regression Analysis," *The Real Estate Appraiser* (September–October 1975), pp. 29–33.

[31]Ronald E. Gettel, "Good Grief, Another Method of Selecting Capitalization Rates," *The Appraisal Journal* (January 1978), p. 90.

[32]James H. Boykin, "Creative Financing in Historical Perspective," *Property Tax Journal* (June 1983), p. 119.

[33]Kenneth M. Lusht, "Inflation and Real Estate Investment Value," *The Real Estate Appraiser and Analyst* (November–December 1979), p. 23.

vestments.[34] For real estate value theorists or practitioners to ignore such findings produces notions and reports of little practical value.

Recent breakthroughs in the field of computers have been astounding, especially with microcomputers. The reasonable prices of desktop computers has allowed increasing numbers of appraisers to use this equipment. The power and variety of repetitive functions performed by computers is impressive. Microcomputers, now prevalent in appraisal offices, can compute, store information, process data as directed by the appraiser, print the results in a variety of formats, and serve as word processors, as well as provide the basis for a bookkeeping system.

Microcomputers are used in each of the traditional approaches to value in increasingly sophisticated ways. Electronic spreadsheets can be used to prepare income-expense statements, comparable sale analyses, depreciated cost approach, and multiyear cash flow projections. The electronic worksheet is best applied to repetitive calculations. Other uses of the computer in appraising are regression analysis for property having similar characteristics to a fairly large number of other properties, and retrieval of replacement cost information via telephone services with such firms as Marshall Swift Publication Company and Bockh Publications.

Unquestionably, the wide availability of microcomputers and software custom designed for real estate analyses will expand appraisal and consulting opportunities over the next decade. Judgment will still be needed by appraisers, but they will have the potential of judging superior data than in the past.

HISTORY OF APPRAISAL ORGANIZATIONS

During the boom years of the 1920s and early 1930s, real estate appraisals were made on a part-time basis by "real estate men." The lack of expertise of these so-called appraisers had contributed to a menacing problem of properties being purchased at prices and mortgaged for amounts bearing little relationship to value. Even after the stock market crash of 1929 and the collapse of real estate values, this appraisal situation still had not improved; persons appointed to appraise properties that had gone into receivership lacked an operational knowledge of value theory.[35]

In an effort to devise national standards of performance and self-regulation as well as development and application of sound appraisal theory, Henry A. Babcock became the first chairman of the National Association of Real Estate

---

[34]James H. Burton, *Evolution of the Income Approach*, citing research by Arnold H. Diamond and Robert J. Wiley in the 1970s; see p. 205.

[35]James H. Boykin, "Real Property Appraisal in the American Colonial Era," *The Appraisal Journal* 44, no. 3 (July 1976), p. 362.

Boards Appraisal Division's Committee on Standards of Practice. In 1929 he published the "Standards of Appraisal Practice for Realtors, Appraisers and Appraisal Committees of Member Boards."[36] This division was chartered on July 1, 1932, as the American Institute of Real Estate Appraisers. Three years later, in 1935, the Society of Residential Appraisers (now the Society of Real Estate Appraisers) was organized.

At about the time Babcock was helping to organize the forerunner of the American Institute of Real Estate Appraisers (1929), the American Society of Farm Managers and Rural Appraisers was founded. Yet probably the first real estate appraisal organization to be created was the Royal Institution of Chartered Surveyors in England in 1863. Twenty years later, the New Zealand Institute of Surveyors was founded. During the 1960s and 1970s a large number of appraisal groups were formed in this country. There is some question how this explosion of organizations has aided the professionalization of this field or protected the public.

INFLUENCE OF VALUE THEORY UPON APPRAISAL PRACTICE

As stated in the introductory paragraph of this chapter, today's appraiser depends heavily on the body of ideas and knowledge created by past thinkers in the fields of value, valuation, and economics. The value theories briefly outlined here have each contributed a link to the chain of value thought. Value theory and practice as taught by leading appraisal societies today are largely a synthesis of the important ideas and economic concepts developed by leaders of the classical, Austrian, historical, neoclassical, and modern schools of value theory. The three approaches to value applied in current appraisal practice indicate especially the impact of value theory as it has developed over the past two centuries. The cost approach to value largely follows the teachings of the classical school, with greater emphasis placed perhaps on replacement cost than on reproduction cost—as was the case at the time of Adam Smith. The income approach in effect is a utilitarian measure of value which yields the present worth of future rights to income without reference to relevant cost of the agents of production. The market sales comparison approach places emphasis on short-run market forces of supply and demand, and yields an index of prevailing prices at a given time and place which may or may not equal a measure of long-term, stabilized, or warranted value. These three approaches to value are really three different ways of measuring the *same* value and are useful as a check one upon the other in judging the accuracy of the end (value) results.

Many of the practices and procedures used today rest on the logical approaches to value problem solving that have been brought forward by practicing appraisers. Courts, clients, academicians, and appraisers continue to im-

[36]*Ibid.,* pp. 362–363.

prove appraisal thought and practice by maintaining an inquiring attitude. To understand these value forces better, a firsthand study of the principal writings of the masters in economic literature, as referenced here, is a "must" for those appraisers seeking attainment of a truly professional status. The evolution of value theory, no doubt, will continue in the future as it has in the past. Alertness and awareness of ever-changing value tendencies must therefore be the watchwords of the appraisal profession.

REVIEW QUESTIONS

1. List and discuss the principal contribution to present-day appraisal practices of each of the early schools of economic thought.
2. Discuss the similarity between the terms "most probable selling price" and "most probable use."
3. Do you agree with the underlying logic of Thurston Ross's band-of-investment method of developing a capitalization rate? Explain your answer.
4. Discuss Frederick Babcock's criticism of the cost approach: "If we find difficulty in applying a correct process, we cannot improve the valuation by using an incorrect one."
5. Discuss the major departures made from prevailing valuation procedure made by Ellwood.
6. List and briefly discuss at least five contributions made to the present practice of appraisal procedures, being certain to identify each contributor.

READING AND STUDY REFERENCES

BABCOCK, FREDERICK M.   *Valuation of Real Estate.* New York: McGraw-Hill Book Company, 1932.

BOYKIN, JAMES H.   "Real Property Appraisal in the American Colonial Era," *The Appraisal Journal* 44, no. 3 (July 1976), pp. 361–374.

BURTON, JAMES H.   *Evaluation of the Income Approach.* Chicago: American Institute of Real Estate Appraisers, 1982.

DILMORE, GENE.   *The New Approach to Real Estate Appraising.* Englewood Cliffs, N.J.: Prentice-Hall, Inc., 1971.

FELDSTEIN, MARTIN.   "The Retreat from Keynesian Economics," *The Public Interest* (Summer 1981). Reprinted in *Annual Editions Economics 82/83,* Glen Beeson and Reuben E. Slesinger, eds. Guilford, Conn.: The Dushkin Publishing Group, Inc., 1982, pp. 121–127.

GREER, GAYLON E., and MICHAEL D. FARRELL.

Chapter 21, "Contemporary Valuation Techniques," *Contemporary Real Estate: Theory and Practice.* Hinsdale, Ill.: The Dryden Press, 1983.

HURD, RICHARD M.   *Principles of City Land Values,* 3rd ed. New York: The Record and Guide, 1911.

RATCLIFF, RICHARD U.   "A Restatement of Appraisal Theory," *The Appraisal Journal* 32, no. 1 (January 1964), pp. 50–67.

WEIMER, ARTHUR M.   "History of Value Theory for the Appraiser," *The Appraisal Journal* 28, no. 4 (October 1960), pp. 469–489.

WENDT, PAUL F.   *Real Estate Appraisal: A Critical Analysis of Theory and Practice.* New York: Henry Holt and Company, 1956.

WENDT, PAUL F.   Chapter 2, "The Development of Appraisal Theory," *Real Estate Appraisal: Review and Outlook.* Athens: University of Georgia Press, 1974.

3

NATURE AND PRINCIPLES
OF PROPERTY VALUATION

Learning Objectives
After reading this chapter, you should be able to:
Appreciate the importance of the legal concept of property value
Understand the principles of real estate valuation and how they are interrelated
Understand how fee simple ownership of real property is restricted by public and private limitations
Discuss the nature and importance of highest and best use as a basis for real estate valuation

Although the history of value thought supports the contention that value is the heart of economics, and that all things of value created or wanted by human beings are objects with which economics as a science is concerned, there are nevertheless valid arguments that "property" valuation as a practiced art is greatly influenced by legal and institutional constraints. The basis for such arguments is the contention that real property and real estate—which are the subjects of valuation—are principally legal and not physical or economic in character. The terms *property* and *estate* denote measures of rights and ownership which are legally identified and constitutionally guaranteed to the true owner under the *allodial*[1] system of land ownership which prevails in the United States. It stands

---

[1]Private land ownership is subject to broad governmental limitations, as opposed to ownership under a state-controlled (communistic) or feudal system, under which absolute ownership of land rests with the king or the sovereign government.

to reason that the larger the rights, the larger the measure of value—all other things remaining equal.

The legal concept of property value and ownership, as will be demonstrated, is very important. Without a thorough understanding of the nature and character of rights in realty as recognized and supported by law, appraising as a professional practice would not be feasible. In the final analysis, no doubt, the appraiser is concerned not so much with the physical aspects of the property under value study but rather with the possible and legal uses to which the property may be put—under competent ownership and effective control.

WEALTH VERSUS PROPERTY

All tangible and useful things owned by human beings which have attributes of economic value are classified as "wealth." Thus an inventory of wealth would include all material and physical things controlled and owned by man to which an economic or monetary scale of value could be applied. Property, on the other hand, is an intangible concept, being the right to own or possess wealth and to put it to legal uses if one wishes. Property thus is a legal right that expresses the relationship between owners and their possessions. To illustrate: A 40-acre farm in North Carolina may possess certain given physical characteristics and measurable natural qualities of fertility. These physical facts are known, and the land can rightly be classified as wealth. The value of this farm, however, depends on the legal and permissible uses (property rights) to which this farm may be put. If only cotton can be grown commercially, one value will result; but under corn or truck farming, another and higher value will accrue to land. If a government allotment makes possible the growing of leaf tobacco, a still higher—and perhaps maximum—farm use value will result. This illustration should make it clear that the appraiser is concerned only secondarily with physical attributes of wealth. His chief and prime interest must be the valuation of rights or property in land and its improvement.

The distinction between wealth and private property can further and more dramatically be illustrated by considering the impact that national decree effects under which the ownership of all land is transferred (confiscated) from the estates of individuals to the nation as a whole. Such a shift of ownership actually did occur in Cuba in 1960, and presently is a matter of national policy in all communistic countries. Confiscation of wealth and the shifting of property rights which control this wealth from one person or persons to another or to the state as a whole does not alter the inventory or magnitude of total national wealth, but it does destroy the value of such property (rights) as were vested in the individual. To safeguard Americans from such governmental decrees the Fifth and Fourteenth Amendments to the constitution provide that no life, liberty, or property may be taken from anyone without due process of law and without just compensation where such taking is for public use and in the public interest.

THE LEGAL CONCEPT OF PROPERTY

Land is the original and basic factor of production. Without land human beings could not exist. No commodity can be produced and no improvement erected without using land. Land as nature provided it consists of the earth's crust, including the underlying soil which provides life-sustaining fertility and supporting power for structures and other human-made improvements. Legally, possession of a given part of this crust of land includes rights to the control of minerals, gas, and oil below the earth's surface as well as the air space above the ground. Thus the boundaries of any parcel of land extend in the shape of an inverted pyramid from the center of the earth upward to the limits of the atmosphere.

Land as originally provided by nature no longer exists anywhere on earth. All land has been directly or indirectly modified by human beings—directly by the construction of improvements on the site and indirectly by improvements related to the site, such as access roads, bridges, canals, and parks. Land, together with its improvements, is designated as *realty*.

The ownership of realty is classified as *property*. Where this ownership is for a term of years, the property (right) becomes *personal* property. Where the ownership of realty extends for a lifetime, or longer to heirs, or forever to assigns, the property (right) becomes *real* property. Thus a lessee possesses personal property in realty, whereas a lessor—to whom the realty reverts at the termination of the lease—owns real property subject to conditions and terms of the lease. Where the term *estate* is used to designate an interest owned, the meaning of real estate and real property are one and the same. *Real estate,* however, as a term is also used to identify the business engaged in by those who conduct commercial transactions in real property. The term "realty" as used in this book includes not only the land and building improvements, but also anything permanently affixed to land or building where the reasonable intent—as supported by the method of annexation and the relationship of the parties involved at the time of annexation—causes the article to be classified as a *fixture:* for example, furnaces, wall-to-wall carpets, built-in cabinets, and similar (fixture) improvements.

THE "BUNDLE OF RIGHTS"

The largest possible estate in real property is known as *fee simple*. Where such ownership exists to the exclusion of all others, the possessor is said to have the complete *bundle of rights.* That is, the "bundle" contains all the individual interests essential to fee simple ownership, including the right to use or not to use the property, the right to lease all or parts of the property (air rights, surface rights, mineral rights, easements, and rights-of-way), the right to sell or not to sell, and the right to donate or grant the property as a gift. Care must be taken by the appraiser to ascertain whether the entire bundle of property rights is to be conveyed by sale or included in the valuation. Since property rights are both separable and divisible it is likely that the bundle of rights is incomplete— whether by partial sale, lease, or by private or governmental limitation—in which case the value of the property is bound to be affected.

OWNERSHIP LIMITATIONS

All land in the United States—whether owned in *fee simple, fee upon conditions, fee determinable,* or as a *life estate*—is subject to certain government limitations on ownership, imposed for the mutual welfare of all citizens. These limitations fall under:[2]

1. The police power of government.
2. The right of eminent domain.
3. The right of taxation.
4. Escheat to the state.

Police Power

The police power is a sovereign power inherent in state government and exercised or delegated by it to the village, city, county, or other governing agency to restrict the use of realty in order to protect the well-being of its citizens. Under police power the rights in property, its use, and occupation may be restricted— without any compensation whatever—when government deems such restrictions necessary in the interest of the welfare, morals, general health or safety of its citizens. It is to this power that citizens take recourse for city planning and zoning as well as for building, urban, and subdivision control. Regulations of rent control authorities and building, fire, and health departments are exercises of the police power and are in fact limitations on the "use" of land.

Eminent Domain

The right of *eminent domain* is the power inherent in the governmental body to "take" an owner's land, or any part of it (air rights, road easements, etc.) by due process of law, when the necessity arises. Only two requirements must be met: the use must be public, and just compensation must be made to the owner. Whether or not the owner wants to surrender the land makes no difference—nor can the owner set his or her own price. The owner's desires are not considered; but a fair value, fixed, as a rule, by expert appraisers, is paid.

[2]For a full discussion of real estate interests and ownership, see Chapter 5 of Alfred A. Ring and Jerome Dasso, *Real Estate Principles and Practices*, 10th ed. (Englewood Cliffs, N.J.: Prentice-Hall, Inc., 1985).

Land is obtained for streets, parks, public buildings, and other public or social purposes through the exercise of this power.

Taxation

Under the right of taxation, the state levies taxes for its support and for the maintenance of all its varied branches which protect and benefit its citizens. It is fair that citizens should pay for the protection and benefit they receive. Land, because of its permanence and accessibility, is a convenient article to tax and is usually the basis for local taxation. If such taxes, when levied, are not paid in due course the owners may lose their land as the result of tax law enforcement. Taxes, too, are a cost of land use and operations. Where such taxes are excessive, the value of land and its improvements are adversely affected.

Escheat

Under the allodial system *escheat* does not limit land ownership but rather provides for the reversion or escheat of land to the state when an owner of land dies, leaving no heirs and not disposing of the land by will. This, however, seldom happens for generally—difficult as it may sometimes be—heirs can be found. Since it is not possible to conceive of land becoming "unowned," the law of escheat to the state provides a logical solution.

In addition to the governmental limitations, real property is often subject to private or contractual limitations on ownership. Such limitations are usually contained in deeds, easements, leases, and in mortgage instruments. Where the bundle of rights is limited, the appraiser must note such restrictions and estimate the effect on value as reflected by typical market operations.

PRINCIPLES OF REAL ESTATE VALUATION

Every field of study and vocation has its principles. These principles provide the underlying basis for each of these fields. Real estate valuation is no different. There are certain principles or rudiments that provide the foundation for the application of knowledge and business experience to valuation situations. It is essential that appraisers master these principles and apply them in their analysis of real property. Although there may be some other influences on the valuation of real estate, the following principles are judged to be of greatest relevance and guidance to its proper valuation.

THE CONCEPT OF HIGHEST AND BEST USE

The principle of highest and best use might well be thought of as the premise or hypothesis upon which an appraisal is based. It is of extreme importance to the accurate valuation of real property. If the appraiser mistakenly judges the property's highest and best use, all subsequent work and analysis in arriving at the property's value is wasted. Suppose, for example, that an appraiser judges the highest and best use of a parcel to be for single family detached homes when, in fact, it has a potential for garden apartments. Consequently, as a result of this initial error, the appraiser would obtain zoning, construction, rental income and expense, and sales information for single-family homes rather than for the more intensive and valuable use as garden apartments. Thus extreme care must be taken to truly analyze a property at its highest and best use rather than simply including a brief and incomplete statement.

Another important aspect of highest and best use is that it is the connecting tissue between external and internal influences on value. That is, in judging a property's highest and best use, it is necessary to consider all pertinent neighborhood and community influences along with the existing or proposed improvements for the site. After having considered these external and on-site influences, an appropriate highest and best use of the site can be reached.

A logical approach to arriving at a site's highest and best use is to begin with the definition of such use. *Highest and best use is defined as that use or succession of available, legal, and physically permitted uses for which there is sufficient demand that produce the highest present site value.* Examining each key word in this definition provides a working guide for the appraiser in his or her property analysis. For example, *succession of uses* implies that there may be an interim or short-term use of the property until such time as market conditions improve sufficiently, possibly rezoning occurs or public utilities are extended to the site. At this time, a higher and better use can be achieved. *Available uses* implies that the use is achievable rather than speculative or remote. Conceivably higher values may be achieved from given uses, but if it is not possible to achieve such uses in the foreseeable future, they should be excluded from consideration. *Legal uses* direct the appraiser to an examination of both public and private limitations on the use of a site. If there is demand for a use such as highway commercial use but the zoning ordinance prohibits such use and it is extremely unlikely that the necessary rezoning can be obtained, the potential highway commercial uses would not be realized. The same constraint applies to private deed restrictions that prohibit certain uses considered to be incompatible with the subdivided land. Also, a long-term lease may constrain a site from realizing its highest and best use. *Physically permitted uses* deal with the suitability of terrain and shape of the site, as well as its subsoil conditions. Thus it is compelling for the appraiser to consider such physical constraints in order to judge whether a prospective highest and best use would likely be achieved at the site in question.

Sufficient demand is often the critical test for determining whether a site realizes its potential highest and best use. If there are no willing and able buyers, investors, or tenants, a proposed use fails the test of highest and best use. It is important to consider all of these factors when judging a property's highest and best use.

Often it is desirable to consider several probable highest and best uses. Some of these uses, although initially seeming reasonable, may quickly be set

aside due to obvious legal constraints or physical difficulties. Once having eliminated some of the more obvious unsuited uses, the appraiser may project income
streams for two or more prospective uses for a given site. As will be considered
later in the land residual technique chapter, highest present income is not always
the most reliable indication of a site's highest and best use. Different remaining
economic lives of the buildings or different building or land capitalization rates
can eventually cause a prospective use with a comparatively high gross income
to have a lower residual income to the land and, when combined with the higher
capitalization rate, also a lower site value.

Duration and Intensity of Site Uses

For any site analysis, it is critical that both the duration and intensity of uses be
specified. Some critics might argue that it is difficult to accurately forecast either
the holding period for the entire property or the remaining economic life of
the site improvements. Although this point is not disputed, nevertheless, the
duration of uses must be eventually addressed in an appraisal. There is no better
time for this than in the highest and best use section. The necessity of specifying
this time period is later considered in the various approaches to value. The
intensity of site use simply means that a specific use rather than a generalized
use should be specified. For example, rather than state that the highest and best
use is residential, the appraiser needs to indicate whether the site has development potential for three dwelling units per acre or 14 units an acre.

It should be remembered that the largest, most expensive improvement
is not necessarily the highest and best use of a site. Importantly, the relationship
of community, neighborhood, site, and improvements must be considered in
order to reach the optimum use and value combination. For example, if the
improvements are excessive for the size or location of the site, the accompanying
expenses may greatly erode the profitability and value of the underlying site.

Improved Site Use

Generally, highest and best use is thought to pertain to the site as if vacant.
There will be instances where the client is interested in knowing the highest and
best use of an improved property, which, of course, involves both the site and
buildings or for other reasons the owner chooses to retain the present buildings.
It may be that the present use cannot be altered due to deed or lease restrictions.
Another very important reason for ascertaining the highest and best use of an
already improved property is to consider several alternative uses of the property
via adaptive use. In such cases, the appraiser will project alternative conversion
expenses and then weigh the resulting income against such expenses in order
to judge the highest and best use of the upgraded property.

Because labor, capital, and entrepreneurial compensations have priority
claims on the income or products of land only the balance remaining after the

due shares to the mobile factors of production (labor, capital, and entrepreneurial compensations) are paid serves as a measure of the earning power of land. Because land receives what is *left* as a *residue* of the total income stream, land earnings are said to be *residual* in character.

The passive nature of land, which causes its income to be residual, makes it of prime importance that land be employed under its *highest and best possible use.* Only under such use can land attain its maximum return of income and hence its maximum value. It must be kept in mind that a given parcel of land may be available for alternative and competitive uses. Nevertheless, a site can have only *one* or one combination of, highest and best use at a given time. The latter condition would apply to a mixed-use development where each part of the total site would be devoted to a particular use. For instance, the highest and best use of an urban site may be to leave it vacant in order that it may "ripen" into an anticipated use that forms a higher present value than it would under the immediate and alternate uses to which the land might be put. This may be the case, for instance, where a tract of land can be developed for apartment purposes, but thorough study has disclosed that the site location will prove ideal as a neighborhood shopping center in three to five years. The proper choice in this instance should be supported by an appraisal study in which the value findings will serve as a guide to appropriate economic action. No doubt the present worth of future rights to income will be higher under a commercial use in this instance although the property is to be idle during the years of ripening. Although a site is limited to one or one combination of land use activities at a given time, there may be a series of uses for a site over a specified period of time.

The determination of the highest and best use of a given parcel of land at a given time requires careful study and expert analysis of the social, political, and economic forces which influence land utilization and land income over the economic life of the improvements. Basically, the amount of net income that can accrue to a parcel of land is essentially limited by the *law of diminishing returns.* Under this law employment of additional units of production will yield an increasing residual (net) income to land until a maximum of income per unit of investment is reached, after which diminishing returns set in until a point is reached at which the last unit of input yields only an income great enough to cover its cost with no return to land. It is at this point that the aggregate income to land is highest. By analysis of the current and hypothetical uses to which a site can legally be employed—now and in years to come—the appraiser is able to select that use which will yield to land its highest present value.

The ability of land to absorb additional units of labor and capital profitably is economically classified as land *capacity.* Capacity refers to the volume of input. Some sites have the capacity to absorb millions of dollars before the point of no return (to land) is reached. Other sites reach maximum capacity on the expenditure of a few thousand dollars. In the illustration shown in Figure 3.1, the capacity of the site is reached on expenditure of labor and material sufficient

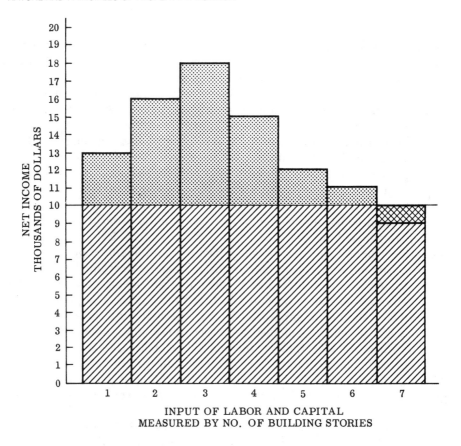

INPUT OF LABOR AND CAPITAL
MEASURED BY NO. OF BUILDING STORIES

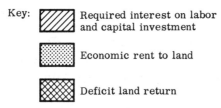

Key:

Required interest on labor and capital investment

Economic rent to land

Deficit land return

Figure 3.1

to erect a six-story building. Construction of less than six stories in this instance would constitute an underimprovement, and construction of a higher structure an overimprovement. Either under- or overimprovement will reduce the overall property value.

The construction of a one-story building as shown in Figure 3.1 results in a net income sufficient to cover not only building operating expenditures, but also required earnings to meet interest payments on labor and capital investment plus an excess or residual return (rent) to land in the amount of $3,000.

The addition of a second-story unit further increases excess rent income by $6,000. A third-story addition yields another $8,000 as excess land income. At this point, and under this selected use, the efficiency of land per unit of labor and capital input is at its highest. As long, however, as added units of labor and capital cover their investment costs and yield excess rent returns, the property warrants further and more *intensive* land utilization. As shown in Figure 3.1, the parcel's capacity to absorb added units of labor and capital is reached with the construction of a six-story building. Adding a seventh floor would result in a deficit land income, thus diminishing both land income and property value. The economic loss caused by an overimprovement of a subject property is chargeable, as will be demonstrated below, as external obsolescence to the building improvements and not to the value of the land. For the latter's value logically is established under the highest and most profitable use.

A study of land capacity by itself, however, is insufficient in a determination of highest and best use. The appraiser need further consider the efficiency of land return in relation to land capacity under alternative types of uses. Two sites with equal capacity may differ in efficiency of land return and hence differ in value. Sites developed for apartment housing have often greater capacity (to absorb construction dollars profitably) than commercial sites in downtown areas. The greater efficiency of business property, too, may more than offset the lack of land capacity. Whereas capacity refers to the ability of land to absorb capital outlays profitably, efficiency refers to a measure of quality as represented by the ratio of dollar land input to dollar land output in terms of income and capital expense. Figure 3.2 is intended to demonstrate a case where alternate land uses provide the same capacity but differ in efficiency, and hence value, as determined by the amount of residual land income.

The more efficient land use, as shown in Figure 3.2, is to improve the property with a six-story office building. Zoning permitting, the residual rent for an office building substantially exceeds that realized for an apartment development. As demonstrated in Figure 3.3, the cumulative market rent under use "A" is $25,000 as compared with $38,000 under the more efficient use "B." The ratio of efficiency per unit of labor and capital input is 38 ÷ 6 or $6\frac{1}{3}$ under the highest and best use and 25 ÷ 6 or $4\frac{1}{6}$ for the next best or alternate use. The higher the ratio of output (return) in relation to input (invested capital), the greater the efficiency of land use. As demonstrated, the highest and best use of a site is not necessarily that use which permits development to the greatest capacity nor that use with the greatest efficiency. It is rather that use in which the composite results of capacity and efficiency of land use brings the greatest net return that forms a basis for the land's highest present value. Capacity and efficiency bear the same relation to the quality of a parcel of land that length and breadth do to the area of a rectangle. An examination of Figure 3.3 shows that the more efficient land use represents an income area of 38 unit squares ($6\frac{1}{3}$ efficiency ratio times 6.0 capacity). The larger the area, other things remaining equal, whether due to greater capacity or greater efficiency of land use,

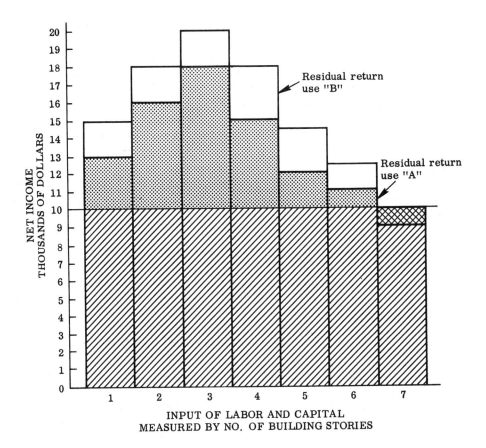

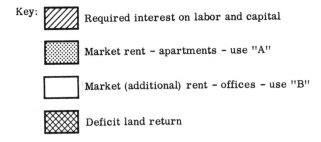

Figure 3.2

the higher the net income and hence value. Only by careful study and analysis of permissible and economically feasible alternative land uses can the appraiser determine professionally the highest present value of a site.

Once the highest and best use of a site has been determined, and the value under such use fixed, it stands to reason that the misuse of a site either through over- or underimprovement cannot subtract from this value. Man-made errors arising from improper land utilization must be charged against the value

CUMULATIVE ECONOMIC RENT
UNDER ALTERNATE DEVELOPMENT

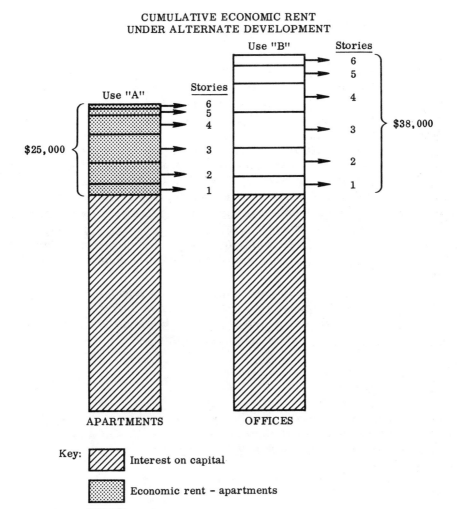

Figure 3.3 Cumulative Economic Rent Under Alternate Development

of the improvements as a form of functional or external obsolescence (depreciation). To illustrate: Assume that there is a two-story apartment building constructed on a site. Assume further that the land value under this use is $100,000. If because of miscalculation the improvement costing $600,000 is placed on this land, and the total value of land and building upon completion proves to be only $650,000, then the value of the component parts is derived as follows:

Total value	$650,000
Value of land under highest and best use	100,000
Value of improvement	$550,000

The difference between building cost of $600,000 and building value of $550,000 is a functional loss (depreciation) in the amount of $50,000 due to an overimprovement.

To restate the land utilization principle: Land value is based on residual land income under the highest and best use of the land. Under any other use both income and value diminish and the value loss incurred constitutes "built-in" depreciation. *Only under the highest and best land use are costs of improvement equal to market vaue of such improvements.*

The income which is ascribable to land under its highest and best use is known as *market rent*. It is that rent which the land is capable of producing when employed to its optimum capacity and efficiency. Any other income or rent agreed on between owner and tenant is known as *contract rent*. Where the contract rent is less than the economic rent, the owner in fact transfers a portion of the land value to the user. Where contract rent exceeds economic rent, the owner realizes a bonus value which is computed by capitalization of these excess earnings at an appropriate risk rate (capitalization rate) as will be demonstrated in Chapter 20.

In addition to the concept of highest and best land use and the principle of increasing and decreasing return resulting from intensive land utilization it is essential for the student of appraising to understand the operations of other principles and market rules of operations as follows:

1. Consistent use.
2. Substitution.
3. Marginal productivity.
4. Supply and demand.
5. Balance in land use and development.
6. Anticipation of future benefits.
7. Conformity.
8. Changes in socioeconomic patterns.

CONSISTENT USE

A corollary of the principle of highest and best use is consistent use. This principle holds that both the site and improvements must be evaluated as the same use. This principle is best applied in transitional neighborhoods, that is, neighborhoods that are changing from one set of land use activities to a set that generally would be of a higher order. A good example of this would be in a residential neighborhood which is traversed by a busy traffic artery. Gradually, the homes are converted to interim uses and then later the land becomes so valuable that the converted residences are demolished and more substantial and properly designed improvements such as retail or office space are constructed. The dilemma facing the appraiser in these changing neighborhoods is the tendency to appraise the land for the more valuable use and the improvements at their higher value (such as residential).

The consistent use principle is violated when the appraiser seeks to assign a value to the land based on one highest and best use and a value to the improvements based on a different highest and best use. Thus sound appraisal theory requires that the appraiser consider the property's single highest and best use on the basis of the transitional nature of the neighborhood. It is permissible to consider time-phased highest and best uses, which recognizes the interim and ultimate highest and best uses. This concept is fairly simply administered by discounting the income available to the property under each of the highest and best uses by time period. For example, the highest and best use may be for home-converted office space for the next five years, followed by a larger office building after this interim period.

SUBSTITUTION

All properties, no matter how diverse their physical attributes or how varied in geographic location, are substitutable economically in terms of service utility or in income productivity. The economic concept of substitution thus sets an upper limit of value that is set by the cost of acquisition of an equally desirable substitute property, provided such can be fashioned without undue (costly) delay.

The principle of substitution is applicable not only to the replacement of a new property of reasonably equal service utility or earnings capacity but also to an existing old or equally depreciated replica. This theory of substitution provides the basis for using substitute (comparable) properties in the direct market, income, and cost comparison approaches to value, which will be demonstrated more fully in the following chapters.

MARGINAL PRODUCTIVITY

The principle of marginal productivity (often called principle of contribution) is concerned with the value that the presence of a property component contributes to the overall value of that property. Conversely, it is the reduction in the overall property value caused by absence of the component. This principle frequently is used in economic feasibility decisions, where it discerns between incremental cost and value or expenses and income. For example, if the addition of a $10,000 air-conditioning system results in an increase in property value of $15,000, the expenditure would probably be judged feasible.

Another important application of this principle involves making adjustments in the market comparison approach. Two examples will illustrate this statement. Suppose that a sale property has a two-car garage and the appraised property has only a one-car garage. The question is not how much more the

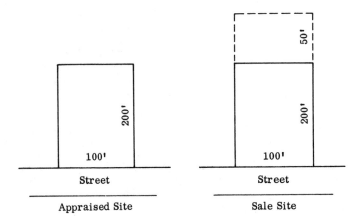

Appraised Site Sale Site **Figure 3.4**

two-car garage will cost but rather how much would it contribute to the value of the sale property. This amount then provides the basis for the dollar adjustment to reveal the estimated value of the appraised property. Another example is shown in Figure 3.4.

The sale site shown sold for $40,000, which in turn reflected its depth of 250 feet. The question now becomes how much did the extra 50 feet of depth contribute to the value of the 250-foot-deep site. If, for instance, it was $2,000, the indicated value of the subject site would be $38,000.

An understanding of the principle of marginal productivity is also important in a determination of highest and best land use. A feasibility study undertaken to test economic advantages of alternate land uses requires a study of marginal productivity at the point where intensive or vertical land use balances output (income) realized at the margin of horizontal or extensive land utilization. When productivity under intensive and extensive land uses are in balance, the two margins merge into one (of equal productivity) in conformity with this principle.

SUPPLY AND DEMAND

In applying the principle of marginal productivity the practicing appraiser essentially makes a comparison between capital input and output under proposed or alternate improvement plans. Since the output of income from rentals or operation is governed by the economic law of supply and demand the value of a given improvement may or may not equal costs, depending on the status of the market and the present and potential quantity of competition. Care must be taken to analyze thoroughly the market operation under *typical* conditions in order to avoid the pitfall of capitalizing excess income, which is temporary in nature and due to consumer time preference as to the moment of purchase, caused by scarcity or transitional monopoly. Like water seeking its natural level, so excess income (profit) will seek its natural level through competition from nearby competitive properties.

Where market forces are competitively free to operate, and where population is unrestricted in movement and migration from farm to urban and from urban to suburban areas, the shift in balance or changes in the interaction of supply and demand for housing causes prices to fluctuate from a high point at extreme scarcity to bargain prices below cost of replacement in a buyers market and generally in areas where supply is superadequate. Economists characterize this trade imbalance by reference to long-range values and short-run prices. Since appraisals are made as of a given date or moment in the overall sequence of time, it is important that market forces which abnormally influence supply and demand for real property in a given community be carefully analyzed and their impact on present value noted and explained.

The principle of supply and demand holds that price tends to vary directly according to demand and inversely proportional to supply, that is, higher prices will be paid when there is strong demand for a good. Alternatively, when the market is oversupplied, prices decline. The importance of this concept is twofold. (1) When analyzing prior market information such as rentals or sales, it is necessary to consider the state of the market before making adjustments to reveal the appraised property's value. For example, if there is a seller's market (possibly resulting from strong demand and low supply) and the current market is not as favorable for sellers, the sales or rental data should be adjusted downward. Similarly, when the prior rentals or sales occurred and there was a buyer's market (some combination of low demand and high supply), an upward adjustment would need to be made to reflect such circumstances if a more positive market occurred today. (2) The other factor to consider would be the state of the current market. Is it depressed or is it a booming market but not likely to be sustained in future years? The appraiser must take this situation into consideration when making his or her appraisal.

BALANCE IN LAND USE AND DEVELOPMENT

An understandable error which many appraisers are prone to make is evaluating property without due consideraton of the principle of *balance*. If the value of a site under the World Trade Center or some other well-known skyscraper has been reasonably established, it does not necessarily mean that the site adjacent to it warrants a like value. A market study may disclose that one skyscraper will amply serve the space needs of a community for many years, while the construction of another may spell economic loss if not disaster to the owners of both. The resulting loss in property value would be a direct measure of the degree to which the principle of balance had been violated. The presence of too many hotels, motels, restaurants, drugstores, or other building facilities brings about a "buyer's market" in which lowered values will reflect the degree of imbalance in relation to demand.

To guard against value losses caused by lack of property balance, an appraiser must know the community and be thoroughly conversant with effective land utilization as well as with community planning policies. This principle relates the neighborhood to the property, the site to the improvements, and each part of the building to the whole building. This will be discussed more fully in Chapter 6.

The principle of balance and its influence on value can also be effectively considered in judging interior design and the efficiency of a floor plan. Too many or inadequate bathrooms, bedrooms, or storage areas; wasted space in kitchen, hall, or living rooms; ceilings which are too high or too low; and over- or undersized heating, piping, or cabinet facilities—all are symptoms of interior imbalance that may be reflected in value losses. The technique used to measure the amount of such losses will be more fully treated in Chapter 13.

ANTICIPATION OF FUTURE BENEFITS

The principle could just as well be referred to as the principle of futurity since the appraiser's responsibility is to interpret attitudes of persons trading in the real estate market. Thus he or she is obligated to consider both the likelihood of future trends and the impact that such trends will have on the reactions of buyers, sellers, and tenants, as expressed in present market transactions. It might be argued that the cost approach (to be discussed in a later chapter) has its roots in the past. The direct market comparison approach, however, reflects the buyer's and seller's attitudes of the past and especially of future expectations for a property. Without question, futurity undergirds the income approach since a person leases a property for future benefit. Leases themselves often go several years beyond the present date. The appraiser must bring future income and expense expectations back to a present value.

It sometimes is said that a home buyer buys the largest home that he or she can currently afford. There is both truth and logic to this observation. A home buyer certainly would not go into debt for 15 to 25 years to acquire a property that served only his or her family's immediate needs. Hence the amenities acquired provide a future benefit.

Market value, although limited in amount by the operation of the forces of supply and demand, nevertheless provides the owner or user of real property a measure of anticipated property utility. Hence it is defined as "the present worth of future benefits." It is the future and not the past with which the appraiser must be concerned. The history of operation of the subject, or, like properties in a market area, is important only in ascertaining a trend in anticipated earnings over the remaining economic life or holding period of the property under valuation. Past operations and other than "typical" management practices may hinder or in the case of accumulated good will accelerate (at least for a time) income production. Such assets or liabilities of a property must be considered in the measure of present value.

Changes in anticipated demand caused by off-site improvements in forms of highways, freeways, bridges, schools, and parkways have an important impact on value even though such improvements are in the planning stage and not visible at the time of the appraisal. The principle of anticipation thus points up the importance of being fully informed of community affairs and with economic changes anticipated in the market area in which the subject property is located.

CONFORMITY

A property's value is maximized when it conforms to the surrounding properties, neighborhood, and tastes and desires of prospective users and purchasers. In a residential sense, conformity refers to compatible but not necessarily monotonous "look-alike" dwellings. Often this compatibility is regulated by subdivision restrictive covenants that specify the architectural design and exterior materials as well as size of dwellings. The old adage of "birds of a feather tend to flock together" has merit in this case. Persons interested in purchasing a two-story, brick colonial design home are unlikely to look in a neighborhood characterized by modern, one-story frame dwellings, and vice versa. Nor will they be attracted to the colonial-designed home in the midst of a contemporary-designed neighborhood.

The same principle pertains to nonresidential structures as well. The nonconforming use generally is a departure from established styles and designs within a particular market. A departure from these architectural, size, or amenity norms often results in adverse market reaction to such properties. The final result is that such properties are not worth as much as surrounding properties.

Conformity is also expressed as *under-* and *overimprovement* of a site. There is a residential condominium development in one of the eastern states where the developer built the maximum number of housing units allowed by the local zoning ordinance. However, the development site was one with unfavorable terrain. When the project was completed, there were parking problems as well as severe street cuts and unusually high site-preparation expenses. The end result was a displeasing visual effect, market resistance, and considerable price discounts that were required to market the condominium units at all.

Another example of an overimprovement would be where a person builds a six-bedroom dwelling with a three-car garage and swimming pool in a neighborhood of three- and four-bedroom homes with one- and two-car garages and no swimming pools. In a six-bedroom, three-car garage, swimming pool neighborhood, the owner would likely recoup all or most of his or her investment. However, this property is incompatible with its existing neighborhood, and consequently, the owner normally cannot expect to recover the full amount of expenditure. Thus in this case the property value tends to seek (regress toward) the neighborhood value norm. The converse of this situation would be where a modest dwelling was built in a neighborhood of expensive homes. In this case, two things might happen. It may be so grossly underimproved there would be no market for the property, or the property value would be pulled up (progress toward) the neighborhood value norm.

Still another example of nonconforming use is where a property fails to conform with the current zoning laws. Often a property may have been built prior to the present zoning ordinance being enacted. For example, a building may contain six apartment units in a zoning classification which currently allows only four dwelling units for a similar site. In this case, the nonconforming use results in the property being worth more than a four-unit site, but since it could not be restored to six units in case of fire, it is reasonable to expect that the property would not realize its full six-unit value as would similar properties that are legally permitted this number of units.

CHANGES IN SOCIOECONOMIC PATTERNS

To the student of appraising it must now be apparent that the principles of property valuation as outlined above are interrelated and that all of them must be considered separately and as a whole if a reliable and accurate estimate of value is to be derived. Perhaps the single greatest error in value judgments is that of inexperienced appraisers taking the present status quo for granted. Next to death and taxes, nothing is as certain as the prospect of change. Change, of course, is a product of technological progress and the resulting shift in socio-economic styles of living. One need only reflect on causes which led to a decline in the value of horses and buggies, bicycles, passenger ships, and railroads. Even once popular land use schemes, such as street car–dependent subdivisions, in-efficient load-bearing walls of earlier office buildings, or strip retail centers have fallen into public disfavor to varying degrees. An appraiser must not only be conscious of the forces of change, but learn to also evaluate their impact. This is essential in measuring the degree of anticipated changes causing functional and possible economic obsolescence as well as the ever-present value losses caused by age, wear, tear, and actions of the elements.

REVIEW QUESTIONS

1. What, if any, relationship exists between realty and fixtures?
2. Explain the terms "police power" and "eminent domain" and discuss how an affected property owner is compensated under each.
3. Discuss why an accurate highest and best use is so important in the appraisal of real estate.

4. List and discuss the importance of the key terms in the concept of highest and best use.
5. How can the marginal productivity concept be applied to the market comparison approach?
6. Distinguish wealth from property and state why the valuator is concerned with the appraisal of property rather than with the appraisal of wealth.
7. It is stated that "where the bulding codes or local conditions make construction more costly in one city than another, the general land values are lower." Is this statement true? Give your reason.

READING AND STUDY REFERENCES

AMERICAN INSTITUTE OF REAL ESTATE APPRAISERS. Chapter 2, "Foundations of Appraisal," *The Appraisal of Real Estate.* Chicago: AIREA, 1983.

BABCOCK, FREDERICK M. Chapter 13, "Axioms of Valuation," *The Valuation of Real Estate.* New York: McGraw-Hill Book Company, 1932.

DERBES, MAX J., JR. "Highest and Best Use—What Is It?" *The Appraisal Journal* 49, no. 2 (April 1981), pp. 166–178.

FLOYD, CHARLES F. Chapter 4, "Private and Public Restrictions on Ownership," *Real Estate Principles.* New York: Random House, Inc., 1981.

KINNARD, WILLIAM N., JR. "Urban Land Economics," *Income Property Valuation.* Lexington, Mass.: Lexington Books, 1971, pp. 22–29.

ORDWAY, NICHOLAS, and JACK HARRIS. "The Dynamic Nature of Highest and Best Use," *The Appraisal Journal* 49, no. 3 (July 1981), pp. 325–334.

RUGGLES, ROBERT K., and JAMES J. WALSH. "Supply, Demand and the Nature of Value," *The Appraisal Journal* 51, no. 2 (April 1983), pp. 190–201.

SHENKEL, WILLIAM M. Chapter 1, "Appraisal Principles and Practice," *Modern Real Estate Appraisal.* New York: McGraw-Hill Book Company, 1978.

VANDELL, KERRY D. "Toward Analytically Precise Definitions of Market Value and Highest and Best Use," *The Appraisal Journal* 50, no. 2 (April 1982), pp. 253–268.

4

IMPORTANCE OF COST, PRICE, INCOME, AND MARKET

Learning Objectives
After reading this chapter, you should be able to:
Distinguish between replacement and reproduction cost
Identify the conditions that must be satisfied before price equates to market value
Understand the meaning of *net operating income*
Recognize special market conditions that can affect property income and the market for real estate

Perhaps no single concept in the theory of value gives rise to greater miscalculations by both nonappraisers and appraisers than the concept of *cost*. Cost and value are confused because sacrifices in terms of dollars or in labor and materials are necessary in order to supply goods or services in demand, and in the long run such sacrifices or costs must equal value if construction (production) is to continue and prove economically rewarding. Then, too, as was explained in Chapter 3, under highest and best use, cost influences the *supply* side of value—and since value without expenditure or cost of production is unthinkable, it would appear that the reliance on cost as a measure of value is justified.

There are a number of reasons, nevertheless, why care must be exercised before accepting costs as a measure of value. First, cost and value are only equal if, among other considerations, the property is new or proposed. Since improvements age physically from the day of construction, and since functional and external forces of obsolescence are operating constantly because of changes in style, use, and demand, depreciation must be accounted for accurately and subtracted from cost as if new in order that *depreciated cost* may reflect a truer measure of value. Second, cost and value are one and the same only where the improvements represent the highest and best use. Since many properties are under- or overimproved—or misimproved—cost and value may differ significantly. Finally, costs must be economically warranted if the sacrifice of the agents of production is to equal value. To illustrate: Digging a hole in the ground for no purpose whatever except to satisfy a whim does not create value. In fact, the hole in the ground may constitute "negative" value because it may have to be filled again in order to make the site economically usable. Costs which are not justified cannot equal value because no "informed" buyer will pay more for a good or service than is warranted at a given time or place and under prevailing economic conditions. The proverbial "hotel built in a desert" is an illustration of this. Cost is always a measure of a past sacrifice either of labor or materials or both, and always represents a measure of *past* expenditures. Value, on the other hand, always lies in the future because value, by definition, constitutes the *present worth* of future rights to income.

REPLACEMENT COST VERSUS REPRODUCTION COST

Even when costs are accounted for and deemed acceptable as an initial measure of value it is *replacement* cost and not *reproduction* cost that must be considered in a determination of value. The valid question facing an informed buyer or a professional appraiser is what it would cost to duplicate the subject improvements. *Duplication* means to recreate the utility or amenities which the property is expected to offer a typical buyer. Where modern methods of construction and design offer savings in both labor and material costs as compared with methods in vogue when the appraised structure was originally built, then present-day replacement costs should be used by the appraiser. Ceilings may be too high or too low, walls excessively thick or not properly reinforced, the floor plan outmoded or simply wasteful in space utilization, and convenient built-ins and energy-saving devices lacking. To reproduce such a structure—even on paper for hypothetical calculation of value—would be a wasteful practice. Only where required by law—as in condemnation trials, where the owner's property is to be left intact—may a reproduction cost estimate be in order. But even here the law in most states requires the owner's property to be left intact in terms of *value*, and only a replacement of like improvements, or what typical buyers value as such in open market transactions, can effectively serve as the final guide to just compensation.

Replacement cost is defined as "the necessary expenditure or sacrifice of the agents of production required to replace the improvements with one having the same utility." Reproduction costs, on the other hand, measure the expenditure necessary to reproduce a replica of the building. There are currently two schools of appraisal thought on this subject. One holds that to apply replacement costs as a measure of value constitutes "lazy" appraising, inasmuch as some forms of functional obsolescence are not accounted for unless a reproduction cost estimate is first obtained. From this estimate of reproduction cost subtraction should then be made for all evidences and forms of accrued depreciation resulting from wear and tear, action of the elements, and all forms of functional and external obsolescence. Thus if the present building walls are of brick 24 inches thick, the reproduction cost adherents would estimate the cost to reproduce these walls even though modern methods of construction call for steel-reinforced walls with a maximum thickness of 12 inches. The other school of appraisal thought (to which these writers subscribe) maintains that it is wasteful to estimate reproduction cost when factual evidence supports the conclusion reached by typically informed buyers that replacement costs set the ceiling of value, and that reference to costs of reproducing an outmoded replica is not a realistic approach to accurate value measurement.

In choosing replacement cost rather than reproduction cost as a measure of value, the appraiser must take care not to double up depreciation losses. Such doubling of value losses takes place when faulty methods of construction or design are eliminated in the calculation of replacement cost and then included again in the estimate of accrued depreciation. To state it differently, where replacement costs are lower than reproduction costs of a subject property the estimate cannot be reduced again for faults which theoretically have been cured by the cost estimator. Such practice distorts the facts and places a property as well as its owner in double jeopardy. The application of the cost approach and the technique of measuring accrued depreciation will be dealt with fully in later chapters.

PRICE AS A MEASURE OF VALUE

Price paid simply represents an expression of market value in terms of dollars. Before accepting a price as bona fide evidence of value, however, it is essential that the appraiser verify the transaction in order to learn how closely the purchase price fulfills the definition of market value. The following conditions must be carefully scrutinized:

1. The relationship of the parties.
2. The terms of sale and the market conditions.
3. The date of sale.
4. The effect of changes in the purchasing power of the dollar.

The importance of the relationship of parties is not always self-evident. Unless the buyer and the seller deal on a reasonably objective and impersonal basis, little reliance can be placed on their transaction as representing *typical* attitudes of market buyers and sellers. Thus a sale from father to son, or brother to sister would hardly represent typical market exchanges. Neither would sales from one corporation to a subsidiary company, nor from an employer to an employee be considered evidence of *market* value. Such sales, even though validly recorded on public records, must be disregarded in favor of impersonally objective transactions by sellers and buyers who have bartered freely and independently in an *open* market in which the sale was offered with knowledge of the property's potential uses and where its availability to all concerned is readily and widely known.

A major cause of differences in the price/value relationship is the underlying conditions, or terms of sale. Where the sale is made on time, where down payments are extremely low, and where the mortgage payments are spread over many years at favorable (below market) rates of interest, the price paid for a property will reflect these favorable terms. In such cases, the buyer has in effect purchased two things: (1) the property, and (2) time preference (terms) for paying conveniently out of future earnings in the years to come. Suppose that two residences, equal in every respect as to location, quantity and quality of construction and valued at $80,000, each sell on terms as follows:

House A   All cash
House B   10 percent cash as down payment and the balance payable
           in equal installments over 20 years at 12 percent interest

House A, if sold objectively at $80,000, represents a price equal to property value. House B will realize a price of $80,000 (property value) plus the value of favorable terms that accrue because of the low cash payment, the high mortgage-to-equity ratio, and the below-market interest rates. Assuming that house B sold for $84,000, the price paid represents the following:

Value of the property	$80,000
Value of favorable terms	4,000
Total transaction price	$84,000

The appraiser, in accepting sale B for market comparison purposes, would have to consider the low down payment and other favorable terms when relying on this sale as evidence of value.

In judging prices as evidence of value, care must also be taken to determine whether the market is *normal*, whether the buyer and seller acted with *typical* care, and had no unusual motivation for buying or selling the property, and whether the buyer was informed as to the present and potential utility (income) which the property can render under the existing and potential uses to which it can legally be put. By normal market is meant conditions when market supply and demand are in balance, or equilibrium, and when prices paid neither reflect a premium, because of scarcity of supply (seller's market), nor a discount, because of oversupply (buyer's market). Furthermore, it stands to reason that, unless the parties to the transactions are mature and well informed as to the present and potential uses of the subject property, the price paid cannot be viewed as evidence of value. At all times it is essential to judge market transactions with typical informed buyers and sellers, acting in a typical market without duress, in mind.

In analyzing market transactions, the date of sale is also of great importance. Appraisers as a rule rely on the date of the transaction as shown on the deed of record as evidence of time of sale. It is essential to recognize that the date of sale, guiding in courts of law, is not the date of deed recording or date of transfer of title but rather the day on which a meeting of minds of the parties to the contract for deed took place. Since it is possible that months, or even years, may elapse between the date of contract and the date of transfer of title by deed, adjustments must be made to account for possible economic effects on market prices occurring during the interval between the date of contractual agreement and the date of appraisal of a given property. However, it is not always possible to obtain this contract date and the deed date is used instead. This date is preferred over the date the deed is recorded since several weeks may pass before a deed is recorded.

Perhaps the most confusing aspect in price adjustment due to lapse of time over either past or future years is attributable to *inflation*, i.e., changes in the purchasing power of the dollar. Assume that a property constructed twenty years ago for $40,000 sold today for $80,000. What has been the change in value? Certainly the price has risen to double the number of dollars; but if the purchasing power of the dollar has shrunk to 35 percent in the time interval, the value of the property today, assuming no depreciation, in terms of constant (uninflated) dollars is $28,000, showing a loss of 30 percent rather than an increase of 100 percent as indicated by inflated dollar prices. This illustration is intended to give emphasis to the economic truth that *market prices* merely provide a measure of the purchasing power of the money (dollars) paid. The economic impact of changes in the purchasing power of money can perhaps be better realized if a parallel situation could be visualized in a nonmonetary field of practice. Suppose that by governmental decree the number of inches in the standard measure of a foot were altered and thus varied from month to month or year to year. The resulting confusion in the construction industry would be almost incalculable. If 24 inches are finally accepted as the inflated parts of a "foot," does that make everyone twice as tall? Conversely, doubling all wages at times when all goods and services have doubled in price does not make a wage earner twice as rich. In effect such price inflation may harm the typical worker where his or her savings melt in power to exchange for other economic goods, and where lagging adjustment to income tax rates exact a higher levy through payroll deductions.

Fortunately, for the appraiser, where the task is to estimate value in *present* dollars, anticipated inflation is of little or no concern provided the sale of property is to be on a cash basis and the bundle of rights to be conveyed is

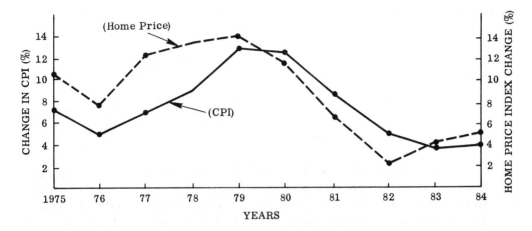

Figure 4.1   Consumer Price Index Versus Median Price of Home Sales

Source: *Federal Reserve Bulletin*, Table 2.14, "Housing and Construction," and Table 2.15, "Consumer and Producer Prices" (Washington, D.C.: Board of Governors, Federal Reserve System); and the U.S. Department of Labor.

typically unencumbered or unimpaired. Like ships which maintain their size and position no matter how high the waves rise, so unencumbered properties in a free economy should retain their purchasing-power position, unaffected by the rising or falling level of prices. During the seven-year period 1975–1982, the annual rate of increase of home prices outstripped the rate of inflation.

Figure 4.1 shows how the price of homes generally outpaced the rise in inflation over one period of time. An important point brought out by this chart is that the rate of value change varies from one period to another. Two other important value trends that are not revealed are that trends for one class of real estate do not necessarily apply to other classes or to other locations. The power of a good to command other goods in exchange, other things remaining equal, cannot logically be affected by inflation. Changes in the level of prices are only significant where they affect the equilibrium of supply and demand for given goods and services. This would occur where savings are wiped out or changes in the pattern of living are altered.

There are, however, circumstances and conditions when inflation, or the threat of it, is of serious concern to the appraiser. This would be the case where the property or its income cannot adjust itself as readily as a ship in a rising sea to changes in the level of prices. Under price or rent control, for instance, the income is "anchored," and rising price levels in effect economically diminish if not "drown" the power of that good to be exchanged for other goods which are free from such controls.

The relationship of changing (inflated) prices to value can effectively be demonstrated by comparing the price/value ratio of a property with the price/ value ratio of another commodity—let's say coffee—in times of inflation. Assuming, all else remaining equal, that the purchasing power of the dollar declined 33⅓ percent, and that as a consequence prices increased threefold, a valid comparison of the property—coffee value/price relationship would be as follows:

Year	Price of Property	Purchasing Power of Dollar in Terms of Coffee
19—	$ 50,000	$ 50,000 at $2.50 per lb obtains 20,000 lb
20 years later	$150,000	$150,000 at $7.50 per lb obtains 20,000 lb

As the table indicates, the price of the property increased in terms of dollars over a 20-year period from $50,000 to $150,000. A relative price change has also taken place with coffee, which went from $2.50 per pound to $7.50 per pound. Although prices for both goods increased 200 percent, the value relationship of one good to another remained the same. The property exchanged for 20,000 pounds of coffee now as it did 20 years ago. This is as it should be where prices of properties are economically free to adjust themselves. Under such circumstances the appraiser need not be concerned with inflation if charged to find present value in present dollars.

The impact of inflation on fixed income can effectively be demonstrated again by using the property–coffee relationship assuming, for purposes of this illustration, an 80 percent nonamortizing first mortgage on a residential property as follows:

Year	Price of Property	Purchasing Power of Dollar in Terms of Coffee
19—	$ 50,000 Total	$ 50,000 at $2.50 per lb obtains 20,000 lb
	40,000 Mortgage	40,000 at $2.50 per lb obtains 16,000 lb
	10,000 Equity	10,000 at $2.50 per lb obtains 4,000 lb
20 years later	$150,000 Total	$150,000 at $7.50 per lb obtains 20,000 lb
	40,000 Mortgage	40,000 at $7.50 per lb obtains 5,333 lb
	110,000 Equity	110,000 at $7.50 per lb obtains 14,667 lb

Here again the exchange value of the property as a whole in relation to coffee has not changed. The property commanded 20,000 pounds of coffee today as it did 20 years ago. The relative value position of the equity and mortgage interests, however, have been materially altered. Whereas the mortgagee could purchase 16,000 pounds of coffee with his holding 20 years ago, his interest today has shrunk to one-third, or 5,333 pounds. On the other hand, the equity interest has increased almost four times, from an equivalent purchasing power of 4,000 pounds of coffee 20 years ago to 14,667 pounds, today.

Whereas in an inflationary market, when prices move upward, purchasing power is shifted from the creditor or mortgagee to the debtor or the equity interests, the reverse takes place in a deflationary market when prices move downward.[1] To illustrate, again using the property–coffee price and value relationship—let's assume a decline in purchasing power from a base of 100 percent to a level of 80 percent. The relative mortgage–equity positions shift as follows:

Year	Price of Property	Purchasing Power of Dollar in Terms of Coffee
19—	$50,000 Total	$50,000 at $2.50 per lb obtains 20,000 lb
	40,000 Mortgage	40,000 at $2.50 per lb obtains 16,000 lb
	10,000 Equity	10,000 at $2.50 per lb obtains 4,000 lb
20 years later	$40,000 Total	$ 6,000 at $2.00 per lb obtains 20,000 lb
	40,000 Mortgage	6,000 at $2.00 per lb obtains 20,000 lb
	Zero Equity	Zero at $2.00 per lb obtains 0 lb

In the illustration above a modest decline of 20 percent in purchasing power caused a fixed debt in dollars to wipe out the equity interest completely, thus transferring value from the debtor to the creditor. During the severe depression in the years 1932–1935, nearly one-fifth of all residential homes in the United States were on the verge of foreclosure, necessitating federal banking and refinancing relief measures to bridge the deflationary gap. With monetary controls now firmly manipulated by federal agencies, deflation and economic busts may be experienced only rarely, but the threat of inflation, high interest rates, and shortages of investment capital are ever-present problems resulting in part from continuing large federal deficits.

In recent years (1973–1983), residential foreclosures have typically remained under 0.20 percent, rising above that level in late 1974 and early 1975 and again in 1982 and 1983.[2] Inflation was not the sole cause of the higher-than-usual rates of foreclosures started. Inflation rose at the rate of 12.2 percent annually in 1974, but fell to 7.0 percent in 1975, and subsided sharply to average 4.0 percent for 1982–1983. The appraiser must, therefore, consider the impact of changes in the level of prices and in the purchasing power of the dollar, and measure the impact on value where rentals or incomes are fixed or where a market comparison study involves sales which were transacted in diverse markets and at different levels of prices.

To summarize, inflation need not concern the appraiser so long as his task is to find value on a "cash" basis of unencumbered property in terms of *present* dollars. However, where the income is fixed or controlled—as may be the case under long-term leases or rent control, or where the property is en-

[1]This relationship does not hold true for adjustable-rate mortgages, which improve the mortgagee's financial position, sometimes causing negative amortization for the borrower. Also, some income participation loans for income properties distort this relationship.

[2]Mortgage Bankers Association of America, "Delinquency Rates of 1- to 4-Unit Residential Mortgage Loans" (seasonally adjusted), *National Delinquency Survey* (Washington, D.C.), quarterly.

cumbered by a mortgage and a split interest is to be appraised—the impact of inflation on risk of ownership must be given careful value consideration as well as the effect of unemployment, high interest rates, and other such influences on the risk and affordability of real estate ownership.[3]

INCOME AS A MEASURE OF VALUE

Although replacement cost under the theory of substitution establishes the ceiling of value, the lower limit of the value range is set by the present or discounted worth of the anticipated net income stream. Investors sometimes refer to these values as "physical value" and "economic value." If the former exceeds the value revealed by the discounted income stream by too great a margin, building costs may be excessive. It is assumed that this net income is reasonably obtainable from the improved property during its economic life span and under typical ownership. Income, therefore, especially for industrial and commercial properties, is an important index of value since income is essentially what an investor buys. Care must be taken to consider only income which is ascribable to the property under typical management. Income that is attributable to superior management or goodwill attaches to people or to the business and not to the property for which an estimate of value is sought. The technique of estimating income and the method of capitalizing it into a sum of present value will be discussed fully in Chapters 14 and 16 through 18. This chapter only introduces the basic principles underlying income forecasting.

Property income in previous references has been characterized as a "stream." The words "income stream" were deliberately chosen to create in the minds of both reader and appraiser a pictorial concept of the ups and downs of dynamic income productivity. Nothing is static, as the principle of change has taught us. Past income experiences may indicate a certain trend, and present income flow may substantiate this trend; nevertheless, the anticipated future income expectancy may radically differ on the basis of important changes in national, regional, and local business activity—of which the real estate market is a part. Income forecasting must not, however, be thought of as crystal ball gazing. The subject property in nearly all instances can be classified as belonging to a certain group of properties for which income experience data are known from prior appraisal analysis or from study data published by management, accounting, or appraisal institutes. If experience data are unobtainable from file or published sources, a rental or income flow study of similar, or *bench mark*, properties (comparable properties from which value indexes are derived) must be undertaken as a guide to income forecasting.

[3]This relationship continues today. Thomas B. Bohm and Joseph A. McKenzie report in "Inflation, Taxes, and the Demand for Housing," *Journal of the American Real Estate and Urban Economics Association* 10, no. 1 (Spring 1982), p. 33, that "inflation adversely affects the probability of home ownership and the amount of housing purchased."

The key income for appraisal purposes is usually *net operating income*, after all operating expenses and contingencies have been accounted for, but as a rule, before deductions are made for mortgage debt service. Also a deduction for accrued depreciation is not made either. This deduction is avoided under the assumption that tenants and landlords already have adjusted the rent in view of the present state of the property. This provision holds true in a determination of total accrued depreciation, but not in estimating the amount of *annual* provisions for future depreciation (recapture). If the recapture *rate* is known, this rate as part of the overall capitalization rate can be applied to the net operating income to determine the annual amount of recapture that should be subtracted from the net operating income to reveal the income left over for the land (I_L). Under this procedure, it would be necessary to separate income to land from income to building, as must be done whenever future depreciation or recapture is treated as a rate rather than as an operating expense under the income approach to value. To illustrate: When an appraiser estimates capital recapture at the rate of 2 percent per year and required earnings (excluding recapture) to be 8 percent per annum, a net operating income of $1,000 would yield a capitalized value of $10,000 ($1,000 ÷ 0.10). In selecting 10 percent as the overall rate of capitalization, the appraiser in effect estimates that 2 percent out of 10 percent or 20 (2 ÷ 10) percent of income represents recapture of capital and 80 percent of the remaining income a return on the invested capital. The income problem can now be restated as follows:

Net operating income	$1,000
Less recapture of capital	
2/10 or 20 percent =	200
Net income after recapture provision	$ 800
Value of property:	
$800 ÷ .08 =	$10,000

Thus whether the appraiser capitalizes $1,000 at 10 percent (8 percent income rate plus 2 percent recapture) or $800 at 8 percent (return on investment only) the estimate of value remains the same. The advantage of the expense method for the provision of recapture of depreciable property is that it conforms to investment practices followed by accountants, lawyers, income tax agents, and the investor for whom presumably the appraiser reports most of his estimated findings. Further and more detailed treatment of the subject of provision for capital recapture will be given in Chapter 16.

THE REAL ESTATE MARKET

To understand more fully the nature and predictability of property income, the appraiser must be aware of the peculiar characteristics of land and how these affect income and the market for real estate. Immobility, indestructibility, and nonhomogeneity of land cause the market for real estate to be *local* in character. As a commodity, real estate cannot be moved from place to place. An oversupply of land in one community cannot be used to balance an undersupply in another. Real estate must be employed where it is, and, because of its fixity in geographic location, it is extremely vulnerable to economic effects caused by shifts in local demand.

Land dissimilarity—nonhomogeneity—further imposes special market conditions. Because of location, no two parcels of real estate are physically alike. Each parcel is geographically fixed and has distinct legal descriptions which as a rule are accurately set forth in public plat book records. Since no one parcel of land may be legally substituted for another without the purchaser's consent, value considerations must reflect this market immobility.

The durability of real estate, too, causes maladjustments in both supply and demand on a local market level. Thus where demand for any reason suddenly falls, the inability to adjust supply will cause real estate prices to fall as well. An oversupply of real estate creates a buyer's market, which in turn results in lower price offerings and hence lower market values. A sudden increase in demand also is difficult to meet. The resultant scarcity causes market prices of realty to rise, creating an upward swing in the real estate cycle.

The appraiser must take great care to study objectively the underlying forces creating supply and demand for real property. Since value, by definition, is a measure of the present worth of future rights to income, temporary booms or depressions must be analyzed to determine their cause and to forecast their duration and effect on typical buyer-seller bargaining power. The real estate cycle, sometimes induced by land speculations, more often reflects the state of general business and housing or construction cycles. The business cycle operates on the demand side, positively or negatively, through increased or decreased overall employment, wage levels, supply of mortgage funds, interest rates, and personal savings. The construction or building cycle, on the other hand, operates on the supply side, reacting to population changes, family formation, vacancy ratios, and cost of land and housing supply in relation to prevailing and anticipated income or rental levels.

Though physically abundant, land which is economically usable is often in short supply. Improvements, in the form of access roads, drainage facilities, water, and other community utilities, must be added to raw land before it ordinarily can be subdivided and offered for sale through marketing channels. Because such improvements are costly and can be successfully carried out only with community sanction and on a relatively large scale, there often is a shortage of land that economically warrants being used. This lack of building sites in turn causes upward pricing of real estate holdings to a point where community development and real estate market activities may be adversely affected. On the other hand, speculative optimism, unchecked by community foresight and planning, may cause potentially valuable land to be developed in quantities too great to be absorbed by prevailing demand, thereby creating an oversupply which may depress the market for real estate for many months or even years.

There is a definite relationship between business booms and depressions on the one hand, and real estate market activity on the other. As a rule the downward swing of the real estate cycle precedes the downward swing of business activity caused by business recession, and lags long beyond the period of general business recovery. As economic adjustments or recessions cast their shadows, typical home and land buyers prefer to wait and to maintain a cash position during periods of adversity. In a like manner, when business recovery takes place, expenditures for fixed investments are undertaken only after all immediate needs for clothing, food, and other necessities are met. Thus the economic inflexibility of real estate as a commodity and its sensitivity to mortgage interest rates is directly accountable for the greater intensity of real estate booms and depressions and the longer life of the real estate cycle as compared with the normal upward and downward swing of general business activity. It is important, therefore, that the appraiser keep his finger on the pulse of business as well as on real estate market activities in order to forecast with reasonable accuracy shifts in market conditions and changes in the anticipated income flow that forms, for a given property and at a given time, the basis of real estate value. The impact of social, political, and economic forces on the market for real estate from a national, state, and community level will be discussed at length in the succeeding chapters.

REVIEW QUESTIONS

1. Why is "replacement cost" favored by appraisers over "reproduction cost" as an initial measure of value?
2. Explain the conditions that must be checked for a sale property before using it as an indication of market value.
3. How can the date of sale of a comparable sale property distort the indicated market value of an appraised property?
4. Discuss how the relative values of the debt and equity positions change in an inflationary environment.
5. Why is a deduction made for accrued depreciation in the cost approach but not in the income approach?
6. Identify the different activities that prevail during the business cycle and the building cycle.
7. Define (a) value, (b) price, (c) cost, and (d) warranted cost.
8. Mr. Baker is asked by his employer to appraise a combination garage and loft building which the owner has offered as security for a $60,000 loan. Mr. Baker proceeds to the site and after careful, detailed inspection estimates that the depreciated replacement cost of this structure plus the site value is $75,000. He reports his valuation and recommends that based on this security, the loan be granted. Do you agree with Mr. Baker? State your reasons.

READING AND STUDY REFERENCES

CARPENTER, MICHAEL D., and DONALD S. SHAN-NON. "The Effect of Inflation on Value," *The Real Estate Appraiser and Analyst* 47, no. 1 (First Quarter 1981), pp. 51–55.

CASE, FRED E. "The Value of a Thing Is the Price It Will Bring," *American Real Estate and Urban Economics Association Journal*, 7 no. 2 (Summer 1979), pp. 265–268.

FRIEDMAN, JACK P., and NICHOLAS ORDWAY. "Real Estate Markets," *Income Property Appraisal and Analysis*. Reston, Va.: Reston Publishing Co., Inc., 1981, pp. 5–8.

LUSHT, KENNETH M. "Most Probable Selling Price,"

The Appraisal Journal 51, no. 3 (July 1983), pp. 346–354.

RATCLIFF, RICHARD U. "Capitalized Income Is Not Market Value," *The Appraisal Journal* 36, no. 1 (January 1968), pp. 33–41.

RATCLIFF, RICHARD U. Chapter 5, "Cost and Depreciation in Price Prediction," *Valuation for Real Estate Decisions*. Santa Cruz, Calif.: Democrat Press, 1972, pp. 94–116.

THOMAS, JAMES G. "The Influence of Environmental Legislation on the Appraisal Process," *The Appraisal Journal* 46, no. 1 (January 1978), pp. 26–31.

SECTION II   External Influences on Property Value

5

IMPACT OF POLITICAL, SOCIAL, AND ECONOMIC FORCES

Learning Objectives
After reading this chapter, you should be able to:

Appreciate the influences on property value resulting from regional, national, and international political, social, and economic forces

Realize how governmental intervention in the economy has both positively and negatively affected real estate markets

Understand the demographic changes and population shifts that have occurred in the United States and their effect on real estate

Discuss how the "political climate" of a state or region within a state can influence economic development

Every parcel of land located anywhere within the United States, no matter how small its dimensions, is subject to political, social, and economic forces which influence its value. In fact, the general forces that influence property values on a local level increasingly come from beyond the borders of our country. Not only are these three forces important to real estate as viewed in the traditional local sense, but increasingly, national and international events have a strong influence on the demand for and value of real estate in local communities. Often it is difficult to distinguish between these forces. For example, a civil war in some foreign country may have an adverse economic impact in the United States. The same cause–effect relationship is true of international politics and economics.

Up until 1973 the United States maintained a very favorable trade balance with its trading partners. But in that year, the Organization of Petroleum

Exporting Countries (OPEC) pushed the price of exported petroleum up to unprecedented levels. The beginning of massive trade deficits began as well as a real estate operating costs soared. The latter factor affected the income and value of oil-heated real estate.

Breaking down racial and sex barriers has greatly broadened employment and housing opportunities for racial minorities and women. The results have been to expand the market for real estate and to make it easier for both of these groups to purchase more expensive and presumably valuable housing. Another social change has been the growing mobility of our population and a resulting greater emphasis on maintenance-free housing. The advent of more two-spouse wage-earning households has further reinforced the market for convenience-designed, smaller homes (often apartments) as well as a stronger demand for recreational properties.

A strong, and not yet fully appreciated political–economic relationship was the phasing out of interest-rate ceilings among savings institutions in 1980. Historically, savings and loan associations held a $1/4$ of 1 percent rate advantage over commercial banks on their savings accounts—but both were subject to interest rate ceilings. The unfortunate result often was that depositors were withdrawing funds when higher yields became available elsewhere. Further deregulation and broadened lending powers were given S&Ls under the 1982 Garn–St. Germain Depository Institutions Act. It is conjectured that the result of the deregulation will reduce the irregular nature of savings and loans' capital flows. However, the higher interest now permitted on savings and money market certificates may push mortgage interest rates to higher levels. The result could unfavorably affect the affordability of real estate, especially housing.

Of course, it is not the appraiser's opinion that counts, but rather the actions of buyers and sellers as reflected by the opinion of political and economic experts who study market operations and who make it their business to publish the effects of world trends and shifts in international relations. A number of national services and others in related economic fields keep an ear to the international ground, warning their readers of probable coming events and their consequent effects on the value of real property. In every valuation it is the appraiser's duty to stipulate whether the value reported does or does not reflect possible and impending changes in international relations and, if so, to what degree and amount. The client or reader of the appraisal report is then in a position to make his or her own value adjustments based on personal observation of market operations and his investment risk position.

POLITICAL FORCES INFLUENCING VALUE

Under our allodial system of property ownership (as opposed to state or feudal control of land and land improvements) property values are derived from property rights. Although these private rights are constitutionally guaranteed to the fee owner they are nevertheless subject to important modification by legislative, executive, and judicial action. Even the form of government and the underlying philosophy guiding political leadership can influence market operations and investment choices made by individuals or corporations. In the USSR and the other communist-controlled nations of Europe and Asia, for example, ownership of land was seized in the name of the "people," and private rights and value in realty for these nations have been liquidated as a result of communist political policy.

In the United States, Great Britain, and many western European nations, attempts have been made to transfer to the state or nation the value increments in land which—as claimed—unjustly accrue to private owners. The so-called unearned land value increment theory reached its popular peak with the effective writing of the American economist Henry George, who in his book *Progress and Poverty*, published in 1879, suggested the "single-tax" remedy whereby value increments in land created by community life and action could be returned to the "people," from whence it came. In America, adherents of the single-tax doctrine made a concerted and powerful effort to have this socialistic theory implemented by legislative action. Since the power to tax, in the hands of unwise or biased government, is tantamount to the power to destroy property values, special safeguards are provided in the U.S. Constitution (the Fifth and Fourteenth Amendments) and by statutory law in the various states to protect property owners.

The political attitude and national policy toward home ownership, urban revitalization, and public housing is also of interest to the appraiser, since changes in national policy as expressed in housing legislation have a direct and often significant effect on property values. To illustrate, passage of the Home Owners Loan Corporation Act as an emergency measure by Congress to prevent disastrous and large-scale mortgage foreclosures during the depression years of 1932–1935 stabilized the real estate market and prevented foreclosure action for about four out of five home borrowers who sought the Corporation's aid. Enactment of rent control during World Wars I and II prevented runaway prices threatened by war-induced home scarcities and limitations of home construction. Retention of rent control, however, beyond the period of an emergency—for political rather than economic purposes—depresses values of property so affected and discourages investment in rental real estate wherever such controls are still operative, as in New York City or overseas in France, Italy, and England to this day. The chronology of events typically associated with rent control has been: (1) the quality of housing suffers and the quantity is reduced; (2) the private ownership sector withdraws; and (3) the government (using tax dollars) attempts to provide replacement housing.[1]

Urban renewal legislation provides a direct subsidy by the federal gov-

---

[1]James H. Boykin, "Mortgage Usury Ceilings—Statutory Denial of Home Ownership," *Real Estate Issues* 5, no. 1 (Summer 1980), p. 45. See also Ron Utt, "Rent Control: History's Unlearned Lesson," *Real Estate Review* (Spring 1978), pp. 87–91.

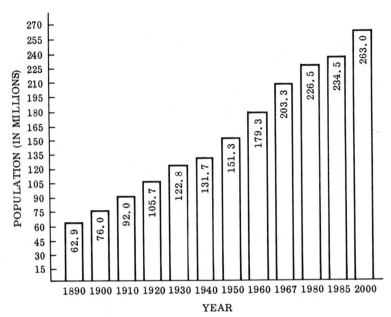

Figure 5.1 Population Growth in the United States

Source: U.S. Department of Commerce, Bureau of the Census, *Statistical Abstract of the United States 1982–83*.

ernment to a given county or city government and indirectly contributes to the enhancement of values of property located adjacent to or in the immediate vicinity of rehabilitated areas. A boon to private rehabilitation of older city properties came about in the mid-1970s when the federal income tax laws were changed. It became profitable to upgrade underutilized and vacant properties. In turn, investors returned to our cities in search of profitable ventures with whole districts often being rehabilitated. Often new uses were created for apparently obsolete structures.

The significant increase in homeownership and home construction everywhere in the United States is directly traceable, in a large measure, to federal financing aids and fiscal policy controls. The Federal Housing Administration and the Veterans' Administration loan programs are largely responsible for the increase in home ownership and home construction during the two decades following World War II. Later, with the advent of the high-loan-to-value conventional loan made possible through use of private mortgage insurance, the market share of these two federal agencies waned. These loan programs, too, have encouraged suburban land development and have thus brought about a shift of urban land values from the central city to outlying residential areas. Government fiscal policies and their effect on money interest rates also must be watched closely by the real estate appraiser in order to measure the effect of rate changes on value of income-producing real property. As a rule, changes in the rate of interest or interest rate structure have an inverse relationship to real property values. A rise in the rate of interest lowers property value, and a fall, for instance, in rates is reflected in higher value. This is due to the direct relationship which income bears to value, with the interest rate serving as leverage for conversion of income into value. For example, a $1,000 income in perpetuity at 10 percent interest is worth $10,000 ($10,000 at 10 percent equals $1,000); whereas a rate of 5 percent interest produces double the value ($20,000 at 5 percent equals $1,000). Moreover, rising interest rates discourage the sale of residential property and cause price concessions. Income property, with an increased mortgage debt burden produces a lower income and in turn a lower value.

SOCIAL FORCES INFLUENCING VALUE

Since people create value it is important to keep abreast of changes in the number, age and income distribution, and household sizes of the total population. A vigorous growth and a positive trend in the national population may not necessarily be reflected in an equally beneficial population pattern on a state or local level. Nevertheless, the impact of local population forces cannot be effectively understood or interpreted unless the national pattern is used as a background for growth comparison. As shown by the chart in Figure 5.1, the total U.S. population steadily increased from approximately 62.9 million in 1890 to 226.5 million in 1980. The forecast for total population by the year 2000 is 263.8 million. This increase of over 163 million people during the past 90 years is also reflected in the increase in population per square mile of land from 21.2 persons in 1890, to 64.0 persons in 1980.

Even more important from a real estate valuation perspective is where this growth has occurred. In the past 40 years, for example, our nation's population has become more urbanized. Where 53 percent of the total U.S. population lived in metropolitan areas in 1940, by 1980 this share had risen to 75 percent. Moreover, during this same period, the share of land area more than doubled in these metropolises (going from 7 percent to 16 percent).[2] The remarkable fact revealed is that three-quarters of the nation's population is housed on just 16 percent of our land. Another important point can be drawn from this trend—population growth creates demand for real estate, which in turn increases the value for vacant land and improved land alike.

Another important influence on real estate demand and its value is the differences in regional population growth patterns. In the last century, and even up through the 1940s, there were huge migrations of population from the rural south to northern and north-central cities. Generally, the motivating force was jobs in these highly industrialized regions. More recently, and certainly in the 1970s, this trend was reversed. As shown in Table 5.1, population shifts were

[2]U.S. Department of Commerce, Bureau of the Census, *Statistical Abstract of the United States 1982–83*, Table 15, p. 14.

Table 5.1 Interregional Migration (Thousands)

	REGION			
Date	Northeast	North-central	South	West
1970–1975	– 1,342	– 1,195	+ 1,829	+ 708
1975–1980	– 1,486	– 1,173	+ 1,764	+ 893

SOURCE: *U.S. Statistical Abstract of the United States* 1982–83, U.S. Department of Commerce, Bureau of the Census, Table 13, p. 14.

from the northeast and north-central regions to the South and West. Moreover, the moves, in all regions except the West, have tended to be from cities to suburbs and nonmetropolitan areas. Although, as stated previously, a greater proportion of the nation's population now live in metropolitan areas, an increasing proportion of that population lives in the suburbs instead of cities. Not only have there been these population shifts, but over the past 190 years, there has been a continual westward movement, as shown in Figure 5.2.

Although the concentration of people took place largely in metropolitan areas, the overall increase in population is nevertheless remarkably related to an increase in the value of all U.S. lands. Over the years, the net increase in U.S. land values generally has been directly proportional to the rise in the overall

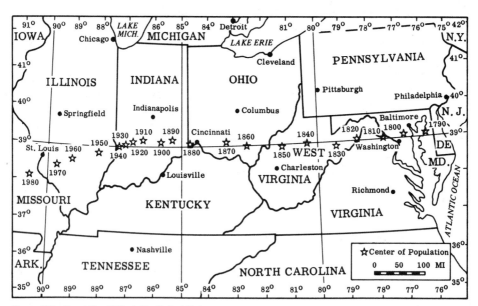

Figure 5.2 Population Shifts in the United States

For dates of admission of the states and changes in areal definition, see "State Origins and Boundaries," *United States Summary, U.S. Census of Population: 1960*, Vol. I. For year of admission to statehood, see Table 338.
Source: U.S. Bureau of the Census, *Census of Population: 1970*, vol. I.

population shown in Figure 5.1. The significance of the population–value relationship is thus of prime importance, and must be considered carefully in appraising the impact on the value of a given property of general economic forces anticipated for future years.

Another significant trend which is important to the appraiser is the steadily increasing demand for dwelling units per 1,000 population as shown in Table 5.2. Dwelling units increased from 12.69 million in 1890, to 88,207 million in 1980—or by 695 percent—compared with an increase in population of 360 percent for the same period. This housing demand, brought about by increasing divorces, delayed birth of children, more single-person households and "undoubling" (where two or more families were living together) has reduced the average population—as shown in Table 5.2—from 4.93 persons per dwelling unit in 1890, to 2.76 persons per dwelling unit in 1980. In effect this means that whereas 493 persons exerted a demand for 100 dwelling units in 1890, the same number of persons demanded and occupied 180 dwelling units in 1980. Even if no growth in population had taken place during the past 91 years, housing on the basis of changes in family formation alone would have increased by over 80 percent. Since the trend toward smaller families is expected to continue, this factor also must be considered in the appraisal of real property, especially in areas where high standards of living prevail.

Another factor of increasing importance in the evaluation of general forces which affect changes in property values is the longevity of life as reflected in the changing age composition of the U.S. population. People not only live longer but, through pension, Medicare and social security plans, are economically and medically better cared for. These aging citizens demand independent dwelling units in increasing numbers, most often seeking retirement opportunities in geographic areas where mild climate keeps housing and related costs at a minimum. As a result, Sunbelt states such as California, Arizona, New Mexico, and

Table 5.2 Total Dwelling Units in the United States, 1890–1980

Year	Dwelling Units (Thousands)	Population per Dwelling Unit
1890	12,690	4.93
1900	15,964	4.76
1910	20,256	4.54
1920	24,352	4.34
1930	29,905	4.11
1940	34,949	3.77
1950	42,857	3.37
1960	58,326	3.33
1970	68,672	3.14
1980	88,207	2.76

SOURCE: U.S. Department of Commerce, Bureau of the Census, *Population Series Reports*, 1960; and *Current Population Reports*, Series P-20, No. 116.

Florida have experienced during recent years greater than average population gains, which have been directly reflected in rapidly advancing market activity and prices of real property. Whereas 6.8 percent of the total U.S. population was 65 years old and over in 1940 (9.0 million persons), this percentage of senior citizens increased to 11.4 percent by the year 1981 (26.2 million).

GENERAL ECONOMIC FORCES INFLUENCING VALUE

Since real estate activity, property price levels, and real estate values are directly influenced by the general economic activity and economic well-being of the country as a whole, the appraiser must be seriously concerned with the general economic forces which influence value. Important indexes that should be observed as a barometer of general economic progress include the following:

> Gross national product.
> Per capita income and real wage levels.
> Unemployment as a measure of full employment.
> Personal savings and investments.
> General business and real estate activity.

Although all the above are related as measures of economic well-being, the year-to-year variations, or lag of one index as compared with another, may provide an important clue to anticipated changes in general economic activities which are bound to influence the value of real property. The measure most widely used as a yardstick for economic progress in the United States is the gross national product (GNP), which aggregates in dollars the annual value of all goods and services produced, consumed, saved, and invested by individuals, business corporations, and government operations. Using 1940 as a base, the GNP has grown from 99.7 billion dollars in that year to 2937.7 billion in 1981. The percentage growth in economic activity from year to year over the 41 years may be observed by study of the chart in Figure 5.3. Attention is called to the fact that general economic activity prior to and during war conflicts is accelerated, and that readjustments following a war cause overall business operations and consumptions to decline. The rise in the GNP from 1946 through 1980 also reflects rising prices caused by dollar inflation and a consequent loss in the purchasing power of the dollar of 85 percent during this time period. The experienced rate of economic progress in constant dollars has averaged 2.7 percent per year over the past decade despite declines in 1973–1974 and again in 1980. Growth at this level over the coming decade depends largely upon the relationship of the political, social, and economic forces discussed earlier in this chapter.

Per capita income and changing level of real wages provide another and more refined measure of economic well-being as seen from the consumer's point of view. Although overall dollar productivity for the country as a whole is of

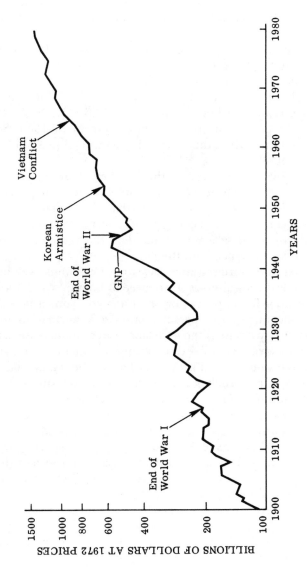

Figure 5.3 Gross National Product—United States

prime importance, the appraiser must temper his value conclusions for given types of real property in accordance with the distribution of this total income flow to the factors of production, including tax payments to government. The steadily rising standard of living is a direct result of increasing productivity and wage increases. Personal income (income before state and federal taxes) has risen from 402 billion dollars in 1960, to 2,160 billion dollars in 1980. This constitutes an increase of 537.3 percent. In constant dollars, based on the purchasing power of the dollar in 1972, the increase is 96.8 percent. Personal income has in effect almost doubled over this 20-year period. It is this continuing rise in the financial well-being of individuals that largely accounts for the significant increase in the number of homeowners from 43.6 percent of all dwelling units in 1940, to 61.9 percent in 1960, to 65.6 percent in 1980. Some observers conjecture that in the future this level of homeownership is not likely to increase significantly, if at all.

This significant increase in the number of owner-occupied dwellings, when coupled with the continual growth in total population, presages a continued and increasing demand for desirable suburban sites suitable for residential and commercial development. As a consequence, overall land values are expected to increase in future years at a rate faster than the value of goods and services invested in the improvements on the land.

Another and more sensitive measure of economic well-being that is important to property appraisers is the degree of unemployment in relation to the total available labor force. Accepting labor analysts' conclusions that labor turnover and willfully unemployed persons comprise a "normal" unemployment rate of approximately 2 percent of the total labor force, an increase in the percentage of idle workers above this rate—discounting seasonal unemployment—will adversely affect the value of real property. This is understandable, since expenditures for ownership of shelter are less important for subsistence than outlays for food and clothing. There is a direct correlation between unemployment, property foreclosures, and property tax delinquencies. When unemployment reached the peak of 24.9 percent of the civilian labor force in 1933, property values also hit the century's lowest ebb; and, as pointed out, government emergency laws were passed to create a debt moratorium to halt the avalanche of foreclosures. In recent years, unemployment has fluctuated from a low of 3.5 percent in 1969 to a high of 9.7 percent in 1982. These changes in the level of unemployment are of national concern because they are accompanied by changes in economic progress and rates of increase in land values throughout the nation. Thus the appraiser should reflect in his or her value estimates the prospect for property demands as based on a forecast of the health of the labor-consumer market as a whole.

Investor confidence and national economic stability can also be judged by the amount of personal savings as related to total disposable personal income after all taxes. Patterns of expenditures change, as does consumer saving philosophy; hence the importance of time preference in consumption. The cause

Table 5.3 Personal Savings as Percent of Total Disposable Income, 1940–1983 (Billions of Dollars)

Year	Disposable Personal Income	Personal Outlays	Personal Savings	Savings as Percent of Income
1940	75.7	71.8	3.9	5.1
1945	150.2	120.7	29.5	19.7
1950	206.9	193.9	13.0	6.3
1955	275.3	259.5	15.8	5.7
1960	352.0	332.3	19.7	5.6
1965	475.8	442.1	33.7	7.1
1970	695.3	639.5	55.8	8.0
1975	1,096.1	1,001.8	94.3	8.6
1980	1,824.1	1,717.9	106.2	5.8
1983	2,340.1	2,222.0	118.1	5.0

SOURCE: *Economic Report of the President*, transmitted to the Congress, Bureau of the Census, February 1968; U.S. Department of Commerce, *Statistical Abstract of the United States 1982–83*, 1982; and U.S. Department of Commerce, *Survey of Current Business 64*, no. 11 (November 1984), p. S-1.

for a decreasing rate of personal savings should be carefully analyzed, for a continued downward trend in savings will decrease investment capital and hence the demand for and value of real property. The percentage relationship of personal savings to disposable personal income for selected years since 1940 is shown in Table 5.3.

Although no fixed percentage of savings to disposable income is recommended as an optimum guide to capital reinvestment, it is apparent that venture capital is dependent on this source for capital funds. A continued rate of savings below 5 percent may foreshadow insufficient capital formation to maintain modern industry, causing our nation to be noncompetitive in a worldwide economy with a resulting rising level of unemployment. An increase, however, in the annual rate of savings above 7 percent may prove equally disconcerting if the increased thrift reflects *underconsumption* or lack of investor confidence in the economic progress and stability of the United States. In any case, changes in this index as a barometer of economic climate call for analysis and value interpretation by professional real estate appraisers.

A composite of all the forces that motivate economic activity within a nation is reflected in the position of the business cycle that measures the intensity of general business operations. A historical study of business cycles in the United States discloses a rhythmic recurrence of business booms and depressions to such a degree that economic forecasts on the basis of past experience with a high degree of accuracy were deemed possible. The Cleveland Trust Company has made studies of general business activity since the year 1850, and has computed business indexes in relation to a "norm" of business activity. A review of their published cyclical business behavior supports the contention that under normal unimpeded economic behavior in a capitalistic nation, business reflects consumer and investor cycles of optimism, overoptimism, caution, or pessimism. Cyclical business behavior, it seems, is attributable to violations of the economic laws of supply and demand and the lack of central business control. In studying past cyclical behavior of business activity to forecast future business operations, the appraiser must keep in mind that in recent years federal government controls have successfully counteracted adverse economic behavior and, with varying degrees of success, have revitalized business operations by means of pump-priming government expenditures in a vast variety of public construction projects and general improvements. The necessity for increased government action is a sign of maladjustment in the private sector of the national economy, and requires careful attention by the real estate appraiser translating the impact of the general national economy, especially in times of extreme booms or depressions affecting real estate activity on a regional, state, and local level.

STATE OR REGIONAL FORCES INFLUENCING VALUE

The same pattern of statistical analysis which guides the real estate appraiser in interpreting the value influence of general forces on a national level should be used in the analysis of state or regional forces which influence property values. Here again the nature, character, and comparative general quality of social, political, and economic forces must be carefully studied and interpreted as a basis for reaching a professionally sound and reliable value conclusion. This is not to suggest that the appraiser conduct a state or regional analysis for every appraisal report. Instead, it implies that there should be a continual awareness of such value-influencing trends.

Unless the population within a state or region increases as favorably as that of the nation as a whole, local property values will reflect—on a broad level—the area's retarded growth. The center of population within the continental United States has steadily shifted west by southwest since the formation of this country. A continued rapid population increase in states such as California, Arizona, New Mexico, and Florida seems assured as long as people and industry, aided by advances in rapid transportation and electric power, seek milder climates and areas where natural resources can more advantageously be exploited. Accelerated growth in these states by necessity is accomplished at the expense of a decelerated growth—if not a decline—of population in other states and regions. Thus, though the nation as a whole may experience a favorable growth in total population, care must be taken to relate this growth to regional prospects and developments.

Although for the country as a whole total population was used as a measure of growth significance, the population analysis of a state or region must give greater emphasis to population quality and characteristics. The influx of people aged 60 and over in search of retirement homes, for example, may create economic problems that far outweigh the economic benefits which normally accrue from favorable immigration. With the aid of federal and state census data, appraisers should keep abreast of population changes and interpret for their clients the long-term effects of regional population trends on the value of real property. Several useful federal sources of population and other data are listed at the end of the chapter.

Equally important as a population factor affecting the value of real properties is the political climate in which people and industry find opportunity to prosper. Many states have passed legislation—often by constitutional referendum—to favor business, industry, or resident homeowners in order to spur state economic growth. The relatively simple and economically favorable laws of incorporation in Delaware, the homestead exemption tax law of Florida, and freedom from state income taxes in Maine and other states are instances where the law has been designed to foster state growth and development. In some states, however, what once was considered beneficial to a growing economy may prove in later years an investment handicap—even a financial burden—to a more mature economy. The rent control laws still in effect under state law in New York City and Chicago discouraged apartment developments for years until such laws—at least for new construction—were made inapplicable. The homestead tax exemption law in Florida, too, has long since outlived its economic usefulness, and the revenue burden which this law places on populous counties often necessitates oppressive indirect and business taxation to offset this outdated legislation.

Since property values reflect the present worth of *future* benefits, the appraiser must not only analyze the nature and character of present state laws and the quality of government but he must interpret the trend of government and legislation for better or worse in the years to come. The stability and quality of government, as will be demonstrated in subsequent chapters, is directly reflected in the rate of interest at which capital for investment purposes becomes available. The higher this rate of interest, as a rule, the greater the risk of investment ownership and hence the lower the investment value for a given anticipated flow of income dollars.

The current economic status and prospects for anticipated economic development must also be given careful attention. To judge effectively the economic status of a given state or region, the appraiser must gather for ready reference and use in his or her office or appraisal plant statistical data from which comparative value judgment conclusions can be drawn. The importance of the state or region to the economy of the nation as a whole should be ascertained. To what extent is dollar or resource competition threatened? Is the state economy sufficiently diversified to withstand rapid technological changes in production and marketing demands? The economic hardships of the "cotton" South, the "shipping" Northeast, the "corn-belt" Midwest, the "cattle" Southwest, and the coal mining and steel smelting regions of the country are still fresh enough in memory to serve as vivid reminders that the principle of change is ever active. No appraiser can hazard a judgment based on an extension of the status quo. Unless a state or region is strong enough to resist strains of powerful economic readjustments caused by changes in technology—as, for example, having the resources to adjust itself to new developments in atomic energy and space—the remaining economic life of property because of anticipated obsolescence is shortened. The possible loss of future productive income years is translated, of course, into lower property values by informed investment buyers.

It is the appraiser's responsibility to gather pertinent social, political, and economic data on a national, state, or regional level, and to interpret the meaning of such data in the light of action taken by *typical* buyers and sellers in the marketplace. Generally, the appraiser should decide whether the outlook for real estate investment over the years to come is good, bad, or uncertain. Data should then be supplied to support the appraiser's conclusions and to aid the reader of the valuation report in reaching his or her own value judgment where circumstances warrant subjective rather than objective considerations.

REVIEW QUESTIONS

1. How has the reduction of racial and sex discrimination barriers affected real estate demand and values?
2. Discuss the likely sequence of events of municipal rent control laws.
3. Briefly describe the changes that have occurred in household size in this country. How have these trends affected the demand for housing?
4. How can the rate of savings eventually influence the well-being of a nation?
5. List the probable advantages and disadvantages of deregulation of savings and loan associations with regard to housing.
6. List and discuss the implications of the apparent leveling off in the rate of homeownership, including those given in the chapter and any that you may think of.
7. Can zoning regulations prevent value decline in residential districts? Discuss.

READING AND STUDY REFERENCES

BAXTER, CHERYL. "The Impact of Government Policies and Programs on Land Values," *The Real Estate Appraiser and Analyst* 45, no. 3 (May–June 1979), pp. 42–45.

'84 SAVINGS and LOAN SOURCEBOOK. Chicago: United States League of Savings Institutions, 1984.

PLATTNER, ROBERT H. "Regional Migration: Its Impact on Land Use," *The Real Estate Appraiser and Analyst* 49, no. 2 (Summer 1983), pp. 5–12.

PUTH, ROBERT C. *American Economic History.* Hinsdale, Ill.: The Dryden Press, 1982.

SCHUSSHEIM, MORTON J. "The Impact of Demographic Change on Housing and Community Development," *The Appraisal Journal* 52, no. 3 (July 1984), pp. 375–381.

U.S. BUREAU OF THE CENSUS. *Census of Retail Trade* (every five years, by groups of counties). Washington, D.C.: U.S. Government Printing Office.

U.S. BUREAU OF THE CENSUS. *Characteristics of Population* (every 10 years, by counties). Washington, D.C.: U.S. Government Printing Office.

U.S. BUREAU OF THE CENSUS. *Housing Authorized by Building Permits and Public Contracts* (monthly, by individual places). Washington, D.C.: U.S. Government Printing Office.

U.S. BUREAU OF THE CENSUS. *Housing Characteristics for States, Cities and Counties* (every 10 years, by large areas and SMSAs), Washington, D.C.: U.S. Government Printing Office.

6

REGIONAL AND COMMUNITY ANALYSIS

Learning Objectives

After reading this chapter, you should be able to:

Appreciate the relationship of regional and community analysis in the valuation of real estate

Understand the motivation for the settlement of villages and how many of these same forces influence urban spatial layout today

Discuss the urban growth models and their relevance to anticipating future growth trends

Explain the fundamental principles of the economic base theory

Discuss the economic measures of community growth

There are several key factors that the appraiser must keep in mind when appraising real property. One is that all parts of the property analysis must lead toward a clear and convincing conclusion of (1) the highest and best use, and (2) the value of the appraised property. As the regional and community analysis is undertaken, the appraiser needs to be a bit of a skeptic, continually raising the question "Does this information assist me in arriving at the highest and best use and value of the appraised property?" If not, then, however interesting the data may be, they should be discarded and the appraiser's efforts redirected to uncover information that will shed light on these two key issues. Another important concern is to ascertain the social, political, and economic implications of the region and community as related to the appraised property's attractiveness and value. Too often there is a tendency to "plug in" irrelevant data simply because it permits the appraiser to quickly complete the regional analysis section. Again, if the information provides no insight as to a property's highest and best use and value, there is no reason for it to be included. It simply clutters the report, increases the cost of the appraisal service, and causes many clients to scoff at the inclusion of superfluous information that has no practical value for business decision making.

There is no set way of analyzing a region and community for all classes of property or for all valuation purposes. The nature of the property and assignment dictate the geographic breadth of regional analysis as well as the intensity with which such analysis is pursued. For example, the appraisal of a single-family residence does not involve consideration of the same regional forces as an appraisal of a factory. Residential value is governed strongly by community and neighborhood concerns. The industrial property value also may be influenced by neighborhood factors, but its value is tied to a larger extent to regional influences such as employment, access to materials, transportation, and markets.

CAUSES OF URBANIZATION

If we are to consider the effects of regional forces on real estate values, we should understand why people have come together to form villages, towns, and cities over the years. We should also understand the spatial evolution and growth of cities. Initially, there was the *tribe*, which, in its earliest stages, was nomadic rather than agrarian. The size of an area controlled by a tribe was a function of its ability to defend it. Later, tribal communities were faced with three choices for survival:

1. Migrate to newer and better hunting grounds.
2. Split the tribe and part of the members move to another place (this same practice was later employed in the Roman city-states).
3. All remain in the same place—with agriculture then becoming the principal vocation rather than relying on hunting as previously.

Villages grew from the third option first. The key to growth of the village was the ability of those who tilled the soil to produce and store and trade the surplus. This specialization of labor freed others to pursue different trades. In fact, this period might be thought of as the beginning of job specialization. Even in these early days of settlement, villages were transitory due to soil and game depletion. Settlers moved every 20 years or so. The size of villages was largely determined by the distance which water could be carried. During this period, more productive plant cultivation and animal domestication occurred, allowing for more permanent settlements.

The next type of human settlement was the *pre-industrial city*, where several different modes of development occurred. During this era, villages and then later medieval cities were created essentially for reasons of government, commerce, culture, religion, courts, and mutual protection.

During the Industrial Revolution (the steam age), greater specialization and subdivision of work occurred. Factories were developed with the wealthy living nearby, often a convenient carriage drive away. The poor lived farther away, sometimes beyond the safety of the walled city. Later, as transportation and communication facilities improved, the wealthy moved to outlying areas and the poor migrated to points within walking distance of factories.

In ancient times the location of cities such as Rome on its seven hills and Paris on an island were chosen largely for defense. In this country examples of such defense settlements or fort communities were Fort Pitt (Pittsburgh), Nashborough (later named Nashville), and Savannah. Trade routes—the lines of least resistance between the sources of products and their final markets—in all ages have prompted commercial cities to situate at places where a break in transportation occurred, such as on rivers and at harbors, breaks in mountain chains, and at the fall line of rivers. The confluence of rivers or the interesection of a river with a bay has also influenced the founding of cities. A favorable elevation has caused cities to be built. Memphis is such an example. The intersection of plains with mountains requires a change in modes of transportation. Cities such as Milan and Munich have developed at such places. Proximity to raw materials has prompted the settlement of many cities, such as Saginaw and Seattle, with proximity to forests or Los Angeles and San Jose, near orchards. Water power, sufficient to generate electricity, has created many cities, such as Fall River and Lowell in New England. Political seats have created other cities, such as Washington, D.C. River cities tend to flourish where there is deep water sufficient for barge transportation.

Comparative Advantage

David Ricardo is credited with articulating the concept of comparative advantage. He argued that economic specialization between countries explained why some areas produced a limited number of goods and then imported other complementary goods. Although comparative advantage cannot always be isolated to a single factor, some of the initial reasons that villages and, later, cities were developed were based on their inhabitants trying to gain an advantage or to make their lives more pleasant by taking advantage of natural resources, climate, and rivers as a source of transportation and power.

City Spatial Form and Growth

Several theories have been set forth over the years to explain the physical form of cities. The balance of this section will identify some of the key urban growth models. These growth theories, for the most part, are static in nature and do not fully explain all the variations of urban growth. Nevertheless, an understanding of these theories is helpful in gaining a better insight into why urban areas have developed as they have over the years. Also, it allows the appraiser to more accurately forecast the probable future nature and rate of urban development.

Concentric Ring Growth Theory

Ernest W. Burgess developed the concentric ring theory of growth in the 1920s.[1] This static model of urban growth can be challenged as to its inability to explain fully contemporary city growth. It is overly simplistic in its giving the appearance that there are distinct zones. Yet this spatial development model gives appraisers systematic means for analyzing growth patterns of a metropolis.

To some extent all cities have grown in a circular fashion except as inhibited by physical, social, or political forces. This circular growth is the result of the maximum land use activities being contained within a minimum surface area. Moreover, transportation routes can be minimized through this form of spatial development. Land use activities throughout a city generally follow some logical pattern. The appraiser should seek this pattern in anticipating the sustained productivity and value of properties.

Burgess divided his model city into fixed zones as shown in Figure 6.1. His model oversimplified actual growth patterns since the various zones would be irregular in shape. The center (or ring 1) is the financial and office district and the retail shopping zone. Generally, the central business district (CBD) forms the central point of this inner zone. It is located at the point with convenient access to people from throughout the city. Burgess recognized the likelihood of satellite business centers, which developed independently of the central business district. These subcenters were generally located at or near subway railroad stations or intersecting points between principal highways.

The transition zone is the second ring, adjacent to the central business zone but usually not entirely encircling it. Scattered throughout this zone are old residential dwellings that form the residential section of an earlier and smaller city. This district provided housing for immigrants until they were financially able to move out to more desirable neighborhoods. This area contained the city's slums. At its outer perimeter were the wholesale and manufacturing activities.

The low-income housing zone (ring 3) was for "working men's" homes. These homes generally did not completely encircle the central part of the city, which might be viewed as a breakdown in the concentric circle theory. Many of these homes were substandard and previously had been large homes. Immigrants from ring 2 tended to move into this zone as they became financially able.

Ring 4 is the middle-to-high-income housing zone. The higher-rent areas

---

[1]See R. E. Park and E. W. Burgess, *The City* (Chicago: The University of Chicago Press, 1925), pp. 47–62.

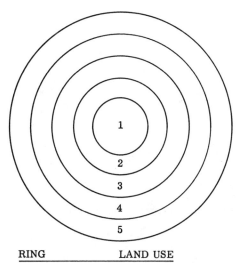

Figure 6.1 Concentric Ring Growth Pattern

RING	LAND USE
1	Central Business District *CBD*
2	Transition Zone
3	Low-Income Housing Zone
4	Middle-to High Income Housing Zone
5	Commuters' Zone

in the residential zone tend to radiate out from the city but do not generally completely enclose the city. More expensive apartments and single-family homes are located here.

The commuters' zone (ring 5) was found beyond the periphery of the city in the form of scattered, isolated communities having diverse values of homes. Lots in ring 5 tended to be comparatively large. This zone formed a buffer between the urban and rural areas. Today we would call this the suburbs.

Axial Growth Theory

Residential areas tend to develop along the fastest transportation routes, according to Richard M. Hurd.[2] These transportation routes frequently elongated the centrifugal development to form the spokes of the starlike urban pattern described in Figure 6.2. Other types of development, such as industrial activities, often developed in a lateral pattern along the shores of a river.

Hurd spoke of axial growth characterizing city growth, based on quick access to or from the business center by way of turnpikes.[3] Chicago is a prime example of a city developed in a spokelike fashion along the turnpikes and later, commuter railroad lines. He observed that there was "a continual contest between

[2]Richard M. Hurd, *Principles of City Land Values*, 3rd ed. (New York: The Record and Guide, 1911) (originally written in 1903).
[3]*Ibid.*, p. 41.

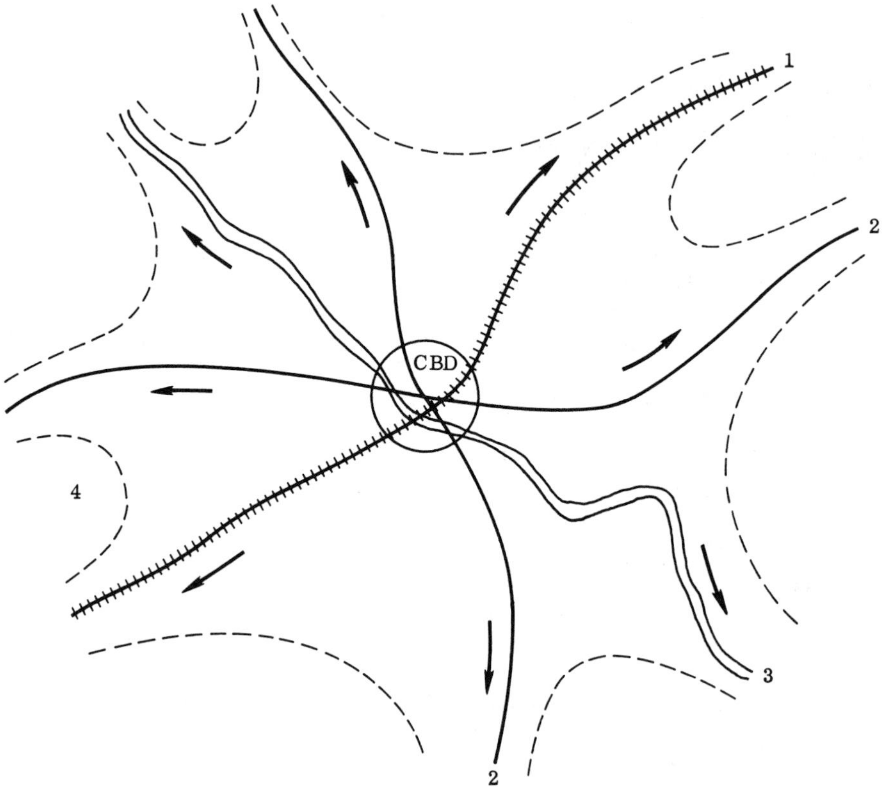

Legend:

CBD	Central Business District
1	Railroad
2	Expressways and Highways
3	Navigable River
4	Boundaries of Major Development
→	Major Paths of Growth

Figure 6.2 Axial Growth Pattern

axial growth pushing out from the center along transportation lines and central growth, constantly following and obliterating it, while new projections are made further out of the various axes."[4]

The normal result of axial and central growth is a star-shaped city. The growth extends first along the main thoroughfares radiating from the center, and later the parts lying between are filled in with land uses not so strongly dependent on immediate access to the main traffic arteries. Varying topography may alter this type of growth somewhat.

[4]*Ibid.*, p. 59.

Sector Growth Theory

Beginning in 1934, Homer Hoyt compiled data on over 200 American cities for the purpose of studying the internal structure and growth of American cities.[5] Nine major observations were drawn from this Federal Housing Administration residential study. This study was conducted to identify residential mortgage lending risks; therefore, it focuses on residential neighborhoods. Some of these growth patterns are not valid today, but nevertheless, this theory provides one more perception of growth in American cities that should be appreciated by real estate appraisers. The sector theory as illustrated in Figure 6.3 holds that the direction and pattern of growth in cities tends to be governed by some combination of the following considerations:

1. High-grade residential growth tends to proceed from a given point of origin, along established lines of travel or toward another existing nucleus of buildings or trading centers.
2. The zone of high-rent areas tends to progress toward high ground, which is free from the risk of floods, and to spread along lake, bay, river, and ocean fronts, where such water fronts are not used for industry.
3. High-rent residential districts tend to grow toward the section of the city which has free, open country beyond the edges and away from "dead-end" sections which are limited by natural or artificial barriers to expansion. It was found that open fields, golf courses, country clubs, and country estates act as a magnet to pull high-grade residential areas in their direction.
4. Higher-priced residential neighborhoods tend to grow toward the homes of the leaders of the community.
5. Movement trends of office buildings, banks, and stores pull higher-priced residential neighborhoods in the same general direction.
6. High-grade residential areas tend to develop along the fastest existing transportation lines.
7. Growth of high-rent neighborhoods continues in the same direction for a long period of time.
8. Deluxe high-rent apartment areas tend to be established near the business center in old residential areas.
9. Real estate promoters may bend the direction of high-grade residential growth. Such developments and communities as Miami Beach, Coral Gables, and Roland Park in Baltimore typically have quality amenities and strong architectural controls.[6]

Multiple Nuclei Growth Theory

In 1945, Chauncey D. Harris and Edward L. Ullman observed clusters of fairly discreet forms of land use activities (see Figure 6.4). From these ob-

---

[5]Homer Hoyt, *The Structure and Growth of Residential Neighborhoods in American Cities* (Washington, D.C.: Federal Housing Administration, 1939).
[6]*Ibid.*, pp. 116–119.

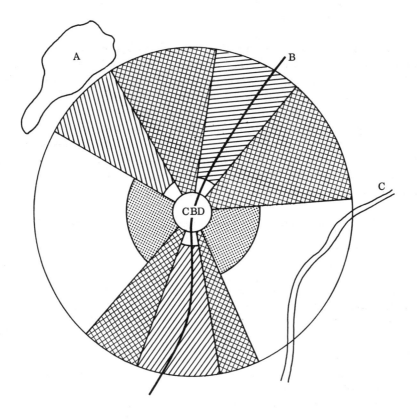

Legend

A   Scenic Lake
B   High Speed Traffic Artery
C   River – Subject to Flooding
CBD   Central Business District

Industrial Activities

Figure 6.3 Sector Theory of Urban Growth

servations they developed the multiple-nuclei theory of urban growth. They found different nodes of development for retail, industrial, residential, and wholesale land use activities.[7] A major feature of this urban land development

[7]Chauncey D. Harris and Edward L. Ullman, "The Nature of Cities," *The Annals of the American Academy of Political and Social Sciences* (November 1945).

model was that the various nodes of development were caused by certain activities requiring specialized facilities. Certain similar activities group together because they benefit from close proximity. Certain unlike activities are repulsed from other unlike activities. Certain activities can afford occupancy only in various districts.

None of these urban development models is universal or infallible. The appraiser, however, should be familiar with each theory to use the appropriate parts to recognize past growth patterns and project future land use development trends.

REGIONAL ANALYSIS

This section presents a generalized approach to regional analysis and is concluded with a discussion of two methods of regional economic analysis. The first

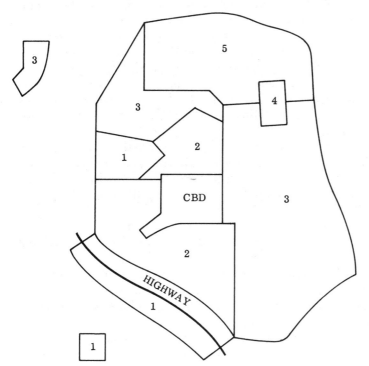

CBD	Central Business District
1	Industrial Cluster
2	Low–Income Residential
3	Middle–Income Residential
4	Business District
5	High–Income Residential

Figure 6.4 Multiple-Nuclei Growth Theory

method is economic base analysis, and the second is input–output analysis. However, virtually all regional analyses begin with employment, which provides the basis for population projections.

General Concerns in Regional Analysis

Although the regional environment is too often neglected in favor of site and building inspection and analysis, it is critically important to the success of any land use activity. Sometimes it is easier to conclude on the structural and design adequacy of a building than the more subtle economic implications of external demographic trends. These trends may not be readily perceptible, but within any region, they are present and the appraiser should identify and convey to the client the implications of regional trends.

One dimension of the economic "health" of any region is its employment opportunities. This includes the diversity of employment as well as the unemployment rate and recent and probable future employment trends. Some of the extreme situations to be alerted to are those regions with few industries or different but closely related and interdependent industries. Such lack of diversity can cause economic turmoil and property value declines if those industries' products fall into disfavor. The same difficulty can exist in areas where the economy is largely dependent on a military base. If the base closes, a calamitous effect is felt throughout the region. Thus employment diversification is an important factor to consider.

Other regional data of interest to the appraiser are the master plan for the jurisdictions within the region. The proposed directions and nature of future growth, when considered along with established development patterns, zoning, and planned utility routes, can greatly assist in judging the probable growth areas for the future.

The comparative supply and demand for real estate is another key component of regional analysis. If, for example, the appraisal is of a residential rental project, it is important to have some idea of the demand for such rental space. This demand estimate will be based in large part on available and competing space, success of competing projects, availability of utilities, and adequacy of transportation and jobs throughout the region. Also, it is important to understand population trends. Is the population getting older or younger? Are households growing or shrinking in size? Are there more two-household wage earners? Are there large percentages of teenagers in households? All this information is beneficial in trying to judge the probable success of and value of projects or individual properties.[8]

[8]A good reference on regional analysis is Lawrence A. Kell, Chapter 5, "Location Analysis," in *Real Estate Counseling*, James H. Boykin, ed. (Chicago: American Society of Real Estate Counselors, 1984).

Regional Analysis Techniques

Two types of regional analysis often used are economic base and input–output analysis. These techniques are too elaborate for most appraisal assignments. Nevertheless, the methodology and regional considerations embraced in each analytical technique are of value to the appraiser.

Economic Base Analysis.

This technique was initially developed by Robert M. Haig and later refined by Homer Hoyt. This method focuses on how a community earns its living. The economic base of a community is broken down into two parts. These are basic (sometimes called export) industries and nonbasic (sometimes called service) industries. A ratio of the number of service jobs created by basic industry jobs sometimes can be developed for short periods of time, but this relationship does not uniformly hold up for all communities. Nevertheless, the important concern is that a community cannot be sustained by "taking in its own laundry" but must sell a product or service to others beyond its region. A regional economic base study typically seeks to:

1. Identify regional export activities.
2. Forecast the probable growth in these activities.
3. Evaluate the impact of export activity on nonbasic activities of the region.[9]

This analysis, which generally is undertaken by local government planning departments, provides a basis for appraisers to judge the nature and size of future population changes within the region.

This once popular method has largely been replaced with available data from the U.S. Census Bureau so that actual output performance of industries can be readily determined. A criticism of this approach is the use of fixed relationships between the basic and nonbasic industries and the assumption that industries in various categories of Standard Industrial Classifications (SIC) are either basic or nonbasic. This relationship is a function of the product and location of an establishment within a region.

A variation of economic base analysis is location quotient. In using this method, regional employment by SIC is listed from published sources such as the U.S. Department of Labor. The percentage of each SIC category is computed and then compared to corresponding national figures. This ratio can be used to project employment for the region when only national employment projections are available. Errors may occur as economic and social shifts take place for the region in comparison to the nation as a whole.

[9]Edgar M. Hoover, *An Introduction to Regional Economics* (New York: Alfred A. Knopf, Inc., 1971), p. 222.

Regional Input–Output Analysis

This technique is used largely by regional economists and planners in trying to trace the impact of demand on a region's income and employment. It sets up a series of "accounts" to describe the relationship of economic activities between the region and area beyond the region as well as among establishments within the region. The basis for input–output analysis is regional businesses, households, all levels of government within the region, the stock of capital in the region and individual activities beyond the region.

The idea underlying regional input–output analysis is to trace industrial output and purchases from producer to consumer in order to show the effect of an increase of output by one industry on purchases by other sectors of the economy. This technique is not one ordinarily used by appraisers.

In using any studies or reports on a region, the appraiser should be concerned with the credibility of the forecaster as well as the purpose of the study. Not all data obtained for use in regional analysis by the appraiser are necessarily unbiased. Hence, if the highest and best use, demand for property, or its value rests on such forecasts, care should be used in discerning the validity of such information. It provides a means to study interregional relationships and the comparative economic soundness and functioning of different regions.

POPULATION TRENDS AND CHARACTERISTICS

Because of the direct correlation between growth of population and rising values of real property, the real estate appraiser must be fully informed as to the history of population changes in his or her community, especially over the preceding two or three decades. In addition, population shifts, deaths, and birth and migratory patterns must be analyzed to forecast the population status over periods extending 40 or 50 years into the future—or, in any case, a period not shorter than the remaining economic life of the property under appraisal. The city's growth pattern, whether favorable or unfavorable, can best be ascertained by comparison with the rate of growth for the state and the nation. Where community population increases faster than that of the nation and the state, real estate values generally will also keep pace with the accelerated growth. A study of the number of people alone, however, is inadequate. A meaningful population study must also consider, among other things, the following:

1. *Age-group analysis*: It is important to know the number of persons aged under 20, 20 to 40, 40 to 60, and 60 and over. A favorable ratio of persons in the 20-to-60 age group provides the work force on which the community depends for economic support. Excessive ratios of young or dependent old people may pose community problems the effects of which, if any, must be known and evaluated.
2. *Income bracketing*: To judge the demand for an appraised residence, it is beneficial

to know the breakdown of the population by income. This information will reveal the probable demand for different-priced apartments and houses as well as for different goods and services.

ECONOMIC MEASURES OF COMMUNITY GROWTH

Although measures of economic growth may be equally applicable in small as in large communities, it must be kept in mind that the hazards of economic forecasting increase with a decrease in community size. An estimate of probable changes in economic standing for a city of 100,000-and-over population can be made with greater certainty than a similar estimate for a community of 25,000-and-under population. The loss of a dominant industry, for instance, due to plant relocation may prove economically disastrous in a small community. A similar loss in a metropolitan city, however, may go wholly unnoticed because of the constant readjustments that take place in the everyday economic life of a large city. For instance, thousands of businesses come and go each year in and around New York City and Chicago without creating a noticeable effect on the balance of their overall economic growth and activity. Indicators of economic growth which warrant observation and provide a basis for judging the quality of investment prospects in a community include, among others, the following:

1. Number of banks, bank deposits, and savings.
2. Postal operations and receipts.
3. Construction and building permits (volume and dollar amounts).
4. Automobile and truck registration.
5. Railroad, airline, and bus passenger traffic.
6. Assessed value of real property.
7. Number of electric meters and telephone service connections.
8. Retail sales and buying income per household.
9. Number of gainfully employed by type of employment.
10. Real estate sales volume.

As a rule, the economic growth of a community can best be judged by comparison with other communities of like size and character within the region or by a per capita or per family basis comparison with similar cities anywhere in the country. The census of housing and population income and characteristics, and the special census of manufacturing, provide excellent source data for such comparative growth studies. Ready access to economic growth data listed above should enable the real estate appraiser to formulate accurate forecasts of what the future holds in store for a given community. The number of banks and their total deposits and savings reflect on a per capita basis the degree of well-being as well as the extent of optimism or pessimism that motivates the general economy. Construction volume in dollars and the number of building permits issued during a given period are excellent measures of speed of growth or retardation. Registration statistics of automobiles and trucks, compared with state or national averages, provide further proof of conclusions supported by commercial indexes. Saturation measures of electric and telephone service on a per household basis are useful in ranking a community on the economic "totem pole." Most informative of all as a statistical measure of community standing, however, are retail expenditures, buying income per household, and number of gainfully employed by type of employment.

Employment data should be analyzed as to number and percent engaged in primary occupations as compared with those employed in secondary or service establishments. A primary source of employment involves a product or service that is exported from the community, and which channels into it purchasing power from outside areas that supports service and community economic life generally. As a rule, each primary worker supports two secondary workers engaged as butchers, tailors, barbers, shopkeepers, and general servicers. Thus a new industry providing jobs for 100 family breadwinners in effect accounts for 200 more families which are needed to provide essential social, educational, economic, and recreational community services.

Generally, it is not too difficult to ascertain the status and past performance record of a city and to keep one's finger, so to speak, on the economic pulse of the community under study. Economic source data as a rule can be obtained from utility companies, which are called on to forecast community needs for many years into the future. State development agencies as well as local and state chambers of commerce take periodic inventories to ascertain the relative impact of economic growth on the city, the region, and the state. Appraisers should keep themselves well informed as to the economic health of their communities and be in a position, when compiling reports for appraisal clients, to support their judgments concerning the prospects for growth, decline, or stability of property values within the confines of a city over the economic life of the realty for which they form value judgments.

Care must be taken not to rely too strongly on past performance. Every effort should be made to forecast accurately, on the basis of past trends, the prospects for continued economic growth as well as the anticipated rate of progress compared with past performance. Value of property, as previously emphasized, lies in the future; and the ups and downs of property income, and hence property worth, are closely tied to the economic strings of the city to which real property is irrevocably attached.

THE NATURE AND CHARACTER OF CITIES

Cities, broadly speaking, may be classified as *primary* and *secondary* urban centers. A primary community is one which has its own economic base, and whose existence is not dependent on the operations or welfare of other communities within the state or the metropolitan region. A secondary community, on the other hand, is in effect a satellite whose length and strength of orbit depends on the principal cities to which it owes its existence. These satellite communities are better known as "bedroom" cities where commuters (people who work where they would rather not or cannot afford to live) reside. The economic strength of a satellite community is entirely dependent on the strength of the primary community, of which it is often an unwilling part. To appraise property in such a community necessitates careful evaluation of the forces which keep the primary community operative.

Primary communities may be subclassified into cities which reflect their cause of urbanization, as follows:

Industrial cities	such as Detroit, Michigan, and Pittsburgh, Pennsylvania.
Commercial cities	such as Chicago, Illinois, and San Francisco, California.
Mining cities	such as Scranton, Pennsylvania, and Wheeling, West Virginia.
Resort cities	such as Miami Beach, Florida, and Atlantic City, New Jersey.
Political cities	such as Tallahassee, Florida, and Washington, D.C.
Educational cities	such as Chapel Hill, North Carolina, and Ann Arbor, Michigan.

Many communities have assumed a diverse economic base and may fall with equal importance into two or more subclassifications. Thus New York City is both industrial and commercial in character. Miami, Florida, which started as a resort city, is presently one of the most important commercial cities in the South, having one of the largest international airport facilities in the country. New Orleans, which served as the fishing and commercial center of Louisiana, is important today as an international shipping center with impressive harbor facilities and shipping tonnage.

In evaluating property within a city, it is important that a clear understanding is had not only of the city's origin but also of the economic base that presently and prospectively will support continued city growth and development. A city with a single dominant industry or service activity, no matter how prosperous currently, must be evaluated with caution. Having all its eggs in one basket is hazardous for a city, and technological changes or competition within the area may cause economic slumps that severely depress its property values. Even though the appraiser is unable to forecast with accuracy future changes in economic patterns, he or she must call potential value hazards to the attention of clients and reflect the concern of informed investors for the required yield which the market will deem necessary to attract investment and venture capital.

THE CITY'S PLAN AND LAND USE PATTERN

City planning is an art more often talked about than practiced. Most cities with a simple village origin grow like Topsy until economically costly growing pains call for hindsight actions which foresight actions could well have avoided. (The growth of Boston along its early cowpaths is a vivid example of this kind of chaotic growth.) Generally, the development of a city should be planned 10 or even 20 years in advance under a comprehensive master plan. Communities, like people, are dynamic in character, and their expanding or changing needs must be served through orderly expansion beyond the city's limits where necessary. Like a business enterprise, a city as a whole must prosper if it is to continue effectively as a going concern.

As a requisite to better understanding of a city's potential growth and development, the appraiser should inventory the physical and economic resources of the subject community and maintain an active file to keep such data up to date. The first step in the collection of pertinent data is to obtain an official city map on which the legal boundaries are delineated and the street pattern shown. Wherever possible, land use data about contiguous county areas should be obtained to observe facilities for street and utility service expansion. A well-planned city, as a rule, reduces per capita urban operating costs and facilitates the ready flow of people and commerce during normal as well as rush hours.

Next in importance is checking the adequacy of land use patterns and city zoning in relation to public needs for sites suitable for improvements as follows:

Residential homes.
Commercial buildings.
Industrial parks and districts.
Public administrative and school buildings.
Recreational parks and playgrounds.

Residential areas should be free from natural or human-made hazards, and should provide the opportunity for privacy and enjoyment of the amenities of home ownership. Through streets should be routed around residential areas to reduce traffic flow and noise, especially during evening hours. Streets should be paved; curbs, gutters, and sidewalks provided; and all essential utilities— including water, electricity, telephone, sanitation, and storm sewerage—made available for service connection. Effective zoning should call for uniform building setback, minimum plot width, and building construction and population-density regulations. Nonconforming uses of an industrial and commercial nature should especially be screened out by natural or artificial buffer zones, such as landscaped plantings. The degree to which good planning is lacking, and the extent to which private or public hazards are permitted to encroach on residential areas, will significantly affect the lifespan of the neighborhood and the duration of economic life throughout which property values are assured freedom from external obsolescence.

Commercial facilities—including retail stores, bank and office buildings, and wholesale establishments—should be grouped together in an orderly pattern, with ample off-street parking to permit uncrowded commerce and safe shopping. Spot and faulty business zoning impede orderly city growth and adversely affect the value of surrounding property. Generally, areas chosen for commercial development are level, of even contour, and readily accessible by surface transportation. Commercial areas should also be strictly zoned and protected by building ordinances to promote public interests and to safeguard private ownership of a city's most valuable investment—the 100 percent shopping district.

Industrial sites, which prior to World War II were given little protection from encroachment by other supposedly higher uses, have often been hampered in potential development and in relation to their highest and best land use. Manufacturing, whether heavy or light, provides for many communities the "bread and butter" resources on which much of the secondary commercial and service industries depend. Planned industrial parks should play an important part in every master plan. Such industrial locations should be situated near major highways, railroad rights of way, waterways, and airports. Ready road and rail access, adequate utility service, and freedom to expand give assurance to established industries that they are wanted and respected for the part they play in the corporate structure of the city. In communities where residential, commercial, and industrial growth complement rather than encroach upon each other, the values of real estate properties will reflect the increased income stability and the stronger holding power of property owners.

Public administration buildings, school buildings, and recreational parks and playgrounds should all be carefully planned and located to serve public needs adequately and efficiently. Even quasi-public buildings such as churches, libraries, museums, and exhibition halls should be placed as near as possible to the community areas they serve. In political, educational, and resort cities, great care must be taken in planning the location of public structures that may influence the character and extent of private building investment and thus indirectly influence the very structure of city growth. Familiarity with the principles of good city and regional planning will better enable the real estate appraiser to judge economic forecasts in the light of regional and state developments in which the subject community plays a part.

REVIEW QUESTIONS

1. How can the earlier causes of urbanization be applied to present regional analysis?
2. Briefly list the basic features of each of the urban growth theories.
3. Identify and discuss the urban growth theories that are useful in analyzing a region today.

4. Explain how the economic base analysis helps you understand regional economy.
5. What is the main purpose(s) of regional economic and population analysis?
6. List economic measures of community growth in addition to those discussed in the chapter. Explain how these economic measures assist in the appraisal of real estate.

READING AND STUDY REFERENCES

BARRETT, G. VINCENT, and JOHN P. BLAIR. *How to Conduct and Analyze Real Estate Market and Feasibility Studies.* New York: Van Nostrand Reinhold Company, Inc., 1982. See Chapter 2, "How to Analyze Real Estate Markets."

GREER, GAYLON E., and MICHAEL D. FARRELL. *Contemporary Real Estate: Theory and Practice.* Hinsdale, Ill.: The Dryden Press, 1983. See Chapter 2, "Urban Growth and Land Use Patterns."

HARVEY, ROBERT O. Chapter 21, "Location Analysis," in *The Real Estate Handbook*, Maury Seldin, ed. Homewood, Ill.: Dow Jones-Irwin, 1980.

HOYT, HOMER. "The Structure and Growth of American Cities Contrasted with the Structure of European and Asiatic Cities," *Urban Land* 18, no. 8 (September 1959).

HURD, RICHARD M. *Principles of City Land Values*, 3rd ed. New York: The Record and Guide, 1911. See particularly Chapters 2 and 5, "Location of Cities" and "Directions of Growth."

ISARD, WALTER. Chapters 1, 6, 7, *Introduction to Regional Science.* Englewood Cliffs, N.J.: Prentice-Hall, Inc., 1975.

KELL, LAWRENCE A. Chapter 5, "Location Analysis," in *Real Estate Counseling*, James H. Boykin, ed. Chicago: American Society of Real Estate Counselors, 1984.

MARTIN, W.B. "How to Predict Urban Growth Paths," *The Appraisal Journal* 52, no. 2 (April 1984), pp. 242–249.

RATCLIFF, RICHARD U. *Urban Land Economics.* Westport, Conn.: Greenwood Press, 1949. See Chapters 2 and 13, "The Economics of Urbanization" and "City Growth and Structure."

RATCLIFF, RICHARD U. *Real Estate Analysis.* New York: McGraw-Hill Book Company, 1961. See Chapters 2 and 4, "The Urban Setting" and "The Locational Basis of Real Estate Value."

TIEBOUT, CHARLES I. *The Community Economic Base Study.* Supplementary Paper 16. New York: Committee for Economic Development, 1962.

TOYNBEE, ARNOLD (ed.). *Cities of Destiny.* New York: McGraw-Hill Book Company, 1967. See especially the chapters entitled "The American City in History" and "The Coming World-City: Ecumenopolis."

7

NEIGHBORHOOD VALUE ANALYSIS

Learning Objectives
After reading this chapter, you should be able to:
Understand the essentials of a neighborhood
Discuss the neighborhood life cycle
Identify the principal ways that neighborhoods are delineated
Appreciate the nature of neighborhood characteristics
Recognize amenities that enhance the appeal of residential neighborhoods
Point out the major attributes of commercial and industrial districts

NEIGHBORHOOD DEFINED

In the past, neighborhood analysis has been distorted by two major misconceptions. The first was an idealized notion of what a neighborhood *should be* rather than what it *actually is*. Such phrases as "homogeneous grouping of people" or "similarity of backgrounds" do not necessarily describe residential neighborhoods as they exist and are not fully accurate for nonresidential districts. People of different backgrounds and different but usually compatible land use activities come together and remain together for various reasons. The other mistake of the past has been perpetuated by appraisers, mortgage lenders, and the federal government through a misunderstanding of the effect on property values by racial minorities. Some earlier "studies" implied with an apparent high degree of precision the negative effect of racial "infiltration," as it was once called.

Today, neighborhood analysis is enhanced through use of a model that universally applies to all land use activities—residential as well as nonresidential. Therefore, a generalized definition of a neighborhood is *a bounded area wherein certain land use activities are attracted and retained by sets of linkages.* Ideally, these activities are compatible, but if they are not, there is still a neighborhood. Unquestionably, a neighborhood's economic and social strength is enhanced if its activities are compatible. This fact may be called its linkages.[1] "Linkages" are the "glue" that hold a neighborhood together. Linkages may be thought of as external economies or centripetal forces. It is the periodic interaction between people or establishments that draw and hold them together. Examples of linkages are where machine work is subcontracted by one business for other nearby business or where close proximity to legal or advertising services makes a particular location attractive for a small business unable to afford such specialized in-house staff. In a residential neighborhood, linkages may exist between the home, shopping, schools, social and religious centers, and place of employment.

Usually, it is not difficult to delineate a neighborhood, because of natural or artificial barriers which enclose it or because of physical attributes or development practices that characterize the area. In most planned communities, neighborhoods come into existence as a result of deliberate platting by subdividers or developers who, with the aid of deed restrictions, control the character, growth, and expansion of neighborhoods. In Figure 7.1, a desirable neighborhood has formed about a spring-fed creek that winds its way alongside a dual-lane, oak-tree-shaded boulevard. Mere size, of course, does not determine a neighborhood. However, the larger the size, the better the protection from infiltration by inharmonious land use influences or detrimental property uses. At the same time land use activities near the center of a large neighborhood or district sometimes are remote from desired supporting services.

THE NEIGHBORHOOD AGE CYCLE

An important step in the valuation process is the determination of a neighborhood's *age-cycle position.* All neighborhoods have a beginning, and most follow an age pattern that reflects growth, maturity, decline, and transition or reha-

---

[1] This concept is amply covered in the literature, but sometimes by different names. See, for example, Robert M. Haig and Roswell C. McCrea, "Major Economic Factors in Metropolitan Growth and Arrangement," *Regional Survey of New York and Its Environs,* Vol. I (New York: New York Regional Planning Committee, 1927), p. 37; Ernest M. Fisher and Robert M. Fisher, *Urban Real Estate* (New York: Henry Holt and Company, 1954), p. 324; R. L. Estell and R. Ogilvie Buchanan, *Industrial Activity and Economic Geography* (London: Hutchinson University Library, 1966), pp. 94–96; Alfred Weber, *Theory of the Location of Industry,* translated by C. J. Freidrich (Chicago: The University of Chicago Press, 1928), pp. 163–167; Edgar M. Hoover, *The Location of Economic Activity* (New York: McGraw-Hill Book Company, 1948), pp. 118, 120; Walter Isard, *Location and Space-Economy* (Cambridge, Mass.: Technology Press, MIT; New York: John Wiley & Sons, Inc., 1956), p. 182.

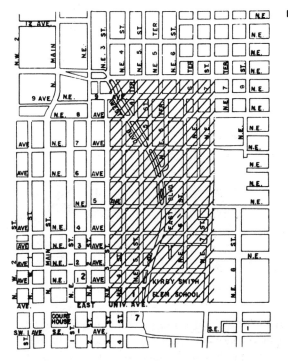

Figure 7.1 Highland Subdivision, Gainesville, Florida

bilitation as influenced by socioeconomic forces that shape community land use patterns. A typical neighborhood age cycle may be diagrammed as in Figure 7.2. It should be noted that there generally are several recurring cycles in the life of a neighborhood. Moreover, the value trend may either be declining or increasing. Frequently, neighborhood property values decline to a point of fostering new uses which reverse the trend of declining values.

As indicated in Figure 7.2, the *development period* of any neighborhood is the period of growth. The length of time to reach neighborhood maturity will vary with the size of the area under development, but 15 to 20 years is generally considered typical. Peak neighborhood values are reached during the period of maturity, when improvements generally are at their prime appearance. The length of the maturity period will vary with the kind and size of the community and the economic well-being of neighborhood residents and businesses. Generally, a period of 20 to 25 years may be regarded as a typical stretch of time during which a neighborhood remains static in quality.

As buildings pass the prime of their economic life, and as a new generation replaces the old, properties that no longer fulfill the needs of the original buyers are placed on the market and a new and generally lower class of buyers infiltrates the area. This is the stage of neighborhood decline. At first, the trend of property values gently turns lower, as shown by the diagram in Figure 7.2.

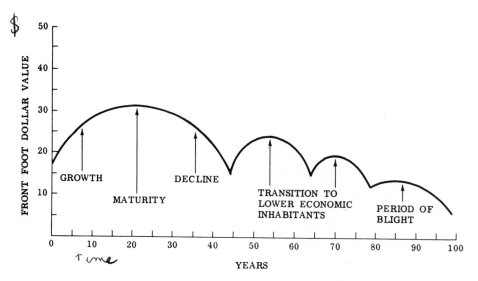

Figure 7.2 Typical Neighborhood Age Pattern

As demand for properties increases with the transition to the new class of residents (who tell their friends and relatives of the better residential district now available at costs they can all afford) property values again rise, but rarely to the heights reached in prior years. This cyclical economic behavior repeats with successions of transitory ownership-clan changes until the neighborhood reaches a status of blight and prospective slum conditon. At this stage, or in prior periods, public or private (renewal) efforts may change the character of a neighborhood to a higher and better use. The same concept applies to nonresidential neighborhoods.

It is the appraiser's responsibility to determine the position of the neighborhood's life cycle and to estimate the effect of neighborhood age and obsolescence on amenities of ownership or income from its use over the remaining economic life of the subject property. As will be demonstrated in Chapter 15, the income productive capacity of a property, as a rule, lessens with age; and under the impact of forces of obsolescence, consideration must be given to the value effect of such contingencies by stabilizing in the appraisal the anticipated declining income flow, by increasing the risk rate at which such prospective diminishing income must be capitalized, or by reflecting the rate of decline in the capitilization rate. There have been many instances where new highways or bypasses have been constructed, causing much of the former business to be diverted from a particular neighborhood. Eventually, alternative uses for these commercial businesses are developed and the buildings are rehabilitated as shown in Figure 7.3.

Figure 7.3 Former Three-Bay Service Station Converted into a Savings and Loan Facility

NEIGHBORHOOD CHARACTERISTICS

In judging the quality of a residential neighborhood the following physical, population, and economic factors warrant analysis:

A. Physical features
  1. Location within the city.
  2. Nature of terrain.
  3. Nature and load-bearing capacity of soil.
  4. Features of natural beauty.
  5. Drainage facilities, both natural and human-made.
  6. Street pattern and street improvements, including essential public utilities.
  7. Type of architecture and quality of housing.
  8. Nature, frequency, and cost of public transportation facilities.
  9. Proximity to schools, stores, and recreational facilities.
  10. Freedom from hazards and adverse influences.
B. Population characteristics
  1. Types of residents—as to income and education.
  2. Living habits and care of homes.
  3. Attitude toward law and government.

    4. Homogeneity of cultural and civic interests.

    5. Age grouping and size of families.

C. Economic data

    1. Extent (percentage) of development.

    2. Percentage of homes owner-occupied.

    3. Professional or occupational means of earning a livelihood and income stability.

    4. Taxation and assessment levels, and tax burdens.

    5. Zoning and deed restrictions.

    6. Investment quality of area for VA, FHA, and institutional mortgage-loan financing.

    7. Price range and rental value of neighborhood homes.

NEIGHBORHOOD BOUNDARIES

It is desirable to define the limits of the neighborhood wherein the appraised property is situated. There are several reasons for this phase in appraising. By knowing the limits of a neighborhood, the search for comparable properties can be concentrated within a defined area. Further, a knowledge of neighborhood boundaries permits the appraiser to determine the present state of the neighborhood. Finally, it is possible to more accurately ascertain the highest and best use of the appraised property. It is important to note that neighborhood analysis is an essential link in the eventual conclusion of an appraised property's highest and best use and its value. It is not an overstatement to say "so goes the neighborhood, so goes the property." The desirability and in turn the value of a property are inextricably intertwined with the soundness of its neighborhoods.

    The question then arises: How can the boundaries of a neighborhood be identified? There are several ways to do this. The most obvious neighborhood boundaries are physical in nature (see Figure 7.1). Examples of physical boundaries are natural features such as rivers, changes in topography such as ravines or hills, or changes in soil conditions or natural growth (e.g., trees). Human-made features can also establish neighborhood boundaries. Examples are railroad rights-of-way, expressways, streets, and major building complexes. Legal and governmental factors sometimes will shape a neighborhood. For example, the limits of a platted residential subdivision can set boundaries as well as can different zoning classifications, municipal boundaries, and the school districts in those cities where there is no forced busing of school-age children. A final type of neighborhood boundary is established by price levels of residences. Generally, residential neighborhoods are fairly similar with regard to the price of lots, which in turn dictates the price of homes built, which finally sets the level of family income needed to live in various neighborhoods. The appraiser needs to consciously identify neighborhood boundaries as an important step in arriving at the value of an appraised property.

LOCATION CHARACTERISTICS

The first step in the analysis of a neighborhood is to delineate the boundaries which encompass the area under value study. This can readily be done by identifying the names of streets which enclose the neighborhood north, south, east, and west. Generally, the boundaries of a neighborhood are not difficult to establish because of physical features—natural or artificial—that distinguish the area characteristically as a unit of development. Normally, the neighborhood is referred to by name as originally recorded on public plat book records or by reference to a distinguishing natural feature that marks the area. Often a neighborhood, because of location within the city, acquires a favorable reputation which to status-seeking buyers enhances the location or status value of the area thus described.

The *nature of terrain*, too, may influence development practices and should be described and noted as to its effect on value. For residential purposes, gently rolling land is preferable to a flat plateau. People, it seems, prefer to live on hillsides, which make possible the enjoyment of a more extensive view of the community's skyline. Elevations, and sometimes valleys, provide a sense of security which attracts residents to that location in preference to others. A flat terrain, on the other hand, is preferable for commercial and industrial development. It is costly and difficult to make building storefronts conform to sloping sidewalks, and an uneven area is hazardous in a wintery climate where ice and snow make travel on sloping streets dangerous. The nature of the terrain may thus, as noted, exact an important influence on the marketability of a given site for a particular type of intended and permissible use.

Many appraisal reports are deficient in that reference to the *quality of soil* has been omitted. The reason for this oversight, no doubt, is ascribable to the fact that a "normal" load-bearing quality of the soil is taken for granted and that quality of soil for other purposes is considered of negligible importance. An appraiser, however, has no right to take anything for granted. It is his or her obligation to gather factual data and to report it without prejudice instilled by custom or personal preference. In commercial uses of land the presence of rock, quicksand, hard pan,[2] and high or low water levels may significantly influence costs of construction and hence—since the income to land under a highest and best use is residual in character—the value of the land. Even for residential use, the quality of soil for lawn development and general landscaping may prove of value significance and of deciding importance to a purchaser.

Features of natural beauty that distinguish a neighborhood also deserve careful attention. Majestic trees which line an avenue or provide welcome shade in summer months add value to the abutting land far beyond the price of cords

[2]Layers of dense sand or limestone that prevent the percolating (penetration) of surface waters to subsurface levels.

of wood that can be realized if the same trees (as is often, sadly, the case) are cut down and sold for lumber. The presence or nearness of creeks, streams, rivers, lakes, or even artificial reservoirs enhances the value of sites to varying degrees, depending on land use, beauty of terrain, and utility of the waterways. In any case, the appraiser in formulating a final value decision should carefully inventory the influencing value features for the use and information of the report reader.

Of increasing importance in suburban developments, where the extension of public sewerage facilities proves too costly, is the adequacy of soil drainage both natural and synthetic. Existence of hard pan or inadequate (safe) soil drainage as based on *percolating soil tests*[3] may cause a site or area to be declared unsafe for installation of sanitary septic tanks, and may result in the denial of building permits in order to safeguard public health. Drainage of surface or flood waters during periods of seasonal rains or storms also must be considered. Failure to do so is a serious omission of factual data, and may subject the appraiser to a lawsuit and court charges for professional negligence.

The impact of neighborhood street patterns and street improvements, including essential public utilities, must next be carefully evaluated. Subdivision cost studies confirm that development expenditures for road grading, paving, curbing, gutter, water mains, storm drains, and sanitary sewage facilities aggregate from a minimum of 60 to as high as 90 percent of the value of a developed site. Conversely, the value of raw land may be as little as 10 and seldom more than 40 percent of the value of a fully developed neighborhood site. The presence or absence of street improvements must therefore be emphasized and evaluated by market comparison studies, as demonstrated in Chapter 8. The street pattern, too, should be noted and its influence on value stressed. The grid street pattern which characterizes older neighborhoods, and which is still favored to this day by economy-minded builders and developers, is frowned on by modern planners and discouraged in proposed subdivisions submitted for loan approval to the VA or the FHA. Curvilinear streets and cul-de-sac avenues cause automobile traffic to slow down and usually limit their use to residents in the immediate area, creating greater enjoyment and safety for neighborhood occupants both young and old. Market prices confirm buyer preference for *safe* lot locations, and the appraiser must recognize this in the adjustment of comparable sales where neighborhood street patterns are unsatisfactory.

In judging the quality of a neighborhood it is essential to observe the type of architecture and the quality of housing. In design, a distinction should be made between "homogeneity" and "monotony." Houses may appear to be alike but yet be different. Pleasing and tasteful exterior dwelling design in an attractive setting enhance the appeal and market value of residences. A good neighborhood will not be marred by irregular setbacks, extremely unorthodox designs, and clashing periods of architecture. The appraiser should be conversant with the features and characteristics of basic architectural styles and be able

---

[3]Soil penetration or drainage tests taken by county, HUD, and other agencies to determine soil fitness for installation of private sanitary sewage tank systems.

to classify the ancestry of a residence at least in terms of its relationship to colonial, English, Latin, contemporary, or native-conventional periods of construction.

Although the automobile has diminished the importance of intracity transportation, nevertheless the quality of a neighborhood is enhanced by the ready availability of public transportation. Pedestrians are still the rule rather than the exception in community life, and the use of public surface transportation to reach schools, shopping, and recreational centers provides an essential convenience. In considering the value added by convenient public transportation, the type, frequency, reliability, and cost of service should be ascertained and reported. Generally, a neighborhood with ready accessibility to good-quality public transportation is preferable and deemed more valuable than one isolated from arteries of public surface travel.

Spreading decentralization, aided by the increasing use of electricity for the performance of essential household chores, has encouraged the development of residential subdivisions far from the public conveniences offered to residents of central urban areas. Although efforts are made to provide essential public conveniences for these outlying developments through the construction of neighborhood shopping centers, schools, parks, and recreation areas, there is nevertheless a considerable time lag from the period of original neighborhood development to the period when neighborhood shopping facilities and schools become a reality. Years often elapse without such public conveniences, and the values of suburban sites will reflect their absence. An appraiser, therefore, must accurately report the distances in blocks or miles from the subject neighborhood to nearby schools, stores, and churches as well as to the central business area. He or she must also estimate the effect that distance from these public service facilities may have on the value of the subject property.

The last, but by no means the least of the physical features that make or break a neighborhood from a value point of view is the relative freedom which residents of the area enjoy from *health hazards and other adverse influences.* The danger of through automobile traffic was mentioned before. Other hazards to be checked are smoke, dust, noise, and the gradual infiltration of nonconforming land uses. A check of area residents, public officials, and the opinions of informed persons, along with a thorough neighborhood investigation, should disclose the absence or presence of neighborhood nuisances. Where evidence points to artificial or natural conditions which presently or potentially will impair the health or peace of area residents, the effects on the present value of neighborhood sites must be ascertained and disclosed in the section on area influences.

SOCIAL FORCES INFLUENCING NEIGHBORHOOD VALUES

People create value—hence the compatibility and congeniality of people in an area are important to sustain and enhance neighborhood desirability and property values. A good-quality neighborhood will disclose compatibility among residents as well as well maintained properties.

The role of the appraiser is to interpret the attitudes of buyers, sellers, tenants, and owners toward real estate in a neighborhood. The appraiser should never inject his or her own value biases or preferences. Also, the appraiser is obligated to reflect actual values in a neighborhood rather than to conjecture on the effect on value of a particular situation. Instead of noting that a neighborhood exhibits "pride of ownership," he or she should document the actual state of maintenance of properties and off-site improvements.

Inspections of the neighborhood by sight and by interrogation will give additional value clues as to the *living habits* of residents and their *care of property*. These external evidences give the neighborhood a character of its own. Well-kept lawns, attractive landscaping, neat and well-maintained buildings, and clean, quiet thoroughfares provide self-supporting evidence of pride of ownership— an important ingredient in the forecasting of value stability.

Attitude toward government is another essential social trait that enters into a neighborhood quality rating. Ownership and possession of property are legally backed and sanctioned. Respect for law and judiciary opinions minimizes vandalism and the violation of constitutional rights to the quiet enjoyment of life, liberty, and property. Law-abiding citizens, too, will refrain from the illegal and illicit use of premises—use that undermines the moral character of the area. A breakdown in moral fiber, respect for law, and law enforcement itself destroys neighborhood value more swiftly than do the physical forces of wear, tear, decay, and the actions of the elements. A statement of the apparent attitude of local residents toward law, order, and government is an essential part of a report on property value.

Another social characteristic lending support to neighborhood stability and value is the relative *homogeneity of cultural interests*. Generally, this homogeneity is evidenced by friendly relations among neighbors, membership in the area's civic and protective organizations, organized neighborhood social and cultural events, the extent of resident participation in social clubs, and the sharing of recreational facilities. This social aspect of neighborhood population is, of course, closely linked to homogeneity of occupational and professional economic interests that will be discussed below.

Racial discrimination in appraisal and mortgage lending practices has occurred from a variety of causes—good intentions in making loans in sound neighborhoods, ignorance of actual economic facts, and slipshod analysis. The term "redlining" was once used by the Federal Housing Administration to indicate residential neighborhoods that had a history of septic tank failures. Later, the term assumed negative racial overtones. Mortgage lenders avoided making loans in such designated racial minority neighborhoods due to perceived high risks which accelerated their physical deterioration.

It is unlawful as well as unethical for an appraiser to discriminate in appraising real estate. The National Fair Housing Act, Title VIII, of the Civil

Rights Act of 1968 prohibits discrimination in the sale, rental, or financing of real estate on the bais of race, color, religion, sex, or national origin.

In addition to avoiding discriminatory approval practices related to individuals as mentioned above, the appraiser must avoid such unwarranted actions regarding a dwelling's age and location. Each property should be considered on its own merits, with the appraiser avoiding any arbitrary judgment that automatically places older residences or those in older neighborhoods at a disadvantage.

With the increasing longevity of life, another point of appraisal interest concerns the neighborhood's *age groupings and size of families*. Extreme age differentials among heads of households is not conducive to neighborhood value stability. Older citizens acquire different habits and modes of living and may find the active and seemingly frivolous conduct of younger neighbors distracting and disquieting. An area devoid of age-group conflicts, of course, will be more appealing than one where consciousness of social and age differences is noticeable. Size of family, too, must be observed and rated, especially in relation to the space availability of the typical home. Young couples wanting families cannot long remain residents of a neighborhood where two- or even three-bedroom houses with single bathroom facilities are typical for the area. Where variation in family size is observed, possible transfers of occupants to quarters where their needs can be better served must be anticipated.

NEIGHBORHOOD ECONOMIC CHARACTERISTICS

A matter of important interest to mortgage lenders, and of prime concern to real estate investors, is the extent or percentage of neighborhood development. The image of investment failures and mass property foreclosures during the early 1930s—although more than a generation removed—is still much talked and read about in informed real estate circles. The danger then and the fear now are based on overexpansion caused by thinly supported hypothetical demands envisioned as a projection of a temporary "boom" psychology rather than a projection based on the analysis of long-term trends and socioeconomic resource studies. An area thinly developed or improved below 50 percent of its land capacity holds investment hazards which must be reflected in value estimates and stressed in appraisal report writing. Undeveloped sites, too, tempt owners and speculators into premature, hasty, and often faulty land utilization that may adversely affect the value of abutting and neighboring properties. The appraiser is duty-bound to remove the "blinds" which cause the uninformed to evaluate an apparent "jewel" of a property without an objective study of its situation.

If the neighborhood is of residential character, it is important to determine the number or percentage of total homes that are *owner occupied*. Tenants, no matter how desirable, are transient in character,[4] and frequent changes in the kind and composition of tenant families create a sense of insecurity and area instability which impairs the investment quality of a neighborhood. Tenants, too, lack a feeling of belonging, and generally their lack of pride of ownership is reflected in lax lawn and home care. Owner-occupancy status can readily be secured from public tax-record data or from tax officials, especially in states where homestead tax exemptions are accorded owner occupants.

Frequency of *property turnover* and percentage of home, apartment, or store vacancies provide another measure of economic rating. As a rule a neighborhood with well-established owner occupants of long standing poses fewer investment risks than one characterized by frequent property transfers. Excessive property sales, no matter how valid the reason, create a feeling of investment insecurity or a climate of speculation, resulting in distorted market prices and often deferred maintenance for the properties involved. Since property values— unless otherwise stated—reflect the present worth of future rights to income, at least over the remaining economic life of property improvements,[5] the appraiser must take into account the influence of temporary price determinants and objectively predict future expectancy under anticipated typical market operations. Vacancies, too, if in excess of normal ratios varying from 2 to 5 percent of total space supply—depending on geographic location and kind of real property—must be analyzed with care. Excessive vacancies may indicate a glutting of the market or its becoming less appealing to owners, tenants, and investors.

The economic status of neighborhood occupants, their means of livelihood, and their income stability are of further economic importance. The predominant professional or occupational interests of area residents should be established. The order generally descends from executives to professionals (doctors, lawyers, etc.), junior executives, white-collar office workers, skilled mechanics, clerks, and skilled laborers. Although a neighborhood can normally be classified as housing one or more of the occupational or professional interest groups, it is the relative income and status of the area occupants (assuming compatible social status) that matter most. Generally, there is a direct relationship between range of annual earnings and range of property values. Executives earning $50,000 to $70,000 annually generally seek homes in the price range $125,000 to $150,000. On the other hand, white-collar workers earning from $16,000 to $20,000 annually create a demand for housing in the $40,000 to $60,000 price range. Of equal significance is income stability. Certain occupations, though lower on the scale of earning power (such as teachers and salaried technicians), enjoy greater job security and stability of income. Neighborhoods occupied by this group, or any similar group—such as retired persons—whose stability of income is relatively certain will experience greater stability in their level of prop-

---

[4]Studies of tenancy in metropolitan areas support the fact that the average tenant moves once each year.

[5]A shorter holding period generally typifies income-producing property resulting from federal income tax laws and mortgage terms.

erty values. However, it is possible that in some neighborhoods of fixed-income residents property values will be adversely affected as rising utility bills prevent normal home maintenance due to lack of income.

The economic impact of property taxation and assessment levels and burdens must be carefully analyzed in the valuation process. Although property taxation is generally a matter for study and analysis as a political policy of county and city goverments, it is a commonly recognized fact that tax differentials exist between most newer and older communities. Initially, new neighborhoods and even communities will have relatively low tax burdens. Fast-growing suburban neighborhoods often fit this pattern. They also are characterized by crowded schools and inadequate public services. Eventually, residents demand improved public services, with the result being tax rates increasing at a faster rate than in older established neighborhoods (or tax districts). The appraiser needs to anticipate such trends. Over the short-term, municipal capital budgets for schools, parks, sewers, and streets provide an indication of these tax rate trends. Where such tax differentials exist, they must be noted and evaluated over the immediate years as being, at best, a form of community "good will". Conversely, neighborhoods may have been overburdened with heavy assessments for road and area improvements that have brought little if any benefits to the properties affected. To illustrate: In a court case, property owners in Miami Beach, Florida, challenged the right of the municipality to levy assessments for the widening of Indian Creek Drive. The property owners contended that the improvements were made to relieve congested traffic on another street, and that as a result of the widening the affected street had turned into a noisy thoroughfare that had caused neighboring values to lessen. The State Supreme Court, in a 4−3 decision, ruled against the city and in favor of the property owners by recognizing that benefits which may accrue from road widening in a residential area are questionable. The majority opinion at one point asked: "Whoever heard of making a traffic count to locate a home?" However, where uneconomic assessments are enforced the appraiser must estimate their effect (considering both amount and duration) on the market value of neighborhood properties.

Since the typical buyer, contrary to accepted opinion, is not especially informed on matters concerning public zoning and private deed restrictions, it is the appraiser's responsibility to evaluate the benefits or detriments constituted by the presence or absence of protective zoning and private deed restrictions. Care must be taken to recognize that zoning by itself does not create value. For example, to zone an area for business counter to good planning or in excess of such land use demands may not only lower the value of the property so zoned but may also lessen the value of surrounding properties in the neighborhood. Zoning is designed to restrict *land* uses. Good zoning, however, does assure uniformity of land use and thus provides protection against inharmonious land uses which exploit the public good for purposes of excessive private gain. The presence, need, and adequacy of deed restrictions must also be evaluated. Zoning ordinances can often be rescinded or adversely amended. Deed restrictions, however, have stronger legal sanctions which attach to and run with the land and cannot be violated without consent of the property owners affected, as well as without compliance to stipulated contractual provisions under which land use exceptions may be made. The period of time during which deed restrictions are effective must be noted along with permissible extension of existing deed restrictions where they are deemed essential to protect the character of the neighborhood over the economic life of the neighborhood improvements.

Of interest to investors and home owners, as well as being of value significance, is whether a neighborhood warrants approval for FHA, VA, or *institutional mortgage-loan financing.* In recent years where an increasing number of marginal home buyers depend on high-ratio mortgage-to-value loans, the unavailability of government-underwritten or institutional loans—especially if caused by a lack of required neighborhood improvements such as sewerage, water, paving, etc.—may curb sales of residential properties to an extent where a buyers' market will reflect in its lower values the absence of liberal financial aid. The loss in property value in a restricted mortgage market is often far in excess of the costs of street and utility improvements the absence of which disqualify the neighborhood for government-approved or conventional mortgage loans.

An important guide to the price quality of a neighborhood is the value range of residential homes. In fact, the first step in classifying a neighborhood is to establish the price range within which typical homes can be exchanged in the open market. It is this price range[6] that guides the appraiser in his or her selection of comparable properties to serve as a market guide for estimating the worth of a particular property in the subject neighborhood. Care must be taken not to attempt a narrowing of the range to the point where "guesstimating" becomes a strong temptation. As a rule, the spread of values may range from a minimum of 25 to a maximum of 50 percent of typical sale values. The appraiser thus may conclude a range, for instance, of from $50,000 to $62,500; or a maximum spread of from $50,000 to $75,000. Although circumstances may warrant exceptions, it should be kept in mind that a typical and not an extreme range is sought in categorizing a neighborhood. The actual, or imputed, rental value per month or per annum of typical neighborhood structures, too, is of interest. This information serves importantly in helping to check market sales estimates against the capitalized value found under the income or earnings approach to value.

No appraisal is complete without a thorough analysis of environmental forces and improvements that affect the value rating of a neighborhood. Every appraisal form in use currently provides for entry of data which aid the field appraiser in reaching a value conclusion concerning the quality of the area under study.

---

[6]The other major consideration is the similarity of comparable properties. This is truly the "yardstick" of value for the appraised property.

NEIGHBORHOOD						Good	Avg.	Fair	Poor
Location	☐ Urban	☐ Suburban	☐ Rural						
Built Up	☐ Over 75%	☐ 25% to 75%	☐ Under 25%	Employment Stability		☐	☐	☐	☐
Growth Rate ☐ Fully Dev.	☐ Rapid	☐ Steady	☐ Slow	Convenience to Employment		☐	☐	☐	☐
Property Values	☐ Increasing	☐ Stable	☐ Declining	Convenience to Shopping		☐	☐	☐	☐
Demand/Supply	☐ Shortage	☐ In Balance	☐ Over Supply	Convenience to Schools		☐	☐	☐	☐
Marketing Time	☐ Under 3 Mos.	☐ 4–6 Mos.	☐ Over 6 Mos.	Adequacy of Public Transportation		☐	☐	☐	☐
Present Land Use ___% 1 Family ___% 2–4 Family ___% Apts. ___% Condo ___% Commercial				Recreational Facilities		☐	☐	☐	☐
___% Industrial ___% Vacant ___%				Adequacy of Utilities		☐	☐	☐	☐
Change in Present Land Use	☐ Not Likely	☐ Likely (*)	☐ Taking Place (*)	Property Compatibility		☐	☐	☐	☐
(*) From ___ To ___				Protection from Detrimental Conditions		☐	☐	☐	☐
Predominant Occupancy	☐ Owner	☐ Tenant	___% Vacant	Police and Fire Protection		☐	☐	☐	☐
Single Family Price Range $___ to $___ Predominant Value $___				General Appearance of Properties		☐	☐	☐	☐
Single Family Age ___ yrs to ___ yrs Predominant Age ___ yrs				Appeal to Market		☐	☐	☐	☐

Note: FHLMC/FNMA do not consider race or the racial composition of the neighborhood to be reliable appraisal factors.

Comments including those factors, favorable or unfavorable, affecting marketability (e.g. public parks, schools, view, noise)_____

Figure 7.4 Neighborhood Analysis Grid Used by FHLMC and FNMA

Figure 7.4 shows the factors that the Federal Home Loan Mortgage Corporation considers important in residential neighborhood analysis. Some of the key concerns revealed in this excerpt from a form appraisal are the demand for homes, development activity and trends, type of occupancy, typical age and price range of homes, proximity and adequacy of employment, neighborhood educational, shopping and recreational facilities, and general appeal of the neighborhood to prospective purchasers.

NEIGHBORHOOD ATTRIBUTES OF COMMERCIAL DISTRICTS

Greater dependence by shoppers on private means of transportation has accelerated the development of suburban shopping centers where ready access and ample parking invite unhurried and carefree shopping. Contrary to hasty predictions made by prominent urban economists, the central city as a commercial entity is, however, far from oblivion. In fact, the downtown shopping areas, which in major cities struck a low point in unit land value in the 1960–1965 period, are now readjusting, modernizing, and effectively competing for their share of the community trade dollar.

It is the appraiser's responsibility to analyze the qualitative importance of the commercial shopping area and to designate the grouping of stores which marketwise constitute the 100 percent trade location. Other locations that radiate from this 100 percent area can then be qualitatively and percentage-wise rated in the process of estimating comparative unit land values.

Neighborhood traffic conditions play a crucial role in the success of retail districts and especially for shopping centers. These centers are largely dependent on a sizable unimpeded flow of vehicular traffic. This traffic should be neither too slow to become congested nor too fast to cause prospective shoppers to miss seeing the center or possibly be deterred by the rapidly moving traffic. A high

Table 7.1 Neighborhood Shopping Centers: Composition by Tenant Group

	Percent GLA	Percent Sales	Ratio: Percent Sales to Percent GLA
General merchandise	6.6	3.6	0.55
Food	27.8	57.9	2.08
Food services	8.6	6.5	0.76
Clothing	5.3	5.1	0.96
Shoes	1.1	0.8	0.73
Home furnishings	2.2	0.8	0.36
Home appliances/music	2.0	1.2	0.60
Building materials/garden	3.1	1.3	0.42
Automotive supplies/service station	2.4	1.1	0.46
Hobby/special interest	2.6	1.8	0.69
Gifts/specialty	2.6	1.7	0.65
Jewelry and cosmetics	0.6	0.7	1.17
Liquor	1.5	2.0	1.33
Drugs	9.3	9.9	1.06
Other retail	3.5	1.5	0.43
Personal services	5.4	2.1	0.39
Recreation/community	3.4	0.7	
Financial	4.3	0.1	
Offices (other than financial)	3.2	0.7	
Other	4.5	0.5	
Total	100.0	100.0	

Source: *Dollars & Cents of Shopping Centers: 1981* (Washington, D.C.: The Urban Land Institute, 1981), p. 296.

volume of traffic may be misleading, especially if it is intercity or commercial traffic.

The shopping center itself must be analyzed in accordance with the principle of balance to ascertain the adequacy in number as well as the variety of essential retail establishments. According to a 1981 survey by the Urban Land Institute, the median size of neighborhood shopping centers was 63,328 square feet. Table 7.1 shows the predominance of food sales, followed by drug and food services.

The kind and number of retail establishments in a subject commercial area depend, of course, on community custom, climate, and the general characteristics of the inhabitants.

INDUSTRIAL DISTRICT ATTRIBUTES

There exist today a large number of industrial districts. These districts often are characterized by older multistoried buildings that front on city streets and alleys. These buildings were individually planned and are individually owned.

The modern counterparts to these districts are planned industrial parks. Generally, there is one developer but numerous tenants and/or building owners. Increasingly, these parks contain office buildings along with the traditional manufacturing and distribution functions.

Some of the district or park attributes that are judged to be important for industrial activities are an ample supply of utilities (water, sewer, and source of power). Accessibility to markets, to sources of materials, subcontractors, a skilled workforce, and adequate circulation and parking for trucks is needed. Access to alternative transportation for certain industries in the form of rail and airlines is required. Adequate public school systems, housing, shopping and recreation and religious facilities are also desirable in order to attract and retain employees. Realistic zoning and building codes are expected to protect the industrial districts from incompatible land uses and from inferior construction.

REVIEW QUESTIONS

1. Briefly discuss two past errors made in neighborhood analysis.
2. Discuss and give examples of the "linkages" concept.
3. Why is it important to accurately perceive the phase of life cycle that a neighborhood is in at the date of appraisal?
4. List the several ways that a neighborhood can be delineated.
5. Drawing from your own observations, describe a neighborhood that has been revitalized. What factors were responsible for its economic upturn?
6. List 10 residential neighborhood characteristics that should be investigated by an appraiser.
7. Discuss the earlier justification for the practice of "redlining" and explain the fallacy of this practice when later applied to minority neighborhoods.
8. Discuss the importance of traffic analysis in residential, commercial, and industrial neighborhoods or districts.

READING AND STUDY REFERENCES

AMERICAN INSTITUTE OF REAL ESTATE APPRAISERS. Chapter 7, "Analysis of Neighborhoods and Districts," *The Appraisal of Real Estate*. Chicago: American Institute of Real Estate Appraisers, 1983.

BLOOM, GEORGE F., and HENRY S. HARRISON. Chapter 6, "Neighborhood Analysis," *Appraising the Single Family Residence*. Chicago: American Institute of Real Estate Appraisers, 1978.

BOYKIN, JAMES H. "Neighborhood Analysis," *Financing Real Estate*. Lexington, Mass.: D.C. Heath and Company, 1979, pp. 433–444.

HANEY, RICHARD L., JR. "Race and Housing Value: A Review of Their Interrelationships," *The Appraisal Journal* 45, no. 3 (July 1977), pp. 356–364.

RAMS, EDWIN M., ed. *Analysis and Valuation of Retail Locations*. Reston, Va.: Reston Publishing Co., Inc., 1976.

RING, ALFRED A., and JEROME J. DASSO. Chapter 11, "Urban-Area Structure and Highest and Best Use," *Real Estate Principles and Practices*. Englewood Cliffs, N.J.: Prentice-Hall, Inc., 10th ed., 1985.

SHENKEL, WILLIAM M. Chapter 5, "Neighborhood Analysis," *Modern Real Estate Appraisal*. New York: McGraw-Hill Book Company, 1978.

SUMICHRAST, MICHAEL, and MAURY SELDIN. Chapter 13, "Location-of-Development Analysis," *Housing Markets*, Homewood, Ill.: Dow Jones-Irwin, 1977.

8

CONSIDERATIONS IN SITE ANALYSIS

Learning Objectives

After reading this chapter, you should be able to:

Understand the purposes of site analysis

Discuss the factors normally considered in analyzing a site

Distinguish among the terms "site," "parcel," "tract," and "land"

Appreciate the different methods used to describe a site

Apply the principle of marginal productivity to site analysis

This chapter focuses on sites and in particular on the physical, legal, and economic analysis of sites. All of this leads to judging the desirability and in turn the value of an appraised site. Although the term "site" is generally used in this chapter, it will be enlightening to the reader if four terms—site, tract, parcel, and land—are defined at this point:

Site: A unit of land that is ready for its intended use. A site generally is a section of a larger holding, such as a subdivision. It has been prepared and serviced. That is, it has been surveyed, cleared, graded, and has the necessary drainage. Streets, curbs, gutters, sewer, water, and other public utilities, such as gas and electric lines, are in place.

Tract: A comparatively large unit of land that has not been prepared for its eventual use. A site may be developed from a tract.

Parcel: This unit of land is part of a larger holding, and under one ownership. It sometimes is used interchangeably with *tract.*

Land: The meaning of this term is evasive even though sometimes it is used synonomously with the other terms above. It may refer to the earth's surface, a region, natural resources, or a property. It is distinguished from *site* in its not having been developed for an intensive use (e.g., farmland versus shopping center site).

SITE ANALYSIS PRINCIPLES

Several of the value principles discussed in Chapter 3 are particularly relevant to site analysis. Determining highest and best use is one of the two major reasons for site analysis. Thus the appraiser must keep his or her objective in mind as the site and off-site influences are considered. Another concern is the principle of marginal productivity, which was previously illustrated using two different sites with varying depths. Although each additional foot of depth adds overall value to a site, its unit value contribution diminishes when the depth of the site extends beyond some optimum use point.

In judging the utility and value of a site, the appraiser should consider the optimum site depth and size for a prospective use. These considerations will guide his or her selection of comparable sales to support the estimated value of the site. It is preferable to develop local depth and corner value relationships than to use depth and corner setback tables that may be empirically derived but for different circumstances at an earlier date in different municipalities, and possibly in another state.

Purpose of Site Analysis

A basic rule of mathematics is that "the sum of the parts equals the whole." This principle is sometimes violated in the case of appraising. Logically, each section of a report should relate to the final value reported. In fact, some of the parts (facts) considered have no relation to the whole (value estimate). Yet a basic premise of real property valuation is that every factor considered should relate to a property's highest and best use and its value. If it does not, it is superfluous and should be excluded. Similarly, the regional analysis should relate to the community analysis and in turn to the neighborhood and site analysis. If the appraiser keeps these interrelationships in mind, the appraisal product will be a coherent and convincing report.

The major purposes of site analysis are to judge a property's highest and best use, its utility for prospective present and future uses, its market appeal, the remaining economic life of the improvements, and finally, its value. All of these factors are influenced by physical, legal, and market constraints. This analysis essentially is undertaken to judge the usefulness of a site, which then may be translated into a measure of its value. Also, the type of analysis is undertaken to identify the boundaries of the property, any encroachments, and also to establish the rights to be appraised.

Site Identification

Every appraisal should include a legal description which definitely and unmistakably fixes the geographic location of the subject property. Where the land is improved, the legal description should be reinforced by street name and building number for added reference. Within the city limits and in suburban subdivisions, a description by lot and block number as shown on a given page in a plat book on official record best serves this purpose. For property locations in suburban or rural areas, or where subdivision designations by lot and block numbers are unavailable, the appraiser should obtain accurate legal descriptions prepared under either the "metes and bounds" or government survey system.

Because of the technical competency required to derive directional bearings north, south, east, and west with accuracy to minutes and seconds of degrees, metes and bounds descriptions should be prepared only by registered land surveyors. In metes and bounds descriptions as shown in Figure 8.1, the bearings or course of a line of direction is the angle which that line makes from the central point of departure parallel with a meridian. As shown below, the bearing of any line cannot exceed 90 degrees. A line running almost due east might have a

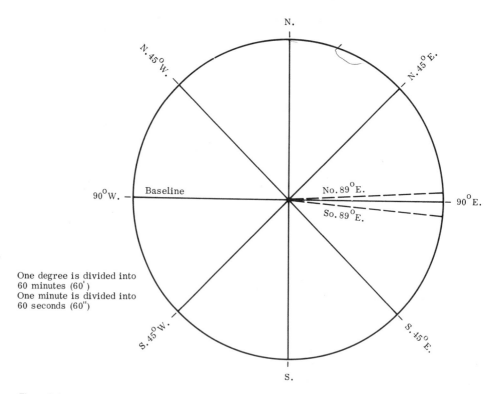

One degree is divided into
60 minutes (60')
One minute is divided into
60 seconds (60")

Figure 8.1

bearing of "north" 89 degrees east. If this same line were rotated 2 degrees in a clockwise direction, its bearing would become "south" 89 degrees east.

Bearings may be measured and described either from the magnetic north and south (in which case they are called *magnetic bearings*) or from a true astronomic meridian north and south (in which case they are called *true bearings*). The bearings of a given line as expressed under the two systems will differ by the amount of the magnetic declination for that date and locality.

Rectangular Survey System

To make available accurate legal descriptions, particularly in rural areas, the federal government adopted in 1785 the rectangular survey of land locations. This system is based on surveying lines running north and south, called meridians, and east and west, called base lines. These are established through the area to be surveyed and each is given a name and number by the land office in Washington, D.C. A map showing the location of the several prime meridians and their base lines in the United States is shown in Figure 8.2.

Beginning at the intersection of the meridian and base lines, the surveyors divided the area between intersections into squares, called "checks," 24 miles on each side. These squares were further subdivided into 16 areas each measuring 6 miles by 6 miles, called "townships." The townships containing an area of 36 square miles were again subdivided into "sections," each a square mile containing 640 acres, and the sections were then divided into halves, quarters, or smaller subdivisions as the need called for to describe individual land holdings.[1]

To identify the various townships, the rows east and west and parallel to the base line were numbered as "tiers" 1, 2, and so on, north or south, of a given base line. The rows north and south and parallel to the meridians were called ranges and were numbered 1, 2, and so on, east or west of a principal or guide meridian. The numbering system is illustrated in Figure 8.3.

Owing to the spherical shape of the earth, the meridians converge as one goes north—the north side of a township is approximately 50 feet shorter than the south side. To correct this error, the government established certain principle meridians and others, called guide meridians, which are changed at each parallel to make allowances for the earth's curvature. This problem really concerns only the surveyor and is mentioned only so that the reader may not be confused in studying the diagram.

In describing a section, it is customary to state first the number of the section, then the township and range: "Section 12, Township 3 North, Range 2

---

[1]For a full explanation of land surveying and property descriptions, see Chapter 4 of Alfred A. Ring and Jerome J. Dasso, *Real Estate Principles and Practices*, 10th ed. (Englewood Cliffs, New Jersey: Prentice-Hall, Inc., 1985).

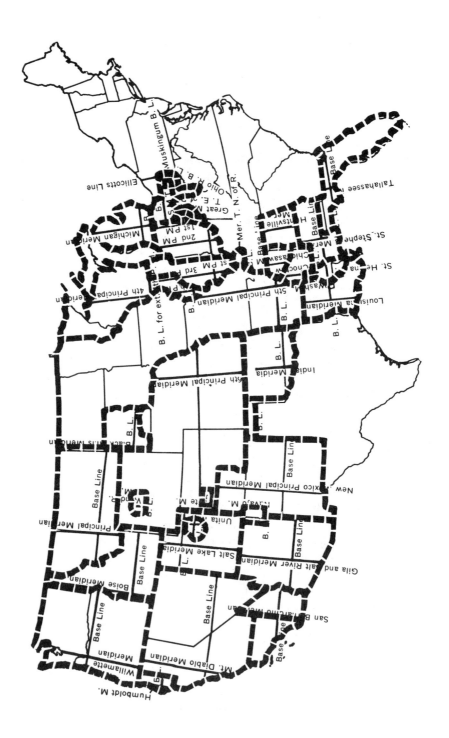

Figure 8.2 Map of Prime Meridians and Their Base Lines Within the United States

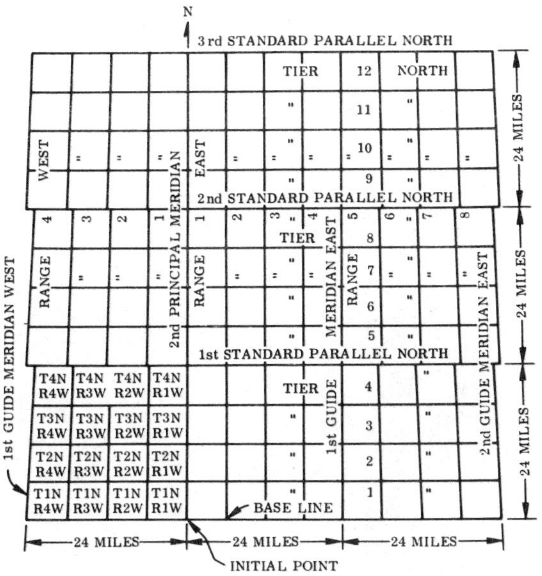

Sections are identified by number as indicated on the following diagram:

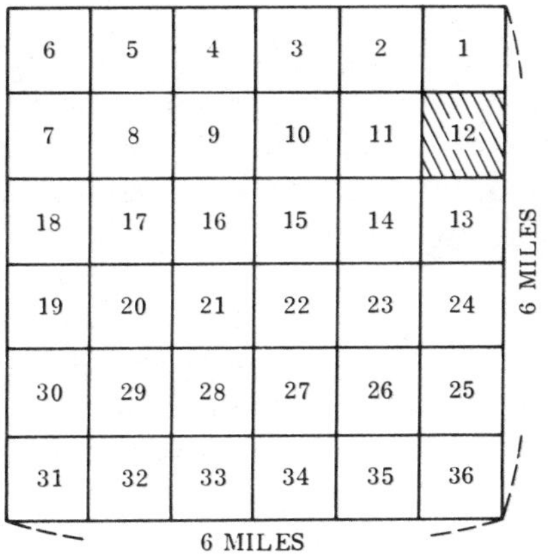

Figure 8.3

East of the principal (named) meridian." It may be abbreviated "Sect. 12 T. 3 N. Rge 2 E, . . . County, State of. . . ."

The description of a part of a section is simple. For example, the plot A shown in Figure 8.4 is "West ½ of Southwest ¼, Sec. 12." The same diagram indicates the description of other parts of the section.

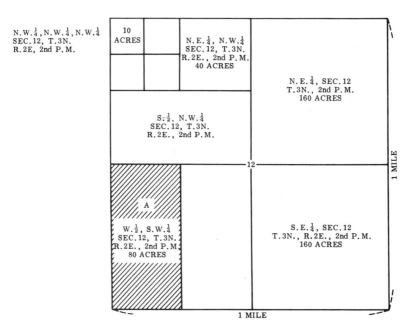

Figure 8.4 Divisions of a Section

Metes and Bounds Method

This method of site or tract identification may be used with any of the other methods. It is especially prevalent in the states that formed the original 13 colonies, the South Atlantic states, and Texas. It describes a property's boundaries by giving the courses and distances. The courses are indicated by compass headings; distances in a given direction generally are measured in feet.[2] This lineal method is based on a boundary survey. It starts at a point of beginning, which usually is some distance from a point extended from a side property line to the center line of the abutting street or road. The boundary is traced around the site's perimeter and eventually returns to the point of beginning. The appraiser should be much more familiar with this technique than the city investor who once asked the owner of a rural tract: "What are these leaps and bounds that you've been talking about?" An example of this metes and bounds method is shown for lot 5 in Figure 8.5.

[2]The following measurements commonly appeared in deeds for properties surveyed prior to this century:

1 link	= 7.92 inches	1 furlong	= 660 feet or 40 rods
1 rod	= 16½ feet or 25 links	1 acre	= 43,560 square feet,
1 chain	= 66 feet		160 square rods, or
			10 square chains

See also, "Land Measurement Table" in Appendix V.

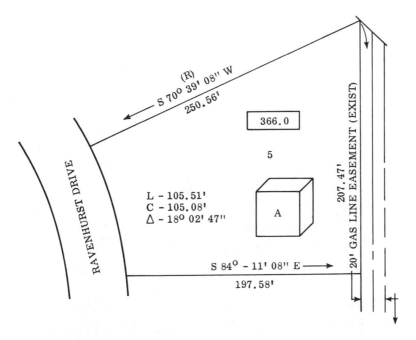

Figure 8.5 Illustrative Legal Description (Using Metes and Bounds)

Monument Method

In many early surveys, a rural property's boundaries were fixed by reference to "monuments." These landmarks were such items as a neighbor's wooden fence or a particular tree, stream, or rock. Such references over time often disappeared or were relocated, causing confusion for later owners of the property. However, a monument may be either natural or fabricated; it is used to indicate a corner or change in direction of a property line. Earlier these were used without any measured distances between monuments. Later, this method included such measurements and greater use of artificial monuments such as iron stakes set by surveyors. An example of an earlier monument system is shown below. This illustration points out some of the potential problems in using the monument system, including changing directions of streams, replaced and relocated rock piles, trees dying over the years, and named and once familiar landmarks being unrecognizable in successive generations.

The following description, taken from the Hartford, Connecticut, Probate Court records for 1812, will illustrate what is often encountered in early metes and bounds (boundary) surveys.

147 acres, 3 rods, and 19 rods after deducting whatever swamp, water, rock and road areas there may be included therein and all other lands of little or no value, the same being part of said deceased's 1280 acre colony grant, and the portion

hereby set off being known as near to and on the other side of Black Oak Ridge, bounded and described more in particular as follows, to wit:—Commencing at a heap of stone, about a stone's throw from a certain small clump of alders, near a brook running down off from a rather high part of said ridge; thence, by a straight line to a certain marked white birch tree, about two or three times as far from a jog in a fence going around a ledge nearby; thence, by another straight line in a different direction, around said ledge and the Great Swamp, so called; thence, in line of said lot in part and in part by another piece of fence which joins on to said line, and by an extension of the general run of said fence to a heap of stone near a surface rock; thence, as aforesaid, to the 'Horn,' so called, and passing around the same as aforesaid, as far as the 'Great Bend,' so called, and from thence to a squarish sort of a jog in another fence, and so on to a marked black oak tree with stones piled around it; thence, by another straight line in about a contrary direction and somewhere about parallel with the line around the ledge and the Great Swamp, to a stake and stone bounds not far off from the old Indian trail; thence, by another straight line on a course diagonally parallel, or nearly so, with 'Fox Hollow Run,' so called, to a certain marked red cedar tree out on a sandy sort of a plain; thence, by another straight line, in a different direction, to a certain marked yellow oak tree on the off side of a knoll with a flat stone laid against it; thence, after turning around in another direction, and by a sloping straight line to a certain heap of stone which is, by pacing, just 18 rods and about one half a rod more from the stump of the big hemlock tree where Philo Blake killed the bear; thence, to the corner begun at by two straight lines of about equal length, which are to be run by some skilled and competent surveyor, so as to include the area and acreage as herein before set forth.

Aerial Photography

A frequently overlooked and potentially valuable means for ascertaining the location of a parcel, especially an outlying tract, is aerial photography. A recent aerial photograph can be used to give an overview of a neighborhood, depict landmarks, and show different classes of land such as pasture and woodland. With the use of a polar plenimeter, it is possible to compute the area of the entire tract as well as individual sections. The scale of the photograph is needed to make these computations.

Figures 8.6 and 8.7 depict the boundaries of a tract. By using the aerial photograph the appraiser can orientate himself or herself to the corners of the property on the road, aid the appraiser in inspecting the property based on landmarks shown on the photogaph, and reveal the location of structures or land features that otherwise may have been overlooked. Some clients find aerial views of property to be informative.

Subdivision Method

Whenever a site is located in a platted subdivision, it should be identified with reference to that subdivision. For example, in Figure 8.8 the shaded lot on Ravenhurst Drive could be generally identified as being a certain distance southwest of Robious Road and so many feet southeast of the intersection of Ravenhurst Drive and Charter Drive. However, a more specific identification would

Figure 8.6 Aerial View of Property

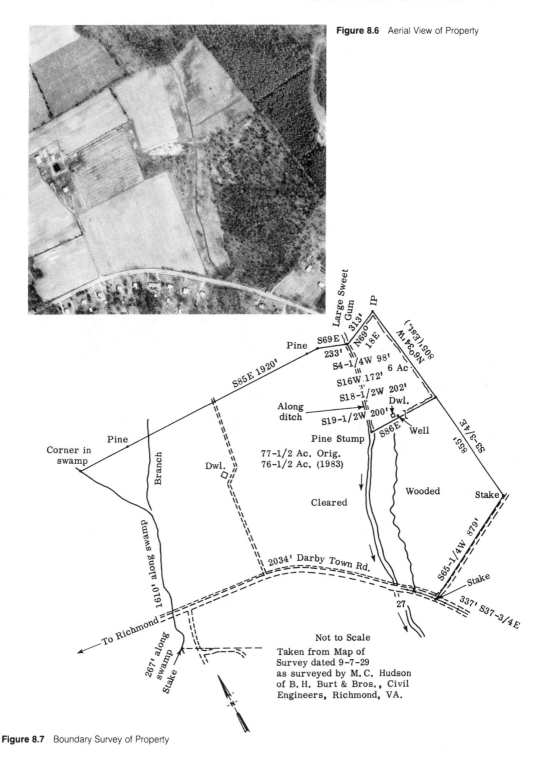

Figure 8.7 Boundary Survey of Property

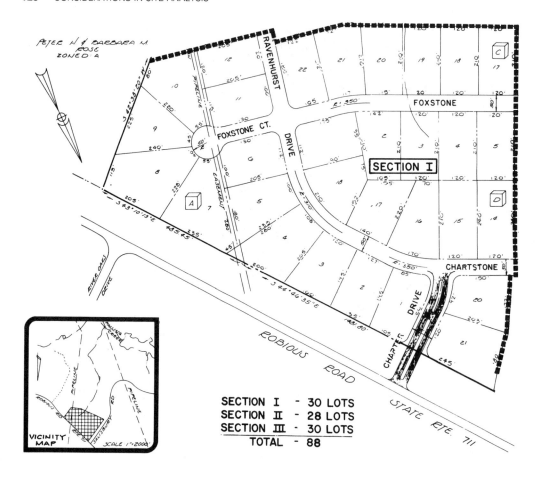

SECTION I - 30 LOTS
SECTION II - 28 LOTS
SECTION III - 30 LOTS
TOTAL - 88

Figure 8.8 Subdivision Plat Showing One of Several Sections

be to identify it as Lot 5, Block A, Section I, Charter Woods, in Midlothian District, Chesterfield County, Virginia. Taking this description a step further, the appraiser would refer to the plat book and page where the lot is recorded in the courthouse of the local jurisdiction.

In addition to the subdivision method, a property is identified by its metes and bounds description on a sketch of the site. Reference to a recorded subdivision plat offers the advantage of giving an accurate measure of the boundary lines, quantity of land, any dedication of streets or easements, sources of title, and a statement of the liens on the property. An example of such reference follows:

> All that certain lot, piece or parcel of land, with all improvements thereon, lying and being in Midlothian District, Chesterfield County, Virginia, known and designated as Lot 5, Block A, Section I, Charter Woods, as shown on a subdivision

plat of Charter Woods, dated May 3, 1985 by J. K. Timmons and Associates, Inc., Engineers, Surveyors, Planners, said plat recorded May 16, 1985 in the Clerk's Office, Circuit Court of Chesterfield County, Virginia, in Plat Book 50, page 29, and reference to which is hereby made for a more particular description thereof.

Condominium Subdivision

Especially where condominiums are housed in a multistoried building, it becomes necessary to identify a property accurately, not only in the customary horizontal manner but vertically as well. The vertical part of the legal description may begin at a datum point on the ground and extends to elevations from the top of a unit's unfinished floor to the bottom of the unfinished ceiling. The space between ceiling and floor is part of the common area. Each unit is described in a master deed for the entire development. Important, too, for identification purposes, is an identification of the common areas owned by each individual condominium owner. The joint ownership and maintenance of these common areas can influence the value of each individual property since ownership is extended beyond the actual residence and maintenance expenses may be burdensome.

Street Address

This method is ordinarily used either by itself or preferably, in conjunction with one of the other methods. It can only be used in municipalities where streets have been numbered. This system is weakened when several streets within a metropolis have the same name. Sometimes streets are renamed and renumbered. A safeguard, in view of these possible events, is to include the U.S. postal zip code along with the street address.

To avoid any possible misunderstanding as to the exact location of the site under value study, it is recommended that a location sketch, such as that shown in Figure 8.9, be made a part of every appraisal report. This sketch should designate a prominent point of reference, such as a courthouse, police station, museum, or other well-known public building, and should indicate by reference to public roads or streets the direction and location of the subject property. With the aid of this sketch, even a stranger to the community should be able to reach the location without fail. As shown, distances in blocks or miles should be noted to avoid further unnecessary delays in pinpointing the subject location.

The location, once accurately established, should then be analyzed in regard to:

1. Nature of terrain and soil characteristics.
2. Size, depth, shape, and corner-lot location influences.
3. Street improvements and availability of essential public utilities.

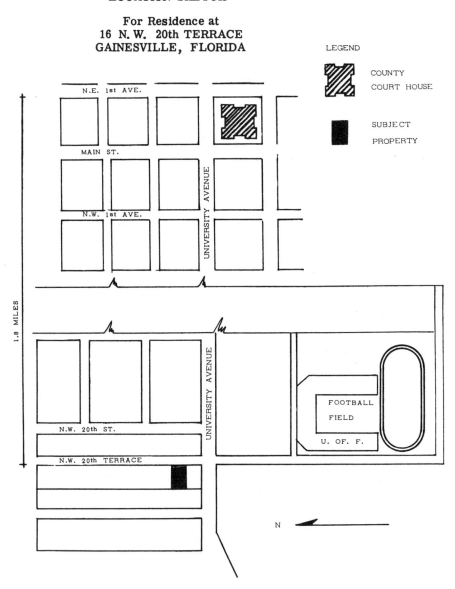

Figure 8.9   Location Sketch

4. Zoning, building, and deed restrictions.
5. Title considerations and encroachments.
6. Adjoining structures and land uses.
7. Landscaping, building, and subsurface land improvements.

NATURE OF TERRAIN AND SOIL CHARACTERISTICS

Site preparations and cost of site developments differ with soil conditions and nature of terrain. Sites below street level may require filling; others, because of subsurface flaws, costly shoring; and still others, terracing to prevent washouts or construction of retaining walls to safeguard building foundations. Rock may have to be blasted or pilings driven where the load-bearing quality of the soil is deemed inadequate. Additional costs of site preparation, over and above those typically incurred in building construction, usually diminish the value of the land. This reduction in land value is in proportion to the extraordinary dollar outlays necessary because of adverse site conditions. Some sites, in fact, may prove so costly to prepare that the land is classified *submarginal* and defaulted in title to the city or county for tax-saving purposes, or deeded to public authorities for utilization—at public expense—as a park or for other recreational or community-use benefits. Conversely, a site, because of favorable orientation or natural terrain features, may bring about savings in construction or offer amenities which result in *situs qualities* (economic characteristics of land made or brought about by popular acceptance) over and above those typical for other neighborhood locations. In such instances it is the appraiser's task to estimate the construction cost savings, or to measure the added value resulting from demand preference for site locations possessing quality attributes ascribable to nature of soil or geographic orientation.

Terrain

Topographical analysis should be used to determine if the site is usable for the intended or prospective use. Is the terrain so irregular and steep as to prohibitively increase the site preparation costs and foundation costs for the building? The relationship of the terrain at street or road grade is important. If it is elevated several feet, steps will be necessary which may reduce the appeal of the site for residential purposes for many prospective users. If, on the other hand, the site is below street grade, it may be equally unattractive and pose some problems in getting a vehicle onto the street. A site with some variation in topography, such as a gently rolling parcel, offers appeal for residential subdivision purposes. The variation in terrain adds interest and variation to the individual home sites. This premise is not true for commercial or industrial sites, however.

A site with some slope gradient facilitates surface water runoff. But if the slope is too great, there may be erosion problems. On the other hand, a flat site eliminates erosion problems but, depending on subsoil conditions, may cause standing water. Water standing under a house may in time cause rotting structural members or leaking basements.

In some areas it is particularly necessary for the appraiser to be aware of both the neighborhood's and the site's history. For example, the subdivision may have been built over coal mines or a sanitary landfill. Both could cause subsidence. Continual house repairs are associated with foundation and footings settling where there may be such unstable subsoil conditions. The additional threat of homes on a landfill site is the possible emission of methane gas. It can cause explosions and the property to be uninhabitable or certainly its value greatly reduced in the future.

Soil

Soil surveys generally are available throughout the country. Although appraisers are not soil scientists, it is important that soil conditions be taken into account in judging the potential use and value of a site. Figure 8.10 is taken from a soil survey in Virginia. The illustration is included to point out the appearance of a soil survey map and to show a preliminary means for determining whether certain soils are fit for developmental purposes. In studying this soils classification map along with a description of the different classes of soil, it can be determined, for example, that WoB (Woodstown) has a seasonal high water table, is moderately suited for septic system drain fields, but is not suited for basements; it has a low shrink-swell potential. The SfA and SfB (Sassafras) is a well-drained soil and permeable; it is only slightly impaired for septic system drain fields and basements. Tm (Tidal Marsh) is generally composed of various combinations and layers of sandy, loamy, clayey, and mucky materials. It is constantly waterlogged and unsuitable for development or septic system drainage fields.

Another key consideration in site analysis is the combined effect of slope and subsoil conditions. A particular subsoil may be marginally suitable for development purposes for a level site. Yet when there is a slope, the same subsoil may be too unstable to support footings for a building.

Flood Hazard

Flood insurance has become important for the financing of residential property. For example, HUD requires flood insurance on single-family properties when they are located in a 100-year floodplain. An appraiser can obtain "flood hazard boundary maps" showing flood-prone areas in most communities. These maps are provided by the Federal Insurance Administration of the Federal Emergency Management Agency in Bethesda, Maryland. A flood-prone area is one where there is a risk of serious flooding at least once every 100 years. An example of a flood hazard map for Ontario, Oregon, is shown in Figure 8.11.

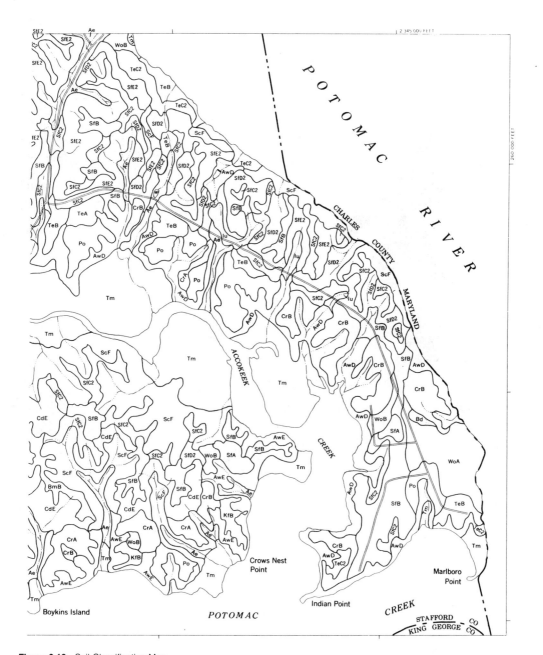

Figure 8.10 Soil Classification Map

Source: *Soil Survey: Stafford and King George Counties Virginia*, U.S. Department of Agriculture in cooperation with Virginia
Polytechnic Institute and State University (Washington, D.C.: Government Printing Office, 1974) sheet no. 30.

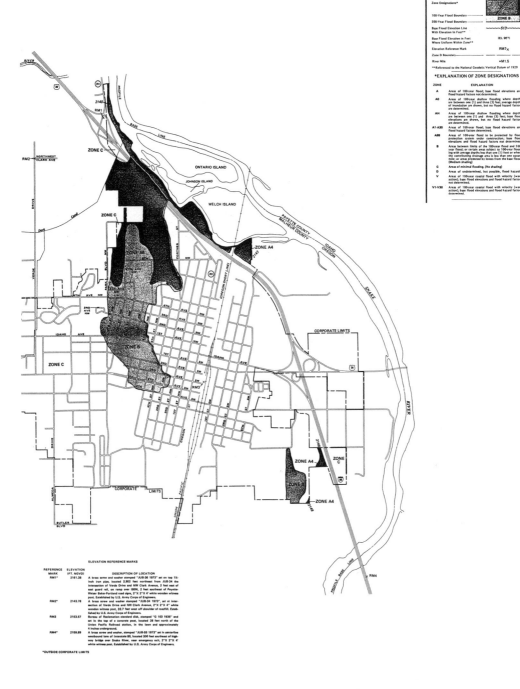

Figure 8.11 Flood Hazard Boundary Map for Ontario, Oregon

STREET IMPROVEMENTS AND AVAILABILITY
OF ESSENTIAL PUBLIC UTILITIES

Street accessibility and extent of street frontage are of substantial value importance for all urban land use activities. This is supported by the fact that the *unit value* for such sites is typically quoted on a front foot rather than on a square foot or acre basis, as is the case with industrial or agricultural land. This front-foot value is considerably enhanced where streets are properly improved and provide for service connections to essential public utilities. Street improvements recognized as adding value include paving, sidewalks, curb, gutter, storm drains, sanitary sewage, and connections for water, gas, telephones, and electricity. Care must be taken to make certain that all improvements are fully paid. The value of a site is generally based on "as is" condition on a given date. If assessments for street and capital improvements are outstanding, the present worth of the future dollar obligations must be subtracted from the site value derived under a "free and clear" assumption of land ownership. To avoid misunderstanding the appraiser should stipulate that the value findings assume the discharge of all outstanding debt obligations and assessments due and payable, including accrued taxes to date of the appraisal. Where essential street improvements or public utilities are lacking, the appraiser must measure with care the "negative value" market reactions that penalize a site, often in excess of cost of such utilities or of road improvements.

The highest and best use and value of a site is strongly influenced by the availability and adequacy of public sewer systems. Alternatively, it should be determined whether the site is capable of supporting an individual septic system if public facilities are unavailable. The review of subsoil conditions, interview of municipal sanitary engineers and a general knowledge of an area will generally disclose the probability of problems due to inadequate subsoil permeability. Sometimes subsoil conditions are such that it is prohibitively expensive either to build an on-site sewerage system or even to construct the building itself. Examples of this would be where there are outcroppings that require expensive and time-consuming rock blasting or unstable subsoil that requires piling or substantial footings.

SHAPE, SIZE, DEPTH, AND CORNER LOCATION INFLUENCES

Shape and Size

Virtually every land use has an optimum site size and shape. In some cases, depth is important, while in other instances frontage is of greater significance. A business that depends on customers arriving in vehicles must have a site with sufficient frontage to allow comfortable braking distance and turning radius for its customers. For example, a service station typically needs at least 200 feet of road frontage.

Another example of the importance of adequate site size is residential sites that lack a community sewage removal and water supply. In such cases the minimum site size is determined by the locally required health department distance between the well and septic system drain field. Further complicating this site size determination is the fact that the well generally needs to be uphill from the drain field and then there must be perhaps 100 feet of separation between any drain fields on adjoining properties. Also, there may be a dwelling setback requirement. In some cases all parts of a site do not have sufficient percolation capacity to allow the drain field being placed where the owner prefers.

The importance of these factors being considered is shown in relation to a situation where a lot was purchased at a lake resort. The current owner had paid $15,000 for a lakefront site 12 years previously. Ordinarily, the value for such property would be considerably greater than the purchase price after 10 years. However, the developer failed to install a public water system, causing each individual lot owner to have to install his or her own well in addition to a septic system. After having considered all the various setback requirements, this particular lot had no value except to an adjoining property owner to assemble two lots in order to create one usable site. Instead of the property value increasing, lots were selling for only $300 to $500.

A site must be of a minimum size and shape to permit effective utilization in conformity with the principle of highest and best use under existing zoning, building, and deed restrictions. A site 10 feet wide and 100 feet deep in a residential area where building restrictions call for a minimum size lot containing 10,000 square feet of area has no value except as it may attract offers from neighboring property owners who may, at a nominal price, be interested in adding this strip of land to their holdings. It is important, therefore, to make certain that a site under valuation meets minimum lot-size requirements. The value of a rectangular site (if residential or commercial in character) depends on the number of front feet, along the abutting street, and on the depth of the lot if the same is deeper or shallower than that considered standard for the neighborhood. The shape of the site also influences its use and value.

To illustrate: Assuming a standard lot depth of 100 feet in a given neighborhood and a front-foot lot value of $150 (as supported by market comparison of similar lot sales), a 100-foot-wide by 100-foot-deep lot is estimated to bring $100 \times \$150$, or $15,000, if exposed for sale. For every street foot added or subtracted from this lot, provided that the lot depth remains 100 feet, the value will increase or decrease by $150 in amount, as long as the same increment of utility is contributed or deducted by each foot added or subtracted for the standard lot. In many instances, however, lots are either substandard or in excess of a depth considered standard for the area. To measure the value influence of depth—in conformity with the principle that the front of a lot (because of street access and utility) is more valuable than the rear—depth rules have been devised to measure changes in value resulting from variations in depth size—all other things remaining equal.

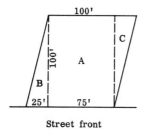

Figure 8.12

In applying depth rules, it should be kept in mind that rules by themselves do not make value but rather reflect the market actions of typical buyers in a community. Then, too, rules applied should merit acceptance by professional appraisers in the area and prove acceptable in court practice.[3] Most of the depth rules have been devised as an aid to tax assessors to permit uniformity of value treatment. For individual appraisals, it is generally better for the appraiser to develop his or her own guidelines regarding the incremental unit of value added or deducted for nonstandard depth sites. Observations need to be made for different types of sites in different locations. To generalize for all categories of land is no better than using standardized depth tables.

Odd-Shaped Lot Valuation

Irregular plots often present a problem in appraising. Assuming no disutility because of odd shape and no impairment of utilization for a particular highest and best land employment program, an irregular site should be evaluated in accordance with the customary unit measure applied in practice for similar and regular-shaped lots, plus value allowance for odd-plot portions as demonstrated in Figure 8.12. Residential and commercial sites are generally evaluated in relation to the number of feet fronting on a city street. Where the shape is a parallelogram as shown in Figure 8.12, usually no value adjustment is necessary for lot irregularity since the two triangles, marked B and C, in effect form a rectangle the combined value of which is equal to a rectangle of like street frontage.

Odd-shaped lots such as those shown in Figure 8.13 are valued as rectangular lots, plus the additional value of the triangular lots. Based on market study, a triangular lot with its base fronting the street, such as Lot 2 in Figure 8.13, is worth 65 percent of a rectangular lot of the same frontage. A triangular lot with its apex on the street, such as Lot 1 in Figure 8.13, is worth 35 percent

[3]During testimony in an Alabama District Court a witness referred to the use of a "New York depth rule in measuring damages for land taken under eminent domain proceedings." Opposing counsel asked, "Why do ya'll use a Yankee rule in the Southland?" The jury got the message, at least so the verdict indicated.

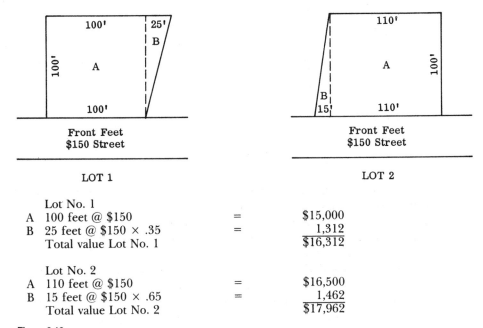

Figure 8.13

of a rectangular lot with a street frontage equal to the base of the triangle. To illustrate, assuming a value of $150 per front foot, the lots illustrated in Figure 8.13 would be appraised as shown below the figure. Importantly, each site must be appraised on the basis of local value patterns.

Corner Lot Valuation

With the increasing width of standard residential lots—from 20 and 25 feet to 100 feet or more in suburban subdivisions—the advantages which corner locations once offered in providing better light, more convenient access, and perhaps, greater privacy have diminished to a point where the additional hazards encountered at corner locations from automobile traffic have completely neutralized corner location advantages. In residential areas, therefore, the recommended appraisal practice is not to ascribe a value increment because of corner location, unless market sales in a community or area clearly demonstrate preference for such locations.

Commercial corner locations, however, do have value advantages over inside lots because of greater accessibility, increased pedestrian traffic, better merchandise display, and store visibility from two street locations. Corner lots typically command better rentals, and the net income to land is higher at corner store locations whether they are under owner or tenant occupancy. Under the income approach—as will be demonstrated in Chapter 18—the added corner

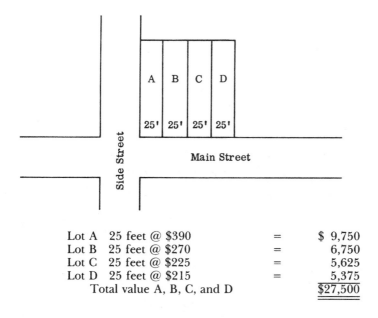

Lot A	25 feet @ $390	=	$ 9,750
Lot B	25 feet @ $270	=	6,750
Lot C	25 feet @ $225	=	5,625
Lot D	25 feet @ $215	=	5,375
	Total value A, B, C, and D		$27,500

Figure 8.14

value is directly accounted for by capitalization of the increased income resulting from a favorable location. Under the market approach, however, comparison sales data generally relate to inside lots, and adjustments are required to account for corner value influences. As stated previously, rules do not create value; nevertheless, they do offer, where tested by field practice, an opportunity to check value findings derived from other approaches to value. After a while, experienced appraisers will develop sufficient data to reveal the extent of corner premiums, if any, for different classes of property.

As a rule, the land closest to the corner benefits most from the corner location influences and the corner value diminishes to a negligible or fractional amount for the last portion of the corner lot. Assuming separate ownership of a corner lot as marked in Figure 8.14 and on the basis of empirical data, the corner value benefits would be derived as shown below the figure. Figure 8.15 shows how market-derived data can reveal value differentials for corner proximity and depth.

Where the assembled lots, because of single ownership and unified control, permit more intensive utilization of the land, the added value increment is known as *plottage*. This plottage value is best measured by capitalizing the actual or anticipated increased income attributable to an assembled property rather than by any arbitrary percentage such as 10, 20, or more percent as was customary in years past. Considerable care must be exercised by the appraiser in using small sites to derive the value of a larger site. Due to plottage, the total

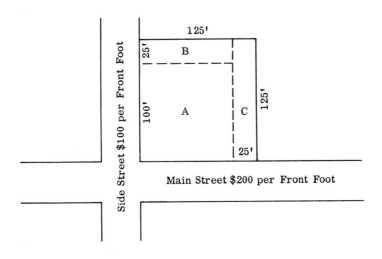

Lot A   100 feet @ $200   = $20,000
           Corner value: 100 feet @
           $100 × .75   =   7,500
           Total Lot A $27,500

Lot B   25 feet @ $100   =   2,500
Lot C   25 feet @ $200 × 1.10 (depth   =   5,500
           factor)
           Total value A, B, and C $35,500

       Alternatively, sales data may be obtained that reveals the value differential for proximity of sites to street intersections. Such data would be presented as shown in Figure 8.13.

Figure 8.15

value may be understated. Conversely, the total value of the smaller, more affordable sites could overstate the value of the larger parcel.

ZONING AND CONTRACTUAL LIMITATIONS ON OWNERSHIP

The highest and best use of land is often limited by the legal and permissible use for which a site may be developed. Again attention is called to the fact that zoning by itself does not create value. There must be a demand for land so zoned. If this demand is lacking, the period of years required for land to ripen into the highest and best use must be estimated and the value as of a future date discounted into a sum of present value at an appropriate (discount) rate.

       Often changes in the character of a neighborhood support a strong possibility that changes in zoning regulations will follow in order that utilization of land be adapted to changing and dynamic community needs. Where this is the case, the appraiser should recognize such added value influences, provided that current prices of similar land indicate investor expectation of higher and better land uses under anticipated changes in zoning or deed restrictions. Arbitrary denial of land use changes may be overruled by judiciary decree in courts of equity, if not in courts of law.

Contractual limitations on ownership are generally noted in deeds of record, and hence are referred to as "deed restrictions." Such restrictions as a rule are initiated by subdividers for the protection of property owners, and are intended to govern future land utilization in conformity with preconceived building plans and in the interest of owners and users as a whole. Deed restrictions which go with or attach to the land may control items as follows: minimum lot sizes, maximum building area, building height, and minimum building value, building setback requirements from front, side, and rear property lines, occupancy by single family, and other customary and reasonable limitations on ownership to safeguard property values.

Other contractual limitations which must be noted and evaluated by the appraiser include easements, leases, and mortgages. Easements are rights extended to others for ingress and egress over the property, or to air or subsurface rights for utility installation, soil removal, flood control, or mining operations. The effects of such easements on property value must be measured and accounted for in appraisal reporting. Leases give tenants or lessees the right to use land and its improvements for certain periods of time. In effect, leases create "split" interests that divide property values among the parties involved. The technique of appraising lease interests will be fully illustrated in Chapter 10. Mortgages in effect encumber a property. Where terms of the mortgage debt are at typical market rates of interest and for typical periods of years, no impact on property value will result. However, where mortgage contract terms are favorable or unfavorable as measured by market loan standards, the resulting plus or minus income adjustments when discounted to present worth will affect the price at which the property will exchange when exposed for sale.

Title Considerations and Encroachments

The appraiser, in seeking values, operates within the field of economics. He or she is cautioned not to usurp the functions or assume the responsibilities that are rightfully those of abstractors, title companies, lawyers, architects, or construction engineers. For appraisal purposes it must be assumed that the title to the subject property is free and clear, unless otherwise and expressly stated, and that no encumbrances restrict the full use of the property except those covered by zoning and deed restrictions as shown on public records. If the appraisal client, in addition to value, seeks assurance that the title is good and marketable or that lot measurements are accurate and the property is free from encroachments, qualified professionals in the respective fields should be consulted and the cost of their services added to the fees deemed compensatory to cover the appraisal service.

Furthermore, the validity of title and the accuracy of survey lines and measurements for appraisal purposes must be assumed to be correct, except for encroachments and property use violations that are apparent at the time of field inspection. Where violations or *easements* (rights for public ingress or egress to or over the site) are apparent, it is the appraiser's responsibility to report them and to estimate their effects on the value and marketability of the property.

Adjoining Structures and Land Uses

As the prospective highest and best use of the site is considered, it is important to visualize it in the context of adjoining properties. Will the prospective use be compatible with other nearby uses? Are the uses likely to cause market resistance to the subject property? Are the structures on adjacent properties inadequately maintained so that the residential or nonresidential potential of the appraised property is impaired? These factors must be seriously considered by the appraiser in a site analysis.

Site Improvements

All improvements classified as *fixtures*, the ownership of which legally "runs" with the land, must be inspected and appraised. To guard against errors and omissions, it is recommended that a plot plan be prepared as a guide for better appraisal reporting. As indicated on the plan shown in Figure 8.8, the lot dimensions and lot improvements are drawn to scale and in proportion to boundary line measurements which enclose the property. The plot plan should further sketch walks, driveways, and roof plans of the various structures that improve the property. This plan, together with pictures of the site and neighboring street and lot improvements, is deemed essential to effective site analysis in the appraisal process.

Other land improvements which should be inventoried and analyzed include landscaping and subsurface land improvements. Not all shrubs are classified as fixtures, and care must be taken to specify in the appraisal report the extent and amount to which landscaping contributed to total value. An allocation of 1, or at most 2 percent of final value for lawn sodding and foundation plantings may prove typical for most residential properties. Amounts expended in excess of 2 percent constitute *costs*, which may or may not be a measure of market value, depending on the circumstances at the time the property is exposed for sale to typical buyers.

Subsurface improvements, too, must be given value influence considerations. Underground utilities such as gas, telephone, sewerage, drainage, water, electricity, and steam piping are assets adding to site value. *Site data* or other on-site improvements to be included in site valuation include paving, curb, gutter, and sidewalk installation. (See the illustrative report in Appendix I.) Especially when comparing comparable land sales for differences in site location, care must be taken to adjust transaction prices to reflect the presence or absence of the various site improvements.

REVIEW QUESTIONS

1. Explain the relationship between chains and acres.
2. How many feet are there on each side of a square acre?
3. List three major concerns in conducting a site analysis.
4. Give an advantage and disadvantage of the monument method of site description.
5. Discuss the importance of a knowledge of soil conditions to a proper site analysis.
6. What do you judge to be an inherent weakness of depth tables?

READING AND STUDY REFERENCES

BABCOCK, RICHARD F., and CLIFFORD L. WEAVER. "Zoning City Neighborhoods," *Real Estate Issues* 5, no. 1 (Summer 1980), pp. 1–15.

BOYCE, BYRL N., and WILLIAM N. KINNARD, JR. Chapter 6, "Property Analysis," *Appraising Real Property*. Lexington, Mass.: Lexington Books, 1984, pp. 135–44.

COOPER, NORMAN L. "Land Use Consequences of Transportation," *The Real Estate Appraiser* 43, no. 3 (May–June 1977), pp. 19–22.

EPLEY, DONALD R., and JOSEPH RABIANSKI. Chapter 2, "Public Controls, Private Restrictions, and the Concept of Value," *Real Estate Decisions*. Reading, Mass.: Addison-Wesley Publishing Co., Inc., 1981, pp. 41–49.

FLOYD, CHARLES F. "Valuation of Flood Plain Lands for Stream Valley Parks," *The Appraisal Journal*, 51, no. 2 (April 1983), pp. 202–10.

GUNTERMANN, KARL L. "The Corner Influence on Value: Some Empirical Results," *The Real Estate Appraiser and Analyst* 45, no. 5 (September–October 1979), pp. 22–26.

HARRISON, HENRY S. "The Residential Appraiser, Site Data and Analysis," *The Real Estate Appraiser* 42, no. 1 (January–February 1976), pp. 47–49.

RING, ALFRED A., and JEROME J. DASSO Chapter 3, *Real Estate Principles and Practices*. Englewood Cliffs, N.J.: Prentice Hall, Inc., 10th ed., 1985, pp. 74–78.

SCRIBNER, DAVID. "The Key to Value Estimation: Highest and Best Use or Most Probable Use," *The Real Estate Appraiser* 44, no. 3 (May–June 1978), pp. 23–28.

SMITH, HALBERT C. and MARK R. MAURAIS, "Highest and Best Use in the Appraisal Profession," *The Real Estate Appraiser and Analyst*, 46, no. 2 (March–April 1980), pp. 27–37.

SMITH, WALSTEIN. "Some Enchanting Easements," *The Appraisal Journal*, 48, no. 4 (October 1980), pp. 527–539.

STRAIN, JOSEPH A. "Appraisal of Flowage Easements—Another Look," *The Appraisal Journal* 49, no. 4 (October 1981), pp. 580–586.

WOODWARD, LYNN N. "The Use of Remote-Sensing Photography and Maps in Appraising," *The Appraisal Journal* 45, no. 1 (January 1977), pp. 85–94.

9

FUNDAMENTALS OF LAND VALUATION

Learning Objectives

Upon reading this chapter, you should be able to:

Understand why separate site appraisals are sometimes required

Distinguish among the four principal land appraisal methods and when each is appropriately used

Recognize the major factors that influence land values

Organize market data analysis on a systematic basis

Since some sites are superior to others because of geographic situation, land improvement, size, shape, and other physical or economic attributes, it is important that the site be analyzed separately and evaluated as if free for development, in conformity with the principle of highest and best use. There are, of course, other reasons why the value of the land, as distinct from the improvements which it supports, must be known:

1. Local tax assessment regulations, in most jurisdictions, require the allocation of total property value to land, buildings, and other land improvements. This division aids the assessor in the allocation of units of value with greater consistency and uniformity. Improvements, too, are made subject to adjustment for loss in value due to depreciation, whereas land historically has shown tendencies to appreciate.

2. Federal internal revenue regulations also require the separation of land from improvement value for purposes of depreciation allowance on the latter.

3. Where land is not improved with structures that constitute the highest and best use, it is necessary to determine the value of land as if free and clear and to charge the improvements with value losses resulting from over-, under-, or faulty improvements.
4. For insurance purposes, a separation of land from value of building improvements (which are subject to fire and other hazards) is essential in order to measure accurately the nature and extent of insurable risks.
5. For investment purposes, a study of shifting land to building value ratio may prove important and useful in measuring changes in the duration of economic building life.
6. Some appraisal techniques, too, as is the case under the cost and building residual income approaches to value, require separate handling of site and improvements in the valuation process.
7. Unimproved or vacant land too must be evaluated as available under a potential and legally permissible highest and best use.
8. Site leases require that the value of a site be specified.

In estimating the value of land, reliance is placed on one or more of the following methods, or approaches:

1. The sales comparison approach.
2. The land residual earnings approach.
3. The land developmental approach.
4. The ratio of site value to total property value.

Generally, only one of these approaches to land value is accepted as guiding, although a second approach, if applicable and appropriate data are available, may prove useful as a check for accuracy. For purpose of clarity, the various approaches to land value will be discussed as independent appraisal techniques. In theory and practice, nevertheless, all valuation irrespective of method or approach is related and imputed to market operations. The interrelationship of the various approaches to value will become apparent from the discussion of recommended appraisal procedure as presented below.

THE SALES COMPARISON APPROACH

The most reliable method of estimating land value is based on a comparison of the subject property with similar properties in like locations which have sold recently. Where the market is active and the sales recent and similar in kind, the comparison approach yields satisfactory value estimates. The mechanics of the comparison approach are relatively simple, and no great skill is required to master the method.

The first and most important requirement in the sales comparison approach to value is ready access to up-to-date sources of real property sale transactions. The sources of sales data in order of availability, accuracy, and convenience are as follows:

1. Abstract or title insurance company records.
2. Tax assessor's record files.
3. County clerk's official public records.
4. Appraiser's personal office files.
5. Real estate brokers' multiple listing or general sales record files.
6. Financial news or newspaper reporting services.

The appraiser may use one or more of these sources for sales data depending on appraisal volume and procedures adopted for maintenance of an appraisal plant file. There are often commercial sources of comparable sales data in most larger cities as well as a national source, the SREA Market Data Center. In many communities copies of official deed records are made available by the county clerk's office at reasonable costs. This information, when promptly posted in geographic order or by alphabetical name of subdivisions, furnishes a ready and convenient source for market sales information. This recommended practice, where available, keeps the appraiser abreast of market operations and thus provides him or her with ready information concerning volume of transfers, price trends, and community growth patterns.

Irrespective of the source from which sales record data are obtained, it is the appraiser's responsibility to verify the price and terms of sale by a personal or telephone interview with the buyer, the seller, or both. Real estate transactions historically are considered private in nature and public records may or may not reveal factual circumstances which "cushioned" or "sweetened" a sale. Interviewing the parties to the transaction, or informed persons such as lawyers or brokers who guided the sales, enables the appraiser to formulate judgments in adjusting market prices paid to the prices obtainable for the subject property were it exposed for sale in the open market. If a sale cannot be confirmed, or where the prices or terms are deliberately held secretive, it is best to disregard the transaction in favor of another and more reliable sale property. When applying the market approach to value, caution must be exercised in accepting state revenue stamps affixed to deeds as reliable evidence of the transaction price. Legally, a deed is considered an instrument of "conveyance" in which the actual consideration agreed on in a prior and unrecorded contract need not be stipulated. Although most state laws require that revenue stamps (or the dollar amount of taxes) based on the exact transaction price be attached to the deed, there are, nevertheless, circumstances under which these stamps do not indicate the price for which the property was exchanged. For instance:

1. A buyer may wish to give the impression that he or she paid an amount greater than the actual purchase price and for that reason affixes more revenue stamps than the law requires. There is no limit to the number or amount of stamps that may be purchased, and the tax agent will gladly sell all the buyer wants. The attaching of excess stamps may be a device to have future buyers believe that

the property is worth a great deal more than the "bargain" price at which it is offered to them.

2. Sellers who must deliver the deed at time of closing—with revenue stamps attached—may attempt, unlawfully, to save on this expenditure by purchasing fewer stamps than the sale price calls for. The county clerk from whom the revenue stamps are obtained does not question the transaction price quoted by the seller, or the intent of the seller in obtaining more or fewer stamps than the law requires.

3. Many states do not have deed revenue stamp laws, and even where such laws are in force the requirements regarding the effects of existing mortgages differ. In some states, only the cash portions of transactions need be considered; whereas in others, state revenue stamps representing the full consideration must be attached to the deed.

4. In the case of property exchanges, the interested parties may understate or overstate the transaction price for tax or other purposes which prove mutually advantageous.

Although in many jurisdictions state transfer tax or grantor's tax reflect fairly well the actual transaction price of the property, the possible exceptions noted above should be kept in mind when accepting state transfer tax data as evidence of market price or value. In most condemnation trials, too, revenue stamp data as evidence of market sale price are inadmissible or subject to challenge when introduced by an expert witness. To aid the appraiser in the analysis of market sales, a data report form such as shown in Figure 9.1 is recommended for use.

In securing information from courthouse or file records for entry on the work form, it should not be taken for granted that the date of title closing represents the date of sale. Often land is sold under a *contract for deed*,[1] in which case months and years may separate the date of contract from the date of title closing. The date of contract, in fact and in law, determines the time at which a meeting of minds took place, and it is that date which ideally serves as a basis for time adjustments reflecting changes in economic or market conditions up to the date of appraisal. Furthermore, the appraiser must make certain that the sale was concluded under objective, impersonal bargaining and that the terms of sale were fully disclosed. Sales from father to son or daughter or from one relative to another, or where circumstances indicate undisclosed terms and conditions, or where prices paid appear unreasonable or questionable should be discarded in favor of other clear-cut, bona fide sale transactions.

Many multiple listing services (MLSs) show the percent of sales price to listing prices. In fact, some of these services report this relationship for different classes of properties, such as townhouses, industrial, and vacant land. During early 1984, a survey of several MLSs in Virginia by the Virginia Real Estate Research Center revealed that all categories of real estate sold for 96 percent of the listed prices. This relationship varies according to the state of the real

---

[1]An agreement under which transfer of title to the land is deferred until partial (periodic) payments aggregate the entire or agreed-upon amount of the purchase price.

Location _____

_____

Seller _____   Type of Instrument _____

Buyer _____

                                        Deed Date _____

Area _____

                                        Date of Record _____

                                        Deed Book _____ Page _____

State Transfer Tax _____

Price Indicated $_____   Price Shown $_____

Price Paid was $_____   or $_____ per _____

_____ as confirmed by _____ to

_____ on _____ at _____ AM/PM

The property was inspected by _____on _____

Zoning _____   Allowable density _____

Utilities _____

Unusual Influences _____

_____

Land _____

_____

_____

Improvements _____

_____

_____

Assessment: County $_____ Year _____ City $_____ Year _____

Remarks and Analysis of Sale (continued on back along with site sketch) _____

_____

MARKET DATA REPORT FORM

Index Sale No. _____

Figure 9.1

estate market and with different classes of property, especially land. Where market data for comparable properties are unavailable, recourse may be had to property listings.

Adjustment of Comparable Sales

Prior to comparatively analyzing the comparable site sales, it should be remembered that the adjustments always are made toward the appraised site. Stated differently, the adjustments are made from the known (sale prices) toward the unknown (market value of subject). Some of the different adjustment techniques, such as percentage versus dollar adjustments, multiplication versus addition and subtraction of adjustments, and cash equivalency, are covered in detail in the following chapter.

Regardless of the method used to make adjustments in arriving at an estimate of the appraised site's value, the appraiser must always seek, first, to discover truly comparable sales, and second, to be thoroughly familiar with each sale. Another factor that is sometimes misapplied in adjusting comparable sales is adjusting for conditions (physical and economic) that existed when the property was sold. Two examples will clearly illustrate the meaning of this statement. A site may have sold as an unfinished parcel, lacking its present zoning and curbs and gutters. Also, it may have sold in a "buyers' market," whereas at the date of appraisal, the market had reverted to a "sellers' market." Thus the appraiser must determine the physical and economic conditions that existed when the property was sold—not those existing on the appraisal date.

Elements of Comparison

To give some reasonable degree of order to the comparative analysis and the related adjustment process, sales analysis should be broken down into four categories. These are:

1. Date of sale.
2. Conditions of sale.
3. Location.
4. Physical features.

Date of sale. Previously, it was stated that the appraiser must be thoroughly familiar with the physical and economic conditions that existed when the property sold. Although it is desirable to make time adjustments from the contract date, this date is not always readily available. The next best date to use is the deed date. Whenever possible, however, the appraiser should adjust from the contract date since this is the date that the buyer and seller had a "meeting of the minds." Unfortunately, too frequently greater effort is expended on making adjustments rather than securing recent sales that require no time adjustments.

The appraiser has several options available in making time adjustments. Generally, it is advisable to use more than one method to ensure that a reasonable adjustment has been made. Perhaps the best indication of value change due to the passage of time is the sale and resale of the sale site. In using this method, care must be taken to ascertain whether any significant change has occurred in the property or neighborhood. Another method is to study several sites that have sold at different times in the same neighborhood. The third method is to consider general land value trends in the market. This observation may lack the precision of the other two methods.

Conditions of sale. Several different factors can influence the price paid for a site. If these influences are too great or canot be substantiated, it is best to delete such sales. Some of these conditions that can influence the price paid for a property are unequal bargaining power of the two parties, favorable or unfavorable financial terms, unusually strong motivation either to buy or to sell a particular site, market conditions that differed sharply from prevailing conditions. An example of buyer motivation that would cause an unusually high price to be paid is when a prospective buyer needs an adjoining site for business expansion purposes. In all likelihood, he or she would pay more for this site than for a similar site a block away.

Location. It might be argued that the best comparable sale is a sale of the appraised site with the second best comparable being the adjoining site. The closer the sale to the appraised site, the possibility of a location adjustment is greatly reduced. In short, more reliable appraisals result from more thorough market analysis and less dependence on "judgment." When making location adjustments the off-site amenities and disadvantages for a given highest and best use must be taken into account.

Physical features. Adjustments are made for any significant differences in physical features that would likely be detected by buyers and sellers of similar sites. The appraiser sometimes may be tempted to make adjustments for insignificant features that are of no consequence to persons trading in a particular class of real estate. To make such unnecessary adjustments places the appraiser in a position of distorting market value. He or she no longer is interpreting the actions of those who make up the real estate market.

A review of Chapter 8 will reveal the physical features for which adjustments *might be* necessary. Some of these are differences in terrain, depth, frontage, soil conditions, shape, and drainage.

After a minimum of four comparable sales has been selected, confirmed, field inspected, and analyzed, the appraiser is in a position to transfer the individual sales data to an adjustment sheet for adjustment and correlation purposes to derive an estimate of market value for the subject property. Table 9.1 shows a sample adjustment sheet on which the derivation of a market value estimate for a residential site is illustrated. The property under appraisal measures 110 feet along the street front and is 150 feet in depth. In this instance, it is compared with four reasonably similar market sale transactions that are adjusted to reflect and equalize for economically better or poorer conditions of the subject property as demonstrated. The standard depth for a typical residential site in the neighborhood is 120 feet.

In following the step-by-step correlation of comparable market sales data as indicated in the market value adjustment sheet, it will become apparent that the accuracy of the final value conclusion reached depends largely on the exercise of sound appraisal judgment. This judgment cannot be gained by textbook reading or classroom study alone, but follows as a result of diligent application of the valuation principles in field practice. Individual maturity and thought discipline based on an inquiring and energetic mind are essential ingredients of good appraising.

Table 9.1 Market Value Adjustment Sheet

	SALES REFERENCE NO.			
	1	2	3	4
1. Date of sale	One month ago	Two months ago	Twelve months ago	Eight months ago
2. Indicated price	$14,000	$12,600	$11,600	$12,400
3. Size of lot	100' × 150'	80' × 200'	90' × 120'	100' × 90'
4. Price per front foot	$140.00	$157.50	$128.89	$124.00
5. Time adjustment factor	1.00	1.00	1.15	1.10
6. Unit price adjusted for time	$140.00	$157.50	$148.22	$136.40
7. Depth adjustment	0.92	0.82	1.00	1.11
8. Unit price adjustment for depth	$128.80	$129.15	$148.22	$151.40
Subject property is rated as follows in regard to:				
9. Neighborhood	Same	Better	Same	Poorer
10. Location	Better	Same	Same	Same
11. Site facilities	Better	Same	Same	Poorer
12. Subject comparative percent rating	1.10	1.05	1.00	0.90
13. Adjusted value	$141.68	$135.61	$148.22	$136.26

Market value correlation:

14. Estimated (correlated) unit value of land $140.00

15. Value of subject site   110' × $140.00 = $15,400   rounded to $15,500

16. Value adjusted for corner or plottage influences   None

17. Final estimated land value $15,500

[handwritten annotations: "Sold", "adjusting to make it like the subject", "Now weighted average"]

The first entry on the summary sheet is the *date of sale* for each comparable property. This entry is important as a measure of elapsed time to date of appraisal, allowing consideration to be given where necessary to changes caused by economic forces which influenced market value during the interval.

The second entry shows the *indicated price* paid for the sale property. This price as a rule is based on state transfer tax data. Where tax stamp information appears to be out of line, and where sale confirmation fails to yield supporting facts and explanations, the sale should be rejected in favor of another and more reliable source of market value evidence.

The third entry notes *size of lot*. With the aid of these measurements the appraiser is in a position to compute the price paid per unit (front foot) of land, and to adjust unit value where necessary to compensate for variation in lot depth. Economic units, such as the number of apartment units permitted by zoning, may be used too.

The fourth entry is the *price paid per front foot of land*. This amount is derived by dividing the total price paid (entry 2) by the number of front feet (entry 3) of the comparable lot.

The fifth entry indicates a *time adjustment factor*. If because of economic conditions, the comparable sale property would bring more or less were the sale to take place today (i.e., on the date of appraisal), an adjustment factor should indicate the percentage of increase or decrease as market conditions warrant. Where no adjustment is necessary, the entry is 1.00. A 5-percent-plus adjustment would be noted as 1.05. Plus or minus adjustments are allowable.

The adjustment factor in entry 5 is then multiplied by the unit foot value given in entry 4, and the resulting *unit price adjusted for time* is then shown in entry 6. This time adjustment must not be made arbitrarily but rather must be based on considered study of market conditions—or at least on the opinions of *informed* persons such as experienced appraisers, builders, and realtors in the community.

Entry 7 provides for *depth factor* consideration. Where all sales are of the same depth as the subject property, this and the following entry can be omitted from the adjustment sheet. However, whenever lot-depth variations influence the price paid, the appraiser must adjust the figures accordingly and in conformity with appropriate depth value guidelines developed in the local market. The resulting calculation is entry 8 and is expressed in this example as sale price per front foot.

Entries 9, 10, and 11 constitute judgment conclusions concerning the relative quality of the subject property as compared with each comparable property in regard to (a) neighborhood, (b) location advantages, and (c) site facilities. Considering the status of the *subject* property as compared with the *sale* property, the appraiser establishes a quality rating for each of the features as being better, poorer, or the same. An overall percentage rating is then reached for the subject property (Entry 12).

In the narrative section of the valuation report as shown in Appendix I—the Illustrative Appraisal Report—the appraiser explains *why* the neighborhood, location, and site facilities of the subject property are deemed better, poorer, or the same, thus justifying the overall comparative percentage rating assigned in the market value summary sheet. Some appraisers prefer to rate each feature on a percentage basis, and to multiply the separate percentage ratings for a weighted or combined average. There is danger, however, in such a practice. Suppose that each of the features (i.e., neighborhood, location, and site) is judged to be 50 percent when compared with the sale property; by multiplying 0.50 times 0.50 times 0.50, an overall average of 12.5 percent is obtained. This method has a tendency to overadjust for comparative deficiencies and to underadjust for superior features. To illustrate: Where one adjustment calls for a 50 percent minus rating and another adjustment calls for a 50 percent plus rating, it would appear logical that the two ratings should cancel out. By multiplying 0.50 by 1.50, the net result is nevertheless 75 percent, which constitutes an overadjustment on the minus side of the rating scale.

Even when percentage adjustments are added—plus and minus—to overcome the errors derived by percentage multiplications, the separate adjustment for each category of variation is fraught with hazards which lead to "guesstimating" rather than "estimating." For this reason it is recommended that ratings be judged descriptively, and that only *one* final percentage quality rating be arrived at and entered as shown under entry 12 of the market summary sheet.

The overall quality percentage rating is then multiplied by the adjusted unit price (entry 8) of the comparable property to derive an estimated value per unit measure of land for the *subject* property. This value is listed in entry 13. The next step calls for correlating the adjusted values derived from four or more sales into a single estimate of unit value. This final unit value is found in entry 14. Correlation does not mean averaging but rather assigning judgment weights to each sale on the basis of compatibility, terms of sale, and reliability of sales data. The correlation procedure should be explained in the narrative section of the appraisal report as follows:

Sale 1 is located in the same block as the subject property, is identical in size, and required no time adjustment. A judgment weight of 50 percent was given to this sale. This weight implies to the client that this sale is of such similarity that 50 percent of the final value component is based on it.

Sale 2 is also located in the same block, but the property depth of this sale is nonstandard. For this reason a judgment weight of only 30 percent was given to this sale.

Sales 3 and 4 are in an adjacent neighborhood, and both sales required time adjustments of 1.15 percent and 1.10 percent, respectively. For these reasons the correlation weight assigned to these sales was 10 percent each.

The value of the subject property for a standard depth of 120 feet is then derived as follows:

INDEX SALES	ADJUSTED VALUE	WEIGHT OF SALE	VALUE COMPONENT
1	$141.68	50	$ 70.84
2	135.61	30	40.68
3	148.22	10	14.82
4	136.26	10	13.63
			$139.97
	Rounded to $140		

The value of the subject site is then derived by multiplying the number of unit feet of land by the unit value as was done under entry 15. Similarly, adjustments for corner locations or plottage if called for should be made and noted under entry 16. The final estimate of land value, rounded to the nearest $500 value bracket (for sites in this value range), should then be listed in entry 17. The market value procedure as outlined,[2] when applied with professional care, should yield accurate estimates that will reasonably reflect the market price that may be anticipated were the subject property exposed for sale in the open market on the date of appraisal.

The Ideal Neighborhood Site Comparison Method

In the conventional market comparison method as demonstrated above, each comparable sale represents a market rating of 100 percent and the subject property is adjusted plus or minus to reflect quantitative and qualitative differences. This approach to value necessitates a reevaluation or recomparison of the sale property each time the index sale is used as a value base in subsequent appraisals involving other subject properties. In order to streamline appraisal practice and to permit instant reuse of rated sale properties a novel market evaluation procedure known as the "ideal neighborhood site comparison method" is sometimes used. Instead of using a variable base—as in the market approach to value explained above, under which each of many comparable sales is used as a standard of comparison—an *ideal* neighborhood is used as a base for com-

[2]An alternative market comparison method provides for direct adjustment of the comparable using the subject property as a "norm" or "standard" in terms of which variations or deviations in the comparables are measured. Either method, of course, if diligently applied should yield identical end results.

parison of all comparable sales as well as for the subject property. The percentage components of the ideal neighborhood are as follows:

FEATURES	PERCENT RATING
1. Location: access, transportation to center of city, nearness and quality of schools and shopping	15
2. Surroundings: percent developed, age, price range of homes, upkeep, quality of neighbors	15
3. Zoning: protection, land use trends	10
4. Traffic: safety, parking, accessibility	10
5. Street improvements and services: paving, sidewalks, curb, gutter, sewer, water, garbage, fire protection	15
6. Lot features: size, topography, shape appeal, landscaping, trees	15
7. Amenities and trends: prestige, popularity, competitive position	20
Total rating	100

The conventional site comparison method discussed above is intended only as a guide in helping the appraiser consider fully the differences in market sales data in order to reach a sound value conclusion. No valuation table, method, or procedure can ever serve as a substitute for diligent data compilation, careful analysis, and sound judgment sharpened by experience. Conversely, it is inconceivable that sound judgment can be exercised without a systematic data adjustment program such as that outlined above.

THE LAND RESIDUAL EARNINGS APPROACH

In the final analysis, the value of all land is based on its productivity or income-producing capacity under a program of highest and best land use. Whenever the market approach is inapplicable, either because of absence of market transactions or nonexistence of unimproved land in the subject or comparable areas, the appraiser may resort to the earnings or income approach to value. Land income, as discussed in Chapter 3, is residual in character. Costs of labor, management, maintenance, operations, and a fair market return *on* and *of* the invested capital in improvements must be met first. What is left, if anything, under a program of highest and best use belongs to land. This residual income, when capitalized at an appropriate rate of interest, forms a capital sum of money that measures the *present* worth of the subject site.

To apply the income approach to land value, the appraiser cannot and must not assume that the existing building improvements necessarily constitute the highest and best use of the land. The appraiser, in fact, must undertake a land utilization study of the area and site and determine what type and size of improvement should be placed on the land in order to reap for it the highest possible return and present value. Since few improvements—even when considered to represent the highest and best use—are in new condition, it is necessary under the income approach to land value to assume first a reasonable highest and best land use, and second that improvements *are* viewed in their current condition (and value).

The procedure for selecting the highest and best use and the process of capitalizing the residual income into a sum of present value can best be illustrated as follows. Suppose that a building site in a given community can be developed for residential purposes only under existing and reasonably anticipated zoning restrictions. Suppose, further, that preliminary analysis of neighborhood characteristics and of housing demand narrows the choice of possible and profitable site improvements to one of the following types of structures:

1. A single-story duplex building, each rental unit containing two bedrooms, dining-living room, kitchen, and tiled bath. Total improvement cost, $42,500.
2. A three-family apartment building, each apartment containing two bedrooms, dining-living room, kitchen, and tiled bath. Total improvement cost, $50,000.

Since the *highest* use of the building site was prescribed by zoning law for residential purposes, the determination still to be made is which of the alternate types of improvements described above constitutes the *best* use. Under the definition of highest and best use, it is necessary to ascertain the income-producing capacity of the land under the alternative types of improvements and to find by the process of capitalization which income yields to the land its highest present value. Based on prevailing rentals of similar residences in comparable neighborhoods at $375 per month per four-room and bath duplex unit, and $325 per month per four-room and bath apartment unit, the procedure to derive land income and land value at a market rate of interest (R_L) of 10 percent is as shown in Table 9.2. This valuation procedure is one generally practiced by informed investors to determine the present worth of land under the income or earnings residual approach to land value. Based on the analysis, as illustrated, the conclusion can be drawn that the highest and best use of the building site under value study is a three-family apartment building to be constructed at a cost of $50,000 and renting at $325 per month per dwelling unit. Under this highest and best use, the land warrants a present value of $12,170. Under the next best type of improvement or utilization, both land income and land value diminish.

The residual techniques of capitalization under the income approach to value are more fully described and demonstrated in Chapter 19.

Table 9.2 Analysis of Land Income and Land Value Under Alternate Types of Improvements

	Single-Story Duplex	Three-Family Apartment
Gross annual income		
Duplex units $375 × 2 × 12 (months) =	$9,000	
Three-family apartment $325 × 3 × 12 (months) =		$11,700
Less vacancy and collection losses at 5%	450	585
Effective gross income	$8,550	$11,115
Less operating expenses		
Management fee (7%)	$ 599	$ 778
Real estate taxes	910	1,100
Maintenance and repairs	470	610
Hazard insurance	160	220
Fuel and utilities	560	700
Janitor service		240
Total operating expenses	$2,699	$ 3,648
Net operating income	$5,851	$ 7,467
Less income attributable to buildings (I_B)		
Duplex $42,500 × 0.125 (0.10 + 0.025)	$5,313	
Apartments $50,000 × 0.125		$ 6,250
Net income remaining to land (I_L)	$ 539	$ 1,217
Value of land at 0.10% rate of capitalization (R_L)		
Duplex $539 ÷ 0.10	$5,390	
Apartment $1,217 ÷ 0.10		$12,170

you care —> about (handwritten annotation next to Net operating income)

THE LAND DEVELOPMENTAL METHOD

Throughout the historical development of appraisal thought, and in the writing of most appraisal literature, the existence of land has been taken for granted. In effect, it is implied that land cannot be produced and hence should not be evaluated via the cost approach to value. This classical theory of land as being permanent, indestructible, immovable, and unique (heterogeneous) is valid only if applied to raw land as God created it. The appraiser, however, is concerned with "economic" land, modified and improved; and in this economic sense, such land *can* be produced, duplicated, and its situs qualities shifted to other locations.

Our ability to modify land and thereby produce land value is illustrated by the following story. A farmer, after years of grueling work cutting trees, pulling stumps, and plowing, had converted an overgrown forest region into a fertile and productive farm. One day while harvesting he was talking with a city cousin who was mightily impressed by the lush appearance of the farm and said: "Aren't you lucky to own this land, which God created and presented as a gift to man." The farmer looked bemused at his calloused hands and replied: "It's true. But you should have seen this land when God had it all to himself."

Today, raw land as nature provided it no longer exists. All land has been directly or indirectly modified by human beings. Direct modification has included the construction of buildings, fences, dikes, drainage canals, land filling and grading, and the conversion of forests into grazing, farming, or building sites. Land has been modified indirectly by the construction of access roads, bridges, canals, modes of rapid transportation, and other means of public improvements which increase land utility.

This appraisal method should be supported by use of the direct market sales approach whenever possible. It can be used in the appraisal of any kind of land as long as it has subdivision potential. That is, it is adapted to residential, industrial, or commercial uses. Further, it does not have to be immediately "ripe" for development, but the probable absorption period should be capable of an accurate estimate. There are reasons that this method produces unrealistic value estimates, including:

1. Inaccurate highest and best use analysis.
2. Failure of analyst to account for all the expenditures necessary to produce the forecast income.
3. Overstatement of income or failure to graduate the sales income as the marketing program progresses.
4. Incorrect selection and application of the discount rate.[3]

Where land is anticipated to ripen into higher economic uses, or where the conversion of farm or rur-urban (land in transition, being neither farm nor suburban in use or character) acreage into suburban building sites is justified by community growth and demand, the appraiser can logically and accurately apply the land developmental approach to value.

The suggested steps in using this method are as follows:

1. Create a sound development plan.
2. Forecast a realistic pricing schedule.
3. Forecast accurately the absorption rate and mix of sites to be sold.
4. Accurately estimate the staging and expense of land development and related expenses.

[3]James H. Boykin, "Developmental Method of Land Appraisal," *The Appraisal Journal,* 44, no. 2 (April 1976), p. 181.

5. Forecast marketing and related expenditures.
6. Estimate the annual real property taxes during the development and marketing periods.
7. Estimate a reasonable overhead and profit allowance.
8. Analyze the market to determine the appropriate discount rate expected by investors for this type of investment.
9. Select a discount factor that properly reflects the timing of the site sales.[4]

An appraisal assignment calls for finding the value of 50 acres of land which a subdivider seeks to purchase and develop into residential building sites. As a result of a highest and best land use study, it appears best to subdivide the 50-acre tract into 150 lots each measuring 100 feet by 120 feet, or three lots per acre. Under this development plan the 150 building lots comprise 82.5 percent of the total land area, while the balance, or 17.5 percent of land, is deemed necessary for construction of access streets, avenues, traffic isles, and other public uses. Based on study and analysis of comparable property sales, it is concluded that the lots can be marketed as follows:

First year: 40 lots at $20,000 each
Second year: 60 lots at $22,000 each
Third year: 50 lots at $24,500 each

The basic question answered by this technique is how much could an investor afford to pay for an undeveloped site today in anticipation of a forecast development and marketing program. An illustration of this appraisal method is shown in Table 9.3. This illustration does not include costs of sidewalks, extension of gas, electric, or telephone utilities, or expenditures for other public or recreational facilities. Should such expenditures be incurred by the developer they must, of course, be added into the land production cost approach to value.

SITE VALUE-TO-PROPERTY VALUE RATIO

Under conditions where the market, income, or land developmental approach to value is not applicable, an estimate of land value may be derived from a study of typical ratios of site value to total property value as indicated by comparable improved property sales. Under highest and best utilization of land, studies disclose certain optimum land/property value ratios on which the appraiser may rely for value guidance. At the outset, stress is laid on the fact that ratios, like depth or corner land value rules, do not *make* value but rather reflect typical land/property relationships which serve a useful purpose in the allocation of total value to the component parts of land and building improvements.

[4]*Ibid.*, p. 186.

Table 9.3 Appraisal by the Land Developmental Approach

Income and Expenses	Year 1		Year 2		Year 3	
Lot sales		$ 800,000		$1,320,000		$1,225,000
Less:						
Engineering	$ 67,500		—		—	
Clearing	26,250		—		—	
Roads and drainage	375,000		$ 90,000		$ 82,000	
Water lines	78,750		61,000		48,000	
Sanitary sewer						
(on- and off-site)	390,000		78,000		72,500	
Entrance	20,000		—		—	
Advertising	3,000		1,500		1,500	
Real estate taxes	3,750		3,000		2,000	
Mortgage interest	85,000		67,500		19,000	
Project management	10,000		8,000		5,000	
Overhead and profit						
(35% of lot sales)	280,000	(1,339,250)	462,000	771,000	428,750	658,750
Value of net sales revenue		$ (539,250)		$ 549,000		$ 566,250

Present Value of Net Sales Revenue
(using a 10% end-of-year factor)

Year 1	$(539,250) × 0.909091 =	$(490,227)	
Year 2	549,000 × 0.826446 =	453,719	
Year 3	566,250 × 0.751315 =	425,432	

Present value of raw acreage $ 388,924 rounded to $390,000

Present value per acre ($390,000 ÷ 50) $7,800

Where land value equals improvement value, the ratio is said to be one-to-one; or the land to property ratio is said to be 50 percent. Commercial land in the downtown area is generally characterized by a low (but efficient) land-to-improvement ratio, and the ratio increases as the land is put to lower (less efficient) uses. Guiding ratios for a typical community may range as follows:

Land Use	Land-to-Property Ratio (%)
Commercial	50
Office	20
Residential	15
Apartment house	10
Industrial	5

Once a study of typical land uses within a community discloses a guiding relationship of site value ratios, the appraiser may use the results as a basis for or check on the accuracy of value findings by other and more direct appraisal methods. For instance, if typical residential properties are improved with buildings so as to create a 12 to 16 percent ratio, a property with a land/value ratio of as little as 5 percent or as high as 25 percent may connote over- or under-development of the site. In either case, faulty improvement will cause a loss in building value reflected by the difference between actual and estimated potential dollar return realizable under a program of highest and best site utilization.

This method seldom can stand by itself as an indication of site value. When used in a built-up, older residential neighborhood, the question that must be answered is: What was the market source of the ratio evidence? The irony of this method is that it is most accurately applied to new residential properties. Whenever ample site sales are available this method is usually superfluous.

The site value results will likely be distorted if site value ratios for new properties are applied to older properties or ratios for properties in one neighborhood to another neighborhood. Nevertheless, it has its place in obtaining an initial idea of a site value. For example, the site value of an appraised site might be estimated as follows. Assuming a typical land/value ratio of 20 percent, and that each of the sale properties is similar to the appraised site:

Sale No.	Sale Price	Land Ratio	Site Value
1	$100,000	× 0.20	$20,000
2	110,000	× 0.20	22,000
3	95,000	× 0.20	19,000
4	108,000	× 0.20	21,600
5	112,000	× 0.20	22,400

Thus the indicated range of values for the subject site is from $19,000 to $22,400. The appraiser, based on similarities in the improved property sales and the appraised property, would be expected to select a value within this $3,400 range.

REVIEW QUESTIONS

1. List five purposes for separate site appraisals being made.
2. Discuss four situations where the stated consideration in a deed may be inaccurate.
3. Explain why it is important for an appraiser to understand thoroughly the conditions that existed when a property sold.
4. Identify and discuss the number and type of adjustments that should be made by the appraiser.
5. Comparatively evaluate site appraisal via the sales comparison and land residual earnings methods.
6. Under what circumstances is it acceptable to use the developmental land appraisal method?

7. Two identical residences are erected on opposite sides of the same street. The same builder and identical building designs are employed. The contract specified that the builder should be compensated at a cost-plus-10-percent basis with a maximum expenditure of $100,000 per structure. The final costs were as follows: building A, $90,000; building B, $95,000. The higher cost of building B was caused by the existence of rock which had to be blasted out of place. The land for each structure (75 feet by 150 feet) was purchased for $10,000 per lot. Based on the data above, discuss the following:
   (a) Have the buildings different values? Explain.
   (b) Are the lots identical in value?
   (c) What is the nature of the expenditure for blasting the rock? Does it add to or detract from the value of (1) the building and (2) the land?

READING AND STUDY REFERENCES

BOYCE, BYRL N., and WILLIAM N. KINNARD. Chapter 8, "Site Valuation," *Appraising Real Property*. Lexington, Mass.: Lexington Books, 1984.

BOYKIN, JAMES H. "Developmental Method of Land Appraisal," *The Appraisal Journal* 44, no. 2 (April 1976), pp. 181–192.

CONSTAM, E. "Methodology of Water Lot Evaluation," *The Appraisal Journal* 45, no. 1 (January 1977), pp. 70–79.

GAINES, JAMES P. "Industrial Land Valuation," *The Real Estate Appraiser and Analyst* 47, no. 4 (Winter 1981), pp. 5–9.

HOAGLAND, GARY. "Are the Mechanics of the Adjustment Process Correct?" *The Real Estate Appraiser and Analyst* 48, no. 1 (Spring 1982), pp. 59–61.

MAES, MARVIN A. "Subdivision Analysis: A Case Study," *The Appraisal Journal*, 50, no. 1 (January 1982), pp. 100–112.

WILLIAMS, SCOTT R. "Problems with Percentage Adjustments," *The Real Estate Appraiser and Analyst* 48, no. 4 (Winter Quarter 1982), pp. 48–55.

Sales Comparison and Depreciated Cost Approaches

10

SALES COMPARISON APPROACH TO VALUE

Learning Objectives

After reading this chapter, you should be able to:

Comprehend the reason for and be able to adjust for nonstandard financing

Appreciate the various methods of adjusting comparable sales to indicate the value of the appraised property

Understand how to use linear regression as a means of adjusting prices of comparable sale properties

Develop and properly use the gross income multiplier technique for estimating property value

Use the assessed value/sale price ratio as an approach to estimating market value

Distinguish between the GIM and EGIM

For standardized goods and services, prices paid at "arm's-length" bargaining in an open and normal market provide a reliable *index* of value. As a rule, little difficulty is encountered in obtaining reasonably accurate estimates of market price quotations for commodities such as wheat, coffee, sugar, corn, eggs, poultry, or for bonds and stocks which are freely traded. The greater the dissimilarity of the product and the less frequent the trading, however, the greater the skill required to adjust for product differences in order to attain price comparability, and the greater the chances for error in the final estimate of value via the market approach.

With real estate, which is heterogeneous in character, exact comparability can never be obtained, if only because of differences in the fixed geographical location of the property. It is possible, nevertheless, through study and analysis of market operations, to adjust for price effects caused by differences in "physical" characteristics in order to obtain "economic" equality essential to an accurate estimate of market value.

The greater the number and the more recent the sales of comparable properties, the greater the accuracy and the more convincing are the results obtained via the market approach to value. Ready access to market transaction source data is, therefore, of first importance. Most active appraisers maintain a market sales-data file as part of their appraisal plant, at least for the geographic community area in which the majority of their appraisal assignments originate. The appraisal report file itself provides an important source of market transaction information. It is a gratifying experience to receive an appraisal request and to find that a comparable property in the same neigborhood, or better still in the same block, was recently appraised. Where office files are insufficient or incomplete, ready access to sales data must be had through abstract companies, county tax or record offices, or through commercial services which computerize sales data for multiuse research purposes. Abstract companies, for title search and title insurance application, maintain accurate records of property ownership and title transfer data which generally are filed in geographic or alphabetical order by legal descriptions for a county area. With aid of these data, abstract companies render specialized services in all matters concerning the acquisition date and type of real property ownership. For appraisal purposes abstract record data are deemed most reliable and, in the long run, most economical when the appraiser's time is an important consideration.

VERIFICATION OF SALES

Market sale transactions should never be used as value source data unless the appraiser personally, or through a responsible assistant, has taken steps to confirm the sale and to inquire into the circumstances causing the sale or affecting the transaction price. The verification, as a rule, can readily be obtained from the seller or purchaser of the property. It is rare that a seller or purchaser refuses information, especially if informed that the sales information was obtained from public records and is to be used as one of many sales transactions in deriving a measure of objective value. Circumstances surrounding and affecting the sale must be known, especially if extraordinary terms or conditions of sale appear likely or if lack of objective, impersonal bargaining or forced-sale motivations are suspected. Where the sale was not clear cut, and when adjustments for conditions or terms of sale cannot readily and accurately be made, it is best to refrain from using the particular transactions and to select another and more reliable guide to market value.

Sales prices, too, should never be deduced from the amount of state transfer tax cited in a deed of record. Real estate transactions are still largely deemed private and confidential in character, and these tax references may be over- or understated deliberately for devious tax or investment gain purposes. State tax data, too, are deemed unreliable and unacceptable as evidence for an index of market value in most court jurisdictions, unless the sales price was directly confirmed with a party to the transaction.

PRICE ADJUSTMENTS TO COMPENSATE FOR TIME AND TRANSFER TERMS

Comparable sales selected for price analysis under the market approach to value must be adjusted, if necessary, to compensate for the effect of economic forces that influenced the real estate market during the time interval elapsed between the date of the comparable sale and the date of subject property appraisal. Market prices of real estate are dynamic in character and move upward or downward with changes in building supply and demand, variations in business and real estate cycles, and changes in the value of money as a result of dollar inflation or deflation. The more recent the index sale, the better and the more reliable are the market comparison results. Sales which are six months old or older must be analyzed in the light of current market conditions (to measure the price effect, if any) that are attributable to the passage of time. The appraiser should ask himself or herself the question: Suppose that the comparable sale were exposed for sale today (on the date of the appraisal)—would it bring the same price at which it sold some time ago? If the answer is in the negative, price adjustments are called for, and the reason for them must be explained in the narrative section of the appraisal report. Adjustments are generally shown in relation to 100 percent and applied as ratios of 1.00—such as 0.95, 1.02, 1.05, etc.—of prevailing market prices.

Where it is known or evident that the terms of sale influenced the price at which the index property exchanged, price adjustments, too, are called for. Value, by market definition, is based on property transfer on a cash or cash equivalent basis. Where the impact of terms is difficult to measure, or where the sale was not on an open and competitive basis, it is best to disregard the transaction and to select another for market comparison purposes.

Adjusting for Financing

Seldom, if ever, does a party buy real estate alone. The decision to acquire and to pay a particular price for real estate may be influenced by the perceived benefits generated by the property, its ability to shelter other earned income from income taxes, and also by the financing terms. Usually favorable financing terms can either inflate or deflate the price that a party is willing to pay. The appraiser's dilemma is twofold: (1) being able to use a mathematical method that will logically account for out-of-the ordinary financing terms, and (2) determining to some reasonable degree of satisfaction whether market participants' behavior is reflected by this adjustment methodology. This adjustment method is known as "cash equivalency." Application of this method departs from actually equating a sale price to the price expected from an all cash purchase. Instead, the process is more accurately described as "prevailing financing equivalency." The appraiser seeks to identify any unusual financing and then to adjust accordingly until the price reflects the price that probably would have been paid had prevailing or normal debt financing been used. In effect, this adjustment is made to determine the price the real estate itself would have brought in a sale involving normal financing. No adjustment is needed if the financing arrangements did not affect the price paid for the comparable property.

There is no universal agreement as to how this adjustment should be handled. The following examples illustrate how this adjustment can be applied.

Sale price	$130,000
Financing terms	$104,000 loan, 30 years, level monthly payments, 11½% interest rate
Prevailing loan terms	25-year term and 13% interest rate with monthly installments

The question is how much would a buyer probably have paid for this property if it had been financed with a typical 25-year, 13% loan. The cash equivalency of the down payment of $26,000 needs no adjustment since this is already cash. The next step is to adjust the $104,000 loan to its prevailing financing equivalence by use of present worth factors. This adjustment is simply a means of computing the installment to amortize of both the favorable and prevailing loans. The subject of present worth and finance mathematics is covered in more detail in Chapters 17 and 18.

Installment to amortize 1 at 11½% for 30 years	$\dfrac{0.009903}{0.011278} = 0.878054$
Installment to amortize 1 at 13% for 25 years	

or the value of the existing loan would be worth $91,318 ($104,000 × 0.878054). Stated differently, the 11½ percent loan would be discounted by 12.19 percent in a 13 percent market. The adjusted sale price of this comparable sale would be

$ 26,000
+ 91,318
$117,318   or $117,000 (rounded)

Adjustment for terms of sale, when known, can readily be made by computing the present worth of savings which accrue to the purchaser. Suppose that a residential property sold for $82,000, subject to a $75,000 existing mortgage which remains to be amortized over the next 20 years at 11 percent interest.

Assuming a current mortgage market rate of 12 percent, the value of the terms of sale are estimated as follows:

1. Savings in mortgage placement and closing costs. These average a minimum of 3 percent of the value of the mortgage,[1] or in this instance 3 percent of $75,000, or $2,250.
2. Savings resulting from existing favorable rate of interest, which is 1 percentage point below prevailing mortgage market rates. A $75,000 mortgage to be amortized over 20 years at 12 percent interest requires monthly payments of interest and principal in the amount of $825.82. A like mortgage at 11 percent interest calls for monthly payments of $774.14. The difference of $51.67 per month, capitalized over a period of 240 months, results in savings to the purchaser of $51.67 × 90.819416 (present worth of an annuity of 1 dollar *per month* at 12 percent per annum for 240 months, or $4,694).

The combined savings resulting from existing and favorable financing in the amount of $2,250 + $4,694, a total of $6,944 (rounded), must be subtracted from the selling price to derive the price that would have been realized had the property been sold on cash or cash equivalent terms.[2]

An important point to remember when using this method is to determine whether the financing terms were known prior to the offer to purchase having been made. In the case of a loan assumption or seller-provided financing, the buyer certainly would be aware of these terms. Sometimes with third-party financing (such as a bank), the buyer does not know the exact terms and often they do not vary significantly from prevailing terms anyway.

MARKET COMPARISON ADJUSTMENT TECHNIQUES

The market approach to value as applied to the appraisal of unimproved land, and the adjustments necessary to equalize for differences in sale prices caused by neighborhood, location, and site advantages was illustrated and explained in Chapter 9. The market data report form shown in Figure 9.1 can with slight modification also be used for entry of improved property sales information from public records. The only suggested change in the form, as shown, is to provide for field entry of a description of the kind and condition of on-site improvements. To adjust for value differences attributable to variations in age, size, and quality of building construction, one of the following techniques may be employed:

1. Construction detail analysis and price rating technique.
2. Overall construction and building condition rating technique.

---

[1]Loan origination fee of 1 percent, title insurance costs of 1 percent, and 1 percent covering legal expenses, appraisal fee, credit report expense, stamp taxes on note and mortgage, and notarizing and recording fees.

[2]Typical financial terms currently available to the typical (accredited) purchaser.

The application of these market comparison techniques as applied to the subject property and to the comparable sales are for purposes of illustration based on building construction data obtained as follows:

Subject property: Frame construction, 1,450-square-foot area. Exterior walls of redwood siding. Three bedrooms, two tiled bathrooms, living room, kitchen, and dinette. One-car garage, screened porch, and concrete patio. Central forced-air ducted gas heating, finish oak flooring over plywood subflooring, asbestos shingle roofing over 4-inch rock-wool insulation. Building condition good, deferred maintenance—none. Effective age eight years. Lot value by market comparison, $13,500.

Index Sale 1: Concrete block structure, 1,650-square-foot area, four bedrooms, three tiled baths, living–dining room combination, kitchen, and utility room. Carport storage area and open entrance porch. Central forced-air–oil-fired heating system. Terrazzo flooring over concrete slab subflooring. Asphalt shingle gable roof. No attic insulation. Building condition good, deferred maintenance (decorating) $1,800. Effective age 10 years. Lot value by market comparison, $15,000. Total sale price: $63,000. Date of sale: one month ago.

Index Sale 2: Brick veneer over concrete block structure, 1,503-square-foot area. Three bedrooms, one tiled bath, living room, sunporch, and kitchen. One-car garage, open porch. Central oil heating and 3-ton air-conditioning system. Oak parquet flooring over concrete slab subflooring. Asphalt shingle roof over 4-inch rock-wool insulation. Floored attic storage area. Condition good, no deferred maintenance. Effective age 12 years. Lot value by market comparison, $12,000. Total sale price: $67,500. Date of sale: current.

Index Sale 3: Cedar-shingled frame structure, 1,400-square-foot area. Three bedrooms, den living-dining room, kitchen, and two partially tiled bathrooms. Two-car garage, open entrance porch. Suspended floor, wall-to-wall carpeting over plywood base and pine subflooring. Built-up roofing covered with marble chits, 4-inch insulation, circulating gas heater, 36-inch attic fan. Built-in reverse-cycle air-conditioning wall unit. Effective age 5 years. Deferred maintenance $600 (repaint kitchen, bath, and hallway areas). Lot value by market comparison, $13,500. Total sale price: $68,500. Date of sale: six months ago.

Index Sale 4: Concrete block structure, stuccoed exterior, 1,550-square-foot area. Three bedrooms, one tiled bathroom, living room, kitchen, utility room, and screened porch. Two-car carport. Suspended oak flooring over pine subflooring. Asphalt shingle roof over 4-inch insulation, hip-roof construction, boxed eaves, 36-inch roof overhang. Central duct oil-fired–forced-air-heating system. Built-in kitchen fan, electric wall heater in bathroom, and garbage disposal unit. Condition good, no deferred maintenance. Effective age 12 years. Lot value by market comparison, $15,750. Total sale price: $61,500. Date of sale: 20 months ago.

CONSTRUCTION DETAIL ANALYSIS AND PRICE RATING TECHNIQUE

After confirmation of the sales prices and terms of sale with respective buyers, sellers, or real estate brokers, the index properties are inspected and inventoried for size and details of construction in order that price adjustment can be made to make each sale as nearly as possible comparable to the subject property. The appraiser, in effect, must ask as he or she considers differences in age, size, and quality of building construction: How much more or less will a typical purchaser pay—as compared with the subject property—because of the presence or absence of major construction features? The successful application of this technique requires:

1. Building construction know-how.
2. Detailed property inspection and keen observation.
3. Knowledge of construction costs and building unit prices.
4. Knowledge of typical buyer preferences and price reactions.
5. Application of sound judgment to obtain reasonable results.

The adjustments required to bring about price comparability of the index sales with the subject property are shown in Table 10.1. The first adjustment equates differences in time of sale. As noted, index properties 3 and 4 would bring $1,500 and $3,000 more if exposed for sale on the date of the appraisal as compared with sale prices realized six months and one year before, respectively. Differences in lot value, based on market sales, are adjusted next. Other adjustments reflect differences in quantity and quality of building construction. Building area was equalized at a current building rate of $22.50 per square foot, exclusive of fixtures, heating, electrical, and plumbing costs in kitchen and bathrooms. Further adjustments were calculated at estimated construction expenditures at time of construction new, less accrued depreciation due to wear and use over the period of economic age of the index property. Differences in economic ages were equated at uniform rates of 2.5 percent per year on the basis of straight line accounting over an economic age period of 40 years. Differences in building conditions were adjusted on the basis of estimated expenditures to cure deferred maintenance. Based on these adjustments and assignment of correlation (judgment) weights, in accordance with the importance of each sale as an index of market value, a final estimate of $67,500 indicates the value for the subject property under the market approach using the construction detail analysis and price rating technique.

The four comparable sales used in the market data approach to value were correlated in accordance with assigned judgment weights as shown in Table 10.1. The reasons that justify the selection of the correlation weights are as follows:

Sale 1 was given a weight of 30 percent because no time adjustment was necessary to update this sale for market changes in the price level of residential properties. This sale is located in a similar setting as the subject property, both being in the same neighborhood. Further, an opportunity to inspect this sale property with care made possible accurate adjustments for variations in building features and construction.

Table 10.1 Market Sale Price Recapitulation Schedule Based on Construction Detail Analysis and Price Rating Techniques

	INDEX SALE NO.			
	1	2	3	4
Indicated price	$ 63,000	$ 67,500	$ 68,500	$ 61,500
Time adjustment	0	0	+ 1,500	+ 3,000
Lot value difference	− 1,500	+ 1,500	0	+ 2,250
Construction variations[a]				
Building area	− 4,500	− 1,600	+ 1,125	− 2,250
Exterior walls	+ 2,325	− 2,250	− 1,050	+ 1,500
Interior finishes	+ 2,400	0	+ 750	0
Number of baths	− 1,050	+ 1,050	0	+ 1,050
Tile in baths	− 825	+ 825	+ 900	+ 825
Roof construction	+ 900	+ 900	0	+ 600
Insulation	+ 525	0	0	0
Heating and cooling	0	− 2,700	+ 1,800	0
Equipment	0	0	− 1,275	− 675
Finished flooring	0	0	− 1,500	0
Attic area	0	− 1,600	0	0
Garage construction	+ 1,500	0	− 2,400	0
Porches and utility rooms	+ 900	+ 900	+ 1,125	0
Building age	+ 1,500	+ 3,000	− 1,500	+ 3,000
Building conditions	+ 1,800	0	+ 600	0
Total adjustment	$ + 3,975	$ + 25	$ + 75	$ + 9,300
Adjusted sale price	$ 66,975	$ 67,525	$ 68,575	$ 70,800
Correlation (judgment) weight	× 0.30	× 0.40	× 0.20	× 0.10
Weighted value	$ 20,092	$ 27,010	$ 13,715	$ 7,080
Correlated value	$ 67,897			
Rounded to	$ 68,000			

[a]Price variations are based on *market* evidence (*not* cost to install) of how much more or less buyers are willing to pay for the presence or absence of construction features.

Sale 2 was given a weight of 40 percent because this property is located in the same block as the subject property, and because this sale represents the most recent transaction of all the sales considered in the market approach to value. Sale 2 also comes reasonably close to the building area of the subject house (1,450 square feet, as compared with 1,503 square feet for the sale property). Similarity of building condition, too, made this sale superior to sales 1 and 3.

Sale 3 is located in a comparable neighborhood, ½ mile from the subject property. The sale took place one year ago and a time adjustment of $1,500 was made to reflect the estimated increase in market prices caused by rising property values in the community. Because of substantial variations in time of sale and location, this comparable sale was given a weight of only 20 percent.

Sale 4, although most comparable as far as physical features are concerned, took place nearly 20 months ago, thus necessitating a time adjustment of $3,000. This sale, too, is located in a similar but distant neighborhood, causing a significant adjustment in the property lot value. Because of the substantial adjustments necessary to make this sale comparable, the weight assigned was judged at 10 percent. (A summary of the sale prices and adjustments is provided in Table 10.2.)

The market approach to value under the construction detail analysis and price rating technique as illustrated is ideal, provided that good reasons are given for the use of the different correlation percentage weights. The appraiser, in deciding on the degree of comparability among sale properties, should not rely on the net adjustments. A better guide of similarity is the number and total dollar amount of adjustments made for the selected sales. A sale may show a nominal net adjustment which resulted from a large number of offsetting plus and minus adjustments. As indicators of the appraised property's value, such sales are inferior to those requiring relatively few adjustments of lesser dollar amounts.

When applied with care, the market comparison method produces accurate appraisal estimates. This method, however, can be used successfully only where the appraiser, through available plant or other source data, has construction features for each sale property readily at hand. In practice, few appraisers can afford the time required to complete a thorough field inspection of each comparable sale (assuming owner's permission) used as an index to market value. Nor do appraisal fees customarily paid for appraisals of residential properties economically warrant the expenditure of effort necessary to secure and analyze essential market and construction data as outlined above. For this reason a less detailed but still sufficiently accurate market comparison technique is recommended for appraisal purposes.

OVERALL CONSTRUCTION AND BUILDING CONDITION RATING TECHNIQUE

Under this approach to value, market comparison is based on an overall judgment as to percentage-price adjustment called for in order to make each index sale comparable with the subject property. The overall percentage applied to each property in turn is justified by a statement that the subject property is

Table 10.2 Market Sales Prices and Adjustment Summary

Index Sale No.	Market Price	Price Adjustment	Indicated Value	Percent Weight
1	$63,000	$+3,975	$66,975	30
2	67,500	+25	67,525	40
3	68,500	+75	68,575	20
4	61,500	+9,300	70,800	10

deemed better, poorer, or the same (comparable) in relation to its construction as to type, size, features, age, and building condition. Since the subject property in every value problem represents X (unknown price), each index sale for comparison purposes is accepted as a measure of market forces of supply and demand equal to 100 percent at a given time and place. By adjusting the index rating upward or downward in accordance with characteristics of the subject property, a market value estimate is derived. The greater the number of truly comparable index sales used for market analysis purposes, the greater, as a rule, the accuracy of the final value estimate. Individual errors in fact or judgment generally cancel out or are at least mitigated in their effect on the end results.

The application of the overall construction and building condition technique is demonstrated in Table 10.3. The judgment ratings shown are supported by property descriptions as detailed earlier, and are based on a general rather than detailed field inspection of the physical property improvements. For the reader's benefit, further explanatory statements can be made in the appraisal report as follows: "The subject property, as compared with index sale 1, is poorer in type of construction because the index property has four bedrooms and three fully tiled bathrooms as compared with three bedrooms and two bathrooms contained in the subject building. The subject also is smaller in size, containing 1,450 square feet of area as compared with 1,650-square-foot area of the index sale. The subject property is deemed better in construction features, age, and condition because it has an asbestos-shingled roof and rock-wool insulation compared with the asphalt-shingled roof without insulation of the index property. The subject property has an effective age of 8 years; the index property age is 10 years. The subject property is in good condition with no deferred maintenance. Index sale 1 requires an expenditure of $1,800 to redecorate the interior. The overall adjustment rating for the subject property is estimated at 110 percent, and the adjusted market price ascribable to the subject property is $67,650." A like comparative analysis of each of the other index sales with the subject property aids the client for whom the report is prepared in following step by step the procedure and logic used by the appraiser in arriving at the final estimate and value conclusions.

Although the percentage adjustment method does not appear as refined as the dollar equalization method, the former method is more realistic and in conformity with thought processes which motivates buyers and sellers when bargaining. It must be kept in mind that appraising is an art and not a science, and that final estimates of value are deemed reasonably accurate if within 5 percent, plus or minus, of actual market value realized by a subsequent and open sale. Then, too, the market approach to value is rarely used alone. Generally, the cost approach and, where applicable, the income approach to value, or both, are used as checks and counterchecks on each other to ensure the accuracy of the final value estimate as certified in the appraisal report.

PERCENTAGE ADJUSTMENTS: THEIR USE AND LIMITATION

To achieve comparability and to adjust for price differences caused by variations in type, size, features, age, and condition of the improvements, most appraising practitioners rather than using the "better, poorer, same" judgment analysis as illustrated in Table 10.3, apply percentage ratings to reflect superior or inferior market factor relationships. The use of a sequence of percentage ratings poses serious pitfalls and limitations. First, to ascribe to a number of structural deviations precise percentage ratings such as 5 percent superior, 10 percent inferior,

Table 10.3 Market Sales Price Recapitulation Schedule Based on Overall Construction and Building Conditions Rating Technique

	INDEX SALE NO.			
	1	2	3	4
Indicated price	$63,000	$67,500	$68,500	$61,500
Time adjustment	0	0	+1,500	+3,000
Price adjustment for time	63,000	67,500	70,000	64,500
Lot value difference	−1,500	+1,500	0	−2,250
Adjusted price	61,500	69,000	70,000	62,250
Subject property rating in regard to:				
Construction:				
Type	Poorer	Poorer	Poorer	Same
Size	Poorer	Poorer	Better	Poorer
Features	Better	Poorer	Same	Better
Age	Better	Better	Poorer	Better
Condition	Better	Same	Better	Same
Subject property percent rating	1.10	1.00	0.95	1.15
Adjusted value	$67,650	$69,000	$66,500	$71,588

INDEX SALES WEIGHTS AND MARKET CORRELATION

Index Sale No.	Adjusted Market Value	Weight of Sale	Value Components
1	$67,650	0.30	$20,295
2	69,000	0.40	27,600
3	66,500	0.20	13,300
4	71,588	0.10	7,159
Correlated market value—total			$68,354
Rounded to $68,350			

and so on, presumes appraising to be a science—which it is not. Then, too, an appraiser would be hard put to justify whether a given quality of construction should be rated exactly 10 percent or perhaps 9 or 11 percent superior, respectively. A jury or even an investor might get the impression that the appraiser is playing a numbers game that borders on "guesstimating" rather than professional estimating. Second, and more serious, is the mathematical distortion that results from giving equal weight to percentage minuses and percentage pluses. A given market value can decline only 100 percent but can possibly increase a million or more percent—perhaps large and long enough to reach the moon. To illustrate, a minus of 50 percent is not offset by a plus of 50 percent, for a multiplication of 0.50×1.50 equals 0.75. Third, use of multiplied separate percentage adjustments presumes an interrelationship that probably does not exist. For example, there certainly is no relationship between the time, location, and conditions of sale adjustments.

In making adjustments, it is recommended that the sale prices of the sale properties be made toward the appraised property in order to *reflect the inferiority or superiority of the appraised property.* An easy way to remember this adjustment process is to make a minus adjustment when the appraised property is inferior to the sale property. Similarly, a positive adjustment is called for when the subject property is superior to the comparable sales property. This logic is illustrated in the following example. A small commercial building sold for $500,000; the subject property has 10 feet less frontage than the sale property. Such frontage is worth $1,000 per front foot. However, the appraised property has a heating and air-conditioning system that is judged to be $50,000 superior to that serving the comparable sale property. Thus these adjustments to the sale property reveal a value for the subject property as follows:

Sale price		$500,000
Frontage	$ – 10,000	
Heat and air conditioning	+ 50,000	+ 40,000
Indicated value of subject property		$540,000

There seems to be no consensus as to how adjustments should be made. Certainly, two initial adjustments should be made before physical or locational adjustments are undertaken. First, a sale should be adjusted to reveal the price that it probably would bring at the date of the appraisal. Generally, a sale and resale of the sale property at fairly recent dates can provide support for this adjustment. Care must be taken to ascertain if any physical improvements occurred in the interim. For example, a good part of the increase in the sales price may have resulted from modernization or perhaps a room having been added to the dwelling. The sale of similar properties can also provide an indication of property appreciation. Next, the conditions influencing the sale such as buyer and seller motivation and financing terms should be considered and appropriately adjusted. Once having adjusted for these items, the appraiser knows the price that the comparable sale would have brought in the current market. The next (and key) question is to determine the probable selling price of the appraised property.

The value caused by the presence or lack of a physical item is the proper adjustment—not its cost. Ordinarily, time adjustments are made on a percentage basis, but physical and locational adjustments are made both on a percentage and dollar basis. Two key points for the appraiser to always remember are that (1) his or her job is to reflect the attitudes of buyers and sellers and not his or her own biases, and (2) if the market participants do not consider certain features in arriving at a purchase price, then neither should the appraiser.

ASSESSMENT RATIOS AS A GUIDE TO MARKET VALUE

A useful check on the accuracy of the market approach is provided by application of the property assessment ratios of the sale properties to the assessed value of the subject property. In every county or parish the tax assessor generally attempts to assess real property for tax "ad valorem" purposes at uniform ratios in relation to market value. It is true that individual properties may be grossly out of line in being over- or underassessed, but where many properties are combined in an assessment-to-market value ratio analysis, the results are often quite accurate. This, it is realized, may be due to compensating errors whereby inequities in individual property assessment are canceled out through the use of a larger sample as a base for study. In many counties, too—especially in the larger and the more progressive smaller ones—responsible appraisal firms are periodically called in to establish equitable assessments based on fair market value.

The application of the assessment ratio method as a guide to market value is a relatively simple procedure. This method, by the way, is facetiously referred to as the "fourth approach to value." In gathering market sales data from public records, the appraiser can readily obtain from tax records in the county clerk's office the assessed value for each of the index sales. The work form shown and recommended for market study use in Figure 9.1 provides for entry of assessment data and computation of sale-to-assessment ratios. By combining the sale/assessment ratios for all index sales used in the market approach to value, a typical or average ratio can be derived and applied to the assessed value of the subject property as a guide to market value. To illustrate: Suppose that the index sales described above yield sale-to-assessment ratios as follows:

Index Sale No.	Assessed Value	÷	Sale Price	=	Assessment/Sales Ratio
1	$ 51,600		$ 63,000		0.82
2	57,400		67,500		0.85
3	54,800		68,500		0.80
4	54,750		61,500		0.89
Totals and average	$218,550		$260,500		0.84

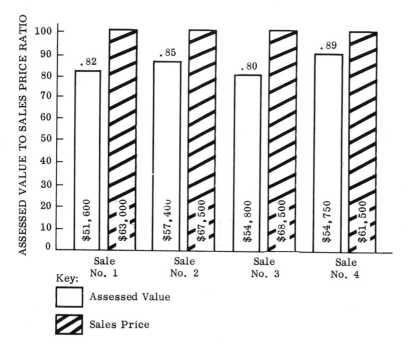

Figure 10.1 Market Comparison Approach Based on Ratio of Sales Prices to Assessed Valuations

Assuming that the subject property is assessed for $56,500, the indicated market value based on the typical sale-to-assessment ratio of 0.84, as computed above, would be $56,000 ÷ 0.84, or $67,260. This appears to compare favorably with the values of $68,000 and $68,350 derived above under the conventional market approaches to value. Should the results obtained under the assessment ratio guide to value be considerably out of line, the appraiser would have good cause to recheck the data for possible errors in the market value analysis. Where no errors are found and the conclusions point to an over- or underassessment of the subject property, this information may also prove of useful interest to the client or owner of the property. On numerous occasions such value findings have brought about a lowering of property assessments and welcome tax savings to the grateful property owners. The sales/assessment ratio method as described above is graphically presented in Figure 10.1.

REGRESSION ANALYSIS

In regression analysis a mathematical expression is developed so that property value can be expressed as a function of another variable or variables. These variables are known as the independent or explanatory variables. The simplest form is when one independent variable is used to explain the value of the dependent variable through the use of a straight line or linear relationship. The statistical method known as *simple linear regression* fits a straight line to a set of data points. In graphical representation the independent or explanatory variable is plotted on the X axis and the dependent variable is plotted on the Y axis. In real estate applications the dependent variable is property value or sales price which depends on the value of some independent variable such as street frontage.

The simple linear regression equation is[3]

$$Y = a + bX$$

where $a = Y$ intercept, the point where the line intersects the Y axis

$b = $ slope of the line, the amount Y would change if the value of X increases one unit

If the value of the slope is positive, then Y would increase as X increases. Correspondingly, if the slope is negative, then Y would decrease as X increases.

One should always plot the data to visually examine how well a straight line will fit the data. A numeric measure of how well the regression line describes the relation between the variables is the coefficient of determination, r^2. Its value ranges from 0 to 1 and measures the proportion of the variability of the dependent variable that is explained by the independent variable. If $r^2 = 0$, the independent variable explains none of the variability of Y. If $r^2 = 1$, the independent variable explains all of the variability of the dependent variable; hence if one knows the value of X, then by using the regression equation the value of Y can be determined exactly. It should be noted that if r has a positive value, then the X's and Y's are positively correlated. That is, Y increases in proportion to increases in X. Conversely, when the X's and Y's are negatively or inversely related, the Y value increases as the X value decreases. The resulting line is said to have a negative slope.

The coefficient of determination (r^2) is the square of the correlation coefficient (r) and can easily be determined on a calculator. For example if $r = 0.5$, then $r^2 = 0.25$ and the simple linear regression line explains only 25 percent of the variability of Y, which is not sufficiently linear to warrant use of a linear equation.

An example of linear regression applied to real estate appraising follows:

Lot frontage, X (ft)	Sale price, Y
150	$18,750
140	15,400
155	17,360
132	15,250
147	17,500
158	19,500
162	19,000
160	17,400
138	17,650
125	14,750

[3]The equations for determining a and b are not included because many calculators have the ability to calculate the values automatically. This line is often called the least squares line because of the method that is used to fit the line to the data.

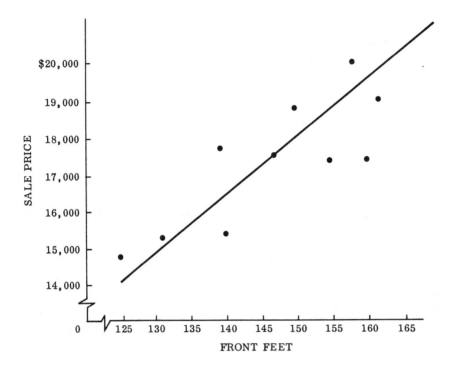

Figure 10.2 Plot of Sale Prices, Frontage, and Regression Line

Plotting these data produces the regression line shown in Figure 10.2. This plotting gives an initial idea as to whether there is a linear relationship between lot frontage and value.

By use of a programmable calculator, it can be determined that for each 1-foot increase in lot frontage, the projected front-foot value increases by $107.07. Also, the Y intercept is $1,548.27 and the regression equation is $Y = 1,548.27 + 107.07X$. Using this equation the value of the appraised site with 152 front feet is estimated to be $17,823. Using a calculator, the value of r^2 is computed to be 0.67, which says that 67 percent of the variability of sales price for these data can be explained by knowing the lot frontages.

The same results occur when using the linear regression equation. If neither method were used, the appraiser could approximate the estimated market value of the appraised site simply by plotting the front footage and sale price of each sale on a chart. The subject site's frontage would be lined up with a corresponding site price (or value).

SP	SP − $\overline{SP}$	(SP − $\overline{SP}$)²	FF	(FF − $\overline{FF}$)	(FF − $\overline{FF}$)²	(SP − $\overline{SP}$)(FF − $\overline{FF}$)
$ 18,750	$1,494	$ 2,232,036	150	3.3	10.9	4,930.2
15,400	− 1,856	3,444,736	140	− 6.7	44.9	12,435.2
17,360	104	10,816	155	8.3	68.9	863.2
15,250	− 2,006	4,024,036	132	− 14.7	216.1	29,488.2
17,500	244	59,536	147	0.3	0.1	73.2
19,500	2,244	5,035,536	158	11.3	127.7	25,357.2
19,000	1,744	3,041,536	162	15.3	234.1	26,683.2
17,400	144	20,736	160	13.3	176.9	1,915.2
17,650	394	155,236	138	− 8.7	75.7	− 3,427.8
14,750	− 2,506	6,280,036	125	− 21.7	470.9	54,380.2
$172,560	0	$24,304,240	1,467	0	1,426.2	152,698.0

$\overline{SP}$ = average sales price
$\overline{FF}$ = average front feet

$$\overline{SP} = \Sigma \, SP/n$$
$$= \$172,560/10$$
$$= \$17,256$$

$$\overline{FF} = \Sigma \, FF/n$$
$$= 1,467/10$$
$$= 146.7$$

$$a = \overline{SP} - (b)(\overline{FF})$$
$$= \$17,256 - (107.1)(146.7)$$
$$= 1,544.4$$

$$b = \frac{\Sigma(SP - \overline{SP})(FF - \overline{FF})}{\Sigma(FF - \overline{FF})^2}$$
$$= 152,698.0/1,426.2$$
$$= 107.1$$

$$MV = a + b \, (SF)$$
$$= 1,544.4 + (107.1)(152)$$
$$= \$17,824$$

Multiple regression is a statistical technique that allows the analyst to take a step beyond simple linear regression in that more than one independent variable can be included in the analysis. When it is found that a variable such as lot frontage does not adequately explain the sale price of property, other variables may be included. For example, studies have found that variables such as the house size, the number of bathrooms, and the physical condition of the dwelling generally predict the probable value of the appraised residential property.

The multiple regression equation is a straightforward extension of simple linear regression. If the number of explanatory or independent variables is n, then the equation is

$$Y = a + b_1 X_1 + b_2 X_2 + \cdots + b_n X_n$$

Solutions for the a and b's can be obtained through the least squares method. Because of the computing power required, a small computer is needed to find the multiple linear regression equation for most problems. Most computer regression packages compute the coefficient of determination, denoted R^2 for multiple regression, in addition to the regression coefficients (i.e., the a and b values). As in simple linear regression it measures the proportion of the variation in Y that can be explained by the independent variables.

Interpreting the value of the regression coefficients for real estate problems is often very tricky. If the intercorrelations among the n independent variables are all zero, that is, they do not vary together, then b can be accurately interpreted as the amount of change in Y that would accompany a one-unit change in X_1. If X_1 is the square footage of a dwelling and X_2 is the number of baths, then these variables would tend to covary. A large value for X_1 would generally be accompanied by a large value for X_2. Hence the correlation would be positive and the line would slope upward to the right. When explanatory variables covary in multiple regression, the data are said to be multicollinear. In the presence of multicollinearity one cannot accurately use the multiple regression coefficients to estimate the value contribution to Y that would accompany a one-unit change in a multicollinear independent variable. The regression equation itself is still accurate for prediction purposes even if multicollinearity exists. The difficulty exists in the interpretation of the coefficients.

The use of regression equations presents a well-established way of formally using a set of past data to help predict the sales price of a property based on the characteristics of the property. For example, consider a hypothetical regression equation

$$Y = 15,000 + 7X_1 + 850X_2$$

where X_1 = dwelling square footage

X_2 = number of rooms

Suppose that a prediction is desired for the value of a property similar to those in the data set that generated the equation above. This property has 1,500 square feet in the dwelling and eight rooms. Then $Y = 15,000 + 7(1,500) + 850(8) = \$32,300$.

THE MARKET DATA APPROACH FOR COMMERCIAL AND INDUSTRIAL PROPERTIES

The larger and more complex the physical improvements, the more detailed and difficult the market comparison approach. Whereas with residential property the structure as a whole served as a basis for comparison, a more detailed and manageable microstructural unit basis now must be devised to permit realistic comparison and logical adjustments for building differences caused by size, age, quality, and quantity of construction.

Market price equalization is generally achieved by the unit comparison approach selecting for comparability one or more of the following:

1. Price per square or cubic foot of building volume.
2. Price per square foot of net rentable area.
3. Price per apartment including land investment.
4. Price per room inclusive of bath, closet, and storage areas.
5. Gross annual or monthly income multiplier.

For industrial, warehouse, or office buildings the cubic foot method of comparison (giving weight to the third dimension, i.e., height of ceilings and depth of basement area) yields more accurate results than the square foot comparison approach to value. Care, however, must be taken to exclude land value from the total market price paid for the property when there is a significant variation in site sizes and to adjust the cubic foot cost of each sale or index property for differences caused by age, quality and condition of building(s), economy of building size, and equipment features compared with the subject property. Where sale properties are selected with care, this market approach to value yields reliable results. The gross income multiplier, as explained below, can also be applied as a check on the direct and usually more accurate unit comparison approach to value. The appraiser should observe the amount and finish of any office space, adequacy of parking and turning radius for trucks, as well as column spacing and overhead clearance in warehouses.

Apartment properties offer greater flexibility in the application of the market or unit comparison approach to value. Because of greater uniformity in construction design and building technique, and competitive demand and supply for apartment housing, it is readily possible to apply the unit comparison method more effectively on the basis of sale price[4] per apartment, per room as well as per square or cubic foot. All these various price unit indexes can then be rechecked by the gross annual multiplier for derivation of a market-correlated index of value for the property as a whole.

Given a subject property that is effectively in new condition and which contains 110 apartments and 374 rooms, and for which the underlying land value was estimated at $300,000, and the effective gross income at $478,200 a sales recapitulation summary schedule for the estimation of market value may be constructed as shown in Table 10.4. The comparative analysis is relatively simple. The price paid for each comparable sale property is adjusted for changes attributed to passage of time from date of sale transaction to date of the appraisal. From this adjusted total the land value, derived by a market comparison approach, is subtracted to obtain the residual value attributable to the building improvements. Next comes an important percentage adjustment that reflects,

---

[4]Where building-to-total property value ratios are markedly different, the appraiser may be justified in using a value unit measure with the land excluded, as shown in the following example.

in the appraiser's judgment, the age and condition of each sale property as compared with the subject property. The adjusted sale prices are then allocated on a per apartment and a per room basis as shown. By correlating the derived units of measurement, giving greater judgment weights to sales which require little or no percentage adjustment, the appraised value of the subject property is obtained as demonstrated.

GROSS INCOME MULTIPLIERS AS A GUIDE TO MARKET VALUE

When using this technique, the appraiser must apply it in the same manner that it is derived. For example, a GIM can be based on either gross potential income (assumes full occupancy) or effective gross income (allows for actual occupancy).

Table 10.4   Market Approach to Value of Apartment Property

	INDEX SALE NO.			
	1	2	3	4
Sale price	$2,450,000	$2,392,000	$2,480,000	$3,025,000
Time adjustment	0	0	0	1.10
Adjusted price	$2,450,000	$2,392,000	$2,480,000	$3,327,500
Less land value	$ 240,000	$ 235,000	$ 295,000	$ 275,000
Building value	$2,210,000	$2,157,000	$2,185,000	$3,052,500
Location adjustment	0.90	0.80	1.00	1.05
Age and condition	0	1.05	0.97	0.88
Adjusted improvement value	$2,455,556	$2,537,647	$2,252,577	$3,282,258
Number of apartments	100	112	95	38
Number of rooms	348	384	312	469
Sale price per apartment	$ 24,556	$ 22,658	$ 23,711	$ 23,784
Sale price per room	$ 7,056	$ 6,608	$ 7,220	$ 6,998
Effective gross income	$ 429,825	$ 410,996	$ 404,565	$ 527,000
Gross multiplier	5.70	5.82	6.13	5.74

Market Value of Subject Property

1. 110 apartments at $23,750	= $2,612,500	
Add land value of	300,000	
Indicated value—based on apartments		$2,912,500
2. 374 rooms at $7,000	= $2,618,000	
Add land value of	300,000	
Indicated value—based on rooms		2,918,000
3. Effective gross income	$ 478,200	
Gross income multiplier[a]	5.75	
Indicated value—based on multiplier		2,749,650
Correlated market value		$2,900,000

[a]Market indexes based principally on sale 1, because no adjustment for age and condition of building was necessary and room and apartment count were close to the subject property.

Thus, if a GIM is based on actual occupancy of a sale building, it should be applied to the appraised property's actual or effective income. Sometimes, this multiplier is abbreviated EGIM. It may be more accurate to use effective gross income data, but not all property owners are able or willing to provide this rental information. Hence gross potential income and sales price are usually used to derive a GIM.

The gross income multiplier (GIM) as a device to convert monthly or annual gross income into an expression of market value has gained popularity as a rule of thumb and as an index of value. Like all rules which are based on the law of averages, the gross income multiplier can serve a useful purpose when applied intelligently and with care.

At the outset, it should be realized that the use of the gross income multiplier should not be considered as part of the income or capitalization approach to value. To capitalize means to convert the estimated *net* operating income anticipated over the remaining economic life of the subject property or some other shorter holding period into a present value. The gross income multiplier does not give weight to amounts of operating expense ratios or to variations in the remaining economic life of properties. In fact, the user of the multiplier may incorrectly assume that all properties within a given classification, such as residential, commercial, or industrial, are identical in operating characteristics and in their economic age span of remaining productive life.

It may be fair to state that, by custom, many appraisers have been compelled to give recognition to the gross income multiplier as an index of value. In many areas, lay investors use the multiplier as a cardinal guide in judging the quality of property purchase offers. The multiplier is unscientific but nevertheless is a market phenomenon that cannot be ignored.

Not only should the GIM not be ignored, it should be used to the fullest extent possible. As with any research methodology, the results can be no better than the quality of data analyzed. It is argued that the gross income multiplier produces inaccurate results when the sale-rental properties possess different operating expense and land value-to-property value ratios, or are used for different aged properties. True, but there is no reason to expect reliable results in any approach to value when dissimilar data are considered. The key, then, is to compile a sufficient quantity of recent and similar transactions that have been confirmed by the appraiser. Instead of two or three comparables, perhaps 10 or 12 would be more in order.

One study revealed that if appraisers in the study had used nothing but GIMs for their final figure, their appraisals, on the average, would have been within 0.1 percent of the final value estimates.[5] This study of real estate price/earnings also found that the average percent difference between predicted sales price and actual sales price varied within a 4 percent and 8 percent range. This range is believed to be acceptable for most appraisers.[6]

[5]Richard U. Ratcliff, "Don't Underrate the Gross Income Multiplier," *The Appraisal Journal* 39, no. 2 (April 1971), p. 264.
[6]*Ibid.*, p. 269.

By custom, the gross income multiplier is used for conversion of monthly rentals in establishing the value of residential properties and is applied to the annual gross income valuation of industrial and commercial properties. Studies disclose that multipliers vary from region to region, often among communities within a region—and conceivably among neighborhoods within a city. The multiplier is simply derived for any given area by relating market prices of a given class of properties which have recently sold to the gross income actually or hypothetically derived from these properties if offered for rent in the open, competitive market at the time of sale. For residential properties—using the four index sales described earlier—the procedure for obtaining and using the multiplier is as follows.

The market analysis detailed in Table 10.5 indicates a monthly multiplier of 135. This multiplier can now be applied to the actual or estimated rental of the subject property to yield a measure of market value. Based on an estimated rent of $500 per month, the resultant market value equals $67,500 ($500 × 135). Conversely, the multiplier may also prove useful in estimating market rentals for residential properties offered for lease. Given a market value of $67,500 and a prevailing monthly rent multiplier of 135, the expected market rent is $67,500 ÷ 135, or $500 per month.

Advantages of the Gross Income Multiplier

The advantages of the GIM are that it typically is used by investors, is easily understood by investors and clients, and perhaps most important, is based exclusively on actual market events. There is no esoteric, complicated, or unrealistic opinion involved in its derivation and use which often characterizes the depreciated and capitalized income approaches. The key to its successful use is in obtaining a sufficient number of truly comparable sale-rental properties that have sold and rented recently. It is important that both the sales and rental transactions be recent. Examples of the under- and over-value distortion created by mismatched data are shown below for 12-unit apartment properties.

Table 10.5   Derivation of Monthly Rent Multiplier for Residential Properties

Index Sale No.	Sales Price	Actual or Estimated Monthly Rental	Gross Monthly Multiplier
1	$63,000	$475	133
2	67,500	510	132
3	68,500	500	137
4	61,500	450	137
Totals and average	$65,125	$484	135

Example A: old sale and recent rent
$250,000/$50,000 = 5.00

Example B: recent sale and old rent
$300,000/$42,000 = 7.14

Example C: recent sale and recent rent
$300,000/$50,000 = 6.00

Carrying these examples further, suppose that the expected or prevailing rental for the subject 12-unit apartment building is $52,000. Applying each of the three GIMs derived above produces the following value results:

A: 5.00 × $52,000 = $260,000
B: 7.14 × $52,000 = $371,280
C: 6.00 × $52,000 = $312,000

Disadvantages of the Gross Income Multiplier

As indicated, in the hands of an informed person the multiplier may prove a useful aid in approximating prevailing market value. The professional appraiser, however, is well advised to use this valuation tool with caution for the following reasons. First, the multiplier converts into value *gross* rather than *net* operating income. It is entirely possible that a property which produces a comparable gross income may yield inadequate or even no net operating income because of excessive operating or maintenance costs due to faulty construction or inequitable contractual commitments written into long-term lease agreements. In either case the existence of gross income gives an illusion of value that could not be justified by an expert appraiser. It is for this reason that users of the gross income multiplier should pay heed to the saying. "The accountant can estimate our gross, but only God can give us our net."

Second, the use of the multiplier assumes uniformity among properties in their operating ratios. Even among residential properties, where operating experience supports claims for relative constancy of expense outlays, individual properties may vary significantly from the norm as a result of differences in construction, quality of insulation, type of heating, amount of built-in equipment, equity of property taxation, and other causes. Again the key to successive use of this method is to compile a sufficient number of truly similar sale–rental properties.

Third, consideration of remaining economic life appears entirely ignored. It is a rare coincidence that properties selected as index sales are identical in relation to effective age, and a rarer coincidence still that the subject property should be of the same age as those of the index sales. Uninformed use of the gross multiplier would ascribe equal value to properties of equal income even though one may be in the last stages of its economic life and the other in new condition. It may be argued that such properties are not comparable; but be that as it may, the gross income multiplier *never* provides for adjustment of differences in properties which are by nature heterogeneous in character.

Fourth, care must be taken not to adjust the gross income, or the "raw" market prices, paid for comparable properties for age, condition, or location of the sale property. To do so will overadjust for physical, functional, or economic factors which both the renters and the investors have already considered in the price paid for rental and in the purchase amount offered for the property in its "as is" condition.

With these limitations in mind, the gross income multiplier may be used as a valuable straw in the bundle of straws to which the appraiser clings in formulating and justifying his or her final judgment of market value.

REVIEW QUESTIONS

1. Compute the cash equivalent for a sale that sold for $125,000 and was financed with a 12 percent, 25-year, monthly installment 80 percent mortgage in a market where the prevailing terms were 13 percent, 20 years, and the same loan-to-value ratio.
2. Explain why a comparatively small net adjustment may not represent the most comparable sale.
3. Why should adjustments be made for time and conditions of sale prior to considering differences in physical and locational features?
4. What weaknesses might be present in the use of the assessed value–sales price appraisal technique?
5. What problem occurs when applying a market-derived GIM to an appraised property's effective gross income?
6. Discuss the relative merits of the gross income multiplier as a means of estimating property value.

READING AND STUDY REFERENCES

CHRISTENSEN, BARBARA. "Take the Guesstimating Out of Adjustments," *The Appraisal Journal* 48, no. 2 (April 1980), pp. 255–60.

DASSO, JEROME J. "Multiple Regression Analysis and the Appraisal Process," *The Real Estate Appraiser* 39, no. 2 (March–April 1973), pp. 4–14.

DELACY, P. BARTON. "Cash Equivalency in Residential Appraising," *The Appraisal Journal* 51, no. 1 (January 1983), pp. 81–88.

FRIEDMAN, JACK P., and BRUCE LINDEMAN. "Cash Equivalent Analysis," *The Appraisal Journal* 47, no. 1 (January 1979), pp. 35–43.

GIPE, GEORGE W. "Developing a Multiple Regression Model for Multi-family Residential Properties," *The Real Estate Appraiser* 42, no. 3 (May–June 1976), pp. 28–33.

GOOLSBY, WILLIAM C., JAMES A. GRAASKAMP, and TIMOTHY N. WARNER. "Cash Equivalent Value of Real Property," *The Real Estate Appraiser and Analyst* 49, no. 3 (Fall Quarter 1983), pp. 43–48.

HARRISON, HENRY S. "The Residential Appraiser: Direct Sales Comparison Approach," Part I, *The Real Estate Appraiser and Analyst* 44, no. 5 (September–October 1978), pp. 61–62.

HARRISON, HENRY S. "Making Adjustments," Part II, *The Real Estate Appraiser and Analyst* 44, no. 6 (November–December 1978), pp. 72–79.

HAUSER, NATHANIEL W. "Simple Comparison Control," *The Appraisal Journal* 45, no. 2 (April 1977), pp. 210–222.

HOAGLAND, GARY. "Are the Mechanics of the Adjustment Process Correct?" *The Real Estate Appraiser and Analyst* 48, no. 1 (Spring 1982), pp. 59–61.

KAMATH, RAVINDA R., and KENNETH R. YANTEK. "Linear Multiple Regression Analysis Applied to Valuation of Single Family Homes," *The Real Estate Appraiser and Analyst* 45, no. 5 (September–October 1979), pp. 36–41.

RATCLIFF, RICHARD U. "Don't Underestimate the Gross Income Multiplier," *The Appraisal Journal* 39, no. 2 (April 1971), pp. 264–71.

SCHWARTZ, ARTHUR L., JR. "Influences of Seller Financing upon Residential Property Sales Prices," *The Real Estate Appraisal and Analyst* 48, no. 4 (Winter Quarter 1982), pp. 35–38.

SHENKEL, WILLIAM M. Chapter 15, "Valuation by Statistical Inference," *Modern Real Estate Appraisal.* New York: McGraw-Hill Book Company, 1978.

SIRMANS, G. STACY, C. F. SIRMANS, and STANLEY D. SMITH. "Adjusting Comparable Sales for Assumption Financing," *The Appraisal Journal* 52, no. 1 (January 1984), pp. 84–91.

SMITH, THEODORE R. "Multiple Regression and the Appraisal of Single Family Residential Properties," *The Appraisal Journal* 39, no. 2 (April 1971), pp. 277–85.

SMITH, HALBERT C., and JOHN B. CORGEL. "Adjusting for Nonmarketing Financing: A Quick and Easy Method," *The Appraisal Journal* 52, no. 1 (January 1984), pp. 75–83.

WILLIAMS, SCOTT R. "Problems with Percentage Adjustments," *The Real Estate Appraiser and Analyst* 48, no. 4 (Winter 1982), pp. 48–53.

11

BUILDING CONSTRUCTION AND PLAN READING

Learning Objectives

After reading this chapter, you should be able to:

Recognize the basic structural components of a residence and be able to distinguish the quality and condition of each

Distinguish among the different roof designs

Understand how roof pitch is calculated

Appreciate the basic design components found in construction plans

Sense the importance of written construction specifications

Discuss the basic attributes of good floor planning

A competent appraiser, to be professionally qualified, must possess a working knowledge of the arts of building design and building construction. As will be demonstrated, this knowledge is essential in the accurate application of each of the approaches to value as well as in deriving a reliable measure of accrued depreciation. Under the cost approach to value, knowledge of construction quantity and quality is essential in order that the applicable unit cost per square foot or per cubic foot can be computed to reproduce or replace the structure in new condition. Under the market approach to value, structural differences between the subject and the comparable properties must be recognized in order to make reasonable qualitative and quantitative value adjustments. Under the income approach, too, an estimate of remaining building life expectancy is sometimes necessary for correct capitalization of building income. Even an estimate of accrued depreciation cannot be made without an estimate of the effective structural age as reflected by a building's condition, its functional and locational obsolescence, and the structural resistance it offers to forces of wear, tear, and action of the elements.

BUILDING COMPONENTS

The anatomy of a building[1] may be studied in the order of its structural components as follows:

1. Footing, piers, and foundation walls.
2. Exterior walls.
3. Sub- and finish floor framing.
4. Partition framing and interior walls.
5. Roof framing and roof cover finish.
6. Windows and doors—kind, quality.
7. Cabinetwork.
8. Plumbing and electric wiring.
9. Heating and air-conditioning systems.
10. Insulation and other improvements.

Footings, piers, and foundation walls as a rule are constructed in accordance with local or national (FHA or VA) building codes. Footings generally consist of reinforced concrete that is poured on undisturbed soil below the frostline, as specified for the geographic area. The width of the footing must be at least twice that of the foundation wall to be supported, and equal to the thickness of the foundation wall in depth, and in no instance less than 6 inches. Foundation walls typically are of concrete blocks 8 by 8 by 16 inches in size. A recent innovation in foundation wall construction is the use of pressure-treated wood trusses. These trusses span each footing to form the floor system. Builders have begun to use this system because it saves time, money, and the problems involved in dealing with masonry subcontractors. Where needed for extra strength, reinforcing rods are placed at corner and wall supporting locations. Waterproofing is a requirement where subfloor or basement areas are subject to surface water penetration. The appraiser, unless informed of structural weaknesses, or unless he sees evidence of excessive settlement at the time of building inspection, assumes proper compliance with applicable construction codes in all foundation work. Where doubt exists, or conditions warrant it, a construction engineer should be called on to inspect the premises for building flaws and to render a certified report on which the appraiser may rely for value adjustments or repair expenditures.

[1]Since the bulk of building construction is residential rather than commercial or industrial in character, emphasis in this chapter for illustration purposes will be placed on the anatomy of a single family building structure.

Exterior walls are constructed in a variety of frame, metal, or masonry materials and generally in conformity with community customs and owners preferences. Again, unless evidence points otherwise, structural soundness must be assumed. The appraiser should chiefly be interested in cost differentials of the materials used, and in the comparative utility (or disutility) of exterior wall construction in relation to expenditures for building maintenance and repair. More expensive exterior wall material may be warranted from a value point of view (brick versus frame) where the additional construction cost—other things remaining equal—does not exceed the present worth of anticipated dollar savings in building management and upkeep. Amenities offered by attractiveness of exterior design or appearance must, of course, be considered as plus items in the value estimate.

Where exterior walls are of frame or of brick or stone veneer, the supporting wood framing consists of studs either 2 by 4 inches or 2 by 6 inches in size that rest on sills which are bolted to the foundation wall. In geographic areas where termite infestation is prevalent, soils enclosed by the foundation walls are poisoned by licensed pest exterminators and metal termite shields are placed on top of foundation walls and piers to safeguard against these wood-destroying subterranean pests.

In checking the kind and quality of *sub- and finish floor construction* the appraiser should make certain that the underlying and surrounding soil shows no evidence of poor surface drainage and moisture in the crawl space or on the underside of the subflooring and that no telltale signs point to the existence of, or possible damage from, subterranean pests or surface varmints. The subsurface building area should be checked for size, quality, and utility of basement area. Many residential buildings today are constructed without basements, and most throughout the South and Far West are built on concrete slab poured directly on the ground without crawl space or excavation of any kind. This type of construction, in milder climates where ground frost presents no danger, offers savings of $1,500 to $3,000 per residential structure depending on size of building area. Where the subfloor is suspended and of frame, a check should be made of the size of girders, size and spacing of floor joists, proper cross bridging of joists (at least every 8 feet apart) to assure floor stability, and creakproof construction. Subfloor plywood sheets generally are ½ to ¾-inch tongue-and-groove plywood. Each sheet should have its longest dimension run perpendicular to the floor joists. The kind and quality of finished flooring should be noted, and inspected for uniformity of placement and appearance. Wall-to-wall carpet should be mounted over ½-inch foam padding for even and longer wear. Where rugs are intended as partial floor covering, the finished wood surface should be of hard clear wood strips or parquet wood tiles nailed over 4 by 8 foot plywood sheets or other subflooring. Kitchen floors generally are covered with grease-resistant vinyl sheet. Bathroom floors, for long lasting use as well as appearance, are recommended to be finished with ceramic tile firmly cemented in place over concrete slab or plywood subflooring. Concrete flooring in basement, commercial or industrial areas, should be four inches in thickness and for reinforcement be poured over continuous wire mesh.

Construction details of *partition framing and of interior walls* should be considered. Particular checks should be made where exterior walls are of metal or masonry to discern whether the inside of these walls are fitted with furred strips of kiln-dried or moisture-treated wood to create airspace between the wall surface and the plaster or other interior wall finishes. This airspace is important wherever climatic conditions cause walls to sweat because of extreme differences in indoor-outdoor temperatures. Most brick walls today are brick veneer that is supported by a wood frame. The combination of the wood and vertical open spaces between bricks (weep holes) allows moisture buildup to be discharged. Where plaster is placed directly on the wall rather than on rock lath over furring strips, the appraiser should reflect this "economy" construction in his or her value estimate and possibly consider penalizing the property under functional obsolescence, especially in areas where lending companies reject such substand-ard construction for mortgage loan purposes. Interior finishes, too, should be noted for quality attributes. Where wood paneling is used, check for quality workmanship in the mitering of joints, and for type and grade of wood and excellence of finish. Height of walls from floor to ceiling are important, and where more or less than standard (8 feet) clearance, a plus or minus adjustment should be made to reflect the lack of, or increase in, resulting amenities to owner-occupants.

Type of *roof construction*, method of framing, and roof shingle or surface finishing should next be given due attention. Depending on the period of architecture, the principal roof types are as follows: flat (built-up), gable, hip, gambrel, mansard, or pyramid, as shown in Figure 11.1. Where roofs are sloped and roof shingles are conventionally nailed (and not cemented), it is important

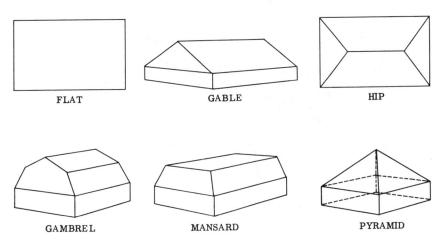

FLAT GABLE HIP

GAMBREL MANSARD PYRAMID

Figure 11.1 Roof Types

Figure 11.2 Roof Slope

that the rise in slope is not less than 3 inches for every 12 inches of roof slope distance, as shown in Figure 11.2

The higher the rise in slope, the costlier the roof construction—but the larger the attic area and the safer and more lasting the roof shingle coverage because of lessened wear and tear from rain, hail, snow, or tornadic winds. A rise in slope below 3 inches in 12 inches permits rain and wind to drive under the shingles, weakening the shingle fastenings and the undercover roof seal. Ceiling joists and roof rafters should be at least 2 inches by 6 inches in size for residential buildings, and placed not less than 16 inches on center (from the center of one joist or rafter to the center of the adjacent joist or rafter). The trend is toward use of 2 by 4 inch wooden trusses, 2 feet on center. The roof extension, or eaves, should be at least 12 inches beyond the exterior wall surface, and larger where protection is sought from sun and rain for windows and exterior finishes. A typical roof section shows details as in Figure 11.3.

Windows and doors should be inspected to ascertain the manufacturer, the kind of wood or metal sash, the quality of fitting, and the extent of trouble-free operation. Weakness of construction or poor lintel support over wall openings manifests itself in plaster and wall cracks at corners of windows and doors. Where cracks are due to structural settlement, inspection of floor beams and

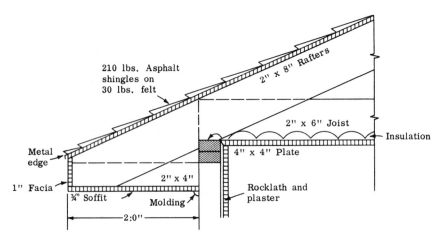

Figure 11.3 Roof Section View

piers should be made to determine the necessity for and cost of corrective repairs. Windows should be tested and checked for airtightness, and exterior doors should be fitted with full-length screens and weatherstripped saddles and frames. Windowsills and stools, where of special construction and finish, should be noted as quality attributes which must be reflected specifically in the cost approach to value.

Windows are either double-hung or casement type and of wood sash in northern and midwestern states, and of jalousie or awning type and of aluminum sash in subtropical climate states. Jalousie windows are largely used in closed-in porches and in industrial and commercial buildings. Better home construction practices confine window types to double-hung, casement or awning manufacture. Triplex-pane windows are seldom justified except in the northern parts of the country. Vinyl-clad wood is a superior type of window construction because the vinyl protects the exterior from deteriorating and the wood protects the interior from sweating. Ease of operation and weatherstripping are further marks of quality noticeable by careful inspection.

Sufficiency in number, size, and quality of *closets, built-ins, and cabinet work* in general should be evaluated and described for the benefit of the report reader. Quality construction is apparent when closets are cedar-lined, fitted with switch-controlled lights, and contain carpentry details such as shoeracks and special shelf-and-rod arrangements. Sliding, louvered, or mirrored closet doors, too, may warrant special value consideration. Built-in vanities, bookcases, mantles, china closets, and extra kitchen cabinets that increase functional utility and amenities of living must be itemized and considered for appraisal purposes.

Adequacy, convenience, and safety of *plumbing and electrical installations* are a *must* in a modern home. Each bathroom, unless back to back with another, should be separately vented with a PVC or polybutilane stack extending through the roof as well as have a window. Similar venting for the kitchen sink is a requirement. Water faucets should have individual valve shutoffs to permit emergency repairs or washer replacements. The piping should be checked as to kind of metal (galvanized or copper) and whether water flow is adequate or impeded by inadequate pipe size or faulty construction. It is important, too, to ascertain whether sewage disposal is by a public, community, or individual septic tank system. In the latter case, the number and size of septic tanks and condition of drain fields should be considered and reported. Increasing reliance on electrically operated household conveniences such as ranges, refrigerators, dishwashers, garbage disposals, and washing machines makes proper and adequate wiring for regular lighting and power use of utmost importance. Modern construction calls for a three-wire (220-volt) panel wiring, of 100-ampere or greater capacity, and fitted with circuit breakers rather than old-fashioned fuses. Wall receptacles, at least three to each room, should be conveniently located. Switches, whether conventional or mercury (silent) type, should be noted. All plumbing and wiring should be concealed, including wiring for telephone outlets to various rooms and television antenna connections.

Most often underestimated is the kind and quality of an adequate *heating and air-conditioning system*. In many southern and far-western homes heat is supplied simply by a single gas, electric, or oil-fired space heater. Such a method of heating—no matter how warm the climate during most of the year—is inadequate and often unhealthy because of faulty venting or inadequate air circulation. The cost of central heating, with adequate duct and register controls, may vary from $2,000 to $6,000, depending on quality of furnace and intricacy of pipe or ductwork installation. This wide cost range is reason enough for an appraiser to confirm the kind and quality of heating, and to reflect the appropriate value attributes in his appraisal estimate. Air conditioning in most parts of our country is still in a luxury classification, and care must be taken to study the demand for homes so equipped in order to reflect market value rather than necessary cost of construction expenditures.

Last but not least, accessory building details should be inventoried. Included in this category are ceiling and wall insulation. The appraiser should note the type and form of insulation installed. It may be mineral wool, fiberglass, or cellulosic fiber and be installed loosely (hand poured or machine blown) or in the form of blankets or batts that fit between the floor joists, wall studs, or ceiling joists. Other choices are foam or rigid board insulation. The latter is usually used on basement walls. The symbol used to measure the insulating quality of the material is "R value." The higher the R value, the better the insulation. Different R values are expected for ceilings and walls and in different temperature zones of the country. For example, in temperate zones the following R values may be expected for fiberglass insulation: walls (R-11, 3½-inch thickness); ceiling (R-19, 6- to 6½-inch to R-30, 9 to 10-inch thickness). Also to be considered is the finished attic space, outdoor flood-lighting, patios, landscaping, driveways, walks, porches, garages, stoves, refrigerators, laundry equipment, disposals, fireplaces, incinerators, elevators, storm sash, fences, wells, water tanks, water softeners, water pumps, sprinkler systems, and other related improvements.

PLAN READING FOR PROPOSED CONSTRUCTION

It is said that the best time to appraise a property is before it is built. Ideally this would give the best protection to builders, investors, and home buyers. In practice, however, this precaution is not generally taken. It is often assumed by the public at large that cost and value are synonymous. Not until a resale takes place do errors come to light as to under-, over-, or faulty improvements and resultant value losses. Fortunately, as a protection to mortgage lenders, the practice of appraising proposed buildings prior to construction is mandatory— at least where governmental agencies or private institutional lenders are involved.

Every appraiser must be capable of analyzing building plans and specifications, and must know how to estimate from architectural specifications the cost of constructing proposed improvements. Whether costs are warranted will depend on the kind and character of the described improvements in the light of prevailing demand and market conditions, as was discussed in preceding chapters and as will be further outlined in chapters concerned with the cost, market, and income approaches to value.

Typical construction drawings, as a rule, contain the following:

1. Foundation plan.
2. Floor plan.
3. Elevations (i.e., front, rear, and side views).
4. Sectional views.
5. Mechanical, heating, and electrical plan layouts.

The *foundation plan* is generally drawn to a scale of ¼ inch to 1 foot and provides the essential details concerning size of footings, size and dimensions of piers, and construction measurements and details of the subfloor area. Where the building foundation is of concrete slab, the plan will show thickness of slab, kind and size of steel wire reinforcement, and areas where foundations are to be thickened for placement of load-bearing interior walls. Location of concrete expansion joints and foundation areas to be termite-shielded are also marked for ease of reference and worker's guide. Where basement area or subfloor crawlspace is called for, the foundation plan will note the exact location and size of girders and beams as well as the kind and quality of floor joists—generally 2 by 8 or 2 by 10 inches in size and placed, as a rule, 12 or 16 inches on center, depending on the type of superstructure and the permissible building codes. A recent innovation in construction techniques is the use of plywood floor joists. They are straighter and easier to handle than conventional wood joists. Fewer joists are needed since they can be spaced on 2-foot centers.

The *floor plan* (see Figure 11.4) is an important guide to accurate building layout. From this plan, measurements are taken for the calculation of square foot or cubic foot space volume that serve as a basis for construction-cost estimating. The floor plan, as shown, indicates wall-to-wall dimensions, room sizes and exposures, and placement of windows, doors, partitions, fireplace, chimney, fixtures, cabinets, patio, breezeway, and attached garage. The floor plan is normally drawn to an exact scale of one-quarter inch to one foot and includes, where separate mechanical drawings are not called for, construction details concerning placement of lighting outlets, telephone jacks, plumbing, and heating fixtures.

Elevations show the exterior sides of a building as it appears after all structural work has been completed. As a rule, each building side is viewed by an elevation and, for identification, marked as north, south, east, and west or by structural designation as front, rear, left, and right side elevation. Symbols on elevation drawings indicate the kind of exterior materials, their placement, and the height of their construction. The type and slope of roof is noted, as well

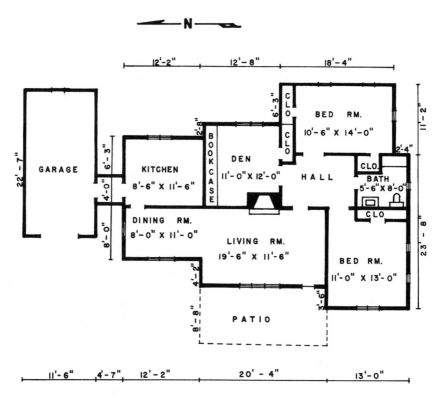

Figure 11.4   Floor Plan for Residential Structure

as the kind and placement of roof shingles. Type and placement of windows are detailed, as are other openings such as doors, dormers, vents, and skylights. Typical elevations, from which an overall view of the finished building can be obtained at a glance, are shown in Figure 11.5

To provide a detailed guide to specific construction practices, sectional views of exterior and interior walls are made a part of every set of building plans. Sectional views permit detailed considerations of specific construction methods, from footings and subflooring to ceiling, attic, and roof construction. Special elevation drawings, too, are provided for built-in items such as bookcases, china closets, and kitchen cabinets.

THE IMPORTANCE OF WRITTEN SPECIFICATIONS

No matter how completely plans, elevations, and related drawings and sketches are prepared, they still would fail to convey an accurate picture of the structural elements to be incorporated in a building without the important and supple-

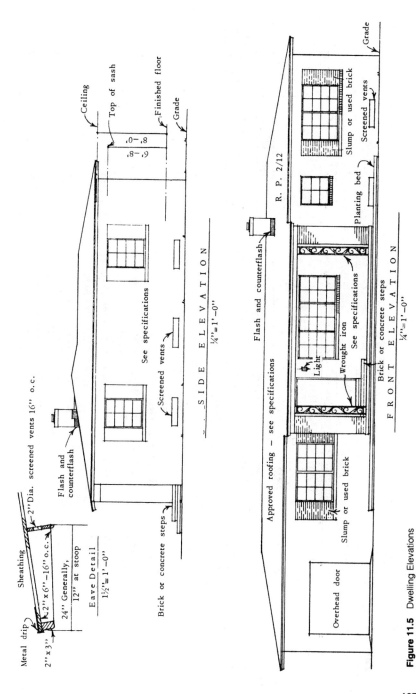

Figure 11.5 Dwelling Elevations

197

PLUMBING:

FIXTURE	NUMBER	LOCATION	MAKE	MFR'S FIXTURE IDENTIFICATION NO.	SIZE	COLOR
Sink	1	kitchen	stainless steel	double bowl	32 x 21	ss
Lavatory	1	1st fl lav	ELJER	E1634	19 x 17	white
Water closet	3	baths	"	E5250	–	"
Bathtub	1	hall bath	"		60"	
Shower over tub	1	"			–	
Stall shower	1	mast. br			48"	
Laundry trays						
Lavatory	1	hall bath	ELJER			
"	1	mast. br	"			

△ ☐ Curtain rod   △ ☐ door   ☐ Shower pan: material _____

Water supply: ☐ public; ☐ community system; ☐ individual (private) system. ★

Sewage disposal: ☐ public; ☐ community system; ☐ individual (private) system. ★

★ Show and describe individual system in complete detail in separate drawings and specifications according to requirements.

House drain (inside): ☐ cast iron; ☐ tile; ☐ other ___ ABS/DWV ___ House sewer (outside): ☐ cast iron; ☐ tile; ☐ other _____

Water piping: ☐ galvanized steel; ☐ copper tubing; ☐ other _____ Sill cocks, number _2_

Domestic water heater type ___ elect. hi-recovery ___ make and model ___ glass lined ___ ; heating capacity _____

___ 36 ___ gph. 100° rise. Storage tank: material ___ glass lined ___ ; capacity _50_ gallons.

Gas service: ☐ utility company; ☐ liq. pet. gas; ☐ other _____ Gas piping: ☐ cooking; ☐ house heating.

Footing drains connected to: ☐ storm sewer; ☐ sanitary sewer; ☐ dry well. Sump pump; make and model _____

___ ; discharges into _____

DESCRIPTION OF MATERIALS
HUD-92005 (6-79)
VA Form 26-1852, Form FmHA 424-2

Figure 11.6 Plumbing Specifications

mentary aid of written specifications (sometimes called "specifications of materials"). In fact, written instructions are deemed of greater importance than graphic illustrations, and where these two are in conflict it is the written word that is guiding and legally binding.

The reason for the importance of written specifications can be readily illustrated. Plans may indicate construction and placement of materials. In the specifications, however, structural quality and quantity is specifically spelled out. Thus the specifications may call for a concrete mix of one part cement, two parts sand, three parts stone, and a minimum supporting strength of 2,400 pounds per square inch at a time interval of 48 hours after pouring. Or the plans may show 2-by-6-inch floor joists placed 24 inches on center. The specifications will indicate the kind of timber—whether pine, oak, or other—and the grade of timber as rated in accordance with quality and manufacturer's tensile strength. Specifications, too, may stipulate whether timber is to be treated, processed for protection against termites, or kiln dried to minimize shrinkage.

Specifications historically have served as a contract document between builder and owner, and are intended to avoid disputes or misunderstandings concerning details of construction. Other and equally important purposes are to permit accurate estimating of required labor, quality of materials, and costing of contractors' and subcontractors' services in accordance with plan requirements. Specifications also safeguard against expensive omissions when construction costs are estimated and minimize construction delays due to misunderstanding of building plans. Written specifications generally are prepared in one of two forms:

1. The narrative or report form.
2. The standard specification form.

For multiple-story residential and for commercial and industrial buildings the narrative or report form is generally used. For a skyscraper, for instance, the specifications contain sufficient pages to comprise a book. An excerpt from a standard specification form for a single family dwelling is shown in Figure 11.6.

COMPUTING BUILDING MEASUREMENTS

Depending on local custom and building practices, construction areas are quoted in terms of square-feet or cubic-feet measurements. The latter method of sizing a building is more accurate, since weight is given to height of structure from 6 inches below the finished surface of the lowest floor to and including the roof and attic area. Where given structures, such as residences, are of uniform height, however, the use and application of the square-foot method of costing a building is justified and does yield accurate results, as will be demonstrated in Chapter

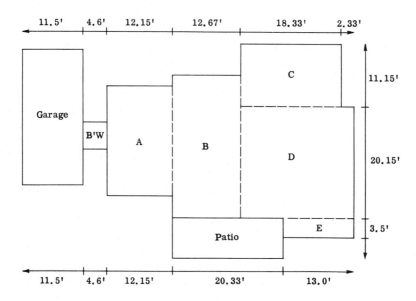

Figure 11.7

12. All building measurements are based on exterior rather than interior wall dimensions. This practice gives consideration to thicknesses of walls which importantly contribute to the cost of building construction.

In illustrating the procedure of "squaring" a building, reference is made to the floor plan shown in Figure 11.7. For computation purposes the floor area is divided into rectangular units.

Where cubic-feet measurements are required, an additional multiplication for each rectangular unit must be made in accordance with the building height taken from 6 inches below the finished basement floor to the outside measurement of a flat roof. Other roof plans must be computed to reflect accurate cubic-foot volume of gable or other types of roof areas. For detailed illustrations and instructions on building measurements, reference can be made to the various cost services, which are identified in Chapter 12.

BASIC ATTRIBUTES OF GOOD FLOOR PLANNING

It is the appraiser's responsibility to develop and use sound judgment in classifying attributes of good or poor floor planning, and to evaluate the effects on the marketability of the property of excellence in layout and design or lack of functional utility. Where the principle of balance in interior space allocation is violated the market will reflect the degree of functional obsolescence in sales resistance that is measurable in dollars, either directly by market comparison or by the extent to which such obsolescence is curable or incurable in estimating this cause of loss in value.

Attributes of good floor planning which increase the amenities of living in residential structures and which make for more efficient use of space include, among others, the following:

1. Orientation of rooms to capture prevailing breezes, sunshine, and beauty of area views surrounding the property.
2. Proper placing of picture window and large window areas to assure adequate light and fenestration for all rooms.
3. Provision for entrance hall or foyer (with guest-closet space) to shield living room from direct view and drafts.
4. Grouping of bed and bathroom areas to assure maximum of privacy. A separate entrance to the bedroom wing or access without a view from or crossing of living room area is considered a must.
5. Proper functional layout of kitchen area to conserve steps in housekeeping.
6. Location of kitchen near entrance and side doors to minimize traffic flow.
7. Adequate bedroom, linen, and storage closets and necessary utility space.
8. Proper wiring and location of household utility equipment and economical but adequate provision for central heating.
9. Accessibility to attic space area via conveniently located hatch or concealed stairway.
10. Minimum room sizes at least equal in square feet area and dimensions as provided by minimum property standards for residential units adopted by local or statewide building codes.

Earlier minimum property standards prescribed by the Federal Housing Administration provided guidelines for room sizes and other architectural features of dwellings. Over the last several years FHA (U.S. Department of Housing and Urban Development) has moved away from establishing such standards and has allowed local requirements and nationally recognized standards to achieve these goals. Examples of current standards follow.

A single-family dwelling shall have at least one room with a minimum of 150 square feet of floor area; other habitable rooms except the kitchen must have at least 70 square feet; the minimum dimension for all rooms except kitchen is 7 feet; bathrooms must be lighted and ventilated by outside windows of not less than 3 square feet[2] (unless mechanically vented); ceiling height, except kitchen, shall have an average height of at least 7 feet 6 inches for at least 50 percent of the required area, no portion shall be less than 5 feet.[3]

[2]*The BOCA Basic Building Code/1981*, 8th ed. (Homewood, Ill.: Building Officials and Code Administrators International, Inc., 1980), pp. 142–43.

[3]*One & Two Family Dwelling Code*, 3rd ed. (Homewood, Ill.: Building Officials and Code Administrators International, Inc. Whittier, Calif.: International Conference of Building Officials, Birmingham, Ala.: Southern Building Code Congress International, 1979), p. 13.

The functional utility of commercial, industrial, or farm buildings can in like manner be tested by the principle of balance. In appraising large and multistory structures—especially if old or intricate in design—professional aid from contractors, builders, architects, or construction engineers may have to be obtained to report in detail on matters such as structural condition, deferred maintenance and repair, adequacy, safety and speed of elevators, and functional conditions which affect the cost of servicing the building. In some court jurisdictions (the New York Supreme Court, for example) appraisers are not qualified to testify as experts on matters concerning construction or costs thereof, unless they are also licensed as building contractors, architects or building engineers. Other matters of structural design affecting revenue, maintenance, management and, possibly, the remaining economic building life include the following:

1. Adequacy of foyer, halls, and public areas to accommodate traffic flow of tenants, employees, and business clientele.
2. Proper washroom facilities assigned where possible for private use to minimize general janitorial services.
3. Modular construction that permits space repartitioning to suit tenant needs.
4. Good lighting and adequate, concealed telephone and electric wiring to serve anticipated maximum service loads.
5. Sufficiency of central heating under individual unit or zone control.
6. Capacity and readiness to supply air conditioning where competitively necessary.
7. High ratio of net rentable area as percentage of total building square foot area.
8. Necessary off-street parking.

In the appraisal of old structures, special care must be taken to recognize functional disutility. For example, structures built of thick masonry walls, which were designed under the old post-and-lintel system to support by sheer dead weight the stresses and strains of tall, multistory buildings, may offer as much as 10 percent less net rentable space than modern structures where exterior walls are built of steel or of steel-reinforced masonry.[4] In such instances, the capitalized income loss due to outmoded type of construction will reflect the amount of accrued depreciation caused by this type of functional disutility.

IMPORTANCE OF CONSTRUCTION KNOWLEDGE

Since improvements on and to land comprise the major portion of total property value, it is important that the appraiser become thoroughly familiar with the essential details of building construction and building-plan reading. In this chapter, an attempt was made to stress the importance of construction principles and practices knowledge in order that the appraiser may effectively differentiate and

---

[4]Construction under the modern *birdcage* building method, where outer walls are mere protection sheaths, may offer further space advantages or construction-cost economies.

evaluate the vast variety of building improvements. Many books have been written on construction subjects, and many colleges and universities throughout the country offer courses in this important field of study. A qualified appraiser who seeks to serve his profession well should familiarize himself with the types of architecture and construction practices which typically prevail in the state or region in which he serves his clients. Reading and course work is important to lay a foundation for appraisal knowledge; but nothing can take the place of field experience gained from the inspection of buildings at various stages of construction. Every appraisal presents a challenge to inventory correctly the details of construction, and to evaluate accurately the utility of building improvements. Effective application of the construction guides discussed above should contribute importantly to accurate consideration of building improvements under the cost, market, and income approaches to value, as will be demonstrated in succeeding chapters.

REVIEW QUESTIONS

1. How can the rise (or pitch) of a roof affect the life of the shingles?
2. What aspect of a building does the "R value" measure?
3. What feature of a building do the elevations show?
4. List six attributes of good floor planning.
5. Of what importance are specifications of materials?
6. List five matters of structural design that affect revenue, maintenance, management, and possibly, the remaining economic life of a building.

READING AND STUDY REFERENCES

ADDLESON, LYALL. *Building Failures: A Guide to Diagnosis, Remedy and Prevention*. London: Architectural Press, 1982.

AMERICAN INSTITUTE OF REAL ESTATE APPRAISERS. Chapters 9 and 10, *The Appraisal of Real Estate*, 8th ed. Chicago: AIREA, 1983.

BLOOM, GEORGE F., and HENRY S. HARRISON. Chapter 10, "Improvement Description and Analysis," *Appraising the Single Family Residence*. Chicago: American Institute of Real Estate Appraisers, 1978.

BOYCE, BYRL N., and WILLIAM N. KINNARD, JR. "Improvements Analysis (Building Analysis)," *Appraising Real Property*. Lexington, Mass: Lexington Books, 1984, pp. 144–59.

DALZELL, J. RALPH. *Plan Reading for Home Builders*, 2nd ed. New York: McGraw-Hill Book Company, 1972.

FOUTE, STEVEN J. "Appraising and Underwriting the Energy Efficient Home: The Energy Mortgage Value Method," *The Real Estate Appraiser and Analyst* 48, no. 1 (Spring 1982), pp. 5–9.

HARRISON, HENRY S. *Houses: The Illustrated Guide to Construction, Design and Systems*. Chicago: National Institute of Real Estate Brokers, 1973.

ISAKSON, HANS R. "Residential Energy Audits: A New Source of Appraisal Data," *The Appraisal Journal* 49, no. 1 (January 1981), pp. 74–84.

MULLER, EDWARD J. *Reading Architectural Working Drawings*. Englewood Cliffs, N.J.: Prentice-Hall, Inc., 1981.

OLIN, HAROLD B., JOHN L. SCHMIDT, and WALTER H. LEWIS. *Construction—Principles, Materials and Methods*, 4th ed. Chicago: Institute of Financial Education, 1980.

WHITE, EDWARD L. "Appraising from Plans and Specifications," *The Real Estate Appraiser* 32, no. 6 (June 1966), pp. 13–26.

12

THE DEPRECIATED COST APPROACH: COST ESTIMATING

⌐

Learning Objectives

After reading this chapter, you should be able to:

Appreciate when and when not to use the depreciated cost approach

Understand the basic steps involved in the depreciated cost approach

Discuss the relationship and differences between cost and value

Explain and give examples of direct and indirect building costs

Contrast reproduction and replacement costs

Explain the different ways that current construction costs can be computed

STEPS IN THE COST APPROACH

The cost approach is a hybrid approach in that it uses the sales comparison approach in combination with the depreciated cost method. The steps involved in this approach are outlined below.

1. Estimate the highest and best use of the site. This initial step provides a basis for selecting comparable site sales as well as later establishing a "yardstick" against which accrued depreciation of the improvements is measured.

2. Find the present cost of reproducing or replacing the building(s). In order to accurately estimate this amount, the appraiser must understand building design and materials as well as be acquainted with cost estimating to a reasonable degree. Techniques for estimating construction costs are covered later in this chapter.

3. Estimate the total dollar amount of accrued depreciation from all causes. This depreciation is broken down into three categories: physical deterioration, functional obsolescence, and external obsolescence.
4. Subtract the dollar amount of accrued depreciation from the present reproduction or replacement cost. This difference, if computed accurately, approximates the present value of the building(s).
5. Estimate the depreciated cost of any minor buildings and other on-site improvements, such as landscaping, fencing, and driveways. The key to this step is estimating the value that these improvements add to the overall value of the property rather than their cost.
6. Add the site value to the depreciated cost of the building(s) and other on-site improvements (steps 4 and 5). The resultant figure is the estimated value of the property via the depreciated cost approach.

PROS AND CONS OF THE DEPRECIATED COST APPROACH

Every method conceived to either measure or predict the value of real estate has its proponents and opponents. The depreciated cost approach certainly has not been spared this divided support. As forthrightly as possible, this section will lay out the alleged advantages and disadvantages of this method. The reader should attempt to recognize that this, and the other approaches to finding value, has its relative strengths and weaknesses and each approach should be used to its best advantage.

Advantages.   The advantages of this approach are as follows:

1. By inspecting a property and subsequently accounting for its cost new and value lost due to accrued depreciation, the appraiser enhances his or her ability to estimate the property's value via the sales comparison and capitalized income approaches.
2. It can be used to estimate the financial feasibility of a proposed property. That is, if the value indicated by the sales and income approaches equals or exceeds the current replacement cost, the property is feasible. The reverse situation implies infeasibility.
3. The same arguments advanced for a separate site value apply to use of this approach, which can provide a separate estimate of building value.
4. It can be used to provide an indication of value for special-purpose properties, newer properties, or in those instances when there is a dearth of similar market transfers or rental data.
5. Sometimes there are insufficient market data for the sales comparison approach to reveal the value differential for such items as differences in building size, heating–air conditioning systems, or roof covering.

Disadvantages.   The major disadvantages of this method are:

1. It requires great diligence in maintaining current data as well as in carefully recognizing differences in cost due to different sizes and quality of materials.

Also, a careful identification and accounting for the various elements of accrued depreciation is required.

2. It fails to provide a truly independent estimate of market value. The site value, comprising perhaps 10 to 40 percent of a property's value, is estimated by use of comparable sales. Deductions for accrued depreciation generally are based on market evidence. Thus a great deal of the reported value is generated by the analysis of sales of comparable sites and improved properties.

3. It is not well suited for old buildings. Appraisers often deplore using comparable sales which require net adjustments in excess of 15 to 20 percent. Yet the "adjustment" or deduction for accrued depreciation for an old building can easily reach 75 percent.

4. It can be an overly complicated approach that is suspect especially when the various deductions for supposed accrued depreciation are backed up by nothing more than such unconvincing statements as "the appraiser's experience" or "unfavorable consumer reaction to a particular building or neighborhood feature." Such practices can only harm the appraisal field.

COST VERSUS VALUE

As discussed in Chapter 2, there has been an ongoing debate over the legitimacy of the depreciated cost approach, which often is called the "cost approach." Earlier reasoning held that the true measure of the worth of an item was the cost of creating it. This notion is not necessarily true. Cost is the amount of money necessary to acquire or to create an item, while value represents its worth. Carrying this reasoning a step further, suppose that a property cost $100,000 to build, but is only worth $80,000; the difference represents the value loss or accrued depreciation. There is merit to claiming that a prudent person would not pay more for a used property than the cost necessary to build the same structure without an unacceptable delay. However, there is absolutely no reason for the estimated depreciated cost of a property to set its upper limit of value. Value may be equal to or more or less than fabrication or acquisition cost.

DIRECT AND INDIRECT COSTS

In estimating the present construction cost, it is important that all associated costs be included. As a matter of convenience, total current construction cost (reproduction or replacement) may be identified as *direct* and *indirect* costs. *Direct costs* are labor and materials, which include:

1. Labor hired by the general contractors and subcontractors.
2. Materials used beginning with site clearance to the final cleanup.
3. Equipment, leased or owned.
4. Temporary electric service.
5. Builder's overhead and profit.

Indirect costs, equally important as direct costs, may not be as apparent to persons unfamiliar with building construction. These costs are supporting costs, such as:

1. Professional service fees, including legal, appraisal, financial feasibility, engineeering, architectural, and surveying.
2. Construction and possibly permanent loan charges.
3. Property management commissions.
4. Project management fees.
5. Land lease rent, if appropriate.
6. Real estate taxes.
7. Project promotion charges.
8. Any other interim carrying costs.

In a normal market, when building supply and demand are in equilibrium, replacement cost in current dollars will set the ceiling of value—provided that the structure is new and conforms in design, size, and mode of construction with the principle of highest and best land use. As a first step in the field-data program it is essential that the appraiser make a detailed inventory of the existing or proposed land and building improvements in order that an accurate estimate can be made of the cost to *replace* the form utility of the structure under up-to-date but generally typical methods of building construction.

Replacement cost is defined as the current cost of building the appraised structure with one providing similar functional utility. Further, it implies that modern materials, methods, and technology are used and as a result all vistages of functional obsolescence are excluded. This cost is less than the amount indicated by the reproduction cost method. It implies that the cost is based on a modern building that affords utility equivalent to that provided by the appraised building.

Reproduction cost is the cost of building the appraised structure in a manner that replicates the materials, design, layout, and quality of workmanship. In short, this cost involves rebuilding the subject structure with any inherent faulty design superadequacies and inefficiencies. It is an unrealistic method for older obsolete structures because virtually no one would waste money erecting such inefficient and expensive buildings. Reproduction costs of a replica building—using current labor and similar materials—rather than replacement costs generally are considered more accurate as an approach to value, but this may not necessarily be true since the appraiser will have to account for any functional obsolescence that has occurred. No doubt the purpose of the appraisal and the nature of the value problem will guide the appraiser in selecting the costing method which, at the proper time and place, will yield the most reliable results. The appraiser must be aware of which of these costs are implied in cost manuals or from any other source. Also, since the current value of a property ordinarily is sought, the appraiser is concerned with the present cost of building the structure, not with some earlier building cost.

The art of cost estimating is taught in vocational schools and in colleges of architecture and building construction. The cost estimator as a technician is generally not concerned with value. It is the appraiser's task to convert cost into value by considering the effect of market conditions and identifying causes of depreciation, as explained in Chapter 13. Cost estimating methods presently in use by architects, builders, and appraisers are classified as follows:

1. Builders' detail inventory method.
2. Subcontractors' or quantity survey method.
3. Unit-in-place construction method.
4. The comparative market method.
5. Cost indexing method.

BUILDERS' DETAIL INVENTORY METHOD

This method is generally used by experienced cost specialists when estimating project expenditures on large-scale construction proposals which are to be completed in accordance with detailed building plans and specifications. Under this method, a detailed cost estimate is made for each major labor and material construction item in the order of specification requirements. Every unit of labor essential in the building process from ground breaking to final decorating and cleaning up is itemized and costed. To this is added the detailed cost of the various quantities of building materials and equipment items. To the summation of the labor and material costs is then added a percentage rate to cover prevailing architect fees and builders' field and general overhead costs and profit. To demonstrate the application of the builders' detail inventory method, a cost breakdown for a 1,000-square-foot block residence is demonstrated in Table 12.1.

The builders' detail inventory method of cost estimating as illustrated yields, when applied with care, accurate results. The application of this method, however, is time consuming and costly. The typical appraiser, in fact, is not technically trained or qualified to undertake such minute and detailed cost studies. For this reason recourse is made to quicker and more suitable methods of applying the cost approach to value.

QUANTITY SURVEY METHOD

This method of cost estimating is simpler in application and less time consuming than the method discussed previously; it is preferred by architects in the costing of residential structures. Under this method, bids for major construction work are obtained by the general contractor from subcontractors and summarized to derive the composite cost estimate. Since each subcontractor is a specialist in a limited field of operation, the resultant economy generally offsets the overlap-

Table 12.1 Construction Cost Estimate Based on Builder's Detail Inventory Method for a Single-Family Residence

Building Description: Two-bedroom, living room, kitchen and bath, concrete-block (painted) residential structure. Interior walls of frame and plaster. Asphalt-shingled roof with 4-inch in 12-inch pitch over 2-inch rock-wool ceiling insulation. Concrete subflooring and terrazzo finished flooring. Aluminum double-hung windows. Equipped with 40-gallon automatic electric water heater, built-in electric stove and oven, and 85,000-btu oil-fired, forced-air central heating system. Construction methods and specifications to meet FHA minimum property standards for one and two living units; contains 1,000 square feet of living area.

COST BREAKDOWN

Specification No.	Type of Construction	Material	Labor	Total
	Water tap			$ 120.00
	Building permit			90.00
	Electric service			105.00
	Site clearing			180.00
	Architect fee			300.00
1	Excavation			
	Layout and batter boards	$ 49.50	$ 33.00	82.50
	Excavation—130 × 1⅓ = 173⅓ ÷ 27 = 6.41 c.y.			
	Labor—6.41 c.y. × $11.25		72.11	72.11
	Backfill—approx. 1 c.y.		5.25	5.25
	Dirt fill—1,000 s.f. × ⅔′ = 667 c.f. ÷ 27 = 24.7 c.y.			
	24.7 c.y. × $5.25	129.68		129.68
	Puddling and tamping—1,000 × $0.24		240.00	240.00
2	Foundation			
	⅝″ rods—364 l.f. × $0.36	131.04		
	Labor—364 × $0.12		43.68	174.72
	Footings—130 l.f. × ⅔′ × 1⅓ = 115.5 c.f. ÷ 27 = 4.3 c.y. × $60.00	258.00		
	Labor—4.3 × $7.50		32.25	290.25
	1 course dapped-out block			
	M. 98 × $0.33	32.30		
	L. 98 × $0.60		58.80	91.10
3	Chimney-masonry			
	Brick	180.00	120.00	300.00
	Flashing	15.00	30.00	45.00
4	Exterior walls			
	Concrete blocks 8 × 8 × 16)—130 × 0.75 = 98 × 12 (tiers) = 1176 × 0.84	987.84		
	Labor—1176 × $0.60		705.60	1,693.44
	Gable ends (8 × 8 × 16)—200 (blocks) × $0.84 × 2	336.00		
	Labor—200 × $0.57 × 2		228.00	564.00
	Steel rods—364 l.f. × $0.36	131.04		
	Labor—364′ × $0.09		32.76	163.80

Table 12.1 Continued

	COST BREAKDOWN			
Specification No.	*Type of Construction*	*Material*	*Labor*	*Total*
	8 × 8 concrete lintel—⅔ × 130 = 57.77 c.f. ÷ 27 = 2.13 c.y. × $63.00	134.19		
	Labor 2.13 c.y. × $7.41		15.78	149.97
	Mortar mix and sand ($0.15 per block)— 1,274 × $0.15	191.10		
	Labor on setting forms and removing—6 hr at $14.85		89.10	280.20
5	Floor construction			
	Membrane (2 15-lb felt, hot mopped)—1,000 × $0.18	180.00		
	Labor—1,000 × $0.75		75.00	255.00
	Wire mesh—1,100 s.f. × $0.14	148.50		
	Labor—1,100 × $0.019		20.46	168.96
	Expansion joint (1″ × 4″)—156 l.f. × $0.29	44.93		
	Labor—156 × $0.06		9.36	54.29
	Concrete slab 4″—1,000 s.f. × ⅓′ = 334 c.f. ÷ 27 = 12.4 c.y. × $60.00	744.00		
	Labor—12.4 × $6.00		74.40	818.40
	Bolts (½″ × 6″)—31 × $0.45	13.95		
	Labor—31 × $0.24		7.44	21.39
	Finishing—$60 l.f. × $0.15	9.00	150.00	159.00
6	Partitions			
	Sole plate (2 × 4 treated)—94 × ⅔ × 2 = 126 l.f. × $0.54	68.04		
	Labor—126 × $0.30		37.80	105.84
	Studs (2 × 4)—94 × 0.75 = 70.5 or 71 + 8 (waste) 79 × 8′ = 632 l.f. × ⅔ = 423 b.f. × $0.39	164.97		
	Labor—423 × $0.22		93.06	258.03
7	Ceiling framing			
	Top plate (2 × 6)—130 s.f. × $0.54	70.20		
	Labor 130 s.f. $0.23		30.00	100.20
	Joists, ceiling (2 × 6)—33 × 0.75 = 24.75 + 4 = 29 × (28 + 2) 30 = 870 s.f. × $0.39	339.30		
	Labor—870 × $0.30		261.00	600.30
	Bridging (1 × 3)—33 × $1.34 = 44.22 l.f. × 2 = 88.44 × 2 = 177 l.f. × $0.12	21.24		
	Labor—177 × $0.18		31.86	53.10
	Rough and finish not otherwise included	330.00		330.00
8	Roof framing			
	Bolts (½″ × 6″)—130 ÷ 4.32 × $0.48	14.40		
	Labor—32 × $0.18		5.76	20.16

Table 12.1   Continued

COST BREAKDOWN

Specification No.	Type of Construction	Material	Labor	Total
	Top plate (2 × 4)—94 × 2 × ⅔ = 126 b.f. × $0.39	49.14		
	Labor—126 × $0.30		37.80	86.94
	Facia (1 × 6)—80 l.f. × ½ = 40 × 2 = 80 × $0.57	45.60		
	Labor—80 × $0.39		31.20	76.80
	Boxed cornice—84 × 1.5 = 126 b.f. × $0.42	52.92		
	Labor—126 × $0.30		37.80	90.72
9	Roofing			
	Rafter (2 × 6)—1,040 b.f. × $0.39	405.60		
	Labor—1,040 × $0.30		312.00	717.60
	Purlins (2 × 4)—35′ × 2 = 70 × ⅔′ = 47 b.f. × $0.42	19.74		
	Labor—47 × $0.36		16.92	36.66
	Bracing (2 × 4's)—4′ o.c. 35 ÷ 4 = 8.6 × 2 = 17.2 × 6 = 103 b.f. × $0.39	40.17		
	Labor—103 × $0.36		37.08	77.25
	Roof decking (1 × 6 or 1 × 8)—35′ × 37 = 1,295 b.f. + (waste) 333 = 1,628 × $0.39	634.92		
	Labor—1,628 × $0.30		488.40	1,123.32
	Roofing (15-lb felt, 2 layers T.T.)—1,628 × $0.06	97.68		
	Labor—1,628 × $0.045		73.26	170.94
	210-lb roofing—13.33 squares × $27.75	369.91		
	Labor—13.33 squares × $17.25		229.94	599.85
	Eave drip (36.4 × 2)—73 × 10% = 7 + 73 = 80 l.f. × $0.23	18.00		
	Labor—80 × $0.075		6.00	24.00
10	Gutters and downspouts (none)			
11	Windows			
	Windows—11 × $99.00	1,089.00		
	Labor—11 × $18.00		198.00	1,287.00
12	Entrance and exterior detail			
	Doors, outside (1 jalousie, 1 comb.)—2 × $130.50	261.00		
	Labor—2 × $30.00		60.00	321.00
	Doors, screen—2 × $36.00	72.00		
	Labor—2 × $15.00		30.00	102.00
	Louvres—2 × $28.50	57.00		
	Labor—2 × $6.00		12.00	69.00
13	Insulation: 2″ rock wool	150.00	90.00	240.00

Table 12.1 Continued

COST BREAKDOWN

Specification No.	Type of Construction	Material	Labor	Total
14	Stairs (none)			
15	Lath and plaster			
	Furring strips (1 × 2 treated 130 × 8)—			
	1,040 l.f. × $0.21	218.40		
	Labor—1,040 × $0.09		93.60	312.00
	Plastering (lath and plaster)—material: 386			
	s.y. × $3.60	1,389.60		
	Labor—386 s.y. × $2.25		868.50	2,258.10
16	Finish flooring: Terrazzo	1,050.00	1,350.00	2,400.00
17	Tile and resilient floor (none)			
18	Interior door and trim			
	Exterior walls			
	Baseboard—130 l.f. × $0.39	50.70		
	Labor—130 × $0.24		31.20	81.90
	Molding—130 l.f. × $0.15	19.50		
	Labor—130 l.f. × $0.09		11.70	31.20
	Interior partitions			
	Baseboard—92 l.f. × 2 = 184 + 18			
	(waste) = 202 × $0.39	78.78		
	Labor—202 × $0.15		45.45	124.23
	Shoe mold—202 × $0.15	30.30		
	Labor—202 × $0.09		18.18	48.48
	Interior doors—10 × $135.00	1,350.00		
	Labor—10 × $37.50		375.00	1,725.00
	Weatherstripping (2 outside doors)—2 ×			
	$6.00	12.00		
	Labor—2 at $10.50		21.00	33.00
19	Cabinet work			
	8′ base—finished with Formica top and			
	splash at $54.00	432.00		
	Labor—8 × $16.20		129.60	561.60
	Wall cabinets—12 lin. ft.—Labor and			
	material at $27.00			324.00
	Medicine cabinet	75.00	15.00	90.00
	Shelves and rods	45.00	45.00	90.00
20	Painting and decorating			
	2 coats undercoat and 1 coat enamel—			
	material: 3,556 s.f. at $0.15	533.40		
	Labor—3,556 s.f. at $0.18		640.08	1,173.48
	11 windows at $27.00			297.00
	Exterior walls and gable			276.00

Table 12.1 Continued

COST BREAKDOWN

Specification No.	Type of Construction	Material	Labor	Total
21	Plumbing			
	Plumbing w/40-gal HWH, 5-yr guaranty	1,200.00		
	Labor		1,254.00	2,454.00
22	Heating			2,250.00
23	Electric			
	Electrical—37 outlets × $18.00 (L & M)			666.00
	Service—100 amp	150.00		
	Labor		180.00	330.00
	Range and heater wiring	60.00	105.00	165.00
	Fixtures			255.00
	Total labor and material cost			$28,990.76
	Add: Field overhead at 3%			869.72
				$29,860.48
				$29,860.48
	Contractor overhead and profit at 12%			3,583.26
	Total construction cost—new			$33,443.74
	Rounded to $33,400.00			
	Cost per square foot of building $33.40			

ping of field and overhead expenditures. An illustration of this costing method as applied to a single-family residence is shown in Table 12.2.

The quantity survey or subcontractors' method, if expertly applied, produces fairly accurate results. The application, however, is often too time consuming and costly to be recommended for use for most appraisal assignments. In fact, it would take thoroughly trained cost estimators, who are conversant with the operational details and technology of the building industry, to apply this method with assurance and relative accuracy. The typical appraiser is by necessity, therefore, referred to still simpler and more objective methods of cost calculation.

UNIT-IN-PLACE CONSTRUCTION METHOD

Under this method only costs of structural units installed in place as charged by the various subcontractors or incurred by the general contractor are itemized and summarized. Under this method, for instance, the number of cubic yards of concrete poured is multiplied by the unit cost per yard in place. The same is

Table 12.2   Construction Cost Estimate Under the Quantity Survey or Subcontractor's Method for a Single-Family Residence Containing 1,000 Square Feet of Building Area

Building Description: Two-bedroom, living room, kitchen and bath, concrete-block (painted) residential structure. Interior walls of frame and plaster. Asphalt-shingled roof with 4-inch in 12-inch pitch over 2-inch rock-wool ceiling insulation. Concrete subflooring and terrazzo finished flooring. Aluminum double-hung windows. Equipped with 40-gallon automatic electric water heater, built-in electric stove and oven, and 85,000-Btu oil-fired, forced-air central heating system. Construction methods and specifications to meet FHA minimum property standards for one and two family living units.

COST BREAKDOWN

Type of Construction	Total, Materials and Labor
Architect's fee	$ 150
Permits and utility connections	300
Site clearing	315
Excavation	180
Foundation	531
Chimney-masonry	645
Exterior walls	345
Subflooring	2,700
Framing, carpentry	1,486
Roofing	5,340
Windows and doors	786
Lath and plaster	1,680
Finished flooring	3,171
Cabinet work	2,400
Insulation	1,065
Painting	240
Plumbing	1,746
Heating	2,454
Electrical	2,250
Fixtures	1,161
Insurance	255
Miscellaneous	90
Field overhead—3%	300
Contractor's overhead & profit	1,880
Total	$31,470

Rounded to $31,500

Cost per square foot of building $31.50

done for the number of squares of roofing of a given type and grade. Typical unit-in-place costs are as follows:

Asphalt shingle roofing	per square (100 sq ft)	$70.50
Plaster in place	per yard (27 cu ft)	4.05

Brick veneer wall	per lineal foot	64.50
Parquet finished flooring	per square foot	2.55
Ceramic tile wall or floor	per square foot	3.45
Vinyl tile flooring—⅛ in.	per square foot	2.10
Gutter and spouts	per lineal foot	4.05

This method of cost estimating is useful for estimating costs of substitute materials, and for estimating construction additions or deletions from given plans and specifications. Because of the difficulty to reduce accurately carpentry and finishing work to a unit basis, this method of cost estimating is only infrequently employed by builders and developers and is not recommended as a valuation tool for real estate appraisers.

SEGREGATED OR TRADE BREAKDOWN METHOD

This method, which is introduced in Figures 12.1, 12.2, and 12.3, generally represents how most residential and small commercial property builders prepare their cost bids. The source of the individual numbers in Figure 12.3 is Appendix VI. It produces a total building cost on the basis of bids received from subcontractors. These subcontractors may be responsible for site clearance (and well

Figure 12.1 Courtesy of Marshall and Swift, Los Angeles, California.

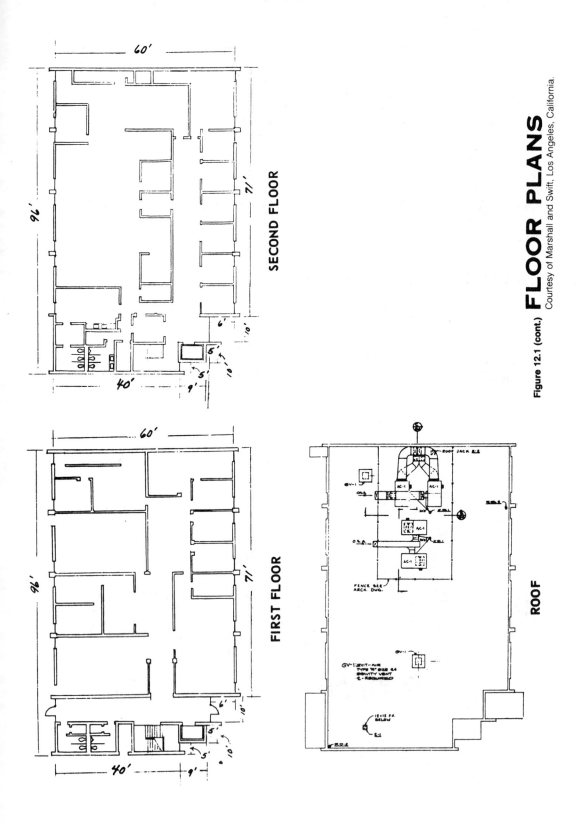

SECOND FLOOR

FIRST FLOOR

ROOF

Figure 12.1 (cont.) **FLOOR PLANS**
Courtesy of Marshall and Swift, Los Angeles, California.

SUBJECT BUILDING DESCRIPTION

OCCUPANCY:	Offices
BUILDING CLASS:	"C"
QUALITY:	Good
NUMBER OF STORIES:	Two
TOTAL HEIGHT:	26 feet
AVERAGE STORY HEIGHT:	13 feet
AVERAGE SINGLE FLOOR AREA:	5490 sq. ft.
FOUNDATION:	Continuous concrete footings and foundation for the bearing walls.
EXTERIOR WALLS:	Grouted 10" reinforced brick with pilasters. The exterior is face brick.
ROOF STRUCTURE:	1/2" plywood sheathing over 2" x 10" rafters 16" o.c.
ROOF COVER:	3 ply composition with tar and gravel.
FLOORS:	First floor: 4" concrete slab on the ground, with a vapor barrier. 25% quarry tile - 10% vinyl asbestos tile. 65% carpet over concrete slab, ceramic tile floors in restrooms. Second floor: 1-5/8" foamed concrete over sheathing. Wood joists and sheathing. 60% vinyl asbestos tile. 40% carpet.
CEILING:	Acoustic tile on a suspended ceiling structure.
INTERIOR CONSTRUCTION:	Drywall construction, taped and spackled. Some Good quality hardwood plywood paneling on wood frame. Some concrete block partitions on first floor only. Ceramic tile wainscoting in restrooms. Wood cabinets with a laminated plastic countertop in employees lounge.
HEATING AND COOLING:	For the purpose of this example the building is considered to be in the central district in a moderate climate. It has a Package A. C. system.
ELECTRICAL:	Flex-conduit, typical outlets throughout. Recessed fluorescent fixtures.
PLUMBING:	Includes four restrooms, 8 toilets, 2 urinals, 6 lavatories, 1 kitchen sink, 2 service sinks, 30 gal. electric hot water heater for restrooms and lounge, 2 drinking fountains.
SPRINKLERS:	Fire extinguishers.
ELEVATORS:	One small office elevator with simple call system and push button control, four passenger cab with 2 stops.

Figure 12.2 Courtesy of Marshall and Swift, Los Angeles, California.

and septic system installation for outlying properties), excavation, foundation and masonry walls, carpentry, roofing, plumbing, and electrical. These trades are broken down even more in the segregated cost example mentioned previously.

Computing costs in this manner is simpler for appraisers to prepare and more readily understood by clients than the builders' detail inventory method or the quantity survey method. There is a similarity between the latter method and the segregated method in that both are based on subcontractors' bids. However, the segregated method is less detailed and more widely used by appraisers. None of these methods will produce acceptable results unless the appraiser thoroughly inspects the appraised building and judiciously compares the nature and quality of the building to the bench mark building in a cost manual or to figures provided by a local contractor. If the initial cost figures are inaccurate, the eventual depreciated cost in turn will be inaccurate.

SEGREGATED COST FORM

For subscribers using the MARSHALL VALUATION SERVICE Segregated Cost

1. Name of building _____ Owner _____
2. Located at _____ Class __C__ No. of Stories __2__
3. Occupancy: Section 1. _OFFICE_____ Section 2 _____ Section 3 _____
4. Subscriber making survey _____ Date _____

	COST RANGE RATING NUMBERS			
	Low No. 1	Average No. 2	Above Average No. 3	High No. 4

5. Quality _GOOD_____ Age _____ Condition _____

FLOOR AREA COSTS

		UNIT COSTS					
		NO.	SECTION I	NO.	SECTION II	NO.	SECTION III
6. Excavation _SITE PREP. @ $.10 ÷ 2 (SITE APT. - 2 STORIES)_		2	$ .05				
7. Foundation _BEARING @ $1.17 X 1.02 (HT.) X .992 (MULTI-STORY)_		2	1.18				
8. Frame _____							
9. Floor Structure _50% CONC. + WTRPRF = $1.23 + 50% WOOD = $1.91 + 50% FORMED CONC.= $.25_		3	3.39				
10. Floor Cover _SEE NOTES_		2/3	2.34				
11. Ceiling _CANE FIBER @ $.96 + SUSPENDED @ $.89_		3	1.85				
12. Interior Construction _80% FRAME = $8.98 + 20% MASONRY $2.44 = $11.42 X 1.05 (HT.)_		3	11.99				
13. Plumbing _OFFICE_		2	2.04				
14. Sprinklers _NONE_							
15. Heating, Cooling, Ventilating _PACKAGE A/c = $4.39 X 1.03 (HT.)_		2/3	4.52				
16. Electrical _OFFICE_		3	5.81				
17. _____ Total floor area unit costs move to line 24			$ 33.17				

WALL COSTS

18. Exterior Walls _10" BRICK @ $13.90 + FACE @ $1.50 + PILASTER @ $.67_ Move to line 25		3	$16.07				
19. Wall Ornamentation _____ Move to line 26							

ROOF COSTS

20. Roof Structure _WOOD JOIST - WOOD DECK_		3	$3.42				
21. Roof Cover _BUILT-UP_		3	1.12				
22. Trusses _____							
23. _____ Total roof unit costs move total to line 27			$ 4.54				

FINAL CALCULATIONS

	from line	SECTION I			SECTION II			SECTION III		
		UNIT COST	X AREA =	TOTAL COST	UNIT COST	X AREA =	TOTAL COST	UNIT COST	X AREA =	TOTAL COST
24. Floor area costs	17	33.17	X 10,980 =	$364,207		X	=		X	=
25. Exterior walls	18	16.07	X 8112 =	130,360		X	=		X	=
26. Wall Ornamentation	19		X	=		X	=		X	=
27. Roof	23	4.54	X 5490 =	24,925		X	=		X	=
28. Section Sub Totals				$ 519,492						
29. Number of Stories Multiplier			X 1.000			X			X	
30. Section Totals				$ 519,492		+			+	

31. Total of All Sections . . . . $ 519,492
32. Architect's Fees (Sec.99/2) 1.069
33. Current Cost Multiplier (Sec.99/3) 1.02
34. Local Multiplier (Sec.99/5) 1.05
35. Final Multiplier (Ln.32 x Ln.33 x Ln.34) . 1.145
36. Line 35 x Line 31 . . . . $594,818
37. LUMP SUMS (Ln.47) 26,908
38. REPLACEMENT COST (Ln.36 + Ln.37) $621,726
39. Depreciation % (Section 97) . . . .
40. Depreciation amount (Ln.39 x Ln.38). . .
41. DEPRECIATED COST (Ln.38 − Ln.40). .

INSURABLE VALUES

%

Insurance Exclusions: Basement excavation. . . .
(Section 96)   Foundation below ground
                     Piping below ground. .
                     Architect's Plans and Specs

42. Total Exclusions − Percentage . . . .
43. Exclusions on New Costs (Ln.38 x Ln.42). . .
44. Insurable Value New (Ln.38 − Ln.43). . . . .
45. Depreciated exclusions (Ln.41 − Ln.42). . . .
46. Insurable Value Depreciated (Ln.41 − Ln.45)

See back of this form for drawings and area calculations

Figure 12.3

218

THE COMPARATIVE MARKET METHOD

The comparative square- or cubic-foot method is used almost exclusively by appraisers and by builders and architects when cost estimates are needed quickly. Under this method, the applicable unit cost per square or cubic foot of a building is derived by dividing the total building costs of similar structures recently completed by the volume of square or cubic feet contained within the exterior wall dimension of the building's structural surfaces—including attics, dormers, basements, and subfloor areas. Where the building to be costed is similar in size, design, quality, and quantity of construction of buildings completed within a three- to six-month period, the results obtained should prove quite accurate. The unit cost thus obtained is then multiplied by the total number of square- or cubic-foot space area, and to this total is added a percentage for architect's fees and builder's overhead and profit.

The principal difficulty and inaccuracy of the comparative costing method is that—except for large developments—no two buildings are exactly alike in type and quality of construction; and unless adjustments are made to reflect these differences, the margin of possible error may prove too great to make the estimate reliable as a guide to building costs. To minimize errors and to perfect this costing method, square- or cubic-foot cost is calculated for a *standard* or *base* building of a given size, exclusive of land costs, and adjustments are then made for differences in size, perimeter, or shape of building as well as for quality and quantity of features such as extra bathrooms, special flooring, fixtures, equipment, ceiling height, and other exceptional improvements. The application of the modified comparative method of cost estimating is demonstrated in Figures 12.4 and 12.5.

ESTIMATING THE STANDARD OR BASE HOUSE

Since a comparison with anything in any field is best attained if a reliable standard of measure is available, a base building typical for a given geographic area is selected and priced under the quantity survey or unit-in-place method by competent, reliable, and active builders. Generally, specifications complying with local or state building codes are set up and given to at least two, preferably three, community builders for detailed cost estimating. The several estimates are then analyzed, checked, and correlated into one composite estimate representative of local building costs for the selected base building. The 1,000-square-foot house as described and estimated in Table 12.1 is used for purposes of illustration. Attention is called to the fact that items subject to frequent variations, such as the size of a house, its perimeter shape, special type or kind of flooring, paneled walls, extra equipment, built-in cabinets, and air conditioning, to name a few, must be separately priced and added to the basic unit cost at the time when adjustments are made to account for differences between the base or standard

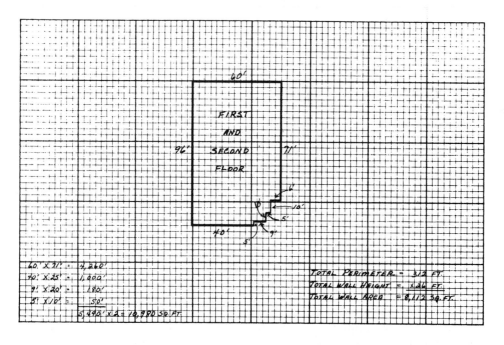

LUMP SUM ADDITIONS for items not priced above add as lump sums: Elevators Sec. 58, Refrigeration Sec. 58, Stained glass Sec. 55, also miscellaneous costs from the segregated cost pages. (Apply architect's fees and appropriate current cost and local multipliers from Section 99, Pages 3 and 5 before transferring total to line 37.)

ONE ELEVATOR - 2 STOPS (SEC. 58) $23,500 X 1.145 (FINAL MULT.)   = | $26,908
FINAL MULTIPLIER: CURRENT COST @ 1.02 X LOCAL @ 1.05 X ARCH. @ 1.069

47. _____ Total Lump Sum Costs Move to Line 37 | $ 26,908

FLOOR COVER: 13% _QUARRY TILE_ (3) @ $ 5.55 = $ .72
              52% _CARPET_   (3) @   2.50 =   1.30
              35% _V.A.T._   (2) @   .90 =   .32
                                                $2.34

Figure 12.4 Comparative Market Method   Courtesy of Marshall and Swift, Los Angeles, California.

OFFICE AND MEDICAL OFFICE BUILDINGS
(CALCULATOR METHOD)

CLASS	TYPE	EXTERIOR WALLS	INTERIOR FINISH	LIGHTING, PLUMBING AND MECHANICAL	HEAT	COST Sq. M.	COST Cu. Ft.	COST Sq. Ft.
C	Excellent office	Steel frame, masonry and glass, stone ornamentation, top quality	Plaster, paneling, carpet and terrazzo, suspended ceilings	*Best fluorescent ceiling panels tiled restrooms, good fixtures	Warm & cool air (zoned)	$766.18	$5.93	$71.18
	Good office	Steel frame or bearing walls, brick/conc. panels, some ornamentation	Plaster or drywall, good partitions, acoustic tile, carpet and vinyl	*Good fluorescent lighting, good restrooms and fixtures	Package A.C.	566.62	4.39	52.64
	Average office	Steel or concrete frame, or bearing walls, some trim	Paint, drywall partitions, acoustic tile, asphalt tile	*Fluorescent lighting, adequate outlets and plumbing	Forced air	405.26	3.14	37.65
	Low cost office	Masonry bearing walls, light rafters, very plain	Paint, few low cost partitions acoustic tile, asphalt tile	Minimum office lighting and plumbing	Wall furnace	280.29	2.17	26.04
	Excellent medical	Steel frame, masonry and glass, ornamentation, top quality	Plaster, paneling, carpet and vinyl tile, acoustic plaster	*Fluorescent panels, air piping, X-ray rooms, good plumbing	Hot & chilled water (zoned)	865.75	6.70	80.43
	Good medical	Steel frame, masonry, best concrete panels, ornamentation	Plaster or drywall, good partitions, acoustic tile, carpet and vinyl	*Good fluorescent lighting, X-ray rooms, good plumbing	Warm & cool air (zoned)	672.64	5.21	62.49
	Average medical	Steel or concrete frame, or bearing walls, some trim	Plaster, drywall partitions, acoustic tile, vinyl asbestos	*Adequate lighting and outlets, adequate plumbing	Package A.C.	523.24	4.05	48.61
	Low cost medical	Masonry bearing walls, light rafters, very plain	Paint, cheap partitions, acoustic tile, asphalt tile	Minimum lighting and outlets, adequate plumbing	Forced air	399.56	3.09	37.12
D	Excellent office	Studs or steel columns, bar or web joists, brick or stone veneer	Best plaster, paneling, carpet and vinyl tile	*Fluorescent panels, many outlets, good tiled restrooms	Warm & cool air (zoned)	709.13	5.49	65.88
	Good office	Best stucco on good frame, brick or stone trim, good front	Plaster or drywall, good partitions, acoustic tile, carpet and vinyl	*Good fluorescent lighting, good restrooms and fixtures	Package A.C.	518.83	4.02	48.20
	Average office	Stucco or wood siding on wood studs, some trim	Drywall, acoustic tile, low cost carpet or asphalt tile	Adequate lighting and plumbing	Forced air	368.99	2.86	34.28
	Low cost office	Light stucco or siding on wood studs, very plain	Drywall, few partitions, acoustic tile, asphalt tile	Minimum lighting and plumbing	Wall furnace	264.69	2.05	24.59
	Excellent medical	Studs or steel columns, bar or web joists, brick or stone veneer	Best plaster, paneling, carpet and vinyl tile	*Fluorescent panels, air piping, X-ray rooms, good plumbing	Warm & cool air (zoned)	796.11	6.16	73.96
	Good medical	Best stucco on good frame, good brick or stone trim	Plaster or drywall, good partitions, acoustic tile, carpet and vinyl	*Good fluorescent lighting, X-ray rooms, good plumbing	Warm & cool air (zoned)	636.15	4.93	59.10
	Average medical	Stucco or wood siding on wood studs, some trim	Drywall, acoustic tile, low cost carpet or asphalt tile	Adequate lighting and outlets, adequate plumbing	Package A.C.	482.66	3.74	44.84
	Low cost medical	Light stucco or siding on wood studs, very plain	Drywall, cheap partitions, acoustic tile, asphalt tile	Minimum lighting and outlets, adequate plumbing	Forced air	371.14	2.87	34.48
	Basement offices	Plaster or drywall interior	Average office finish, acoustic tile, vinyl asbestos	Typical office lighting and plumbing	Forced air	293.64	2.27	27.28
	Basement storage	Painted interior	Paint only, few partitions	Minimum lighting, drains	None	127.12	.98	11.81
C–D S	Basement parking	Unfinished interior	Plaster or drywall ceiling, concrete floor	Minimum lighting, drains	Ventilation	156.40	1.21	14.53
	Mezzanine office	Not included	Enclosed, average office finish, acoustic tile soffit	Average office lighting and plumbing	In building cost	240.25	—	22.32
	Mezzanine open	Not included	Open, finished floors and soffit	Average lighting, no plumbing	In building cost	129.81	—	12.06

MULTISTORY BUILDINGS
Add .5% for each story over three, above ground, to all base costs, excluding mezzanines.

SPRINKLERS
Add for sprinklers from Section 45.

*ELEVATORS — Buildings with elevators included in the base costs are marked with an asterisk (*). If none are found, deduct the following from the base costs for buildings on this page which are marked.

	Sq. M.	Sq. Ft.		Sq. M.	Sq. Ft.
Excellent	−$23.14	$2.15	Good	−$13.46	$1.25
			Average	−$8.07	$ .75

Basements and mezzanines: add the cost of additional stops from Section 58.

Figure 12.4 (cont.) Courtesy of Marshall and Swift, Los Angeles, California.

CALCULATOR COST FORM

For subscribers using the **MARSHALL VALUATION SERVICE** *Calculator Cost Method*

SQUARE FOOT COSTS

1. Subscriber making survey _____ Date of survey _____
2. Name of building _____ Owner _____
3. Located at _____

	SECTION I	SECTION II	SECTION III	SECTION IV
4. Occupancy	OFFICE			
5. Building class and quality	Cls _C_ Qual _GOOD_	Cls ____ Qual ____	Cls ____ Qual ____	Cls ____ Q.a ____
6. Exterior wall..............	FACE BRICK			
7. No. of stories & height per story ..	No. _2_ Ht _13'_	No. ____ Ht ____	No. ____ Ht ____	No. ____ Ht ____
8. Average floor area	5490 SqFt.			
9. Average perimeter...........	312 LIN.FT.			
10. Age and condition..........	Age ____ Cond ____	Age ____ Cond ____	Age ____ Cond ____	Age ____ Cond ____

	SECTION I	SECTION II	SECTION III	SECTION IV
11. **Base Square Foot Cost**	$52.64			

SQUARE FOOT REFINEMENTS

12. Heating, cooling, ventilation... PACKAGE A/C	BASE			
13. Elevator deduction				
14. Miscellaneous				
15. .... Total lines 11 through 14	$52.64			

HEIGHT AND SIZE REFINEMENTS

16. Number of stories-multiplier	1.000			
17. Height per story-multiplier (see Line 7)...............	1.023			
18. Floor area-perimeter multiplier (see Lines 8 and 9)	.988			
19. .... Combined height and size multiplier (Lines 16 x 17 x 18)	1.011			

FINAL CALCULATIONS

	SECTION I	SECTION II	SECTION III	SECTION IV
20. Refined square foot cost (Line 15 x Line 19)	$ 53.22			
21. Current cost multiplier (Sect. 99 p. 3)	1.00			
22. Local multiplier (Sect. 99 p. 5 and 6)	1.05			
23. Final sq. ft. cost (Line 20 x Line 21 x Line 22)	$ 55.88			
24. Area (Back of this form).................	10,980 SqFt			
25. Line 23 x Line 24.......................	$ 613,562			
26. Lump sums (Line 32).................				
27. **Replacement Cost** (Line 25 - Line 26)........	$ 613,562			
28. Depreciation % (Sect. 97).................				
29. Depreciation amount (Line 27 x Line 28)........				
30. **Depreciated Cost** (Line 27 – Line 29)				

TOTAL OF ALL SECTIONS

31. Replacement cost _$ 613,562_ Depreciated cost _____ Insurable value _____

FORM 1003 (Calc. Cost)

Figure 12.5 Courtesy of Marshall and Swift, Los Angeles, California.

house and the subject house under cost study. This is similar to the practice of pricing automobiles where the costs of extras are added to the factory price of a "standard" model as quoted f.o.b. at the factory location.

As shown in Table 12.1, the total cost of the described standard or base house in a given geographic area is $31,500 inclusive of contractor's overhead and profit calculated at the rate of 12 percent. This amount, divided by the size of the base house of 1,000 square feet, equals a market unit cost of $31.50 per square foot. The next step is to adjust the unit cost of the base house to a unit cost applicable to a specific or subject house under cost study.

Variations in unit cost most frequently encountered are caused by the following:

1. Differences in community construction costs and standards.
2. Differences in building size.
3. Quality of design and construction.
4. Added construction cost of built-in features.
5. Built-in fixture and appliances.

Unit costs per square foot or cubic foot of building construction are generally available for metropolitan areas as well as for principal cities with populations of 100,000 persons and over from individual sources or commercial cost valuation services. For communities of lesser size, or where unit-building cost quotations are unavailable, it is necessary to adjust the best available and most reliable cost index for a given community in accordance with cost differentials known to exist between it and the community in which the subject property is located. As a rule, cost variations are ascribable to differences in wage rates, costs of locally delivered materials, local construction standards, and labor practices enforced in given areas. Assuming a cost average of 1.00 for the United States as a whole, location cost differentials for selected cities have been calculated by the *Marshall Valuation Service* as follows:[1]

Metropolitan Area	Local Cost Modifier
Atlantic City, N.J.	1.13
Augusta, Me.	0.99
Baltimore, Md.	0.99
Baton Rouge, La.	0.98
Bismarck-Mandan, N.D.	0.97
Boston, Mass.	1.12

[1]*Marshall Valuation Service*, Class S, Section 99, January 1985 insert (Los Angeles: Marshall and Swift Publication Company).

Metropolitan Area	Local Cost Modifier
Chicago, Ill.	1.09
Cleveland, Ohio	1.11
Dallas-Fort Worth, Tex.	0.97
Denver, Colo.	1.02
Detroit, Mich.	1.08
Flint, Mich.	1.02
Greenville, S.C.	0.85
Hartford, Conn.	1.10
Indianapolis, Ind.	1.00
Jacksonville, Fla.	0.90
Lansing, Mich.	1.05
Las Vegas, Nev.	1.12
Manhattan, N.Y.	1.25
Milwaukee, Wisc.	1.07
Minneapolis, Minn.	1.08
Montreal-Laval, Quebec	1.14
New Orleans, La.	1.00
Oklahoma City, Okla.	0.97
Omaha, Nebr.	0.94
Philadelphia, Pa.	1.10
Portland, Me.	0.98
Portland, Ore.	1.01
Raleigh-Durham, N.C.	0.85
Richmond, Va.	0.94
Sacramento, Calif.	1.14
Winnipeg, Manitoba	1.25

ESTIMATING THE SUBJECT HOUSE

As a prerequisite to the application of the cost approach it is essential that an accurate and detailed word picture of the building and related improvements under value study be obtained. Without full and firsthand knowledge of building construction features it is not possible to compare effectively the subject house with the standard house, and to adjust applicable construction unit costs to reflect the differences. To illustrate the application of the comparative market method of cost estimating where the square foot of building volume is accepted as a unit of construction cost, it is assumed that the property under appraisal consists of a building site 100 feet by 125 feet valued by comparison at $12,000, and that the building improvements (new) are described in Figure 12.6. Based on the

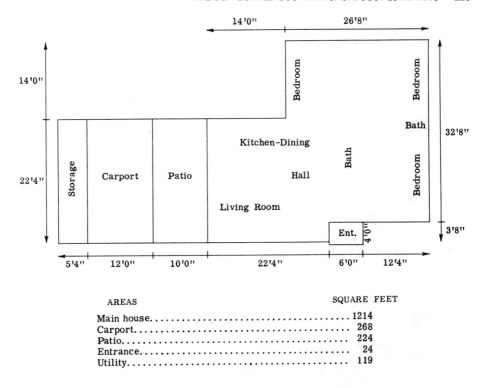

AREAS   SQUARE FEET

Main house...................................... 1214
Carport... 268
Patio... 224
Entrance..   24
Utility... 119

Figure 12.6 Floor Plan   Courtesy of Marshall and Swift, Los Angeles, California.

building data, property value under the market comparison cost approach is derived in the following manner:

Cost Approach to Value

Base cost per square foot of standard (1,000 sq ft) house =	$31.50
Base cost of subject house[2] (1,214 sq ft) = $31.50 × 0.95 =	29.93
Adjustment for cost variation due to location =	None

All cost data are provided to illustrate application of the cost approach to value (Table 12.3). In practice the appraiser must consult applicable local builders' services or employ current national building cost references and adjust same to reflect local cost variations. For items not listed, the appraiser should contact a building contractor or a building supply agency to obtain needed cost data. Attention is called also to the necessity of adjusting the base cost per square foot of a building to account for variations in building size. Since certain basic construction costs are relatively inelastic (plumbing, electrical equipment, and bathroom and kitchen facilities), the principle of decreasing unit cost is operative with an increase in building size. The percentage relationship of building size

[2]See Table 12.4 for variations in base costs due to building size.

Table 12.3 Cost Adjustments for Variation from Standard Construction

Item	Amount
Built-up roof	$ 375
Extra bathroom with full tiling	2,025
Perimeter wall adjustment 7 ft at $41.40	290
Sliding glass doors (2)	540
Extra windows 2 at $165.00	330
Extra interior door 2 at $173	346
Garbage disposal	270
Kitchen fan, 10 in.	240
Bathroom fan, 8 in.	180
1,000-watt bath wall heater	345
Built-in bookcase	600
Built-in vanity	330
Double kitchen sink	135
Washing machine connections	375
Wind wall 4 ft at $16.50	66
Extra kitchen cabinets and counter	360
Extra closet	240
Gutters and spouts	120
Exterior construction details and finishes	675
Total extras	$ 7,842
Cost of extras per square foot = $7,842 ÷ 1214 =	$ 6.46
Adjusted square foot cost—subject house ($29.93 + $6.46)	36.39

Cost Calculations

Cost of:			
	Main house	1,214 sq ft at $36.39 =	$44,177
	Carport	268 sq ft at $12.00 =	3,216
	Patio	224 sq ft at $ 8.25 =	1,848
	Entrance	24 sq ft at $18.00 =	432
	Utility	119 sq ft at $16.50 =	1,964
	Total costs of improvements		$51,637
Add:	Cost of venetian blinds		$ 600
	Landscaping		750
	Walks and driveway		675
	Value of land—by comparison		12,000
	Total value via cost approach		$65,662
	Rounded to $65,650		

to building unit costs is shown in Table 12.4, where information is also given as to the number of perimeter feet of exterior walls contained in typical houses of varying building size. The base or standard house, as a rule, is rectangular in shape. Where architectural design calls for an elongated L-type or a ranch-type residence, the extra number of feet of perimeter wall must be reflected in the cost estimate. To illustrate: A structure 20 feet by 20 feet and a structure 40

Table 12.4   Variation in Base Unit Cost and Perimeter Wall Dimensions Resulting from Changes in Building Size[a]

Building Size (Square Feet)	Percentage of Base Cost	Exterior Walls Perimeter (Feet)
700	115	105
750	110	109
800	108	113
850	106	117
900	104	121
950	102	125
1,000	100	130
1,050	99	134
1,100	97	138
1,150	96	142
1,200	95	147
1,250	94	151
1,300	93	155
1,350	92	159
1,400	91	163
1,450	90	167
1,500	89.5	171
1,550	89	175
1,600	88.5	180
1,650	88	184
1,700	87.5	188
1,800	86.5	197
1,900	85.5	205
2,000	85	213

[a]For buildings in excess of 2,000 square feet, use maximum adjustment for 85 percent of cost of standard house. For quality workmanship, add 5 to 10 percent to final cost estimate. For poor workmanship, subtract 5 percent or more as justified.

feet by 10 feet both contain 400 square feet of building area. However, the latter requires 100 feet of perimeter wall as compared with 80 feet of perimeter wall of the former. The cost of the perimeter wall per lineal foot (inclusive of exterior and interior wall finishes) varies depending on the type of construction.

The comparative building cost method, as demonstrated, provides a speedy and fairly accurate means for obtaining value estimates for appraisal purposes. Where variations in ceiling heights or building practices necessitate cost quotations on a cubic-foot rather than a square-foot basis, this costing method can be converted by adding the third, or height, dimension and dividing total building costs by the number of cubic-foot units contained in the base house.

With experience and years of appraisal practice, an ever-expanding file of building cost material and construction data can be accumulated. This, as part

Table 12.5 Cost Approach Format

Current replacement cost: all building improvements inclusive of all direct and indirect costs	$_____
Less: Accrued depreciation (see Schedule)	
1. Deferred maintenance	$_____
2. Reserve for replacement of major units—roof, heating, etc.	_____
3. Incurable loss due to age of structure	_____
4. Functional obsolescence, curable	_____
5. Functional obsolescence, incurable	_____
6. External obsolescence	_____
Total accrued depreciation	$_____
Depreciated replacement cost	_____
Add land value—by comparison	_____
Landscaping	_____
Walks and drive	_____
Other land improvements	
(fences, etc.)	_____
Total value via depreciated cost approach	$_____

of the overall appraisal plant, should prove a valuable aid in perfecting appraisal cost estimates. It is important, of course, to keep building construction costs up to date. It is suggested that a check of overall labor and material costs and practices be made at least every six months, or preferably every three months.

From the replacement or reproduction cost estimate, as is the case with existing structures, a deduction must be made for accrued depreciation caused by age, wear, tear, and action of the elements. For a detailed study of the causes of depreciation, and the various methods in use for estimating and accounting purposes, the reader is referred to Chapter 13.

The format of the cost approach for existing buildings is recommended as outlined in Table 12.5

COST INDEXING METHOD

Some assignments may involve buildings for which it is difficult to estimate the current construction cost. If the original date of construction and the cost of construction are known, the appraiser can index the original cost to the date of appraisal to provide a check on the current replacement or reproduction cost.

Care must be exercised in ascertaining the accuracy of the original cost. Cost information provided by building permits usually is inadequate and tends to understate actual costs.

Suppose, for example, that the appraised dwelling was built in 1962 at a cost of $38,360. A check on building cost indexes (usually included in commercial cost services) shows that the 1962 index was 324.7; the present index is 1,218.8. Thus, by comparing the two indexes, the present reproduction cost is estimated to be $144,000.

$$\left(\frac{1,218.8}{324.7}\right) (\$38,360) = \$143,989$$

COMMERCIAL COST SERVICES

The cost approach, as a measure of value, becomes increasingly tenuous as the size and age of a structure increases. In fact, the cost approach is the least reliable measure of market value and is recommended for use primarily as an overall check of the reliability of other market measures of value or where the cost approach—as is the case with fire insurance or with special-purpose properties—represents the principal if not the only measure of value.

Few appraisers, unless they also are a trained cost specialist, a contract builder, or a construction engineer, are capable of estimating with any degree of accuracy the costs of proposed construction or the replacement costs of existing structures where the same are of complex commercial, industrial, or special-purpose use and architectural design. In such cases, it is best for an appraiser to rely on comparative cost studies made available on a periodic updated subscription basis by commercial cost services such as the *Building Cost Calculator and Valuation Guide*, published by the McGraw-Hill Information Systems Company at 1221 Avenue of the Americas, New York, New York, a looseleaf service covering different types and sizes of buildings; the *Boeckh Building Valuation Manual*, published by the American Appraisal Company at 525 East Michigan Street, Milwaukee, Wisconsin, three volumes covering residential and agricultural, commercial, and industrial and institutional buildings; *Marshall Valuation Service*, published by Marshall and Swift Publication Company at 1617 Beverly Boulevard, Los Angeles, California, a looseleaf service giving replacement cost of buildings and improvements; or *Residential Cost Handbook*, also published by Marshall and Swift Publication Company. The latter is a looseleaf presentation of localized square foot and segregated replacement costs. Both Boeckh and Marshall and Swift offer telephone-accessible computer-based cost routines. The preparation of a single-family dwelling cost estimate may take less than three minutes and cost under $5. An example of one of these computer printouts is shown in Figure 12.7. In these and other more regionally or localized cost

AMERICAN APPRAISAL ASSOCIATES, INC

8/6/85

```
POLICY NUMBER:      7123-A-347 AD                    07/86
PROPERTY OWNER:     JOHN JONES                       COST AS OF:  3/85
PROPERTY ADDRESS:   100 MEADOW LANE
                    DALLAS,                 TX 75221
```

```
RESIDENCE DESCRIPTION
     CONSTRUCTION:    CLASS C 100%
     # OF STORIES:    1-STORY     30%    2-STORY     70%
     OCCUPANCY:       SINGLE-FAMILY
     EXTERIOR WALL:   CATEGORY I    100%
     AREA:            2975 SQUARE FEET OF LIVING AREA
     BASEMENT:        1200 SQUARE FEET
```

```
                         BASE RESIDENCE WALL CATEGORY I        83,776
                         ADD FOR BASEMENT                       4,712
                         ADD FOR ROOF MATERIAL                  1,820
                              100% WOOD SHAKES
                                                             -----------
                         BASE RESIDENCE COST                   90,308
                         AREA/PERIMETER RATIO FACTOR             1.00
                                                             -----------
                         ADJUSTED BASE RESIDENCE COST          90,308
```

```
ADDITIONAL FEATURES
     PORCHES                                 5,460
     HALF BATH                                 850
     FULL BATH                               1,850
     GARAGE(S)                               5,625
     AIR CONDITIONING                        3,964
     BUILT-INS
        INCLUDED ARE
           MICROWAVE, DISHWASHER,
           RANGE HOOD
     ADDITIONAL BUILT-INS                    2,715
           COUNTER COOKTOP, OVEN, DISHWASHER
           GARBAGE DISPOSAL, BATHROOM HEATER
           POWER ATTIC VENTILATOR
           SECURITY FIRE ALARM
                    TOTAL ADDITIONAL FEATURES               20,464
```

```
                         TOTAL BASE COST                     110,772
                         LOCATION MULTIPLIER                    1.35
                         LOCAL REPLACEMENT COST              149,542
```

```
                                   TOTAL                     149,542
```

```
                         INSURED AMOUNT                       82,000
                         % OF INSURANCE TO REPLACEMENT COST      55%
```

```
BOECKH SYSTEM, A PRODUCT OF AMERICAN APPRAISAL ASSOCIATES, INC.
```

```
ABOVE COSTS INCLUDE LABOR AND MATERIAL, NORMAL PROFIT AND OVERHEAD AS OF
DATE OF REPORT. COSTS REPRESENT GENERAL ESTIMATES NOT TO BE CONSIDERED A
DETAILED QUANTITY SURVEY.
```

Figure 12.7   Computerized Building Cost Estimate (Courtesy of E.H. Boeckh Company, Milwaukee, Wisconsin)

services, information is published for typical industrial and commercial buildings as follows:

> Apartments.
> Hotels, motels, and clubs.
> Offices, banks, and lofts.
> Stores and shopping centers.
> Warehouses.
> Garages and service stations.
> Theaters.
> Educational and public buildings.
> Industrial structures.
> Hospitals and churches.
> Restaurants, bowling alleys, and stadiums.
> Other special-purpose buildings.

The commercial cost units generally are quoted on a base cost (i.e., cubic-foot) basis exclusive of foundation and excavation costs and exclusive of architects' fees and builders' overhead and profit allowances. The latter costs generally average 20 percent of quoted base costs, which must be further adjusted to reflect local conditions, which vary due to differences in labor, material, sales tax, insurance and finance costs, and building construction regulations. It is possible to obtain this cost data from computerized services, saving the appraiser considerable time. Nevertheless, the appraiser must check the figures for reasonableness.

It is deemed a "must" that every appraiser subscribe to at least one major cost service, and further subscribe to a competent market newsletter or economic business publication that keeps the appraiser informed of national and state laws and general market conditions which are bound to have an impact on building construction costs.

Building cost services, at best, serve as a guide to the establishment of replacement costs when the building is in "new" condition. The difficult task of estimating accrued depreciation remains a valuation weakness. For a more detailed study of the causes and measures of accrued depreciation, the reader is referred to Chapter 13.

REVIEW QUESTIONS

1. Briefly explain how the determination of a site's highest and best use relates to the estimated depreciated cost of the building.
2. (a) List the single most important advantage and disadvantage of the depreciated cost approach.
   (b) Explain your reasoning for these choices.
3. Give a short definition of accrued depreciation.

4. What is the principal difference between direct and indirect construction costs?
5. Give the respective advantages of replacement and reproduction costs.
6. List one advantage and one disadvantage of each of the five methods of estimating the current construction cost of a building.

READING AND STUDY REFERENCES

AMERICAN INSTITUTE OF REAL ESTATE APPRAISERS. Chapter 19, "Building Cost Estimates," *The Appraisal of Real Estate*. Chicago: AIREA, 1983.

DERBES, MAX J., JR. "Is the Cost Approach Obsolete?" *The Appraisal Journal* 50, no. 4 (October 1982), pp. 581–90.

ENTREKEN, HENRY C., JR., and STEVEN D. KAPPLIN. "More Applications of The Cost Approach," *The Real Estate Appraiser* 43, no. 6 (November–December 1977), pp. 13–15.

SACKMAN, JULIUS L. "The Limitations of the Cost Approach," *The Appraisal Journal* 36, no. 1 (January 1968), pp. 53–63.

WENDT, PAUL F. Chapter 8, "The Replacement Cost Method," *Real Estate Appraisal: Review and Outlook*, Athens: University of Georgia Press, 1974.

ZIMMERMAN, PAUL. "Reproduction Cost New Is "Cute," *The Real Estate Appraiser* 40, no. 4 (July–August 1974), pp. 43–47.

13

THE DEPRECIATED COST APPROACH: MEASURING ACCRUED DEPRECIATION

Learning Objectives
After reading this chapter, you should be able to:
Define and give examples of each of the forms of accrued depreciation
Distinguish between accrued depreciation and amortization
Understand the difference between economic life and physical life
Compute accrued depreciation using several different methods

A *loss* in value—from any cause—as measured by the difference between replacement cost (or reproduction) new of a property in current dollars and the market value of the same property is classified as *accrued depreciation*. In fact, it is possible that a property may appreciate rather than depreciate, as is the case when abnormal scarcity exacts a market premium for possession or where uniqueness (classification as antique) makes the property a collector's item. Appreciation may also be apparent rather than real where inflation has diminished the purchasing power of the dollar. Nevertheless, appreciation is the exception rather than the rule and its causes and measures will not be dealt with in this chapter.

In appraisal practice, it is an established maxim that an estimate of value via the depreciated cost approach is no more accurate than the underlying estimate of depreciation through which measures of cost are converted into measures of value. The difficulties encountered in obtaining accurate dollar expressions of accrued depreciation are ascribable, generally, to lack of sound appraisal judgment, faulty cost estimate, incorrect methodology, or insufficient research essential to an evaluation of the causes of a loss in value of a given property at a specific time and place. Judgment is a subjective mental attitude difficult to teach and which generally must be developed through experience and maturation of thinking. In this chapter an attempt is made to outline and discuss the theory underlying causes of accrued depreciation and to explain and demonstrate the methods most suitable in measuring the resultant losses in value.

DEPRECIATION VERSUS AMORTIZATION

It is the appraiser's task to estimate the amount of accrued depreciation without concern as to whether depreciation reserves have been established to compensate the owner for losses in the value of the original investment. It is on this point that recognition should be given to the differences in functions of, and responsibilities assumed by, the accountant versus the appraiser. The accountant, with the aid of effective bookkeeping, traces and records the *history* of dollar expenditures for capital outlays and those spent for maintenance and operation of an enterprise or property. The accountant is principally concerned with *original cost*, and his or her interest in value (in current dollars) is, as a rule, incidental and secondary. The appraiser, on the other hand, is principally interested in the *present worth* of future rights to income which flow from the productive use of the subject property. The original or historical cost of the property are data that may be gathered by the appraiser in order to be fully informed, but the importance of such data is secondary, if not negligible, in the valuation process. What someone pays for a property may or may not be equivalent to value. In fact, the property may have been given to the present owner, or purchased at a token price from a friend or a relative at an earlier date.

Once an estimate of value is ascertained and certified to by an appraiser, his or her task, generally, is completed. The accountant may take over from here to check the book value against the economic value reported by the appraiser, and to make or recommend changes in accounting procedure to accelerate or decelerate depreciation reserve provisions.

It would prove less confusing and contribute to greater clarity of thinking if in practice and in literature all reference to reserve provisions for the recapture of investment capital be classified as *amortization* rather than *depreciation*. The term "future depreciation" is a misnomer. The best that one can do is provide for the recapture of anticipated value losses in accordance with a preselected schedule of capital amortization which at the investment rate of interest will equal in amount the replacement cost of the subject property at the end of its economic life. A schedule of amortization of an investment of $50,000 over an economic investment life of 30 years is illustrated in Appendix V. The cumulative amount of capital recapture, computed at an investment interest rate of 10 percent, represents at the end of a given period of years depreciation as an *amount* or *book depreciation* derived under the annuity or debt amortization method, as will be explained more fully below. This concept may be applied to the systematic reduction of mortgage debt or in structuring lease payments for retiring a capital investment. Accrued depreciation as an economic *fact* at any given time first necessitates an estimation of value. Thus if we know that the present replacement cost of a residential property is $80,000, and that market sales of like properties in "as is" condition are exchanging for $60,000, accrued depreciation as a market fact is $20,000 or 25 percent.

It is important to recognize that accrued depreciation is a loss in market value from *all* causes and that this loss, measured in a lump sum, is automatically reflected in the prices that comparative properties sell for in the open market. The same holds true when value is derived under the income approach. Old properties, as a rule, produce less net operating income than like properties when in new condition. The income from old properties, too, must be capitalized at a higher rate. As in the market approach, the difference between the dollar amount as represented by present replacement cost and the value derived by capitalization of income for the property in an "as is" condition measures the loss in value (accrued depreciation) from all causes. Thus under the market and income approaches to value, the appraiser is freed from the responsibility to measure accrued depreciation independently as a loss in value. The market, through lower prices and reduced rentals or income, automatically reflects the property's diminished utility from all causes, be they age, wear, tear, actions of the elements, or human-made, functional, or external obsolescence. Only under the depreciated cost approach to value is the appraiser compelled to estimate independently and directly the amounts ascribable to the various causes which have lessened value as a result of age, and so on. For this reason the cost approach is deemed the least accurate measure of value. The accuracy of the depreciated cost approach in fact, as explained in Chapter 4, is no more reliable than the appraiser's judgment estimates which are basic to an accurate measure of accrued depreciation.

DEPRECIATION THEORY

Accrued depreciation is defined as a *loss in value from any cause*. The principal causes are recognized as follows:[1]

1. Physical deterioration.
2. Functional obsolescence.
3. External obsolescence.

[1]A more detailed list of causes of accrued depreciation is given in Table 13.1. It is based on a speech by Robert V. McCurdy, MAI, CRE in Atlantic City, New Jersey, in 1958. The source of this list is William S. Harps, Chapter 15, "Value Analysis: The Cost Approach," in The Real Estate Handbook, Maury Seldin, ed. (Homewood, Ill: Dow Jones–Irwin, 1980), pp. 243–245.

The forces within these causes may be further subclassified for purposes of identification as follows:

Physical Deterioration

1. Wear and tear through use.
2. Action of the elements (including ravages of storms and extreme temperatures), age, and destruction by termites and other varmints.
3. Structural impairment through neglect, fire, water, explosion, and vandalism.

Functional Obsolescence

1. *Faulty design*: ceilings too high or too low; improper location of kitchen, bathroom, bedrooms, and so on; wasted space; and general disutility arising from poor floor planning.
2. *Inadequacy of structural facilities*: ceilings and walls not insulated; inadequate wiring, plumbing, heating, fenestration, and other functional deficiencies which limit effective utilization of the property as a whole.
3. *Superadequacy of structural facilities*: oversized heating or cooling systems; oversized plumbing and electric wiring; excessive number of closets, bathrooms, and built-in facilities; and exterior walls built in excess of normal building uses.
4. *Outmoded equipment*: old-fashioned cast-iron tub and kitchen sink; exposed wiring and plumbing; coal-burning kitchen stove; manual control water heating; etc.

External Obsolescence

1. *Neighborhood hazards and nuisances*: heavy traffic flow; smoke; dust; noise; offensive odors; or the intrusion of incompatible land uses.
2. *Change in zoning and highest and best land use classification*: lower land uses and less stringent zoning and building regulations impair utility of use and ownership.
3. *Over or underimprovement of land*: a $100,000 home in a $50,000 neighborhood or a $50,000 home in a $100,000 neighborhood lessen overall property value as a result of violation of prevailing site (land)-to-property value ratios.
4. *Decreasing demand*: population shifts; depression, or other economic factors that lessen demand cause external obsolescence as reflected in lower property values.

ECONOMIC LIFE VERSUS PHYSICAL LIFE

Since a property, to be productive, must produce an income commensurate with dollar investments in land and building improvements over and above the expenditures necessary to operate and maintain the property, it stands to reason that when a property ceases to be productive it may have reached the end of its economic life. A structure thus may conceivably be physically sound but economically dead and constitute a financial burden on the land on which it rests. Experience has demonstrated that more properties are torn down to make room for more economically productive replacements than fall down.

Economic life is the productive life of a building measured from when it was built to when it economically encumbers the site. That is, at the end of a building's economic life, the building has no value and its presence reduces the site's value. Typically, the economic life of a well-constructed improvement is approximately 50 years. It is true that many buildings reach chronological ages well beyond that age figure; but experience discloses that most buildings at the ripe old age of 50 years must be overhauled, modernized, and generally rejuvenated to warrant their continued existence. Capital improvements generally extend the remaining economic life of a building or, conversely, lower its effective age. Properties, too, with identical chronological age, may differ significantly in their effective age depending on quality of construction, maintenance practice, operational care, and expenditures made for capital improvements or modernization. Thus it may be concluded that the *effective age* of a building is based partly on its actual age, but more important, on its comparative utility, physical condition, and remaining life expectancy. These determinants of effective age are based on other similar properties. If, for example, the appraised property has been unusually well maintained, is in a promising neighborhood, or if it has been rennovated, its actual age could be 40 years, but its effective age is only 25 years. The converse is true of a building that has suffered hard use or been neglected. A term used to describe a building's remaining productive life is *remaining economic life* (REL).

To determine the effective age on which calculations of accrued depreciation are based, the appraiser subtracts from the total (typical) economic life for the type of building under value study his or her estimate of the remaining economic life over which the structure is deemed to be productive. This estimate, as a rule, is derived after careful field inspection and a conclusion of the extent of condition new ascribed to the building improvements. To illustrate: Assuming a total economic life of 50 years and an estimated remaining economic life of 35 years[2] (based on a degree of newness, judged to be 70 percent), the effective age employed in depreciation calculations is 15 years. These data are shown as follows:

Total (average) economic building life	50 years
Remaining (estimated) economic building life	35 years
Effective age of building	15 years

In using the effective age to estimate accrued depreciation, it should be noted that in its simplest form, this method accounts for all forms of physical deterioration and obsolescence. For example, suppose that the reproduction cost of a building is $140,000, the remaining economic life is 26 years, and the total economic life is judged to be 45 years. Then the total accrued depreciation is

---

[2]Remaining economic life can also be measured by the period over which a competitive net return is anticipated by typical buyers.

computed as follows:

$$(\$140,000)(19/45) = \underline{\underline{\$59,111}}$$

The actual or chronological age of the structure is, of course, of interest to the appraiser. *Actual life* of a building is simply the time that has passed from the date of its completion to the date of the appraisal. If, for instance, judgment based on field study supports an effective age of 15 years, but building history discloses a chronological age of 30 years, evidence should be gathered to support the reason and justification for this difference. In this case, no doubt, structural improvements were added or substantial rehabilitation must have taken place.[3] Chronological age, too, is important in giving effect in depreciation calculations to structural decrepitude resulting from wear and aging of the building's supporting structures, and for estimating the effective age of component building parts such as roof shingles, plumbing, electrical wiring, and heating equipment— which have a limited service life, shorter than the remaining economic life of the property as a whole, and for which a replacement reserve must be established under the category "physical deterioration: deferred curable," as demonstrated below.

THE ENGINEERING OR OBSERVED METHOD FOR MEASURING ACCRUED DEPRECIATION

There are two principal methods of measuring accrued depreciation:

1. The engineering, or observed condition breakdown, method.
2. The age-life method.

[3]An alternative technique for estimating the actual age of a building depicts the age of the original section of a building plus any subsequent additions. This method is called the "weighted average age" method, lists the ages of each of a building's various sections, and assigns a weight in proportion to the ratio of that section's area to the building's total area. It is uniform, objective, and simple in comparison to "effective age" and can also be used in the sales comparison method. An example of this method, taken from James H. Boykin, *Industrial Potential of the Central City* (Washington, D.C.: Urban Land Institute, 1973), pp. 27–29, follows:

(a) Year Section Completed	(b) Age of Section	(c) Area of Section (sq ft)	(d) Ratio of Section to Building Area	(e) Weighted Age of each section (b) × (d)
1925	60	10,000	0.22	13.33
1975	10	25,000	0.56	5.60
1980	5	10,000	0.22	1.10
Total area		45,000	1.00	20.03 or
Weighted average age of building as of 1985				20 years

The *engineering*, or *observed condition breakdown*, method is so named because (1) the method is frequently used by engineers in structural analysis, and (2) field inspection and observation are essential in the gathering of depreciation data. The engineering method is an *applied* method that yields informative and accurate results if professionally compiled. Under this method the causes of depreciation (see Table 13.1) are analyzed as follows:

Table 13.1 Classification of Depreciation and Obsolescence

Physical–Curable[a]
  Worn roof covering
  Rusted downspouts and gutters
  Broken or worn walks and drives
  Poor maintenance of exterior walls
  Worn trim
  Worn floors
  Worn wall finish
  Worn trim finish
  Worn bath fixtures
  Worn kitchen fixtures
  Worn plumbing and water supplies
  Worn and overaged heating and ventilating equipment
  Worn electrical switches and fixtures
  Cracked basement floor
  Badly maintained garage
  General wear and tear that is economically curable
Physical–incurable
  Loss in value resulting from the wearing out of irreplaceable items
  Damage to concealed foundations, exterior walls, load-bearing members of roof
  Structural defects
Functional obsolescence–curable[a]
  Crack or failure in foundations having other causes than structural defects or poor workmanship
  Undersized and weak roof members
  Insufficient downspouts and gutters
  Walks and drives not in place or insufficient
  Inadequacy or absence of baths
  Obsolete bath fixtures
  Fixtures or finish below neighborhood standards
  Poor kitchen layout
  Inadequate kitchen cabinets
  Obsolete kitchen fixtures
  Obsolete plumbing and water supply system
  Inadequate plumbing and water supply system
  Inadequate or insufficient heating and ventilating system
  Obsolete heating and ventilating system
  Inadequate electrical wiring
  Outdated electrical fixtures
  Insufficient electrical service
Functional obsolescence–incurable
  Oversized foundations
  Cracked foundations

Table 13.1   Continued

Oversized roof members
Roof covering substantially better than those of neighborhood
Roof covering substantially worse than those of neighborhood
Eccentric trim
Poor workmanship in structural framing, oversized or undersized structural framing
Poor workmanship in floor and roof slabs, oversized or undersized floor and roof slabs
Overimprovement or poor quality of workmanship in finished floor
Poor quality and workmanship in walls
Poor quality and workmanship in trim
Bath fixtures above neighborhood standard
Kitchen equipment above neighborhood standard
Plumbing and water supply system above neighborhood standard
Superadequacy in heating and ventilating
Superadequacy in electrical wiring
Garage too small or superadequate
Architecture poor or unusual—bad floor plan, excessive ceiling height, poor plot plan
Overadequacy or underadequacy of capacity of plant
Excessive wall thickness
Any functional characteristic of a building which has become nonfunctional by reason of new materials, new techniques, or decreased costs, such as ventilation furnished by monitor roofs prior to the economic feasibility of mechanical ventilation systems
External Obsolescence
Architectural overimprovement or underimprovement for neighborhood
Nuisances such as smoke, dirt, noise, odor, traffic, zoning, change in use, rent control, excessive taxes, and inadequate transportation, shopping, schools, and parks
Local, regional, and national legislation

aThese items are curable only if economically justified. Therefore, economic feasibility is the crucial test, not physical possibility.

Physical Deterioration–Curable

Under this heading, based on careful and detailed inspection, a listing is made of all deferred maintenance and repairs necessary to bring the structure into first-class operating order. The test of curability is based on (1) necessity to cure defects to provide for efficient (economical) operation, and (2) the cost to cure relative to value added or the increase in net operating income for the property as a whole. Provision is also made for depreciation reserves necessary to cover anticipated expenditures for capital items and major units of maintenance which must be replaced or refurbished periodically. The latter items include heating, roofing, plumbing, electrical wiring, and periodic painting and refinishing of exterior and interior surfaces. Prices for maintenance and repair work need to be obtained from service personnel and subcontractors who typically engage in this type of work. (For illustration of this and other sections of the observed depreciation schedules, see Table 13.4.) In addition to deferred maintenance which requires immediate attention, another form of curable physical deterioration is *curable postponed*, which is measured as a percentage of cost new.

Physical Deterioration—Incurable

Under this part of the depreciation schedule, an attempt is made to measure the accrued loss in dollars due to wear and tear of long-lived structural load-bearing parts of the building improvements. Since the supporting parts of a structure such as footings, foundations, and supporting walls and partitions are economically as well as mechanically incurable (without tearing the building down) the appraiser must establish a pro rata estimate of the expired portions of the various substructures in relation to their total unit replacement cost—in place. This can be accomplished by one of two alternative suggested methods:

1. The overall component value method.
2. The individual component value method.

Under the overall component value method, the appraiser applies the estimated accrued percentage loss of the substructural component parts to the replacement cost estimate of such parts as shown in Table 13.2.

The individual component method is similar to the method above except that it applies a depreciation rate to each of the components considered. Often, this method is applied only to short-lived items of a structure. Examples are roofing, carpeting, electrical, plumbing and the mechanical parts of heating and air-conditioning systems. Using the information above plus data on short-lived items, this method might appear as shown in Table 13.3.

Table 13.2 Overall Component Value Method

Component—Structural Parts	Replacement Cost	
Excavation	$1,200	
Footings	2,400	
Walls	9,900	
Partitions	3,600	
Roof construction	2,100	
Beams and joints	2,850	
Piers	660	
Total		$22,710
Add: 8% Architectural costs		1,817
12% Overhead and profit		2,725
Total components replacement costs		$27,252
Estimated observed incurable physical deprecia- tion 15%[a]		$ 4,088

[a]Based on ratio of effective age to normal life span of building improvements.

Table 13.3 Individual Component Value Method

Component– Structural Parts	Replacement Cost	Effective Age	Normal Life Span	DETERIORATION	
				Percent	Dollars
Excavation	$ 1,200	9	60	15	$ 180
Footings	2,400	9	60	15	360
Walls	9,900	9	60	15	1,485
Partitions	3,600	9	60	15	540
Roof construction	2,100	9	60	15	315
Beams and joists	2,850	9	60	15	428
Piers	660	9	60	15	99
Roof cover	1,450	10	20	50	725
Heating–air conditioning	2,600	8	15	53	1,378
Carpeting	2,000	10	12	83	1,660
Total replacement cost	$28,760				
Total physical deterioration–incurable					$7,170

As demonstrated, the direct component value method of measuring accrued physical deterioration–incurable and the liability to replace methods can be effectively applied as measures of physical–incurable depreciation.[4]

Functional Obsolescence–Curable

Under this heading, the appraiser lists recommended modernization and improvements which are essential and economically justified (or feasible) and which would be found in a new and comparable building. Into this category generally fall expenditures for modernization of bathrooms, kitchen, insulation, central heating, additional closets, and other built-in fixtures. Whether such improvements are warranted and thus curable depends on market demand and on compliance with the principle of contribution. Cost estimates to cure items subject to modernization are obtained from building contractors or subcontractors who specialize in the areas of construction involved. Care must be taken not to duplicate estimated outlays. If, for instance, it is considered that the bathroom and kitchen are subject to modernization, and the cost of painting and decorating of these rooms is included in the modernization estimate, this expenditure must be excluded from items covered under physical deterioration–

[4]Whichever computational process is employed for measuring incurable physical deterioration, great care must be taken in the selection (estimation) of the total as well as of the remaining economic life of the improvements that are under value study.

curable, under which category repainting of the entire structure may have been called for.

Functional Obsolescence–Incurable

This item of the depreciation schedule rests heavily on the application of sound appraisal judgment. An attempt is made here to reflect the sales resistance encountered from typical buyers as a result of flaws deemed economically incurable such as poor floor planning, lack of privacy, or low ceilings. This sales resistance is generally measured in rounded dollars—$100, $500, $1,000, etc.—or as a percentage of total replacement costs new—1 percent, 5 percent, 10 percent, and so on.

The test of whether a structural component suffers from incurable functional obsolescence is the economic feasibility of taking such corrective measures.

External Obsolescence–Incurable

Losses resulting from external obsolescence are always caused by forces outside of the structure and within the immediate or market environment of the property. Since the typical property owner cannot control these outside forces, the resultant losses are classified as "incurable." The economic loss ascribable to the subject location, as compared with an ideal, like a neighborhood free from such environmental hazards or nuisances, is determined by capitalizing the actual or estimated rental or income loss through the use of a rent multiplier for residential buildings (see Chapter 10) or through the use of the capitalization process for income-producing properties as explained in Chapter 18. Since the schedule of depreciation should aggregate losses ascribable only to the building improvements, care must be taken to exclude losses attributable to the land. This is accomplished by multiplying the capitalized income loss (depreciation) resulting from external forces by the typical ratio that building improvements bear to the value of the property as a whole, including the land. To do otherwise would penalize the land twice—once here and again under the market comparison approach to land value, under which the environmental hazard or nuisance would also be reflected. For application of the depreciation procedure to reflect external obsolescence, see the demonstration schedule in Table 13.4.

MARKET EXTRACTED DEPRECIATION

This method accounts for all aspects of accrued depreciation. It might be argued that it is not as precise as the engineering breakdown method. However, in reality it probably is potentially as accurate but offers the advantage of being

Table 13.4 Demonstration Schedule of the Observed Method for Measuring Accrued Depreciation

Building statistics based on field observation indicate the following:

Effective age		15 years
Remaining economic life		35 years
Replacement cost—new		$55,500

Physical deterioration
Curable
Deferred maintenance

Exterior painting	$ 900	
Repair porch screening	120	
Paint kitchen, bath, and hall	360	
Scrape and refinish floors	405	
Replace linoleum in kitchen	240	
Total deferred maintenance		$ 2,025

Postponed

Roof shingles 20% of $1,050	$ 210	
Interior painting 40% of $750	300	
Heating unit 40% of $1,125	450	
Plumbing and wiring 20% of $1,800	360	
Total reserves for replacement		$ 1,320

Incurable

Based on overall component method	$ 4,088	
Total physical deterioration		$ 7,433

Functional obsolescence
Curable

Modernize bathroom (exclusive of painting)	$ 660	
Insulate ceiling	345	
Total functional–curable		$ 1,005

Incurable
Sales resistance due to low 7.5-foot ceilings and poor floor plan
(lack of privacy in bedroom areas) 10% of cost to replace

Total functional–incurable		5,550
Total functional obsolescence		$ 6,555

External obsolescence
Incurable
Rental loss due to heavy traffic and road hazards and noise
$45 per month. $45 times monthly rent multiplier for area =
$45 × 135 = $6,075
Ratio of land value to property value is 17 percent. Loss of
rental value attributable to building is 83% of $6,075

		5,042
Total estimate of accrued depreciation		$19,030

Percent accrued depreciation
$19,030 ÷ $55,500

		34.29%

Table 13.4 Continued

Value via depreciated cost approach		
Estimated replacement cost new (buildings)	$55,500	
Less accrued depreciation	19,030	
Depreciated replacement cost		$36,470
Add: Land value by market comparison		9,000
Walks and driveway		300
Landscaping		450
Total value via cost approach		$46,220
Rounded to $46,200		

market derived and easily understood by clients. This method is particularly well adapted to larger projects where a large number of similar properties are being appraised.

The steps in this method are outlined below.

1. Locate, throughly inspect, and confirm sales of comparable improved properties.
2. By use of lot sales, estimate the value of each underlying site; this value is deducted along with the estimated value of minor site improvements.
3. Compute the area of each sale building and then estimate the current reproduction or replacement cost.
4. Deduct the sale price allocated to the building from the current construction cost; this difference is the total accrued depreciation.
5. Divide the total accrued depreciation by the reproduction (or replacement) cost of the building to find the overall rate of depreciation.
6. Divide the overall depreciation rate by the physical age to give the annual rate of depreciation. This annualized depreciation should be applied only to properties of similar age and physical characteristics.

This method is illustrated below:

1.	Sale price	$100,000
2.	Less site value (and minor on-site improvements)	20,000
	Building value	$ 80,000
3.	Current reproduction cost (2,800 sq ft at $50/ sq ft)	140,000
4.	Total accrued depreciation ($140,000 − $80,000)	60,000
5.	Overall rate of depreciation ($60,000 ÷ $140,000) =	42.86%
6.	Annual rate of accrued depreciation (42.86% ÷ 17 years) =	2.52%

DEPRECIATION ESTIMATES: THEIR LIMITS OF USE

Fortunately for the professional appraiser, estimating accrued depreciation directly is usually of secondary importance.[5] In fact, depreciation cannot accurately be determined until value is known. Then, by comparing present worth with estimated cost new, the amount of accrued depreciation is fixed with certainty. However, this "back door" approach fails to reveal the current value of a property. Under the market and income approaches to value, as will be explained in succeeding chapters, depreciation as a separate measure is of little importance. The appraiser's problem is to find the value of the subject property by comparison with comparable properties which have sold in recent times, or by capitalizing the rights to net operating income derived from the subject property over the remaining economic life of the property or some generally accepted holding period. Once this value is found, the appraiser's task is, as a rule, completed. Only where the depreciated cost approach is deemed of importance must accrued depreciation—as a separate calculation—be taken into account. The depreciated cost approach is a most useful tool in the appraisal process, but in the hands of uninformed or unskilled appraisers it can result in grossly misleading calculations. A closing precaution: Use depreciation estimates with care. Apply the observed method for measuring accrued depreciation whenever possible.

REVIEW QUESTIONS

1. Discuss the similarity and differences between accrued depreciation and amortization.
2. List three causes of each of the different forms of accrued depreciation. How do you think a prospective property owner or tenant would account for each of these deficiencies in terms of rent or sales price?
3. For investment purposes why is economic life more important than physical life?
4. Compute the value of a property with a lot worth $15,000; current replacement cost is $120,000; effective age is 15 years, and remaining economic life is 45 years.
5. What is the principal criterion used to determine whether a building suffers from curable versus incurable physical deterioration?
6. Define and give five examples of functional obsolescence—curable.
7. Outline the steps involved in estimating market value via the engineering or observed method.
8. Find the depreciated cost and dollar amount of depreciation of a comparable sale dwelling based on the following facts: sale price, $125,000; value of site and minor on-site improvements, $28,000; current reproduction cost, $135,000. If the dwelling was built 14 years ago, what is the annual depreciation rate?
9. A real estate investor sold two parcels of property; one was an office building for which she received $175,000 and on which she made a capital gain of 25

[5]The relative merits of the depreciated cost approach, covered in Chapter 12, should be reviewed now.

percent; the other was an apartment building for which she received $175,000 and on which she suffered a loss of 25 percent. How much did the seller gain or lose? Show all computations.

READING AND STUDY REFERENCES

AMERICAN INSTITUTE OF REAL ESTATE APPRAISERS. Chapter 20, "Accrued Depreciation," *The Appraisal of Real Estate*. Chicago: AIREA, 1983.

CORGEL, JOHN B., and HALBERT C. SMITH. "The Concept of Economic Life in the Residential Appraisal Process: A Summary of Findings," *The Real Estate Appraiser and Analyst* 48, no. 4 (Winter 1982), pp. 4–11.

EPLEY, DONALD R., and JAMES H. BOYKIN. Chapter 5, "Estimate of Value by the Cost Approach," *Basic Income Property Appraisal*. Reading, Mass.: Addison-Wesley Publishing Co., Inc., 1983.

GORDON, WILLIAM S. "Incurable Functional Obsolescence due to the Lack of an Item: Is It Possible?" *The Real Estate Appraiser and Analyst* 48, no. 2 (Summer 1982), pp. 32–35.

HARPS, WILLIAM S. Chapter 15, "Value Analysis: The Cost Approach," *The Real Estate Handbook*, Maury Seldin, ed. Homewood, Ill.: Dow Jones-Irwin, 1980.

HEALEY, F. H. "Does the Cost Approach Suffer from Obsolescence?" *The Real Estate Appraiser* 36, no. 7 (November–December 1970), pp. 44–45.

KIRBY, THOMAS R. "Functional Obsolescence: The Nemesis of the Demonstration Report Writer," *The Real Estate Appraiser and Analyst* 47, no. 2 (Summer 1981), pp. 19–21.

WELDRON, WILLIAM D. "Toward an Honest Cost Approach," *The Appraisal Journal* 39, no. 3 (July 1971), pp. 370–73.

14

INCOME FORECASTING AND ANALYSIS

Learning Objectives
After reading this chapter, you should be able to:

Sense the fallacy of using average rather than actual income in estimating value

Understand why typical management is assumed in conducting market value appraisals

Appreciate the necessity of recognizing the probable future income pattern for both comparable and appraised properties

Distinguish between potential gross income and effective gross income

Be aware of the need for the appraiser undertaking a comprehensive lease analysis

Recognize different conditions that can distort rental income

One of the basic characteristics that a commodity must have to possess value is *utility*.[1] Everything else remaining equal, the greater the utility, the greater the value. One of the best measures of utility is the amount of income or rental which a property can earn or command in an open and competitive market for the space facilities it offers at a given time and place.

As emphasized previously, valuation, especially under the capitalized income approach, necessitates a determination of an estimate of the present

[1]Utility as used here refers to the power of a good to satisfy human wants or to render service or to produce income to its owner. See pages 6–8 for a discussion of value characteristics.

worth of future rights to income. The term *future* in this definition of value imposes on the appraiser an obligation to forecast with reasonable accuracy the pattern of income expectancy that may be anticipated over the remaining economic life of the subject property, or in most instances, a shorter holding period. Forecasting in any enterprise is fraught with hazards, as is testified by the thousands of business failures and bankruptcies reported every year. But forecast the appraiser must, or change to another profession in which he or she can search the annals of history, looking backward with reasonable certainty rather than forward into a realm of economic uncertainty. Every business venture requires prediction of future operations, and every property is improved in anticipation of estimated revenue from rental or owner use.

The quality of prediction of an anticipated income flow varies directly with the proximity of future estimates to the date of the appraisal. As a rule, income for the year ahead can be established with a high degree of certainty. Income for the second, third, and fourth years ahead can be forecast with reasonable dependability; but thereafter, and to the end of the economic life of a property (extending up to 50 or more years) the accuracy of the forecast becomes tenuous. Fortunately, under the capitalization process the early and relatively accurate years of income forecasting are accorded substantial weight in the valuation process, with the importance of latter years diminishing as indicators of value. To illustrate this point, let's assume that two properties, *A* and *B*, are estimated to yield equal annual net operating incomes of $1,000 each, but that property *A* has an economic life of 50 years and property *B*, one of 100 years. At 8 percent interest, applying the present worth of an annuity of 1,[2] property *A* is worth $1,000 × 12.233, or $12,233, while property *B* is valued at $1,000 × 12.494, or $12,494. The difference is $261, or approximately 1 percent of the value of property *A*. In this instance, a 100 percent difference in the span of the economic life causes no practical impact on the value estimate of the two properties as a direct result of the discounting process.

ACTUAL VERSUS AVERAGE INCOME

Reliance on *average* rather than on *factual* anticipated income may, under the income approach to value, result in substantial errors in the appraisal estimate. This is clearly demonstrated in the analysis of two income producing properties as shown in Table 14.1.

In this illustration two income-producing properties with identical total and average incomes were discounted over a period of 10 years to a sum of present worth at a rate of 10 percent interest. Property A, with a total income of $5,500, and an average income of $550 ($5,500 ÷ 10), yields a capitalized value of $2,903.56. Property B, though experiencing the same total and average

[2]Present and future worth functions are covered in detail in Chapter 17.

Table 14.1   Analysis of Present Worth of Two Income-Producing Properties—Having Identical Total and Average Incomes—Under Divergent Income Assumptions

Years	NET INCOME		Present Worth Factor 10 Percent	PRESENT VALUE	
	Property A	Property B		Property A	Property B
1	$ 100	$1,000	0.9091	$ 90.91	$ 909.10
2	200	900	0.8264	165.28	743.76
3	300	800	0.7513	225.39	601.04
4	400	700	0.6830	273.20	478.10
5	500	600	0.6209	310.45	372.54
6	600	500	0.5645	338.70	282.25
7	700	400	0.5132	359.24	205.28
8	800	300	0.4665	373.20	139.95
9	900	200	0.4241	381.69	84.82
10	1,000	100	0.3855	385.50	38.55
Total	$5,500	$5,500		$2,903.56	$3,855.39
Average	550	550		100%	133%

income—but derived from a reversed income experience, as compared with property A—yields a present worth of $3,855.39, or a sum over 30 percent greater than that derived from property A. The difference in valuation is a direct result of the nature of the income flow and the degree of time preference expressed in the rate of capitalization. A dollar due one year from today has a greater value than one due ten years from today because the early dollar may be put to work for a period of nine years, and the wages which this capital amount earns are reflected in the higher present value.[3] The difference in value estimate of the two diverse income-producing properties will vary directly, of course, with the rate of capitalization employed in the income approach—increasing with higher rates, and decreasing with lower rates until equality in present worth is reached at a rate of zero percent.

It may be argued that the illustration offered is extreme in nature and that it does not conform to general practice or experience. Perhaps so. But insistence on the use of unweighted income averages in the process of capitalization is dangerous and may, as demonstrated, result in a substantial error in the value estimate. It is well to keep in mind that as a rule realty, because of its heterogeneous nature and fixity of location, varies in revenue productivity and hence in quantity and quality of income flow. Some income from realty is ascending because land and, indirectly, its improvements are ripening into higher use. Other properties may exhibit declining yields due to transition into lower uses, particularly during the last stages of their economic life cycle.

[3]This example introduces the discounted cash flow concept which will be developed more fully later in the book.

MARKET VERSUS CONTRACT RENTS

Too much importance is often placed, especially by amateur appraisers and "guesstimators," on past or present income or lease commitments. The present, it must be remembered, is merely a fleeting moment dividing the past from the future. Properties may be underimproved, overimproved, or faultily managed, or income may be attributable to personal skill or business operations rather than to the property itself.

It is the appraiser's duty when seeking market value to evaluate a property as if owned under fee simple title, free from all encumbrances except for use limitations imposed by public authorities and deed restrictions shown on public records. The property, too, must be considered in the light of its earning capacity in conformity with the principle of highest and best use. After value under these normal conditions has been established, appropriate adjustments should be made to reflect economic advantages or disadvantages ascribable to limited contractual agreements or temporary managerial operating policies.

Market rent, which should form the basis of value, is defined as *that amount of rent the appraised property probably would command at the date of appraisal.* It may be revealed by rentals being paid for similar space.

Market rent may also be thought of as the "ought to" rent; that is, the rent that the appraised property ought to bring in the current market. *Contract rent,* on the other hand, is that rental income ascribable to the property as a result of contractual commitments which bind owners and tenants for a stipulated future time. As stated, this contract rent may be greater or lesser than the prevailing market rent under the highest and best—and legally permissible— use of the property.

IMPORTANCE OF TYPICAL MANAGEMENT

All property must be considered to be under some form of management, either by the owner himself or by a professional manager. In either case, operating expenses must reflect a charge—whether or not incurred—for the expenditure of time and effort customarily employed in operation and property supervision. Such managerial costs, as will be shown in the following chapter, are generally considered a percentage of revenue and vary from 5 to 10 percent of realized revenues or rent collections.

In forecasting income, it is important to consider property productivity under the operation of *typical* management. To do otherwise would ascribe to the property a value that is influenced by personal characteristics of the management. By *typical* management is meant that which most frequently prevails in the ownership and use of given types of properties. Income considerations, too, are based on typical future managerial practices. This does not mean that effects of past managerial control and operation which linger on are not to be considered under the income approach to value. Exceptional management during past years may, like business good will, be the cause of surplus income extending over two or more years depending on the degree of exceptional property maintenance and the amount of excess rentals under existing lease terms. *Excess rent* is defined as the amount that contract rent exceeds market rent. Poor management during past years, on the other hand, may burden future operation as a result of deferred maintenance, or may reduce income because of unfavorable tenant commitments such as rental concessions.

ESTIMATING THE QUANTITY OF INCOME FLOW

The amount of income, all else being equal, will vary with the quantity or volume of land and its improvements. Industrial property offered under land use contracts will produce revenue in proportion to the number of square feet of area offered for lease. The presence or absence of railroad siding, highway access, and proximity to market and to community facilities will affect directly the quantity of payments offered per unit of space. The unit of income and value for commercial property is based on the number of either square feet or front feet of land in the property—depending on business use and land location—and the number of square feet of building area contained within the improvements. Apartment buildings produce revenue on a per room or per apartment basis depending on local market customs. Single residences are rented on a "property" basis of stated dollars per month. The amount of revenue generally varies with the size of the building, quality of construction, neighborhood, location and site characteristics, and amount and quality of furnishings and fixtures. The procedure for adjusting the estimated income of a subject property by analysis of income derived from comparable but dissimilar properties will be explained below in connection with the preparation of a rental schedule.

Income takes different patterns, as will be discussed later in the section "Future Payment Provisions." These patterns may be level, straight-line change, step-up or step-down variable such as in a percentage lease, or may occur at the end of a holding period when the property is sold and the seller receives the net proceeds from the sale. The appraiser's initial task is to recognize and forecast the future income pattern that the appraised property will probably experience. This task becomes complicated for a large multitenant office building where rents vary by size and location of space within the building and according to lease termination dates. An electronic spreadsheet can be especially helpful with this task. Next, he or she must be prepared to convert the forecast income pattern into an estimate of present value. The latter topic will be covered in a subsequent chapter.

Attention is also called to the fact that income generally declines as building age advances. It stands to reason that, per space unit (all other things remaining equal), more will be offered for a property in its early, or prime of, economic life than for a similar property in the middle or late period of its economic life. How to adjust for anticipated decline (or rise) in the revenue flow is a controversial matter. Many appraisers follow teachings that advocate the selection of a higher rate of amortization under the straight line method of capital recapture to compensate for loss of revenue due to property aging. Based on an investment of $100,000, a remaining economic life of 20 years, a 10 percent annual rate of return, and straight line amortization at 5 percent per year, computations for declining income are demonstrated below. The formula used for computing the annual income decline under the method demonstrated below is

$$\Delta I = \frac{R \times D}{R + D}$$

Investment beginning of first year	$100,000	
Income during first year:		
10% annual return on $100,000		$10,000
5% recapture on $100,000	5,000	5,000
Remaining investment	$ 95,000	
Total income first year		$15,000
Investment beginning of second year	$ 95,000	
Income during second year:		
10% annual return on $95,000		$ 9,500
5% recapture on $100,000	5,000	5,000
Remaining investment	$ 90,000	
Total income second year		$14,500
Investment beginning of third year	$ 90,000	
Income during third year:		
10% annual return on $90,000		$ 9,000
5% recapture on $100,000	5,000	5,000
Remaining investment	$ 85,000	
Total income third year		$14,000

In this equation, R is the interest rate and D the rate of recapture. Substituting the rates used above, the percentage annual income decline is found to be

$$\frac{0.10 \times 0.05}{0.10 + 0.05} = \frac{0.0050}{0.15} = 0.0333 \quad \text{or} \quad 3.33\%$$

The logic employed to forecast the amount of depreciation or appreciation to offset an anticipated loss or rise in the flow of income appears highly questionable. Extreme care must be taken in forecasting future changes in income patterns as a basis for judging the present worth of a property. A fundamental question is: How can future income be more accurately predicted than the present rent or value of a property? The selection of the appropriate rate of future depreciation or appreciation must be based on the characteristics of the property, its quality of construction, and market practices for depreciation in typical use. The rate of amortization logically has no relationship to the quantity, quality, or pattern of the income stream. Since the value formula is designated as $V = I/R$, where I represents capitalizable income and R the rate of capitalization, it is mathematically incorrect and logically indefensible to adjust the denominator in an equation (the rate of capitalization in this instance) to reflect anticipated changes (decline of income) in the numerator. Furthermore, an income decline based on an equal percentage curve suggests a precision in income forecasting that is insupportable in the light of real estate market operations. If the income flow—on the basis of study of similar properties—is expected to change, then it is the appraiser's clear-cut responsibility to forecast the pattern of this change and to capitalize the changing returns accurately and professionally. Often, too, attempts are made to stabilize future returns by arithmetic averaging. Such a procedure is both unscientific and unrealistic, since early dollar returns under discounting procedure have greater weight in relation to present value than equal dollar returns in late property life.

It is possible, however, to stabilize accurately a declining income stream implicit in the straight line method of capitalization, to derive a present value equivalent to that of an ordinary annuity by use of the following formula:

$$I\left(\frac{1/a_n}{i + D}\right)$$

where

$$
\begin{aligned}
I &= \text{first year income} \\
1/a_n &= \text{annuity rate of capitalization (reciprocal of Inwood factor)} \\
i &= \text{effective interest rate} \\
D &= \text{annual straight-line rate of recapture}
\end{aligned}
$$

Example: An income of $1,000 per year declining under straight-line assumption over a period of 40 years at 7 percent interest equals a value of

$$\$1,000 \div 0.095 = \$10,526$$
$$(0.07 + 0.025)$$

To stabilize this income stream, we derive a ratio by the formula noted above as follows: $\$1,000 \times (0.075 \div 0.095) = \$789.47.$[4] Thus whether we

---

[4]This amount was derived with the aid of the formula above as follows:

$$\frac{I}{13.33171} \div (0.07 + 0.025) = 0.075009 \div 0.095 = 0.78947$$

$$\$1,000 \times 0.78947 = \$789.47$$

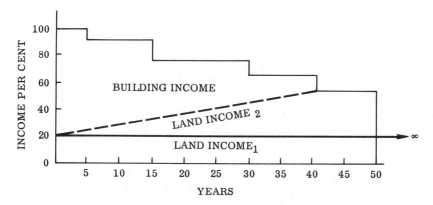

Figure 14.1 Typical Income Flow for an Apartment Property Over an Economic Life Period of 50 Years

capitalize a declining income beginning with $1,000 under the straight-line method or capitalize a stabilized income of $789.47 under the annuity or Inwood method of capitalization the answers are identical. To prove:

1. Straight-line capitalization: $1,000 ÷ 0.095 = $10,526.
2. Inwood method of capitalization: $789.47 × 13.33171 = $10,525.

An early and noteworthy attempt to measure income decline by classes and kinds of real property was made by Frederick M. Babcock in *The Valuation of Real Estate.*[5] The reader is referred to Chapter 27 of this book for an excellent discussion of the development of income decline premises. In practice, the mathematical theory underlying Babcock's premises proved difficult to explain and more difficult for practitioners and laymen alike to understand. Consequently, little is currently known—and still less is applied—of Babcock's declining income premise findings. A more direct and mathematically less cumbersome method of accounting for income flow variations is explained below.

Study of income behavior of various types of properties over past years should enable an appraiser to forecast income expectancy as affected by building age and the space competition of new construction. The diagram shown in Figure 14.1 illustrates an anticipated income pattern of a 16-unit apartment building in a moderate-size commercial community.

This diagram, supported by income experience data of comparable buildings, indicates that earnings on completion of improvements and full occupancy will remain stable for an operating period of about five years. Building age and obsolescence as well as anticipated building competition are expected to cause a decline in building income at that life stage of approximately 10 percent. Income at this lower level is expected to prevail for a period of another 10 years, at which time continued obsolescence and space supply competition

[5]Frederick M. Babcock, *The Valuation of Real Estate* (New York: McGraw-Hill Book Company, 1932).

will cause a further drop in income of about 15 percent, or to a level of 75 percent of the income earned during initial years of property life. This level of income expectancy, as shown, is to prevail for a period of 15 years, or until at building age 30 (midlife). At this time, and again at building age forty, a decline of 10 percent, respectively, is anticipated in rental receipts. The income level during the last, or late building life, period is at a rate of 55 percent of the amount earned during the early years after building completion. Had the market land rent risen as shown by the dashed line instead of remained stable, the economic life of the building would have been shortened. In this example, the building life would have been reduced from 50 years to 40 years.

To capitalize this changing income flow does not require special mathematical skill or the use of special capitalization tables. Each level of future income is merely converted into a sum of present worth and discounted to the date of the appraisal. The recommended procedure for capitalizing this declining and rising income will be demonstrated and explained in Chapter 18.

The accurate construction of a schedule of anticipated income, on which the value of a property is to be based, is a responsibility which the appraiser cannot evade by hiding the process of income forecasting behind a straight-line method of capital recapture. For long-lived properties the application of straight-line accounting to appraisal theory becomes increasingly more difficult to justify, especially in the light of ever more sophisticated market investment practices.

QUALITY AND DURATION OF INCOME

The value of property varies not only with the quantity or amount of dollars, but also with income quality and its duration. The quality of income generally is dependent on the kind and character of tenants, the type of long- or short-term leases, the degree and extent of space competition (both current and anticipated) over the economic life or holding period of the subject property, and the stability of economic conditions in the subject market area. As a matter of practice, differences in the quality of income among properties should not be reflected in upward or downward adjustments of the amount of anticipated income. Quality differentials should rather be a matter for separate and analytical considerations in the selection of the applicable interest rate at which the net income flow is to be capitalized. The analysis and correlation of market rates of interest for purposes of selecting or constructing rates of capitalization will be demonstrated and discussed in Chapter 16.

The duration of income is directly proportional to the remaining useful or economic life of the land improvements.[6] The income attributable to land

---

[6]The remaining economic life employed here should be the same as that used for estimating accrued depreciation in the cost approach.

under fee simple ownership is sometimes thought to extend into perpetuity. In actuality, it has generally been found to rise over a period of time. Improvements, however, are subject to physical wear, tear, and the forces of obsolescence, and income to be derived from employment of depreciable assets will cease when their value reaches zero. In predicting the economic life span of property improvements, the appraiser must consider.

1. The physical and functional characteristics of the building improvements.
2. The external economic forces which operate on the demand side for the kind of utility or amenity offered by the subject improvement.

The physical characteristics set the outer limit of duration of useful life. Therefore, the type of architecture, the quality of materials used, the workmanship employed, and the physical conditions of maintenance and repair must be considered in establishing the maximum number of years of utility life. More important as a mortality factor, however, are the environing economic forces which bring about building obsolescence. Otherwise identical improvements will have different economic lives depending on their location within or among communities. In rapidly growing cities, building obsolescence is accelerated as a result of important changes in land use and consequent significant increases in land value. For example, the 100 percent business location in a city may shift a distance of several blocks as a result of new and redevelopment construction activity. The impact of the automobile, community decentralization, development of suburban shopping centers, and location of new industries in suburban areas are largely responsible for shifting land values and increased economic mortality of building improvements in central business locations.

Where buildings are relatively new, errors in the prediction of remaining building life have a generally minor effect on the overall estimate of total property value. This is true for two reasons: first, because of the relatively minor weight given to the value of distant future income in the discounting or capitalization process; and second, because increased building obsolescence has historically been accompanied by rising land values which often more than compensate for the economic sacrifice of remaining building life. Where buildings are in middle or late life, however, an error in the anticipated duration of income may importantly affect the value estimate. To predict accurately remaining economic building life requires judgment based on intimate knowledge of community and neighborhood forces affecting property value, as detailed in Chapters 6 and 7. It is for this reason, among others, that property appraising as an applied art is largely limited to local practitioners who keep their fingers on the economic pulse of their community. Also, the difficulty of accurately making such long-term forecasts is another reason that appraisers often prefer using a shorter holding period that reflects investor practices.

RENTAL SCHEDULE CONSTRUCTION AND ANALYSIS

In forecasting income for existing or proposed properties, the appraiser must look to the market for income experience data of properties comparable to the one under appraisal. Through cooperating broker-appraisers or property management firms, it is possible to secure rental amounts paid on a per room, per apartment or square-foot basis for residential properties, and a square-foot or front-foot basis for commercial or business properties. With the aid of this information, the appraiser can construct a rental schedule which—after adjustments for differences in building age, construction, and attributes of neighborhood, location, and site facilities—can serve as a basis for rental estimates of the subject property.

Rental schedules for the various units of space to be offered are most realistically established on a market comparative basis. This is effectively done by rating the subject property in relation to like properties in similar neighborhoods for which accurate rental data are available. The comparison approach, though simple in application, relies on sound judgment for effective use. Comparison is generally made with a number of typical space units, and price adjustments for the subject property are based on quantitative and qualitative differences. For example, in the pricing of an apartment unit consideration should be given to the following: area of floor space, number of bathrooms, quality of construction, amount of decorative features, efficiency of interior layout, type and quality of elevator service, nature and quality of janitorial services, reputation of the building, adequacy of on-site parking, recreational facilities, and characteristics of tenants. In addition, the location of the building in relation to public conveniences and the quality rating of neighborhood and trends must both be considered. Assuming that a standard unit in an ideal neighborhood rents for $400 per month and the comparative rating for the subject property is 90 percent, then the estimated fair rental is judged to be $360 per month. If a detailed comparison is made for each space unit with four or more selected and comparable units, a fairly accurate and reliable rental schedule for appraisal purposes can be established.

LEASE ANALYSIS

The ability to conduct a comprehensive lease analysis is an essential skill that should be mastered by any competent appraiser. This analysis can become quite tedious for a large multitenant office building such as that depicted in Figure 14.2. Investors generally ascertain the strength of each tenant and his or her obligation to pay rent for a specified term. When sophisticated owners and tenants understand the intricacies of an executed lease agreement and the ap-

Figure 14.2 High-Rise Office Building (Courtesy of Federal Reserve Bank of Richmond)

praiser only knows the property rents for so many dollars a square foot, then the appraiser is incapable of providing a fully informed service.

For an appraiser to understand completely the responsibilities of the parties to a lease and be able to accurately note exactly how much a tenant pays, he or she must study the executed lease, accompanying exhibits, and any amendments. Some of the major lease provisions that affect the amount paid by tenants are covered in the following examples. One of the first chores to be undertaken by the appraiser is to array the leases according to expiration dates. This will show the distribution of rental revenue according to date of lease, the percentage increase in rentals, as well as the rents paid by the most recently made leases.

Area of Leased Premises

Different classes of buildings and those in different regions tend to be measured differently. The following examples will demonstrate the importance of the appraiser fully understanding how the demised premises are measured.

Otherwise, the income applied to the appraised property probably will either be under- or overstated.

1. A multitenant office building with several tenants on a given floor would probably have the rentable area exclude exterior and corridor walls as well as public washrooms, halls, stairways, elevator, and mechanical shafts.
2. For a tenant occupying an entire floor, the area might be computed as within the exterior walls but exclude areas common to other tenants, such as elevator and stairway space.
3. If the leased area is computed from exterior walls, the *building efficiency* or ratio of occupied space to gross area becomes a consideration.
4. It is possible for one office building to include exterior wall dimensions in computing leasable square footage where area for offices in another building may include one-half the thickness of exterior or interior partition walls.

Factors Influencing Rental Levels

In addition to carefully ascertaining the actual leased area for the comparable and appraised properties, the appraiser should be aware of other conditions that distort rentals. The following list contains examples of some conditions that, if not recognized by the appraiser, could result in an erroneous income being applied to the subject property:

1. Part of the rental income diverted away from the lessor may go to the mortgagee as the result of a participation loan. Thus consider rent paid rather than net rent received by owner.
2. Tenant improvements may cause an apparently low rental.
3. Managerial competence can affect the level of vacancies, income, expenses, and maintenance.
4. Netness of leases and expense "stops" can give the illusion of different rental levels.
5. Concessions given up by either the lessor or lessee can affect rental levels. Examples are radius requirements or special features being provided by the lessor such as free draperies.

Netness of Lease

Every lease is different. Nevertheless, the appraiser should be familiar with certain generalized leasing practices. For instance, short-term leases (up to one year) tend to be gross leases. This means that the owner pays all the operating expenses. At the other extreme, the expense burden tends to shift from the owner to the tenant for long-term leases (in excess of five years). Although the following schedule does not hold true in all cases, it outlines the conventional means of identifying expense responsibilities under leases.

Type of Lease	Expense Responsibility
Gross	Owner pays all expenses.
Net	Tenant pays all or part of future real estate tax increases after the base year.
Net net	In addition to taxes, the tenant pays all or part of insurance expenses; these premiums may be plate glass, boiler, fire, and extended coverage or public liability.
Net net net (also called absolute net)	In addition to taxes and insurance, the tenant agrees to pay all or part of the maintenance costs, which may be interior, exterior, or both.

Never should the appraiser assume that he or she understands "who pays what and when" or the netness of a lease simply from the interviewed party stating that it is a net or some other type of lease. Sometimes a net lease is confused with an absolute net lease.

Future Payment Provisions

A truism in commercial property is that virtually every lease is different. This section presents the basic ways that lease payments are structured. It should be remembered, however, that a lease may combine several of these future payment clauses. Most of the following payment provisions are included to minimize erosion in the owner's profits after the initial year of a multiyear lease.

Flat rental. This type of lease typically is used for small commercial properties and apartments. It usually is for a one-year term. To extend the fixed rental beyond one year is inequitable for either the owner or the tenant. This type of lease, which at one time enjoyed wide use and popularity, has come—at least for long-term leasing—into gradual disuse. The reason, no doubt, is the steadily declining purchasing power of the dollar. Whereas in selling a property the owner can reinvest his or her equity in another type of property, in a lease payments are due over a series of future years, and—where rentals are fixed in amount—a declining dollar value deprives the property (or fee) owner of a fair return in proportion to the value of his or her property as measured in terms of constant dollars.

Graded rent clause. This multiyear lease actually is a series of flat rental payments, rising in stair-step fashion as shown on the next page. Thus it sometimes is called a step-up lease. This form of lease is intended to give the land user an opportunity to lighten operating expense burdens during the early formative years of his or her business enterprise and to give the landlord an opportunity to participate in future business growth through successively higher rental payments. Such lease agreements must be cautiously evaluated, since excessive rental payments historically have proved a prime cause of business failure and resultant bankruptcy.

Occasionally, it may be fashioned in a step-down manner for a property that is losing its appeal or for one in a deteriorating neighborhood. A variation of this lease is one where future-year payments are scheduled to increase by a predetermined percentage amount.

Years	Monthly Rental
1– 5	$1000
6–10	1200
11–15	1500
16–20	1800

Index clause. This provision allows the owner to enjoy the benefits of inflation by having rentals track some specified price index, such as the Consumer Price Index. Rental income is periodically adjusted in accordance with such a published index. Tenants sometimes criticize this rent adjustor because it bears little relationship to actual building operating costs. An example of an index clause follows.

> . . . commencing on the first year of the renewal term and yearly therafter shall be $15,152.17 (for improvements) plus an amount determined by multiplying the sum of $53,060.00 by a fraction, the numerator of which shall be the Consumer Price Index for the last month of the previous lease year, and the denominator of such fraction shall be the Consumer Price Index for March 1985 (when original lease began), less one-half of the increase over $53,060.00. In no event shall the application of the Consumer Price Index reduce the monthly rental to be paid during the extended term below $4,421.67.

Escalator clause. An escalator clause increases the tenant's operating expense burden. Conversely, it arrests the amount of expense paid by the owners. Hence it is sometimes called an "expense stop" and was previously covered in the discussion of netness of leases. Often, the tenant will require that a ceiling be placed on the amount of expenses shifted to him or her from the owner. An example of a real estate and utility expense stop for an apartment project follows.

> The tenant agrees that the monthly rent stipulated in the lease shall be adjusted to reflect any increase in the cost to the landlord for increases in real estate taxes and utilities. The cost shall be prorated monthly one-two hundred and twenty-ninth of the cost increase to the project.

Percentage clause. This type of rent provision usually applies to retail businesses, including restaurants. It is made up of two parts: (1) base rent and (2) percentage rent. Ordinarily, the base rent will be paid regardless of the volume of the tenant's business. The percentage rent, as shown in the following example, varies according to the level of the tenant's sales. The appraiser should disregard any potential income from percentage or overage rentals unless there is convincing evidence provided by operating histories of the subject or similar retail businesses. Percentage rentals may range from as low as 2 percent of gross sales for department stores or supermarkets to as high as 75 percent for parking lot operations.

Minimum annual rental:

Year	Rental
1	$22,800
2	24,000
3	25,200

Plus percentage rental at 5½% of gross annual sales in excess of:

Year	Gross Annual Sales
1	$414,545.45
2	436,363.64
3	458,181.82

Also includes as additional rental common area maintenance and merchants' association promotion fund.

Sale and lease-back. The "sale and lease-back" contract agreement has gained wide popularity with owners of large industrial and commercial properties. Under this form of agreement the owner, in return for full value, conveys title to his or her property by deed to a real estate investor or an institutional lender—generally an insurance company or pension fund—and leases back the property for a long term.

Under provisions of the lease the former owner becomes the lessee and agrees to pay a net rent as well as all operating expenses, including taxes, insurance, maintenance, and essential replacements.

The sale and lease-back transaction has many advantages as a mode of real estate ownership and tenant operations:

1. The seller (user of realty) obtains the full cash value of the property which, as a rule, is twice the amount that could be obtained under mortgage financing and this without the burdensome provisions of mortgage debt clauses and the possible threat of foreclosure in case of nonpayment of interest or principal.
2. The seller is able to reinvest the cash in his business enterprise in which as a "specialist" he has greater skill to increase net operating earnings. The sale, too, increases flexibility of capital investment and mobility of the enterprise in case expansion or relocation becomes necessary.
3. The seller, often, secures substantial tax advantages. If the sale yields a price less than book value of the property, the loss can be reflected in income tax reporting. Also, the entire amount paid for rent becomes a business expense,

whereas under mortgage borrowing only the interest portion of the debt and accrued depreciation are tax-deductible items.

The purchaser also gains advantages which make the sale and lease-back transaction financially profitable to her:

1. Since the lessee assumes all operating expenses and burden of management, the net income (rent) provides a rate of return generally more favorable than that obtainable under a mortgage debt in investment.
2. Equity ownership provides an excellent hedge against inflation. If the property enhances in value during its investment life, it is the investor who will benefit in the long run.

The advantages to buyer and seller under a sale and lease-back transaction as outlined above are not all-inclusive, but are sufficiently substantial to make consideration of this type of real estate financing worthy of serious and profitable consideration.

OWNER'S INCOME STATEMENTS AND ADJUSTMENTS

In the appraisal of existing properties from which income experience data is obtainable, it is customary to request that the owner furnish an operating statement for at least three years previous. This statement can then be analyzed and reconstructed in conformity with income expectancy under typical managerial operating care and sound appraisal practices.

The income data supplied by the owner are generally labeled *as reported*. The average shown for the three-or-more-year income period is then modified to reflect typical operations, and the amounts used for appraisal purposes are labeled *as adjusted*.[7] Where adjustments reflect more than the rounding of dollar amounts, it is essential that a full explanation be given in the body of the valuation report or added as a footnote. Typical adjustments may show rental income for the owner- or janitor-occupied apartment, or they may reflect increases or decreases in existing rentals where such rentals are out of line with market rental comparisons.

Owners' statements also generally reflect rentals on an as-is basis and thus include built-in vacancies and rent-collection losses, if any. To indicate operation under typical management, it is preferable to estimate gross revenue collectable under 100 percent occupancy and then to subtract for normal vacancy and collection losses that prevail for this type of property in the community market area. Generally, vacancy and collection deductions are calculated as a percentage of gross revenue, varying from a minimum of 2 percent to as high as 50 percent in summer resort areas. In college town or neighborhoods, where

[7]See Chapter 15 for suggested method to adjust reported operating incomes and expenses.

school enrollment declines during the summer months, vacancy ratios in apartments that cater to students and faculty personnel must be calculated to indicate *realizable* rather than *potential* income.

In appraisal terminology, the amount left after deductions for vacancy and collection losses are made is referred to as *effective gross revenue*. Even in rare instances where owners report no vacancies or collection loses over past years, the appraiser must provide for such contingencies in accordance with typical loss ratios reported for similar properties in the community. The exception, of course, would be where an entire property is under firm lease to a responsible tenant over a period of years.

In forecasting income for capitalization in the determination of value of proposed construction, or in the determination of land value under a hypothetical highest and best use, care must be taken to account for land income and capital investment losses (income forgone) during the period of construction. The present worth of such losses, discounted at the rate of interest applicable to the type of property, must be subtracted from the present worth of estimated future income to derive a net value as of the date of the appraisal. Consideration, too, must be given to high vacancy ratios during initial months or years of the property's operation. Typical sound management calls for careful tenant selection, and larger office and business properties may require periods of two or more years to reach full occupancy. Such revenue losses also must be accounted for in the valuation process via the income approach.

INCOME ADJUSTMENT FOR CHANGES IN THE PURCHASING POWER OF THE DOLLAR

Fortunately for the real estate appraiser, the anticipated income stream forecast over the economic life of a property need not be adjusted for possible changes in the purchasing power of the dollar. As previously indicated, future income, through the process of capitalization, is converted into a sum of present dollars for which the property is to be exchanged in the open market. Assuming freedom from mortgage debts and other financial encumbrances as well as freedom from restrictions on income such as rent control, a property is deemed competitively free to adjust itself to future changes in the purchasing power of the dollar. However, in a study of income performance over many past years, or in accepting the historical income flow of similar properties as a guide to the forecasting of an anticipated income flow for a given property, it is necessary to adjust past income to reflect changes in the purchasing power of the dollar. This can readily be done with the aid of price level indices published by the U.S. Bureau of Labor Statistics. Thus a rising income stream over thirty or more elapsed years may actually, after dollar purchasing power adjustment, disclose a declining trend in real operating income. Care must be taken, however, to restrict the use of dollar purchasing power adjustment factors to past income only. Where future income is sluggish in adjusting itself to market dollar forces of inflation or deflation—as in the case of long-term lease arrangements—it is best to reflect this rigidity in income flow as a factor of negative income quality, and to adjust the rate of capitalization by an appropriate increase in the risk factor component of the rate of capitalization. A study of the income-to-price relationship of similarly afflicted properties will disclose directly the rate of capitalization applied by investors to like properties in the open market. For a full discussion of the derivation of the capitalization rate, the reader is referred to Chapter 16.

REVIEW QUESTIONS

1. Define market and contract rent. Under what conditions may they be equivalent?
2. Using the equation

$$\Delta I = \frac{R \times D}{R + D}$$

   compute the annual income decline when $R = 10\%$ and $D = 2.5\%$.
3. Review Figure 14.2 and explain how rising land income and declining building income can shorten the remaining economic life of a building.
4. List at least five items that should be considered by an appraiser in deriving market (economic) rent for an apartment property.
5. Why should the appraiser recognize unusually high vacancy levels during the "rent-up" period for new properties if a 3 to 7 percent vacancy level can be expected a year after completion?
6. How can a failure to account accurately for the actual leased area for comparable rental properties distort the economic rental used for the appraised property?
7. Give the general expense responsibility pattern between lessor and lessee for short- and long-term leases.
8. How can a knowledge of future payment provisions in leases improve the accuracy of an appraisal report?
9. Brown bought a building from which he anticipates, at the time of purchase, $8,000 in net operating income (per annum). Ten years later, having maintained the building in full repair, his operating income remained at $8,000 per annum. He anticipates the same level of income throughout the future service life of this building. Has the passage of time, assuming all other things remain equal, affected the value of this building? Explain.
10. Why must the appraiser under the income approach to value consider past managerial practices? Explain.
11. In the valuation process what significance should the appraiser attach to (a) present income, (b) past income, and (c) anticipated income?

READING AND STUDY REFERENCES

BOYKIN, JAMES H. "Future Payment Clauses" in "Lease Financing," Chapter 19, *Financing Real Estate*. Lexington, Mass.: D. C. Heath and Company, 1979, pp. 495–500.

BOYKIN, JAMES H. Chapter 12, "Property Income,"

The Real Estate Handbook, Maury Seldin, ed. Homewood, Ill.: Dow Jones-Irwin, 1980.

ELLWOOD, L. W. "The Income Forecast: Straight Line or Curve?" *The Appraisal Journal* 39, no. 2 (April 1971), pp. 51–55.

FRIEDMAN, JACK P., and NICHOLAS ORD-WAY. Chapter 8, "Income Estimating and Forecasting," *Income Property Appraisal and Analysis*. Reston, Va.: Reston Publishing Co., Inc., 1981.

HALLOCK, JAMES A. "Lease Analysis and Appraisal Review," *The Appraisal Review* 39, no. 3 (July 1971), pp. 338–45.

SHIPP, ROYAL. "Property Income Streams—Measuring and Evaluating Their Size and Certainty." *The Appraisal Journal* 38, no. 3 (July 1970), pp. 357–75.

SINGER, BRUCE. "New Methods of Income Analysis," *The Appraisal Journal* 39, no. 3 (July 1971), pp. 327–37.

WENDT, PAUL F. "Inflation and the Real Estate Investor," *The Appraisal Journal* 45, no. 3 (July 1977), pp. 343–55.

15

OPERATING EXPENSE FORECASTING AND ANALYSIS

Learning Objectives
After reading this chapter, you should be able to:

Distinguish between income deductions and operating expenses

Understand how net operating income can and sometimes needs to be derived for an appraised property without having the actual real estate taxes

Be familiar with the major published sources of income–expense data for different types of real estate

Reconstruct an owner's operating expense statement

Discern the difference between capital and operating expenditures

Understand the pros and cons of using reserves for replacements and be familiar with several ways of setting up such reserves

The development and use of the gross income multiplier (see pages 182–186) seems to bypass completely the need for operating expense forecasting and analysis. Professional appraisers nevertheless should not neglect this important phase of the income approach to value. Further study of the reasons first noted in Chapter 10 will disclose that failure to analyze expense schedules and operating property performance may be the cause of substantial errors in the final estimate of value. Moreover, it is not always possible to use the GIM due to lack of comparable sales and rental data.

The apparent neglect of operating expense data and their analysis is accounted for by acceptance of the belief that properties of given classifications— residential, apartment house, office buildings, and so on—are characterized by similar expense-to-income ratios. To assume this is to ignore differences in types of buildings, quality of construction, building volume, age of improvements, architectural design, building features, vacancy ratios, location characteristics, and types of tenants. Since net operating income is the basis of value, under the income approach, failure to forecast anticipated operating expenses accurately is bound to be reflected in grossly unreliable appraisal reporting.

INCOME DEDUCTIONS VERSUS OPERATING EXPENSES

An understanding of accounting procedure proves helpful in identifying and classifying expenditures which are personal in character, or which are of the nature of income deductions as opposed to expenditures that are essential to the operation of a property. Confusion often arises because of differences in treatment of certain expenses under conventional profit and loss accounting as compared with income and expense classification of expenditures for appraisal purposes. To illustrate: Two of the most important outlays incurred in connection with ownership of real property are (1) mortgage interest and mortgage amortization payments, and (2) allowances or expense charges for investment losses due to depreciation (amortization) of the property. There is no question concerning the fact that under conventional accounting both of these expenditures—i.e., mortgage interest as well as depreciation charges—are costs of ownership. But in the appraisal of real property, mortgage interest charges are considered operating costs only when evaluating the *equity* (i.e., the owner's interest in the property exclusive of the mortgage lien). When borrowing funds, an investor, as a rule, engages in *trading on the equity*. Under such circumstances he finds it profitable to borrow funds at interest rates lower than the property is expected to earn as an operating entity. In deriving gains from interest differentials between the rate of property earnings and the cost of borrowing money, the owner is assuming investment risks for which—if his efforts are successful—he is being duly compensated. But such financial dealings are personal in character (a business venture within itself) and must be classified as income deductions and not as expenditures essential to the operation of a property. A commodity, as has been pointed out in foregoing chapters, can logically have only one value based on f.o.b. delivery at a given time and place. The price of a given commodity may and generally does vary with the terms and conditions of sale; but commodity value must necessarily and consistently be measured in relation to net income derived under typical management, free and clear of all encumbrances, including mortgage liens.

Once the value of a property has been established, free and clear of all encumbrances, due price allowance must be made for favorable or unfavorable terms of sale which attach to the subject property. Because of the importance of "tax shelter" opportunities that enable an owner to convert operating net income into a category of long-term capital gain which for individuals is taxed at a maximum of 40 percent the rate applicable to earned income, a separate chapter will deal exclusively with equity financing and the methods by which equity yields realized can be computed under varying assumptions and conditions. More and more the tax bracket into which individual investors fall influences their price decisions personally and the market value of income-producing properties which attract given classes of buyers, generally. For more on this subject, the reader is referred to Chapter 21.

INCOME TAX AND PROPERTY TAX CONSIDERATIONS

Personal and corporate income taxes, too, must be excluded as costs of operation. Income tax payments vary with the income brackets into which the taxable earnings of individuals and corporations fall. Such payments are important to a purchaser of property and may influence his decision as to whether to buy a given property; but the value of the commodity (property) must be found free and clear of such variable and personal considerations. Otherwise, the art of real estate appraising would lose its general applicability as a guide to market value. That is, market value would vary according to the particular financial status of each prospective purchaser.

Real estate (property) taxes are correctly classified as an operating expense. The omission of property taxes would overstate the net operating income used for capitalization purposes and, as a consequence, the answer sought in the valuation problem. On important occasions, however, the value to be used for tax purposes is at issue, as in the case of a *tax certiorari* proceeding.[1] To include as an operating expense a tax payment made on what is believed to be an excessive assessment would lower both net operating income and value, as compared with the market value that would prevail under equalized tax assessment practices. Where value for tax purposes is at issue—and this is an exception rather than a rule—property taxes as an amount can also be excluded from the operating expense schedule, and taxes as a rate (percent per hundred dollars of assessed value) can be added to the rate of capitalization. In such instances the appraiser must not put into the problem an operating expense amount which depends on the value sought. Thus, if the rate of capitalization is 8 percent and the rate of taxation based on market value is 20 mills, or 2 percent, value for tax purposes can be derived by capitalizing net operating income before property taxes by a combined rate of 10 percent. This method also is applicable for proposed construction where the real estate taxes are unknown. Suppose, for instance, that the forecast net operating income (excluding real estate taxes) for a proposed property is $28,000 annually. Further, the market-derived overall

---

[1] If an owner believes that the assessed value of her property is too high, and is unable to secure a reduction upon protest to the tax officials, she can appeal to the courts. Such a court case is known as a *certiorari* proceeding.

capitalization rate is 12 percent. If the tax rate is 2 percent, the estimated value is as follows:

$$\$28,000 \div 0.14 = \$200,000$$

The application of a *certiorari* tax valuation problem will be demonstrated in connection with problem 10 at the end of the chapter.

CLASSIFICATION OF OPERATING EXPENSES

In nearly all appraisal assignments it becomes necessary to reconstruct operating expense schedules and to adjust—over the forecast income period—expenditures in accordance with those estimated to be incurred under typical management and operation. This requires knowledge of property care and maintenance, as well as the analysis of operating performance of comparable properties in similar locations.

Operating expense schedules generally are arranged to provide for recording of costs under the following headings:

1. Fixed charges.
2. Variable expenses.
3. Reserves for replacements.

Fixed charges are those which as a rule vary little, if at all, with occupancy from year to year. In this category fall property taxes and insurance for fire, theft, and comprehensive hazards.

Variable expenses include expenditures for periodic maintenance, management, janitorial care, heating, utilities, repairs, and miscellaneous building supplies.

Reserves for replacement cover outlays on a pro rata basis of the estimated service life of furnishings and fixtures. For instance, if an apartment building contains 20 refrigerators each having an estimated service life of 10 years, the reserve for replacement in this case would call for expense provision equal to costs of two refrigerators annually. Similarly, if each of the 20 apartments is decorated once every fourth year, annual provision would include the cost of 20 divided by four—or five apartments typically during any one year. Where exterior fronts, roofing, and plumbing are replaced at service-life intervals, like provision would be made, generally on a straight-line accounting basis.

It is recommended that operating expense schedules be reconstructed in accordance with the accounting procedure followed by a group such as the National Association of Building Owners and Managers. This permits comparison of expense estimates with those typically incurred for similar properties and as reported annually by the Association in its *Building Experience and Exchange*

Reports, available through the Washington office of the Association. A listing of several income–expense sources is listed at the end of this chapter. Cost comparisons for office buildings can readily be made from these reports on a per-square-foot basis of rentable space for the following items:

> *Operations:* Cleaning; electrical system; heating and ventilating; plumbing system; elevator; general expenses for offices; and general expenses for the entire building.
>
> *Construction:* Alterations; repairs and maintenance; and decorating costs.
>
> *Fixed charges:* Fire and other hazard insurance; taxes; and depreciation. Allowance for depreciation, although not used as an expense in the capitalization process, gives a clue to the length of economic lives of buildings, as well as to the methods and market rates of depreciation employed under typical management.

A good source for apartment income–expense data is the *Income/Expense Analysis—Apartments,* which is published annually by the Institute of Real Estate Management. This publication presents trends in apartment building operations and includes income and operating cost data and tenant turnover data for various types of apartment buildings by selected metropolitan areas, region, and by age. An example of an income–expense presentation is shown in Table 15.1.

Typical income and operating expenditures for garden apartment buildings, based on an annual survey by the Institute of Real Estate Management, are classified by square feet of rentable area and median percent of gross possible total income in Table 15.1.

For operating expense data and comparative performance statistics of hotels, informative reports are published by Harris, Kerr, Forster and Company, accountants and auditors.[2]

Detail data for major cities are given for average hotel expenditures as follows:

> Administrative and general expenses.
> Payroll taxes and employee benefits.
> Advertising and promotion.
> Heat, light, and power expenditures.
> Repairs and maintenance.
> Replacements, improvements, and additions.

This report provides statistics for 1,000 hotels and motels in the United States. This publication emphasizes trends of hotel and motel income and expenses, earnings on capitalization, occupancy ratios, room rates, and disposition of the hotel dollar. These facilities are analyzed according to type and operations, showing 20-year trends. For purposes of hotel and motel appraising, this pub-

---

[2]*USA Edition 1983, Trends in the Hotel Industry* (Houston, Texas: Harris, Kerr, Forster and Company).

Table 15.1 Comparison of Median Income and Operating Costs for Garden Apartment Buildings Unfurnished, United States and Canada, 1983

	Med. $/sq ft (Rentable Area)	Med. Percent of GPTI
Income		
Rents		
Apartments	4.79	97.6
Garage/parking	0.07	1.5
Stores/offices	0.06	1.4
Gross possible rents	4.81	97.8
Vacancies/rent loss	0.23	4.7
Total rents collected	4.44	92.7
Other income	0.11	2.4
Gross possible income	4.94	100.0
Total collections	4.59	95.3
Expenses		
Management fee	0.23	4.8
Other administrative	0.28	5.7
Subtotal administrative	0.50	10.2
Supplies	0.02	0.4
Heating fuel		
CA only	0.04	0.9
CA and apartments	0.31	6.4
Electricity		
CA only	0.08	1.7
CA and apartments	0.24	4.6
Water/sewer		
CA only	0.09	1.7
CA and apartments	0.13	2.7
Gas		
CA only	0.03	0.7
CA and apartments	0.14	2.6
Building services	0.05	1.1
Other operating	0.02	0.5
Subtotal operating	0.50	10.2
Security	0.02	0.3
Grounds maintenance	0.09	1.9
Maintenance–repairs	0.21	4.4
Painting/decorating	0.11	2.2
Subtotal maintenance	0.44	9.2
Real estate taxes	0.33	7.0
Other tax/fee/permit	0.01	0.2
Insurance	0.06	1.2
Subtotal tax–insurance	0.41	8.5
Recreational/amenities	0.02	0.5
Other payroll	0.23	4.8
Total all expenses	2.06	41.9
Net operating income	2.33	48.5
Payroll recap	0.43	8.8
Number of buildings in sample	2,926	2,971

Source: *Income/Expense Analysis—Apartments* (Chicago: Institute of Real Estate Management, 1984), p. 32.

lication offers important statistical data which are most useful in a study of comparative income and expense performance.

OPERATING EXPENSE SCHEDULE RECONSTRUCTION

An owner's typical expense statement for a 20-unit apartment house may contain information as shown in Table 15.2. A reconstructed owner's operating expense statement for appraisal report analysis and valuation of the subject property is presented in Table 15.3. The reference numbers noted in the reconstructed operating expense statement are a guide to explanatory footnotes as follows:

1. Revenue was adjusted upward in the amount of $3,900 to include rental value of $325 per month for an apartment occupied by the resident janitor.
2. Vacancy and collection losses, based on a community rental study and records of the local board of Realtors, typically amount to 5 percent of gross income at 100 percent occupancy. This rental loss was provided to cover vacancy contingencies over the forecast income period for the property.

Table 15.2 Owner's Operating Expense Statement for the Year 19—

Revenue			$74,100
Operating expenses:			
Taxes		$7,500	
Insurance			
Fire	$900		
Theft	150		
Liability	120		
		1,170	
Maintenance			
Janitor—exclusive of apartment		3,000	
Heat—oil		3,600	
Water		450	
Electricity		675	
Repairs—miscellaneous		600	
Elevator—contract		1,200	
Replacements			
1 refrigerator		750	
1 stove		1,200	
Decorating—six apartments		2,700	
Mortgage—interest		1,800	
Amortization		1,500	
Paving assessment		3,000	
Depreciation		6,675	
Total operating expenses			$35,820
Net operating income			$38,280

Table 15.3 Reconstructed Operating Expense Statement for the Year 19—

	As Reported	As Adjusted	Reference
Potential gross income	$74,100	$78,000	1
Vacancy and collection losses 5%		3,900	2
Effective gross income		$74,100	
Operating expenses			
Fixed expenses			
Taxes	7,500	7,500	
Insurance	1,170	1,425	3
Maintenance costs			
Management 6%		4,446	4
Janitor	3,000	6,900	5
Heat	3,600	3,600	
Water	450	450	
Electricity	675	675	
Miscellaneous—supplies		300	6
Elevator—contract service	1,200	1,200	
Miscellaneous—repairs	600	2,340	7
Replacements			
Refrigerators	750	1,400	8
Stoves	1,200	700	9
Decorating	2,700	2,250	10
Roof replacement		1,800	11
Plumbing and electrical		3,600	12
Furniture—lobby and halls		600	13
Other expenses	12,975		14
Total operating expenses	$35,820	$39,186	
Net operating income	$38,280	$34,914	15

Operating expense ratio $39,186 ÷ $74,100 = 53%

Operating expense ratio (using PGI) $39,186 ÷ $78,000 = 50%

3. Insurance coverage was increased to 80 percent of coinsurance requirements.
4. Management costs for comparable properties equal 6 percent of effective gross revenue (sometimes called collectible rent). Subject building is owner-managed.
5. Janitorial expenses were adjusted to include cost (income forgone) of apartment furnished for his use.
6. Miscellaneous supplies for cleaning were estimated at a cost of $15 per apartment.
7. Miscellaneous repairs increased to equal typical expenditures estimated at 3 percent of potential gross income.
8. Refrigerator expenses adjusted to provide for two per year. Service life is 10 years, or 20 ÷ 10 = 2.
9. Stove replacement adjusted to provide for purchase of two per year.
10. Decorating expenses were adjusted to provide for refurbishing each apartment once every four years at a cost of $150 each.

11. Roof replacement required once every 20 years at a cost of $36,000 (5 percent of $36,000 = $1,800).

12. Plumbing and electrical replacements based on the service life of fixtures of 20 years, or 5 percent of $72,000 = $3,600.

13. Lobby and hall furnishings at a cost of $6,000 are replaceable every 10 years, or at a cost of $600 per year.

14. Other expenses shown in the owner's statement were omitted as follows:
    (a) Mortgage interest and amortization payments are income deductions, not property expenses. Financing arrangements benefit the owner and not the subject property.
    (b) Paving assessments are capital improvement outlays which increase the value of land.
    (c) Depreciation is included as a rate of return to the property owner in the building rate of capitalization. To include it here would provide a dual return.

15. It is recommended that the net operating income used be that income expected for the appraised property as of the date of appraisal. Operating expenses should be as of the same date. Use of "stabilized net operating income" is an unclear concept since it may be for the early years of a loan, the typical investor's holding period, or for some other future period.

RESERVES FOR REPLACEMENTS

This is a troublesome part of the appraisal process. In this section the issues are explored and the relative merits of the different ways of handling this phase are presented. Each reader will need to decide on the most applicable handling of replacement reserves. The opposite positions on this issue are:

1. (*Pro*) Any wasting asset with a useful life less than the remaining life of the building will need to be replaced—maybe more than once. If the operating expenses fail to recognize these future expenses on an annualized basis, the net operating income and in turn the appraised value of the property will be overstated.

2. (*Con*) Most investors do not include an entry for replacement reserves. In fact, one study revealed that 58 percent of real estate investors did not include such provision for replacements.[3] This argument goes on to say that if investors do not recognize this future expense in their statements, but only pay for such replacements when they occur, then appraisers are not faithfully representing the real estate market when this "artificial" entry is made in their appraisal reports.

One point certainly is clear: Appraisers should know whether income-expense records for comparable income and sale properties either include or

---

[3]Robert H. Zerbst and Gary W. Eldred, "The Specification of Net Operating Income," *The Real Estate Appraiser and Analyst* 45, no. 6 (November–December 1979), p. 43, citing Kenneth M. Lusht, *The Behavior of Appraisers in Valuing Multifamily Property*, unpublished report sponsored by the Society of Real Estate Appraisers Foundation.

exclude replacement reserves. Ignorance of this information will distort the expense ratio, net operating income, and appraised value of the subject property.

If replacement reserves are included, there are three basic ways of handling them.[4]

Method 1. Identify the short-lived items that must be replaced during the remaining economic life of the building; determine how many times the item will need to be replaced; estimate its cost; determine the total cost; and finally determine the annualized average replacement cost as follows:

Item	Expected Life (Years)	Number of Replacements	Cost per Replacement	Total Cost	Average Replacement Cost
Roofing	20	2	$5,000	$10,000	$200[a]

[a]$10,000 ÷ 50 years.

Method 2. It can be argued that method 1 is illogical since it places as much weight on an item to be replaced in 40 years as one requiring replacement in 20 years. Thus a more appropriate means would be to recognize the time value of money by finding the present worth of these future replacements via the sinking fund factor. This process only considers the first replacement, but it could just as well include the present worth of subsequent replacements. Applying a 10 percent discount rate to the example above produces the following annual roofing replacement reserve requirement, which is considerably less than by the previous method.

Item	Expected Life (Years)	Cost of Replacement	Sinking Fund Factor	Annual Requirement
Roofing	20	$5,000	0.017460	$87.30

Method 3. Consistent with the trend of analyzing income streams over typical investors' holding periods, it seems reasonable to forecast reserve replacements over a like period instead of the remaining economic life of the improvements. It seems far more reasonable to include income, expenses, and reserves over a 5- to 10-year holding period than to go beyond this time frame. Why include a replacement reserve for 20 to 40 years if the investor will likely sell it prior to the end of this longer period. To make the inclusion of these reserves even more realistic, a sinking fund method is preferable to an average annual cost method. This method then would exclude such longer-life items as a 20-year roof, but include replaceable building components.

[4]For more detail, see Jay C. Troxel, "Replacement Reserves Reviewed," *The Real Estate Appraiser* 40, no. 5 (September–October 1974), pp. 44–47.

Item	Expected Life (Years)	Cost of Replacement	Sinking Fund Factor	Annual Requirement
Refrigerators	7	$3,500	0.105405	$368.92

For greater accuracy in appraisal reporting and to provide assurance that income and expense forecasting reflects feasible performance capacity of the subject property, it is recommended that the appraiser analyze, whenever possible, income and expense accounting statements for a period of at least three full years. Income or expenditures in any one year may not prove to be indicative of normal operations. Analysis of several years of property operating performance will enable the appraiser to "normalize" operating expense trends and to forecast with greater accuracy the anticipated income stream for the forecast income period of the appraised property.

THE SIGNIFICANCE OF OPERATING EXPENSE RATIOS

Although revenue and operating expenses are independently estimated, a definite relationship exists between them. The amount of rental income for given types of properties varies directly with the amount and quality of services, furnishings, and facilities offered the tenants. Increased revenue from superior conveniences and amenities provided occupants is in turn based on higher operating outlays to supply these services. Characteristically, however, while gross revenue rises and falls in proportion to percent of occupancy, operating expenses are relatively inflexible. Property taxes and insurance payments do not diminish, even where the property at times is 100 percent vacant. Heating, cooling, and janitorial services, too, remain relatively constant. Except for managerial service cost—which is considered a percentage of the effective gross revenue—other expense charges are relatively inflexible.

The inelasticity of operating expenses impairs the quality of net operating income which is derived from properties with high operating expense ratios. To illustrate: Suppose that two properties, A and B, each yield a net operating income of $20,000 as follows:

	Property A	Property B
Effective gross income	$100,000	$40,000
Operating expense	80,000	20,000
Net operating income	$ 20,000	$20,000

Property A, as shown, has an operating ratio (operating expenses divided by effective gross revenue) of 80 percent. The operating ratio for property B is 50 percent. A decline in gross revenue of only 10 percent will, for property A, cause a decrease of 50 percent in the available net operating income. A decrease of 20 percent in revenue will wipe out property A's net operating income entirely. Property B, however, will experience a much less drastic decline in its net income. A decrease of 10 and 20 percent in revenue causes only a drop of 20 and 40 percent, respectively, in the net operating income of property B. High operating ratios thus impair the quality of anticipated income. Increased risk of operation as measured by high operating ratios necessitates, as will be explained more fully in the following chapter, a selection of a higher rate of capitalization—which in turn results in a lower value estimate of the property. Everything else remaining equal, the income stream of $20,000 from property B is worth more than the identical income anticipated from property A, the difference in value being a direct reflection of the investor's unwillingness to gamble with economically sensitive income returns.

Knowledge of typical operating expense ratios is helpful in judging efficiency of operating performance. If typical residential properties indicate prevailing operating ratios between 35 and 45 percent of effective gross income, an operating ratio of 55 percent for a subject property should be cause for inquiry to ascertain the reason for such poor performance. Many factors such as poor construction, mismanagement, and neighborhood decline may underlie the increased economic hazards reflected by the excessive operating ratio.

Typical operating expense ratios for various types of properties may fall into the following percentage ranges:

Residential, single-family structures	35–40%
Apartment buildings—walk-up	40–50%
Apartment buildings—automatic elevator	50–60%
Apartment buildings—manual elevator	55–65%
Office buildings	40–50%
Store and loft buildings	50–60%

These expense ratios vary from area to area with local rental customs and community building use regulations. Like other rules of thumb, operating ratios should not be used as a prime measure of value, but rather should serve as an indicator to judge the reasonableness of the results obtained through reconstruction of owner's income and expense operating statements. An excessively high—or unusually low—operating ratio may be a warning sign that reanalysis of income–expense data is warranted to safeguard against errors through acts of omission or commission.

Several caveats are in order regarding use of operating-expense ratios. First, the appraiser must understand how it was computed for a comparable property. Was it based on the ratio of operating expenses (with or without replacement reserves) to potential gross income or to effective gross income? Once having determined how it was computed, it should be applied to the appraised property in the same manner. For example, if it was based on the comparable property's effective gross income, it should then be applied to the subject's effective gross income. For some buildings, such as office buildings, it may be more accurate to rely on operating expenses per square foot of leaseable area rather than expense ratios.

Without some knowledge of the comparable property, a sizable error could occur when applying the derived operating ratio to the subject property. Some factors that could distort the ratio are:

1. Different building designs can cause different expense ratios.
2. Buildings of different ages or in different locations can experience different income levels but the same square-foot expenses.
3. The netness of leases can alter the share of expenses borne by the lessor and in turn affect the operating expense ratio.

CAPITAL EXPENDITURES

Care should also be taken in the analysis of operating expenses to exclude outlays or investments for capital improvements. Additions of porches, bathrooms, carports, or utility rooms, for instance, increase property value. As a rule improvements of this kind also increase the service utility of the property and produce greater amounts of rentals or amenities to the occupying owner. The test of whether an expenditure is a true operating expense or not rests on the nature of the expenditure and the necessity of the outlay in relation to the operating care and maintenance of the property. Intimate knowledge of operating performance of the various property types for which appraisal opinions are to be rendered is a prerequisite to sound and professional appraisal practice.

REVIEW QUESTIONS

1. List three items that may appear in an owner's income–expense statement that should be disallowed for appraisal purposes.
2. Briefly distinguish between fixed charges and variable or maintenance expenses.
3. List arguments for and against inclusion of reserves for replacements.
4. Prepare an example of how the value of a property can be estimated via capitalized net operating income using the real estate tax rate in lieu of real estate taxes expressed in dollars.
5. Give three ways that an inaccurate operating expense ratio can distort the estimated net operating income of an appraised property.
6. Identify the several methods of setting up replacement reserves. Select a method that you prefer and explain the reasoning for your choice.
7. Two properties have the following income schedules:

	Property A	Property B
Revenue	$100,000	$40,000
Operating expense	80,000	20,000
Net operating income	$20,000	$20,000

Which property has greater value? Why? Explain your reasoning.

8. Based on the facts detailed below, determine via the income approach the value of the apartment property:

1. Building contains 40 apartments renting at $275.00 (average rental) each month. Remaining building life is estimated at 40 years.
2. The land—via market approach—is valued at $120,000
3. Interest rates in the area are 10 percent.
4. The following expenses are listed for the calendar year:

Taxes on land and building	$14,400
Power and light	1,200
Depreciation provision	9,600
Repairs	4,800
Renovating and painting	7,200
Janitor expense	1,200
Extermination	360
Replacements:	
40 ranges (8-year life)	18,000
40 refrigerators (12-year life)	36,000
New roof	6,600
Legal fees	720
Corporation tax	1,800
Income taxes	2,100
Mortgage interest	7,200
Mortgage amortization	6,000
Management fees	7,200
Water	2,700
Fire insurance (three-year policy)	3,600
Paving assessment	2,400
Promotion and advertising	1,500

9. In estimating capitalizable net operating income for office or apartment properties, should depreciation expense be subtracted from effective gross revenue? Explain your reasons fully.
10. A skyscraper office building on Madison Avenue in New York City was assessed for $20,500,000, and the property tax at 30 mills per dollar based on this value was set at $615,000. The owners claimed overassessment and instituted certiorari proceedings to reduce taxes in conformity with fair market value. Assuming a land value of $5,000,000, a net income before interest and amortization but after taxes (as billed) of $1,600,000, a discount rate of 9.0 percent, and an annual recapture rate of 2.5 percent, determine the following:
    (a) The capitalized value of the property.
    (b) Property taxes based on this value.
    (c) Net income after (fair) taxes.

READING AND STUDY REFERENCES

AMERICAN INSTITUTE OF REAL ESTATE APPRAISERS. "Operating Expenses," *The Appraisal of Real Estate*. Chicago: American Institute of Real Estate Appraisers, 1983, pp. 362–383.

EPLEY, DONALD R., and JAMES H. BOYKIN. Chapter 8, "Estimate of Net Operating Income, I.," *Basic Income Property Appraisal*. Reading, Mass.: Addison-Wesley Publishing Co., Inc., 1983.

HANFORD, LLOYD D. "Expense Ratios and Their Use," *The Appraisal Journal* 41, no. 1 (January 1973), pp. 100–103.

HINES, MARY ALICE. Chapter 11, "Income Approach: Estimation of Revenue and Expenses," *Real Estate Appraisal*. New York: Macmillan Publishing Company, 1981.

SLACK, THEODORE C. "How to Find the Real Estate Taxes When You Don't Yet Know the Assessment," *The Real Estate Appraiser and Analyst* 50, no. 3 (Fall 1984), pp. 19–20.

TROXEL, JAY C. "Replacement Reserves Reviewed," *The Real Estate Appraiser* 40, no. 5 (September–October 1974), pp. 44–47.

ZERBST, ROBERT H., and GARY W. ELDRED. "The Specifications of Net Operating Income," *The Real Estate Appraiser and Analyst* 45, no. 6 (November–December 1979), pp. 39–43.

LISTING OF PUBLISHED INCOME–EXPENSE SOURCES

BUILDING OWNERS and MANAGERS ASSOCIATION INTERNATIONAL. *Downtown and Suburban Office Building Experience Exchange Report.* 1221 Massachusetts Avenue, Washington, DC 20005 (published annually by region and selected cities).

INSTITUTE OF REAL ESTATE MANAGEMENT. *Income/Expense Analysis: Apartments.* 430 North Michigan Avenue, Chicago, IL. 60611 (annual operating costs by region, metropolis, and building type).

INSTITUTE OF REAL ESTATE MANAGEMENT. *Income/Expense Analysis: Office Buildings (Downtown and Suburban)* (annual operating data for different categories of building area by national, regional, and metropolitan areas)

INSTITUTE OF REAL ESTATE MANAGEMENT. *Expense Analysis: Condominiums, Cooperatives and PUDs* (annual data on over 40 expense categories; metropolitan, regional, and national statistics).

LAVENTHOL & HOWATH. *Lodging Industry.* 1845 Walnut Street, Philadelphia, PA 19103 (annual income, expense, and profit data).

LAVENTHOL & HOWATH and National Restaurant Association. *Restaurant Industry Operations Report* (annual income–expense data and operating ratios).

NATIONAL RETAIL MERCHANTS ASSOCIATION, CONTROLLERS' CONGRESS. *Department Store and Specialty Store Merchandising and Operating Results.* 100 West 31st Street, New York, NY 10001 (annual merchandising results such as financial ratios, operating data, and merchandising data).

PANNELL, KERR, FORSTER & CO. *Trends in the Hotel Industry International and USA Editions.* 1155 15th Street, NW, Washington, DC 20005 (annual income–expense data and operating ratios by region).

URBAN LAND INSTITUTE. *Dollars and Cents of Shopping Centers.* 1090 Vermont Avenue, Washington, DC 20005, 1984 (published every three years and contains income–expense data by type of shopping center and tenant).

16

DETERMINING THE RATE OF CAPITALIZATION

Learning Objectives
After reading this chapter, you should be able to:

Appreciate the primary motivation for real property being purchased

Recognize and discuss the relationship among the various rates of return

Define and give examples of each rate of return

Compute an overall capitalization rate using any of the different techniques presented herein

Distinguish between interest rates and capitalization rates applied to physical and financial components of real estate.

Develop and properly use capitalization rates applied to net operating income and before-tax cash flow

The most important, perhaps the most controversial, and often the weakest phase of property valuation revolves about the procedure for the determination of a market rate of capitalization through which estimated future net operating income can be converted into an estimate of present value. The rate of capitalization acts as a conversion mechanism to convert periodic income into present value.

The lower the rate of capitalization, the higher the value per dollar of income. The conversion power—as in all interest functions—is geometric in character, as is demonstrated in Table 16.1 by the capitalization of an income of $1.00 at selected rates of interest.

As indicated in Table 16.1, an increase in the rate of interest from 2

Table 16.1 Geometric Impact of Rates of Capitalization on Conversion of Income into Value

Income	Rate (%)	Reciprocal Factor	Value
$1.00	0.01	100.00	$100.00
1.00	0.02	50.00	50.00
1.00	0.04	25.00	25.00
1.00	0.08	12.50	12.50
1.00	0.16	6.25	6.25

percent to 4 percent lowers capitalized value by 50 percent. If 4 percent is the correct rate and 2 percent is used, the increase in capitalized value is 100 percent. Again, the difference between a 5 percent and a 6 percent rate of capitalization is only 1 percentage point; but the value impact of this difference is one-fifth (20 percent) or one-sixth (16.67 percent), depending on which rate forms the correct base for the conversion of income into value.

The basic relationship of income to value through the use of a rate or reciprocal conversion factor is expressed by the formulas $V = I/R$ or $V = I \times F$. To find present value, income is divided by a rate and multiplied by a factor.

In these formulas the symbols used represent the following:

V = present worth of future benefits
I = property income
R = rate of capitalization applicable to the conversion of income (over holding period, limited property life, or in perpetuity) into value
F = reciprocal of rate of capitalization (a convenience factor employed to convert income into value by process of multiplication rather than division; usually, a factor is used to convert gross income to value and a rate is used to convert net operating income to value)

Whenever two of the factors represented by the symbols in the foregoing formulas are known, the third or unknown factor can be calculated mathematically. Thus if value and income amounts are known, the rate of capitalization or the reciprocal rate factor can be calculated by application of the formulas $R = I/V$ or $F = V/I$. Similarly, applicable income is ascertained by use of the formulas $I = V \times R$ or $I = V/F$. Figure 16.1 provides handy memory tools for ready appraisal reference.

Appraisers often spend hours if not days in the analysis of income and operating expense statements in order to derive with accuracy the potential net operating income essential to a measure of market (investment) value. By comparison, relatively little time is employed in the selection of the applicable and essential rate of capitalization even though an error of only 1 percentage point (use of 8 percent in place of a 7 percent rate of interest) causes an error of 12.5 percent in the final estimate of value. It seems advisable, therefore, to spend less time on auditing of minor accounts and more time on the study of market indexes which offer an insight into investors' risk rate motivations.

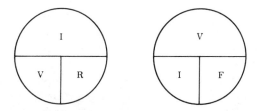

Figure 16.1

Why is it so difficult to derive a correct rate of capitalization? This is a question often raised. The answer evolves about the problems encountered in ferreting out accurate information for objective analysis of the varied and numerous subjective reasons motivating buyers to purchase properties at given prices and times. But even if buyer motives were known, it is still essential to extract reliable and accurate information concerning the net operating income of a subject property.

Generally, real property is purchased for one of the following reasons:

1. *Investment:* In this classification fall all buyers who intend to hold property for its income or, if vacant land, to develop it into an income-producing investment.
2. *Owners' use or pleasure:* Under this category fall homeowners, store owners, and other individuals who acquire property for purposes other than investment or speculation. In such cases property utility in terms of income-producing capacity must be estimated (imputed).
3. *Speculation:* This classification includes those whose principal motive in buying is to profit from the resale of the property at some future time. Properties purchased for speculation, such as vacant land, may produce no income at all; in fact, the income may be negative, in the form of outlays for taxes and related costs of ownership.
4. *Investment and Speculation:* This type of purchase is often motivated by the desire to improve the income tax position of the buyer.

Where speculation or motives other than investment buying are prime reasons for a purchase, the sale price of the property in relation to its income, if any, is of little aid to the appraiser in his or her search for applicable market rates of capitalization. In fact, such sales, if used, may prove highly misleading as indicators of prevailing yields on real estate investment. This can be illustrated by a hypothetical sale as follows:

Suppose that 40 acres of rur-urban property is purchased at a price of $1,000 per acre in anticipation that it will increase to $4,000 per acre in 10 years' time. Suppose, further, that the land is rented for cattle-grazing purposes and produces a rent just equal to taxes and miscellaneous outlays, leaving a zero operating income. Under traditional analysis where the appraiser relates current income to current market prices, the resultant rate of capitalization would be zero since no net income is realized by the purchaser. Should this property, however, sell for $4,000 per acre as anticipated 10 years later, the resultant increment in value represents a yield of nearly 15 percent per annum. Reference to a compound annuity table will confirm that $1.00 invested at 15 percent compound interest will grow to $4.05 in 10 years' time. The necessity to consider both appreciation and depreciation of the investment during the period of ownership is most essential and will be given further and more detailed consideration in Chapter 21.

Most appraisers would find themselves at a loss if the application of the capitalized income approach and the selection of a rate of capitalization had to be substantiated solely by analysis of investment sales in the community. Real estate transactions are traditionally private and confidential in nature and factual income data are often difficult to obtain. More difficult still is selecting those sales that could be usefully employed for statistical income analysis.

Although real estate as a commodity is local in character, the financing and purchase of real estate—both for investment and speculative purposes—have characteristics of a national market. The mobility of credit and the flexibility of investment buying with income reserves and surpluses accumulated by insurance companies, investment firms, and labor union pension funds has—as is the case with "arbitrage" in the stock and commodity markets—channeled funds into community areas where the investment returns in relation to capital risks are highest. The existence of a national real estate investment market makes available for real properties national income and rate-of-return statistics which are compiled by investment firms and real estate analysts. These national indices of investment yields, when adjusted for community and regional risks for given classes of real properties, can be used as effective guides in judging the reasonableness of rates of capitalization secured from market analysis of comparable sales.

Although an appraiser may not readily translate capital market trends into capitalization rates, a familiarity with these markets, inflationary trends, and federal monetary and fiscal policy are desirable to providing astute services to clients. Since institutional investors, such as life insurance companies, are primarily obligated to protect the financial interests of their investors or policyholders, they seek investments that balance risk and yield. As a consequence, they invest in real estate only when it is competitive with stocks, bonds, and securities. Therefore, competition exists between real estate and nonrealty alternatives. If an appraiser is aware of the yields on these alternative investments, he or she has a basis for developing real estate capitalization rates.

Historically, mortgage lenders have sought a "real" earnings rate of about three percentage points over the anticipated rate of inflation. Thus mortgage interest rates ordinarily would be pegged to the *expected* inflation rate. An understanding of inflationary trends as related to mortgage interest rates assumes major significance since most of the capital involved in real estate investments is debt capital. A fairly close pattern generally exists between prevailing mortgage constants and overall capitalization rates. Similarly, since federal monetary policy, as administered by the Federal Reserve System, strongly influences interest rates, it behooves appraisers to be able to anticipate conditions that will probably prompt intervention in the nation's economy by the Federal Reserve System.

TYPES OF RATES OF RETURN

It may prove helpful to enumerate and briefly explain the types of and purposes served by various types of rates in common use today. Appraisers should recognize and differentiate among the following:

1. Interest rate, i.
2. Capitalization rate, R.
3. Overall capitalization rate, R_O.
4. Building capitalization rate, R_B.
5. Land capitalization rate, R_L.
6. Investment recapture, or amortization rate, $1/S_{\overline{n}|}$.
7. Mortgage rate, R_M.
8. Equity dividend rate, R_E.
9. Equity yield rate, Y_E.
10. Property yield, Y_0.
11. Composite rate.

The *interest rate* is in effect a measure of the cost of money and represents "wages" paid for the use of capital. It is a return on the investment and must be high enough to attract capital to a particular kind of investment. The interest rate as here defined is based on the continued and unimpaired existence of the property as an investment entity. The rate does not include any provision for depreciation or recapture. The interest rate is a market phenomenon and varies in amount with the supply and demand of money, and with the quality characteristics of the investment property. The interest rate as a composite annual return per dollar of investment is influenced by the following market forces:

1. Rate of interest on government bonds on guaranteed bank deposits.
2. Burden of management or cost of maintaining the investment, including bookkeeping, collecting, inspection, and fund supervision expenses.
3. Relative liquidity of the investment for conversion into cash.
4. Risk of loss of income and investment due to competition or operation of economic forces as reflected by the position of the business cycle.

The *capitalization rate* expresses in percentage form the relationship between the net operating income of a property and the value or price at which the property sold. The rate of capitalization is always a composite of (1) the rate of interest, and (2) the rate of amortization of the investment when the future value is expected to decline. In instances where the investment or any part of it will maintain its level of value into perpetuity, the rate of amortization for that part or for the investment as a whole, as the case may be, is zero.

The interest rate (or risk rate) and the capitalization rate are often used interchangeably as if their meaning were one and the same. It is this kind of loose thinking which confuses the uninformed and leads to erroneous value conclusions. It is true that in all instances where amortization of the investment need not be provided for, the rate of interest and the rate of capitalization are identical. But even in such cases it is best to be consistent and to speak of a rate of capitalization rather than a rate of interest when converting income into value. The latter term should be used only when reference is made to a return on the investment representing "wages" paid for the use of capital. It would also contribute to clarity of thinking if the term *rate of capitalization*, whenever used in appraisal practice, were modified to indicate whether use is made of this rate as an overall (R_O), a building (R_B), or a land (R_L) rate of capitalization.

The *overall capitalization rate* is a ratio indicating the relationship (R_O) of net operating income of the entire property (land and building) in relation to value or price of the entire property. The overall rate of capitalization is, as a rule, always greater than the land rate of capitalization and less than the building rate of capitalization. To illustrate: If a building valued at $80,000 produces a net income of $9,600, the building rate of capitalization is $9,600 ÷ $80,000, or 12 percent. If the land on which this building stands is valued at $20,000 and yields an income of $1,800, the land rate of capitalization is $1,800 ÷ $20,000, or 9 percent. The overall capitalization rate would be obtained by dividing the combined land and building (property) income by the combined land and building (property) value. In this illustration the overall rate equals $11,400 ÷ $100,000, or 11.4 percent. This overall rate can then be checked by weighting the building and the land (split) rates of capitalization on the basis of a building-to-property ratio of 80 percent and a land-to-property ratio of 20 percent as follows:

Building capitalization rate, 0.12 × 0.80 =	0.096
Land capitalization rate, 0.09 × 0.20 =	0.018
Total property, or overall, rate of capitalization =	0.114, or 11.4 percent

When property income (for both land and building) is converted directly into value by use of an overall rate of capitalization, the method of valuation is called *direct capitalization*. The direct method of capitalization is not recommended for use when other and more precise methods of capitalization, as will be demonstrated in the following chapters, are available. The use of an overall rate assumes that the subject property is identical in building characteristics, building age, and land-to-building value ratio to the comparable properties from which the overall rate was derived. This in practice is rarely the case.

The building capitalization rate is a ratio of building net operating income (R_B) to the value of the building. Since building income must cover both a return on the investment and amortization of the building investment over the remaining economic life of the building or the forecast holding period, the rate of capitalization applicable to the building must also be a composite of a rate on and a rate of the investment. The rate of amortization generally is based on one of the theoretical methods of depreciation explained in Chapter 12. To illustrate: If the rate of interest for a building investment is 9 percent and the rate of amortization is 2 percent (straight-line depreciation based on 50-year remaining life), the building capitalization rate is 9 percent plus 2 percent, or 11 percent. As the remaining building life shortens, the building rate of capitalization will increase—assuming no change in the rate of interest. To illustrate: Where the remaining economic life is estimated at 20 years, the straight-line rate of amortization is 5 percent. This rate, when added to the 9 percent rate of interest, equals a 14 percent building rate of capitalization.

The *land capitalization rate* (R_L) is a ratio of net operating income derived from land to the value or price paid for the land. Where property rights are held in fee simple ownership, income from land is assumed to extend into perpetuity, and no provision need be made for depreciation of the land investment. However, where land is subject to depletion of its mineral or other resources, or where ownership is for a period of years as in a leasehold estate, a rate of depreciation or amortization must be calculated and added to the rate of interest to provide for a return of the land investment over the terminal years of ownership. In some instances, the value of the site is expected to increase over the forecast income period, causing a lowered overall capitalization rate (R_O). In appraisal problems in which the capitalization of land income involves perpetuity, the land rate of capitalization and the land rate of interest are one and the same.

The *amortization rate* $(1/S_{\overline{n}})$ provides for a return or recapture of the investment over the economic life of the property. This is sometimes known as the sinking fund factor and may be applied over a shorter period than the economic life. This annual rate of recapture is based, as a rule, on one of the theoretical, or age-life, methods explained in Chapter 12. The selection of the appropriate rate at which an investment is to be amortized is most important because of the impact that differences in rates have on capitalized value. This is illustrated by the amortization provisions necessary to return an investment over a 25-year-life period under capital recapture methods as follows:

Method	Rate of Amortization
Straight line	0.040
Sinking fund (4%)[1]	0.024

The straight-line method of providing for future depreciation as compared with the annuity method, as shown above, requires nearly two times the dollar provisions necessary under the latter method. Considering the important

[1]See the calculator keystroke sequence in Chapter 17.

differences in leverage that small differences in rates of capitalization cause in the results obtained under the income approach to value, it is evident that the selection of the method and rate of amortization must be undertaken with great care.

In practice, the sinking fund method of capital recapture is rarely used. Where the straight-line method of recapture is applied to reflect a declining income stream over the life of the investment, it is recommended to "stabilize" the declining income and to capitalize under the annuity, or Inwood method, for correctly applied and identical appraisal results.[2] Except for short-lived properties or for provision of reserves for the replacement of furniture and fixtures, the use of the straight-line method of capitalization is not recommended.

The *mortgage rate* (R_M), frequently called mortgage constant, is a term associated with level payment mortgages. It, however, can apply to variable payment mortgages as well. It expresses a constant relationship between annual mortgage payments (including interest and amortization) and the original amount of a loan; an example of this, using dollars, is

$$R_M = \frac{\text{monthly mortgage payments} \times 12}{\text{original mortgage principal}}$$
$$= \frac{\$1,000 \times 12}{\$100,000}$$
$$= 0.1200$$

The *equity dividend rate* (R_E) complements the debt or mortgage rate. Two different equity rates exist and will be discussed at length in Chapter 21. The equity dividend rate is a post-debt service rate, that is, it relates cash flow income to the original equity or down payment made by an investor and sometimes is called "cash on cash."

The other equity rate is the *equity yield rate* (Y_E), which accounts for "cash on cash" plus any forecast future change in value, such as might occur upon sale of the property.

The *property yield rate* (Y_0) equals the overall capitalization rate (R_O) when there is no change in value during the projection period. This rate (Y_0) combines the rate derived from NOI/SP and future changes in value.

The *composite rate of capitalization* is of relative recent origin. This rate is applied in the capitalization of an income stream over a relative short period of ownership of about 10 to 15 years at a preselected yield to the equity owner rather than a rate applicable to the property as an investment entity. The composite rate, as will be more fully demonstrated in Chapter 21, is precalculated to provide the desired equity yield—as influenced by mortgage interest rates and amortization terms, and anticipated percent depreciation or appreciation of the property as a whole over the ownership period. In effect, the equity yield as reflected in the composite rate is that yield or rate of interest at which the

---

[2]See Chapter 14 for the mathematical procedure to stabilize declining income streams.

present worth of the stabilized income stream plus the present worth of the equity reversion at time of sale equals the equity (cash) value of the property, exclusive of the mortgage debt, on date of purchase. Composite rates of capitalization for selected yield and mortgage interest rates over typical mortgage terms and ownership life periods earlier were precomputed and published as "Ellwood tables."[3] Today, similar results are achieved by use of calculators.

CAPITALIZATION RATE SELECTION METHODS

To have any relevance or credibility, rates used to convert periodic income into an estimate of value reliance must be placed on market analysis. To find the basic rate of interest or any of the capitalization rates, the appraiser must analyze market transaction data under one or more of the following rate-selection methods:

1. Banker's rate selection method.
2. Band of investment method.
3. Mortgage terms method.
4. Market extracted capitalization rate.
5. Gross income multiplier derivation of R_O.
6. Overall capitalization rate with different income–value patterns.
   (a) Level income with changing value.
   (b) Straight-line change in income and value.
   (c) Constant income and value change.
7. Market extracted building and land capitalization rates.
8. R_O via simplified mortgage equity analysis.

Banker's Rate Selection Method

An opportune and useful procedure for the selection of interest rates applicable to various classes of property is provided by a back-door approach to investment risk analysis. Investment bankers and lending institutions generally base approval of mortgage loan applications—among other credit requirements—upon favorable and relatively risk-free earning capacity of the property offered as collateral. Depending on the kind and character of the income-producing property—residential, apartment, commercial, industrial, or farm—lenders stipulate the rate of mortgage interest to be charged and set the maximum value of the mortgage loan in relation to guiding safety margins that anticipated earnings must provide as cover for the interest (debt) charges that are due periodically. To assure sufficient income for payment of mortgage interest during the ups and downs of business cycle periods, interest coverage, at certain

---

[3]L. W. Ellwood, *Ellwood Tables for Real Estate Appraising and Financing* (Chicago: American Institute of Real Estate Appraisers, 1977).

loan-to-value ratios, may be set conservatively as follows for different classes of property:

Class of Property	Interest to Be Earned	Loan Ratio (%)
Residential	2 times	75
Apartment	2½ times	70
Stores—100% location	2 times	60
Industrial	3 times	55
Special-purpose	4 times	50

With the aid and knowledge of investment loan practices, the appraiser can derive a rate of interest applicable to a property as a whole as follows: Suppose loan requirements for an apartment property stipulate that:

1. Mortgage interest to be earned 2½ times.
2. Ratio of loan to value to equal 60 percent.
3. Rate of mortgage interest 12 percent.

Suppose further that an analysis of past earnings over a period of three to five years supports net operating income expectations in the amount of $18,000 annually. The property interest rate is then derived mathematically by solving for imputed loan data as follows:

1. Amount of maximum interest payment:

   income of $18,000 ÷ 2.5 (interest coverage) = $7,200

2. Amount or value of mortgage loan:

   $$V = \frac{I}{R} = \$7,200 \div 0.12 \text{ (mortgage interest)} = \$60,000$$

3. Value of entire property:

   mortgage of $60,000 ÷ 0.60 (loan-to-value ratio) = $100,000

4. Earnings rate for entire property:

   $$R = \frac{I}{V} = \$18,000 \div \$100,000 = 0.18, \text{ or } 18\%$$

5. Rate of equity earnings:

   $$R = \frac{I}{V} = \$10,800 \div \$40,000 \text{ (equity interest)} = 0.27, \text{ or } 27\%$$

The accuracy of the findings can now be proven by weighting the fractional rates as follows:

Mortgage rate of 12% times 0.60 (mortgage ratio) =	7.2%
Equity rate of 27% times 0.40 (equity ratio) =	10.8%
Property earnings or interest rate =	18.0%

Band-of-Investment Method

Until recent years, this technique was used to compute the interest rate—the rate that measures the return on the investment in the land and improvements. Added to this rate was the annual recapture rate for the improvements. The recapture period generally was the forecast remaining economic life of these improvements over which the "return of" the investment would occur. An example of this method involves a property for which the available mortgage financing is: 12 percent interest, 75 percent loan-to-value ratio, 25-year first mortgage; a 15-year 14 percent second mortgage due in 5 years, with a 20 percent loan-to-value ratio; the owner's desired equity return is 10 percent; the expected remaining economic life of the building is 50 years.

Therefore, the building (not property) capitalization rate (R_B) is computed as follows:

$0.75 \times 0.12 =$	0.0900
$0.20 \times 0.14 =$	0.0280
$0.05 \times 0.10 =$	0.0050
Total interest rate	0.1230
Plus recapture rate (1/50 years)	0.0200
Building capitalization rate	0.1430

This same information can be used to calculate an overall capitalization rate (R_O), assuming that the land and building value-to-property value ratios are known. To continue this example, assume that 20 percent of the total property value is allocated to the site. The R_O is then computed as follows:

$$0.20 \times 0.1230 = 0.0246$$
$$0.80 \times 0.1430 = \underline{0.1144}$$

$$R_O \qquad 0.1390$$

A variation of the foregoing version of the band of investment method is to add the weighted yields for the debt and equity positions for an investment. The mortgage rate (R_M) or loan constant, which provides for a return on and of the mortgage, is substituted for the mortgage interest. The return of the debt capital is provided through amortization. Added to this mortgage rate is the equity dividend rate (R_E), which includes a return to the borrower after all property operating expenses have been paid and mortgage debt service has been satisfied. The key to this phase is for the appraiser to determine from surveying investors involved in the type and age of property being appraised the equity rate expected before and after mortgage debt service. Using the same information used previously, and assuming that investors usually expect a 10 percent equity dividend rate on cash flow, the overall capitalization rate is computed as follows:

$$0.75 \times 0.1264^4 = 0.0948$$
$$0.20 \times 0.1598 = 0.0320$$
$$0.05 \times 0.1000 = \underline{0.0050}$$

$$R_O = 0.1318$$

Rounded to $\underline{0.1320}$

Mortgage Terms Method

A method developed in the late 1970s by Ronald E. Gettel fully recognizes all aspects of mortgage financing for the class of property under consideration. That is, it accounts for the loan-to-value ratio (M), mortgage rate (R_M), and the debt coverage ratio (DCR), which is expressed as NOI/DS, with DS being the annual mortgage payments. The equation is $R_O = (M)(R_M)(\text{DCR})$. Although this equation indirectly accounts for the equity position, it has been criticized as being lender dominated and failing to account for future equity benefits.[5]

This method can be illustrated by an example that assumes a 75 percent loan-to-value ratio, a 13.50 percent monthly installment 30-year loan with a 5-year balloon, and a debt coverage ratio of 1.30. The R_O then is found to be

$$R_O = (0.75)(0.1374)(1.30)$$
$$= 0.1340$$

Market Extracted Capitalization Rate

This form of direct capitalization is based on the appraiser obtaining accurate rental information on recently sold comparable properties. This method has several variants. Ideally, the net operating income data are available as of the date of sale. Sometimes, it is not possible to obtain this needed information,

---

[4]R_M, allowing for interest and amortization; the keystroke sequence given in Chapter 17.
[5]For example, see Kenneth M. Lusht, and Robert H. Zerbst, "Valuing Income Property in an Inflationary Environment," *The Real Estate Appraiser and Analyst* (July–August 1980), p. 14, and Roy C. Schaeffer. "DCR: An Appraisal Gate Crasher," *The Appraisal Journal*, 50, no. 2 (April 1982), pp. 195–203.

so the appraiser must begin with the potential gross income, apply vacancy and collection loss factor that the buyer or seller generally can provide, and then apply an operating expense ratio in order to produce an estimate of the sale property's net operating income.

In obtaining these market data, comparables should be used that are similar to the appraised property with respect to:

1. Building age.
2. Operating expense ratio.
3. Building design.
4. Building usage.
5. Land-to-property value ratio.

Two examples of this method follow:

Example 1:

Sale	NOI	Sale Price	R_O
1	$41,500	$350,000	0.1186
2	38,090	325,000	0.1172
3	50,635	410,000	0.1235
4	46,460	383,000	0.1213

Example 2:

Sale	PGI	−	Vacancy and Collection Ratio	=	EGI	×	1 − OER	=	NOI	÷	Sale Price	=	R_O
1	$52,000		0.05($2,600)		$49,400		0.55		$27,170		$260,000		0.1045
2	61,500		0.04($2,460)		59,040		0.50		29,520		287,150		0.1028
3	47,360		0.10($4,736)		42,624		0.55		23,443		221,600		0.1058

The equity dividend rate can also be derived by a variation of this method. Discussion of this technique will be covered generally later in this chapter and in detail in Chapter 21.

Gross Income Multiplier Derivation of R_O

Seldom, if ever, are appraisers blessed with an abundance of perfect market data from which to derive an estimate of market value. In fact, if such information were readily available, there would be little need for the appraiser's skills of compiling and analyzing real estate market data. Faced with imperfect and often scant information related to market value, appraisers need a variety of means to accurately appraise real property. One such method is available when the appraiser is unable to obtain more information on a property than its sale price, date and terms of sale, physical description, operating expense ratio (OER), and effective gross income (EGIM). From this information the appraiser can derive an overall capitalization rate (R_O). The equation for this computation is

$$R_O = \frac{I - OER}{EGIM}$$

Suppose, for example, that a comparable property with an effective gross income of $145,500 recently sold for $800,000. An operating expense ratio (OER) of 45 percent is typical for this type and age of property. The overall capitalization rate is

$$EGIM = \$800,000/\$145,500$$
$$= 5.5$$
$$R_O = \frac{1 - 0.45}{5.5}$$
$$= 10.0\%$$

Overall Capitalization Rates with Different Income-Value Patterns

The inevitable task of the appraiser is to understand attitudes and concerns of real estate investors and users concerning real estate. These concerns pertain to both the measurement and prediction of value. Also, to measure value competently, the appraiser must be able to anticipate future trends since investors and homeowners consider real estate in such terms. This section contains three possible ways that future income and value patterns can occur. Based on these future patterns, overall capitalization rates can be derived.

Level income with changing value. The lease terms may specify a fixed rental (flat rental) over a specified term while the value of the property itself changes. This change could be either positive or negative due to the lease impairing the value. Prospective purchasers would pay a discounted price, reflecting submarket contract rentals that are caused by adverse neighborhood or general market conditions.

The basic equation to account for change is $R_O = Y_0 - \Delta$, with R_O the overall capitalization rate; Y_0 the property yield rate,[6] which reflects current income, future income, and value changes; and Δ the annualized value change. Modifying this basic equation to reflect a level income stream and changing

---

[6]The reader is cautioned to avoid incorrectly mixing equity and property yield rates with overall capitalization and equity dividend rates. The proper combinations are $R_O = Y_0 - \Delta a$ and $R_E = Y_E - \Delta a$.

future value results in the following equation:

$$R_O = Y_0 - \Delta a$$

where R_O and Y_0 are as defined above, but Δ is the total expected value change during the forecast income period (n), and a is the sinking fund factor $(1/S_{\overline{n}|})$ computed at the yield rate over the forecast income period.

An application of this method would be as follows. The appraised property is subject to a 10-year lease that specifies absolute net annual income of $80,000; the property value is forecast to increase by 40 percent during this 10-year period; and market analysis shows that investors typically expect a 10 percent property yield.

$$
\begin{aligned}
R_O &= Y_0 - \Delta a \\
&= 0.10 - (0.40)(0.062745) \\
&= 0.10 - 0.025098 \\
&= 0.074902
\end{aligned}
$$

> *Note:* $R_O < Y_0$ when the property is expected to appreciate. $R_O > Y_0$ when the property is expected to depreciate. The reason that R_O is lower than when there is no appreciation is because the owner can recapture a part of his investment through resale of the property instead of solely from rental income.

Suppose now that the same property is expected to decline in value by 40 percent during the 10-year forecast period. Notice the difference in R_O in the two examples:

$$
\begin{aligned}
R_O &= 0.10 - (-0.40)(0.062745) \\
&= 0.10 + 0.025098 \\
&= 0.125098
\end{aligned}
$$

Straight-line change in income and value.   A variation of the foregoing income change pattern would apply to a step-up lease where the rental income

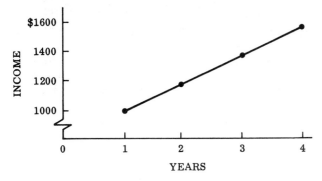

YEARS

Figure 16.2

increases by the same dollar amount each successive year. Similarly, the value is expected to trace a parallel path. Figure 16.2 depicts this expected change.

Instead of using a sinking fund factor as in the previous example, the annualizer (a) is now the reciprocal of the forecast income period (n). Using the figures above, the overall capitalization rate is found as follows:

$$R_O = Y_0 - \Delta a$$
$$= 0.10 - (0.40)(1/10)$$
$$= 0.10 - 0.04$$
$$= 0.06$$

Constant income and value change. When both the property income and value are expected to change at a constant (exponential) rate of change, the solution for R_O is quite simple. This income–value change curve is nothing more than the same percentage rates of change each year for a predetermined time, such as an annual increase of 2 percent for 10 years. The annualizer is then the annual rate of change, as follows:

$$R_O = Y_0 - \Delta a$$
$$= 0.10 - 0.02$$
$$= 0.08$$

Market Extracted Building and Land Capitalization Rates

Inaccurate valuations can occur from the use of overall capitalization rates. Such misleading results are associated with comparable properties that are dissimilar to the appraised property in size, age, land-to-total property value ratio, and building usage. This problem can be avoided by extracting either the building (R_B) or the land (R_L) capitalization rates from an overall rate and then applying either of these to the subject property. The following example illustrates how this procedure operates.

Assume that the following four comparable property sales are being analyzed.

Improved sale 1: Sale price, $250,000; NOI, $30,000; estimated site value ratio, 25 percent.

Improved sale 2: Sale price, $300,000; NOI, $36,900; estimated site value ratio, 15 percent.

Improved sale 3: Sale price, $260,000; NOI, $30,212; estimated site value ratio, 40 percent.

Land sale 1: Sale price, $450,000; NOI, $45,000.

Land sale 2: Sale price, $75,000; NOI, $7,500.

The R_B may be solved for by use of the equation $R_B = [(Ip) - (V_L \times R_L)]/V_B$, or if the value of the building is unknown, the following grid may be used.

Sale	Component	Value Ratio		Cap Rate		Weighted Rate
1	Property	1.00	×	0.1200	=	0.1200
	Land	0.25	×	0.1000	=	0.0250
	Building	0.75		R_B		0.0950
	$R_B = 0.0950/0.75$					
	$= 0.1267$					
2	Property	1.00	×	0.1230	=	0.1230
	Land	0.15	×	0.1000	=	0.0150
	Building	0.85		R_B		0.1080
	$R_B = 0.1080/0.85$					
	$= 0.1271$					
3	Property	1.00	×	0.1162	=	0.1162
	Land	0.40	×	0.1000	=	0.0400
	Building	0.60		R_B		0.0762
	$R_B = 0.0762/0.60$					
	$= 0.1270$					

A building capitalization rate of 12.70 percent and a land capitalization rate of 10.00 percent are thus indicated for the subject property.

R_O via Simplified Mortgage Equity Analysis

An overall capitalization rate can be extracted from market data in a manner similar to that described previously for the physical value components, land and building. In this case, the initial step is to ascertain an appropriate equity dividend rate (R_E), based on an overall capitalization rate and prevailing mortgage terms for a given type of property. Once having computed several market-derived equity dividend rates (R_E), the appropriate mortgage terms are determined for the appraised property. Next, an overall capitalization rate is derived and applied to the appraised property's before-tax cash flow (BTCF).

This method is illustrated with the following example.

Sale 1: Sale price, $1,000,000; BTCF, $120,000; mortgage loan terms, 75 percent first mortgage (or deed of trust); 25-year term; monthly installments; 13 percent interest.

Sale 2: Sale price, $900,000; BTCF, $104,490; mortgage loan terms, 75 percent first mortgage, 30-year term with a 10-year balloon, monthly installments, 12.75 percent interest.

Sale 3: Sale price, $875,000; BTCF, $109,290; mortgage loan terms, 80 percent first mortgage, 30-year term, monthly installments, 13.50 percent interest.

Sale	Component	Value Ratio		Cap Rate		Weighted Rate
1	Property	1.00	×	0.1200	=	0.1200
	Mortgage	0.75	×	0.1353	=	0.1015
	Equity	0.25		R_E	=	0.0185
		$R_E = 0.0185/0.25$				
		$= 0.0740$				
2	Property	1.00	×	0.1161	=	0.1161
	Mortgage	0.75	×	0.1304	=	0.0978
	Equity	0.25		R_E	=	0.0183
		$R_E = 0.0183/0.25$				
		$= 0.0732$				
3	Property	1.00	×	0.1249	=	0.1249
	Mortgage	0.80	×	0.1374	=	0.1100
	Equity	0.20		R_E	=	0.0149
		$R_E = 0.0149/0.20$				
		$= 0.0745$				

It is possible to secure a 75 percent loan-to-value, 25-year 12.50 percent loan for the subject property. Based on these loan terms and the market-derived equity dividend rate, an overall capitalization rate is computed as follows:

Component	Value Ratio	Cap Rate	Weighted Rate
Mortgage	0.75	0.1308	0.0981
Equity	0.25	0.0740	0.0185
Property	1.00	R_O	0.1166
	$R_O = 0.1166$		

REVIEW QUESTIONS

1. Distinguish between and relate amortization rate and mortgage rate.
2. Explain how a capitalization rate is applied differently from a factor in estimating value.
3. Modify the equation $V = I/R$ to find R and I.
4. Explain the basic difference between an equity dividend and equity yield rate.
5. Given mortgage terms of 75 percent loan-to-value, 13.5 percent interest, monthly payments, 20-year term, and a market-determined equity dividend rate of 7 percent, solve for R_O, indicating whether it should be applied to NOI or BTCF.
6. Using the same mortgage terms given in question 5, and NOI of $46,000 and annual debt service of $36,800, compute R_O.
7. A client has asked you to indicate the appropriate R_O for a property for which the potential gross income is $25,000, vacancy and collection losses are 6 percent, operating expense ratio is 40 percent, and the sale price is $117,500.
8. What is the R_O for a property for which both the income and value are expected to decline by 20 percent over the next 10 years? Investors in this type of property usually expect a property yield of 11 percent.

9. Derive the R_B from the following two sales transactions. Improved sale—price $550,000; NOI, $77,000; site value ratio, 15 percent. Land sale—price $100,000; NOI, $12,000.

10. Assume that the net income from the ownership of land is $2,000 and that the current rate of interest (capitalization rate) is 10 percent. Assume further that a tax of $200 is levied on this land, which reduces the net income to $1,800. Compute the following:
    (a) The land value prior to imposition of the tax.
    (b) The land value after the tax levy.
    (c) The amount of capital levy (value reduction) imposed by this tax if the capitalization rate falls to 8 percent.

11. Explain what is meant by (a) overall capitalization rates, and (b) fractional rates.

12. Compute the overall capitalization rates from the following data:

Property A	Land value	$ 2,500	Capitalization rate	6%
	Building value	7,500	Capitalization rate	8%
	Total value	$10,000	Capitalization rate	?
Property B	Land value	$ 5,000	Capitalization rate	6%
	Building value	5,000	Capitalization rate	9%
	Total value	$10,000	Capitalization rate	?
Property C	Land value	$ 7,500	Capitalization rate	7%
	Building value	2,500	Capitalization rate	9%
	Total value	$10,000	Capitalization rate	?

13. Assume the following:

    (a) Income of $25,000 per annum.
    (b) A 60 percent mortgage on the value of the property.
    (c) Mortgage interest at 10 percent.
    (d) Mortgage interest is earned (required) 2.5 times.

    Based on these facts, determine the overall rate of capitalization.

14. Briefly explain the difference between overall capitalization rate and property yield rate.

READING AND STUDY REFERENCES

AKERSON, CHARLES B. Lessons 5, 8, and 10, "Direct Capitalization," "Discounting Procedures and Income/Value Patterns," and "Applied Discounting," *Capitalization Theory and Techniques Study Guide.* Chicago: American Institute of Real Estate Appraisers, 1984.

AMERICAN INSTITUTE OF REAL ESTATE APPRAISERS. Chapter 17, "Yield Capitalization," *The Appraisal of Real Estate*, 8th ed. Chicago: American Institute of Real Estate Appraisers, 1983.

BROWN, RALPH J., and DENNIS A. JOHNSON. "Inflation, Valuation, and the Discount Rate," *The Appraisal Journal* 48, no. 4 (October 1980), pp. 549–555.

EPLEY, DONALD R., and JAMES H. BOYKIN. Chapters 9–11, *Basic Income Property Appraisal.* Reading, Mass.: Addison-Wesley Publishing Co., Inc., 1983.

FISHER, JEFFREY D., and ANTHONY B. SAUN-

DERS. "Capitalization Rates and Market Information," *The Appraisal Journal* 49, no. 2 (April 1981), pp. 186–198.

GIBBONS, JAMES E. "Financial Views," *The Appraisal Journal* 51, no. 4 (October 1983), pp. 600–609.

MASON, ROBERT C. "Present Worth in Present Dollars," *The Appraisal Journal* 51, no. 3 (July 1983), pp. 415–421.

PASCHALL, ROBERT H. "Stock Market Derivation of Discount Rates," *The Appraisal Journal* 42, no. 2 (April 1974), pp. 236–250.

PETERSON, CHARLES H. "Are Capitalization Rates Obsolete?" *The Appraisal Journal* 49, no. 2 (April 1981), pp. 179–184.

WENDT, PAUL F. "Selection of Capitalization Rates," *Real Estate Appraisal: Review and Outlook.* Athens: University of Georgia Press, 1974, pp. 127–144.

17

COMPOUND INTEREST AND DISCOUNTING

Learning Objectives

After reading this chapter, you should be able to:

Compute all present and future worth functions as a means of estimating value or amortized installments

See the interrelationships among the present and future worth functions

Solve problems involving compound interest and discounting via tables or financial calculators

Become generally familiar with several special-purpose tables

Understand how mortgage installments are allocated between principal amortization and interest on remaining principal

Interpolate numerical results in order to reach more accurate findings

An understanding of mathematics as applied to compound interest functions is an important basic tool of property appraising. The entire concept of value is based on a determination of the present worth of future (dollar) rights to income. To convert future income, or, for that matter, future commitments (liabilities) into a sum of present worth or present liability requires not only the application of mathematics but also a knowledge of the functions and purposes served by established financial tables.

There are several types of special-purpose financial tables in current use. Each table is designed as an aid in solving often-repeated problems and to save the user the laborious work and time that basic calculations would otherwise require. In recent years, it has become possible to conveniently derive the financial factors via financial calculators. In succeeding chapters, reference will be made to calculator keystroke sequences to facilitate calculations of present and future values. Reference will also be made to special-purpose tables of which a professional appraiser should have knowledge as an expert in his or her field— even though he or she may never apply such tables or may even disagree with the underlying theory that caused the author to develop the table in question. Among the special tables often used for professional appraisers are the following:

1. Inwood (coefficient) table.
2. Hoskold (sinking fund) premise table.
3. Ring capitalization (straight-line) table.
4. Babcock (declining income) premise tables.
5. Ellwood (investment) tables.

A brief description of the derivation and function of each of the above-named special-purpose tables will be given following a detailed explanation and demonstration of standard tables which are in general use and which serve as basic tools in appraisal practice. These standard tables are as follows:

1. *Compound amount of 1, S^n:* This future value function answers the basic question: How much will a dollar invested today grow to in n periods at a given rate of interest? The equation used to express this relationship is

$$S^n = (1 + i)^n$$

2. *Future worth of 1 per period, $S_{\overline{n}|}$:* This future value function answers the question: To what amount will a dollar deposited at the end of each period grow in n periods at a given rate of interest? This relationship is expressed symbolically as

$$S_{\overline{n}|} = \frac{S^n - 1}{i}$$

3. *Sinking fund factor, $1/S_{\overline{n}|}$:* This future value function answers the question: How much must be deposited at the end of each period at compound interest to accumulate a dollar in n periods? The expression for this factor is

$$\frac{1}{S_{\overline{n}|}} = \frac{i}{S^n - 1}$$

4. *Present value of 1, V^n:* This present value factor, sometimes called a reversion factor, provides an answer to the question: What is the present worth of the right to receive a dollar in n periods in the future at a given rate of interest? The equation expressing this function is

$$V^n = 1/S^n$$

5. *Present value of 1 per period $a_{\overline{n}|}$:* This present value factor, also known as the Inwood factor, answers the question: How much is the present worth of the right to receive a dollar at the end of each period for n years at a given rate of interest? The equation for this function is

$$a_{\overline{n}|} = \frac{1 - V^n}{i}$$

6. *Installment to amortize 1, $1/a_{\overline{n}|}$:* This present value factor, also called mortgage rate or annual mortgage constant, answers the question: How much must be paid in annual payments to amortize a dollar, including principal and interest, in n periods at a given rate of interest? It is expressed in equation form as

$$\frac{1}{a_{\overline{n}|}} = \frac{i}{1 - V^n}$$

Before examining each of the future and present value functions, the reader should note the interrelationship among them. The basis of all these functions is the compound amount of 1. Knowing the equation for this function $(1 + i)^n$ permits the reader to solve for all the others. It should further be observed that functions 1 and 4, 2 and 3, and 5 and 6 above are reciprocals of one another. For example, referring to Table 17.1, it can be seen that S^n for 15 years is 4.177248. The reciprocal $(1 \div 4.177248)$ is the value of V^n, which is 0.239392.

Another important relationship to be remembered is I = *nominal annual interest rate*, which is the annual interest rate, and i = *effective periodic interest rate*, which is the nominal annual interest rate divided by the number of payments per year [e.g., $0.10 \div 4$ payments a year = $0.025(i)$].

COMPOUND AMOUNT OF 1

This compound interest function (table) rightfully may be called the mother function, from which all basic future and present worth functions used in appraisal practice are derived. An understanding of this function and its derivation is most important, for it will permit the ready computation of rates and factors contained in all the other five functions named above. The ability to construct a compound interest or discount factor, too, may fill a vital need—especially at times when prepared tables at required interest rates are not available. At the outset, the reader is cautioned to keep in mind that interest tables do not make valuations; they are merely tools in the appraisal process, furnishing, as needed, ready-made calculations.

The compound amount of 1 interest table is based on the premise that $1 deposited at the beginning of a period—usually a year—earns interest that accrues during the period and which becomes part of the principal at the end of that period or the beginning of the second year (or interest) period. The

Table 17.1 Future and Present Value Using 10 Percent Annual Interest

	1 Compound Amount of 1 $S^n = (1 + i)^n$	2 Future Worth of 1 per Period $S_{\overline{n}|} = \dfrac{S^n - 1}{i}$	3 Sinking Fund Factor $1/S_{\overline{n}|} = \dfrac{i}{S^n - 1}$	4 Present Value of 1 $V^n = \dfrac{1}{S^n}$	5 Present Value of 1 per Period $a_{\overline{n}|} = \dfrac{1 - V^n}{i}$	6 Installment to Amortize 1 $1/a_{\overline{n}|} = \dfrac{i}{1 - V^n}$	
Months							Months
0	1.000000	—	—	1.000000	—	—	0
1	1.008333	—	—	0.991736	—	—	1
2	1.016667	—	—	0.983607	—	—	2
3	1.025000	—	—	0.975610	—	—	3
4	1.033333	—	—	0.967742	—	—	4
5	1.041667	—	—	0.960000	—	—	5
6	1.050000	—	—	0.952381	—	—	6
7	1.058333	—	—	0.944882	—	—	7
8	1.066667	—	—	0.937500	—	—	8
9	1.075000	—	—	0.930233	—	—	9
10	1.083333	—	—	0.923077	—	—	10
11	1.091667	—	—	0.916031	—	—	11
Years							Years
1	1.100000	1.000000	1.000000	0.909091	0.909091	1.100000	1
2	1.210000	2.100000	0.476190	0.826446	1.735537	0.576190	2
3	1.331000	3.310000	0.302115	0.751315	2.486852	0.402115	3
4	1.464100	4.641000	0.215471	0.683013	3.169865	0.315471	4
5	1.610510	6.105100	0.163797	0.620921	3.790787	0.263797	5
6	1.771561	7.715610	0.129607	0.564474	4.355261	0.229607	6
7	1.948717	9.487171	0.105405	0.513158	4.868419	0.205405	7
8	2.143589	11.435888	0.087444	0.466507	5.334926	0.187444	8
9	2.357948	13.579477	0.073641	0.424098	5.759024	0.173641	9
10	2.593742	15.937425	0.062745	0.385543	6.144567	0.162745	10
11	2.853117	18.531167	0.053963	0.350494	6.495061	0.153963	11
12	3.138428	21.384284	0.046763	0.318631	6.813692	0.146763	12
13	3.452271	24.522712	0.040779	0.289664	7.103356	0.140779	13
14	3.797498	27.974983	0.035746	0.263331	7.366687	0.135746	14
15	4.177248	31.772482	0.031474	0.239392	7.606080	0.131474	15
16	4.594973	35.949730	0.027817	0.217629	7.823709	0.127817	16
17	5.054470	40.544703	0.024664	0.197845	8.021553	0.124664	17
18	5.559917	45.599173	0.021930	0.179859	8.201412	0.121930	18
19	6.115909	51.159090	0.019547	0.163508	8.364920	0.119547	19
20	6.727500	57.274999	0.017460	0.148644	8.513564	0.117460	20
21	7.400250	64.002499	0.015624	0.135131	8.648694	0.115624	21
22	8.140275	71.402749	0.014005	0.122846	8.771540	0.114005	22
23	8.954302	79.543024	0.012572	0.111678	8.883218	0.112572	23
24	9.849733	88.497327	0.011300	0.101526	8.984744	0.111300	24
25	10.834706	98.347059	0.010168	0.092296	9.077040	0.110168	25

Table 17.1 Continued

	1 Compound Amount of 1 $S^n = (1 + i)^n$	2 Future Worth of 1 per Period $S_{\overline{n}|} = \dfrac{S^n - 1}{i}$	3 Sinking Fund Factor $1/S_{\overline{n}|} = \dfrac{i}{S^n - 1}$	4 Present Value of 1 $V^n = \dfrac{1}{S^n}$	5 Present Value of 1 per Period $a_{\overline{n}|} = \dfrac{1 - V^n}{i}$	6 Installment to Amortize 1 $1/a_{\overline{n}|} = \dfrac{i}{1 - V^n}$	
26	11.918177	109.181765	0.009159	0.083905	9.160945	0.109159	26
27	13.109994	121.099942	0.008258	0.076278	9.237223	0.108258	27
28	14.420994	134.209936	0.007451	0.069343	9.306567	0.107451	28
29	15.863093	148.630930	0.006728	0.063039	9.369606	0.106728	29
30	17.449402	164.494023	0.006079	0.057309	9.426914	0.106079	30
31	19.194342	181.943425	0.005496	0.052099	9.479013	0.105496	31
32	21.113777	201.137767	0.004972	0.047362	9.526376	0.104972	32
33	23.225154	222.251544	0.004499	0.043057	9.569432	0.104499	33
34	25.547670	245.476699	0.004074	0.039143	9.608575	0.104074	34
35	28.102437	271.024368	0.003690	0.035584	9.644159	0.103690	35
36	30.912681	299.126805	0.003343	0.032349	9.676508	0.103343	36
37	34.003949	330.039486	0.003030	0.029408	9.705917	0.103030	37
38	37.404343	364.043434	0.002747	0.026735	9.732651	0.102747	38
39	41.144778	401.447778	0.002491	0.024304	9.756956	0.102491	39
40	45.259256	442.592556	0.002259	0.022095	9.779051	0.102259	40
41	49.785181	487.851811	0.002050	0.020086	9.799137	0.102050	41
42	54.763699	537.636992	0.001860	0.018260	9.817397	0.101860	42
43	60.240069	592.400692	0.001688	0.016600	9.833998	0.101688	43
44	66.264076	652.640761	0.001532	0.015091	9.849089	0.101532	44
45	72.890484	718.904837	0.001391	0.013719	9.862808	0.101391	45
46	80.179532	791.795321	0.001263	0.012472	9.875280	0.101263	46
47	88.197485	871.974853	0.001147	0.011338	9.886618	0.101147	47
48	97.017234	960.172338	0.001041	0.010307	9.896926	0.101041	48
49	106.718957	1057.189572	0.000946	0.009370	9.906296	0.100946	49
50	117.390853	1163.908529	0.000859	0.008519	9.914814	0.100859	50

interest earned during the second year is again added to become part of the principal on which interest is earned during the third year (or interest) period. This continues for the number of required periods of interest compounding called for in the appraisal problem. The interest earned and added to the principal during each period increases in geometric progression, as is evident from the equation $S^n = (1 + i)^n$. The symbols in this equation represent the following:

S^n = original investment plus the compound interest accumulations
i = rate of interest used per period (effective interest rate)
n = periods of compounding

A compound amount of 1 table at 10 percent is displayed in Table 17.1. The derivation of this table is illustrated in Table 17.2.

If the appraiser is interested in knowing the amount to which $1.00 will

Table 17.2 Derivation of Compound Amount of 1 at 10 Percent Interest

n Periods	Amount at Beginning	Interest at 10 Percent	Amount at End	Progression Formula
1	1.000000	0.100000	1.100000	$1 + i$
2	1.100000	0.110000	1.210000	$(1 + i)^2$
3	1.210000	0.121000	1.331000	$(1 + i)^3$
4	1.331000	0.133100	1.464100	$(1 + i)^4$
5	1.464100	0.146410	1.610510	$(1 + i)^5$
. . .				
49	97.017234	9.701723	106.718957	$(1 + i)^{49}$
50	106.718457	10.671896	117.390853	$(1 + i)^{50}$

grow at 10 percent compound interest over a five-year period, he or she merely refers to the compound interest rate table at that rate and for that period and finds the amount as 1.610510. If the original amount is $200, the compounded principal and interest equals $200 × 1.610510, or $322.10.

Typical Use of Compound Interest Table

An investor purchased a property five years ago for $10,000. If this property is to be sold today, how much must the owner realize in order to have his original investment returned plus 10 percent compound interest? Assuming for purposes of this illustration no other capital or expense outlays and no change in the purchasing power of the dollar, the answer is $10,000 × 1.610510, or $16,105.10. The value would have been even higher if the compounding occurred more frequently than annually.

Calculator Solution

Rather than rely on financial tables, the appraiser often will find it more convenient to use a financial calculator to compute present and future worth functions. In solving for the future worth of 1 at 10 percent for five years the keystroke sequence (this and subsequent keystroke sequences are compatible with the Hewlett-Packard 12C and 38C calculators) is

5 | n | 10 | i | 1 | CHS | | PV | | FV |

The answer is 1.610510. The squares above represent the calculator keys, beginning with n which represents the number of years; i is interest; CHS is pressed to change the sign, representing a capital outflow—it also allows the final answer to be positive; PV is the present value; and FV is the future value. The required interest rate (10) and number of years (5) must be entered by pressing the appropriate keys.

The future worth of 1 can be computed still another way by calculator, using the exponential factor. Begin with the basic expression of $(1 + i)^n$, which in this example is $(1.10)^5$. The keystroke sequence is

1.1 | ENTER | 5 | y^x |

It should be noted that any answer found for the future worth of 1 can then be substituted into the equations for the other functions—assuming that the same term and interest rate are used.

FUTURE WORTH OF 1 PER PERIOD

The function explained above applies to a single sum either invested at the beginning, or anticipated at the end, of a given time. The remaining tables to be explained and demonstrated apply to periodic payments called annuities. An *annuity* is defined as a *series of periodic payments usually, but not necessarily, equal in amount*. Annuity payments or earnings can occur either at the beginning of each period (advance rental payments) or at the end of each period, such as amortization payments or business earnings accounted for at the end of the fiscal period. An annuity payment made at the beginning of each period is called an *annuity due*. An annuity payment made at the end of each year is called an *ordinary annuity*. Since advance income payments are the exception rather than the rule, emphasis is given here to the development and explanation of the future worth of an *ordinary annuity* table. Such a table is in effect an addition of the compound interest amounts of each *payment* over the periods (years) that each payment remains invested. To illustrate: Suppose that periodic payments of $1.00 are made annually at the end of each period for five years. If the interest rate at which these annuity payments are to be compounded is 10 percent, the total sum of these payments, plus interest earned, can be derived with the aid of the compound amount of 1 table, as shown in Figure 17.1.

The last payment under an ordinary annuity is made at the end of the last period and thus accumulates no interest, as shown in Figure 17.1. The next-to-the-last payment is invested for a one-year period, the one before that for a two-year period, and so on. As an equation, the sum total of the compound amount of an ordinary annuity may be expressed as follows:

$$S_{\overline{n}|5} = 1 + (1 + i) + (1 + i)^2 + (1 + i)^3 + (1 + i)^4$$

The construction of a future worth of an ordinary annuity table in relation to the compound amount of 1 table is shown in Table 17.3.

Typical Use of Future Worth of 1 per Period Table

Suppose that operating costs on a vacant property covering taxes, insurance, and related maintenance amounted to $500 per annum over a five-year period. How much must the property owner add to the compounded

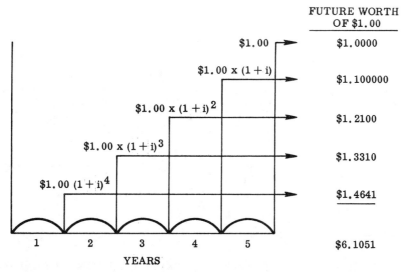

FUTURE WORTH
OF $1.00

$1.00 ➤ $1.0000

$1.00 × (1 + i) ➤ $1.100000

$1.00 × (1 + i)^2 ➤ $1.2100

$1.00 × (1 + i)^3 ➤ $1.3310

$1.00 (1 + i)^4 ➤ $1.4641

1   2   3   4   5 $6.1051

YEARS

Figure 17.1 Construction of Future Worth of an Ordinary Annuity of $1 over a Five-Year Period—At 10 Percent Compound Interest.

amount of his original investment to recover these expenditures plus 10 percent interest? By reference to the future worth of 1 table the answer is derived by simply multiplying the periodic outlays of $500 by the fifth-year factor of 6.1051. This equals a sum of $3,052.55.

To illustrate further: Suppose that a person has an opportunity to purchase a property in five years. The required downpayment will be $10,000. This prospective investor is able to deposit $1,500 at the end of each year in an account paying interest at the rate of 10 percent annually. Will he have accumulated the $10,000 down payment? The answer is found by multiplying the annual deposit by the five-year future worth of 1 per period factor:

$$\$1,500 \times 6.1051 = \$9,157.65$$

Hence the person will be unable to purchase the property.

Table 17.3 Derivation of a Future Worth of 1 at 10 Percent Interest under Ordinary Annuity Payments

n Periods (End of Period)	Compound Amount of 1	Cumulative Amounts Future Worth of 1
1	1.000000	1.000000
2	1.100000	2.100000
3	1.210000	3.310000
4	1.331000	4.641000
5	1.464100	6.105100
. . .		
49	97.017234	1057.189572
50	106.718957	1163.908529

Calculator Solution

Substituting a financial calculator, such as the HP 38C or HP 12C, for Table 17.1, it is possible to solve for $S_{\overline{n}|}$. Suppose that you desire to find how much you would have accumulated at the end of 15 years if you deposited $1 per year and it earned 10 percent annually. The proper keystrokes are as follows:

$$15 \quad \boxed{n} \quad 10 \quad \boxed{i} \quad 1 \quad \boxed{CHS} \quad \boxed{PMT} \quad \boxed{FV} \quad = 31.772482$$

If the periodic deposit was some other amount, such as $1,000, the answer would be $1,000 × 31.772482, or $31,772.48.

SINKING FUND (AMORTIZATION) FACTOR

In all valuation problems in which buildings or other types of property have limited economic lives, provisions must be made for the amortization of that portion of the investment which is consumed annually by use or lessened in value by other causes of depreciation. In instances where the annual provisions for amortization can be set aside in a sinking fund to accumulate at a given rate of interest over the economic life of the property, or where the periodic amortization provisions can be reinvested in like or similar investment properties at risk rates of interest, it is necessary to calculate the amount of annual provisions for amortization—or to know the rate per dollar of investment that must be set aside to provide for a return of capital. A useful and ready-made table, known as a sinking fund or amortization table, gives annuity amounts at various rates of compound interest whose future value is 1. To illustrate: If an amount of $1.00 is to be accumulated at 10 percent compound interest over a period of four years, how much must be set aside annually? The amount whose future value is $1 at 10 percent can be found by reference to the Sinking Fund Factor column of Table 17.1. The amount as indicated opposite the fourth-year period is 0.215471 or $0.215471 per dollar of investment value. The accuracy of this rate or amount can be proven by use of the Future Worth of 1 column in Table 17.1 per period. An annuity of $1 over four years at 10 percent compound interest equals $4.641. By multiplying this accumulation factor by the sinking fund rate of 0.215471, a sum of $1,000 is obtained. If the property is worth $10,000, the amount to be set aside annually over a four-year period at 10 percent interest to equal this sum is $10,000 × 0.215471, or $2,154.71.

The sinking fund or amortization rate table has a reciprocal relationship to the future worth of 1 per period table. Thus any factor at a given rate shown in the future worth of an annuity table, when divided into 1, will yield a sinking fund factor of 1 at the same rate of interest. This reciprocal relationship and derivation of the sinking fund function at 10 percent interest is demonstrated in Table 17.4.

Table 17.4   Derivation of a Sinking Fund at 5 Percent Compound Interest

n Periods (End of Period)	Future Worth of Annuity of 1	Reciprocal of Future Worth or Sinking Fund Rate
1	1.000000	1.000000
2	2.1000000	0.476190
3	3.310000	0.302115
4	4.641000	0.215471
5	6.105100	0.163797
. . .		
49	1057.189572	0.000946
50	1163.908529	0.000859

Typical Use of Sinking Fund Table

A building worth $20,000 is to be amortized over a period of 40 years at 10 percent interest. For appraisal purposes, the following answers may be required:

1. The rate of annual provision.
2. The amount of the annual provision.
3. Proof that the amount computed is correct.
4. The amount of amortization that will be accumulated at the end of 30 years of building life.
5. The percent accrued depreciation at the end of 30 years.

Solutions:

1. The rate of annual provision is found in the sinking fund column (see Table 17.1), and the rate indicated under 10 percent opposite 40 years is 0.002259.
2. The amount of the annual provision is $20,000 × 0.002259, or $45.18.
3. Proof: $45.18 × 442.592556 (future worth of an ordinary annuity over 40 years at 10 percent interest) equals $20,000.
4. The amount of amortization at the end of 30 years will be $45.18 × 164.494023 (future worth of an annuity of 1 over 30 years at 10 percent interest), which equals $7,431.84.
5. The percent accrued depreciation can be derived by (a) dividing $7,431.84 by the total value of $20,000, or (b) multiplying the sinking fund rate of 0.002259 (40-year factor) by the future worth of an annuity of 1 rate of 164.494023 (30-year factor). Either method of calculation will yield identical answers of 37.16 percent.

Calculator Solution

Greater flexibility and speed can generally be achieved through use of a hand-held calculator in seeking a sinking fund value. For example, to determine the amount that would have to be set aside at the end of each year in order to accumulate $25,000 at the end of 12 years in an account earning 10 percent annually, the calculations would be as follows:

12 [n] 10 [i] 25,000 [CHS] [FV] [PMT]

The annual deposit is found to be $1,169.08. This answer can be checked by dividing $1,169.08 by $25,000, which equals 0.046763 (see Table 17.1).

PRESENT WORTH OF 1

In appraisal practice, it is often known that a certain amount will become due or will be realized a given number of years from now. The question confronting the appraiser then may be: What is the present worth of this amount today? The present worth of 1 column shown in Table 17.1, provides the answer at selected years for the amount of $1.00. If X dollars are involved, the amount shown for $1.00 is merely multiplied by X. The present worth of a sum due in the future may be defined as that amount today which if invested at compound interest over the period involved will grow to that sum at the interest rate specified.

The present worth of 1 table in effect bears a reciprocal relationship to the compound amount of 1 table. To illustrate: If $1.00 at 10 percent will grow to $1.10 at the end of one year, then $1.00 due one year from a given date has a present worth at 10 percent interest (discount) of $1.00 × 1/1.10 = $1.00 × 0.909091, or $.91. If $1.00 is due two years from today at 10 percent, the answer is secured by multiplying $1.00 × 1/1.21 or $1.00 × 0.826446 = $0.83. The equation for the present value of an amount then becomes $PV = S/(1 + i)^n$. In this equation, PV is the present worth in dollars and S is the sum due at a future time. The construction of the present worth table is illustrated in Table 17.5.

Typical Use of Present Worth of 1 Table

Suppose at the time of purchase of a property it is known that the porch floor must be replaced five years hence. The cost of this replacement is estimated at $2,000. The question is: How much should be subtracted from the purchase price to provide for this future expenditure? If the interest rate is 10 percent, the answer is $2,000 × 0.620921, or $1,241.84. Proof: If $1,241.84 is invested today at 10 percent compound interest, this amount at the end of the five-year period will grow to $1,241.84 × 1.610510 (compound amount of 1 at 10 percent), or $2,000.

To illustrate further: Supposing that a property is under a 50-year lease and will at the expiration of the lease period have an estimated worth of $50,000, what is the present value of this reversionary right at a rate of 10 percent interest? The answer is $50,000 × 0.008519, or $425.95. To prove this answer: If $425.95

Table 17.5 Derivation of Present Worth of 1 at 10 Percent Compound (Discount) Interest

n Periods	Compound Amount of 1	Present Worth of 1[a]	Factor Formula
1	1.100000	0.909091	$\dfrac{1}{1 + i}$
2	1.210000	0.826446	$\dfrac{1}{(1 + i)^2}$
3	1.331000	0.751315	$\dfrac{1}{(1 + i)^3}$
4	1.464100	0.683013	$\dfrac{1}{(1 + i)^4}$
5	1.610510	0.620921	$\dfrac{1}{(1 + i)^5}$
. . .			
49	106.718957	0.009370	$\dfrac{1}{(1 + i)^{49}}$
50	117.390853	0.008519	$\dfrac{1}{(1 + i)^{50}}$

[a]Reciprocal of compound amount of 1.

is multiplied by the compound amount of 1 at 10 percent interest for 50 years (117.390853), the total will equal a sum of $50,000.

Calculator Solution

The reversionary value of a future single amount can be found via calculator. Assume that a party wants to know how much should they pay today for the right to purchase a property for $100,000 in eight years; a 10 percent discount rate would be appropriate for this type of property. The process is as follows:

8 | n | 10 | i | 100,000 | CHS | FV | PV |

which equals $46,650.74. Still another way of solving for this value would be as follows:

1.1 | ENTER | 8 | y^x | 1/x | 100,000 | X |

This alternative method provides the reciprocal of the future worth of 1.

PRESENT WORTH OF 1 PER PERIOD

This table is used more than any other in appraisal practice. It provides factors indicating the present worth of an ordinary annuity of 1. Most income payments or earnings obtained from the use of real property have the characteristics of an annuity. To find the present worth of an income stream under the earnings approach to value, it is merely necessary to convert (capitalize) the estimated annual earnings into a sum of present value by use of this table. The procedure for converting estimated net operating income into value and the techniques of capitalization will be explained in succeeding chapters. In this chapter, effort will be made to explain the derivation of the present worth of 1 per period table and to demonstrate its use.

It will be recalled that the present worth of 1 table provided (discount) factors for the measurement of present value of a single payment or sum of money due at some future time. In effect an annuity is merely a series of future income payments, and the sum total of the present worth of all payments can be derived as demonstrated in Figure 17.2. Assuming an annual income of $1.00 at the end of each year for a period of five years and an interest rate of 10 percent, the present worth of this annuity can be computed as shown in Figure 17.2.

The equation for deriving the present value of an annuity may be constructed as follows:

$$a_{\overline{n}|} = (1 + i)^{-1} + (1 + i)^{-2} + (1 + i)^{-3} + (1 + i)^{-4} + (1 + i)^{-5} + \cdots$$

This equation is mathematically reduced to

$$a_{\overline{n}|} = (1 - i)^{-n}, \text{ or } \frac{1}{(1 - i)^n}$$

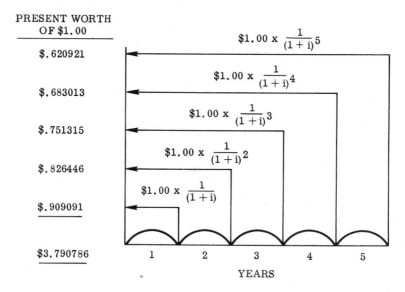

Figure 17.2 Construction of Present Worth of an Ordinary Annuity of $1.00 Over a Five-Year Period—at 10 Percent Compound Interest

The present worth table of 1 per annum at compound interest can be constructed in relation to the present worth of 1 function in Table 17.1.

Inspection of Table 17.6 will disclose that the increase in the present worth of an annuity is at a diminishing rate as future and equal periodic payments are added.

Table 17.6 Derivation of Present Worth of 1 per Annum at 10 Percent Interest Payments at End of Period

n Periods	Present Worth of 1	Cumulative Present Worth of 1 per Annum
1	0.909091	0.909091
2	0.826446	1.735537
3	0.751315	2.486852
4	0.683013	3.169865
5	0.620921	3.790787
. . .		
49	0.009370	9.906296
50	0.008519	9.914814

The expectancy of $1.00 due 50 years from the present date increases the present value of a 49-year annuity (at 10 percent rate of interest) by less than 1 cent ($0.0085). Even if an annuity should be expected to be forthcoming for thousands of years, the present value of such an annuity will never quite equal the sum obtained by capitalizing such an annuity into perpetuity through use of the formula $V = I/R$. At a rate of 10 percent interest, the present worth of an annuity of $1.00 extending into perpetuity equals 1/0.10, or $10. Proof: If a sum of $10 is invested, or deposited with a bank that pays 10 percent interest, the annual income as long as the deposit is kept intact (into perpetuity) is $10 × 0.10, or $1.00. The perpetuity factor for a sum of $1.00 at any rate of interest is merely the sum of $1.00 divided by the rate of interest as in Table 17.7.

Thus where income (as is the case with most land) is anticipated to extend unendingly into the future (i.e., perpetuity), the value of such income is obtained by dividing it by the applicable market-determined rate of interest or, conversely, multiplying same by the perpetuity (rate reciprocal) factor as demonstrated above.

Table 17.7

Income	÷	Rate of Interest	=	Perpetuity Factor
$1.00		0.06		16.67
1.00		0.08		12.50
1.00		0.10		10.00
1.00		0.12		8.33

Typical Use of Present Worth of 1 per Period Table

Suppose that a five-year lease calls for net rental payments at the end of each year in the amount of $1,000. If this lease is offered for sale and the rate of interest is 10 percent, what is the present value of this series of income payments? The answer is $1,000 × 3.790787 (present worth of 1 per period, see Table 17.1), which equals a sum of $3,790.79. Or, suppose that a property in new condition is estimated to yield $10,000 net annually over a remaining building life of 50 years: What is the present value of this level annuity? Answer: $10,000 × 9.914814, or $99,148.14.

Calculator Solution

Instead of finding the present worth of a level annuity by use of financial tables and then substituting the value of the present worth of 1 into the equation $(1 - V^n)/i$, the calculator can be used to find $a_{\overline{n}|}$. Suppose, for instance, that an appraiser has been asked to find the present value of an annual net rental income of $2,500, discounted at 10 percent for the next 25 years. The current value would be computed as follows:

$$25 \boxed{\text{n}} \quad 10 \boxed{\text{i}} \quad 2,500 \boxed{\text{CHS}} \quad \boxed{\text{PMT}} \quad \boxed{\text{PV}}$$

The present value of this level income stream is found to be $22,692.60. The answer is proven correct by comparing the calculation $22,692.60/$2,500 (9.077040) to the present value of 1 per period for 10 percent and 25 years in Table 17.1.

INSTALLMENT TO AMORTIZE 1

Frequently, an appraiser is asked how much net operating income a property of a given value must produce in order to provide a fair return on the investment and amortization of the investment over the economic life of the property, or for the lease term, at market rates of interest. Whenever a mortgage loan is applied for, it must be calculated in advance how much the periodic payments amount to in order to yield interest on the mortgage and a return of the loan principal over the term of the mortgage. Where the value of a property or the amount of a loan is known, the annuity income—or loan payment per dollar of present value—can be obtained from a special table in which the amounts, whose present value is 1, are calculated at selected rates of interest. A table of this type is shown in Table 17.1.

The annuity payment table for an installment to amortize 1 has a reciprocal relationship to the present worth of an annuity of 1 table and may be constructed as in Table 17.8.

Table 17.8   Derivation of Annuity Payment for an Installment to Amortize 1 at 10 Percent Interest

n Periods (End of Period)	Present Worth of 1 per Period	Reciprocal of Present Worth of 1 per Period
1	0.909091	1.1000000
2	1.735537	0.576190
3	2.486852	0.402115
4	3.169865	0.315471
5	3.790787	0.263797
. . .		
49	9.906296	0.100946
50	9.914814	0.100859

Typical Use of Installment to Amortize 1 Table

Suppose that a property is worth $30,000 and has an economic life of 50 years. How much must this property return as net operating income annually to provide interest and amortization at 10 percent interest? The annuity necessary to warrant an amount whose present value is 1 at 10 percent interest is 0.100859 (see Table 17.1). Multiplying this amount by $30,000 gives the answer of $3,025.77. The rate of 0.100859 used in this illustration is in fact a composite of the effective interest rate on the investment, or 0.10 plus the sinking fund rate for 50 years at 10 percent, or 0.00859. To derive the amount whose present value is 1 for a four-year period at 10 percent interest, all that is necessary (if this special table is not available) is to make reference to a sinking fund table and to add the effective rate of interest to the rate shown as follows: Sinking fund rate for four years at 10 percent = 0.215471 + 0.10 interest equals 0.315471, which is the annual amount necessary to provide a return *on* and *of* an investment of $1.00 for a four-year period at 10 percent interest.

A table showing the installment to amortize 1 is especially useful in connection with mortgage-loan financing. This table provides the exact amounts which must be repaid over the loan period at given rates of interest for every dollar borrowed. Attention is called to the fact that interest and amortization payments on mortgage loans are generally computed over monthly rather than annual periods of time. When this is the case the interest rate must be divided in the same proportion that the year is divided into smaller parts. To illustrate: If a $10,000 mortgage is made at 6 percent over 20 years and is to be amortized monthly, the 20-year loan period is multiplied by 12 (months of the year) to obtain 240 monthly payment periods. Similarly, the annual interest of 0.06 must be divided by 12 to obtain the rate per payment period, which in this case is 0.005, or ½ of 1 percent. By reference to a table showing the amount whose present value is 1, the payment per $1.00 is obtained opposite 240 (*n*) periods under the "½ percent interest" column. This amount is 0.007165. Multiplying this rate of payment per $1.00 of loan by $10,000 indicates that monthly payments of $71.65 will be necessary to pay interest at the annual rate of 6 percent

Table 17.9 Amortization Schedule of a Mortgage Loan of $10,000 Providing Monthly Amortization over a 20-Year Period at 6 Percent Interest

Year and Month	Monthly Payment	Interest at 0.005 per Period	Amortization of Loan	Remaining Loan Balance
				$10,000.00
0–1	$ 71.65	$ 50.00	$ 21.65	
0–2	71.65	49.89	21.76	9,978.34
0–3	71.65	49.78	21.87	9,934.72
. . .	. . .	. . .	. . .	. . .
Total	$17,196.00	$7,196.00	$10,000	

(½ percent each month) and to amortize the $10,000 over a period of 240 months. An amortization schedule for the first three months of this loan would show entries as in Table 17.9.

The various interest and annuity tables discussed in this chapter must be thoroughly understood by all professional appraisers. A complete book of financial tables[1] and a good financial (preferably printing) calculator should be part of every appraisal office. Increasingly, small electronic computers are becoming an integral part of real estate appraisal offices. Further illustrations and applications of the various interest and annuity tables will be encountered in the chapters dealing with capitalization methods and techniques.

Calculator Solution

Three different calculator methods are shown below to determine the periodic installment required to amortize a capital investment—either debt, equity, or total property value. The first method is best applied to annual installments as shown below, assuming that the mortgage term is 25 years, the installments are made annually, the mortgage is for $100,000, and interest compounds at the annual rate of 10 percent. Thus the annual principal and interest payment is

25 | n | 10 | i | 100,000 | CHS | PV | PMT | = $11,016.81

Had the installments been payable on a monthly basis, one of the two following methods could have been used:

(1)
25 | ENTER | 12 | X | n | 10 | ENTER | 12 | ÷ | i |
100000 | CHS | PV | PMT | = $908.70

---

[1]*Financial Compound Interest and Annuity Tables*, 6th ed. (Boston: Financial Publishing Co., 1980), and James J. Mason, ed. and compiler, *American Institute of Real Estate Appraisers Financial Tables* (Chicago: American Institute of Real Estate Appraisers, 1981).

or
(2)

25 | g | | 12x | 10 | g | | 12 ÷ | 100000 | CHS |

| PV | | PMT | = $908.70

THE IMPORTANCE OF LOGARITHMIC FUNCTIONS

At the outset of this chapter, it was stated that the basic compound interest table derived by the formula $S^n = (1 + i)^n$ is the mother table from which all other interest tables explained above can be readily derived. It is important, therefore, that professional appraisers learn how to compute the compound amount of 1. Occasions arise when prepared tables at required percentages are not available, or where unusually long property life spans go beyond the number of compound periods covered in available table publications. The capitalization of income from a power dam, or the computation of its reversionary value when its economic life is judged to be 300 or more years, may be such an instance.

To find the compound amount of 1 requires raising the amount of 1 plus the rate of interest (at which 1 is to be compounded) to a power equal to that of the number of interest periods involved. To find the compound amount of 1 at 10 percent interest over a period of five years—$(1 + i)^5$—it is necessary to raise 1.10 to the fifth power, as follows:

$1.00 \times 1.10 = 1.100000$ $1.331000 \times 1.10 = 1.464100$
$1.10 \times 1.10 = 1.210000$ $1.464100 \times 1.10 = 1.610510$
$1.21 \times 1.10 = 1.331000$

To raise 1.10 to a power of 50, or 500, or higher by simple arithmetic would be a most laborious if not an impossible task. A number, however, can be raised to any conceivable power with relative ease through the use of logarithmic tables or with a calculator having natural and common logarithm keys.

It is not intended in this chapter to teach the use of logarithmic tables or to explain the principle underlying the theory of logarithms or its geometric functions. All that is intended is to state briefly the purposes which logarithmic tables serve and to recommend that interested students or professional appraisers unacquainted with these tables acquire a set, together with instructions for their use, through a bookstore or library.

A logarithm expresses a number in decimals of the power of 10. Adding the log of 1.10 to the log of 1.10 has the same effect as raising 1.10 to the second power; 20 times the log of 1.10 in effect raises 1.10 to its 20th power. To find the compound amount of $(1.10)^{50}$ merely requires looking up the log of 1.10, multiplying by 50, and looking up the antilog to obtain the answer sought. To illustrate:

Log of 0.10 = 0.041393
Log 0.041393 × 50 = 2.069634
Antilog 2.069634 = 117.390853

The amount of 117.390853 thus obtained equals the amount shown under the compound amount of 1 table at 10 percent interest opposite the n, or time period of 50. Possession of a calculator with logarithmic capability, working knowledge of its application, and familiarity with logarithmic tables are highly recommended, if not essential, to all practicing appraisers.

SPECIAL APPLICATIONS OF COMPOUNDING AND DISCOUNTING

No table, however complete, will handle every situation confronting the real estate appraiser. This section is included to expand the scope of these present and future worth functions. Presented herein are techniques for:

1. Solving for intermediate period values.
2. Extending functions beyond the capacity of tables.
3. Interpolating for intermediate values.
4. Converting end-of-year to beginning-of-year payments.
5. Valuing deferred payments.
6. Solving mortgage problems.

Intermediate Period Values

There will be times when the value of an intermediate or odd period is required. For example, the appraiser may want to know the present worth of $100,000, discounted at 10 percent annually for 25½ years. In using the tables to solve for this value, it must be remembered that the *rule of exponents* states that exponents are added and factors are multiplied. Exponents may be thought of as years, for example $(25 + 0.5)$, and factors are the value under a particular present or future worth function for a given year and specified interest rate. For 10 percent, this would be 0.092296 (25 years) and 0.952381 (6 months). By multiplying these factors, the present worth of 1 at 10 percent for 25½ years is determined to be 0.087901. A visual inspection of Table 17.1 shows that this factor lies between the 25- and 26-year factors.

A *very important point* to remember when trying to find intermediate values or in extending the tables for the present worth of 1 per period is that the initial computations must be for the present worth of 1 or its reciprocal, compound amount of 1. That factor then is substituted into the equation

$$a_{\overline{n}|} = \frac{1 - V^n}{i}$$

The same process applies for the future worth of 1. The initial calculations must be made for the compound amount of 1. This computed factor is then substituted into the future value of 1 per period equation. Illustrating this method for the present value of 1 per period with the previously computed factor, we see that the 25½-year 10 percent value of $a_{\overline{n}|}$ is

$$\frac{1 - V^n}{i} = \frac{1 - 0.087901}{0.10} = 9.120990$$

A quick perusal of Table 17.1 reveals that this factor is midway between the present value of 1 per period factors for 25 and 26 years.

Extending Table Functions

The above-mentioned law of exponents applies to tabular extensions. Also, the initial calculations should be made for the compound interest of 1 and future value of 1 with the answers then being substituted into the future or present value of 1 per period tables. Assume, for example, a client wants to know the present value of a 75-year $10,000 annual income stream discounted at 10 percent annually. Any combination of reversion factors totalling 75 years will provide the first step. In this case, factors for 50 and 25 years are used.

Step 1:

$$V^n = 0.008519 \times 0.092296$$
$$= 0.000786$$

Step 2:

$$a_{\overline{n}|} = \frac{1 - 0.000786}{0.10}$$
$$= 9.992137$$

Step 3:

$$PV = 9.992137 \times \$10,000$$
$$= \$99,921.37$$

Interpolating Intermediate Values

In some instances, it may not be possible to derive intermediate values via tables. Still, more precision is desired than simply giving a range of values. This is where a knowledge of interpolation is beneficial. This method sometimes is called the rule of proportional parts.

Suppose that a property sold for $400,000 and at date of sale had a net operating income of $53,342, which is expected to continue for the next 15 years. From this information, a present worth of 1 per period factor of 7.498781 is computed ($400,000 ÷ $53,342).

You are interested in the exact discount rate that pertains to this situation. This first step is to bracket the computed $a_{\overline{n}|}$ Next, you solve for the discount rate that corresponds to the $a_{\overline{n}|}$ for a particular property as shown below.

	Discount Rate		$a_{\overline{n}|}$
	0.09	8.060688	8.060688
	Target factor	7.498781	
	0.11		7.190870
Difference	0.02	0.561907	0.869818

$$D.R. = 0.09 + 0.02\,(0.561907/0.869818)$$
$$= 0.09 + 0.02\,(0.646005)$$
$$= 0.09 + 0.012920$$
$$= 0.102920 \quad \text{or} \quad 10.29\%$$

Converting EOP to BOP Payments

Present and future worth tables are traditionally set up on the basis of payments being received at the end of a period (EOP). This rationale fits the premise under which mortgage payments are made. However, rental payments usually are paid at the beginning of a period (BOP). To convert EOP payments to BOP payments, the steps are as follows:

1. Compute EOP present worth of 1 per period factor.
2. Convert EOP factor to BOP factor by multiplying it by $1 + i$, remembering that i is the effective interest rate or the nominal interest rate divided by the number of installments per year.

Assume that an investor wants to know the present worth of a level income stream of $1,000 annually, received at the beginning of each year over 20 years, and discounted at 10 percent. The solution is as follows:

$$PV = \$1,000 \times 8.513564 \times 1.10$$
$$= \$9,364.92$$

If the rental income were received monthly in advance, the present value would be

$$PV = (\$1,000/12)(103.624619)(1 + 0.10/12)$$
$$= (\$83.33)(103.624619)(1.008333)$$
$$= \$8,707.00$$

The calculator solution is as follows:

g	BEG	20	g		n	10	g		i

83.33 | CHS | | PMT | | PV |

The first two keystrokes are done to convert the payments to the beginning of the period.

Some financial calculators allow for BOP payments simply by shifting a key to denote this form of payment rather than EOP.

Valuing Deferred Payments

A type of lease discussed in a previous chapter is one in which future payments are staged in stair-step fashion. Since the income stream is irregular, customary use of the present value of 1 per period is negated. However, a variation of the level annuity method is possible. That is, future income at different levels can be discounted to reveal the present value.

Assume, for example, that a property is subject to a lease where the rent payments are received at the end of each year; for the first 5 years the annual rental is $2,000; for the next 5 years, it advances to $2,500 annually; the discount rate is 10 percent.

The present value is found by using the Table 17.1 factors as follows:

$$
\begin{array}{lr}
3.790787 \times \$2,000 = & \$\ 7,581.57 \\
+\ (6.144567 - 3.790787)(\$2,500) = & \underline{5,884.45} \\
\text{PW of 1 per period for years 1 to 10} & \$13,466.02
\end{array}
$$

The procedure in using this method is to first multiply the present worth of 1 per period for the first period (e.g., first five years) by the annual income to be received during this period. Next, the annual income for the next period is multiplied by the difference in the factor for the last year of the second period and the factor used for the first period. Proof of the correctness of this second-period calculation is shown by calculating the present worth of 1 factors for years 6 through 10 and comparing the total to the difference of the present worth of 1 per period factors for years 10 and 5. The comparative results follow:

1. Present worth of 1 (years 6 through 10):

$$
\begin{array}{r}
0.564474 \\
+\ 0.513158 \\
+\ 0.466507 \\
+\ 0.424098 \\
+\ \underline{0.385543} \\
2.353780
\end{array}
$$

2. Present worth of 1 per period (year 10 −
year 5):

$$
\begin{array}{r}
6.144567 \\
- 3.790787 \\
\hline
2.353780
\end{array}
$$

One other comment is in order regarding the present value of deferred income. The simplest way of converting end-of-period income to beginning-of-period income in order to estimate present value is to (1) solve for present value under the premise that the income is received at EOP; (2) adjust the preliminary answer in (1) by multiplying it by $1 + i$. Applied to the example above,

$$
PW = \$13,466.02 \times 1.10 = \$14,812.62
$$

Mortgage Problems

A problem often occurs when a party prepares to sell its property. That is, before it can judge the net proceeds from a sale, the remaining balance of the loan must be ascertained.[2] Several methods can be used, but all stem from the amount of the mortgage payments. For each of the methods used below, assume annual installments; 10 percent interest; original principal, $80,000; original loan term, 25 years; remaining loan term, 15 years.

1. Remaining loan balance
$$
\begin{aligned}
&= (\$80,000) \left(\frac{0.110168}{0.131474} \right) \\
&= \$80,000 \times 0.837945 \\
&= \$67,035.61
\end{aligned}
$$
   This step compares the installment factor for the full loan term to the remaining loan term.

2. Find annual mortgage payment for 25-year and for 15-year loan terms; next divide the annual payment for 15 years into that used for 25 years;[3] this percent is then multiplied by the original amount of the mortgage.

Annual payment for 25-year loan $= \$80,000 \times 0.110168$
Annual payment for 15-year loan $= \$80,000 \times 0.131474$

$$
\begin{aligned}
\text{Remaining loan balance} &= (\$80,000) \left(\frac{\$8,813.44}{\$10,517.92} \right) \\
&= \$80,000 \times 0.837945 \\
&= \$67,035.61
\end{aligned}
$$

[2]Equity buildup via loan amortization is the complement of the remaining loan balance.
[3]The same results could be derived by getting the monthly dollar payment ratios had these been monthly installment loans.

SPECIAL-PURPOSE TABLES

To permit ready and more rapid conversion of operating income into value, a number of special-purpose tables have been developed and published for use by property appraisers. Although all value problems can be solved without reference to precomputed tables and it is often advisable not to employ or rely on special-purpose tables, especially when testifying in court as an expert witness,[4] nevertheless, there may be certain assignments in which the appraiser will find it advantageous to be acquainted with such tables, their derivation, and with circumstances under which such tables may be correctly applied.

The Inwood (Coefficient) Table

This is the oldest, best known, and most frequently applied capitalization table. This table in essence is a summation of the present worth of $1.00 for each of the future years in which a level income (same amount each year) is expected over the remaining economic life of the property. The Inwood factor, which is the same as the present value of 1 per period covered earlier, for a sum of $1.00 to be received over a period of 40 years at 10 percent is 9.779051. This factor is precomputed as shown in Table 17.1 and is obtained by addition of the present worth of $1 at 10 percent $1/1.10 + 1/(1.10)^2 + 1/(1.10)^3 + \cdots + 1/(1.10)^{40}$ or by the shortcut method under which the rate of interest is added to the sinking fund factor at the same rate for the number of years over which the income is to be capitalized. This rate combination is then divided into the sum of 1.00. The reciprocal thus obtained is the Inwood factor. To illustrate: Interest rate of 0.10 plus sinking fund factor at 10 percent for 40 years 0.002259 equals a capitalization rate of 0.102259. The reciprocal of this rate is 1/0.102259, which equals the Inwood factor of 9.779051. To capitalize an estimated level income of $1,000 per year for a period of 40 years under the Inwood method at 10 percent interest requires only the multiplication of $1,000 by the Inwood factor of 9.779051 to obtain the present value of the property in the amount of $9,779.05.

The Hoskold Factor Table

The Hoskold annuity factor is constructed in a fashion similar to the Inwood annuity factor. The only difference between these two methods of capitalization is that the sinking fund rate of depreciation or recapture is always at a lower, lesser, or "safer" rate than the rate of interest employed as a return on the invested capital. To illustrate: If the rate of interest is found to be 10 percent and the "safe" rate of capital recapture is 5 percent, the rate of capitalization for an income stream over a period of 40 years is 10 percent plus 0.008278 (5%

[4]Experience has shown that laypersons and jurors have difficulty in understanding the use and purpose of complex mathematical tables and as a result become wary of the findings and judge the person's integrity rather than the accuracy of the mechanisms of valuation.

SF) or 0.108278. The Hoskold factor is merely the reciprocal of the rate of capitalization or $1 \div 0.108278$, which equals 9.235486. Thus an income of $1,000 due each year over a period of 40 years is worth, under the Hoskold method of valuation at the rates stated above, the sum of $1,000 × 9.235486, or $9,235.49.

The Ring Factor Table

Another method of capitalization calls for straight line depreciation of invested capital. The rate of recapture is obtained by dividing 100 percent by the number of years of remaining building or property life. For an investment life of 40 years the rate of recapture per year is 100 percent divided by 40, or 2.5 percent. This rate, when added to the interest rate, forms the rate of capitalization. Thus if the interest rate is 10 percent, and the straight-line recapture rate is 2.5 percent, the rate of capitalization is 12.5 percent. To permit use of the value formula $V = I \times F$ and to provide a table that is similar in construction and use as the Inwood and Hoskold tables of capitalization, one of the authors has precomputed reciprocals of straight-line rates of capitalization for years of one to 50 and at interest rates from 6 to 10 percent. These reciprocal rates comprise the Ring Factor Table. The 10 percent section of this table is shown in Appendix 3 page 00.

The Babcock Premise Factor Table

This precomputed capitalization table was developed by Frederick M. Babcock and first published in book form in 1932.[5] In essence, Babcock established curves for declining income streams based on patterns as follows:

1. Premise 1 assumed the income before depreciation to occur in *equal* installments over a given economic life without decline. Discounting this income represented by a sum of $1.00 at compound interest rates resulted in factors (under premise 1) identical to and equal in all respect to the Inwood factors at the identical rates of interest.

2. Premise 2 assumed a gradual decline of an income stream equal to a curve, as shown in Figure 17.3. Discounting this declining income stream beginning with 1.00 at the end of year 1 and reaching zero in year n plus 1, to a present worth at selected rates of interest yielded a Babcock premise 2 factor for ready use. To illustrate: Based on an interest rate of 8 percent and an economic life of 40 years, the Inwood or premise 1 factor is 11.9246. For a declining income in accordance with premise 2, the Babcock factor is 10.9702 or 92 percent of value under premise 1, where the interest rate is 8 percent and the income life is 40 years.

3. Premises 3 and 4 are similarly computed by discounting to present worth at various rates of interest, income streams that decline as shown in Figure 17.3 for properties with a remaining economic life of 40 years. For an income stream declining over 40 years at 8 percent compound interest, the Babcock factors are 9.8134 and 8.7736 under premises 3 and 4, respectively.

[5]Frederick M. Babcock, *The Valuation of Real Estate* (New York: McGraw-Hill Book Company, 1932).

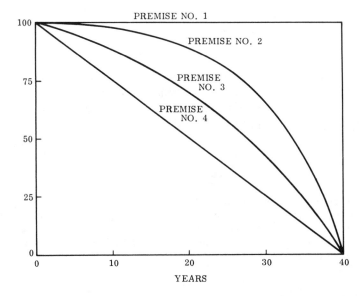

Figure 17.3 Babcock Declining Income Premises

Although Babcock factors are rarely used in practice today, the principle of income decline was firmly established by Babcock and newer and, perhaps, simpler methods for handling changing income and value are illustrated in Chapter 18.

Ellwood Tables

These precomputed rates or coefficients were derived under the "band of investment" rate method to reflect mathematically varying combinations of mortgage and equity ratios over investment or ownership life periods of one to 30 years at preselected mortgage interest and equity yield rates. Ellwood tables were not intended to be applied in the conventional valuation of real property, where the sale represents a cash or cash equivalent transaction. Rather, the Ellwood tables were intended for use in the valuation of *equity* investments where a major part of the total property is encumbered with a level-payment mortgage which is scheduled to be amortized monthly over a number of years at a stipulated rate of interest. With the aid of the Ellwood tables, an appraiser can readily compute the cash outlay that is warranted for the purchase of the equity interest in a property. This cash outlay must equal at stipulated (market determined) equity yield rates the present worth of future rights to income and capital payments as follows:

1. The present worth of the stabilized cash flow—left after mortgage payments covering interest and amortization of principal are met—during the ownership period of the property.

2. The present worth of the cash reversion to which the owner is entitled. This is the selling price less the amount of the remaining mortgage principal that is due at the time of sale.

The derivation and application of the precomputed Ellwood tables will be more fully explained and illustrated along with other equity capitalization techniques in Chapter 21. With the availability of reasonably priced microcomputers, appraisers increasingly have become independent of these tables.

REVIEW QUESTIONS

1. Given a 10 percent annual interest rate and a 22-year term, compute the future worth of 1 per period and sinking fund factor by substituting the compound amount of 1 factor into each of these two equations.
2. To compute an intermediate (odd period) value or extend the tables from the future–present worth table, either of two factors must first be computed. Identify both of these factors.
3. How much must be deposited at the end of each year, compounded at 10 percent annually, to grow to $10,000 at the end of 12 years?
4. If an investor were to deposit $5,000 today, assuming 10 percent annual compounding, to what amount would this grow at the end of 16 years?
5. Would your client have accumulated $10,000 through loan amortization on a 25-year, $75,000, 10 percent annual installment mortgage at the end of the eighth year? How much equity would have been built up?
6. Compute the present value of a property available for purchase in 65 years for $600,000, discounted at 10 percent annually.
7. What is the present worth of a $4,000 annual income stream receivable at the beginning of the year over the next 15 years? Assume that a 10 percent annual discount rate is applicable.
8. Find the current value of the following lease income that is received at the end of the year and discounted at 10 percent annually: years 1 to 3, $10,000; years 4 to 6, $12,000; years 7 to 9, $13,500.
9. B has paid $100 in taxes each year on a vacant lot which he purchased 10 years ago for $3,000. Assuming interest rates at 6 percent, how much is his total investment to date?
10. (a) Explain what is meant by "present value of annuity."
    (b) What is the present value of $1.00 due each year for a period of three years, discounted at 10 percent annually?
11. Capitalize the following at 10 percent:
    (a) An income flow (annuity) of $500 per annum for 15 years.
    (b) An income flow (annuity) of $500 per annum for 100 years.
    (c) An income flow of $500 per annum in perpetuity.
12. If $1,000 is to be accumulated under the sinking fund method over a period of 20 years, how much must be placed annually into the fund if the compound interest rate is 10 percent?
13. Set up a schedule of amortization for an 8 percent, eight-year, $10,000, monthly installment mortgage and show *all* captions, headings, and entries for a two-month period.
14. An apartment house which represents the highest and best use has been completed at a cost of $750,000. The land has been owned by the developer for

many years and its value is unknown. The anticipated net operating income from this improvement, which has an estimated economic life of 40 years, is as follows:

First year	$47,500
Second year	60,000
Third year and thereafter for 37 years	70,000

Based on an interest rate of 10 percent for the entire property, determine the appraised value of this property. Use the Inwood method of capitalization.

READING AND STUDY REFERENCES

ELLWOOD, L. W. *Ellwood Tables for Real Estate Appraising and Financing,* 4th ed. Chicago: American Institute of Real Estate Appraisers, 1977.

EPLEY, DONALD R., and JAMES H. BOYKIN. Chapter 6, "Discounting and Compounding," *Basic Income Property Appraisal.* Reading, Mass.: Addison-Wesley Publishing Co., Inc., 1983.

FRIEDMAN, JACK P., and NICHOLAS ORDWAY. Chapters 2 and 3, *Income Property Appraisal and Analysis.* Reston, Va.: Reston Publishing Co., Inc., 1981.

MASON, JAMES J. (ed. and compiler). *American Institute of Real Estate Appraisers.* Chicago: American Institute of Real Estate Appraisers, 1981.

MASON, ROBERT C. "Present Worth in Present Dollars," *The Appraisal Journal* 51, no. 3 (July 1983), pp. 415–421.

SHENKEL, WILLIAM M. Chapter 11, "Capitalization Tables," *Modern Real Estate Appraisal.* New York: McGraw-Hill Book Company, 1978.

SPRECHER, C. RONALD. Chapter 4, "Present and Future Values," *Essentials of Investment.* Boston: Houghton Mifflin Company, 1978.

WENDT, PAUL F., and ALAN R. Cerf. "Appendix 3B: Development of Compound-Interest Tables," *Real Estate Investment Analysis and Taxation,* 2nd ed. New York: McGraw-Hill Book Company, 1979, pp. 88–103.

18

INCOME CAPITALIZATION METHODS

Learning Objectives

After reading this chapter, you should be able to:

Understand the reciprocal relationship between processing property income via capitalization rates and discount factors

Capitalize an income stream that is forecast to extend into perpetuity

Use several methods for capitalizing income over a specific time period

Explain how periodic recapture is set up via the straight-line and annuity methods

Appreciate the complementary nature of the present worth of the income to the land user and the fee owner's reversionary interest

Use the discounted cash flow technique in deriving an equity yield rate

Appraising, under the income approach to value, calls for aptitude and skill in applying the capitalization process. To capitalize income means to convert or to process earnings anticipated from typical operation of a property into a sum of present worth (capital value). Mathematically, the basic relationship of income to value is expressed by the formula

$$V = I/R \quad \text{or} \quad V = I \times F$$

The symbols used in these alternate capitalization formulas have meaning as follows:

V = present worth of future rights to income
I = net operating income *before* providing for interest on the investment and amortization payments of the investment
R = rate of capitalization—a summation of the rate of interest plus the rate of amortization $(i + r)$
F = valuation or capitalization factor—a reciprocal of R

Whether to use the formula $V = I/R$ or $V = I \times F$ is optional, as far as the appraiser is concerned, since both equations will yield identical value conclusions. However, it is recommended that in the selection of a capitalization formula, consideration be given to the technical level of understanding of the valuation report reader and to present income and capitalization data in logical sequence and simple mathematical style.

The basic value formula $V = I/R$ is applicable to all appraisal problems involving capitalization of future rights to income. Care, however, must be taken to match income and rates of capitalization in relation to the value problem at issue. Thus, if the value of an entire property in fee simple ownership is sought, I_p in the capitalization formula must represent total property income and R_o the total (or overall) property rate at which a fair return *on* and *of* the investment is anticipated. Similarly, if the value of a fractional interest is at issue, both income and the rate of capitalization must be consistently related to that portion of the entire property, as will be demonstrated below.

CAPITALIZATION OF INCOME EXTENDING INTO PERPETUITY

The generally indestructible physical characteristics of land permit consideration of income derived from use of land as extending on and on into perpetuity, without termination. There are times when land loses its value due to physical deterioration, such as from erosion or soil depletion. Other value losses may result from economic causes such as traffic rerouting. Improvements placed on land have finite economic lives; but new improvements can replace old ones, and the cycle of replacement for all practical purposes can be conceived as extending on into infinity.

To illustrate the application of the capitalization process to income extending into perpetuity, it is assumed that a constant, or level, flow of income in the amount of $1,000 annually is to be converted into value at an interest rate of 10 percent. Applying the formula $V = I/R$, the value obtained equals $1,000 \div 0.10 = $10,000. The correctness of this answer can be proven by transposing the basic value formula to find income, or I. In this instance, $I =$

Table 18.1   Perpetuity Factors for Capitalization of Net Operating Income at Selected Rates of Interest

Rate	Perpetuity Factor
0.04	25.00
0.05	20.00
0.06	16.67
0.07	14.29
0.08	12.50
0.09	11.11
0.10	10.00

$V \times R = \$10,000 \times 0.10 = \$1,000$, or the amount necessary annually (into perpetuity) to support a value of \$10,000 at a risk (interest) rate of 10 percent. The value of \$10,000 could also be obtained by use of the formula $V = I \times F$. Since F is the reciprocal of R, the valuation factor is obtained by dividing 1.00 by the rate at which the income is to be capitalized. In this instance $1.00 \div 0.10$ equals a perpetuity factor of 10. Thus $\$1,000 \times 10 = \$10,000$, a sum equal to that obtained under the alternate capitalization formula used above.

Perpetuity factors at any rate of interest or fraction thereof are derived by simply dividing 1.00 by the rate used for capitalization purposes. With the aid of these valuation factors, land value is readily obtained by a simple process of multiplication, as demonstrated above. Perpetuity factors at selected rates of interest are indicated in Table 18.1.

CAPITALIZATION OF NONPERPETUITY INCOME

In the valuation of building improvements or property interests with terminal lives, provision must be made to write off, or amortize, the investment over the economic life period of the property. The methods of capitalization used in appraisal practice are named in accordance with the method under which future depreciation, or amortization, is to be provided. When depreciation is calculated under the formula $V = I/R$, the capitalization methods most frequently applied are known as:

1. Straight-line capitalization.
2. Sinking fund capitalization.
3. Annuity capitalization.

When use of the reciprocal formula $V = I \times F$ is deemed more practical or convenient, specially prepared factor tables can be applied. In such instances, the capitalization factor method used takes its name from the person who compiled or who popularized the use of the ready-made factor table in question. Using the same order as the capitalization methods listed above, the reciprocal or income conversion methods available for valuation of nonperpetuity income are as follows:

1. Ring factor table of capitalization.[1]
2. Hoskold factor table of capitalization.
3. Inwood factor table of capitalization.

The various methods of capitalization yield value conclusions that differ importantly from one another, as will be demonstrated below. Consequently, great care must be taken to select the appropriate method that reflects market actions of typical investors. Under no circumstances must the selection of a method of capitalization be contingent on the value to be found or on preferences voiced either by the appraiser or his or her client. Identical income produce different values under the methods of capitalization named above because of differences in the amount of income set aside under each method to recapture (amortize) the investment value. Everything else remaining equal, the greater the amount that is set aside out of a fixed sum of annual income for amortization purposes, the less total income that remains for the interest earnings on which property value in the final analysis depends.

To illustrate the traditional use of capitalization methods, a simple valuation problem will be assumed, based on the following property and income data:

1. A net operating income of $5,000 per year.
2. A remaining economic life of 40 years.
3. A 10 percent rate of interest.
4. A sinking fund rate of 5 percent.
5. An annuity rate of 10 percent.
6. A straight-line rate of depreciation of 2½ percent over a period of 40 years.

The Straight-Line Method of Capitalization

Based on this method, and using the formula $V = I/R$, the value of a $1,000 net income (net before interest on capital and amortization of capital) estimated to be derived over an investment life period of 40 years and capitalized at an interest rate of 10 percent is derived by first substituting income and rate data for the symbols in the value formula. The capitalization equation is then $V = \$5,000$ divided by 0.125 (0.10 interest plus 0.025 rate of amortization), giving a present worth of $40,000. The accuracy of this value is proven by

---

[1]This factor table, for selected rates of interest, was developed by one of the authors and first published in the April 1960 issue of the *Appraisal Journal*, American Institute of Real Estate Appraisers. An excerpt from this table is given in Appendix V.

application of the interest and amortization rates as follows:

10% return on $40,000 =	$4,000
2.5% amortization allowance on $40,000 =	1,000
Total required annual income	$5,000

The recapture allowance of $1,000 per year without interest over a period of 40 years will equal the value of the original investment of $40,000. Using the Ring factor table of capitalization, and the formula $V = I \times F$, the appraiser can obtain identical value results. Reference to this table (see Appendix V, page 607) discloses under the 10 percent rate of capitalization, and opposite 40 years, a present worth factor per dollar of income of 8.00000. Multiplying the income expectancy of $5,000 by the Ring factor of 8.00000 (1 ÷ 0.1250) produces a value of $40,000, which is identical to the value found under the $V = I/R$ rate formula above.

An alternative method of capitalization under which identical results can be obtained—but where depreciation under the straight-line theory of capital recapture is provided as an *expense* of operations rather than as a *rate* applied to the net operating income—is demonstrated as follows:

Net operating income	$ 5,000
Depreciation allowance—straight line (40 years)	
$\frac{0.025}{0.125} = 0.20$, and 0.20 × $5,000 =	1,000
Net income after depreciation	$ 4,000
Value of property, $4,000 ÷ 0.10 =	$40,000

As the illustrations above demonstrate, the appraiser has an option to either capitalize income *before* recapture at the selected rate of capitalization, or to capitalize income *after* providing for recapture at the rate of interest only. Based on the income data given above, the appraiser can either divide $5,000 by 0.125 or net income after recapture of $4,000 by the interest rate of 0.10. Both capitalization options will yield identical value results of $40,000.

It is well to emphasize that the appraiser selects by way of market analysis the applicable rate of interest as well as the method and rate of recapture. Since value is always a proportional relationship of income to the rate of capitalization, the net operating income can be divided into interest income and recapture income by the percentage relationship that the interest rate and the recapture rate bear to the combined rate or rate of capitalization. In the illustration above, the rate of capitalization is 12.5 percent, of which 10 percent divided by 12.5 percent, or 80 percent of total income represents interest return on invested capital and 2.5 percent divided by 12.5 percent represents recapture or depreciation return equal to 20 percent.

Since it is readily feasible to separate that portion of net operating income which must be set aside for recapture, it is possible to do so and to include this amount as an operating expense. This is in full accord with accounting practices followed by CPAs, investors, tax consultants, and agents of the Internal Revenue Service. No matter which method of capitalization is selected by the appraiser, the ratio that the rate of recapture bears to the combined rate of capitalization always represents the percentage of net operating income that should be labeled "provision for recapture" in the operating expense schedule.

Under the straight-line method of capitalization, amortization of the investment is provided in equal annual amounts—but as increasing percentages of the remaining value. This can be observed in the table of amortization and the entries derived over the first three years of income life for the investment of $40,000 as shown in Table 18.2.

In appraisal practice, the use of the straight-line method of capital recapture is often justified by the assumption that income from the investment will decline as the property ages in direct proportion to the reduced interest earnings derived from the remaining value of the investment at the end of each year. Thus if the remaining value decreases by $1,000 annually, as shown in the schedule above, income is expected to decrease annually by 10 percent of $1,000, or in the amount of $100 over the 40-year economic-income-life period. Based on declining income under this assumption and under the straight-line method of capitalization, a schedule of amortization would show entries as shown in Table 18.3.

The assumption that net operating income will decline in precise amounts, as indicated in the schedule above, is difficult to substantiate. Furthermore, it is not orthodox mathematical practice to reflect an anticipated decline in the numerator of the equation above ($V = I/R$) by an upward adjustment of the denominator of the value equation. If income is expected to decline over the life of the investment, why not stabilize the future income stream to reflect this decline rather than tamper with the interest or annuity rate by means of which *all* income should be capitalized? To illustrate: If an income of $1,000 per year

Table 18.2   Amortization for an Investment of $40,000 over a 40-Year Period at 10 Percent Interest Under the Straight-Line Method

End of Year	Annual Income	10 Percent Interest	2.5 Percent Amortization	Remaining Value
1	$ 5,000	$ 4,000[a]	$ 1,000	$40,000
2	5,000	4,000	1,000	39,000
3	5,000	4,000	1,000	38,000
. . .	. . .	. . .	. . .	. . .
40	5,000	4,000	1,000	0
Total	$200,000	$160,000	$40,000	

[a]0.10 × $40,000; similarly, the annual amortization figure is based on 0.025 × $40,000.

Table 18.3 Declining Income under Straight Line Capitalization

Year	Annual Income	10 Percent Interest on Value Balance	2.5 Percent Amortization	Remaining Value
				$40,000
1	$5,000	$4,000	$1,000	
2	4,900	3,900	1,000	
3	4,800	3,800	1,000	

over a life period of 40 years is expected to decline annually over its remaining economic life, many appraisers at present capitalize this income flow by dividing $1,000 by the rate of interest plus the straight-line rate of recapture, or given a rate of 10 percent and a rate of recapture of 2.5 percent the indicated value is obtained as follows: $5,000 ÷ 0.125 = $40,000.

The same value, however, can be obtained by stabilizing this declining income stream to an amount of $4,090.40. Capitalizing this *stabilized* income of $4,090.40 by use of the 10 percent Inwood factor for 40 years of 9.779, or the annuity rate of 0.102260, an identical value of $40,000 is obtained. To stabilize a declining income stream (under the straight-line premise) all the appraiser needs to do is to divide the annuity rate of capitalization at the selected interest rate by the straight-line rate of capitalization. In the illustration shown above, the 10 percent annuity rate for 40 years is 0.102260, and the straight-line rate of capitalization is 0.125. Dividing the former rate by the latter yields a quotient of 81.808 percent. This is the stabilized income flow per dollar of income, which, when capitalized by the Inwood factor or the annuity rate (reciprocal of Inwood factor), will give identical value results as those obtained under straight-line capitalization. An even more accurate procedure for forecasting a declining income stream and for capitalizing same will be demonstrated under the annuity method of capitalization as demonstrated below.

Further and thoughtful consideration will lead the appraiser to realize that most properties are purchased and financed up to 80 or more percent of value by means of a mortgage which is always amortized under the compound interest or annuity Inwood method of financing. If the Inwood or annuity method is applicable to 80 or more percent of property value, one must seriously question the accuracy of straight-line recapture and straight-line capitalization when applied to the property as a whole.

The use of the straight-line method of capitalization, however, may be justified for income to be realized over comparatively short periods of an investment life, or where typical investment practices clearly warrant the use of straight-line amortization. For income-producing properties with economic life periods extending over more than 10 years, and where declining incomes can be estimated or stabilized with a fair degree of accuracy by market comparison study, the use of the straight-line method of capitalization is not recommended nor is it professionally defensible.

The Sinking Fund Method of Capitalization

This method of capitalization is based on the premise that the investor has no access or control over the amounts set aside for amortization of the investment and that provisions for capital replacement can be accumulated in a fund, earning compound interest at a safe, or bank, rate of interest. Employing the same valuation data as that used under straight-line capitalization, the value of a $5,000 income for a period of 40 years at 10 percent interest is derived under the sinking fund (3 percent) rate method as follows: $V = I/R = \$5,000$ divided by 0.1132624 (0.10 interest plus 0.0132624[2] amortization at 3 percent interest), which equals a present worth of $44,145.28. The accuracy of this value is proven by the application of interest and amortization rates as follows:

10% return on $44,145.28 =	$4,414.53
1.32624% annual sinking fund requirements on $44,145.28 =	585.47
Total required annual earnings	$5,000.00

The annual depreciation allowance of $585.47, if invested at compound interest at a 3 percent rate over a 40-year period, will equal an amount of $44,145.28 ($585.47 × 75.401260).

A table of amortization showing the income distribution and value decline of an investment of $44,145.28 over the first three years of income life appears in Table 18.4.

Under the sinking fund theory of capital recapture, identical results can be obtained by application of the expense rather than the rate method of capitalization, as follows:

Net income (before interest and amortization)	$ 5,000.00
Depreciation allowance 3% sinking fund (40 years) $\frac{0.0132624}{0.1132624} = 0.117094$, and 0.117094 × $5,000 =	585.47
Net income (after depreciation)	$ 4,414.53
Value of property, $4,412.53 ÷ 0.10 =	$44,145.30

The sinking fund method of capitalization appears designed to serve accounting rather than appraisal purposes. As a rule investment buyers of real

---

[2]This rate was obtained from a sinking fund table at 3 percent interest. (See Chapter 17 for calculator solution.)

Table 18.4 Amortization for an Investment of $44,125.28 over a 40-Year Period at 10 Percent Interest Under the 3 Percent Sinking Fund Method

Year	Annual Income	10 Percent Interest	3 Percent Sinking Fund Annual	Interest	Total	Remaining Value
						$44,125.28
1	$ 5,000	$ 4,412.53	$ 585.47	$ —	$ 585.47	43,539.81
2	5,000			17.56	1,188.50	42,936.78
3	5,000			35.66	1,809.63	42,315.65
. . .	. . .	. . .	. . .	. . .	. . .	. . .
40	. . .	. . .	. . .	. . .	. . .	. . .
Total	$200,000	$176,501.20	$23,418.80	$20,726.38		

property have access to all the net operating income derived from operation of such property and typically do not set up a fund for amortization of equity interests. The sinking fund method also does not provide for declining income as a property ages. It is possible, of course, to consider that the amounts accumulated in the sinking fund are available for reinvestment and that the annual income will decline in proportion to interest earnings on the remaining value, as was the case under straight-line amortization. The assumption, however, to consider accumulated depreciation returns, under this method of capitalization, as available for reinvestment violates the concept of a "fund" on which the sinking fund or Hoskold method of capitalization is founded.

The Annuity Method of Capitalization

This method of capitalization is similar in all respects to the sinking fund method except that no fund is established in which the annual amortization provisions are to accumulate. Instead, the periodic payments for amortization of investment capital are made available to the property user or owner for immediate reinvestment in similar or other types of property. The rates of earning for both the property as a whole, and for portions of the investment returned each year through amortization provisions—and which are available for reinvestment—are considered as one and the same.

To illustrate again by use of the formula $V = I/R$, the value of a $1,000 income for a life period of 40 years at 7 percent interest is $1,000 divided by 0.075009 (0.07 percent interest plus 0.005009, the amortization rate at 7 percent), which equals a present worth of $13,331.71. The accuracy of this value conclusion can be proved as follows:

7% return on $13,331.71 =	$ 933.22
0.005009 amortization allowance on $13,331.71 =	66.78
Total required annual earnings	$1,000.00

The annual depreciation allowance of $66.78, if reinvested at a compound interest of 7 percent over a 40-year period, will equal the original investment of $13,331.71.

The application of the annuity method, too, can be simplified by use of the formula $V = I \times F$ and the Inwood table method of capitalization (covered in Chapter 17). By reference to the Inwood table, a factor of 13.33171 is obtained under the 7 percent interest column opposite 40 years of income life. Alternatively, the following keystroke sequence produces the same results:

40 [n] 7 [i] 1000 [CHS] [PMT] [PV]

Multiplying this factor by the income of $1,000 gives a present value of $13,331.71, which is identical with that obtained under the annuity method of capitalization. The Inwood premise table and the present worth of an annuity of 1 table are one and the same. Amortization of the investment value of $13,331.71 derived under the annuity, or Inwood, method of capitalization is provided as indicated by entries over the first three years of investment life as shown in Table 18.5.

Study of the amortization schedule shown above will reveal that although the income before depreciation remains stable, the interest or net income on which value in the final analysis is based is declining annually. To say, therefore, that the Inwood method of capitalization should be used when the income flow is constant or stable is a misnomer; for if net operating income really were stable, then value would not decline as shown in the amortization schedule above. As demonstrated with the straight-line and sinking fund methods of capitalization, it would, therefore, be more accurate to extract the amount of recapture (depreciation) and to capitalize the remaining (true) net operating income by the investment or interest rate as follows:

Net operating income	$ 1,000.00
Recapture allowance at 7% annuity over 40 years, $\frac{0.005009}{0.075009} = 0.06678$, and $0.06678 \times \$1,000 =$	66.78
Net operating income (after recapture)	$ 933.22
Value of property, $933.22 \div 0.07 =$	$13,331.71

Table 18.5 Amortization for an Investment of $13,331.71 over a 40-Year Period at 7 Percent Interest Under the Annuity Method

Year	Annual Income	7 Percent Interest	Amortization	Remaining Value
				$13,331.71
1	$ 1,000	$ 933.22	$ 66.78	13,264.93
2	1,000	928.55	71.45	13,193.48
3	1,000	923.54	76.46	13,117.02
. . .	. . .	. . .	. . .	. . .
40	. . .	. . .	. . .	. . .
Total	$40,000	$26,668.29	$13,331.71	

It is often and erroneously held that the annuity method of capitalization should be applied only to a constant or "level" income flow, or to annuities which are equal in amount throughout the economic life of the investment property. As will be demonstrated, the annuity, or Inwood, method of capitalization can effectively and accurately be applied whether the income flow is increasing, decreasing, or a combination of both. Even deficit income occasionally incurred—as during initial stages of investment operation—can be capitalized by the annuity method and amortized out of future earnings.

To illustrate the application of the annuity method to capitalization of a declining income expectancy from a typical apartment property, it is assumed that field studies of comparable properties support a conclusion that a most probable pattern of income over the economic life expectancy of 50 years will be as follows:

First 5 years	$10,000
Next 15 years	9,000
Next 10 years	7,500
Next 10 years	6,500
Last 10 years	5,500

The present worth of this declining income stream at 7 percent interest is capitalized with the aid of conventional interest and discount tables as shown below.

The same value conclusion can also be obtained by application of the Inwood factors exclusively, as shown in Table 18.6.

Table 18.6 Capitalization of Declining Income via Inwood Premise Using Two Different Methods

Income Period	Income Expectancy	×	Present Worth of Annuity of 1	×	Deferment Factor (PW of 1)	=	Present Value
1–5	$10,000		4.1002		1.0000		$ 41,002
6–20	9,000		9.1079		0.7130		58,445
21–30	7,500		7.0236		0.2584		13,612
31–40	6,500		7.0236		0.1314		5,999
41–50	5,500		7.0236		0.0668		2,580
Total present value							$121,638

Income Period	Income Expectancy	Inwood Factor	Fractional Factors	Present Value
1–5	$10,000	—	4.1002	$ 41,002
6–20	9,000	(10.5940– 4.1002)	6.4938	58,445
21–30	7,500	(12.4090–10.5940)	1.8150	13,612
31–40	6,500	(13.3317–12.4090)	0.9227	5,999
41–50	5,500	(13.8007–13.3317)	0.4690	2,580
Total: Inwood factor			13.3317	
Total present value				$121,638

Where appraisers prefer to stabilize income rather than report detailed valuation results in stages of declining or increasing amounts as shown above, this stabilization can readily be accomplished by transposing the formula $V = I/R$ to $I = V \times R$. By multiplying the present value derived from the declining income flow in the amount of $121,638 by the 7 percent capitalization annuity rate of 0.07245985 (0.07 interest plus 0.00245985 amortization at 7 percent for 50 years), a level income flow of $8,813.87 is obtained. A schedule of amortization can now be established using the declining income estimates—or the stabilized income amount—as computed above. In both instances the income flow over the 50-year economic life period will yield an income of 7 percent on the remaining value balances and amortize the investment value of $121,638 under the annuity method of capitalization.

The annuity, or Inwood, method of capitalization is almost always used in connection with capitalization of land income where the period of land ownership does not extend into perpetuity, as is the case under leasehold operation. When the reversionary interest of the fee owner (to whom the land reverts at the end of the lease period) is discounted at the same rate at which the income received by the tenant is capitalized, the value of the parts (into which land ownership is divided) will always equal the value of the land as a whole. Assuming a land value of $100,000 and a discount rate of 6 percent, the value of the split interests at 10-year intervals over a 100-year period is derived as shown in Tables 18.7 and 18.8.

The importance of early years of income life as compared with ownership and income privileges that lie in the distant future can be judged effectively by inspection of the foregoing tables. At 6 percent interest, and under the annuity method of capitalization, the present worth of the income flow over the first 20 years equals 68.8 percent of total property value as compared with 100 percent for income rights that extend into perpetuity. The first 40 years represent 90.3 percent of total property value, and rights extending beyond 80 years and into perpetuity have a present worth of less than 1 percent of total value.

Table 18.7 Present Worth of Income Flow to Land User

Years	Income	Inwood Factor	Present Worth of Income	Percent of Total Value
10	$6,000	7.360087	$44,161	44.2
20	6,000	11.469921	68,820	68.8
30	6,000	13.764831	82,589	82.6
40	6,000	15.046297	90,278	90.3
50	6,000	15.761861	94,571	94.6
60	6,000	16.161428	96,969	97.0
70	6,000	16.384544	98,307	98.3
80	6,000	16.509131	99,055	99.1
90	6,000	16.578699	99,472	99.5
100	6,000	16.617546	99,705	99.7

Table 18.8 Present Worth of Fee Owner's (Reversionary) Interest

Years	Value of Land	Present Worth Factor	Present Value of Reversion Land	Percent of Total Value
10	$100,000	0.558395	$55,840	55.8
20	100,000	0.311805	31,181	31.2
30	100,000	0.174110	17,411	17.4
40	100,000	0.097222	9,722	9.7
50	100,000	0.054288	5,429	5.4
60	100,000	0.030314	3,031	3.0
70	100,000	0.016927	1,693	1.7
80	100,000	0.009452	945	0.9
90	100,000	0.005278	528	0.5
100	100,000	0.002947	295	0.3

DISCOUNTED CASH FLOW

Capitalization is a process for converting periodic future income into an estimated present value. This income conversion process can occur in a variety of
ways such as discussed earlier in this chapter as well as in Chapters 16 and 17.
It is essential that the appraiser be familiar with a variety of methods as well as
know when to apply each method. Earlier, the discounted income from a graduated or step lease was explained. Other variations of irregular income streams
require that a substitute for the Inwood factor used to discount level income
streams be found. Several possible situations require this alternative analysis. It
may be that the appraiser is required to find (1) the present worth of an income
stream that changes annually, (2) the present worth of a changing income stream
as well as the need to account for the down payment and eventual net sales
proceeds, or (3) whether a prospective investment is likely to fulfill an investor's
criteria.

Well over one-half of all institutional real estate investors now use DCF,
particularly internal rate of return (IRR) before taxes. An even higher proportion use this form of DCF on an after-tax basis.[3] Appropriately, increasing
numbers of appraisers have begun to include DCF analysis in reports on income
properties. With greater accessibility to microcomputers and well-designed software, appraisers can be expected to perform both before- and after-tax analyses.
The latter is very important for investment and financial feasibility analyses.

The initial example involves computing the present worth of an income
stream that is scheduled to change annually. It can be computed by use of the
present worth of one (reversion) factors. Assume that the appropriate discount
rate is 10 percent, as shown in Table 17.1. The annual cash flows (could just as
well have been net operating income) are as follows: year 1, $10,000; year 2,

[3]Page, Daniel E. "Criteria for Investment Decision Making: An Empirical Study," *The
Appraisal Journal*, 51, no. 4 (October 1983), pp. 498–508.

Table 18.9 Present Worth via Discounted Cash Flow Method

Year	Cash Flows	×	PW of 1	=	Present Worth
1	$10,000		0.909091		$ 9,091
2	20,000		0.826446		16,529
3	30,000		0.751315		22,539
4	40,000		0.683013		27,321
5	50,000		0.620921		31,046
6	60,000		0.564474		33,868
7	70,000		0.513158		35,921
Total present worth					$176,315

$20,000; year 3, $30,000; year 4, $30,000; year 5, $40,000; year 6, $30,000; year 7, $10,000. To find the present value of these individual cash flows, each must be discounted by the corresponding present worth factor (see Table 18.9). Assume that the income is received at the end of each year.

As can be seen in the example above, an advantage of the discounted cash flow (DCF) method is its ability to be sensitive to the time value of money. That is, it measures the present worth of variable income when it is received rather than on the less accurate average income basis. At the same time, an inherent weakness of this method is that it is usually based on subjective future forecasts of income and expenses. As in all capitalization techniques, diligence is required in selecting the discount rate(s).

Now suppose that the property being analyzed is a proposed structure and consequently is not expected to achieve a stabilized occupancy until the third year. Also, the buyer must make a down payment of $25,000 when the property is purchased. At the end of the fifth year, it is forecast that the net sales proceeds will be $200,000. A 10 percent annual rate of return is necessary to attract investors to this type of venture. The annual income is: year 1 ($50,000); year 2 ($15,000); year 3, $60,000; year 4, $65,000; year 5, $70,000.

The estimated value of this property is shown in Table 18.10.

Table 18.10 Present Worth of Investment with Positive and Negative Cash Flows

Year	Cash Flow	×	PW of 1	=	Present Worth
0	$(25,000)		1		$ (25,000)
1	(50,000)		0.909091		(45,455)
2	(15,000)		0.826446		(12,397)
3	60,000		0.751315		45,079
4	65,000		0.683013		44,396
5	$200,000[a] + 70,000		0.620921		167,649
Net present value					$174,272

[a]Rather than multiply the PW of 1 for five years by the cash flow and net sales proceeds separately, the dollar values of each have been combined.

Table 18.11 Investment with Downpayment and Mixed Cash Flows

Year	Cash Flow	×	PW of 1	=	Present Worth
0	$(75,000)		1		$(75,000)
1	(50,000)		0.909091		(45,455)
2	(15,000)		0.826446		(12,397)
3	60,000		0.751315		45,079
4	65,000		0.683013		44,396
5	120,000		0.620921		74,511
	($50,000 + $70,000)				
Net present value					$ 31,134

Suppose that the investment above required an initial equity contribution of $75,000 and the expected net sale proceeds were $50,000. Would this be a financially acceptable investment if the investor required a 10 percent equity yield? The answer is "yes." Look at Table 18.11.

The net present value (NPV) concept might be thought of as a "go–no go" test of financial feasibility. Certain prescribed conditions, such as projected income, expenses, initial and final equity, as well as the investor's desired equity yield rate, are applied. If under these preset conditions the NPV is equal to or greater than zero (as found above), the investment is feasible. If not, it is judged to be infeasible. In the example above, the investment would be acceptable to the investor.

Upon receiving this information the client may now decide that he would like to know the exact return on his investment. The process for finding the exact investment return is called "internal rate of return" (IRR). Since the NPV is greater than zero, the total return rate or IRR is known to be in excess of 10 percent. Finding IRR is an iterative or trial-and-error process. This iterative process is simply repeating calculations until a more refined answer occurs. The objective of internal rate of return is to find that discount rate that causes the outflows to equal the inflows. If the discounted cash flows exceed zero, a higher discount should be used. The reverse procedure applies when the discounted cash flows are less than zero.

It may be necessary to interpolate to determine the exact IRR, as shown below. Also, a financial calculator can be used. This alternative is illustrated below as well. A higher discount rate must be selected since the NPV is greater than zero.

By using the foregoing process, or a financial calculator, the net present value at 18 percent can be found:

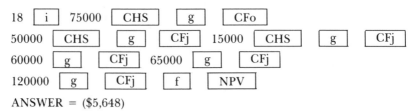

ANSWER = ($5,648)

Thus the IRR lies between 10 and 18 percent, but much closer to 18 percent than 10 percent. By use of interpolation the *approximate* answer can be found. It should be remembered that more accurate results will occur when the trial run rates are relatively close to the actual rate, such as 10 and 11 percent.

	Rate		NPV
	0.10	$31,134	$31,134
	IRR	0	
	0.18		(5,648)
Difference	0.08	$31,134	$36,782

$$\text{IRR} = 0.10 + 0.08\ (\$31{,}134/\$36{,}782)$$

$$= 0.10 + 0.08\ (0.8464)$$

$$= \underline{\underline{0.1677}}$$

Similarly, the IRR can more easily be found by financial calculator by continuing the keystroke sequence above as follows:

| f | | IRR | ANSWER = 0.1654

SUMMARY

The income approach to value calls for application of the capitalization process and use of the basic formula $V = I/R$ or $V = I \times F$. The first formula gives the appraiser a choice of three methods of capitalization, commonly known as:

1. The straight-line rate method.
2. The sinking fund rate method.
3. The annuity rate method.

Where the latter formula is applied, specially prepared factor tables are available. These factor tables are reciprocals of the rates found under the straight-line, sinking fund, and annuity rate methods of capitalization and are in the order given above:

1. The Ring factor table.
2. The Hoskold factor table.
3. The Inwood factor table.

To illustrate the application of the rate and factor methods of capitalization, the following data are assumed: a net operating income of $1,000 per annum over an economic life period of 40 years, a rate of interest of 7 percent, and a 3 percent sinking fund earnings rate. Based on these income rate and property life data, value results were obtained as follows:

Straight Line

1. Straight-line rate capitalization:

$$V = I/R = \$1,000 \div 0.095 = \$10,526.32$$
$$(0.07 + 0.025)$$

2. Ring factor capitalization:

$$V = I \times F = \$1,000 \times 10.52632 = \$10,526.32$$
$$(1/0.095)$$

Sinking Fund at 3 Percent

1. Sinking fund rate capitalization:

$$V = I/R = \$1,000 \div 0.0832624 = \$12,010.22$$

2. Hoskold factor capitalization:

$$V = I \times F = \$1,000 \times 12.01022 = \$12,010.22$$

Annuity Method

1. Annuity method rate capitalization:

$$V = I/R = \$1,000 \div 0.07500913 = \$13,331.71$$
$$(0.07 + \text{sinking fund factor})$$

2. Inwood capitalization:

$$V = I \times F = \$1,000 \times 13.33171 = \$13,331.71$$
$$(1/\text{annuity rate})$$

The values obtained under the respective methods of capitalization vary from a low of \$10,526.32 under the straight-line method to a high of \$13,331.71 under the annuity method for identical income streams of \$1,000 capitalized at 7 percent rate of interest. The difference in value is entirely due to differences in the amounts of income (expressed as a rate per dollar) set aside under each capitalization method for amortization purposes. The greater the portion of net operating income that is reserved for depreciation anticipated over the economic life span of the property, the lesser the amount that represents interest earnings—and, as a consequence, the smaller the capital value.

In appraisal practice, only one method of capitalization can logically be applied. The selection of the appropriate method of capitalization should not be made haphazardly, nor should the choice be influenced by attempts to obtain high, low, or conservative value estimates. Rather it is the appraiser's duty to study earnings-to-price relationships at which comparable properties have exchanged in the open market and to use rates as well as methods of capitalization which reflect typical market practices and operations.

REVIEW QUESTIONS

Given the following information, solve for the present value of a property using the methods called for in each question. Use financial calculators whenever possible (see Chapter 17):

Forecast income period	25 years
Discount rate	10%
Annual net operating income	$10,000
Owner's reinvestment rate	
(for sinking fund)	5%

1. Find the present value via Ring factor capitalization.
2. What is the value of this property using the sinking fund premise?
3. Calculate the value of the income stream above using the annuity method of capitalization.
4. Discuss the reasoning behind the different values found by use of the sinking fund and annuity capitalization methods.
5. Compute the value of the property above using the present worth of 1 per period factor (Inwood) and compare the results to the answer found in question 3.
6. Explain how the NPV concept is similar to as well as different from IRR.
7. A building 40 years old is located in a strong central business district and has shown profitable operating returns throughout its entire history. It is now proposed to modernize the structure at a cost of $150,000. The land has a value of $200,000. Taxes are estimated at $14,500 per annum after modernization. An appraisal of the structure made from plans indicates that after modernization, the building will be worth $250,000. Depreciation has been charged in the past at 2½ percent and will be charged at the same rate in the future. The present owner, who has owned the property since the building was originally constructed, expects to hold the property and seeks a return of 9 percent net on her investment.
   (a) On the basis of a land investment of $200,000, what is the owner's net investment after remodeling?
   (b) What is the net rental required to pay 9 percent and to liquidate the owner's depreciable investment in 40 years?
   Assuming that the property is placed on the market and is sold at its value, not its cost:
   (c) What net rental would a prudent buyer require assuming a 9 percent return and liquidation of her depreciable investment in 25 years?
   (d) Explain how a prudent buyer would establish an equitable *net* rent.

READING AND STUDY REFERENCES

GRISSOM, TERRY V., and JAMES L. KUHLE. "An Alternative Cash Flow Method for Real Estate Analysis," *The Real Estate Appraiser and Analyst* 49, no. 4 (Winter 1983), pp. 52–58.

HINES, MARY ALICE. Chapter 12, *Real Estate Appraisal*. New York: Macmillan Publishing Company, 1981.

KORPACZ, PETER F., and MARK I. ROTH. "Changing Emphasis in Appraisal Techniques: The Transition to Discounted Cash Flow," *The Appraisal Journal* 51, no. 1 (January 1983), pp. 21–44.

RING, ALFRED A. "Streamlining the Income Approach to Value," *The Real Estate Appraiser* 35, no. 1 (January–February 1969), pp. 43–47.

SMITH, HALBERT C. Chapter 5, *Real Estate Appraisal*. Columbus, Ohio: Grid Publishing Inc., 1976.

STRUNG, JOSEPH. "The Internal Rate of Return and the Reinvestment Presumptions," *The Appraisal Journal* 44, no. 1 (January 1976), pp. 23–33.

WENDT, PAUL F. Chapter 6, *Real Estate Appraisal: Review and Outlook*. Athens: University of Georgia Press, 1974.

19

PHYSICAL RESIDUAL TECHNIQUES OF CAPITALIZATION

Learning Objectives
Afer reading this chapter, you should be able to:

Determine which of the physical residual techniques of capitalization is most applicable in determining an estimate of value under given circumstances

Be more aware of the comparative strengths and weaknesses of each of the physical residual techniques

Outline the steps involved in each residual technique

Use the appropriate residual technique along with the different future income and value premises to fit a particular appraisal assignment

Understand why a given future income–value change assumption produces higher or lower values than do alternative methods

In the foregoing chapter, discussion of the income approach to value was limited to application of methods of capitalization. Separate treatment was given to valuation procedure for perpetuity income derived from land and nonperpetuity income derived from either land or building improvements. To promote better understanding of the different methods of capitalization, it was assumed that income from land and income from buildings and their respective values can readily be obtained as separate entities, and that summation of the values of the parts will yield an estimate of the value of the whole—i.e., for the entire property.

In everyday practice, when improvements are placed on land to make land productive in conformity with the principle of highest and best use, an economic merger takes place that weds the investment parts into an economic unit, or property, as a whole. Physically, we can describe the nature and character of land, and, separately, the amount, kind, and quality of the improvements—but income derived from operation is a product of the joint property and not an aggregate of its parts. Yet in valuation procedure it does become necessary to isolate the income attributable to the parts in order to ascertain whether land, in fact, is developed to its highest and best use, and if not, the extent to which value losses are ascribable to the human-made improvements as a measure of functional or external obsolescence; there are other instances where, for example, the value of the mortgage can more readily be ascertained than the equity—the complementary part. This subject will be considered later in Chapter 21.

In all appraising problems where land and building improvements form an integral whole from which revenue and capitalizable net operating income is derived, the appraiser has available the income approach to value (1) the land residual, (2) the building residual, or (3) the property residual techniques of valuation. Which appraisal technique to apply is not a matter of arbitrary selection but rather one dependent on the nature of the valuation data. Where land is developed under a program of highest and best use, and where the improvements are in new condition, it is logical to determine the amount of net income necessary to yield a prevailing (market) risk rate on the value of the building—plus the amounts which are necessary to amortize periodically the depreciable part of the building investment. The amount of income left is then residual to the land and forms the basis for an estimation of land value via the capitalization, or income, approach. Where land is vacant and available for use, the land residual technique permits study of alternative (hypothetical) land uses in order to determine which use over a period of years produces the highest residual land income and hence the highest present value of the land.

When land is developed with improvements considered to be in middle or late economic life, or which do not represent the highest and best use of the site, it is logical to ascertain first wherever possible the value of the land by either the market comparison method or by a hypothetical analysis of land uses and capitalization of land income under a highest and best program of land utilization. Once the value of land is known, the income attributable to land at going rates of interest can be determined, and the balance of the net operating income becomes residual to the building improvements. By capitalization of the residual income under the appropriate method of income conversion, the value of the building is obtained. The building residual technique of capitalization also serves a highly useful purpose in cases where community growth or shifting land uses cause rapid increases in land value and, conversely, accelerates building obsolescence. Where, under this technique of valuation, the net operating income barely covers the income necessary to yield a fair return on the rising value of the land, the appraiser can report the approaching end of a building's economic life and the necessity to plan for reconstruction or rehabilitation to maintain a future flow of income and to preserve the financial integrity of the property as a going investment.

In some instances where buildings are old and land is of specialized nature, or in a location where neither market transactions nor income analysis makes possible a reasonably accurate estimate of land value, it is necessary to treat the property as an integral whole and to apply the property residual technique of valuation. In such instances care must be taken not to use the straight-line or sinking fund methods of capitalization, since both of these methods for the duration of the property life apply to land a rate of amortization which is inconsistent with basic theory and practice underlying the valuation of land. If the property residual technique is deemed applicable, the appraiser should estimate with care the pattern of income flow anticipated over the economic life span of the property and convert this income stream into a sum of present value under the annuity method of capitalization. To the capitalized value of the property income must then be added the present, or reversionary, worth of the land based on land value when such land is free for sale or use at the end of the economic life of the subject property. Since only the present or reversionary worth of estimated future land value is added to the capitalized value of property income, errors in the estimated land value are minimized under this technique of capitalization.

THE RESIDUAL CHARACTER OF LAND

As explained in Chapter 9, the value of land is dependent on its use in combination with labor and capital investment; and the highest value of land is reached at a point when expenditures for land improvements are in accordance with the principle of highest and best land use. Although value can be assigned to land by studying similar sites which are effectively utilized or which have sold recently in the open market, economic comparability via the sales comparison approach is based on judgment and is difficult to achieve—especially where land is found to be best suited for agricultural, industrial, or special-purpose commercial uses. But even where market transactions are considered as reliable indices of value, a check on the accuracy of market forces generally necessitates the application of the capitalized income approach to value.

Economically, land is residual in character. This means that the factors of labor and capital, when combined with land, must be compensated first or they will cease to function and the balance of income which remains is thus residual (left over) to land. It is this residual income which, under highest and best utilization, forms the logical basis for land value.

In appraisal practice, land is found either vacant and available for immediate or prospective use or in different stages of utilization. Because of this, various capitalization techniques had to be developed to strengthen the order of income priority of the production factors, as warranted under given and ever-changing socioeconomic circumstances. The techniques of capitalization which are generally applied in appraisal practice, and which will be fully explained and demonstrated below, are the:

1. Land residual technique.
2. Building residual technique.
3. Property residual technique.

LAND RESIDUAL TECHNIQUE

Where buildings are new and their values are known or can be estimated with reasonable accuracy, the land residual technique is used for estimating land value and for obtaining the value of the property as a whole. Also, it is well applied to such newer properties where the building makes up a large part of the total value. Hence, any possibility of error occurring in the land value estimate will have only a minimum effect on the overall estimated property value. Generally this technique of separating property net operating income into sums attributable to land and buildings is used either when the land is vacant—or assumed to be vacant—and available for development under its highest and best use, or is actually improved with a new building that constitutes the highest and best utilization of property.

Where the property is vacant or assumed to be vacant, it is the appraiser's responsibility to visualize, specify, and support the kind of land improvements which will yield to land a residual income stream that, when appropriately capitalized, results in the highest present value of the land. This generally involves appraising for highest and best use purposes, since the specified improvements in fact may not be built at the time of valuation—or even in the immediate future. Nevertheless, if this capitalization technique is to be accurately applied, the appraiser must carry out the following steps:

1. Describe and justify the type (architecture), kind (materials used), and quality of improvements that are recommended for construction under a program of highest and best land use.
2. Accurately estimate, or ascertain, dependable bids for construction costs of building and related land improvements complete in all respects and ready for operation as of a given date.
3. Estimate the effective gross revenue that can reasonably be obtained under typical management and operation.
4. Estimate the operating expenses to be incurred under typical management, and by subtracting these from the effective gross revenue derive the net operating income before interest and amortization payments.
5. Derive by market study and analysis the risk rate[1] at which land and building income is to be capitalized.
6. Select the method of capitalization and determine the period of economic life expectancy of the building investment or holding period based on the market actions of typical investors who have purchased like or similar properties.
7. Estimate the amount that must be subtracted from the capitalized value of land

---

[1]Risk rate is defined as that rate required by investors; it provides for a periodic return on an investment.

to account for loss of interest earnings and costs incurred during the period of land development.

Where the land is already improved under a program of highest and best use, and where the buildings are in new condition and in operating order, steps 1, 2, and 7 above may be eliminated. To illustrate the application of the land residual technique under straight-line and annuity methods of capitalization, the following assumptions are made:

1. Value of building improvements	$100,000
2. Estimated remaining economic life	50 years
3. Risk rate	10%
4. Net operating income	$ 15,000

1. Land Residual Technique: Straight-Line Capitalization

Net operating income		$15,000
Building capitalization rate (R_B):		
Interest rate	0.10	
Amortization rate (100% ÷ 50)	0.02	
Total building rate	0.12	
Building income (I_B):		
$I = V \times R = \$100,000 \times 0.12 =$		$12,000
Land income (I_L):		$ 3,000
Land capitalization rate (R_L) 0.10		
Land value, $V = I/R = \$3,000 \div 0.10 =$		$30,000
Property value:		
Land	$ 30,000	
Building	100,000	
Total	$130,000	

2. Land Residual Technique: Annuity Method Capitalization

Net operating income		$15,000
Building rate of capitalization:		
Risk rate	0.10	
Amortization rate (SF table 10%)[2]	0.000859	
Total rate	0.100859	
Income attributable to building:		
$I = V \times R = \$100,000 \times 0.100859 =$		10,086
Income attributable to land:		$ 4,914
Land rate of capitalization 0.10		
Land value, $V = I/R = \$4,914 \div 0.10 =$		$49,140
Property value:		
Land	$ 49,140	
Building	100,000	
Total	$149,140	

[2]See Table 17.1 as well as other sections of that chapter for calculator keystrokes for finding present and future value factors.

Note that a higher value results from use of the annuity method, which is based on a level income stream. On the other hand, the straight-line capitalization method assumes that both the building value and income will decline.

3. Land Residual Technique: Changing Income and Value Premise

There are instances when neither the income nor the value of the land and building are expected to remain level over a given forecast period. It is also possible that the income will remain constant while the land value increases (or declines) and the building value declines (or increases). Moreover, it may be that the change in land or building value will occur on either a linear or exponential basis. When change occurs on a linear (or straight-line) basis, it increases or decreases by the same dollar amount each year. Alternatively, exponential change implies the value changes by the same percentage amount each period.

The generalized equation used to account for these changes in arriving at a capitalization rate is

$$R = Y = \Delta a$$

where R = capitalization rate, such as R_O, R_L, or R_B
Y = equity or property yield rate (allowing for anticipated future value changes)
Δ = overall value change during the forecast period
a = annualizer (factor that converts overall change to annual change)

The three major possibilities regarding changing incomes and values are:

1. Income stream remains level while value changes.
2. Both income and value will change linearly.
3. Both income and value will change exponentially.

Level income and changing value. This income-value pattern necessitates annualizing the overall value change by use of a sinking fund factor computed at the equity yield rate. The equation then becomes

$$R = Y - \Delta(1/S_{\overline{n}|})$$

An example of this method follows.
Find the value of a property under the following circumstances:

Level annual net operating income	$ 15,000
Yield rate	10%
Forecast period	20 years
Expected land value change	+100%
Expected building value change	−20%
Estimated building value	$130,000

Net operating income $(I_L + I_B)$		$ 15,000
− Building income (I_B)		
($130,000)[0.10 + (0.20 × 0.017460)]		13,454
= Land income (I_L)		$ 1,546
Capitalized at R_L		
($1,546 [0.10 − (1 × 0.017460)]		
= Land value	$ 18,730	
+ Building value	130,000	
= Property value	$148,730	

Income and value changing linearly. If both the income and value of a property are expected to change on a straight-line basis, the capitalization equation is modified as follows:

$$R = Y - \Delta(1/n)$$

That is, the annualizer (a) is the reciprocal of the forecast period. Thus the property value would now be estimated as follows:

Net operating income $(I_L + I_B)$		$15,000
− Building income (I_B)		
($130,000)(0.10 + 0.20 × 0.05)		14,300
= Land income (I_L)		$ 700
Capitalized at R_L		
($700/0.10 − 1 × 0.05)		
= Land value	$ 14,000	
+ Building value	130,000	
= Property value	$144,000	

Income and value changing exponentially. When the income and property value are forecast to change at the same annual percentage rate, that rate of change replaces both Δ and a. Thus the capitalization equation can be restated as

$$R = Y - CR$$

with CR being the annual compounded rate of change. Under this premise, the property data above would be processed as follows:

Net operating income		$15,000
− Building income $(I_B)^3$		
($130,000)(0.10 + 0.009091)		14,182
= Land income (I_L)		$ 818
Capitalized at R_L		
($818/0.10 − 0.033333)		
= Land value	$ 12,270	
+ Building value	130,000	
= Property value	$142,270	

It can readily be seen that varying expectations of future income and value produce different present value estimates. Therefore, considerable care must be given in the forecasting of these future outcomes.

Somewhat different values were indicated by each of the methods above, which were based on different income and value assumptions. These estimated values varied as follows:

Level income and changing value	$148,730
Income and value changing linearly	144,000
Income and value changing exponentially	142,270

These variations again point up the professional necessity of selecting with great care the method under which an income flow is to be capitalized. It is not consistent with operating experience to assume that income will remain constant over the entire period of economic life, nor is it appropriate to provide for income decline through a rate of amortization. Where the income flow pattern and value changes can be estimated with reasonable certainty, one of the alternative methods of capitalization suggested in sections 2 and 3 can be counted on to produce consistent, logical, and professionally defendable value estimates.

BUILDING RESIDUAL TECHNIQUE

Where land value is known—or can be established with reasonable certainty under the market approach to value or under the capitalization of ground lease income—the appraiser can determine the portion of total net operating income that is attributable to the *known*, the land, and make the balance residual to the *unknown*, which in this instance is the building. Generally, the building residual technique of capitalization is applicable when the building improvements are substantially depreciated, do not conform to standards which represent the highest and best use of the land, or the cost new of the building as well as the depreciated cost are difficult to estimate.

To apply the building residual technique, the appraiser must obtain or estimate the following:

1. The land value by market, income, or preferably both approaches to value.
2. Estimate the effective gross revenue obtainable under typical management.

$$\frac{^3\Delta I \times Y,}{\Delta I + Y} \quad \text{or} \quad \frac{(0.20/20)(0.10)}{0.20/20 + 0.10} = 0.009091$$

3. Estimate the operating property expenditures and derive the net operating income—net, as always, before interest and amortization charges.
4. Derive the risk rate at which land and building income is to be capitalized.
5. Select the method of capitalization, and determine the remaining economic life expectancy of the building improvements or the income forecast period.

To illustrate the application of the building residual technique under straight-line and annuity methods of capitalization, the following assumptions are made:

1. Value of land	$50,000
2. Estimated remaining economic life	30 years
3. Rate of land and building interest	10%
4. Net operating income	$15,000

1. Building Residual Technique: Straight-Line Capitalization

Net operating income		$15,000
Income attributable to land:		
$I = V \times R = \$50,000 \times 0.10 =$		5,000
Income attributable to building =		$10,000
Building rate of capitalization:		
Interest rate	0.10	
Amortization rate (100% ÷ 30)	0.033333	
Total rate	0.133333	
Building value:		
$V = I/R = \$10,000 \div 0.133333 =$		$75,000
Property value:		
Land value	$ 50,000	
Building value	75,000	
Total	$125,000	

2. Building Residual Technique: Annuity Method of Capitalization

Net operating income		$15,000
Income attributable to land:		
$I = V \times R = \$50,000 \times 0.10 =$		5,000
Income attributable to building =		$10,000
Building rate of capitalization:		
Interest rate	0.10	
Amortization rate (SF 10%)	0.006079	
Total rate	0.106079	
Building value:		
$V = I/R = \$10,000 \div 0.106079 =$		$94,269
Property value:		
Land value	$ 50,000	
Building	94,269	
Total	$144,269	

3. Building Residual Technique: Straight-Line Expense Method of Capitalization

Net operating income	$ 15,000
Income to land $50,000 × 0.10 =	5,000
Income to building—before depreciation	$ 10,000
Depreciation on building: $\frac{0.033333}{0.133333} = 0.249998$	
and $10,000 × 0.249998 =	2,500
Building income—after depreciation	$ 7,500
Residual value of building, $7,500 ÷ 0.10 =	$ 75,000
Add value of land	50,000
Total property value	$125,000

4. Building Residual Technique: Annuity Expense Method of Capitalization[4]

Net operating income	$ 15,000
Income to land $50,000 × 0.10 =	5,000
Income to building—before depreciation	$ 10,000
Depreciation on building: $\frac{0.006079}{0.106079} = 0.057306$	
and $10,000 × 0.057306 =	573
Building income—after depreciation	$ 9,427
Residual value of building, $9,427 ÷ 0.10 =	$ 94,270
Add value of land	50,000
Total property value	$144,270

As illustrated, under the building residual technique the land value of $50,000 is held constant and the building value varies depending on the method of capitalization employed. The straight-line method, again, results in the lowest value—in this case, $125,000—for the building, and the annuity method in the highest value, $144,270. Logically, an identical income stream should not produce different values. Again, the reasons for the differences are found in the methods used for providing for future building depreciation, or amortization. The higher amounts set aside under straight-line amortization leave less net income available as interest earnings, hence the lower value. For long-lived properties, there can be only one correct method of amortization. The choice

[4]This expense method deducts an annual depreciation expense from the building income (before depreciation) to give the building income after expenses. The annual depreciation rate is determined by dividing the sinking fund factor by the corresponding partial payment factor (at 10 percent for 30 years).

of four different methods has long proved confusing to laypersons and real estate practitioners alike. Where a reasonably accurate estimate of future earnings can be made either on a declining, rising or a stabilized income basis, the annuity method of capitalization gives results which are consistent with monetary compound interest theory and practice (see Chapter 18).

5. Building Residual Technique: Changing Income and Value Premise

Level income and changing value. Continuing with the example used previously under the land residual technique, we can find the present value of a property using the building residual technique. Initially, it is expected that the income will remain level (probably due to lease requirements) while the value of the property's land and building components are forecast to change during the forecast period.

The same data used previously apply to this example except that the value of the site is judged to be $18,750; the building value is unknown. The value of the property is estimated as follows:

Net operating income ($I_L + I_B$)		$15,000
− Land income (I_L)		
($18,750)(0.10 − 1 × 0.017460)		1,548
= Building income (I_B)		$13,452
Capitalized at R_B		
($13,452/0.10 + 0.20 × 0.017460)		
= Building value	$129,981	
+ Land value	18,750	
= Property value	$148,731	

Income and value changing linearly. This example is similar to the previous land residual except that now the value of the land has already been estimated at $14,000, and the value of the building is now sought as follows:

Net operating income ($I_L + I_B$)		$15,000
− Land income (I_B)		
($14,000)(0.10 − 1 × 0.05)		700
− Building income (I_B)		$14,300
($14,300/0.10 + 0.20 × 0.05)		
= Building value	$130,000	
+ Land value	14,000	
= Property value	$144,000	

Income and value changing exponentially. Assume that both the income and values will change on a compound interest basis. Beginning with an estimated value of $12,270, the residual building value remains to be ascertained, as follows:[5]

Net operating income		$15,000
− Land income		
($12,270)(0.10 − 0.033333)		818
= Building income		$14,182
Capitalized at R_B		
($14,182/0.10 + 0.009091)		
= Building value	$130,002	
+ Land value	12,270	
= Property value	$142,272	

PROPERTY RESIDUAL TECHNIQUE

Occasionally, valuation problems arise in which total property income is difficult to allocate to either land or building. This may be the case where building improvements are old and where there is doubt as to whether they constitute the highest and best land use. Then, too, market sales of comparable sites may not be available, and hypothetical analysis of land income and land value may be of doubtful validity because of the location or specialized character of the land. Under such circumstances the appraiser may find the application of the property residual technique a useful tool of valuation.

This method is frequently used without being identified as the property residual technique. Instead, it is called the Inwood plus the reversion method. However identified, the total present property value is the addition of the present value of the presumed level income stream and the present value of the land and possibly building value at some future date. It often is used to estimate the leased fee value of property under a long-term lease.

In view of the extreme uncertainty of estimating the future income and value at the end of a building's remaining economic life, a shorter forecast term has been substituted in recent years. This alternative forecast period generally coincides with the period that investors tend to hold a particular class of property. Additionally, this method has become more realistic by providing for several possible future income and value patterns. A criticism of this technique is the dependency of the present value estimate on a long-term future value estimate (i.e., the reversionary value).

[5]Land and building incomes were computed previously under land residual example.

To employ the property residual technique, the appraiser must secure or make the following:

1. An estimate of the effective gross revenue that is obtainable under typical management.

2. An estimate of the net operating income—net before interest and amortization charges.
3. The rate at which the property income is to be capitalized.
4. The method of capitalization to be applied over the remaining economic life of the property or the shorter holding period.
5. An estimate of the probable property value at the end of the forecast income period. This may include land and building or just the building.

With the aid of these data, the property residual technique can be applied. For illustration purposes the following initially will be assumed:

1. A risk rate of 10 percent.
2. A building economic life of 30 years.
3. A net operating income of $15,000.
4. An estimated reversionary land value of $40,000.

Based on these assumptions, the property residual technique will be applied under straight-line and annuity methods of capitalization. Later, different assumptions will be used.

1. Property Residual Technique: Straight-Line Capitalization

Net operating income		$ 15,000
Property rate of capitalization:		
Interest rate	0.10	
Amortization rate	0.033333	
Total rate	0.133333	
Property value of property income:		
$V = I/R = \$15,000 \div 0.133333$		$112,500
or $V = I \times F = \$15,000 \times 7.500019$ (Ring factor)		
Reversionary value of land:		
$\$40,000 \times 0.057309 =$		2,292
Property value:		
Value of property income	$112,500	
Present reversionary value of land	2,292	
Total	$114,792	

2. Property Residual Technique: Annuity Method Capitalization

Net operating income		$ 15,000
Property rate of capitalization:		
Interest rate	0.10	
Amortization rate (SF 10%)	0.006079	
Total rate	0.106079	
Value of property income:		
$V = I/R = \$15,000 \div 0.106079 =$		$141,404
or $V = I \times F = \$15,000 \times 9.426914$ (Inwood)		
Present worth of land:		
$\$40,000 \times 0.057309 =$		2,292
Property value:		
Value of property income	$141,404	
Present reversionary value of land	2,292	
Total	$143,696	

The property residual technique, too, produces value results which differ importantly, depending on the method of capitalization used to provide for amortization of the nonperpetuity property investment. Again, the low value under the straight-line provision results because this method subtracts the highest annual amounts from the income stream for estimated losses due to future depreciation.

Appraisers are cautioned against careless or inopportune use of the property residual technique of valuation where a straight-line rate of amortization is combined with the risk rate to form a rate of capitalization. The application of a straight-line amortization rate to total property income in effect applies a rate of depreciation to the land in excess of that sanctioned by sound appraisal practice for a period extending over the life of the building. Thus the longer the economic life of the property, the greater the error in the estimate of value under the straight-line (and sinking fund) method of capitalization. The built-in errors can readily be detected by reference to the value results obtained above under the building residual and property residual techniques. It will be noted that for both techniques the basic income, building, and land value data are identical as follows: net operating income, $15,000; building or property life, 30 years; land value, $50,000; and 10 percent risk rate. The value results obtained on the basis of these identical assumptions compare as follows:

Method of Capitalization	Building Residual	Property Residual
Straight line	$125,000	$114,792
Annuity	144,270	143,696

Only under the annuity method of capitalization are similar value results consistently obtained using both residual techniques, where the underlying income and property data remain equal. The substantial error under the straight-line method points up, once more, the fallacy of mixing an interest-bearing rate of capitalization with a noninterest-bearing rate of amortization.

Nevertheless, the property residual technique under the annuity, or Inwood, method of capitalization serves a useful appraising function. There are occasions when neither land nor building value can be obtained with reasonable accuracy. Under such circumstances the application of either the land or building residual techniques is inappropriate. If these techniques are used, they will magnify the basic error where value of land or building is assumed. The property residual technique, it may be pointed out, also assumes a land or property value in the distant future. Does not such an unreliable forecast invalidate the use of this method also? It does not, because in the property residual technique only the reversionary (present worth)—not the full—value of the land (or property) is included in the appraisal estimate. The effect of a possible error in computing the future value of the land is thus minimized, if not neutralized. To illustrate: Assume that in the problem used above the land value as applied proved to be $40,000 instead of $50,000. What is the impact of this $10,000 error on the present value estimate? The answer is as follows:

I. Assumed land value of $40,000.
    1. Value of property income (see page 362) = $141,404
    2. Reversionary land value ($40,000 × 0.057309) =   2,292

       Total property value $143,696

II. Assumed land value of $50,000.
    1. Value of property income as above = $141,404
    2. Reversionary land value ($50,000 × 0.057309) =   2,865

       Total property value $144,269

The difference in the two appraisals is $573, or approximately $\frac{4}{10}$ of 1 percent of the present value estimate. Since appraisals of such magnitude as those derived above are generally rounded off to the nearest thousand dollars, the present value effect of the error of $10,000 in the assumed land value, 30 years removed from the date of the appraisal, is of little present-worth consequence.

3. Property Residual Technique: Changing Income and Value Premise

The previously presented equation, $R = Y - \Delta a$, also can be applied to the property residual technique. The results are more likely to represent actual investor behavior when a typical holding period is used instead of the longer remaining economic life of the improvements.

Level income and changing value.   The same income and yield rate used previously are used here. However, a shorter forecast period is used along with an overall future property value.

Level annual net operating income	$15,000
Yield rate	10%
Forecast period	8 years
Expected property value change	+25%

$$R = 0.10 - 0.25 \times 0.087444$$
$$= 0.078139$$
$$V = \$15,000/0.078139$$
$$= \$191,966$$

Income and value changing linearly.   Suppose now that the same first-year NOI, yield rate, and forecast period apply. However, the annual change in income is expected to average $750 during the forecast period. At the end of this eight-year period, the property is expected to be worth $250,000. Using preprinted tables or the following equation, the present worth of the income stream can be computed. Initially, the present worth of 1 factor is found:

$$a_{\overline{n}|} = (1 + hn)a_{\overline{n}|} - \frac{h(n - a_{\overline{n}|})}{i}$$

where h = annual increase or decrease after year 1
$\quad\quad\quad n$ = number of years in forecast period
$\quad\quad\quad a_{\overline{n}|}$ = present worth of 1 per period for a level annuity
$\quad\quad\quad i$ = effective interest rate

$$a_{\overline{n}|} = (1 + 0.05 \times 8)(5.334926) - \frac{0.05(8 - 5.334926)}{0.10}$$
$$= 7.468896 - 1.332537$$
$$= 6.136359$$
$$PW = 6.136359 \times \quad \$15,000 = \$ \ 92,045$$
$$+ \ 0.466507 \times \$250,000 = \underline{\quad 116,627}$$
$$\underline{\underline{\$208,672}}$$

Income and value changing exponentially.[6]   The previous data are used again, but now assume that the income and value are expected to rise 5 percent compounded over the eight-year forecast period. Again, preprinted tables may be used to find the present worth of 1 per period factor, assuming a compound

[6]Variations of the exponential and the previous linear equations also are found in Charles B. Akerson, *Capitalization Theory and Techniques Study Guide* (Chicago: American Institute of Real Estate Appraisers, 1984), pp. 154–155.

growth rate, or the following equation can be used to produce the same results:

$$a_{\overline{n}|} = \frac{1 - [(1 + x)^n/(1 + i)^n]}{i - x}$$

where x is the annual rate of change.

$$a_{\overline{n}|} = \frac{1 - [(1 + 0.05)^8/(1 + 0.10)^8]}{0.10 - 0.05}$$

$$= \frac{1 - [1.477455/2.143589]}{0.05}$$

$$= \frac{0.310756}{0.05}$$

$$= 6.215120$$

$$PW = 6.215120 \times \$15,000 = \$\ 93,227$$
$$+ 0.466507 \times \$250,000 = \underline{\ \ 116,627}$$

$$\$209,854$$

Accurate Forecast of Income Period Required

As mentioned previously, it is usually difficult to accurately forecast that future time when the improvements may become worthless. Neighborhoods often change as a result of unanticipated changes in zoning, traffic and land use patterns, and construction materials and technology. Thus one of the most important aspects of the property residual techniques is to accurately forecast the holding period or the remaining economic life of the improvements. A crucial part of this estimate is the probable value of the property (land or land and improvements). Of course, a longer term produces a higher present value of the income stream.

The following two examples show how quite different value estimates can result from using different forecast periods. Different future values would produce even more noticeable variations in present value estimates.

Assumption 1

Net operating income (level)	$ 15,000
Forecast period	10 years
Future property value	$100,000
Discount rate	10%
Present value of 10-year level income stream	
$15,000 × 6.144567	$ 92,169
+ Present value of 10-year reversion	
$100,000 × 0.385543	38,554
= Total property value	$130,723

Assumption 2

Net operating income (level)	$ 15,000
Forecast period	40 years
Future property value	$100,000
Discount rate	10%
Present value of 40-year level income stream	
$15,000 × 9.779051	$146,686
+ Present value of 40-year reversion	
$100,000 × 0.022095	2,210
= Total property value	$148,896

REVIEW QUESTIONS

1. List the relative merits of the three physical residual techniques of capitalization.
2. Find the present worth of a property under the following conditions: current NOI, $25,000; present value of improvements, $150,000; expected remaining economic life of improvements, 20 years; typical risk rate, 10 percent.
3. Compute the current value of a 15-year level annual rental income of $50,000, plus the value of the same property that will be available for purchase in 15 years for $300,000. The appropriate yield rate is 10 percent.
4. What is the present value of a property under the following conditions? NOI, $75,000; forecast period, 10 years; yield rate, 10 percent; building value is expected to increase by 10 percent and the site by 80 percent as a straight line basis during this period; the building currently is judged to be worth $100,000.
5. What would be the estimated current value of a property which has a site worth $200,000 and current net operating income of $90,000? Other relevant information is: remaining lease period, nine years; expected yield rate, 10 percent; land value is forecast to increase by 30 percent while the building value should increase by 3 percent. Both income and values are expected to change on a compounded basis.
6. Advise your client as to the present market value of the following property: annual first year NOI, $50,000; yield rate, 10 percent; holding period for investor, 12 years; annual income is set by the lease to rise an average of $2,500 during the holding period.
7. There are three physical residual methods of processing the net operating income from a property. Assume that you are appraising an old four-story brick-and-frame, furnished apartment property, on a $20,000 lot, and that you have found that the property for some time to come should produce a net operating income of $12,000. Further assume that the furnishings in use in the building have a 10-year remaining useful life, that 10 percent is to be earned on their present value of $11,000, that 8 percent is an acceptable rate of interest return, and that the building has a remaining economic life of 25 years.
   (a) Which one of the residual methods do you use in arriving at an estimate of the value to assign to the structure?
   (b) What is the indicated value of the structure? Show your computations. Use the straight-line method of capitalization.
8. An improved property sold for $150,000. Of this, $25,000 was imputed to land. The stabilized net operating income was $14,000 per annum. The building has

a remaining life of 20 years; 6 percent is required to attract capital to land investment of this type. Problem: Find rates applicable to the building as follows:
(a) Building rate of capitalization.
(b) Interest rate under straight-line recapture—for building only.
(c) Interest rate under Inwood premise valuation—for building only.

READING AND STUDY REFERENCES

AMERICAN INSTITUTE OF REAL ESTATE APPRAISERS. *The Appraisal of Real Estate*, 8th ed. Chicago: American Institute of Real Estate Appraisers, 1983, pp. 395–398.

EPLEY, DONALD R., and JAMES H. BOYKIN. Chapters 14–16. *Basic Income Property Appraisal*. Reading, Mass.: Addison-Wesley Publishing Co., Inc., 1983.

FRIEDMAN, JACK P., and NICHOLAS ORDWAY. Chapter 6, *Income Property Appraisal and Analysis*. Reston, Va.: Reston Publishing Co., Inc., 1981.

SHENKEL, WILLIAM M. Chapter 12, "Residual Capitalization Techniques," *Modern Real Estate Appraisal*. New York: McGraw-Hill Book Company, 1978.

WALL, NORBERT F. "A Case Study—Land Residual Technique," *The Real Estate Appraiser* 33, no. 2 (February 1967), pp. 22–26.

WENDT, PAUL F. "The Residual Approaches," *Real Estate Appraisal: Review and Outlook*. Athens: The University of Georgia Press, 1974, pp. 153–158.

20

LEASEHOLD ESTATES AND LEASED FEE APPRAISING[1]

Learning Objectives

After reading this chapter, you should be able to:

Distinguish among leased fee, leasehold estate, and fee simple interest

List the expenses that property income should cover before a tenant enters into a long-term ground lease

Understand how to value a leased fee interest in a property under different conditions

Appraise a leasehold estate in real property

Understand how a sandwich lease is comprised and how to appraise this interest in real property

Owners of income-producing real estate often find it profitable to permit others to hire the property at a stipulated fee, or *rental*. Where this is the case, the parties to the transaction enter into an agreement, called a *lease*, which establishes the landlord and tenant relationship. When properly drawn and executed the lease becomes a legal contract binding the parties in accordance with specified

---

[1]The term *leased fee* as used in this chapter refers to the owner's interest and rights in the property subject to conditions and terms of a written or oral lease agreement. The term *leasehold estate* refers to the tenant's right—over periods of months or years—to benefit from the use of the property in accordance with a written or oral agreement and the payment of a stipulated periodic rental. The *fee simple interest* is the unencumbered value of a property or the value suggested by prevailing market rentals rather than by any value imposed by existing leases.

terms as to length of possession, use of property, and payments due at periodic intervals.

Broadly speaking, leases are classified as either *short-term* or *long-term* in duration. This division, based on length of time and terms of use, is rather arbitrary. Generally, however, leases extending over ten or more years may appropriately be referred to as having long-term lease characteristics. Such leases, as a rule, are lengthy documents containing many special provisions and land-lord-tenant covenants.

Lease agreements are further subclassified as to type, depending on the methods used to determine the amount of periodic rent payments. The most frequently used types of leases are the following, which are covered in detail in Chapter 14.

1. Flat, straight, or fixed rental leases.
2. Step-up, or graduated rental, leases.
3. Reappraisal leases.
4. Percentage-of-gross-sales leases.
5. Sale and lease-back contract.

IMPORTANCE OF LEASE PROVISIONS

To appraise a leasehold interest or a leased fee estate requires careful study of lease provisions in order to establish the respective rights of parties and their obligations concerning costs of property maintenance and operation. The land-lord, for instance, may own both land and building improvements and agree to pay property taxes, hazard insurance, and expenditures for maintenance of building improvements. Interior costs of decorating, repair, and costs of utilities, on the other hand, may be borne by the tenant.

Many long-term leases are for the rental of unimproved land and are called *ground leases*. Agreements of this type usually provide for construction of a building by the tenant. Under ground-lease terms, the tenant as a rule pays all taxes and other maintenance charges, leaving the landlord's rent as *net*. Ground leases generally provide for disposition of the building at the end of the term. The building, although erected at the expense of the tenant, legally becomes real property and is—unless otherwise provided for—the property of the land-lord, subject to the tenant's right of possession for the term of the lease. At the end of the lease term the building improvements revert to the landlord or the landlord generally, as agreed on, either pays the tenant a stipulated or appraised value for the building or renews the lease at his option. Before a tenant proceeds under a long-term ground lease, he must make certain that his income from use of the property covers the following items:

1. The ground rent payable to the owner.
2. Taxes of all kinds and assessments for local improvements.

3. Premiums on policies of insurance against fire, liability suits, workers' compensation claims, and plate-glass damage.
4. Charges for water, heat, light, and power.
5. Labor and repairs—including all charges for upkeep, maintenance, and service to tenants.
6. Interest on capital invested—that is, on the amount expended in erection of the building.
7. An amount sufficient to amortize the cost of the building during the term of the lease or by the end of the last renewal of the lease.
8. A sufficient amount over and above all the foregoing charges to compensate the operator for his services and the risk involved in the enterprise.[2]

SPLIT INTEREST VALUATION

A lease in effect splits the *bundle of property rights* and transfers the rights to use for a designated period of time from the owner to the tenant. Often the tenant in turn subleases a part or all of his lease interests and thus becomes sandwiched between the owner—to whom he is obligated under the terms of the basic, or original, lease—and the user, or subtenant, of the property, from whom he obtains rental payments for the term of the sublease. In fact, the secondary, or subsidiary, leases between tenant and subtenant are actually called *sandwich leases* and are evaluated under the income approach in the same manner as other nonperpetuity rights to income.

Valuation of leased fee and leasehold interests are in appraisal practice restricted to the annuity, or Inwood, method of capitalization. It is held that contract rent as specified by lease terms provides a definite and thus predictable income flow, to which neither the straight-line nor the sinking fund method of capitalization can be applied with accuracy. Although the same cannot be said for the income flow derived from operation of the property and out of which the tenant discharges his contract rent obligations, the leasehold interest by common agreement in appraisal practice is also capitalized under the Inwood, or annuity, method. This is a step in the right direction, for the logic which sanctions use of the annuity method for appraisal of leasehold interests will probably some day cause also the abandonment of straight-line and sinking fund methods of capitalization for fee appraising.

In the appraisal of split interests, it is found that as a general rule the value of the sum of the parts of a property equals the value of the property as a whole. There are exceptions to this rule, and the appraiser must be alert to recognize conditions under which the value of the sum of the parts may be more or less than the value of the entire property—under free and clear ownership.

---

[2]For a detailed analysis of leases and leasing, refer to Alfred A. Ring and Jerome J. Dasso, *Real Estate Principles and Practices*, 10th ed. (Englewood Cliffs, N.J.: Prentice-Hall, Inc., 1985), Chapter 24.

The summation value of split interests is greater where the contract rent agreed on by a financially strong tenant exceeds the economic rent which the property is estimated to produce at the time of appraisal. Such excessive income nevertheless may have to be separated and capitalized at higher risk rates of interest, for even financially strong tenants seek to correct inequities. Where lease terms are restrictive to the point that the tenant is unable to make effective use of the property, the reduced income flow would cause the value of the parts to be less than the value of the property as a whole.

In all lease appraisal assignments it is advisable to derive the value of the entire property first, as if unencumbered and free for operation under unrestricted fee simple ownership. This total value can then serve as a bench mark against which the reasonableness of the value of the parts can be judged. Failure to follow this procedure deprives the appraiser of necessary checks and balances.

It is also of interest to point out that when the contract rent and economic rent are one and the same—assuming for purposes of illustration that the landlord furnishes both land and building improvements—the tenant's interest in the property is of zero value. One might ask why would anyone want to lease a property if the rental paid leaves no monetary interest or value to the leasehold. The answer is obvious: The land or improved property is leased merely as a vehicle for other business operations (selling merchandise, for instance) from which the tenant makes his profit. In all equity, the landowner should get the full return equal to the economic rent attributable to his property investment. Many large business concerns in fact prefer to lease rather than own in order not to tie up thousands of dollars in real estate investments. Such money generally can be more profitably invested in operations in which management has the know-how and skill to make higher interest returns on capital investment.

LEASED FEE VALUATION

The rights of a landlord under the terms of a lease are basically twofold:

> *First,* he is entitled to receive the contract rent agreed on under terms of the lease for the duration of the lease period.
>
> *Second,* he is entitled to repossession of the land and all permanent improvements thereon in accordance with lease terms. The right to repossess, better known as the reversionary right, reunites the split interests into fee simple ownership on termination or breach of the lease.

In all leased fee valuations, both of these interests or rights of the fee owner must be considered even though the reversionary rights under traditional long-term (99 years) leasing may prove of little value consequence.

To demonstrate appraisal practices in leased fee and leasehold valuations, three types of long-term leases will be presented for analysis as follows:

1. A *fixed-rental* lease with a nationally known company. Under terms of this lease, contract rents specified exceed warranted market rent attributable to the property if free and clear.
2. A *step-up ground* lease, under which contract rentals prove inadequate to yield a fair return on the market value of the property.
3. An *advance-payment* lease, providing for reversion of land and building improvements at termination of the lease.

Illustration 1. A building site in the downtown area of an industrial community was leased 20 years ago to a national concern for a period of 40 years at a fixed rental of $32,000 per year. The current market value of the land is estimated at $300,000, and the rate of capitalization for similar land investments is established at 10 percent. The building, which was erected by the tenant, is considered of no value at the end of the lease term. Based on these facts, the value of the leased fee is derived as follows:

Value of the land by market comparison		$300,000
Land rate of capitalization, 10%		
Contract rent	$ 32,000	
Market rent, $I = V \times R$ ($300,000 × 0.10)	30,000	
Excess rent	$ 2,000	
Present worth of economic rent for the remaining 20 years at 10% $V = I \times F$ (Inwood) = $30,000 × 8.513564 =		255,407
Present worth of excess rent for 20 years at 12%[3] $V = I \times F = \$2,000 \times 7.469444$		14,939
Reversionary land value	$300,000	$270,346
Present worth factor—20 years at 10% = 0.148644		
Present worth of reversion ($300,000 × 0.148644)		44,593
Total value of leased fee		$314,939

In this illustration the value of the leased fee exceeds the market value of the land precisely by the capitalized amount of the excess rentals. Based on the present value of the market rent and the present value of the reversion, the sum total of the parts equals the value of the property as a whole. Attention is also called to the fact that the excess rental, though committed for payment by a reliable national concern, was capitalized at a 12 percent rate of interest to indicate the greater risk attached to this excess income. National concerns of

[3]The likelihood that excess rent may not continue for the period of lease term (e.g., lessee may become bankrupt) warrants application of a higher risk rate to this portion of the total income.

good repute—yes, even banks—have closed down in times of stress. Bankruptcy, for instance, would terminate the lease, and in such a contingency only the market rent could be counted on to support property value. The selection of the risk rate is a matter of judgment based on general economic conditions, the reputation and history of the leasing firm, and the extent and nature of product and space competition.

Increases in the reversionary land value which are due to inflation must be ignored since the appraiser finds value in *present* dollars. Increases in value which are due to supply–demand-influenced market conditions, should be considered only where such increases or decreases can be substantiated with a high degree of certainty.

Illustration 2. A city block measuring 200 feet by 200 feet was leased thirty years ago for a period of 99 years. The step-up lease calls for rental payments as follows:

First 25 years	$16,000
Next 25 years	18,000
Next 20 years	20,000
Last 29 years	22,000

The site on the date of appraisal has a market value of $200,000. It is estimated that this value will remain stable and that this amount may be anticipated at time of land reversion. The rate of interest for similar investments is determined at 10 percent. Based on these facts, and using the Inwood factor method of capitalization, the value of the leased fee is obtained as shown:

Value of land by market comparison	$200,000
Land rate of capitalization, 10%	
Present worth of rental income (69 remaining years):	
$18,000 for first 20 years at 10 percent interest equals:	
$18,000 × 8.513564 =	153,244
$20,000 for next 20 years at 10 percent interest deferred for 20 years equals:	
$20,000 × 8.513564 = $170,271 × 0.148644 =	25,310
$22,000 for balance of 29 years at 10 percent interest deferred for 40 years equals:	
$22,000 × 9.369606 = $206,131 × 0.022095	4,554
Present worth of contract rent	$183,108
Add: Reversionary rights to land value of $200,000, 69 years removed at 10 percent, equals:	
$200,000 × 0.001393 =	279
Total value of leased fee	$183,387

The value above can also be obtained by use of the 10 percent Inwood factors exclusively without reference to the deferment factors:

Present worth of $18,000 per year for 20 years at 10% =		
$18,000 × 8.513564 =		$153,244
Present worth of $20,000 per year from 21st year to 40th year:		
40-year factor	9.779051	
Less 20-year factor	8.513564	
Factor for next 20 years	1.265487	
$20,000 × 1.265487 =		25,310
Present worth of $22,000 per year from 41st year to 69th year:		
69-year factor	9.986071	
Less 40-year factor	9.779051	
Factor for last 29 years	0.207020	
$22,000 × 0.207020 =		4,554
Present worth of contract rent		$183,108
(Add land reversion as above)		279
Total value of leased fee		$183,387

In this second illustration the lease as originally drawn covered a period of 99 years. On the date of appraisal, 30 years of the total lease period had elapsed and no consideration was given either to past rights or past obligations. The value of the leased fee interest as derived above reflects only the present worth of future rights to income. Attention, too, is called to the fact that the value of the lessor's interest of $183,387 is less than the value of $200,000, which this property would warrant if free from lease obligations. The loss in value in this instance is entirely due to lease term provisions under which the contract rent paid is less than the economic rent which the property can produce under a program of highest and best land use. The lessor's loss is, of course, the lessee's gain whenever the value of the sum of the parts equals the value of the property as a whole.

Illustration 3. A single-story building containing three stores in an 80 percent business district is leased for a period of 30 years. The net rent payable annually in advance is $9,540. The tenant is to pay all taxes, insurance, and related costs of maintenance and repair, and to return the property in operating condition subject only to ordinary wear and tear from building age and use. The value of the land free and clear is $40,000 and the replacement cost new of the building is $60,000. At the termination of the lease period, accrued building depreciation is estimated at 60 percent. Based on these facts, and an interest rate of 10 percent, the value of the leased fee is derived as follows:

Contract rent (for 30 years)		$ 9,540
Present worth of 1 per annum		× 10.369605
(advance payment) at 10% interest		
(9.426914 × 1.10)		
Present worth of contract rent		$ 98,926
Add revisionary value:		
Land	$40,000	
Building (40%)	24,000	
Total	$64,000	
Present worth of 1 at 10%	× 0.057309	
Present worth of reversion		3,668
Total value of leased fee		$102,594

In this illustration, although the contract rent and the economic rent are approximately identical, the value of the leased fee exceeds the value of the land and building by $2,594. This excess value is entirely caused by contract provisions, which call for annual rental payments in advance.

VALUATION OF LEASEHOLDS

Theoretically, in a free and competitive market the lessee's interest in the property should be of zero value. Its profits, as previously explained, should be derived from operation of the business in which it specializes. In practice, however, lease terms are relatively inflexible and, as a consequence, contract rent is greater or lesser than the prevailing market rent the property yields under highest and best use and unencumbered fee simple ownership. To the extent that contract rent exceeds market rent, the lessee is transferring value from property he owns in buildings or business to the landlord or fee owner. Conversely, where contract rent is less than market rent the landlord transfers part of his property-value interest to the tenant.

In appraisal practice the value of a leasehold is often obtained by subtracting the value of the leased fee from the value of the property as if free and clear from contract obligations. This shortcut procedure for leasehold valuation is not recommended, because an error in calculation of the leased fee interest automatically transfers this error to the leasehold estate whenever value of the parts is considered equal to the value of the whole. For this reason efforts should always be made to establish leasehold values independently by separate discounting of the future rights to leasehold income (positive or negative) into a sum of present value.

The tenant or user of the property has the right to employ the property in accordance with lease terms and to receive the economic rent which the property produces under its highest and best use. Out of this market rental or income, the tenant pays the contract rent; that which remains, if anything, over the lease period forms the basis for the value of the leasehold estate. To demonstrate the application of leasehold valuation, reference is made to the three illustrations cited above as follows:

Illustration 1

Market rent of property	$30,000
Contract rent per lease	32,000
Deficit rent from property	($ 2,000)
Capitalized value of deficit leasehold income:	
$V = I \times F = \$2,000 \times 7.469444 =$	($14,939)

The deficit income was capitalized at an interest rate of 12 percent. (The rate used must be supported by market analysis of yields for comparable properties.)

To prove the accuracy of the leasehold valuation, a check can now be made as follows:

Valuation of leased fee (see page 372)	$314,939
Add value of leasehold estate (*deficit*)	(14,939)
Value of entire property	$300,000

Illustration 2

Remaining term of leasehold	69 years	
Market rental	$20,000	
First 20 years:		
Market rent	$20,000	
Contract rent	18,000	
Excess rent	$ 2,000	
Capitalized at risk rate of 11%[4]		
$V = I \times F = \$2,000 \times 7.963328 =$		$ 15,927
Next 20 years:		
Market rent	$20,000	
Contract rent	20,000	
Excess rent	None	
Capitalized value		None
Last 29 years:		
Market rent	$20,000	
Contract rent	22,000	
Deficit rent	($ 2,000)	
Capitalized at rate of 11% interest		
69-year (Inwood) factor	9.084128	
40-year (Inwood) factor	8.951051	
29-year factor—used	0.133077	
Value = $I \times F = \$2,000 \times 0.133077 =$		($ 266)
Value of leasehold estate		$ 15,661
Value check:		
Appraised leased fee value (see page 373)		$183,387
Appraised value of leasehold estate		15,661
Value of entire fee		$199,048

[4]The rate of interest applied to the tenant's (lessee) interest in this illustration was selected for demonstration purposes. In practice a study of leasehold sales or market interest rates at which tenants are attracted to comparable investment properties is necessary to support the applicable rate of interest.

The combined value derived above is slightly lower than the value of the property under fee simple ownership. This discrepancy is caused by selection of interest rates—rounded to the nearest quarter of 1 percent—used in the capitalization of split property interests. In appraisal practice the values reported are generally rounded to comply with market practices under which offers to buy and sell are quoted in units of $100, $500, or $1,000, depending on the value of the investment. In the case above, appraisal findings would probably be reported as follows:

Leased fee	$184,000
Leasehold estate	16,000
Total value of property	$200,000

Illustration 3.   In this illustration, lease provisions held the contract rent and economic rent in balance. Under ordinary circumstances in such instances the value of the leasehold estate would be zero. However, business custom and accounting practices typically provide for rental payments at the end of the payment period. This shift in the payment period results in a present worth gain for the leased fee, and a consequent loss to the leasehold estate, as follows:

1. Contract rent for 30 years paid annually in advance	$ 9,540
Present worth—advance—of annuity of 1 at 10%	× 10.369605
Present value of contract rent	$98,926
2. Contract rent for 30 years paid annually at end of year	$ 9,540
Present worth—end-of-year factor (10%)	× 9.426914
Present value of contract rent	$89,933
Deficit (negative) value of leasehold estate	($ 8,993)

SANDWICH LEASE VALUATION

In instances where a leasehold interest is subleased to a third party, the original lessee becomes a sublandlord in his or her own right, and legally as well as economically is sandwiched between the fee owner—to whom the property reverts at the termination of the original lease—and the user, or subtenant, to whom the leasehold was transferred under separate and specific contract provisions. Investors may find it profitable to acquire long-term ground leases, develop the land, erect building improvements, and sublease the property to one or more tenants for part of or the entire period of the original lease term.

The contract rights and obligations of the sandwich leasehold estate normally are clearly spelled out, and the rights to income are capitalized under the annuity, or Inwood, method in the same manner as demonstrated in the three illustrations shown above. Care must be taken to derive the net rental to which the sandwich owner is entitled and to capitalize this net income (the difference between the contract rent received from the subtenant and the contract rent paid to the fee owner) at the appropriate risk rate. Splitting a fee into one or more leasehold interests also splits property value in accordance with terms of income distribution and relative risk of the split ownership. The general rule that the sum of the parts equals the whole prevails. Differences in rates of interest applied to different levels of ownership merely reflect a redistribution of the risk of rights to income under terms of the lease agreements. The fee owner, like a first mortgagee, occupies a preferred risk position. The sandwich leaseholder has a contractual position similar to that of a second mortgagee, and the rate of interest assigned to this second priority of income is appropriately higher. The user of the property must rely on income from operations of the property, and he assumes all the risks that accompany equity ownership.

To illustrate the application of the income approach to value a property under sandwich lease agreement, the following data will be used as a basis for appraisal purposes:

A lease from Stem to Bloom was made 30 years ago, for a term of 80 years. Rental payments were agreed upon as follows:

First 20 years	$2,000
Next 20 years	2,500
Last 40 years	3,000

Ten years after the date of original lease, Bloom completed a building at a cost of $80,000 and subleased the property to Petal for a period of 70 years. Rental payments on a step-up basis were agreed upon as follows:

First 25 years	$9,000
Next 25 years	10,000
Last 20 years	11,000

The property on a free-and-clear basis is estimated to have a market value on the date of appraisal of $70,000 for improvements and $80,000 for land, a total of $150,000. The prevailing market rent is estimated at $12,000. Market analysis indicates risk rates of interest of 7 percent for the leased fee, 8 percent for the sandwich leasehold, and 10 percent for the top leasehold. The lease and improvements have a 50-year remaining life. Based on these data the value of the respective interests is derived as shown below:

1. *Leased fee* at 7 percent rate of interest:

Contract rent for 10 years, $2,500 × 7.0236	
(PW factor for 10 years) =	$17,559
Contract rent for 40 years, $3,000 × 6.771 (50-year factor	
minus 10-year factor or 13.8007 − 7.0236) =	20,331
Present worth of reversion	
$80,000 × 0.03395 =	2,716
Total value of leased fee	$40,606

2. *Sandwich lease* at 8 percent rate of interest:

Net contract rent for first 5 years, $6,500 ($9,000 − $2,500)
Net contract rent for next 5 years, $7,500 ($10,000 − $2,500)
Net contract rent for next 20 years, $7,000 ($10,000 − $3,000)
Net contract rent for last 20 years, $8,000 ($11,000 − $3,000)
Value:

$6,500 × 3.9927 (PW factor—first 5 years) =	$25,953
$7,500 × 2.7174 next 5 years (6.7101 − 3.9927) =	20,381
$7,000 × 4.5477 next 20 years (11.2578 − 6.7101) =	31,834
$8,000 × 0.9757 last 20 years (12.2335 − 11.2578) =	7,806
Total value of sandwich leasehold	$85,974

3. *Top leasehold* at 10 percent rate of interest

Net income for 5 years, $3,000 ($12,000 − $ 9,000)
Net income for 25 years, $2,000 ($12,000 − $10,000)
Net income for 20 years, $1,000 ($12,000 − $11,000)
Value:

$3,000 × 3.7908 (PW factor—5 years) =	$11,372
$2,000 × 5.6361 next 25 years (9.4269 − 3.7908) =	11,272
$1,000 × 0.4879 last 20 years (9.9148 − 9.4269) =	488
Total value of top leasehold	$23,132

Combined value of lease interests:

Leased fee	$ 40,606
Sandwich leasehold	85,974
Top leasehold	23,132
Total	$149,712

In appraisal practice the value results above would be rounded and reported as follows:

Leased fee	$ 40,750
Sandwich leasehold	86,000
Top leasehold	23,250
Total	$150,000

SUMMARY

A lease agreement is a formal, legally binding contract between two or more parties providing for a definite split of the bundle of rights between the owner of the fee, or landlord, and the leasehold user, or tenant. Under lease terms, definite or determinable rental payments are agreed on and paid at designated time intervals monthly, quarterly, semianually, or annually, in advance or at the end of the time period.

The landload, or fee owner, generally is entitled to the contract rent for the duration of the lease and to the reversion of the land and improvements—the latter as specified under lease contract terms. The tenant, or leasehold estate owner, is entitled to the market rent, out of which he pays the contract rent. The difference between the market and contract rent constitutes the net income upon which the value of the leasehold is based. Under a sandwich lease agreement a further split of the leasehold interest is agreed upon and a third, or sandwich leasehold, interest is established. The value of this interest is based on the difference between the contract rent obtained from the top leaseholder and the contract rent paid to the owner of the leased fee.

It is the appraiser's responsibility to examine the lease agreements carefully, to evaluate the property under free-and-clear ownership, to establish the risk rates of interest applicable to the split property interests, and to determine, by capitalization of income under the annuity, or Inwood, method, the value of the various interests or rights to the property. Under typical circumstances, the combined value of the various interests should equal the value of the property as a whole—unencumbered. Where the sum of the parts does not equal the whole (property), an explanation must be offered to substantiate the validity and accuracy of the value findings. As in all valuation problems, accuracy of factual data and soundness of appraisal judgment—rather than mathematical skill—are basic to accurate and reliable value conclusions.

REVIEW QUESTIONS

1. Explain why it is desirable to calculate the value of the unencumbered fee interest prior to estimating the value of either the leased fee or leasehold interest.
2. Identify the two rights of a landlord under a lease.
3. Find the value of the leased fee under the following conditions:

Sale price of property at end of lease	$100,000
Risk rate for comparable properties	10%
Risk rate for excess rent	13%
Contract rent	$ 15,000
Market rent	$ 14,000
Lease term	10 years
Inwood factor for 10%, 10 years	6.144567
Inwood factor for 13%, 10 years	5.426243
Reversionary factor for 10%, 10 years	0.385543

4. Compute the present worth of a property under the following conditions:

Discount rate	10%
Value of property at end of lease	$200,000
Income received at beginning of each year	
Annual rental income:	

Year 1	$1,000
Year 2	1,200
Years 3–5	1,500
Years 6–10	2,200

5. (a) Compute the value of the leasehold estate under the following conditions:

Market rent	$10,000
Contract rent	$8,000
Discount rate	10%
Lease term	5 years

(b) Assuming that the value of the leased fee is $90,293, what is the overall property value?

6. (a) Define a sandwich leasehold.
   (b) Calculate the value of the (1) leased fee interest, (2) sandwich leasehold, and (3) sublessee's interest under the following lease provisions:

Present property value	$ 70,000
Value of land at end of lease	$100,000
Remaining lease term	7 years
Annual net end-of-year rental income	$ 2,000
Expected rate of return	10%
Annual rent paid by subtenant	$ 3,000
Discount rate for sandwich lease	12%

7. X leased a vacant lot which he is using as a commercial parking lot. The lease calls for an annual payment of $600 per annum. X has been paying on this leasehold for a period of five years. If the interest rate is 7 percent, what is the full cost of this leasehold to date?

8. Mrs. A is the fee owner of a vacant lot. She enters into a ground lease with Mr. B for a term of 50 years. The net ground rental reserved in the lease by Mrs. A is

$ 9,000 per year during the first five years.
  10,000 per year during the next 10 years.
  12,000 per year during the remainder of the term.

Mr. B, the lessee, erected a building on the leased land at a highest and best use cost of $200,000. Assume that you have appraised the market value of the freehold (that is, the market value of the entire property—land and building as a unit) lease-free 10 years later and found the total market value of the property to be $400,000. You are to appraise the market value of the leased fee (the interest of the lessor, Mrs. A) and also appraise the value of the leasehold (the lessee's interest, Mr. B) as of today, 10 years after date of lease. After having made an analysis of the site, you have concluded that the land, if vacant, as of the date of the appraisal has a market value of $240,000, and that ground leases for 25 years or more in this vicinity are customarily based on a net interest return of 6 percent. What is the indicated market value of

(a) The lessor's interest?

(b) The lessee's interest?

Assume that the building has a total economic life of 40 years from the date of its completion and that its value will decline at 2½ percent of its cost for each year of its life.

9. Mrs. A, the owner of the fee in a parcel of vacant land, leased the property to Mr. B for a term of 50 years at a net rent of $3,000 per year. Mr. B immediately erected a commercial building on the lot and five years later, subleased to Mr. C at a rent of $8,000 per year net, for 45 years. The vacant lot has a market value of $75,000. The market rental value of the property is $12,000 per year net. As of today (15 years after date of original lease from A to B) on a 10 percent basis for all three parties' interests, and assuming the building to be valueless at the end of the lease:

(a) What is the value of the interest of Mrs. A?

(b) What is the value of the interest of Mr. B?

(c) What is the value of the interest of Mr. C?

Show your computations.

READING AND STUDY REFERENCES

EPLEY, DONALD R., and JAMES H. BOYKIN. *Basic Income Property Appraisal*. Reading, Mass.: Addison-Wesley Publishing Co., Inc., 1983, pp. 385–87.

FREE, ROBERT L. "The Appraisal of Sandwich Leases," *The Appraisal Journal*, 26, no. 3 (July 1958), pp. 354–59.

HINES, MARY ALICE. Chapter 15, *Real Estate Appraisal*. New York: MacMillan Publishing Company 1981.

PALFIN, RICHARD A. "Lease and Fee-Hold Price Differentials in Hawaii," *The Appraisal Journal* 47, no. 2 (April 1979), pp. 227–242.

RING, ALFRED A., and JEROME J. DASSO. Chapter 24, *Real Estate Principles and Practices*. Englewood Cliffs, N.J.: Prentice-Hall, Inc., 1985.

SHENKEL, WILLIAM M. "Valuation of Leased Fees and Leasehold Interests," *The Appraisal Journal* 33, no. 4 (October 1965), pp. 487–98.

21

EQUITY APPRAISING AND FINANCING

Learning Objectives

After reading this chapter, you should be able to:

Distinguish between a market value appraisal and a mortgage–equity appraisal

Appreciate both the potentially positive and negative effects of leveraged financing

Determine the difference between equity dividend rate and equity yield rate

Understand how an anticipated future value change alters equity yield rates

Discuss the fundamentals of the Ellwood method of mortgage–equity capitalization

Ever since the introduction of *Ellwood Tables for Real Estate Appraising and Financing* in 1967, a keen interest has developed among professional appraisers in the application of a more sophisticated method of capitalization that will give effect to profitable equity yields which accrue to investors under mortgage debt financing of real property. Although Ellwood's precomputed tables for mortgage–equity financing are of relatively recent origin, the concept of "leverage" or trading on the equity for purposes of increasing owners' interest earnings on cash investment is as old as civilization. In fact, mortgage lending and equity investment practices date back to Biblical days (see Nehemiah, Chapter 5, verses 1 to 7). Extensive use of credit, however, as a major source of real estate financing did not become popular until the beginning of the twentieth century.

TRADING ON THE EQUITY

Apart from the necessity to borrow funds, probably the greatest justification for incurring indebtedness is to be found in the principle of trading on the equity. In conformity with this principle, it is economically advisable to borrow funds when the use of such funds brings a higher rate of return than the rate, or cost, of borrowing.

Two similar terms should be clearly understood. *Equity dividend rate* is the investor's earnings rate that often is known as a "cash on cash" rate. This rate is based on either the investor's down payment or subsequent equity buildup divided into the annual cash flow. The investor's equity can be expected to increase as the mortgage principal is periodically reduced with each payment. The divisor may also include value increases resulting from appreciation. *Equity yield rate* accounts for the cash on cash return above plus the anticipated net sale proceeds when the property is sold. Sometimes the forecast extends instead to the time the property is expected to be refinanced, and these net financing proceeds to the owner are included in the rate calculation.

The steps involved in computing an equity dividend rate are as follows:

Step		Computation
1		Potential gross income
2	minus	Vacancy and collection losses
3	equals	Effective gross income
4	minus	Operating expenses
5	equals	Net operating income
6	minus	Annual mortgage debt service
7	equals	Cash flow (before taxes)

Equity dividend rate =
cash flow (step 7) divided by owner's equity

To illustrate: Assume that a property costing $100,000 brings in a gross rental of $20,000 per annum and that this property was purchased for all cash and thus is free and clear of monetary encumbrances. If the taxes, repairs, and other operating expenses amount to $7,000 annually, the net operating income is $13,000 or 13 percent on the owner's investment. Now suppose that the owner mortgages the property for $50,000 at 12 percent interest per annum. The annual mortgage payments on $50,000[1] amounting to $6,172 would reduce the net income to $6,828; but since the owner's equity investment is now only $50,000, his equity rate of return has increased from 13 percent to 13.7 percent per annum. Suppose, further, that a mortgage in the amount of $75,000 was obtainable at 12 percent. The annual debt service on this indebtedness would increase to $9,258 ($75,000 × 0.1234) and, conversely, would decrease the cash

---

[1]Assumes a $50,000, 30-year, 12 percent, monthly installment mortgage which results in an annual mortgage constant of 12.34 percent.

flow to equity to $3,742. This income, however, in relation to the equity investment of $25,000, represents an equity dividend—as a result of trading on the equity (often called leverage)—at a rate of 15 percent per annum. To recapitulate:

	Case 1	Case 2
Investment value	$100,000	$100,000
Net income to property	$ 13,000	$ 13,000
Overall rate of earning	13%	13%
Mortgage loan	$ 50,000	$ 75,000
Loan debt service at 12%	$ 6,172	$ 9,258
Equity value	$ 50,000	$ 25,000
Equity net income	$ 6,828	$ 3,742
Equity dividend	13.7%	15.0%

The illustration above was offered to emphasize at the outset of this chapter the distinction that need be made between the earnings capacity of a property under free and clear ownership and equity dividends (cash on cash) obtainable under favorable mortgage debt financing or "trading on the equity." Thus, although a given property earns a maximum rate of 13 percent per annum, the equity yield through increased leverage can be increased as noted above. More favorable loan terms would have increased the equity return even more. From an economic point of view, trading on the equity does not increase the earnings of the property but rather compensates the borrower for the additional risks assumed in securing the safety of borrowed funds and in guaranteeing the priority of interest and amortization payments to which the lender—under the financial mortgage agreement—has a legal claim.

When property is unimproved, or inadequately improved, borrowing to erect a suitable improvement is invariably an advantage. An annual loss or a very small annual return may be turned into an annual income commensurate with the value of the property. The land may be valuable, but it will yield its economic rent only when improved with a building; and it is often a financial advantage to obtain a mortgage loan to pay all or part of the cost of such building. Suppose that a parcel of unimproved land is worth $100,000. The taxes amount to $2,000, and the loss of interest on the money invested in land is 10.0 percent or $10,000, a total annual loss of $12,000 to the owner. To save this loss, the owner puts up a building costing $300,000, and she borrows this whole amount on a mortgage at 10.0 percent.[2] The land and building together produce a rent income of $67,000, and the taxes and other operating charges are $27,000, leaving a net rental of $40,000. Out of this net rental, $31,593 is annual debt service on the money borrowed, leaving $8,407 for the equity owner—this being

---

[2]Assumes a 10 percent, 30-year, monthly installment mortgage, resulting in an annual mortgage constant of 10.53 percent ($31,593/$300,000).

8.4 percent on her cash investment, which is still $100,000. She has, therefore, stopped her loss and now has an income of $8,407.

It is probable that in cases of this kind, the amount of depreciation recapture of the building would be represented by a corresponding annual payment to reduce the amount of the mortgage over the years of the indebtedness. More likely, the amount of depreciation permitted as a write-off under the Internal Revenue Code will provide a tax shelter (tax-free income) to the extent that allowable deductions exceed mortgage amortization. This excess write-off, or at least to the extent to which mortgage amortization as dollar amounts exceed accrued depreciation as a loss in value, increases the equity portion of the total investment and thus converts the excess amount that reverts to the owner at the time of property sale into a "capital gain." The total amount of equity realized or recaptured at the time of property sale, if greater than the original equity investment, further increases the equity yield.

PROPERTY APPRAISING VERSUS EQUITY APPRAISING

Prior to illustrating the application of the mortgage–equity method of capitalization, it is essential that the appraiser fully realizes the distinction that must be made between valuation of real property as an economic whole or entity, and valuation of the "equity investment" under market regulated mortgage–equity methods of financing.

Market value is best defined as the "present worth of future rights to income." To be accurate, market value must be based on income produced under:

1. Fee simple ownership, irrespective of financial encumbrances.
2. Typical property management.
3. Utilization of property under a program of highest and best use.

Once market value has been established, on the basis of typical financial terms, the "price" that the investor is warranted in paying for the property can be ascertained by adding or subtracting from market value the benefits or detriments attributable to personal or financial attributes such as reputation of, or extraordinary management (goodwill), title encumbrances (good or bad leases, easements, and so on), and favorable or unfavorable financial terms of sale. To do otherwise would inject price-influencing personal causes into the capitalization process and cloud, if not prevent, objective analysis and price adjustment of comparable sales in order to derive an accurate measure of present worth of the subject property.

Those who apply and defend the mortgage-equity method of capitalization as a means for estimating property value reject the idea that property should be appraised as though free and clear of financial encumbrances. Instead it is claimed that the investor will secure as much of the purchase price as the "traffic will bear" through mortgage debt financing at rates and terms prevailing in the market. Further, it is refuted that value must be based on income derived over the economic life of the property; rather it is deemed an accepted and observable fact that the customary period of ownership is short lived—eight to 12 years—and that income projections should therefore be of equal short-term duration. At the termination of the investment life, the property is sold, the remaining equity investment (sale price less remaining mortgage debt) reverts back to the owner, and the cycle of ownership from cash-in to cash-out position is completed.

Failure to differentiate between the mortgage–equity "price" methods of capitalization and the more conventional income "value" methods of capitalization, as explained above, is responsible for the confusion found not only among earnest students of appraising but also among most professional appraisers who find themselves lost in mathematical equations. Semantics, too, aggravate the issue at hand. Whereas value should represent the "present" worth of future rights to income and be free·from influences of dollar inflation or deflation (income and value when unencumbered will rise and fall like a ship at sea with the level of prices), the mortgage–equity approach to value yields a "price" that includes the benefits of terms of financing, the impact of leverage, and the inflationary or deflationary effects on equity investment which result in capital gain. Further complicating matters is the fact that under the conventional method of income capitalization, the appraiser is given the option to use, as he or she deems best applicable, the straight line, curved line, or annuity residual techniques of determining land and building value as demonstrated in Chapter 19. Under the mortgage—equity method of capitalization, the appraiser is restricted to the use of an overall rate of capitalization and to the conversion of a "stabilized" or level income derived for the property as a whole rather than for land and improvements as separate and distinct value parts.

To illustrate the application of the mortgage–equity method of capitalization, the following appraisal problem is presented:

A department store property has been leased to a national chain for a term of 10 years at a rental of $25,000 per annum. Owner's taxes, insurance, and exterior maintenance costs total $6,000 per year, leaving a net operating income in the amount of $19,000. Mortgage money of $135,000 can be obtained to finance the purchase of this property at 11.5 percent interest with full amortization over 25 years payable monthly in the amount of $1,372, or $16,467 per year covering mortgage interest and amortization. The property is anticipated to increase in value over the 10-year ownership period, rising from $180,000 to $200,000. The owner seeks an appraisal of this income property specifying an equity yield of 10 percent.

Solution:

1. Net operating income			$ 19,000
2. Mortgage interest and principal—annual			16,467
3. Equity income—cash flow			$ 2,533
4. Present value of equity income of $1.00 at 10% compound interest—Inwood factor, 10-year period			6.1446
Present worth of equity income for 10-year period = $2,533 × 6.1446 =			$ 15,564
5. Sale price of property			$200,000
6. Remaining value of mortgage:			
(a) Monthly mortgage payments		$ 1,372	
(b) Remaining payment period—15 years—Inwood factor for 180 months at rate of 11.5% per annum		85.603	
(c) Mortgage balance on date of sale $1,372 × 85.603			$117,447
7. Value of equity on date of sale			$ 82,553
8. Reversionary value:			
(a) Present worth of $1.00 at 10% for income due 10 years from date of appraisal =			0.3855
9. Present worth of reversion $82,553 × 0.3855 =			$ 31,824
10. Total present value of equity at 10% interest =			47,388
11. Add mortgage loan value on date of appraisal			135,000
12. Total value of property			$182,388

13. Overall rate of capitalization
$R = I/V = \$19,000 \div \$182,388 = 10.42\%$

Proof:

Value of property		$182,388
Mortgage loan		135,000
Equity cash value		$ 47,388
Net income flow	$19,000	
Annual-level mortgage payments	16,467	
Equity cash flow	$ 2,533	
Present worth of cash flow at 10% $2,533 × 6.1446 (Inwood factor for 10 years)		$ 15,564
Present worth of equity reversion ($47,388 − $15,564) =		$ 31,824
Future worth of $31,824 at 10% $31,824 × 2.594 (FW of $1.00) =		$ 82,551
Add remaining value of mortgage loan at time of sale		117,447
Value of property on date of sale		$199,998

The $2.00 difference in the property value is due to rounding off intermediate dollar amounts and present worth factors.

The distribution of net operating income to equity and level mortgage payments, and the changing relationship to the mortgage amortization and mortgage interest components over the 10-year ownership period, are shown graphically in Figure 21.1. By the end of the tenth year the loan amortization has grown to 17.2 percent of the annual mortgage payment. The pattern of changes in capital formation caused by property appreciation, declining mortgage debt balances, and increasing equity over the ownership period are presented in Figure 21.2.

In the example above the equity yield was obtained from the investor. The yield rate can also be obtained from market study of comparable properties. Where a sale price is firm and the mortgage terms and rate are known, the equity interest yield rate can be obtained by analysis as follows.

Suppose that a property was bought eight years ago for $300,000. Of this purchase price, $200,000 was financed by a 25-year mortgage at 10 percent interest. The level mortgage payments totaled $21,804 per year. The average annual net operating income produced by this property during the term of ownership was $30,000. The property brought on date of sale—eight years from date of purchase—a price of $275,000. What is the yield on the equity's investment?

Solution:

1. Original purchase price	$300,000
2. Mortgage loan	200,000
3. Original cash investment	$100,000
4. Sales price—8 years later	$275,000

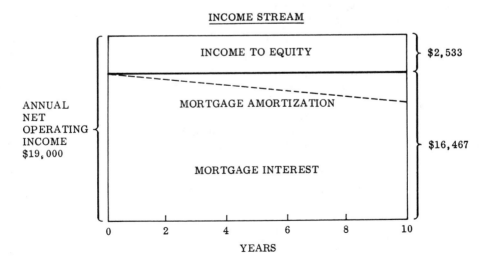

Figure 21.1

Figure 21.1

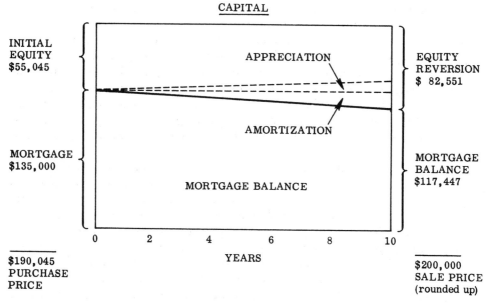

CAPITAL

INITIAL
EQUITY
$55,045

APPRECIATION

EQUITY
REVERSION
$ 82,551

AMORTIZATION

MORTGAGE
$135,000

MORTGAGE BALANCE

MORTGAGE
BALANCE
$117,447

0   2   4   6   8   10

YEARS

$190,045
PURCHASE
PRICE

$200,000
SALE PRICE
(rounded up)

Figure 21.2

5. Mortgage balance—8 years later:
   (a) Monthly level payments $ 1,817
   (b) Inwood factor 10% for 17 years =   97.9230
   Mortgage balance $1,817 × 97.9230 = $177,926
6. Reversion to equity on date of sale $ 97,074
7. Income from property   30,000
8. Mortgage loan payments   21,804
9. Income to equity (cash flow) annually $ 8,196
   "Trial" interest yield rate of 7%
10. Present worth of income stream at 7%
    $8,196 × 5.9713 (Inwood factor for 8 years) = $ 48,941
11. Present worth of reversion at 7%
    $97,074 × 0.5820 (PW of $1.00—8 years) =   56,497
12. Total value of equity indicated by yield rate of 7%
    = $105,438
13. Present worth of income stream at 8%
    $8,196 × 5.747 (Inwood factor for 8 years) =   47,102
14. Present worth of reversion at 8%
    $97,074 × 0.5403 (PW of $1.00—8 years) =   52,449
    Total value of equity indicated by yield rate of 8% $ 99,551

To determine the precise yield rate that falls between 7 and 8 percent, it is necessary to interpolate as follows:

Value of equity at 7% interest =	$105,438
Value of equity at 8% interest =	99,551
Difference caused by 1% rate of interest =	$ 5,887
Value of equity at 7% interest	105,438
Value of equity at X% interest	100,000
Difference of 7% over X%	$ 5,438

Thus the actual rate is 5,438 ÷ 5,887 of 1 percent above the yield rate of 7 percent or 0.00924. This fractional rate when added to the trial rate of 0.07 determines an exact yield rate of 0.0792 or 7.92 percent.

Suppose that the appraiser is called on to ascertain the amount that the property for which a yield rate of 7.92 percent was computed above should have sold for in order to yield a 10 percent rate of interest to the owner. The answer would be derived as follows:

1. Value of income stream at 10% $8,196 × 5.335 (8-year Inwood factor at 10%) =	$43,726
2. Present value of property reversion = $100,000 less $43,726	56,274
3. Future worth of property 8 years hence is $56,274 × 2.144 (FW of $1.00 at 10%) =	120,651
4. Add mortgage loan balance on date of sale (see illustration above)	177,926
5. Sale price of property to yield 10 percent interest to owner	$298,577

Conversely, it could be asked how much should the owner have paid for the property on date of purchase to yield an interest rate of 10 percent where the anticipated sale price of $275,000, the equity reversion of $97,074, and all other factors given in the problem above remain constant.

Solution:

1. Present value of income stream at 10% as above ($8,196 × 5.335) =	$ 43,726
2. Present worth of reversion at 10% $97,074 × 0.4665 (PW of $1.00) =	45,285
3. Value of equity cash investment to yield an interest rate of 10% =	$ 89,011
4. Add amount of original mortgage loan of	200,000
5. Purchase price of property to yield 10% of equity investment	$289,011

The illustrations above support the fact that the equity yield which comparable sales support or which an investor demands is that rate at which the stabilized cash flow to equity when capitalized to present worth over the years of ownership plus the present worth of the equity reversionary interests (sale price less mortgage balance) at time of sale equal the cash value[3] of the equity on date of purchase. It should be held clearly in mind that since a property's income-producing capacity is unaffected by terms of financing, the interest yield to an owner will vary with his ability to obtain the best bargain possible by "trading on the equity," that is, by obtaining the largest possible mortgage in relation to total property value at the lowest possible rate of interest over the longest possible years which are short of the economic life of the property.

As demonstrated above, given a level income and a stated purchase price at appraised value, the equity yield rate will increase or decrease with appreciation or depreciation of the property over the ownership period. The impact on equity yield rates resulting from property price increases or decreases can best be visualized by graphic presentation as shown in Figure 21.3.

Assume that your client has expressed interest in a property currently available for sale for a price of $200,000 and will be rented under an absolute net lease for the next eight years for $15,000 annually. You have been asked to advise her of the expected equity yield under the following projected sale prices: (1) $240,000 (+20%); (2) $200,000 (no change); (3) $190,000 (−5%); (4) $180,000 (−10%).

One method of solving this problem is by use of a financial calculator, using the following key stroke sequence, beginning with the first projection:

$Y_E = 8$ | n | 200000 | CHS | | PV | 240000 | FV | 15000

| PMT | | i | = 9.29%

Equity yields for all four projections are:

Yield for Eight-Year Holding Period

+20% change in value	9.29%
No change in value	7.50%
−5% change in value	7.01%
−10% change in value	6.51%

Another way of looking at this situation is the property would have to increase in value by 20 percent over the next eight years in order to achieve a 9.29 percent equity yield. Yet a yield of 6.51 percent could be realized even if the property declined in value by 10 percent.

An investor may ask advice on still two other sets of conditions. What yield would be realized if the property changed at the same average rate of value

---

[3]Cash value of equity is the cash amount paid for the property over and above the existing mortgage debt on date of purchase of the subject property.

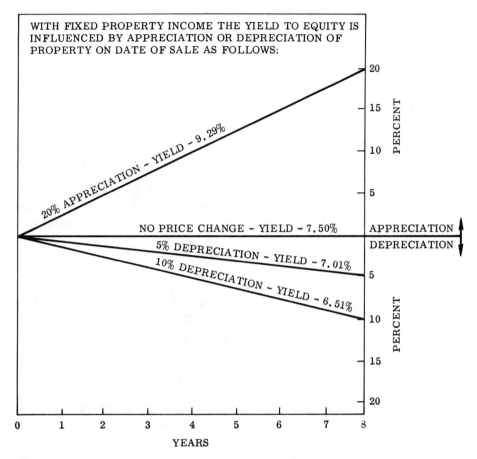

Figure 21.3 Prospects for Yield on Equity Investment Based on Five- and Eight-Year Holding Periods

as shown above, but was only held for five years? What sale price would be necessary to produce a desired yield of 12 percent over five years?

Using the same keystroke sequence as presented above, the forecast yield rates would be as shown below as well as in Figure 21.3.

Yield for Five-Year Holding Period

+12.50% (2.50%/yr)	$Y_E = 9.57\%$
No change in value	$Y_E = 7.50\%$
−3.13% (−0.63%/yr)	$Y_E = 6.96\%$
−6.25% (−1.25%/yr)	$Y_E = 6.40\%$

For all four projected future sale prices, it appears more profitable if the property is sold after five years. The widest yield margin is under the 2.50 percent annual appreciation.

The second question asked was what sale price would be required to produce a 12 percent equity yield over five years.

The answer is $257,176, computed as follows:

5 | n | 12 | i | 200000 | CHS | | PV | 15000 | PMT | | FV |

MORTGAGE LOAN BALANCE

Sometimes it is necessary in appraising real estate to ascertain the loan balance(s), especially when estimating equity yield upon sale of the property. Another question that is sometimes raised is: "How much interest did I pay on my mortgage in a given year?" Answers can be provided to both of these questions as follows.

Example 1. Find the loan balance on a 25-year, $100,000 mortgage at the end of 10 years. The interest rate is 10 percent, and payments are made on an annual basis.

There are several ways to solve for a loan balance. The one suggested here uses the installment to amortize one (loan constant) found in Table 17.1. The numerator is the factor for the full term, and the denominator is the factor for the remaining loan term (15 years). The latter factor should be easy to remember by associating it with the remaining loan balance.

$$\text{Loan balance} = \$100,000 \times \frac{0.110168}{0.131474} = \$83,795$$

The solution to this problem using a financial calculator is

| f | CLEAR | FIN | 25 | n | 10 | i | 100000 | CHS | | PV |
| PMT | 10 | n | | FV | = \$83,795

Example 2. Suppose now that same client wants to know (a) how much equity was accumulated during the same year as a result of loan amortization, and (b) how much interest was paid during the tenth year of the loan.

(a) Total annual loan payment
($100,000 × 0.110168) $11,016.80

Loan balance at end of year 9
(same as beginning of year 10)[4]
$\dfrac{0.110168 \; (1/a_{\overline{n}|} \; 25 \text{ yr})}{0.127817 \; (1/a_{\overline{n}|} \; 16 \text{ yr})}$ =   0.861920

minus loan balance at end of year 10:
$\dfrac{0.110168 \; (1/a_{\overline{n}|} \; 25 \text{ yr})}{0.131474 \; (a/a_{\overline{n}|} \; 15 \text{ yr})}$ =   0.837945

equals loan amortization in year 10   0.023975
times original loan amount $100,000
Equity accumulation   = $2,397.50

[4]The 16-year factor complements the nine-year factor to equal the total loan term of 25 years.

   (b) If the total annual level mortgage installment (principal and interest) is $11,016.80

(b) If the total annual level mortgage installment (principal and interest) is	$11,016.80
and the principal reduction is	2,397.50
then the interest paid in year 10 is	$ 8,619.30

ELLWOOD'S TABLES FOR CAPITALIZATION

The solutions to the equity yield problems, as demonstrated above in the mortgage-equity method of capitalization, were obtained without aid of any formulas or specially derived coefficients or factors other than those found in the standard compound interest tables such as presented and illustrated in Chapter 17 or by use of a financial calculator. Special-purpose tables such as those named Babcock, Inwood, Hoskold, Ring, and Ellwood do, however, play an important role in the valuation process, for they are intended to save considerable work time in the appraisal process by offering precomputed rates, factors, or income derivations applicable to an amount or percentage of $1.00. Once we establish the impact of a method of capitalization on the value of an income stream of $1.00, the appraiser can readily compute the value of X dollars by multiplication or division, as the case might be, by simple reference to the appropriate factor table.

    L. W. Ellwood, who for many years served as supervisor in the Mortgage Loan Division of the New York Life Insurance Company, developed, by following essentially the same mathematical steps as illustrated in the equity value problems above, precomputed "overall rates of capitalization" which permit ready and instant capitalization of a stabilized income stream over specified years of ownership periods at market-determined mortgage loan terms and prevailing equity yield rates applicable to the subject property.

    The basic formula applied by Ellwood[5] in the development of precomputed (mortgage-equity leveraged) rates of capitalization is as follows:

$$R = Y - MC + (\text{dep. } 1/S_n) \text{ or } (- \text{ app. } 1/S_n)$$

where R = overall rate of capitalization
      Y = equity yield rate demanded by prudent investors
      M = ratio of mortgage to total investment (i.e., 70%, 80%, etc.)
      C = mortgage coefficient (This coefficient is derived by the formula $C = Y + (P \times 1/S_n) - f$. Here Y represents the equity yield; P, the percentage of the loan paid off;[6] $1/S_n$, the sinking fund rate at the

[5]L. W. Ellwood, *Ellwood Tables for Real Estate Appraising and Financing* (Chicago: American Institute of Real Estate Appraisers, 1967).

[6]P also can be computed by use of the equation

$$P = \frac{R_m - I}{R_{mp} - I}$$

with R_m the mortgage rate for full loan term, R_{mp} the mortgage rate for the projection or holding period, and I the nominal interest rate.

equity yield rate for given or n years of ownership; and f, the annual level mortgage loan payment per dollar of debt.)

$1/S_n$ = sinking fund factor at equity yield rate, which is multiplied by the percentage of appreciation or depreciation estimated to occur over the years of ownership (This derived portion of the sinking fund factor is added in case of depreciation and subtracted in case of property appreciation.)

To demonstrate the development of a "band of investment" mortgage-equity weighted rate of capitalization, the following market-derived data are applied:

1. Mortgage loan funds available over 25-year loan period for 70 percent of value at 10 percent interest compounded monthly.
2. Equity yield is 12 percent on cash investment.
3. Ownership period from date of purchase to date of sale is 10 years.
4. Net operating income is $57,360.
5. Depreciation is estimated at 1.5 percent per year or a total of 15 percent over the 10-year period.

Solution:

$$R = Y - MC + dep.\ 1/S_n$$
$$= 0.12 - (0.70 \times 0.019754^*) + (0.15 \times 0.056984)$$
$$= 0.12 - 0.013828 + 0.008548$$
$$= 0.114720$$
$${}^*C = Y + (P^7 \times 1/S_n{}^8) - f$$
$$= 0.12 + (0.154387 \times 0.056984) - 0.109044^9$$
$$= 0.12 + 0.008798 - 0.109044$$
$$= 0.019754$$

Value of property = $57,360 ÷ 0.114720 =	$500,000
Mortgage loan at 70% =	350,000
Equity cash investment =	$150,000

Proof:

Total income	$57,360
Debt service payments $350,000 × 0.109044 (mortgage constant)	38,165
Cash to equity	$19,195

[7]1.00 − (monthly mortgage payments of 0.0090870 per $1.00 of loan times Inwood factor for 180 months at 10% of 93.057439 = 0.845613 remaining mortgage principal, or 0.154387 per dollar of loan paid off in 10 years.
[8]Sinking fund factor for 10 years at 12% = 0.056984.
[9]Mortgage constant payment per month of 0.009087 times 12 = annual constant of 0.109044.

Present worth of cash flow at 12% = $19,195 × 5.650223
(Inwood factor) = $108,456
Present worth of reversion, 12%, 10 years = $425,000
($500,000 less 15%) less mortgage balance of
(.845613 × $350,000) $295,965 =
$129,035 × 0.321973 (PW of $1.00 at 12%) =   41,546

Total present value of equity $150,002

  Rounded to $150,000

The value of $500,000 as obtained above, based on an income stream of $57,360 per annum to be derived from a property to be owned over a period of 10 years where 70 percent mortgage funds can be obtained at 10 percent interest over 25-year loan periods and where equity yields must bring 12 percent to the owner-investor, could have been capitalized directly by reference to an Ellwood table for real estate appraising and financing or could be computed by the long method or formula method as demonstrated above. The important thing is that the appraiser "knows" the means and ways for computing value under the mortgage-equity method of capitalization, and understands the difference between "property appraising" free and clear of debt encumbrances and mortgage equity valuation to reflect leveraged income derived from "trading on the equity."

SUMMARY

It is most important that a clear distinction be made between property appraising on the one hand, and mortgage–equity appraising on the other. In the former case, the appraiser is charged with the responsibility to estimate "objectively" the present worth of a property which is or can be employed under a program of highest and best utilization and which is managed in accordance with practices deemed typical in the market area. A property thus utilized can conceivably have only one market value but may, because of available alternate means of mortgage–equity financing and wide differences in buyers' abilities to trade on the equity, have a substantial range of subjective values to individual or corporate owners.

  Much of the confusion in appraisal practice is due to the failure to distinguish between objective value as measured in present worth and number of "current" purchasing power dollars and subjective value (price) which gives weight to terms of the sale, entrepreneurial skill of trading on the equity, tax position of the buyer, and price increments or decrements caused by inflation or deflation. For the sake of clarity as well as for professional purity in appraisal theory and practice, it is strongly recommended that value be estimated objectively first on a free-and-clear basis (i.e., free of all encumbrances); and second, that price of adjustments be made and identified to reflect available terms of financing, tax shelter opportunities, and other tax or ownership benefits which accrue to a specific owner or a group of owners. Such value report presentation will then enable the client or report reader to accept, reject, or modify the appraisal expert's conclusions.

The impact of trading on the equity caused by increasing mortgage loan levarage can cause a diminished equity yield where there is insufficient net operating income to support adequately the loan payments, as follows:

	EXAMPLE			
	1	2	3	4
Market value	$100,000	$100,000	$100,000	$100,000
Net operating income	$ 10,000	$ 10,000	$ 10,000	$ 10,000
Overall rate	10%	10%	10%	10%
Mortgage loan	$ 60,000	$ 70,000	$ 80,000	$ 90,000
Annual debt service at 10.90% constant	$ 6,540	$ 7,630	$ 8,720	$ 9,810
Debt coverage ratio	1.53	1.31	1.15	1.02
Income to equity	$ 3,460	$ 2,370	$ 1,280	$ 190
Cash value of equity	$ 40,000	$ 30,000	$ 20,000	$ 10,000
Equity yield	8.6%	7.9%	6.4%	1.9%

Thus, although the property income and property value remain constant, equity yields can decrease from 8.6 percent to 1.9 percent depending on mortgage–equity ratios or leverages. If the interest rate applicable to the mortgage loan can be lowered because of an owner's increased security status, the equity yield will grow inversely higher.

Perhaps the greatest pitfall in appraisal practice is to include in the measure of current equity yields the impact of price inflation that is estimated to incur 10 or more years from date of appraisal. The constant erosion of the purchasing power of the dollar is also dramatically evident from the diagram presented in Figure 21.4. Also applying future depreciation or appreciation estimates to the total property (both land and building) is counter to conventional accounting and appraisal practices.

On the plus side, the tables for mortgage–equity appraising are most useful in measuring quickly by reference to a precomputed table the effects of "leverage" or trading on the equity and in ascertaining the income tax impact as well as the financial investment cash requirements of the equity owner. Care, however, must be taken not to confuse equity appraising with property appraising where "present worth" of land and building improvements are to be the measure of market value.

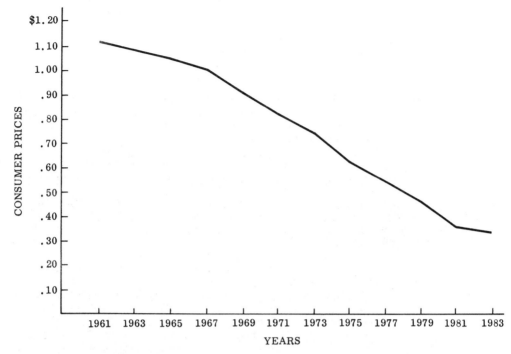

Figure 21.4 Purchasing Power of the Dollar

SOURCE: U.S. Department of Commerce, *Business Statistics, 1982*, 23rd ed. (Washington, D.C.: U.S. Government Printing Office, November 1983), p. 29; and *Survey of Current Business* 64, no. 11 (November 1984), p. S-5.

REVIEW QUESTIONS

1. Explain how the term "equity yield rate" differs from equity dividend rate.
2. Outline the steps necessary to compute equity dividend rate.
3. Solve for the present property value under the following conditions: Investor seeks a 10 percent equity yield rate; level annual net income to owner is $50,000 for the next 10 years; at the end of this period, the property is expected to rise from the beginning value of $200,000 to $300,000; a 25-year, 75 percent loan to value, annual installment loan with 10 percent interest is available. Use the mortgage–equity method in solving for the value.
4. Compute the amount of equity built up by a borrower on a $90,000, 30-year, 10 percent annual installment loan after the first six years.
5. How much interest would have been paid on the mortgage in problem 4 during the fifteenth year?
6. Using a financial calculator, determine which of the following two investments would produce the highest equity yield:

Property A: current purchase price, $500,000; forecast net sales price at the end of 10 years, $600,000; annual gross income, $90,000; forecast average annual operating expenses, $36,500.

Property B: purchase price, $425,000; expected net sale proceeds at the end of eight years, $500,000; annual net operating income, $31,000.

7. By use of the Ellwood capitalization rate formula, find the present value of a property that is subject to the following conditions: loan terms—25 years, 80 percent loan ratio, 10 percent interest rate, annual installments; expected equity yield, 14 percent; holding period, five years; net operating income, $48,000; appreciation during holding period, 10 percent.

8. Define: (a) effective gross revenue; (b) occupancy ratio; (c) collection losses; (d) net operating income (earning expectancy); (e) operating ratio (expense ratio); (f) fixed charges; (g) equity income; (h) trading on the equity; (i) yield on equity investment.

9. An 8 percent first mortgage in the amount of $10,000 is to be amortized monthly over eight years. How much is due per month?

10. A commercial property producing a stabilized annual income of $60,000 is offered for sale to the Goodrich Investment Corporation. The purchase is subject to an existing 25-year amortizing mortgage of $300,000 financed at 12 percent interest. The monthly level mortgage payments amount to $3,160. The Goodrich Investment Corporation seeks an equity return of 10 percent over an ownership period of 10 years. The property is estimated to realize $500,000 on date of sale. The unpaid mortgage balance 10 years from now will be $263,400. Problem: Find the purchase price that will yield a 10 percent return.

11. A property is offered to the Upland Corporation for $400,000. There is an existing 20-year $280,000 mortgage at 10 percent interest. Level debt service payments equal $2,702.06 per month. The property is scheduled to be held for a period of five years. The annual stabilized property income is $45,000. Depreciation is estimated at 1.5 percent per year. Problem: Find the yield to the Upland Corporation.

12. How much of the original loan principal of $110,000 would have been paid off on a 10 percent, 25-year mortgage after 15 years? Assume annual installments.

READING AND STUDY REFERENCES

AKERSON, CHARLES B. Chapters 11–13, *Capitalization Theory and Techniques Study Guide*. Chicago: American Institute of Real Estate Appraisers, 1984.

BOYKIN, JAMES H. Chapter 9, *Financing Real Estate*. Lexington, Mass.: D. C. Heath and Company, 1979.

CUNNINGHAM, TIMOTHY M. "Valuation Theory and Mortgage-Equity Analysis," *The Appraisal Journal* 42, no. 2 (April 1974), pp. 188–199.

EPLEY, DONALD R., and JAMES H. BOYKIN. Chapters 9 and 10, *Basic Income Property Appraisal*. Reading, Mass.: Addison-Wesley Publishing Co., Inc., 1983.

GIBBONS, JAMES E. "Equity Yield," *The Appraisal Journal* 48, no. 1 (January 1980), pp. 31–56.

GIBBONS, JAMES E. "Mortgage Equity Capitalization: Ellwood Method," *The Appraisal Journal* 34, no. 2 (April 1966), pp. 196–202.

ROBERTSON, TERRY, and GLENN RUFRANO. "Equity Yields: A Cash Flow Verification," *The Real Estate Appraiser* 42, no. 2 (March–April 1976), pp. 42–45.

SIRMANS, C.F., and BOBBY NEWSOME. "After-Tax Mortgage Equity Valuation," *The Appraisal Journal* 52, no. 2 (April 1984), pp. 250–269.

Special Appraisal Assignments and Professional Reporting

22

CONDEMNATION APPRAISING PRACTICES AND PROCEDURES

Learning Objectives

After reading this chapter, you should be able to:

Discuss the nature and limitations of the power of eminent domain

Recognize the due process of law associated with the use of eminent domain

Appreciate the meaning of "just compensation" as related to the process of eminent domain

Explain the basic steps involved in the appraisal of a property subject to a partial taking

Understand the causes of monetary damages to a remainder property when there is a partial taking

Ownership of real property is widely distributed, and is cherished by millions of American homeowners and real estate investors. This right to use and control property is legally recognized and is given express protection by the U.S. Constitution. As explained more fully in Chapter 3, property ownership is conceived of as a *bundle of rights* in which the individual sticks that make up this bundle confer on an owner the following privileges:

1. To enter upon the premises or decline to enter.
2. To use the realty or decline to use it.
3. To sell the property rights wholly or separately or refuse to dispose of them.
4. To lease or decline to lease.

5. To donate, dispose by will, or give away the property interest—partially or totally.
6. To peaceful possession and quiet enjoyment.

These rights to the control and enjoyment of property under allodial ownership are inviolate and exclusive, except for superior and sovereign rights of government exercised for the mutual welfare of the community, state, or nation. These sovereign powers are exercised to safeguard the health, welfare, and morality of the public at large and are enforced as needed by taxation, police-power regulations, and the acquisition of property under the sovereign right of eminent domain.

POWER OF EMINENT DOMAIN

In the final analysis, the strength of private ownership is derived from the strength and power of a sovereign government formed to enforce and protect such rights as are vested in the individual under constitutional guardianship. It is fundamental, therefore, that rights essential to the maintenance and welfare of society must be paramount to those claimed by individuals in the pursuit of their separate interests. The right to expropriate private property for public use is legally known as the power of *eminent domain*. This power is well defined in 10 Cal. Juris. Sec. 2 as follows:

> Eminent domain is the right of the people or government to take private property for public use, whenever the exigencies of the public cannot be adequately met and provided for in any other way. . . . Eminent domain is justifiable only because the power makes for the common benefit.

To prevent arbitrary and confiscatory taking of private property by legislative or executive decree, the drafters of the U.S. Constitution have provided safeguards which U.S. courts throughout history have zealously enforced. These safeguards read as follows:

1. *Fifth Amendment*, ". . . nor shall private property be taken for public use, without just compensation."
2. *Fourteenth Amendment*, Section 1. ". . . nor shall any state deprive any person of life, liberty, or property without due process of law . . ."

Individual states, generally, have patterned their respective constitutions to safeguard against the taking of private property except where (1) public necessity has been shown, (2) due process of law is followed, and (3) just compensation is paid to the owner.

DUE PROCESS OF LAW

The acquisition of private property in a condemnation action must conform to legal processes established under law. Procedures vary among states and within federal jurisdictions, but generally petition for taking of private property must provide more or less for the following:

1. Authority and necessity of taking.
2. Indication of public use for which land is condemned.
3. Survey of land and description.
4. Complaint and summons of owners.
5. Interest to be acquired.
6. Necessary parties defendant.
7. Legal testimony before proper tribunal.
8. Petition that property be condemned.

Unless the prescribed legal steps are carefully followed, due process may be declared lacking, and the condemnation action invalidated on account of error or omission of proceeding. Constitutional or statutory provisions by the various states further detail due process to include the following:

1. Process, service, and publication of public action.
2. Trial procedures.
3. Form of verdict by court in jury trials.
4. Appeal and review by court appeal.
5. Allocation of cost of proceedings.
6. Payment into court prior to taking.

JUST COMPENSATION

The payment of just compensation for the taking of property under eminent domain proceedings is assured by constitutional guaranty. The right to such payments is not questioned. The crux of the problem is a determination of the amount of payments due and the valuation procedure on which such payments are based.

Compensation generally is restricted to the value of the property physically taken, and to offset a loss in value, if any, to the remaining parcel on account of severance of a part from the unity of a whole property. In evaluating just compensation, care must be taken to exclude losses incurred by the exercise of the police power of government, which in most states and legal jurisdictions are not compensable. Thus losses incurred through changes in zoning, change in level or grade of roads, construction, or elimination of public improvements and business losses in general are not compensated unless specifically provided for under statutory law or permissible under court instruction. Only losses attributable to the property as a result of physical taking, and as measured by a loss of value subsequent to the taking, are generally permitted as evidence for a court determination of just compensation.

MEANING OF VALUE

Value has many meanings to many persons (see Chapter 1). Because of the failure of the appraisal profession to establish a clear-cut definition of value based on the laws of economics (specifically, the law of supply and demand) higher courts filled the void and interpreted value for purposes of litigation. Most courts have held value to mean *market value* or its equivalent—a warranted market price obtainable as a result of open and free bartering between willing, ready, and informed buyers and sellers.

The definition of market value most frequently quoted in court proceedings and accepted for publication is based on a California court decision and reads:

> Market value is the highest price estimated in terms of money which a property will bring if exposed for sale in the open market, allowing a reasonable time to find a purchaser who buys with knowledge of all the uses to which it is adapted and for which it is capable of being used.[1]

The emphasis placed on market price as evidence of market value is further shown by another court decision which reads as follows:

> The market value of land taken for a public use is the price for which it could have been sold by a person desirous of selling to a person willing to buy, neither acting under compulsion and both exercising intelligent judgment.[2]

The "willing buyer, willing seller" concept so frequently stressed in conventional appraisal practice has little practical application in condemnation proceedings. This is so because the seller as a rule is *not* willing and, in fact, is seeking relief in court.

Court decisions appear to sustain the principle of equity in condemnation under which the property owner is to be left whole in terms of dollars. It is the court's intention to leave his cash position, as measured by the value of his property before and after the taking, intact.

---

[1]Based on *People v. Ricciardi,* 23 Cal.2d 390, 144 p. 2d 799 (1943).
[2]*Baltimore and Ohio Railroad Company v. Bonafield's Heirs,* 90 SE 868, 79 W.Va. 287.

MEASURES OF VALUE

Where, as a result of condemnation for public use, an owner is deprived of *all* his real property holdings at a given location, the loss in value must equal the value of the entire property. Little difficulty, as a rule, is encountered by professional appraisers in estimating the market value of an entire property in accordance with prevailing appraising principles and practices and as outlined in preceding chapters. Generally, the things to be considered in a determination of market value, and as gleaned from a condensation of court decisions, include among others the following:[3]

1. A view of the premises and its surroundings.
2. A description of the physical characteristics of the property and its situation in relation to the points of importance in the neighborhood.
3. The price at which the land was bought, if sufficiently recent to throw light on present value.
4. The price at which similar neighboring land has sold, at or about the time of taking.
5. The opinion of expert witnesses.
6. A consideration of the uses for which the land is adapted and for which it is available.
7. The cost of the improvements less depreciation, if they are such as to increase the market value of the land.
8. The net income from the land, if the land is devoted to one of the uses to which it could be most advantageously and profitably applied.

It is in *partial* taking that substantial differences arise among opposing expert witnesses as to value losses resulting from expropriation plus losses inflicted on the remainder of the property because of property *severance*.

The steps essential to a measurement of value losses in case of partial taking of real property are as follows:

1. Estimate the value of the property under consideration as a whole, free from encumbrances and restrictions imposed by the proposed facility. This market value is to be based on a cash or cash equivalent market transaction.
2. Estimate the value of the part taken. If these are individual parts of the property, such as bushes or sheds, the value that these objects add to the property is the basis for compensation—not their replacement cost.
3. Deduct item 2 from item 1 to reveal the value of the remaining property as if unaffected by the proposed public improvement.
4. Estimate the damages, if any, caused to the remainder property as a result of severance of the part taken under the power of eminent domain.
5. Add the value of the part taken to any damages the remainder suffered; this will be the total just compensation.

[3]Julius L. Sackman, *Nichols' The Law of Eminent Domain* (New York: Matthew Bender & Company, Inc., 1981), Vol. 4, Secs. 12.2–12.3142.

The value of the part taken, plus damages resulting from severance, comprises the amount due the owner as fair compensation. This amount, however, cannot logically exceed the value of the entire property prior to taking as calculated under the first step above. In the valuation of the part taken, courts have ruled that the part under appraisal must be evaluated as a part of the whole and not as a free-standing and separate parcel. A strip of land 5 feet deep and 100 feet long may have little value if offered for sale and use; but the same strip of land may make an important contribution to value if added to a parcel 95 feet deep in an area where a minimum depth of 100 feet is necessary under zoning regulations for a given highest and best land use. In considering what constitutes the whole property where several parcels are under one ownership at a given location, the appraiser should be guided by court-proved rules which establish economic unity in accordance with:

1. Contiguity of location (a continuous, unbroken tract).
2. Unity of ownership.
3. Unity of use as evidenced by economic unity (utility) rather than physical unity).

In the estimation of value for the property as a whole, land and improvements must also be considered as an integral whole and not as independent and unrelated parts. Only after value for the entire property has been ascertained can allocation logically be made to fractional portions of the land or to land and buildings as respective parts. To illustrate: Where one-half of a tract of land is taken, and where the value of the entire tract is estimated to be $20,000, the value of the part taken—as a part of the whole—is deemed to be $10,000. However, if the two halves of the tract of land under value consideration were offered for sale as separate parcels, each may bring only $6,000 because of size and the resultant change in the economically feasible highest and best land use. Courts have consistently ruled that an owner's property must be left economically whole in terms of value and in the illustration cited above would rule on—or instruct the jury to consider—the value of the land taken as a part of the whole and not as a separate parcel unrelated to the owner's entire property from which it is taken. The methods used most frequently in the valuation of property where there is partial taking are:

1. The equal-unit-value (plus severance damages, if any) method.
2. The before-and-after valuation method.

The *equal-unit-value method*, often referred to as the *square-foot method* of land valuation, is a compromise designed to distribute the value of the whole over the physical units contained in the entire parcel affected by the taking. Otherwise, in the condemnation of a strip of land for street-widening purposes, it may be argued that the front part of a lot is more valuable than the rear portion which is remote from access and thus considered less serviceable. Opponents, on the other hand, may argue—and rightfully so—that the economic effect of condemnation of a strip of land for road-widening purposes is simply to reduce the lot in depth, leaving street rights and frontage intact. The economic effect of taking thus is deemed to be from the rear of the property rather than from the front area where the physical severance is to take place. Under the equal-unit-value method the value of the part taken to the value of the whole is intended to be in the same ratio that the physical units of land taken bear to the total land units of the property as a whole.

The *before-and-after method* of land valuation appears to be more equitable in measuring value losses sustained by the condemnee. This method, however, may unavoidably include benefits accruing to a property as a result of the proposed public improvements. For this reason, this method of valuation is used more often as a check on the accuracy of valuation obtained by the equal-unit-value (plus severance damages, if any) method rather than as an independent measure of just compensation. In practice, the procedure generally followed is to compare the property values before and after the effects of the partial taking, allowing for the net difference between the benefits and damages. In some state jurisdictions, such as in Florida, consideration of benefits resulting from proposed public improvements is specifically ruled out by constitutional or statutory provisions. The appropriate measure of just compensation payable to the landowner is the loss in value to his property and not the benefits gained by the condemning authority.

The taking of a part of an owner's property often causes value losses to the remainder property as a result of *severance*. To minimize such severance losses, legislation in many states permits condemning authorities to offset damages caused by severance against benefits (value increments) brought about by the public improvements (for which the property was partially taken). Under no circumstances, however, should value benefits be given consideration in es-

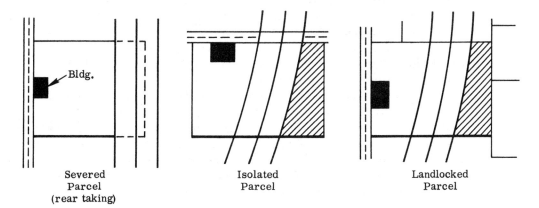

Severed	Isolated	Landlocked
Parcel	Parcel	Parcel
(rear taking)		

Figure 22.1 Types of damaged parcels

timating the value of the part (or whole) of a property taken under eminent domain proceeding. Figure 22.1 illustrates three types of damaged remainder parcels.

SEVERANCE DAMAGE

In brief, *severance damage* constitutes a loss in value of the part of a property remaining after taking as compared with the value of the remainder when considered as a part of the whole. Severance damage in essence is a measure of depreciation attributable to a remainder property as a result of one or more of the following:

1. Change in highest and best use of the property subsequent to the taking.
2. Expenditures necessary to restore or protect the property from hazards caused by the taking of property.
3. Increased cost of operation or, conversely, a lowering of net income on which value is based.

Where a strip of land is taken for construction of a limited access highway across an industrial property and the remainder land is cut off from railroad sidings and road access, a change in the highest and best use to a lower and possibly agricultural land use is likely. The difference in value under the prevailing use prior to land taking, as compared with the highest and best use subsequent to the land taking, constitutes the amount of severance to which the owner is entitled as just compensation in addition to the value of the land taken.

Where, as a result of the taking, expenditures are incurred to make repairs on remaining improvements—or where, for instance, fencing is necessary to guard cattle against the hazards of a proposed railroad right-of-way—such expenditures are recognized as severance damage for which compensation is due. It is important to recognize that severance damages claimed against the building improvements because of road hazards or the destruction of amenities caused by increased proximity to a new road right-of-way can logically be incurred only for the useful (economic) life of the building and cannot extend into perpetuity as is the case with damage to land.

Without actual case studies of similar situations, appraisers unfortunately are forced to rely too much on "judgment." Figure 22.2 shows an example of a partial taking at a proposed interstate highway interchange in the state of Washington. Construction of the interchange caused enhancement rather than damages to the remaining property. In fact, the "after" value of the 27.36 acres exceeded the value of the original 36 acres. Therefore, the appraisal provided unwarranted compensation to the landowner.

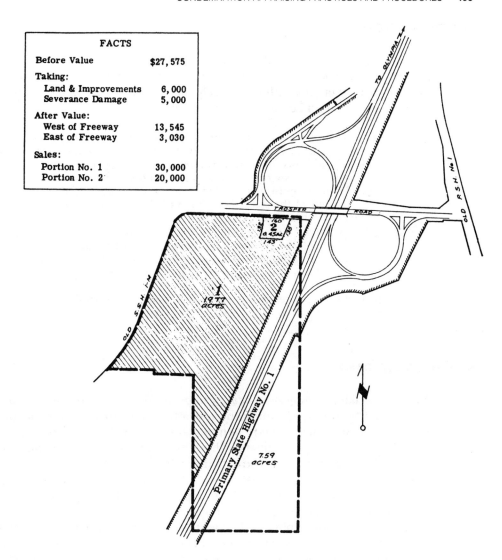

FACTS	
Before Value	$27,575
Taking:	
Land & Improvements	6,000
Severance Damage	5,000
After Value:	
West of Freeway	13,545
East of Freeway	3,030
Sales:	
Portion No. 1	30,000
Portion No. 2	20,000

Figure 22.2 Severance Damage Study Interchange

Source: American Association of State Highway and Transportations Officials, *Acquisition for Right-of-Way* (Washington, D.C.: 1962), p. 660.

TREATMENT OF BENEFITS

Public improvements generally are intended to create benefits for the community as a whole, and specifically for the area in which the improvements are directly located. These benefits, although rarely mutually exclusive, must for purposes of court presentation be identified as follows:

1. Benefits which accrue to the community as a whole, and which in a few states such as Alabama, New Mexico, New York, North Carolina, South Carolina, Virginia, and Wisconsin, are permitted as "offset" against damages claimed as a result of the taking of private property. In other state jurisdictions, however, general benefits must be excluded from consideration in the determination of both the value of the part taken and in the loss of value suffered as a result of the taking by the remainder property.
2. Special benefits which accrue to the adjoining properties, and particularly to the property for which severance damages are claimed. In some states special benefits may be set off against both the value of the part taken and the damages claimed to the remainder property. In other states only the damages to the remainder or severed land may be reduced by the value of such special benefits as are directly related to the public improvements for which the taking of property was authorized.

CONSEQUENTIAL DAMAGE

Broadly speaking, *consequential damage* to property includes all damages suffered by a property owner, including the loss attributable to severance. In practice, however, the term has come to denote damage suffered by owners as a result of proposed public improvements where no real property is physically taken. A change in road grade, the construction of a bridge, the bypassing of a town, the relocation of a road, the construction of a sewage treatment plant—all are instances where neighboring or abutting property owners may suffer losses due to a diminution in the value of their property. Such losses, if ascribable to the exercise of the police power of government, are not compensable. It seems inequitable that some owners, where there is some taking of physical land, are being compensated for consequential damages where such contribute to a lowering of value of the remainder property, while other owners suffering like damage—but where there is no taking of property—are left without recourse for compensation. Often suit is brought by owners so affected, and their action at court is termed *inverse condemnation.* That is, suit is instituted by them for relief under the laws of equity rather than by the condemnor as is the case in usual eminent domain court action. It is seldom that compensation is judicially ordered in such instances unless property losses can directly be linked to the physical taking of an owner's property.

EXCESS CONDEMNATION

Public improvements in general, and road improvements in particular, create benefits that often reflect substantial increment in the value of abutting and neighboring lands. When such value increments are substantial, an attempt is made, where permissible under law, to channel the benefits for disposition by public authority for the good of all within the state or community. Construction of parks, parkways, recreation centers, and planned public buildings are instances of this. In New York State, excess condemnation is permissible under state law. Thus, if it is estimated that the value benefits of a proposed garden parkway may extend up to 500 feet on either side of a 100-foot limited access roadbed, condemning authorities may acquire by eminent domain action a strip of land 1,100 feet in width. After completion of the parkway, the adjacent land may be leased for concessionary use by restaurant and gas station chain operators; or the land may be resold to private owners at prices which may recoup the increment in land value. Such gains may go far to offset the costs of construction, betterments, and capital improvements. The entire theory of excess condemnation is still in the development stage. Wisely used, this practice could prevent windfall gains by land speculators and place much-needed public improvement programs on a self-liquidating, pay-as-you-go financial basis.

THE EXPERT WITNESS

Increasingly, professional appraisers are called on to testify as expert witnesses in condemnation trials. Many facetious definitions of an "expert" are given. He has been called "a person 50 or more miles away from home," or, "someone who has learned to carry a briefcase with dignity." Such definitions are offered to belittle professional skill that usually can be acquired only through years of hard work and study, field experience, careful preparation, and training. The dean of appraisers, the late George Schmutz, defined an expert witness as

> one who is possessed of peculiar knowledge and experience that are not common to persons generally, and who has an opinion based upon such knowledge and experience that is peculiarly fitted for assisting the court, or jury, in determining an issue, such as the amount of damage measured in terms of dollars.[4]

This definition implies that the appraiser, as an expert, merely testifies as to his *opinion* of value. It is the court or jury that *determines* value. This the appraiser must firmly keep in mind, or he will jeopardize his case by being

---

[4]George L. Schmutz, *Condemnation Appraisal Handbook* (Englewood Cliffs, N.J.: Prentice-Hall, Inc., 1963), p. 360.

accused of usurping the functions of both court and jury. Whereas an expert can express opinions and conclusions based on facts, laymen as a rule are restricted to confining their testimony to recitation of statements concerning facts.

Before accepting an assignment to serve as an expert witness, the appraiser must make certain that he will be allowed to testify as an *independent* agent, free from bias and pressure to produce a "favorable" opinion. Unfortunately, many clients through their advocate attorneys shop around for "experts" whose judgment can be swayed. Professional appraisers are subject to censure on ethical and moral grounds if they serve as advocates rather than as free and independent analysts. Appraisal fees, too, should be based on time, expense, and degree of professional responsibility assumed, and should *not* be made contingent on the value reported, the amount of the verdict, or the winning of the case.

PRETRIAL PREPARATION

Testimony to be offered by an expert witness should be backed by a detailed appraisal report in which the value conclusions reached are fully documented. The report need not be and generally is not submitted as a court exhibit, and it cannot be demanded for inspection by the opposing counsel unless the report is referred to and used as a basis for testifying under direct examination. Comprehensive appraisal preparation permits the client's lawyer to familiarize himself with factual details and the technical terminology peculiar to the case. Visual aids, where possible, should be employed. Subdivision maps, photographs, plot plans, market, cost, and income summary sheets should be submitted for court exhibit and to facilitate data presentation at the time of the trial.

It is well, too, for the appraiser and trial attorney to agree on the order of data presentation, and to outline the questions and answers to be asked and given during direct examination. The sequence of questions asked generally falls into categories pertaining to:

1. Qualifications of witness.
2. Examination of subject property.
3. Method used in arriving at an estimate of value.
4. Opinion of value.

Care should be taken to present in a simple but impressive manner the qualifications of the expert witness. Even when opposing counsel stipulates that, in the interest of time, he accepts the witness as qualified to testify as an expert, the client's lawyer should nevertheless—if only for the court's benefit—qualify the witness as an expert in his field. It is the jury or court that sets the value, and the witness's testimony bears greater weight if extensive experience and knowledge in the field of property appraising back up the expert's findings.

Qualifying questions should inform the court as to the expert's background and experience on such points as:

1. Occupation.
2. Place and geographic extent of business or profession.
3. Education and degrees earned.
4. Membership in professional associations.
5. Years of experience as an appraiser.
6. Types of clients served.
7. Types of properties appraised.
8. Appraisal courses completed or taught.
9. Publication of appraisal articles.
10. Experience in related fields of real estate brokerage and property management.

The questions asked pertaining to the examination of the subject property should establish a thorough familiarity with details of land and site improvements. Here the direct testimony should bring forth answers to such questions as:

1. Please describe and clearly identify the subject property.
2. When did you last inspect the property?
3. Have you examined the building plans and specifications for estimating cost of reproduction of the improvements?
4. What is the age of the structure and what methods were used to determine accrued depreciation?
5. Have you compared the subject property with other similar properties that have sold in recent times?
6. Did you verify the income experience of this property? Have expenditures been verified?
7. What is the present and foreseeable future highest and best use of the subject property?

The next group of questions under direct examination explores the method used in arriving at an estimate of value. Since any testimony offered at this stage of the court proceedings is subject to rebuttal during cross-examination, the appraiser should be careful not to present details of estimating that later may be questioned to pinpoint errors of judgment or of facts. Care must also be taken so as not to testify that value was derived by the summation method; that is, an estimation of the value of the lot separately, to which was then added the value of the improvements less accrued depreciation. Land and buildings thereon are merged as an operating unit and any division of the whole into arbitrary parts in some state jurisdictions may be charged as constituting *hypothetical* appraising, which is contrary to accepted valuation theory and practice.

It is best to generalize and to explain in simple, nontechnical words the methods used in estimating value. The appraiser, for instance, may state: "I have examined the property; considered its location within the neighborhood; inspected the site; checked public records for legal description and zoning, deed restrictions, and assessment data; studied comparable sales and analyzed other general and specific factual data deemed essential to the formation of a professional opinion of value."

It is advisable, too, at this point for counsel to request that the witness describe and explain the comparable sales which he or she considered in formulating an estimate of market value. The witness should request permission to refer to a large subdivision map, which should be marked for identification as a court exhibit that jurors may study and to which they may refer during their deliberation. On this map the subject property should be prominently marked in color and the sale properties clearly numbered and marked in different colors. As each sale property is identified, the transaction price should be stated, the seller and buyer named, the date of sale specified, and the terms of sale at which the transaction closed given. The appraiser should make certain that each sale was verified with the purchaser, seller, or real estate broker as to date of sale, transaction price, and terms of sale. Under no circumstances is it wise to rely on the state transfer tax as evidence of market prices at which the comparable sales exchanged. Even if this tax information posted in the deed book is considered accurate, the jury or court could be adversely influenced by lack of sale confirmation and by admission from the witness that revenue stamps can readily and legally be overstated to deliberately mislead those who rely on such evidence as a guide to market value.

The final category of questions concerns the *opinion* of value. Counsel as a rule asks: "As a result of your investigation, and by reason of your experience, have you formed an opinion of value for the subject [identify by name] property as of a specified date [date of taking]?" The witness, of course, answers in the affirmative. Counsel then may ask witness to state his or her professional opinion concerning:

1. Value of the entire property as a whole.
2. Value of the part taken when considered as a part of the whole or as a separate parcel when such testimony is deemed advantageous to the interests of the condemnee.
3. Value of the remainder considered as part of the property as a whole.
4. Value of the remainder as a separate parcel subsequent to the taking of a part of the property as constituted prior to the taking.
5. Severance damage attributable to the remainder property (the difference between items 3 and 4 above).

Where permissible, expert opinion may relate directly to the value of the entire property before the taking and the value of the remainder after the taking. This simplifies proceedings and yields directly the amount of compensation (the difference between before-and-after value as a result of condemnation) to which the owner is entitled to cover both the taking of a part of his or her property and the severance damages caused to the remainder. As explained above in the discussion of severance damages, care must be taken to exclude benefits which may accrue as a result of the road or public improvements at issue. The appraiser must, of course, be prepared to testify as to the extent and possible effects of potential benefits caused by the public improvements, provided such questions are raised with the permission of the court (and undoubtedly over the objection of counsel for the condemnee).

Following the statement of value opinion, the expert witness generally is called on to give a reason for the conclusions reached either as to the value of the property as a whole or the allocation of this value to the parts and the severance damages effected as a consequence. The answer merely calls for a summary of the important conclusions reached as a result of the appraisal investigation and a reemphasis of market cost or income data which support the expert opinion.

CROSS-EXAMINATION

It is under cross-examination that the competence of the appraiser and his or her quality as an expert witness come to light. Many appraisers—although thorough, diligent, and accurate in their value findings—lack personality, experience on the witness stand, diction, and the ease that flows from a broad educational background. Such witnesses, through indecision, lack of confidence, and inability to think quickly while on their feet may undo in a few minutes the work of many days or weeks of preparation. Other witnesses have an oversized ego which causes them to falter or to explode when—directly or by implication—their integrity or competence is questioned. Fear of seeing their findings exposed to ruthless analysis and their community reputation jolted by clever lawyers who go all out to destroy the effectiveness of their testimony keeps many otherwise qualified professional appraisers from accepting assignments that require as a condition subsequent defense of these findings in court.

Yet those who enter the appraisal profession should be trained to take the stand as expert witnesses. As a first step, personal fear must be overcome and confidence acquired that due care was taken in the process of estimating value as a means of aiding the court in reaching a just decision. The court and jurors usually frown on personal abuse and on tricky behavior unbecoming to the legal profession. The witness should remind himself that his counsel is his silent partner, that unfair or misleading questions will be objected to when raised, and that the court and jurors are intelligent observers seeking truth rather than entertainment by a pyrotechnical display of legal skill.

The witness should listen to questions earnestly and carefully. Where the intent of the question is not clear, a clarification should be asked for. Answers should be short, simple, polite, and directed to the jury or court. When yes or no answers are requested, the witness should comply but ask permission to explain his answer when clarification is deemed essential. To illustrate, a series of yes or no questions may be as follows:

1. Are you representing the condemnee?
2. Have you served him or her professionally previously?
3. Are you paid by him or her for your services?
4. You would not be testifying without promise of pay, would you?
5. Your opinion of value is bought, is it not?

Certainly, questions 4 and 5 should be explained, since bias is implied that may influence the court's decision. To question 4 the witness should add that as a member of the appraisal profession he is not accustomed to volunteering his services, and that as an independent fee appraiser he gladly serves all who call on him for professional aid. To question 5 the witness, after a firm "no," should state that although his services are paid for, his opinion of value is based on facts gathered and studied during the course of the investigation, and that the findings and opinions stated would be the same no matter who engaged his services or agreed to defray professional costs and fees.

The cross-examiner must be expected to do all in his or her power to attempt to weaken or even discredit the value testimony of the opposing expert witness. Questions asked are generally designed to cast doubt where possible on such matters as:

1. Adequacy of experience or education.
2. Familiarity with the subject property or subject area and neighborhood.
3. Adequate preparation or omission of relevant data.
4. Freedom from bias or incompetence.
5. Correctness of computations or validity of valuation premises.

In preparing his or her valuation report and in planning the sequence of testimony, the appraiser, with the aid of a lawyer, should anticipate probable questions that may be raised during cross-examination and be ready to offer clear and convincing answers. The following 10 guides can be invaluable as to the proper conduct of appraisers giving expert testimony in court:

1. Never lie or be evasive.
2. Never exaggerate the "highest and best use."
3. Never testify to a dictated appraisal.
4. Carefully examine and evaluate all comparable sales.
5. Avoid capitalizing hypothetical income on vacant land.
6. Judiciously exercise your right to explain your answer.
7. Avoid giving the false appearance of infallibility.
8. Always remember that you are an impartial witness, not an advocate.
9. Your testimony should be the same if appearing for the opposing party.
10. Always remember to control your temper on cross-examination and retain a sense of humor.

REVIEW QUESTIONS

1. Explain why public bodies have been given the power of eminent domain.
2. List six legal requirements that generally must be followed by governmental bodies to protect private property rights when the power of eminent domain is used.
3. Define the term "just compensation."
4. Explain how the conventional definition of market value is inapplicable to eminent domain cases.
5. Give your interpretation of the court-proved rules used to establish economic unity of a condemned property.
6. Briefly explain the before-and-after rule for valuing land for eminent domain purposes.
7. How do consequential damages relate to just compensation for a property owner?

READING AND STUDY REFERENCES

AMERICAN ASSOCIATION OF STATE HIGHWAY AND TRANSPORTATION OFFICIALS. *Acquisition for Right-of-Way.* Washington, D.C.: Association Committee on Right-of-Way, 1962.

CHRISTENSEN, BARBARA. "How to Be a Winning Witness," *The Real Estate Appraiser and Analyst* 47, no. 3 (Fall Quarter 1981), pp. 23–24.

COMMITTEE FOR SPECIAL RESEARCH (AMERICAN INSTITUTE OF REAL ESTATE APPRAISERS). *Divergencies in Right-of-Way Valuations.* Washington, D.C.: Highway Research Board, National Academy of Sciences, 1971.

CONDEMNATION SUBCOMMITTEE OF NATIONAL EDUCATION COMMITTEE. *Condemnation Appraisal Practice* Vol. II. Chicago: American Institute of Real Estate Appraisers, 1973.

EPLEY, DONALD R., and JAMES H. BOYKIN. Chapter 19, *Basic Income Property Appraisal.* Reading, Mass.: Addison-Wesley Publishing Co., Inc., 1983.

HUXTABLE, RICHARD L. "Eminent Domain Is Traced to Biblical Times," *Right of Way* (May 1979), pp. 24–27.

KELLOUGH, W. R. "Impact Analysis of Electrical Transmission Lines," *Right of Way* (December 1980), pp. 19–25.

KENNER, GIDEON. "Remedies in Inverse Condemnation: A New Ball Game?" *Right of Way* (July 1979), pp. 9–10.

ROBERTS, THOMAS L. "Valuation of Project Enhancement in Eminent Domain," *The Appraisal Journal* 50, no. 2 (April 1982), pp. 220–227.

WISE, FLOYD. "Steps Given for Trial Preparation," *Right of Way* (April 1981), pp. 20–22.

23

AD VALOREM TAX VALUATION OF RAILROADS AND PUBLIC UTILITIES

Learning Objectives

After reading this chapter, you should be able to:

Understand the logic for appraising railroads and public utilities under the unit rule

Discuss how regulatory controls affect the value of railroads and public utilities

Appreciate how external obsolescence caused by rate setting is calculated

Compute capitalization rates via a blending of secured and equity debt

Allocate a multistate's system's value to a particular state

Compare different views on the proper handling of such important subjects as development of capitalization rates

APPRAISAL OF RAILROADS AND PUBLIC UTILITIES UNDER THE UNIT RULE

Unit Valuation: Its Meaning

Since the principles and practices of property appraising as outlined in this text apply to all goods and services whether real or personal, whether publicly or privately owned, the reader may wonder why railroads and public utilities are singled out for special consideration in the application of the appraisal process. The explanation rests on the fact that the vast majority of market sales of goods and services involve readily transferable properties that may be sold or exchanged without prior governmental approval. These properties also are free from state or federal controls except for general limitations that fall under the police power, the right of eminent domain, and the right of taxation as explained in Chapter 4.

The properties owned by railroads and public utilities, although composed of separate and identifiable assets such as locomotives, freight cars, railroad tracks, right-of-ways, buildings, power plants, pipelines, transmission lines, and so on, are operationally interdependent and the value of one part cannot effectively or accurately be estimated except as a part of the unit value of the enterprise as a whole. Realization of this fact paved the way for the now generally accepted and court-sanctioned practice of appraising railroad and public utility property as an *operating whole* under the "unit rule."

Unit valuation gained authoritative prominence with publication known as the "Chapman Report," authored by the Committee on Unit Valuation of the National Association of Tax Administrators.[1] Reading of the full report is highly recommended to students of appraising and *must* reading for those who seek professional status as appraisers of railroads and public utilities for ad valorem tax purposes. To quote from this report, unit valuation is aptly described as follows:

> This is an appraisal of an integrated property as a whole without any reference to the value of its component parts. It is to be distinguished from fractional appraisal, which is a valuation of one of the parts without reference to the value of the whole, and from a summation appraisal, which is a valuation of the whole derived by adding two or more fractional appraisals.[2]

Railroads and public utilities are more than a summation of lumber, steel, brick, and mortar. They are going concerns that succeed or fail as a "whole." Thus value of the *unit* is primary and value of the parts inferred by allocation secondary. The concept of unit valuation was given further and more recent support by the Western States Association of Tax Administrators in a report of the Committee on Railroad and Utility Valuation. This report states:

> The unit appraisal means valuing the total properties as *one thing*—an item in the complex array of many property items practically defies individual or suggested valuation. Segments of the total property can be valued by allocation or apportionment of the total unit value when required by statutory law—as the usual rule, however, no attempt is made to assign values in a unit appraisal to individual items of property unless it is a legal requirement.[3]

[1]*Chapman Report* (Chicago: National Association of Tax Administrators, June 1954).
[2]Ibid., p. 2
[3]*Report to National Association of Tax Administrators*, Chicago, October 6, 1971, p. 3.

What Constitutes the Unit

Railroads and public utilities are complex in character and operate their plant as well as render public service as an integrated whole. Basically all property that is owned or used as an operating corporate entity constitutes a "unit" that is subject to appraisal. As indicated in prior chapters, an appraiser must operate within the law and comply with statutory provisions of the government that exercises the "power of taxation." Some states require separate assessments for operating, as distinguished from nonoperating properties. Other states, for utilities engaged in intrastate commerce, require all property under common ownership, or use, to be included in the unit.

As a rule, it is recommended appraisal practice to evaluate the two categories of property, operating and utility owned nonoperating properties, separately. This practice is essential for railroads or utilities engaged in interstate operations in order that equitable shares of the unit value can be distributed to various tax jurisdictions with aid of an allocation formula. The derivation of a "fair" allocation formula will be given further and more detailed consideration in later pages of this chapter.

It is common practice for many railroads and for some utilities to use properties, owned by others, under short- or long-term lease agreements. It is recommended appraisal practice, the law permitting, to consider leased properties as a part of the "unit" and to include the depreciated value of leased properties directly in the cost indicator of value. The income and stock and debt indicators of value reflect of course indirectly the operational worth of all property, whether it is owned, leased, or purchased with reserve funds or with funds contributed by customers or others in "aid of construction." Opinions differ whether, for ad valorem tax purposes, property should be assessed to the owner rather than the user. Contractual agreements between lessor and lessee, as a rule, provide that the latter assume ad valorem tax liability. For this reason, unless mandated otehwise by law, all operating property, whether owned or leased, should be appraised as part of the unit.

THE EFFECT OF REGULATORY CONTROL
ON VALUE OF RAILROADS AND PUBLIC UTILITIES

Railroads and public utilities, because of their unique nature, are subject to statutory and comprehensive federal and state regulatory commission controls that affect not only their day-to-day operations, but their value both for rate-making (tariff) and ad valorem tax purposes. The valuation for rate-making purposes is not a function of the "market" place but rather a semijudicial regulatory process under which, based on a *test* year accounting period, the railroad or public utility is authorized to set rates that are intended, but not guaranteed, to yield sufficient revenues to cover operational costs including a return "of" and a fair return "on" the original or book cost of capital investment in railroad or utility property. The process by which value for rate-making purposes or rather the rate base is periodically fixed will not be detailed or explained in this chapter. To the appraiser the rate base is a fact, which like zoning or deed restrictions, places a limit on income through property use and thus must be accepted as value influencing data in the appraisal process.

Following is a summary of why railroads and public utilities are subject to fairly rigid federal and state regulatory controls, and why such controls have a direct and limiting effect on the market value of the regulated company. Some public services, such as water, sanitary disposal, and police and fire protection, are so vital to the health, welfare, and safety of the public that such services, with the aid of, and under indirect federal control, are rendered directly by local county, town, or municipal governments.

The effect of regulatory controls on operating revenue and especially on net railroad or utility operating income is of vital interest to the appraiser or assessor in the determination of fair market value for ad valorem tax purposes. To illustrate, an established railroad or utility cannot limit nor abandon service— no matter how unprofitable it may be—or extend services beyond territorial limits or sell the corporation's operating assets without specific approval by the regulatory commission. Railroads and utilities, too, are subject to strict accounting system control and must file periodic audited reports to federal and, as a rule, to state regulatory agencies as well.

These annual reports, because of their uniformity and operational details, provide significant factual data on which the appraiser may rely in the application of the traditional—cost, income, and market—approaches to value, for ad valorem tax purposes. In fact, these detailed annual reports prepared under constraint of law provide not only accurate historical and current operational data but enable the appraiser to forecast with reasonable accuracy relevant cost, market, and income performance data that serve as foundation for the estimate of fair market value.

Some assessors as well as appraisers take issue with established regulatory, managerial, and operational policies and as a result substitute their judgment as to the amount a given railroad or utility should generate as net operating income. This is accomplished by adjusting (decreasing) annual allowances for accrued depreciation, by adding back to the income stream the reserve for deferred federal income taxes,[4] and/or by disallowing those portions of rental payments for leased equipment which are judged to measure interest payments on the value of the leased property. It should be kept in mind that the typical appraiser or assessor is rarely qualified to substitute his or her judgment for

---

[4]For income tax purposes a railroad or utility company is allowed to accelerate depreciation write-offs, and the postponement of tax payments resulting from straight-line versus accelerated depreciation is set aside in a deferred tax account for future book adjustment purposes to cover increased tax payments due in future years when straight-line depreciation exceeds allowed book depreciation under accelerated cost accounting.

that of professional engineers, certified public accountants, attorneys at law, or highly specialized railroad or utility officials who serve as treasurers or comptrollers of corporate finances. An appraiser is not an engineer, or a certified acccountant, attorney, or any other designated railroad or utility specialist. He is a market analyst who must employ standard and professionally approved appraisal theory and practices. For an appraiser to usurp managerial functions and to stipulate how a railroad or utility is to be operated, or how books of accounts are to be kept, is presumptuous. Values resulting from hypothetical book adjustments are, no doubt, the cause for the unusual number of tax litigations in which judges, unfortunately, are cast into the role of property appraisers.

RECONCILIATION OF VALUE INDICATORS

Cost as an Indicator of Value

In a normal, open, and competitive market, production costs incurred by an informed and prudent investor are presumed to equal market value; otherwise, it is claimed, the expenditures would not have been made in the first place. This appears true when a plant is new and as a "unit" constitutes the highest and best use, as defined in Chapter 5. For this reason, undoubtedly, the cost indicator of value has been widely used and given maximum weight in the final estimate of probable market value.

Cost, because of passage of time, technological changes, external obsolescence, and last but not least, overregulation, no longer provides an accurate measure of value. It is generally accepted, too, that costs, which serve as a basis for rate-making purposes, at best, set a ceiling of value.

There are varying types of costing techniques in use by appraisers and cost engineers that yield an estimate of plant cost "new" on date of the appraisal. These costing techniques are identified as follows:

1. Original cost of the good or service when first put into production.
2. Original, acquisition, or book cost. This cost may be higher or lower than the "first cost" of production.
3. Reproduction cost. This is the cost to produce a replica of the good or service on date of appraisal.
4. Replacement cost. This is the cost to produce a good or service that yields the same utility as the subject under appraisal, at a given time and place.
5. Trended costs. This is original cost adjusted to reflect cost changes caused by the passage of time, changes in the purchasing power of the dollar, as well as changes in costs of materials and labor.

An appraiser will not apply all the various costs in any one appraisal. Reason dictates that no matter which costing technique is applied, if true and accurate consideration is given to *all* causes of accrued depreciation, as explained in Chapter 13, value cannot logically exceed depreciated book or original cost accepted by regulatory commissions for rate (tariff)-making purposes. It is an economic truism that only costs that yield an income can serve as a base for value to a willing, informed, and prior to purchase, "free" (unregulated) investor. For ad valorem tax purposes, "nonearning" plant (to be identified below), if part of the operating unit, must in accordance with statutory provisions be included in the cost indicator as a measure of value.

It is the appraiser's professional responsibility to exclude from the cost indicator of value property that is subject to either exemption or to separate taxation under law, or classified as nonoperating investments. The former includes such properties as lands held for future use, motor vehicles, aircraft, or motorcraft licensed in lieu of taxation, working cash, accounts receivable, and property under exclusive federal jurisdiction. The latter may include property or lands leased to others, lands not used for utility purposes, investments in subsidiaries, and generally property classified as "nonoperating."

Property nonearning on date of the appraisal and property used, but owned by others, that are deemed assessable include the following:

1. Construction work in progress.
2. Material and supplies.
3. Contributions in aid of construction.
4. Leased or rented property.

The treatment for ad valorem tax purposes of properties that are owned by others or deemed nonearning are "problem areas." Difference of opinions concerning them will be detailed more fully in later pages.

The subject of depreciation and its treatment as negative value has been described fully in Chapter 13. For railroads and public utilities, book depreciation, calculated as a rule, under age-life, straight-line decline in value, is generally accepted as reflecting losses in book value resulting from physical and functional causes.

One technique used to measure obsolescence in railroads is the "blue chip method." Under this method the appraised railroad is compared to the better railroads using the following three steps:

1. Selection of the "blue chip" railroads.
2. Selection of a number of recognized operating quality and efficiency factors in a railroad transportation system.
3. Comparison of each of the quality or efficiency factors for the railroad being appraised with the same factor for the standard or "blue chip."[5]

[5]Robert H. McSwain, *Appraisal of Utilities and Railroad Property for Ad Valorem Taxation*, Tax Institute of America and the Center for Management Development, Wichita State University, 1983.

Most railroads and practically all public utilities incur a third and often severe loss in value due to external obsolescence. This loss in value, as demonstrated below under the cost approach to value, is caused by the difference in the *rate* of return allowed by regulatory agencies and the rate of return that the investment market indicates as competitive to attract a willing, able, and informed purchaser (investor).

The application of the cost approach to value is illustrated as follows:

Book value of gross plant	$250,500,250
Current assets	15,220,150
Construction work in progress	45,300,000
Materials and supplies	12,420,800
Total value of gross plant in operation	$323,441,200
Add: Depreciated value of leased properties	85,358,300
Total book value before depreciation	$408,799,500

Less: Accrued depreciation		
Physical — per book	$115,420,000	
External = 17.4% of		
depreciated plant value[6]		
or 0.174 × $293,379,500 =	51,048,033	
Total depreciation		$166,468,033
Value via cost approach		$242,331,467

External depreciation is calculated as follows:

Market rate of capitalization	11.5%
Allowed rate of return	9.5%
Loss in earnings	2.0%

Loss in earnings of 2% ÷ market rate of 11.5% = 17.4% external obsolescence.

The Income Approach to Value

The income approach for unregulated or nonutility properties was explained fully in Chapters 15 through 18. For railroads and public utilities the standard and recommended approach to value under income capitalization is to take net operating income as reported to the regulatory commission for the last available year and to trend it upward or downward in accordance with "experienced" revenue trends over a 5- to 10-year period. For example, if income has increased at an average annual rate of 5%, it appears reasonable to conclude that current income generated from *existing* plant, and from plant to be placed

[6]Depreciated plant value is difference between total book value — before depreciation of $408,799,500 and accrued physical book depreciation of $115,420,000 or $408,799,500 − $115,420,000 = $293,379,500

in service during the taxable year, will increase at the same rate for the assessment year. Similarly, the rate of capitalization must reflect *current* cost of capital on date of the appraisal. This rate of capitalization cannot logically be lower than the rate or cost of bonded debt or higher than the cost of raising equity capital. Some assessors make use of embedded or existing capital cost to the subject company under appraisal. Since stated or embedded interest costs as a rule are lower than current cost of capital, this practice is viewed as a device to increase value artificially for ad valorem tax purposes. Use of embedded capital cost is justified by some appraisers and tax administrators on the grounds that the hypothetical purchaser takes over the bonded debt and thus benefits from the low interest rate. Thus it is concluded that the resulting interest savings constitute an intangible value which is best reflected in a lower (than current cost) rate of capitalization. This assumption ignores the fact that low-interest bonds can be purchased in the open market at discounted prices that reflect *current* cost of capital instead of coupon rates of interest.

In accordance with professionally approved appraisal principles and practices, value under the income approach, for ad valorem tax purposes, is demonstrated as follows:

Net railway or utility operating income	$ 25,650,000
Market rate of capitalization	11.5%
Income indicator of value	$223,043,478

The market rate of capitalization is a composite of rates which the market indicates that investors demand as interest for secured (bonded or mortgaged) capital and rates which the market indicates as necessary to attract equity or ownership (unsecured or risk) capital.[7] To illustrate, based on an average yield of 9% for bonded debt and for preferred stock, and a range of 14 to 15 percent for equity capital, the rate of capitalization is derived as shown in Table 23-1.

Table 23-1 Determination of the Rate of Capitalization

XYZ Utility	Percent of Capital Structure	×	Current Cost of Capital (%)	=	Weighted Rate (%)
Bonded debt	50.0		9.0		4.50
Preferred stock	5.0		9.0		0.45
Common stock	45.0		14.5		6.53
Weighted rate					11.48
Rounded to:					11.50

[7]For more on this topic, see John C. Goodman, "Use of Stock and Debt Approach Valuing Railroad or Utility Property Owned by A Conglomerate," Proceedings of the 1981 Public Utilities Workshop, Wichita State University, July 27–30, 1981.

The Market Indicator of Value

Prices that result from the interaction of demand and supply as reflected by informed buyers and sellers acting without coercion and allowing for such a selling period as may be dictated by the character of the property offered for sale, are the best evidences of value, in fact such prices *are* value. The marketplace is the final economic authority, but under many circumstances the authority of the market is not reflected. Railroads and public utilities are not freely sold and resold. Comparative sale evidence is scarce or nonexistent.

Although sales of railroads and public utilities or of component parts are most infrequent, and rarely comprise identical or even similar properties, attempts have been made to equate for differences and thus to derive market value. Equating for differences among railroads and public utilities is quite a different matter than equating for differences in six-room houses. The adjustments needed for complex corporations or segments of same would be too complex and subjective in nature to prove meaningful or reliable.

It appears logical that since there is seldom available objective market evidence as to the price that railroads or public utilities would command if offered for sale, the next best alternative is the market price of the stocks and bonds of the enterprise owning the property. Under accounting practices the liability side of the balance sheet must equal the asset side of the balance sheet. It is therefore assumed that the market value of the securities plus short-term debts and other liabilities is a measure of the market value of the tangible and intangible assets of the corporation under appraisal. This assumption is unfortunately not true, and the value of stocks, bonds, and other liabilities of an enterprise is generally dubious and unreliable evidence of the value of the assets that are subject to assessment for ad valorem tax purposes for the following reasons.

First, regulated enterprises commonly own assets and have sources of income from other than the assessable tangible and intangible operating properties. These may be securities in subsidiaries or affiliates or just investments.

Second, the market value of common stock is reflective of value of non-assessable assets under the *unit* procedure and also reflects speculative expectations and normally reflects a substantial valuation of capital gains. Funded debt, too, fluctuates in value depending on the interest or coupon rate on date of an issue. Thus long term bonds issued at a 4.5 percent rate of interest will sell for 50 cents on the dollar if current cost of money is above 9.0 percent, all other factors remaining equal. There is no reliable relationship between the constantly fluctuating market of stocks and bonds and the tangible and intangible assets reflected by such securities. Although knowledgeable assessors and appraisers give little weight to the stock and debt approach as an indicator of value, appraisal practice does sanction this method as a possible check on the reasonableness of the final estimate of value. For this reason an illustration of the application of the stock and debt (market) approach is set forth below.

Based on analysis of a utility's accounting records and market quotations—the average high and low for the prior year—of its securities, the data shown below support an index of value:

Liabilities and Capital	Reported Number of Shares	Average Market Value
Common stock	5,750,250 at $39.25 =	$225,697,312
Preferred stock	420,200 at $53.00 =	22,270,600
Long-term debt	$200,495,400[8]	165,460,500
Total liabilities and debt		$413,428,412
Utility nonoperating assets factor 42%[9]		173,639,933
Market value based on stock and debt		$239,788,479

Reconciliation of Value Indices

It is in the reconciliation or correlation of the value estimates under the cost, income, and market approaches to value that the experience, skill, and judgment of the appraiser can find no substitute. Applying judgment, however, assumes *knowledge* of that to be judged. Thus a reconciliation of the value indicators is not a mathematical or statistical exercise but rather a matter of considered judgment wherein the professional experience and educational training of the appraiser is called upon to determine the final conclusion of value. There might be occasions where only one approach to value is guiding, but generally two or all three approaches contribute in the formulation of the appraiser's judgment. Logic dictates that as a rule the income approach offers the best guide to value since, in the final analysis, value is the "present worth of future rights to income." Where cost and income yield relatively close estimates, it appears appropriate to give equal weight to these indicators of value. Since income, however, is the motivating factor for business activities, reason warrants that as a rule the income indicator of value be given the greatest weight, cost lesser weight, and stock and debt the least weight in the final estimate of value. As stated before, reconciliation is not an exercise in statistical weighting, but rather a serious attempt wherein the appraiser allows his or her experience, knowledge, and analysis of economic data to finalize his or her value judgment.

[8]Based on discounted market prices of bonds on date of the appraisal. Lower prices are due to stated interest rates that are below current rates of new issues.

[9]The nonoperating utility factor was derived as follows:

Total income available for fixed charges and capital	$20,500,300
Nonoperating utility income	$ 8,610,126
Ratio of nonoperating to total income (line 2 ÷ line 1) =	42%

In a professional appraisal report, or in defending an estimate of value as an expert witness in court, the appraiser may elect *not* to stipulate or to defend specific percentage weights assigned to the indicators of value. Instead, he or she may deem it preferable just to state the values derived under each approach and based on all evidence submitted, certify a final value. As stated, some appraisers do and others do not apply percentage weights to the indicators of value. Those who do not, fear that use of specific percentages is subject to scrutiny and challenge as to their accuracy. Finalizing an estimate and expressing it as the appraiser's best judgment of probable value is an accepted professional privilege.

Nevertheless, courts have sanctioned the use of percentage weights that are deemed judicious or reasonable under the circumstances. Applying percentage weights judged applicable to the indices of value derived in the illustrations set forth above, the final probable market value of the utility under appraisal is reported as follows:

Index of Value	Amount	×	Weight	=	Component Value
Income	$223,043,478		60%		$133,826,087
Cost	$242,331,467		30%		72,699,440
Market	$239,788,479		10%		23,978,848
Final estimate of value					$230,504,375
Rounded to:					$230,500,000

ALLOCATION OF SYSTEM VALUE TO A STATE

Railroads and public utilities whose operations are classified as "interstate" and whose plant, equipment, and services thus transcend state lines are faced with the task of allocating the system (unit) value to respective states and where required by law, to tax jurisdictions within a state. Although much has been written on the subject of valuation, per se, there is a void in authoritative literature on the subject of allocation.[10]

Perhaps allocation of system value has not posed a problem because of narrow interpretation of statutory requirements of "situs" of plant and equipment as a basis for ad valorem taxation. Since situs refers to physical location of tangible property, it appears logical that allocation of system value on a cost basis gained wide acceptance. Railroads and utilities, too, did not challenge

---

[10]An exception is the article by L. J. Eastman, *National Tax Journal* (June 1972), pp. 321–330.

allocation practices as long as allocation factors when summarized did not exceed 100 percent.

With the advance of technology and ever greater capital investment in terminal stations and switching yards for railroads and nuclear power plants and gas pumping stations for public utilities, some taxing authorities have questioned the equity of cost allocation and applied a weighted cost/revenue ratio as more representative of "value" allocation. For example, Pacific Power and Light Company challenged in court an allocation factor derived by the Department of Revenue of the state of Montana as a weighted average of plant in service and revenue.[11] The Supreme Court of Montana upheld the allocation factor computed by the Department of Revenue on the basis that the unitary method requires consideration of the worth of the Montana property as part of an ongoing enterprise. The court concluded that the *cost* of Pacific's plant in service in Montana, under the facts of the case, was not an appropriate indicator of this plant since although the plant represented only 1.6% of Pacific's total utility property, it generated 2.37% of the company's revenue. The court thus concluded that a weighted average of percent of plant in state to total system plant, and percent of revenues generated by such plant to total system revenues, is not improper.

Railroad trackage per mile has widely been used in the state of Texas for allocation of a railway system's value. Although the actual mileage of track within a geographic area is important, it is deemed that the percent of total revenue generated by the area under study is of equal importance. Thus in the derivation of taxable value to be allocated to the city of Dallas for the tax years in question, weight was given to both measures—cost and revenue—as shown below:

Percent of track miles within the tax district	2.97%
Percent of revenue generated based on freight origination and destination	5.99%
Total percentage weight	8.96%
Allocation factor 8.96% ÷ 2 =	4.48%

The allocation factor of 4.48% is then applied to the unitary system value to determine taxable value for the years in question.

Since system value is derived by judgment weighting of the cost, income, and market indicators of value, it seems fair and reasonable to "allocate" this system value by giving like considerations to quantity (cost) and quality (revenue) of unitary parts located in separate and distinct tax jurisdictions.

---

[11]*The Department of Revenue of the State of Montana v. Pacific Power & Light Company,* Montana Supreme Court Case No. 13273, December 1976.

Figure 23.1 Richmond, Fredericksburg and Potomac Railroad Company's Potomac Yard in Alexandria, Virginia. Note office buildings in background (Crystal City), a large office complex built on RF & P land.

(Lewis Longest/Action Photo)

PROBLEM AREAS IN VALUATION AND DIFFERING OPINIONS

The treatment of specific accounts, and reserves, as well as the derivation of capitalizable income and rates of capitalization, are still the cause of litigation in many courts throughout the nation. To avoid pitfalls in the valuation of railroads and public utilities for ad valorem tax purposes, it has been suggested by both independent appraisers and tax administrators that the most common divergencies in appraisal theory and practice be clarified. An attempt is made below to present the pros and cons of differing opinions, to analyze same, and to offer solutions to further the cause of unitary valuation for ad valorem tax purposes.

No doubt, the problem areas result from "honest" differences among professionally competent people whose views are influenced by the economic environment that surrounds them. Tax administrators invariably are conscious of the ever-increasing need for higher tax revenues, whereas railroad and utility officials strive hard to minimize their tax and operational expenditures. Since the art of valuation must be "objective" in character and free from conflicts of interest, it is apparent that rational solutions to stated problems can be offered if not resolved. Wide deviations in value estimates are caused by variation in treatment, as well as inclusion or exclusion of one or more of the following:

1. External obsolescence, its cause and measurement.
2. Means and ways of estimating capitalizable income.
3. Development of capitalization rates and influence on same from embedded capital debt.
4. Capitalizing net operating income, as reported or capitalizing income before taxes and/or depreciation expense.
5. Use of straight-line versus sinking fund method of capital recapture.
6. Impact of deferred federal income taxes: its treatment in unitary valuation.
7. Treatment of rental payments for leased property.

Discussion and suggested solutions for these problem areas are offered in the order listed above.

External Obsolescence

It is generally agreed that depreciation as charged to railroad and utility books of account reflect in accordance with uniform accounting practice the age-life loss of capital—as a rule on a straight-line depreciation basis. Most railroads and utilities, because of regulatory lag or overregulation, do not earn the market-determined rate of return. The difference between the earning per dollar of investment that like competitive but unregulated capital can earn, and the rate per dollar of investment that the railroad or utility can or is allowed to earn, is a loss in earnings that when capitalized as illustrated under the cost approach measures the negative value of external obsolescence. To illustrate, two identical apartment houses are equal in every respect as to age and tenant use, but one is under rent control while the other is free to charge the market rate per room or per square foot of living area. The loss in operating income of the rent-controlled property when capitalized measures the impact of external obsolescence. The absence of, or minimizing the effects of external obsolescence will account for divergence between appraisers and assessors in their final estimate of unitary value. Failure to account for this obsolescence is bound to overstate the cost indicator of value.

Because of variance in the application of methods that best measure external obsolescence, the cost approach, in recent years, has lost dominance as a measure of value. Original cost, too, as a result of technological advances and effects of galloping inflation cannot realistically provide an insight into current market price levels for railroads and utility operations. To quote from a Wisconsin Court of Appeals decision on this subject:

The original cost of a railroad has little if any relation to its present value. Attempts to adjust original cost for obsolescence appear to be little more than mathematical exercises in speculation.[12]

Estimating Capitalizable Operating Income

For a railroad or utility that has a long operating history and one that is deemed to be under typically good management, an analysis of income and expense statements for a period of five or more years should permit, by trending of past performance, an accurate forecast of operating net income from plant and equipment *existing* on date of the appraisal. It is true that operating income or expenditures may be abnormal for any given year, but the trending process by the "least squares" statistical method is designed to even out the hills and valleys and to forecast normalized operation. In this respect it should be kept in mind that appraising for ad valorem tax purposes is not as critical as appraising for a transfer or sale of property. An error for tax purposes can readily be corrected within a year's time since valuation returns must be filed annually.

There is a school of thought, though, adhered to by some specialists and tax administrators, that holds that performance ratios, designed for the railroad or utility under appraisal, provide more accurate estimates of the probable income stream. Performance ratios are widely used in feasibility studies and are recommended for use in forecasting operations for *newly* formed utilities or corporations. However, for railroads or utilities of long years' standing, analysis of past operations is judged to be more realistic and reliable as a guide to future performance.

Developing Capitalization Rates

It is generally agreed that the "band of investment" method provides the best approach for the development of capitalization rates applicable to railroads and public utilities. There are sharp differences of opinion, however, as to whether the resultant rates should reflect (1) cost of capital on date of the appraisal, (2) costs based on an average of rates prevalent over the past three to five years, or (3) the weight to be given to existing or embedded costs of debt capital of the subject corporation.

Advocates of the embedded cost of capital theory hold that the hypothetical purchaser need not, nor will not, refinance existing low-interest debt and thus gain financial benefits that must be reflected in the construction of a band of investment rate of capitalization. These advocates, however, seem to lose sight of the fact that under the stock and debt approach to value, the low-interest-bearing bonds are evaluated at discount market prices that in effect convert stated or embedded capital costs to a yield reflecting current costs.

---

[12]*Soo Line Railroad Company v. Wisconsin Department of Revenue*, Court of Appeals Wisconsin District III, Order filed March 29, 1979, Case No. 77-658.

Appraisers who employ embedded costs of capital thus set themselves up as "Indian givers," taking away under the income approach to value what they are willing to grant under the market approach.

Those who claim that averaging costs of capital for a period of three to five years past are more representative than current capital costs also find themselves on weak logical grounds. One cannot very well average past indicators of capital costs without averaging the income stream realized over an identical time period. Reason, and no doubt justice, dictates that the use of *current* income requires its capitalization at *current*, not past costs of investment capital.

Capitalizing Net Operating Income Versus Income Before Taxes and/or Depreciation Expense

Logically, the final value estimate obtained by use of the formula, value equals income divided by the rate of capitalization, should not be affected no matter at what stage operating income (before or after taxes and depreciation) is capitalized provided that the adjustments made to the income side of the equation are equally reflected on the rate side of the equation. Capitalization either before or after depreciation expense, if correctly applied, will yield identical value results. The same, of course, is true with capitalization before or after tax expenditures. In view of this, it appears that appraisers should avoid complicating the capitalization process and employ where possible net operating income—adjusted if needed to reflect *typical* management—in deriving an estimate under the income approach to value.

Straight-Line Versus Sinking Fund Method of Capital Recapture

In accordance with professionally endorsed appraisal theory and practice, the straight-line method of capital recapture is usually employed in developing the income indicator of value for railroads and public utilities. Professional real estate appraisers ordinarily make use of sinking fund or annuity methods of capitalization *only* where the anticipated (future) income stream from *existing* property is either contractually guaranteed or not subject to decline because of use, wear, or other causes of depreciation. Since public utilities as well as railroads must constantly replace worn-out plant to maintain quantity and quality of service, straight-line provision for capital recapture is, as a rule, prescribed by regulatory commissions on both state and federal levels. However, in recent years, some states, including California, Wisconsin, and Oregon, have through their departments of revenue introduced the annuity method of capitalization on grounds that the depreciation reserves could be invested in either safe or risk-bearing sinking funds, and yield an income that increases the worth or fair market value of the subject corporations. This logic, however, goes counter to the uniform system of accounts prescribed under regulation. Further, too, railroads or utilities are not free to reinvest depreciation reserves nor can such reserves be distributed as dividends without specific state or federal commission approval, which to the knowledge of the authors has never been granted.

In the Soo Line Railroad case the Court of Appeals spoke as follows:

> The actual use of a sinking fund would probably destroy the company by failing to provide enough operating income. This is because both internal and external investment of the fund would not generate a sufficient high rate of return. . . .[13]

Impact of Deferred Federal Income Taxes in Unitary Valuation

Ever since Congress ruled that corporations may, for income tax purposes, accelerate their depreciation or recapture of capital allowances, the immediate reductions in federal income taxes (to be repaid in future accounting years) were set up by most railroads and utilities in a reserve shown on the balance sheet as "deferred federal income taxes." Some appraisers and tax administrators hold that the cash generated by this reserve can be and is generally reinvested in plant and equipment and thus adds additional value that must be recognized in the appraisal process. From the railroad and utility point of view, it is contended that plant purchased with such reserve funds is reported on the asset side of corporate records and is appraised for tax purposes under the cost approach to value. Such plant, however, when purchased with reserve funds, is classified as nonearning property under state and federal accounting regulations and thus generates *no* capitalizable income.

Treatment of Rental Payments for Leased Property

Leasing of equipment, particularly rolling stock, among railroads is a common and generally accepted practice. By agreement as well as in compliance with statutory requirements, in most states ad valorem taxes for leased property are assessed to the user. No problem is encountered in the valuation of leased property under the cost approach to value, nor for that matter under the stock and debt approach, which reflects the unitary value of all corporate operations. There is a question, however, raised by some appraiser-assessors as to whether the rental payments are chargeable in their entirety as an operating expense. Those raising this question hold that the rental payments include a return "on" capital (interest on the capital value of the property) which, if the property were owned rather than leased, would not be charged as an operating cost. Thus if 20 percent of the total rental payments are calculated as interest on the value of leased property, this amount is then added back to operating income to cause an increase in the value derived under the income approach.

[13]*Soo Line Railroad Company v. Wisconsin Department of Revenue*, p. 14.

Those who oppose this view and practice hold (1) that leasing, especially with railroads, is a "way of life" and contributes to operating income by its use. Without leased equipment many more railroads would be driven into bankruptcy. (2) Leasing companies, because of volume of equipment purchases, can obtain or manufacture property at substantially more favorable prices than can corporations who rent these properties. It is thus pointed out that it is good business to lease certain equipment rather than to own same outright. (3) Further it is noted that all property acquired by purchase yields a return on capital to the manufacturer or prior owner. Thus to single out leased property for adjustment of payments (that is allowed by regulatory commission) is illogical and designed to create fictitious values for ad valorem tax purposes.

The authors are inclined to lean toward the latter point of view. A national rent-a-car agency equips many corporations with leased delivery fleets that prove more economical than outright ownership of such vehicles. The income generated by leased equipment is already reflected in the income stream and to add further income that hypothetically could have been earned appears to be double counting and a substitution of appraiser's judgment for that of management operating in accordance with typical corporate industry practices.

SUMMARY

This chapter, to the best of the authors' knowledge, represents the first attempt to set forth in narrative form a recommended procedure for the valuation of railroads and public utilities for ad valorem tax purposes.

The first part of this chapter addressed the question of whether railroads and public utilities are corporate entities operating as a "unit" or whether they are merely an aggregation of physical, tangible parts that should be assessed on a one-by-one basis. Appraisers, tax administrators, and courts now strongly support the logic that railroads and utilities are a corporate "whole" and that the system value is best ascertained under the "unitary" rule.

Next, we described the peculiar economic nature and character of railroads and public utilities and the effects of regulatory controls on values for ad valorem tax purposes. It is pointed out that railroads and utilities are affected with "a public interest," that they, for prescribed geographic areas, are granted a service monopoly. To simulate "free" market pricing and operations of their services, railroads and utilities operate under strict regulatory controls by state and where interstate commerce is involved, by federal agencies. Railroads and utilities must comply with a uniform system of accounting and submit comprehensive annual reports detailing their assets, liabilities, income, and expenditures and changes in the various accounts on a year-to-year basis. It is the availability of these detailed reports and the comparison of a subject utility with others of its kind that enables the appraiser-assessor to gather and analyze the evidence that support the final opinion of value.

Our discussion of generally accepted appraisal theory and practice illustrates how indicators of value are derived under the cost, income, and stock and debt (market) approaches to value. It is pointed out that depreciated historical, original, or book cost, depending on regulatory requirement, forms the rate base from which a fair return for the railroad or utility is calculated. Since that return, because of regulatory lag, inflation, and rising costs rarely equals the market return of like—but unregulated—business enterprises, cost (depreciated) for regulated corporations sets the ceiling of value. The income approach generally follows appraisal theory and practice applicable to other income-producing enterprises. The rate used for capitalization of current income must also be a measure of current costs of capital. The market approach—since railroads and utilities are not freely sold—is limited to a valuation of stock and debt. This is deemed valid on the assumption that purchase and ownership of all liabilities and stock must equal the assets of the corporation under double entry book accounting. The reconciliation or correlation of the indicators of value was also discussed and illustrated.

Next, we outlined the allocation of unitary or system value to the states where railroads or utilities are engaged in interstate commerce. In past years because of the weight given to situs (location) of property, cost of fractions of property located in the various states or tax jurisdictions was used as a guide for equitable allocation. In recent years, however, revenue generated within a given state or tax jurisdiction was deemed of equal importance. A test case decided by the Montana Supreme Court ordered allocation of unitary value on a weighted cost and revenue formula. Since system value is a hybrid of cost, income, and market factors, the weighting of the same influences for allocation purposes is deemed fair and reasonable.

Problem areas in the valuation of railroads and public utilities were also discussed. Differing opinions were cited in connection with controversial practices involving divergencies in the derivation of rates of capitalization, influence, if any, of embedded debt on the development of rates, and capitalization using straight-line versus sinking fund methods of converting a future stream of income into a sum of present value.

Decisions by the Oregon Tax Court, the Supreme Court of the State of Oregon and the State of Wisconsin Court of Appeals were quoted to highlight such matters as treatment of deferred federal income taxes in the valuation process, use of performance ratio in calculating capitalizing income, use of a sinking fund versus straight-line capital recapture, and correlation of the evidences of value. Finally, differences of opinion concerning leased properties were cited and solutions were suggested to assist the appraiser in evaluating the consequences of choices in resolving these divergencies.

REVIEW QUESTIONS

1. Define the term "unit valuation."
2. Explain why in recent years cost no longer provides an accurate measure of the value of railroads and public utilities.

3. Outline the steps involved in measuring railroad obsolescence via the blue chip method.
4. Discuss why embedded interest costs are criticized for ad valorem tax purposes.
5. List five possible causes of deviations in appraisal estimates of railroad and public utility property.
6. State when use of sinking fund or annuity method of capitalization is preferable to the straight-line method of capital recapture.

READING AND STUDY REFERENCES

GOODMAN, JOHN C. "Use of the Stock and Debt Approach Valuing Railroad or Utility Property Owner by Conglomerate." Proceedings of the 1981 Public Utilities Workshop *Appraisal of Utilities and Railroad Property for Ad Valorem Taxation Program.* Cosponsored by the Tax Institute of America and the Center for Management Development, Wichita State University, July 27–30, 1981, pp. 57–65.

GUNN, RICHARD L. "Comparable Sales: What Are the Elements of Comparability." Proceedings of the 1982 Public Utilities Workshop *Appraisal of Utilities and Railroad Property for Ad Valorem Taxation Program*, Wichita State University, August 2–5, 1982, pp. 67–76.

McKELVEY, MACY A. "Influence of the Cost Approach on Valuation." Proceedings of the 1981 Public Utilities Workshop, pp. 82–84.

McSWAIN, ROBERT H. *Appraisal of Utilities and Railroad Property for Ad Valorem Taxation* (course syllabus). Co-sponsored by the Tax Institute of America and the Center for Management Development, Wichita State University, 1983.

OHARENKO, JOHN. "Selecting Valuation Techniques for Appraising Bankrupt Railroad Real Estate Property," *The Real Estate Appraiser and Analyst* 48, no. 4 (Winter 1982), pp. 28–30.

PATTERSON, JAMES E. "Validity of Reproduction/Replacement Cost Considering Economic Factors." Proceedings of the 1981 Public Utilities Workshop, pp. 171–175.

ROSS, JUDITH G. "The Use of Embedded Versus Current Cost of Debt in the Valuation Process." Proceedings of the 1982 Public Utilities Workshop, pp. 156–162.

SHANK, DAVID W. "The Appraisal of a Natural Gas Transmission Pipeline." Proceedings of the 1982 Public Utilities Workshop, pp. 166–205.

STEELE, JAMES M. "Reasoning the Use of the Current Cost of Capital for the Capitalized Income Indicator of Value." Proceedings of the 1982 Public Utilities Workshop, pp. 234–242.

24

PROFESSIONAL STANDARDS IN REPORT WRITING

Learning Objectives

After reading this chapter, you should be able to:

Understand the steps involved in planning and performing an appraisal assignment

Discuss several purposes for which appraisals are made

Explain the logic of the value reconciliation stage of an appraisal report

Outline the essential parts of a narrative appraisal report

Comparatively discuss the similarities and differences between a narrative and preprinted form report

Recognize the essentials underlying professional conduct

Appreciate the purposes of standards of professional conduct

Discuss the appraiser's rules of conduct

During the past half century, real estate appraising has developed into a well-defined practice engaged in professionally by thousands of qualified appraisers. Owners and investors in real property—including banking institutions, insurance companies, government agencies, brokerage firms, and commercial and industrial institutions—have come to rely on this profession as a reliable guide to property value. Annually, thousands of business men and women attend appraisal seminars and extension courses conducted under the auspices of the American Institute of Real Estate Appraisers and the Society of Real Estate Appraisers. An ever-increasing number of colleges and universities offer courses in real property valuation for degree credit and on an extension and short-course basis.

APPRAISAL PROCESS

Real estate appraising is patterned in accordance with well-defined ground rules, which as a whole are contained in an orderly plan of action known as the *appraisal process*. It is with the aid of this process that the professional appraiser seeks to reach a sound conclusion or estimate of value. The orderly steps and considerations of the appraisal process include the following:

1. Determine the appraisal problem.
2. Determine the purpose which the appraisal is to serve.
3. Secure a full and accurate description of the property to be appraised.
4. Make a preliminary estimate of the time, labor, and expense involved in the completion of the appraisal assignment, and secure a written request for the appraisal services in which should be stated the fee agreed on for services to be rendered.
5. Plan the appraisal, assign the work details, and assemble the essential appraisal data.
6. Make a study of the general economic, social, and political influences which bear on the value of the property to be appraised.
7. Analyze the appraisal data, and reach a value conclusion under each of the following approaches to value: depreciated cost, market comparison, and capitalized income.
8. Reconcile the value findings.
9. Submit the appraisal report.

The first and most important step in the process is to determine the appraisal problem. Some owners, buyers, or investors are not only interested in ascertaining an accurate estimate of value but also expect information regarding ownership or title interests, rights of tenants, property encroachments, claims of mortgagees and other lienors, conditions shown by accurate survey, tax liens, violations, and so on. The appraiser should not acccept the valuation assignment unless the client clearly understands the limits of the appraiser's professional responsibility and the area of study to which his specialized knowledge is confined. The appraiser, in essence, practices in the field of land economics—for value is in fact the heart of economics. Appraisers should not consider themselves lawyers, architects, builders, engineers, surveyors, or title abstractors. If their clients request information in these specialized fields, authority should be secured to engage such qualified experts as the problem necessitates, arranging for independent compensation of the outside firms or individuals called on for the specified service. Unless otherwise stated, appraisers must assume (1) that a title is held in fee simple and that no legal claims, easements, restrictions, or other rights affect the title or use of the property except those stated to the appraiser by the applicant; (2) that the title and valuation are subject to corrections which an accurate survey of the property may reveal; (3) that the sale of the property will be on a cash or cash equivalent basis, since good or cumbersome financial arrangements do affect the price at which the property may sell in the market; and (4) that no responsibility can be taken by the appraiser for matters legal in character.

Some valuation problems, too, require special owner or tenant cooperation or aid from neighboring property owners, or users. Where such is the case, the assignment must be accepted contingent on the cooperation of the parties involved. Only when the problem is clearly defined, and its limits are known and understood, should an appraiser proceed further with the steps of the appraisal process.

Next, it is essential that the appraiser be provided with a clear statement as to the purpose which the appraisal is to serve. Even though only one value can exist for market purposes at a given time and place, different valuation purposes may warrant greater stress being laid on one or the other of the three value approaches—or the inclusion of special appraisal details in the final report of value. It can readily be seen that different interests are served if the valuation is for one or the other of the following purposes:

1. Purchase, sale, or exchange of property.
2. Fire insurance or hazard underwriting.
3. Valuation for utility rate determination.
4. Investment or mortgage loan security.
5. Inheritance tax, property tax, or assessments.
6. Inventory or accrued depreciation.
7. Equity appraising or financing.

In each instance a different interest is served, and different valuation details warrant emphasis and inclusion in the appraisal report. For instance, a report for fire insurance purposes would principally stress replacement costs as evidence of value, and the report would detail with great accuracy the construction features and material elements that make up the property improvements. For mortgage loan purposes, on the other hand, property income, its remaining economic life, and its ready marketability would receive major stress—with replacement cost, less depreciation, merely serving as a ceiling of value beyond which lenders, as a rule, are restricted or unwilling to go.

To avoid possible misunderstanding or claims that the purpose of the appraisal influenced the value found, the professional appraiser should not only include a clear statement of the purpose which the appraisal is to serve but also a clear-cut definition of the term *value* as used in his report. Failure to do so may cause serious misunderstanding and, where warranted, even disciplinary action under the code of ethics to which all professional appraisers, as members of their respective appraisal societies, subscribe. The date of the appraisal, too, should be fixed and prominently stated. Values are subject to constant shifts because the laws of supply and demand operate in a dynamic society which experiences sudden and often unexpected changes. Then, too, value for specific purposes may have to be stated as of a given day in the past.

A full and accurate description of the property is next in order. Not only must the exact limits of the physical area under appraisal be known, but the full legal property description must be cited in order to leave no doubt as to the precise location and identity of the realty covered in the valuation report. Although various kinds of property descriptions may be used, it is best to rely on one shown in the last deed of record. Should property analysis disclose encumbrances which limit in any way an owner's rights under fee simple title or impede in any way the utilization of the property under a program of highest and best use, then such financial encumbrances on ownership or use limitations must be clearly identified and the impact on value of such limitations made clear to the reader of the appraisal report.

Before proceeding with the valuation assignment, it is essential that the appraiser make a preliminary but careful estimate of the time, labor, and expense involved in completing the appraisal request. This preliminary estimate should serve as a guide in setting a fair appraisal fee commensurate with the responsibility and service requirements assumed. Never should the fee be a percentage of the value findings. Where the recommended fee, for instance, is one-half of one percent of property value, the warranted appraisal fee on a $20,000 property would be $100. This method of service fee determination, however, appears illogical and is subject to censure on ethical grounds. The temptations would indeed be great to boost value findings as a means of increasing service fees. The ethics code of the American Institute of Real Estate Appraisers specifically condemns this practice and stipulates that it is unethical for appraisers to accept an engagement to appraise a property if the employment or fee is contingent on reporting a predetermined or specified amount of value, or is otherwise contingent upon any finding to be reported.

Once a fair fee has been ascertained, the client should be so informed. If the fee, as generally is the case, proves acceptable, the appraiser should request written confirmation of the professional assignment and the fee should be stipulated in the letter of request or should be noted by the appraiser in his letter of acceptance. The fee seldom covers any appearance or testimony by the appraiser before any court, commission, or other body; to avoid later dispute, this should be clearly understood at the time of engagement and stated in the appraisal report itself.

Once the appraisal assignment and service fee are mutually agreed on, steps are taken to plan the work details and to assemble the essential appraisal data. Much of the necessary general data pertaining to social, political, and economic influences on value are directly obtainable from office (appraisal plant) files or may be taken from previous appraisal reports in which the general value comments are deemed sufficiently recent and applicable to be of interest to the case at hand. Automated data retrieval systems have greatly enhanced this phase of the appraisal process in recent years. General data bearing on value of the subject property and not available from the appraisal plant should be secured whenever possible from primary sources. Data applicable to the site, improvements, and immediate environment must be obtained through personal inspection and through a detailed inventory of neighborhood, site, and improvement data that bear directly or indirectly on property values. Many forms have been devised by private firms and governmental agencies to aid the appraiser in the laborious task of gathering field data to ensure that no important matter pertaining to the property is inadvertently omitted.

VALUE RECONCILIATION

Once the general and specific data applicable to the subject property are assembled, the appraiser proceeds with an analysis of the data under each of the value approaches—market, income, and cost. Although the importance of each of the three approaches to value may vary, depending on the kind and nature of the property and the purpose which the appraisal is to serve, nevertheless it is important to consider each approach to value as a separate entity under the appraisal process and to reach independent value conclusions in relation to replacement costs less accrued depreciation, market sales of comparable properties, and capitalization of net operating income derived from property operation under typical ownership and management. These independent but related estimates of value must then be reconciled (correlated) into a sum representing the appraiser's considered judgment of final value conclusion.

Reconciliation of the value estimates should under no circumstances be considered as a mathematical process involving mere averaging of the estimates derived under the independent value approaches. Rather, care must be taken in weighing the results on the basis of accuracy and completeness of data and in the light of market conditions that prevail on the date of the appraisal. Whenever significant differences exist in the estimates derived under the three value approaches, the appraiser, as a first step, should review the data assembled under each approach and check the mathematical procedures which underlie the answer. Under the cost approach, for instance, a recheck should be made of the size of the structure and the volume of square or cubic feet reported. The cost factor, too, may be in error or inapplicable to the type and kind of structure under appraisal. More likely than not, the error may rest in the derivation of the amount of accrued depreciation. The economic age may have been misstated or an omission may have been made in the listing and weighing of the causes which account for total accrued depreciation. Under the market approach, judgment errors are easily committed. The transaction prices of the comparable properties may not reflect true property values, or the properties selected may not represent real comparability. Too, the judgment weights assigned may warrant a careful recheck. The income approach is also fraught with appraising pitfalls. The revenue flow may be over- or understated, allowances for vacancy and collection losses may have been omitted, operating expenses may not reflect operation under competent and efficient management, the remaining life of the property may be in error—and so may be the rate of capitalization—which especially warrants close inspection as to its appropriateness. The application of a rate of 8 percent instead of 9 percent may not appear serious to the uninformed, but the value results would differ by approximately 11 to 12.5 percent depending on which rate is the appropriate one.

If, after careful recheck of the various steps in each approach, significant differences still exist in the value estimates under each approach, the appraiser must consider the results in the light of the problem and the purposes which the appraisal is to serve. Thus, for mortgage loan purposes, the income-producing capacity of the property is all-important. For inheritance tax, condemnation, or sale purposes, the market data (provided the market is sufficiently active to prove guiding) should be given greatest stress. For fire insurance or protection against other hazards, the replacement cost may prove all-important. It is in the reconciliation of the value estimates where there can be no substitute for the experience, skill, and judgment of the appraiser. It is the human factor in the equation which causes real estate appraising to be more of a personal art than an objective science.

THE APPRAISAL REPORT

The final step in the appraising process is the preparation of a comprehensive appraisal report. At one time an oral opinion or a letter of valuation sufficed. Such practices, however, are frowned on today and professional appraisers are advised to furnish their clients with a narrative appraisal report in which their value findings, along with the contingent conditions on which the appraisal is based, are clearly set forth. No particular style of report is copyrighted, nor is any one form recommended. A good report, nevertheless, is one in which the data presented are so convincingly analyzed that the reader inevitably is led to the same value conclusions as those reached by the appraiser. As a rule, the data should be sufficiently self-explanatory to permit judgment adjustment by the reader or client if he or she so chooses.

Figure 24.1 lists essentials for a well-written and comprehensive appraisal report.

Section I: Introduction

1. A letter of transmittal in which the value findings and the effective date of the appraisal are recorded. This letter, too, should state the number of pages contained in the report in order to forestall possible deletion of important pages or data by unauthorized persons.
2. A table of contents which permits quick reference to particular report material.
3. Two clear and preferably large (8 by 10 inch) photographs showing front and side views of the property appraised.
4. A statement as to the purpose of the appraisal and definition of the term *value* as used by the appraiser.

Section II: Description of Relevant Facts

5. A statement of the rights appraised.

6. A statement of highest and best use of the property, and whether the present improvements meet the test.

7. A summary statement of important conclusions, particularly those in which the report reader has a prime interest: taxes, assessments, operating income, operating expenses, and so on.

8. A complete and accurate legal description.

9. An analysis of the general social, political, and economic influences on value, particularly in reference to the region, the city, and the neighborhood or environing area.

10. A factual presentation of site, building, and property data. An inventory should be presented of the important site utilities and building construction features.

Section III: Analyses and Conclusions

11. An explanation of the appraisal process and the methods by which the value conclusions were derived.

12. An analysis of the cost approach to value, followed by schedules showing unit cost deviations and depreciation calculations.

13. An analysis of the market approach to value. Separate comparative tables should be included showing sales considered in arriving at the market value of (1) the land and (2) the property as a unified whole.

14. An analysis of the income approach to value, showing sources of revenue, allowances due to anticipated vacancies and collection losses, operating expenses, rates of capitalization, and process employed in the discounting of the anticipated income into a present sum of value.

15. A reconciliation of the value estimates derived under the cost, market, and income approaches to value. The weights, if any, assigned to each approach or the methods of selection of one estimate in preference to another should be clearly set forth and explained.

16. A statement of limiting conditions in which the appraiser sets forth the areas— as in fields of surveying, engineering, or law—in which he or she disclaims liability.

17. A certification of value in which the appraiser professionally warrants his or her findings and disclaims any personal interest in the property that could possibly influence his or her value findings.

18. A statement of qualifications of the appraiser, setting forth briefly his or her educational, professional background, and experience qualifications allowing him or her to render value opinions.

Section IV: Addenda

19. Addenda material containing some or all of the following: location sketch of the property, a plot plan, floor plan, and a subdivision map and city map on which markings indicate the subject property in relation to important business and civic centers; also, where deemed of interest, additional photographs of neighboring properties and street views, showing improvements north, south, east, and west of the subject property.

Figure 24.1 Essentials for a narrative appraisal report

THE ANALYTICAL, OR DEMONSTRATION, APPRAISAL REPORT

Students of real estate appraising at many colleges and candidates who seek professional affiliation with the American Institute of Real Estate Appraisers or the Society of Real Estate Appraisers are required to submit in partial fulfillment of prerequisites for the respective professional membership designations,[1] fully documented narrative appraisal reports of various types of real property to demonstrate their competence and soundness of judgment in the compilation and interpretation of valuation data and the logical presentation of such data in report form.

The difference between a demonstration and a professional narrative appraisal report lies mainly in the requirement that all data sources, sequence, and analysis of pertinent facts and value conclusions must be documented and justified in a demonstration appraisal report. Whereas the professional appraiser may, on the basis of experience and reputation, reach certain conclusions or make certain assumptions, the student appraiser must follow step-by-step orderly reporting and miss no link in welding the chain of value conclusion. A professional appraiser may categorically stipulate that a rate of capitalization of 10 percent is deemed applicable to the subject property, or that the cost of reproduction of building improvement is estimated at $6.88 per cubic foot, and offer no documentary evidence to support these statements. It nevertheless is advisable that professional reports contain such supporting data. A student appraiser cannot rely on personal skill, maturity of judgment, or years of appraisal experience to justify assumptions or conclusions. The reader of the demonstration report must literally be led along the path of the appraisal process and given an opportunity to judge the technical skill of the writer on the basis of sufficiency of report data, soundness of data interpretation, and extent to which the value conclusions reached are warranted.

NARRATIVE APPRAISAL REPORT

Appraisers often are required to prepare narrative appraisal reports such as presented in Appendices I and II. These reports customarily are written for nonresidential appraisals. Well-prepared reports are characterized by:

1. Being logical and orderly.
2. Being clear, direct, yet comprehensive.
3. Being readable.

[1]Prevailing professional designations offered are as follows: A.S.A., Member American Society of Appraisers; R.M., Residential Member, American Institute of Real Estate Appraisers; M.A.I., Member, American Institute of Real Estate Appraisers; S.R.A., Senior Residential Appraiser, Society of Real Estate Appraisers; S.R.P.A., Senior Real Property Appraiser; S.R.E.A., Senior Real Estate Analyst, Society of Real Estate Appraisers.

4. Avoiding use of the first person.
5. Using appropriate words, summaries, and illustrations.
6. Using positive rather than noncommittal language.
7. Using thorough research that is convincingly and accurately presented.
8. Using language that is readily understood by the client.

It is highly desirable to have another person proofread an appraiser's report. A second person is more likely to spot arithmetical errors as well as unclear phrases. In writing, the appraiser should always concentrate on "expressing" rather than "impressing." A sample of undesirable and preferred words and phrases is listed below:[2]

Undesirable	*Preferred*
Utilize	Use
Inundate	Flood
Attached please find	Attached is
Exact same	Same
In the neighborhood of	About
In view of the fact that	Because
Arrive at	Reach
Subsequent to	After
Whether or not	Whether
Viz	Namely

LETTER REPORT

A letter report generally fails to qualify as a true appraisal report because it does not include the steps leading to the appraiser's value conclusion. Even a form report contains this background information. Often the motivation for preparing such "reports" is that the client wants a report at the lowest possible cost. After having received such a report, the client may find it unusable for loan or sale purposes. In effect, he or she is told that it is inferior, which casts an unfavorable light on both the appraiser and the profession. Thus this form of appraisal digest is discouraged. If, for some reason, it is used, the appraiser should retain in his or her files all the pertinent calculations and analysis that would support the reported value and permit writing of a full narrative or form report.

LETTER OF OPINION

This is not a genuine appraisal report, but instead, it is a preliminary opinion based on limited analysis. The value estimate usually is expressed as a range of values. A difficulty with the letter report is that the reported value range may

---

[2]For further suggestions on proper appraisal report writing, see William C. Himstreet, *Writing Appraisal Reports* (Chicago: American Institute of Real Estate Appraisers, 1971).

be altered upon a more thorough investigation. If used, the appraiser must clearly indicate that this is a (1) preliminary finding, and (2) it may change once a complete appraisal has been prepared.

SHORT-FORM APPRAISAL REPORTING

Government agencies and lending institutions prefer standardized form reports in connection with routine appraising of properties offered as loan collateral. Although such forms leave little room for justification of appraisal judgment, uniformity of data reporting facilitates loan processing and supervision on the basis of comparability of report features in relation to minimum standards which properties must meet to prove acceptable. An appraisal form widely used for reporting on residential properties by mortgage lenders is the FNMA Form 1004 (see Figure 24.2 on pp. 448–450).

In using this standardized appraisal form, the appraiser has an opportunity to include additional explanatory material such as a dwelling's floor plan. Notice the important information that is included in this appraisal report. For instance, the appraiser is able to describe the neighborhood and its growth trends. A brief physical description of the appraised property is allowed, followed by a brief depreciated cost approach. The most space is allotted for the direct market comparison approach. Minimal emphasis is assigned to the income (gross income multiplier) approach, which often lacks sufficient data to permit use of this method.

PROFESSIONAL STANDARDS AND RESPONSIBILITIES

Appraising has come a long way since value judgments were chiefly rendered by real estate brokers to facilitate the meeting of minds in connection with buyer-seller transactions. Today there exists an ever-increasing demand for accurate valuation and general appraisal services on the part of industry, business, civic and public organizations, and related professions. This growth and development of technical appraising is in no small measure due to the individual efforts of leading appraisers who have won great respect for their profession by insistence that value findings be expressed in detailed, logical, and comprehensive narrative reports. Nevertheless, no matter how great the technical skill ascribable to a given field of specialization, the ingredients that cause an individual, or the profession served, to become favorably recognized are to be found in the human element of service to an ideal.

The older professional callings in the fields of medicine, law, and the chemical and biological sciences have conclusively demonstrated that worthwhile achievements—and public acceptance of the status of members as experts or scientists—are founded on unselfish devotion to a cause. Basically, the essentials

RESIDENTIAL APPRAISAL REPORT

File No.

To be completed by Lender

Borrower: Preston E. & Sarah C. Childress — Census Tract: 2001.11 — Map Reference: 20 E-6
Property Address: 2015 Chamblee Road
City — County: Henrico — State: Virginia — Zip Code: 23234
Legal Description: Lot 16, Block E, Section B of Essex Woods
Sale Price $ 89,150 — Date of Sale — Loan Term — yrs — Property Rights Appraised [X] Fee [ ] Leasehold [ ] DeMinimis PUD
Actual Real Estate Taxes $ — (yr) Loan charges to be paid by seller $ — Other sales concessions: Seller to pay $3200 of purchaser's closing costs
Lender/Client: Investors Savings & Loan — Address
Occupant: New — Appraiser: J. L. Sullivan — Instructions to Appraiser: Market Value

NEIGHBORHOOD

Location	[ ] Urban	[X] Suburban	[ ] Rural
Built Up	[X] Over 75%	[ ] 25% to 75%	[ ] Under 25%
Growth Rate [ ] Fully Dev.	[X] Rapid	[X] Steady	[ ] Slow
Property Values	[X] Increasing	[ ] Stable	[ ] Declining
Demand/Supply	[ ] Shortage	[X] In Balance	[ ] Over Supply
Marketing Time	[X] Under 3 Mos.	[X] 4–6 Mos.	[ ] Over 6 Mos.

Present Land Use 100 % 1 Family ___% 2–4 Family ___% Apts. ___% Condo ___% Commercial ___% Industrial ___% Vacant ___%
Change in Present Land Use [X] Not Likely [ ] Likely (*) [ ] Taking Place (*)
(*) From ___ To ___
Predominant Occupancy [X] Owner [ ] Tenant ___% Vacant
Single Family Price Range $ 75,000 to $ 110,000 Predominant Value $ 85,000
Single Family Age new yrs to 2 yrs Predominant Age 1 yrs

	Good	Avg.	Fair	Poor
Employment Stability	[ ]	[X]	[ ]	[ ]
Convenience to Employment	[ ]	[X]	[ ]	[ ]
Convenience to Shopping	[X]	[ ]	[ ]	[ ]
Convenience to Schools	[X]	[ ]	[ ]	[ ]
Adequacy of Public Transportation	[ ]	[X]	[ ]	[ ]
Recreational Facilities	[ ]	[X]	[ ]	[ ]
Adequacy of Utilities	[X]	[ ]	[ ]	[ ]
Property Compatibility	[X]	[ ]	[ ]	[ ]
Protection from Detrimental Conditions	[ ]	[X]	[ ]	[ ]
Police and Fire Protection	[ ]	[X]	[ ]	[ ]
General Appearance of Properties	[X]	[ ]	[ ]	[ ]
Appeal to Market	[ ]	[X]	[ ]	[ ]

Note: FHLMC/FNMA do not consider race or the racial composition of the neighborhood to be reliable appraisal factors.

Comments including those factors, favorable or unfavorable, affecting marketability (e.g. public parks, schools, view, noise): Subject is located in an attractive and well planned new subdivision of very similar style and size contemporary homes in a developing area of popular western Henrico County (approx. 20 miles from downtown Richmond); easy access to roads and interstate highway systems; approx. 50 homes now built and owner-occupied; several other homes now under contract for sale and presently under construction.

SITE

Dimensions: approx. 1/4 to 1/3 acre = 1/4 to 1/3 XXXXXor Acres [ ] Corner Lot
Zoning classification: single family residential — Present improvements [X] do [ ] do not conform to zoning regulations
Highest and best use: [X] Present use [ ] Other (specify)

	Public	Other (Describe)
Elec.	[X]	
Gas	[ ]	
Water	[X]	
San. Sewer	[X]	
[X] Underground Elect. & Tel.		

OFF SITE IMPROVEMENTS
Street Access: [X] Public [ ] Private
Surface: tar/gravel
Maintenance: [X] Public [ ] Private
[X] Storm Sewer [X] Curb/Gutter
[ ] Sidewalk [ ] Street Lights

Topo: fairly level
Size: normal for this subdivision
Shape: rectangular
View: average to good
Drainage: no apparent problems
Is the property located in a HUD Identified Special Flood Hazard Area [X] No [ ] Yes

Comments (favorable or unfavorable including any apparent adverse easements, encroachments or other adverse conditions): usual utility easements

IMPROVEMENTS

[ ] Existing [ ] Proposed [X] Under Constr. — No. Units 1 — Type (det, duplex, semi/det, etc.): detached — Design (rambler, split level, etc.): contemporary — Exterior Walls: cedar siding
Yrs. Age: Actual new Effective new to — No. Stories $1\frac{1}{2}$
Roof Material: cedar shakes — Gutters & Downspouts [X] None: roof overhang — Window (Type): dbl. hung wd. thermo. [ ] Storm Sash [ ] Screens [ ] Combination — Insulation [ ] None [X] Floor [X] Ceiling [ ] Roof [X] Walls
[ ] Manufactured Housing
Foundation Walls: brick/block
[ ] Slab on Grade [X] Crawl Space

BSMT: 0 % Basement — [ ] Outside Entrance — [ ] Concrete Floor — ___ % Finished — [ ] Floor Drain — [ ] Sump Pump — Finished Ceiling — Finished Walls — Finished Floor
Evidence of: [ ] Dampness [ ] Termites [ ] Settlement

Comments: New home under construction is approximately 75% complete at this time.

ROOM LIST

Room List	Foyer	Living	Dining	Kitchen	Den	Family Rm.	Rec. Rm.	Bedrooms	No. Baths	Laundry	Other
Basement		NONE									
1st Level		x	area	x				2	2		
2nd Level		plus	finished	room on	2nd	floor	(could be	used as	office	or den,	etc.)

Finished area above grade contains a total of 5 rooms 2 bedrooms 2 baths. Gross Living Area 1336 sq. ft. Bsmt Area 0 sq. ft.

Figure 24.2

INTERIOR FINISH & EQUIPMENT

Kitchen Equipment: [ ] Refrigerator [X] Range/Oven [X] Disposal [X] Dishwasher [X] Fan/Hood [ ] Compactor [ ] Washer [ ] Dryer [ ] _____

HEAT Type duct Fuel elec Cond. new AIR COND. [X] Central [X] Other heat pump [X] Adequate [ ] Inadequate

Floors	[ ] Hardwood [X] Carpet Over sub-flooring
Walls	[X] Drywall [ ] Plaster [ ] _____
Trim/Finish	[X] Good [ ] Average [ ] Fair [ ] Poor
Bath Floor	[ ] Ceramic [X] vinyl
Bath Wainscot	[ ] Ceramic [X] fiberglass tub/shower

Special Features (including energy efficient items) 2 panel solar system (integrated hot water heater); insulated windows & doors

ATTIC: [X] Yes [ ] No [ ] Stairway [ ] Drop-stair [X] Scuttle [ ] Floored

Finished (Describe) _____ [ ] Heated

CAR STORAGE: [ ] Garage [ ] Built-in [ ] Attached [ ] Detached [ ] Car Port

No. Cars NONE [ ] Adequate [ ] Inadequate Condition _____

PROPERTY RATING

	Good	Avg.	Fair	Poor
Quality of Construction (Materials & Finish)	X			
Condition of Improvements	X			
Room sizes and layout	X			
Closets and Storage	X			
Insulation—adequacy	X			
Plumbing—adequacy and condition	X			
Electrical—adequacy and condition	X			
Kitchen Cabinets—adequacy and condition	X			
Compatibility to Neighborhood	X			
Overall Livability	X			
Appeal and Marketability	X			

Yrs Est Remaining Economic Life 50 to 55 Explain if less than Loan Term

FIREPLACES, PATIOS, POOL, FENCES, etc. (describe) fireplace in living room; front & rear salt treated decks (approx. 250 sq.ft.); attached outside storage shed

COMMENTS (including functional or physical inadequacies, repairs needed, modernization, etc.) Other new homes built in this same subdivision (all built by the same builder and inspected by this appraiser) appear to be well built with good quality materials and craftmanship.

VALUATION SECTION

Purpose of Appraisal is to estimate Market Value as defined in Certification & Statement of Limiting Conditions (FHLMC Form 439/FNMA Form 1004B). If submitted for FNMA, the appraiser must attach (1) sketch or map showing location of subject, street names, distance from nearest intersection, and any detrimental conditions and (2) exterior building sketch of improvements showing dimensions.

COST APPROACH

Measurements		No. Stories		Sq. Ft.
42' x 28' x		1	=	1176
x	x		=	
16' x 10' x		1	=	160
x	x		=	
x	x		=	
x	x		=	

Total Gross Living Area (List in Market Data Analysis below) 1336*

Comment on functional and economic obsolescence: *does NOT include FINISHED room on 2nd floor (approx. 180 sq. ft.)

ESTIMATED REPRODUCTION COST – NEW – OF IMPROVEMENTS:

Dwelling 1336 Sq. Ft. @ $ 42.50 =	$	56,780
2nd fl. (finished) Sq. Ft. @ $ _____ =		5,000
Extras fireplace =		2,500
=		
Special Energy Efficient Items 2-panel solar sys. =		2,500
Porches, Patios, etc. decks; storage shed =		2,500
Garage/Car Port _____ Sq. Ft. @ $ _____ =		
Site Improvements (driveway, landscaping, etc.) =		1,000
Total Estimated Cost New . . . . =	$	70,280

Less	Physical	Functional	Economic	
Depreciation $ --	$ --	$ --	= $ (--)

Depreciated value of improvements . . . . . . =	$	70,280
ESTIMATED LAND VALUE = (If leasehold, show only leasehold value)	$	18,500
INDICATED VALUE BY COST APPROACH . . .	$	88,780

The undersigned has recited three recent sales of properties most similar and proximate to subject and has considered these in the market analysis. The description includes a dollar adjustment, reflecting market reaction to those items of significant variation between the subject and comparable properties. If a significant item in the comparable property is superior to, or more favorable than, the subject property, a minus (-) adjustment is made, thus reducing the indicated value of subject; if a significant item in the comparable is inferior to, or less favorable than, the subject property, a plus (+) adjustment is made, thus increasing the indicated value of the subject.

MARKET DATA ANALYSIS

ITEM	Subject Property	COMPARABLE NO. 1	Adjustment	COMPARABLE NO. 2	Adjustment	COMPARABLE NO. 3	Adjustment
Address	16-F-B Essex Woods	10-F-B Essex Woods		20-C-E Essex Woods		3-A-C Essex Woods	
Proximity to Subj.		same subdivision		same subdivision		same subdivision	
Sales Price	$ 89,150	$ 88,000		$ 98,950		$ 96,960	
Price/Living area	$ 66.73	$ 65.87		$ 72.92		$ 72.57	
Data Source	observation	observation		observation		observation	
Date of Sale and Time Adjustment	3-84	10-83	+2400	2-84		9-83	+2500
Location	good	good		good		good	
Site/View	good	good		good		good	
Design and Appeal	contemporary	contemporary		contemporary		contemporary	
Quality of Const.	good	good		good		good	
Age	new	new		new		new	

ITEM	Subject Property	COMPARABLE NO. 1	COMPARABLE NO. 2	COMPARABLE NO. 3
Condition	new	new	new	new
Living Area Room Count and Total / Gross Living Area	Total 5 | B-rms 2 | Baths 2 — 1336 Sq.Ft.	Total 5 | B-rms 2 | Baths 2 — 1336 Sq.Ft.	Total 6 | B-rms 3 | Baths 2 — 2500 — 1357 Sq.Ft.	Total 5 | B-rms 2 | Baths 2 — 1336 Sq.Ft.
Basement & Bsmt. Finished Rooms	+finished rm- 2nd floor	+finished rm. 2nd floor	+finished rm- 2nd floor	+finished rm- 2nd floor
Functional Utility	good	good	good	good
Air Conditioning	heat pump	heat pump	heat pump	heat pump
Garage/Car Port	none	none	none	none
Porches, Patio, Pools, etc.	decks; storage shed	decks; storage shed	decks; storage shed	decks; storage shed
SOLAR Special Energy Efficient Items	2 panel system insulated windows&doors	none insulated windows&doors +2500	6 panel system insulated windows&doors −4500	6 panel system insulated windows&doors −4500
Other (e.g. fireplaces, kitchen equip., remodeling)	fireplace range-oven d/w & disposal	fireplace range-oven d/w & disposal HOT TUB −2500	fireplace range-oven d/w & disposal security system −2500	fireplace range-oven d/w & disposal HOT TUB −2500
Sales or Financing Concessions	conv	conv	conv	conv
Net Adj. (Total)		[X] Plus [ ] Minus $ 2400	[ ] Plus [X] Minus $ 9,500	[ ] Plus [X] Minus $ 4500
Indicated Value of Subject		$ 90,400	$ 89,450	$ 92,460

Comments on Market Data: All three comparables are fairly recent sales of very similar (style, room count, features, quality of construction) homes as the subject, and they are all located in the same subdivision as the subject.

INDICATED VALUE BY MARKET DATA APPROACH . . . . $ 90,500

INDICATED VALUE BY INCOME APPROACH (If applicable) Economic Market Rent $ n/a /Mo. x Gross Rent Multiplier _____ = $ n/a

This appraisal is made [ ] "as is" [ ] subject to the repairs, alterations, or conditions listed below [X] completion per plans and specifications.

Comments and Conditions of Appraisal: FINAL INSPECTION REQUIRED
The practice of the seller paying discount points and/or closing costs for the purchaser is common and customary in this area and does not affect the final estimate of the market value.

Final Reconciliation: Both the market data (readily available) and the cost approach (new construction) were considered in arriving at the final estimate of value for this property.

Construction Warranty [X] Yes [ ] No   Name of Warranty Program HOW warranty   Warranty Coverage Expires 10 years

This appraisal is based upon the above requirements, the certification, contingent and limiting conditions, and Market Value definition that are stated in

[ ] FHLMC Form 439 (Rev. 10/78)/FNMA Form 1004B (Rev. 10/78) filed with client _____ 19 _____ [X] attached

I ESTIMATE THE MARKET VALUE, AS DEFINED, OF SUBJECT PROPERTY AS OF March 23 19 84 to be $ 89,500

Appraiser(s) John L. Sullivan, MAI, SRA   Review Appraiser (If applicable) _____
[ ] Did   [ ] Did Not Physically Inspect Property

FNMA #110A206

that underlie worthwhile professional conduct include the following:

1. Integrity.
2. Intellect.
3. Education.
4. Judgment.

The Bible asserts that man cannot live by bread alone. This implies that economic activities in any field of human endeavor need to be supplemented and guided by social and moral considerations. *Integrity* is an inner force that flows from a wholesome personal and professional philosophy of life which inspires trust and confidence in others. Integrity is akin to honor and service, and both are basic to a genuine display of sincerity of purpose in the discharge of professional responsibility. It is integrity that propels people to render their

best service, independent of the financial reward offered to solve a given problem or to report on findings or investigations.

The service motive, to be fruitful, must be reinforced with *intellect*. This is the power of reasoning as distinguished from the faculty of absorbing knowledge. Without intellect, the power of knowing gained from study and experience remains limited. Some people are by nature blessed, it seems, with more intellect than are others. But unless such talents are put to use, atrophy—a form of mental rigor mortis—may rob the possessor of this native advantage.

Important as these sources of professional strength are, integrity and intellect cannot stand alone. Both of these qualities must be supplemented by education. One must consciously make efforts to discipline his or her mind through study and instruction. The art of learning is essential in order for professionals to keep abreast with modern developments in theory and in practice. Education, it should be emphasized, need not be formal in character. Although study in college or trade school is economical and time saving in the long run, informal education can be gained through experience, intensive reading, attendance at seminars, workshops, and through related organizational and professional activities. It is in this area of self-study that professional groups render their most valuable service to fellow members.

Judgment, the final ingredient that characterizes a professional person, is the ability to consider and weigh relevant data in order to reach a sound and reasonable conclusion. Of the qualities that go to make up a professional person, judgment is the most difficult to cultivate. Judgment cannot readily be transferred from one person to another. Experience, it is agreed, has proved to be the best teacher of judgment.

IMPORTANCE OF PROFESSIONAL CONDUCT

The more specialized a given activity and the greater the required personal skill, the less the public appears to know about the quality and technical phases of the service rendered. To safeguard the general public against the malpractices of the few, and to promote the general interest of its members, professional societies are formed. Through them, intensive efforts are made to develop and maintain high standards of conduct.

As an organized profession, appraising dates back only to the year 1932, when the American Institute of Real Estate Appraisers was founded. In 1935, another group of specialists organized the Society of Real Estate Appraisers. Both organizations are international in scope, with cooperating chapters in Europe and Canada. Since 1935, other organizations which embrace valuation on a broader scale have been founded. For example, the members of the American Society of Appraisers are interested in the technical appraising of industrial plant equipment, securities, intangibles, and chattel fixtures.

Although real estate appraising has developed during the past 30 years into the most specialized branch of the real estate business, relatively few practitioners have achieved true professional standing. This is because relatively few real estate firms or individuals devote their working time exclusively to real estate appraising. Many members of the two leading appraising organizations depend on other income from collateral interests in brokerage, investment, management, or mortgage-financing fields of the real estate business. The collateral activities are by no means deemed a handicap, for the best known and most respected appraisers are those who have had a broad background in related real estate activities and whose judgments are tempered by wide and personal experience in all the varied phases of the real estate business. Having achieved, however, the experience and perception essential to the makeup of a qualified appraiser, professional status can be claimed only by those who devote their full time and specialized energies to activities which sharpen their value judgments, strengthen their value know-how, and enhance the integrity and quality of their services to clients and to the general public.

PROFESSIONAL QUALIFICATIONS

Although ever-greater stress is laid on adequate selection and analysis of appraisal data, the value conclusions reached by real estate practitioners constitute at best an informed estimate, the soundness of which largely depends on the quality of judgment possessed by the appraiser. To perfect the practice of real estate appraising and to safeguard against incompetence, appraisal societies are setting ever higher standards as requisites for membership. For instance, to be eligible for membership in the American Institute of Real Estate Appraisers, and thus be privileged to use the M.A.I. designation after his or her name, a candidate must have a minimum of five years of creditable appraisal experience, possess a four-year college education, submit acceptable appraisal reports covering different classes of income-producing real estate, and must pass several written examinations in order to demonstrate the ability to cope with valuation theory questions and case study problems. There are several alternatives to writing one of the two narrative reports, such as a doctoral dissertation or published article. Even when meeting these requirements, a candidate may still be short of the points required for membership unless he or she has a college education, more than five years' appraising, and collateral business experience, and unless he or she submits additional appraisal reports or requests additional examinations to satisfy the credit points set as a minimum by the admissions committee of the Appraisal Institute. These stringent admission requirements account for the fact that the Institute has less than 5,000 M.A.I's as members. Many times more than the number of professional appraisers now practicing are needed, however, if the demand for competent real property valuation services is to be met adequately. To this end, a comprehensive nationwide educational program is sponsored by the American Institute of Real Estate Appraisers and the Society of Real Estate Appraisers in cooperation with leading universities and colleges throughout the nation.

STANDARDS OF PROFESSIONAL CONDUCT

All professional societies have established rules of conduct or codes of ethics. Generally, rules of conduct are intended not only to safeguard the interests of individual members from one another but also to assure the public of professional services that will instill confidence and bring honor to the organization at large. To assure this, membership is restricted to those of proven technical competence who are known for adherence to high moral standards and a display of unquestionable personal integrity. Rules of conduct, by and large, are promulgated to promote and protect the common good as follows:

1. The interest of the public.
2. The interest of the client.
3. The interest of fellow members and the profession at large.

The *interest of the public* is deemed adversely affected whenever the appraiser fails to act as an independent agent. It is true that the appraiser must be hired by someone, and that he or she owes loyalty to the principal, but the value findings must not be slanted or biased because of it. Value found must be objective and independent of the client's cause or the compensation paid for services rendered. Based on premises clearly set forth in the body of the appraisal report, the value conclusions reached must be independently supportable no matter whose cause is being served.

In the interest of the public, the appraiser must be careful to base value on factual and reliable data and not on hypothetical assumptions or on questionable and uncertain future benefits. To ignore legal property-use restrictions, or to base value on hoped-for changes in area zoning, is a violation of public trust. The appraisal report must be written for the benefit of the uninformed reader, who will act on the findings in good faith. Care must also be taken not to appraise fractional parts of a property, especially where the sum of the parts appraised as if independent property units does not equal the value of the entire property when appraised as an integral whole. Fractional appraising is deemed unethical whenever the report—intentionally or otherwise—misleads the reader.

The appraiser would also be guilty of professional misconduct if he or she should accept an assignment for valuation of a property in which he or she has an undisclosed financial interest. No one can serve two masters and serve them well, especially where a conflict of interests beclouds the independence of action on which objective value must rest to be publicly acceptable.

The *interests of the client* impose further obligations on the professional appraiser. The most important of these is not to reveal the value findings to anyone unless specifically authorized to do so by the client or compelled to do so by court order. Communications between appraiser and client are not privileged under common law as are those of physicians, clergy, and lawyers. Nevertheless, every precaution must be taken to keep a client's trust confidential and to protect his or her interests at all times.

Clients, too, have a right to expect that an appraiser will not accept an assignment for which he or she has no previous experience or for which he or she is not qualified professionally. It would be considered a violation of professional trust for an appraiser to accept an assignment to evaluate a citrus grove or an industrial park if his or her previous appraisal experience was limited to urban residential properties. Appraisers can, of course, affiliate themselves with other members of the profession who are qualified to render the specialized service, provided that the client is duly informed and the appraisal report discloses the cooperative efforts of the parties involved.

Appraisers must take care to keep their client's relationship above-board. The fees charged should bear a reasonable relationship to quantity and character of service, and to professional responsibility assumed in the discharge of the assignment. As a rule, fees should be calculated on a per diem basis for personnel employed (professional responsibility assumed), plus direct and indirect expenses chargeable to the assignment. It is considered unethical to accept a commission in lieu of a stipulated fee or to accept gifts and services or undisclosed payments. To do so destroys the standing of appraisers as independent members of their profession in the eyes of the public. Such conduct, of course, casts a shadow on all who strive diligently to uphold and enhance the dignity of this specialized calling.

The interests of the members and the profession at large, too, are guided by written and implied rules of conduct. Most professional organizations deem it unethical for members to conduct themselves in such a manner as to prejudice the professional status or reputation of other members or that of the association under whose auspices they practice. Appraisers thus should not solicit assignments or advertise professional attainments or services except as authorized and in a dignified manner. Generally, announcements are limited to business cards, directory listings, and newspaper notices containing only the member's name, professional designation, telephone number, and business address.

Regulations caution members of the appraisal profession not to enter into competitive bidding for appraisal assignments. It is considered undignified to offer services when it is known that the assignment will go to the lowest bidder. Service is two-dimensional: qualitative as well as quantitative. Bidding suggests uniformity of product service which in practice does not exist. Experience, judgment, skill, integrity, and education are intangible ingredients which are difficult to subject to measurement under standard specifications in accordance with which service is to be performed. Some government agencies are still guilty of requesting bids and assigning appraisal service on the basis of cost, without due consideration of the experience, skill, and reputation which affect the quality of the service sought.

APPRAISER'S RULES OF CONDUCT

Whether or not a real estate appraiser belongs to one or more of the leading appraisal institutes or societies, he or she should be aware of and adhere to the guiding rules of conduct on which the growth and development of appraisal service as a professional calling depend. Under these rules, the appraiser must:

1. *Willingly share knowledge and professional experiences.* No one can live unto himself or herself alone. Exchange of experiences and knowledge enriches performance, creates mutual trust, and inspires public confidence. Cooperation, especially through affiliation with professional organizations, has increased the demand significantly for specialized appraisal service during the past 10 years. Members are urged to publish research findings and to participate in educational seminars and workshops in which new theories and practices can be explored and tested. It is in the field of education that professional organizations have made their greatest contributions.

2. *Encourage higher standards and service performance.* The transition from oral and letter reporting to preparation of lengthy and detailed narrative reports in which value conclusions are logically derived and supported is largely due to friendly competition encouraged among professional appraisers to promote higher performance standards. Professional service, if worthy of its name, should be documented and rendered with pride. It is facetiously said that doctors bury their mistakes, but appraisers exhibit theirs for all to see. Increased stress on higher standards and service performance will weed out the incompetent and create interest among the college-trained to share in the challenging opportunities that appraisal service promises to offer in the years to come.

3. *Never speak ill or disparagingly about a fellow appraiser.* Greatness cannot be achieved by pulling others down. One does not become taller by making others smaller. Disparaging talk—even when warranted—leaves a bitter taste, often traced to envy. How much more cheerful and impressive it is to subscribe to the theory that all persons, including fellow competitors, are striving to do well in accordance with their talents and abilities. In the long run, reputation based on quality performance standards will bring the best people to the top in a free and competitive society.

4. *Seek no unfair advantage.* It is disappointing that many otherwise informed people still subscribe to the erroneous philosophy that the goods of the world or of a nation, or the income derived from a service, are all as limited in quantity as is the size of a given pie. To secure a larger slice, those who hold to this philosophy must necessarily connive to shrink the shares of others, or freeze them out entirely. Progress in all phases of life, as well as our high standard of living, is proof that bigger pies—and not more slices of an existing pie—increase the wealth of a nation. This is apparent in most professions, too, where despite increasing membership, work loads and work opportunities have not diminished.

5. *Avoid controversy.* Do not wash soiled linen in public. There is a saying that you may win an argument, but you may lose a friend. The professional person should

avoid arguments; but when unavoidable, disputes should not be aired in public. More often than not, differences of opinion arise because of misunderstandings, statements of half-truth, or quotations taken out of context. Where differences of opinion do arise they can generally be talked out in gentlemanly fashion and under circumstances wherein honorable persons can agree to disagree.

6. *Abide by rules and regulations, and encourage opportunities for professional education.* Most people are understandably rebellious at heart and inclined to disregard rules and regulations when such seem to work against them. We naturally seek to be free from fetters. We want to enjoy rights, but we object to obligations. Yet rights cannot exist without obligations. The right to live imposes the obligation not to kill. The right to free speech imposes the obligation to allow others to do likewise. Rights without obligations lead to anarchy and chaos. Rules and regulations are intended to maximize the common good either of a people or of a given clan or profession. Every individual gain is obtained at a sacrifice of social costs. Control of some sort is needed to keep a balance between incentive (profit) motives and those aimed at the exploitation of the weak, uninformed, or the public at large. Violations of rules and regulations and unprofessional conduct are often traceable to ignorance or lack of understanding. Enlightenment through education has proved the bulwark of professionalism. Every support should be given to efforts intended to spread the gospel of professional truth and know-how.

7. *Keep confidential matters entrusted in good faith.* Every code of ethics, from the oldest to the youngest professions, stresses the importance of "privileged communication." It seems to bolster one's ego to possess information that others long to know, and it is the devilish urge to be magnanimous by sharing such important matters with others that inclines the weak to discuss private matters with the wrong people. The Golden Rule should have special meaning to persons of professional status. Once a trust is violated, it is difficult to regain public confidence. Worse still, a breach of conduct undermines strength of character and may lead to misfeasance in client relations that may have serious repercussions to individual practitioners and to the profession.

8. *Never undermine a fellow practitioner's professional relations with others, or attempt to create exclusionary appraisal practices in one's community.* Experience in all parts of the country supports the conclusion that the demand for qualified appraisers outruns the available supply. Commercial banks, insurance firms, business establishments, investors, and industry rely increasingly on independent appraisers for guidance in their loan and investment policies. Healthy competition is good for trade as well as for professional growth and development. In a progressive society, standing still means going backward. An attempt to keep qualified practitioners from serving the community is a sign of weakness and stagnation. A "let-the-best-person-win" philosophy is essential to keeping good people at the top.

9. *Never solicit employment of a fellow practitioner's office or field personnel without his or her full knowledge and permission.* It is considered poor practice to encourage transfer of working personnel from one office to another. Employees are not subject to the same stringent regulations or codes of ethics that bind their professional employers, and inevitable comparison of office policies and practices may cast doubts on uniformity and quality of service that may adversely affect the integrity of the profession as a whole. Where a spirit of friendly cooperation rather than competition prevails, employees, too, will find their working environment more congenial. Instill a feeling of belonging and a sense of loyalty

among those who serve you. Where such feelings prevail, employment problems cease to exist.

10. *Conduct work so as to achieve a high regard in one's community and make fellow members of the appraisal profession thankful for one's wholesome influence.* There are many things in life which money cannot buy, and reputation is among them. Unfortunately, too many people consider short-run monetary gains without thoughtful deliberation as to the long-term effects of their actions. Where love of work, interest, and service are prime considerations in the discharge of professional duty, success is bound to follow. The sense of a job well done in an atmosphere of confidence and public recognition provides the lasting compensation that is reflected in a firm's shield of honor. It is the hope of all to carry this shield on without blemish from one generation to another.

APPRAISAL POLICY OF INSURED SAVINGS ASSOCIATIONS

In addition to the professional standards of the two appraisal societies discussed previously in this chapter, a Federal Home Loan Bank Board memorandum has affected the practices of real estate appraisers in the United States. This memorandum,[3] popularly known as R-41(b) was distributed in early 1984 to insured savings associations and service corporations.

The principal appraisal policies and procedures set forth in this memorandum are summarized below:

Each appraisal report must:

1. Be totally self-contained so that when read by a third party, the appraiser's logic, reasoning, judgment, and analysis in arriving at a final conclusion indicate the reasonableness of the market value reported.
2. Contain all recognized approaches to market value unless the appraiser fully explains and documents the rationale for eliminating one or more of the approaches to value.
3. Consider and make provision for all appropriate deductions and discounts for any development type property. This pertains to new multi-unit property as well as the conversion of existing property to another use.
4. Address the market/economic feasibility prospects for any proposed major loan/investment real estate project, in sufficient detail to support the appraiser's forecast of the probable success and the conclusion(s) of the highest and best use. If the market/economic feasibility analysis is done by someone else, the appraiser must explain his reasoning for acccepting or rejecting the report.
5. Contain for major loan/investment properties in highly speculative local markets which have experienced dramatic price increases relative to regional norms, a sales history analysis of the appraised property covering the speculative time period.
6. Be based on "market value" which is defined as the most probable price in terms of money which property should bring in a competitive and open market under

[3] D. James Croft, *Guidelines Regarding Appraisal Procedures and Management*, Memorandum # R-41 (b), FHLBB Office of Examinations and Supervision (March 12, 1982).

all conditions requisite to a fair sale, the buyer and seller, each acting prudently, knowledgeably, and assuming the price is not affected by undue stimulus.

7. Under no circumstances permit the appraiser to further qualify or, by assumptions, erode the impact of the definition of market value.

8. Be couched in terms of "cash or its equivalent" and "typical financing" for that particular property type.

REVIEW QUESTIONS

1. (a) Define the term "appraisal process."
   (b) How does an understanding of this process benefit the appraiser?
2. List four assumptions that appraisers will ordinarily make regarding appraisals.
3. Explain why an appraiser should define the appraised value in his or her report.
4. Discuss the nature of the reconciliation process in an appraisal report.
5. Briefly outline the steps involved in the "Analyses and Conclusions" section of an appraisal.
6. List several characteristics of a well-written appraisal report.
7. Why is use of the letter report discouraged by professional appraisers?
8. Distinguish between the terms "certification" and "limiting conditions."
9. How does education play a role in professional conduct?
10. Explain the real estate appraiser's responsibility to the public.
11. Why should an appraiser avoid speaking disparagingly of a fellow professional?
12. Why do you think an appraiser is obligated to maintain a confidential relationship with his or her clients?
13. Why do you think R-41(b) requires an appraiser to explain his or her reasoning for either accepting or rejecting a market/economic feasibility report upon which his or her appraisal report is based?

READING AND STUDY REFERENCES

ADMISSIONS COMMITTEE, "The Written Appraisal Concept," *The Real Estate Appraiser* 43, no. 1 (January–February 1977), pp. 10–17.

AMERICAN INSTITUTE OF REAL ESTATE APPRAISERS. Chapter 22, "The Appraisal Report," *The Appraisal of Real Estate*, 8th ed. Chicago: American Institute of Real Estate Appraisers, 1983.

BOYCE, BYRL R., and WILLIAM N. KINNARD, JR. "Professionalism and Ethics," *Appraising Real Property*. Lexington, Mass.: Lexington Books, 1984, pp. 400–403.

GRAFTON, PETER. "The Institution and Society," *The Appraisal Journal* 48, no. 2 (April 1980), pp. 182–193.

HAGOOD, WAYNE D. "Reconciliation Analysis (Formerly Called Correlation)," *The Real Estate Appraiser* 44, no. 1 (January–February 1978), pp. 42–44.

HEINRICH, ROBERT J. "A Candidate's Guide to Writing a Passing M.A.I. Demonstration Appraisal Report," *The Appraisal Journal* 47, no. 4 (October 1979), pp. 561–573.

HINES, MARY ALICE. Chapter 21, "The Appraisal Report," *Real Estate Appraisal*, New York: Macmillan Publishing Company, 1981.

KOKUS, JOHN, JR. "Ethics for the Real Estate Appraiser," *The Appraisal Journal* 51, no. 4 (October 1983), pp. 540–545.

LENNHOFF, DAVID C. "Why All the Ruckus over R-41b?" *The Appraisal Journal* 52, no. 3 (July 1984), pp. 443–447.

NEILSEN, DONALD A. "Certification of Appraisers: Issues, Dilemmas, and Prospects," *The Appraisal Journal* 49, no. 2 (April 1981), pp. 259–270.

PYLE, CHESTER R., III. "Letters of Opinion: Should We or Shouldn't We," *The Real Estate Appraiser and Analyst* 45, no. 4 (July–August 1979), pp. 4–12.

REYNOLDS, ANTHONY J. "Theoretical vs. Practical

Appraising (1982)," *The Appraisal Journal* 50, no. 1 (January 1982), pp. 20–24.

RYNDERS, LEO J.   "Photography for Appraisers," *The Real Estate Appraiser and Analyst* 46, no. 2 (March–April 1980).

SMITH, HALBERT C.   Chapter 10, "Appraisal Reports, Conclusions and Standards" *Real Estate Appraisal*, Columbus, Ohio: Grid Publishing, Inc., 1976.

STELLMACHER, H. BOB.   "Real Estate Appraisal: The World's Newest Profession," *The Appraisal Journal* 47, no. 1 (January 1979), pp. 99–125.

WOODWARD, LYNN N.   "Is the Appraisal Profession Dying?" *The Real Estate Appraiser and Analyst* 47, no. 4 (Winter 1981), pp. 25–28.

APPENDIX I

VALUATION REPORT FOR SINGLE-FAMILY RESIDENCE

VALUATION REPORT

FOR

SINGLE-FAMILY RESIDENCE

PREPARED FOR

MR. JOHN B. HOPEFUL

16 N. W. 20th TERRACE

GAINESVILLE, FLORIDA 32603

1908 N. W. 7th Lane
Gainesville, Florida 32603
January 15, 19--

Mr. John B. Hopeful
16 N. W. 20th Terrace
Gainesville, Florida 32601

Dear Mr. Hopeful:

In compliance with your request the undersigned has completed an appraisal of residential property owned and occupied by you at 16 N. W. 20th Terrace in Gainesville, Florida. This property is legally described as follows:

> Lot 3 and the North five feet of lots 1 and 2 and the South fifteen feet of lot 4, Block 2 College Court Subdivision as recorded in public records of Alachua County, Florida.

A careful and personal inspection was made of this residential site and its building improvements and due consideration was given to all factors and forces that influence property value at the subject location.

The attached report contains an analysis of general and specific data which was deemed essential to support the estimate of value as reported herein under the cost, market, and income approaches to value.

As a result of my investigation and finding it is my considered and professional opinion that your residential property, as described above, warrants a market value as of January 12, 19-- in the amount of

Mr. John B. Hopeful
Page 2
January 15, 19--

               Sixty-Seven Thousand Dollars

                    ($67,000)

     Should questions arise in connection with this report
or if I can be of further assistance in this or other
matters, please feel free to call upon me.

                         Respectfully submitted,

                         Alfred A. Ring, M.A.I.,
                         S.R.P.A.
                         Consultant - Appraiser

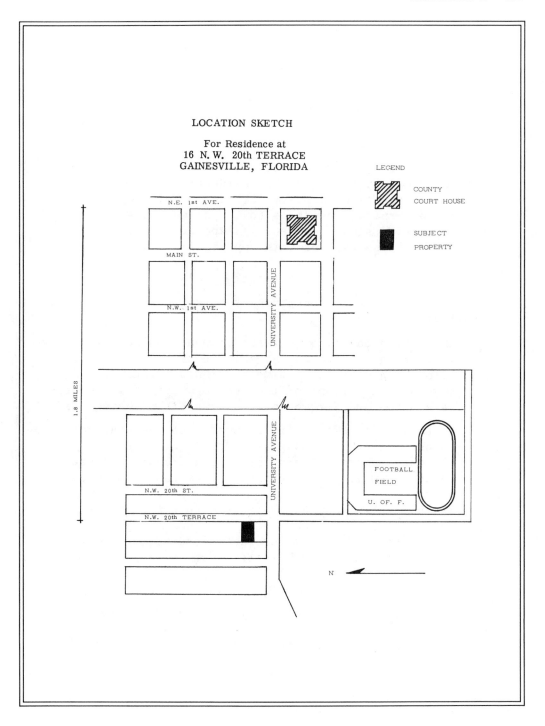

LOCATION SKETCH

For Residence at
16 N. W. 20th TERRACE
GAINESVILLE, FLORIDA

Purpose of the Appraisal

The purpose of this appraisal is to establish an estimate of market value of the residential property described herein as of January 12, 19--. This report is prepared to furnish a guide as to the sales price that the subject property should command if exposed for sale in the open market on the date of this appraisal.

Definition of Market Value

Market value, for purposes of this report, is defined as follows:

> The estimated price in terms of money which a property will bring if exposed for sale in the open market, allowing a reasonable time to find a purchaser who buys with knowledge of the use to which this property is adopted and for which it is capable of being used.

In this definition it is assumed that the transaction is based on cash or cash equivalent considerations. Favorable or unfavorable terms of sale are bound to affect the transaction price which this property can command in the open market.

It is further assumed that title to the property is good and marketable and that fee simple ownership is to be transferred free from all encumbrances except for those specified in the deed of public records.

Legal Description

Lot 3, and North 5 feet of lots 1 and 2 and South 15 feet of lot 4, Block 2, College Court Subdivision, as recorded in the public records of Alachua County, Florida.

Statement of Highest and Best Use

It is the appraiser's opinion that the subject property as found on the date of inspection, January 2, 19--, was improved in accordance with the principle of highest and best land use.

By highest and best use is meant that program of land use which will preserve the utility of the land and yield a net income flow that forms, when appropriately capitalized, the highest present value of the land.

Assessment and Tax Data

The subject property, bearing Tax No. 6460-94, is assessed for ad valorem tax purposes, by city and county governments and by school and water district agencies, for the current year as follows:

Agency	Assessed Value	Tax Millage	Tax Amount
County	$50,600.00	0.00871	$ 440.73
City	50,600.00	0.00564	285.38
School	50,600.00	0.00794	401.76
Water	50,600.00	0.00032	16.19
Total tax			$1,144.06

Neighborhood Data:

The subject property is located in a fully developed neighborhood that enjoys an air of quality and social refinement. The homes are 25 to 35 years of age, of varied but pleasing architecture, well set back from the street line, and in excellent physical condition. A wide double-lane boulevard, divided by an attractively landscaped parkway, separates the community homes on opposing sides. The lots are of generous size, varying from 75' to 100' in width and 120' to 140' in depth. The homes are well placed, assuring a maximum of privacy and quiet enjoyment.

The neighborhood encompasses an area of six square blocks and is well protected geographically, as well as by zoning and deed restriction, from detrimental influences. The physical boundaries of the neighborhood are University Avenue on the south, N. W. 5th Avenue on the north, N. W. 22nd Street on the west, and N. W. 17th Street on the east.

All public utilities -- gas, water, telephones, sewerage (both drain and sanitary), and electricity -- are available. The area is frequently patrolled, assuring adequate fire and police protection. City bus lines servicing this neighborhood at 30-minute intervals come within one block of the subject property.

There is an excellent grade school within four blocks of the property, and ample opportunities for recreational activities are found on the campus of the University of Florida, which adjoins the neighborhood and extends south and eastward over an area comprising more than 300 acres. The main shopping center is reached by bus or car in a few minutes' drive. The distance is about one and one-half miles; however, small shops catering to neighborhood customers are located within a half mile distance. Two excellent high schools are located within one and a quarter miles from the subject property and land has been acquired within four blocks by school authorities, who contemplate the erection of a modern high school to serve this neighborhood.

The city has twenty-two churches, mostly of Protestant denomination, all of which are centrally located within a radius of two miles, and readily accessible by public or private transportation.

The neighborhood population is wholly professional, and College Court is occupied almost entirely by University personnel. The street often is referred to as "Professors' Row." The income averages about $30,000 per annum. The stability of this income is well reflected in pride of home ownership as shown by housing and lawn care. Owner occupancy is rated at 95 per cent. Property turnover is at a minimum.

Continued growth of the University of Florida and of Gainesville proper assures this neighborhood of an active demand for residential housing far beyond the remaining economic life of the subject property described below.

Site Data:

Subject site is geographically situated on the west side of Northwest 20th Terrace, approximately 125' north of University Avenue. It is rectangular in shape, having a frontage of 70' on a paved street and a depth of 130'.

Northwest 20th Terrace is a dual-lane thoroughfare, divided by an attractively landscaped parkway. Concrete curbing and gutters facilitate surface drainage. The building site is fairly even in contour, slightly above street level, with a natural slope toward the rear. The sandy soil permits ready absorption of normal rainfall.

The plot is serviced by both sanitary and storm sewers. City water, electricity, and gas are available and connected to the site. Mail is delivered daily and bus transportation is within a few hundred feet. Exceptionally well-maintained landscaping and desirable shade trees provide very pleasant surroundings.

Although the adjoining lot on the south is unimproved, it is zoned for lower residential purposes, which permits the erection of four-unit-type multiple dwellings. There is a fraternity house directly across the street from the subject site. In the appraiser's opinion the nearness of student housing facilities does not create a detrimental influence. Investigation disclosed that the neighborhood occupants are mostly University professors who do not find fraternity and student housing objectionable. It is further reasonable to assume that the subject property, if offered for sale on the open market, would attract University personnel who no doubt share the opinion of the other residents.

Property Data:

The Building

The lot is improved with a one-story bungalow-type house of 1427 square feet area containing three bedrooms, a dining room, a living room, a study, a hall, a kitchen, one and one-half baths, and a screened-in porch. The residence is a detached wooden structure, shingled with cypress, conforming in design and size with the surrounding residences and with accepted architectural standards. It is so placed that ample privacy is obtained; the front door opens south of the porch so that entrance from the street is indirect. The garage, completely detached from the house, is located at the rear of the lot.

The house is squarely placed on a continuous brick foundation extending to a mean height of eighteen inches above grade. Adequate ventilation is provided through screened openings, and metal shields are provided to prevent termites from reaching the joists. The house is in good condition; the structural members are sound; no evidence of rot, sagging, or uneven settling is present.

The gable-type roof is of asphalt shingle in excellent repair. All gutters, conductors, and flashings are of copper. All windows are frame-sash-type and double hung. Outside steps are made of brick.

Interior walls and ceilings are of sand-finish plaster and in very good condition. The floors are of a good-quality hardwood oak throughout over pine subflooring. All closets provide for air circulation through built-in screened ventilators in the ceiling. The attic, which is accessible through two large trap doors (hall and study closet), is sufficiently high to serve for storage of light furniture and household goods.

The effective age of this structure is 30 years. The remaining economic life is estimated to be 20 years. Equipment includes a 36-inch attic fan, an 85,000-Btu thermostat-controlled gas space heater, and two gas space heaters each of 20,000-Btu rating. Hot water is supplied by a G.E. 40-gallon electric heater. The kitchen is wired for an electric stove. Hot and cold water connections are piped for an automatic washing machine.

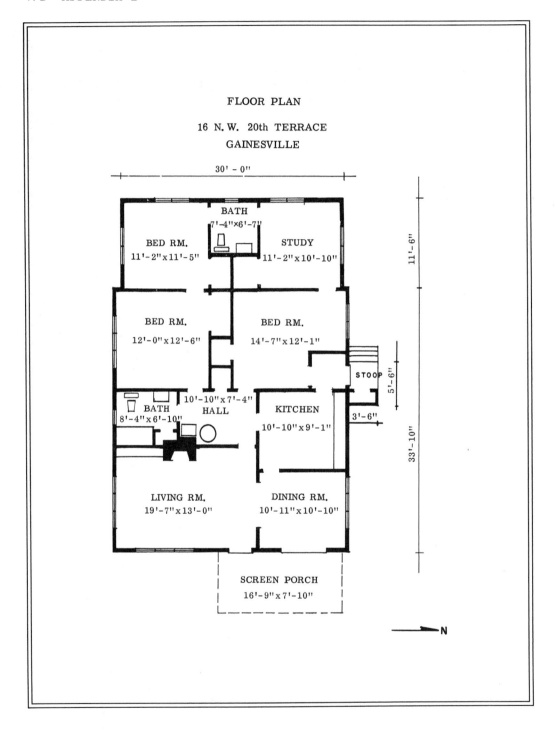

FLOOR PLAN

16 N. W. 20th TERRACE
GAINESVILLE

Market Approach to Value

comparable properties

In the determination of value via the market approach, four sales were analyzed as follows:

Sale No. 1 is located in the same block as the subject property and is identified by the street address of 208 N. W. 20 Terrace. This property sold a year ago for $69,000 and was purchased by B. F. Meter and wife. The lot size is identical to the subject property. Time adjustment due to inflation is judged to be plus 10%. The overall rating for the subject property is 95% because of differences in effective age. All other building features appear comparable. The adjusted sales value is $65,550.

Sale No. 2 is also located within the subject block at 123 N. W. 20th Terrace. This property has an 80-foot frontage as compared with 70 feet for the subject property. This property was purchased by K. L. Mitch and wife six months ago for $80,000. The subject property is smaller in building size by 285 square feet. The subject property rating is 85%, which includes a lot value adjustment of minus $2000. The adjusted sales price is $68,000.

Sale No. 3 is better located at 1717 N. W. 7th Place on a larger lot which is priced $6,500 more than the lot value estimated for the subject property. The property sold three months ago to E. G. Folk and wife for $75,000. Time adjustment was rated at plus 2% and the overall comparability for the subject property because of better construction features is 90%. The adjusted price is $67,500.

Sale No. 4 is also better located at 1730 N. W. 11th Road causing an estimated land value differential of $8,750. The subject property is larger by 127 square feet and is better in construction features and condition. The sale property was bought four weeks ago by C. F. Cain and wife for $78,000. There is no time adjustment, however, the rating for the subject property is 85%. The adjusted price is $66,300.

The four sales were correlated giving a value weight of 50% to sale no. 1, 30% to sale no. 2, and 10% each to sales 3 and 4. The correlated market value on the basis of these sales is $66,500.

The Cost Approach to Value

Determination of Base Unit Cost Factor:

Based on the unit-in-place cost method of building construction, the subject property—free of special features—would require an expenditure of $38.00 per square foot. This basic cost factor is verified by special cost studies recently concluded by local builders.

Cost factor derivation:

Basic unit cost per square foot		$38.00
Add special features:		
Brick fireplace	$1,500	
Tile work in kitchen and bath	850	
Additional millwork allowance	650	
Additional half-bath	750	
Additional closets	250	
Total extras	$4,000	

Extra costs per square foot

$4,000 ÷ 1,427 sq ft =	2.80
Adjusted cost per square foot	$40.80

The Cost Approach to Value

Estimated replacement cost, new:

Main dwelling

1427 sq ft at $40.80	$58,222
131 sq ft screened porch at $25.00	3,275
19 sq ft side stoop at $15.00	285
500 sq ft garage at $21.50	$10,750

Total replacement cost, new $72,532

Plus depreciated cost of landscaping, walk,
drive and equipment:

Attic fan	$ 600
Gas space heater	1,125
Venetian blinds	520
Aluminum awning	200
Landscaping	400
Walks and drives	300
Total extras	3,145
Total replacement cost	$75,677
Less accrued depreciation (see schedule)	19,101
Depreciated replacement cost	$56,576
Add value of land—by comparison	11,000
Value via cost approach	$67,576

Rounded to $67,600

...what it would cost to replace these things

Depreciation Schedule

Physical deterioration

Curable:

Refinish floors	$1,200
Repair window screens	375

Incurable:

$$\frac{\text{effective age} \quad (30)}{\text{economic life expectancy (50)}} \times \$12,547* \quad \underline{7,528}$$

Total physical deterioration	$9,103

Functional obsolescence

Curable:

Install air-conditioning system	$1,600
Relocate hot water tank from hallway to attic	480
Replace two outmoded light fixtures	350

Incurable:

Loss due to poor floor plan. This estimate is based on 10% sales resistance of replacement cost new	<u>7,568</u>

Total functional obsolescence	9,998
External obsolescence	None
Total accrued depreciation	<u>$19,101</u>

*Includes long-lived structural components such as foundation and walks. For more on this topic, see "Physical Deterioration—Incurable" in Chapter 13.

Income Approach to Value

— what the income property will be rented

The income approach to value is of minor significance in the valuation of single-family residential properties. This is the case because most properties of this type are under homeowner occupancy and amenities (or "psychic income") derived from ownership do not lend themselves readily to economic measurement.

An attempt, however, was made to determine what comparable properties rent for in similar locations. Rentals ranged from $600 per month for homes in relatively new condition to $450 per month for homes in late life. A market income of $500 per month reflects the current income-producing capacity of this property. This rental estimate was confirmed and judged accurate by leading Realtors in the Gainesville community.

The monthly rent multiplier for Gainesville based on sale of comparable properties is 120. — ?

Value based on rent multiplier

$$120 \times \$500 = \underline{\$60,000}$$

Correlation of Value Estimates

The current market conditions in Gainesville reflect an active demand for residential homes. An informed seller, however, would consider the depreciated replacement cost of similar property as a ceiling of value. The income approach for residential property was given little weight.

In consideration of all the forces which influence value, the appraiser has applied the following judgment weights in the derivation of the final estimate of value:

	Value Estimate	Value Weight	Value Influence
Market	$66,500	0.60	$39,900
Cost	67,600	0.40	27,040
Income	60,000	0.00	
Total			$66,940
Final estimate of value			$67,000

Explanation of Value Weights:

The value weights as applied above are justified as follows: The market is active for new homes which sell at replacement cost new. Hence the cost approach is of greatest present influence as a market price determinant for new rather than older properties such as the appraised property. The weight assigned for this measure of value is 40%.

The demand for older homes in this neighborhood remains relatively strong. The comparable sales analyzed were within this neighborhood and required comparatively small adjustments. The assigned weight is estimated at 60%.

The income approach is of negligible importance in the value of residences--hence no weight was assigned to this index of value.

Certification

This is to certify that the undersigned has made a careful personal inspection of the property legally described herein and that all findings, statements and opinions submitted in this report are correct to the best of his knowledge.

This appraisal was prepared for demonstration purposes and the valuation estimate certified below is not contingent on any monetary fees or interests whatsoever.

The appraiser has no present or prospective interest in the subject property and the fee agreed upon is in no way related to or contingent upon the value reported.

It is further certified that this appraisal has been made in conformity with the professional standards of the American Institute of Real Estate Appraisers and the Society of Real Estate Appraisers, of which the undersigned is a member.

The market value of the property as described herein is certified as of January 15, 19-- to be:

Sixty-seven Thousand Dollars

($67,000)

Certified by

Alfred A. Ring, M.A.I.,
S.R.P.A.
Consultant - Appraiser

Statement of Limiting Conditions

This appraisal is subject to the following limiting conditions:

1. The property is free and clear of all liens and encumbrances other than those listed in the deed of record.

2. The appraiser did not search validity of title nor does he assume responsibility for corrections which a survey of the property may reveal.

3. The sale of this property will be on an all-cash basis -- since financial arrangements, good or cumbersome, are bound to affect the price at which this property may sell in the market.

4. The information contained herein is not guaranteed, but it was gathered from reliable sources which are believed to be accurate.

5. No responsibility is assumed for matters legal in character.

6. Sketches are accurate only for purposes of approximation.

7. This report is not to be reproduced in part or as a whole without written consent of the appraiser.

APPENDIX II

APPRAISAL REPORT AND ANALYSIS OF THE SANDCASTLE II APARTMENT COMPLEX

APPRAISAL REPORT AND ANALYSIS OF
THE SANDCASTLE II APARTMENT COMPLEX
Located at
6717 Everhart
Corpus Christi, Texas

Prepared for:

MR. W. J. SOUTHWELL
S & M Properties
S & M Building
McAllen, Texas 78288

Prepared by:

LOVE AND DUGGER
Real Estate Consultants and Appraisers
111 Soledad, Suite 890
San Antonio, Texas 78205

—Partners—
Scruggs Love, Jr., MAI
Richard L. Dugger, MAI
R. Don Canaday, MAI

Love & Dugger

Real Estate Consultants & Appraisers
111 Soledad/Commerce Plaza Bldg.
San Antonio, Texas 78205
(512) 227-6229

Kenneth F. Fisher
Debra A. Schuch
Hal A. Coon
Gerald Burke Schulz
Nicole M. Love
Christine M. Pellett
Mary Jo Hutton-Smith
Jerry Anooshian
C. Dub Suttle
Martin Bryant
Clyde O. Davis
Anne Woodriff
Ted A. Moore
Raymond T. Hatch
Bobby Mealer
Wes Foster

June 15, 1984

Mr. W. J. Southwell
S & M Properties
S & M Building
McAllen, Texas 78288

Dear Mr. Southwell:

In response to your authorization, we have conducted the
required investigation, gathered the necessary data, and
made certain analyses that have enabled us to form an
opinion of the market value of the Sandcastle II Apartment
complex located at 6717 Everhart, Corpus Christi, Texas.

Based on the inspection of the property, and
investigation and analyses undertaken, we have formed the
opinion that, as of June 10, 1984, subject to the
assumptions and limiting conditions set forth in this
report, the Sandcastle II Apartment complex has a market
value of the fee simple title of $7,200,000. As the
contract rental under the existing leases is the same as the
prevailing market rental, it is our opinion that the value
of the leased fee estate is the same as the value of the fee
simple title to the appraised property. We have concluded
that the leaseholds created by the various apartment leases,
in effect, have no value.

It often is advisable to indicate the total number of pages in a report to reduce
the chance of subsequent alterations by unauthorized persons.

Martin Bryant assisted in the preparation of this
report. We certify that we physically inspected the subject
property on June 10, 1984.

The narrative appraisal report that follows sets forth the identification of the property, pertinent facts about the Corpus Christi apartment market, comparable data, and the results of our investigation and analysis.

Respectfully submitted,

Scruggs Love, Jr.

Scruggs Love, Jr., MAI

Mary Jo Hutton Smith

Mary Jo Hutton-Smith

/ceg

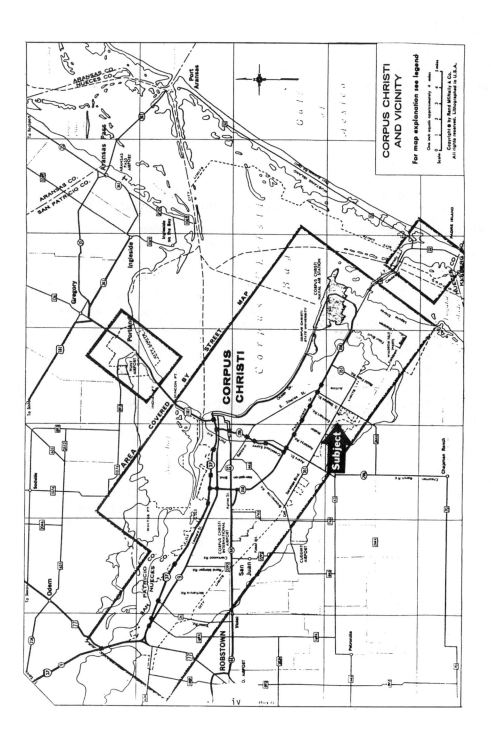

SUMMARY OF IMPORTANT FACTS AND CONCLUSIONS

This section gives a client an opportunity to gain an overview of the appraisal report prior to a detailed reading.

Property Identification:

The Sandcastle II Apartment complex is a 216-unit apartment development legally described as Lot 1, Block 1, Country Club Estates, Nueces County, Corpus Christi, Texas.

Objective of the Appraisal:

The purpose of the appraisal is to estimate the market value of the fee simple title of the Sandcastle II Apartment complex. The function of the report is to be of assistance in making a decision to acquire the property for investment.

Define and relate the terms fee simple title, leased fee, and leasehold estate (see Chapter 20).

Location:

The subject property is located on the north side of the 6000 block of Everhart Road, in the southeasterly portion of the City of Corpus Christi, Texas.

Land:

A survey prepared by Urban Engineering shows the site to contain 378,576 square feet of land area or 8.69 acres.

Improvements:

The Sandcastle II Apartment complex is a 216-unit, garden, brick veneer and frame apartment development. The improvements are in excellent condition. The building was constructed in 1983.

The Cost Approach:

Estimated reproduction cost new of the improvements	$6,505,737
Less: Accrued depreciation	− 188,364
Estimated depreciation reproduction cost new of the improvements	6,317,373
Site value: 378,576 SF at $2.50 per SF rounded	946,500
Value indicated by the cost approach:	(R) $7,264,000

Market Date Approach:

Unit of comparison:

Sales price per SF	$ 50
Indicated cost per unit	$33,000
Gross rent multiplier	7.05
Effective gross income multiplier	7.70
Indicated overall rate	9.5%

Value indicated by the market data approach:	(R) $7,000,000

The Income Approach:

Gross potential income	$ 991,680
Less: Vacancy and credit loss (8%)	− 79,334
Effective gross potential income	912,346
Operating expenses: 143,056 SF at $1.50 per SF	214,703
Net operating income:	697,643
Overall capitalization rate of 0.095	7,343,611
Less: Estimated rent loss year 1	− 188,364
Value indicated by income capitalization after rent loss:	(R) $7,155,000

FINAL ESTIMATE OF VALUE:	(R) $7,200,000
Allocated: Land: 378,576 SF ($2.50/SF)	$946,500
Improvements:	$6,253,500

TABLE OF CONTENTS

A table of contents should precede any report in excess of 5 to 10 pages. Importantly, each page should be numbered to facilitate reference to particular pages. Pagination is especially helpful when a client and appraiser discuss a report by telephone. It also reduces the possibility of pages being placed out of order.

LIST OF TABLES

PURPOSE OF THE ANALYSIS AND THE PROGRAM OF USE CONSIDERED

The purpose of this appraisal is to estimate the market value of the Sandcastle II Apartment complex located at 6717 Everhart Road, Corpus Christi, Texas, as of the current date, June 10, 1984. The appraised property is located in the Country Club Estates Subdivision in Nueces County, Texas.

PROPERTY RIGHTS APPRAISED

The property rights appraised are those constituting the unencumbered fee simple title to the subject property subject to the existing leases. Liens and encumbrances, if any, have not been considered.

DEFINITION OF MARKET VALUE

The definition of Market Value is as follows: "The most probable price in terms of money which a property should bring in competitive and open market under all conditions requisite to a fair sale, the buyer and seller, each acting prudently, knowledgeably, and assuming the price is not affected by undue stimulus.

Implicit in this definition is the consummation of a sale as of a specified date and the passing of title from seller to buyer under conditions whereby:

1. Buyer and seller are typically motivated.
2. Both parties are well informed or well advised, and each acting in what they consider their own best interest.
3. A reasonable time is allowed for exposure in the open market.
4. Payment is made in cash or its equivalent.
5. Financing, if any, is on terms generally available in the community at the specified date and typical for the property type in its locale.
6. The price represents a normal consideration for the property sold unaffected by special financing amounts and/or terms, services, fees, costs, or credits incurred in the transaction."[1]

---

[1]American Institute of Real Estate Appraisers and Society of Real Estate Appraisers, Real Estate Appraisal Terminology, revised edition, ed. Byrl N. Boyce (Cambridge, Mass.: Ballinger Publishing Company, 1981), pp. 160-161.

CLASS DISCUSSION: What is the relationship between conditions 4, 5, and 6 of this definition of market value? Is there any conflict among these three conditions?

AREA ANALYSIS

Corpus Christi is located in Nueces County on the Gulf of Mexico. The city is approximately 210 miles southwest of Houston, 145 miles southeast of San Antonio, and 160 miles north of Brownsville. The Corpus Christi area comprises an area of 392.1 square miles of which 275.5 square miles are covered by water. The city government was incorporated in 1852 and is currently ruled by a council manager form of government.

The 1970 census for Corpus Christi showed a population of the city of 204,525. The 1980 census noted a population of 231,999, for a growth of 13% percent. The 1984 estimated population for the city is 253,780.

Table II-1, prepared by the Corpus Christi Chamber of Commerce, illustrates growth in the employment and residential housing markets and highlights major factors affecting apartment occupancy.

The appraiser should be careful to explain the meaning of any tables or charts included in a report. Also, he or she should exclude from the report any regional data that fail to relate to the highest and best use and value of the appraised property.

Table II-1

CORPUS CHRISTI ECONOMIC TRENDS

	MARCH 1984	FEBRUARY 1984	% CHANGE	MARCH 1983	% CHANGE	1984 TO DATE	1983 TO DATE	% CHANGE
ECONOMIC ACTIVITY INDEX*	109.2	106.6	+2.4%	112.0	-2.6%	107.4	108.4	-1.0%
TOTAL EMPLOYMENT	151,500	148,701	+1.9%	152,000	—	148,934	152,217	-2.2%
UNEMPLOYMENT (%)	9.2%	8.4%	+9.5%	10.5%	-12.4%	9.2%	10.1%	-8.9%
BANK CLEARINGS	$424,094,729	$410,825,854	+3.2%	$433,959,250	-2.3%	$414,820,424	$402,041,425	×3.2%
TOTAL VALUE BUILDING PERMITS**	$19,372,241	21,384,500	-9.4%	$22,805,775	-15.1%	$53,560,536	$79,237,443	-32.4%
RESIDENTIAL DWELLING UNITS**	313	423	-26.0%	332	-5.7%	889	1,133	-21.5%
RESIDENTIAL ELECTRIC CONNECTIONS	82,989	82,779	—	79,097	+4.9%	82,727	78,911	+4.8%
PORT TONNAGE**	4,683,523	4,061,472	+15.3%	2,819,727	+66.1%	13,234,860	8,465,483	+56.3%
AIRLINE PASSENGERS**	69,453	60,946	+14.0%	71,605	-3.0%	191,359	187,728	+1.9%
MAIN STATION TELEPHONE CONNECTIONS								
Residential	80,565	80,309	—	80,445	—	80,353	80,340	—
Commercial	31,769	31,592	—	29,190	+8.8%	31,571	29,025	+8.8%

*1980 = 100
** Year-to-date figures are cumulative
—Less than 1% change
+TEC revised figures
1/84

(The ECONOMIC ACTIVITY INDEX is a composite of four values indicative of current business activity. These forces are weighted and averaged to form an Index number based on the year 1980.)

(Compiled by the Economic Research Department, Corpus Christi Chamber of Commerce)

The city has varied employment and numerous financial institutions, including 19 banks with deposits of more than 1.6 billion dollars and 9 savings and loans with deposits in excess of 612 million dollars. Access in and out of the city is provided by air, bus, rail, motor freight, water, and highways running to or through the city, which include U.S. Highways 77, 181 and IH-37. Steamship agencies representing dry cargo carriers and bulk cargo carriers provide daily service in and out of Corpus Christi for a number of industrial interests in the city. The Port of Corpus Christi is the deepest port on the Gulf of Mexico; it is currently authorized to a depth of 45 feet.

Publications in the Corpus Christi area include one morning newspaper, one evening newspaper, and four weekly papers. There are 17 radio stations in the central business area and 6 major television stations. Utilities are provided to the City of Corpus Christi by Central Power and Light Company. Water is distributed by the city from Lake Corpus Christi at Mathis, approximately 30 miles north. Natural gas is provided to the city by the City Natural Gas Service.

Excellent academic opportunities are available from several resident and extension programs, including Del Mar College, Corpus Christi State University, Texas A&M University Marine Science Institute, and Howard Penn University at Corpus Christi.

The basic industries in the surrounding area include agriculture, fishing, manufacturing, the U.S. Naval Air Station, Corpus Christi Army Depot, oil, port traffic, ranching, and tourism. Principal manufacturing products in the Corpus Christi metropolitan area include petroleum refining products, primary metals, stone, clay, and glass products, including chemicals and allied products. Electronic components and metal fabrication have been a recent addition to the manufacturing output of the city. Due to the recent decline in oil and related energy exploration, activity in the heavy manufacturing industries has declined markedly. This has resulted in an increase in unemployment in these specific fields. The decline is expected to be of a temporary nature. However, the diversfied economic base of Corpus Christi is not easily affected by a single industry.

Corpus Christi has long been known as the recreation-entertainment center for South Texas. The city offers six golf courses and a public auditorium and coliseum with 6,000 seats. There are over 170 parks within the city, featuring picnic facilities, fishing piers, swimming pools, bike trails, and playgrounds. All of these are offered in addition to the excellent year-round weather, with a mean temperature of 71.2° Fahrenheit.

In the 1983 U.S. News and World Report Review of Growing Cities, Corpus Christi is identified as one of the primary growth communities of under 500,000 people. The ample natural resources and labor supply indicate that Corpus Christi will continue to be a growth city during the 1980s.

NEIGHBORHOOD ANALYSIS

The Sandcastle II Apartments are located in a mixed-use neighborhood in the southeasterly portion of the City of Corpus Christi. In the immediate area of the Sandcastle II Apartments there are good-quality single-family residences, apartment buildings similar in quality and amenities to the Sandcastle II Apartments, and a condominium/garden home development. There are also a variety of commercial and retail shopping developments, including a large H.E.B. grocery store and a mixed-use suburban community shopping center.

The Sandcastle II Apartment site is bound on the east by the Sandcastle I Apartments, on the north by a residential development, on the west by a drainage right-of-way, and on the south by Everhart Road, a paved, publicly maintained major thoroughfare. Directly across the street to the east of the subject is a high-quality condominium/garden home complex which is over 70% sold to individual purchasers. The intersection of Everhart and Saratoga Roads is one and one-half blocks north of the subject property. Both of these roads are major, high-volume traffic arteries. The apartment site has direct access from Everhart Road on the southern boundary across a drainage right-of-way. Everhart Road provides excellent access in and out of the subject site.

One block south of the subject is a 300-unit apartment complex under construction by Ryan Construction Company. This company has a proven history of quality developments and will no doubt provide direct competition for the subject complex. The new complex is scheduled to start renting in November 1984.

All the improvements in the neighborhood of the Sandcastle II Apartments are of good-quality construction. The neighborhood is among the fastest growing and one of the most desirable, prestigious areas of Corpus Christi.

See Chapter 7 for additional discussion of neighborhood analysis.

ZONING AND DEVELOPMENT REGULATIONS

The Sandcastle II Apartment complex is zoned by the City of Corpus Christi as "A-2," or apartment house. The specific limitations under this zoning are noted in the Apartment House District Regulations on page 549 of this report.

The access agreement pertaining to the subject site stipulated that the access to this tract be from Everhart Road across a drainage right-of-way. It further stipulated that the culvert necessary to allow crossing the right-of-way be constructed at the expense of the landowner and at no cost to the City of Corpus Christi in accordance with plans and specifications approved by the City Engineering Department. The terms of this agreement were met prior to the issuance of the building permit for the construction of the subject property improvements. A copy of this original agreement is included on the plat shown on page 24 of this report.

The subject improvements have been built in accordance with the uses defined under the Corpus Christi zoning and applicable development regulations.

HIGHEST AND BEST USE

The economic principal of highest and best use is that use at the time of the appraisal which is most likely to produce the greatest net return to the land and buildings over a given period of time. It is that use that will maximize the owner's wealth by being one of the most profitable uses.

The subject improvements have been constructed to conform with the guidelines outlined by the City of Corpus Christi zoning regulations. The improvements are new and exhibit no deferred maintenance or functional obsolescence. A slight amount of external (economic) obsolescence is indicated due to the temporary oversupply and underdemand for apartment units in this area. The site is located in a

rapidly growing section of Corpus Christi. Improvements,
including residential and commercial development in the
neighborhood, are being constructed at a rapid rate and
compare favorably with the subject property. Access to the
apartment project from all parts of the city is good. The
units are well designed and have excellent appeal.

In our opinion, the use of the subject site as an
apartment complex reflects a use that develops the land to
its fullest potential and highest market value. Even though
the improvements suffer a small amount of obsolescence,
there is still sufficient entrepreneurial profit, in our
opinion, to warrant a typical apartment developer to
construct the improvements. For this reason we believe the
improvements represent a reasonable and proper use of the
site.

After reading the "Highest and Best Use" section in Chapter 3, would you have
changed this section of the appraisal report? Explain.

FEASIBILITY/MARKETING AND ABSORPTION

The Sandcastle II Apartment complex is located in a rapidly
developing area of Corpus Christi which has a large variety
of residential improvements. These vary from 20-year-old
apartment complexes to $250,000 custom homes under
construction. We have conducted a survey of the most
similar apartment complexes marketed in the past 12 months
considered to be in competition with Sandcastle II. Table
II-2 illustrates the current occupancy and absorption of
these rental units.

The analysis of all the complexes which have been
completed in the past twelve months illustrates that better
quality complexes in good locations have no difficulty
obtaining high stabilized occupancy rates in a reasonable
period of time. The marketing strategy of these complexes
has ranged from rental rebates of two weeks to one month,
free plane tickets to a U.S. destination, or a discounted
ski vacation. None of these better quality complexes have
waived the security deposit requirements.

This survey reveals that there is a strong demand for
apartments in Corpus Christi. Although at least 800 new
units are currently under construction in Corpus Christi,
the demand remains strong. Absorption has been steady and
the demand appears to remain high in the foreseeable
future. In our opinion, the Sandcastle II Apartment complex

Table II-2   OCCUPANCY AND ABSORPTION CHART

Property/Address	Total Units	Occu-pancy Rate	No. Units Occu-pied	No. Mos. on Market	No. Units Leased/ Month
Chandler's Mill 6350 Meadow Vista	248	92%	228	8	28.5
Sugar Tree 8050 S. Padre Island	250	96%	240	8	30.0
The Rafters 11325 IH-37	250	52%	131	2	65.5
Sandcastle II 6717 Everhart	216	82%	177	6	29.5

is feasible and will be readily absorbed in a reasonable period of time provided that competitive marketing techniques are utilized.

A discussion of marketing techniques, occupancy, and absorption levels for competitive properties should be a part of any income property appraisal assignment.

The current occupancy rate for the subject is 82% and occupancy has risen steadily since initial marketing of the units for rent. Sandcastle Phase I, adjacent to the subject, is currently 98% occupied. Phase I has been rented utilizing the same techniques as the subject property. This is by offering one month's free rent for a six-month lease. For this reason, we anticipate Sandcastle II to be fully leased by the end of year 1 and to have achieved a stabilized occupancy of approximately 92%. Because of the large number of apartment units coming on the market, we believe that higher than a 92% average occupancy would not be forecasted by a typical investor. The allocation for the loss of income due to free rent and the temporary vacancy rate has been calculated and is shown on page 518 of this report. This loss in value has been deducted from each value indication as external (economic) obsolescence. As the existing leases are short term and at the prevailing market rental rates, there is no rent advantage to either the lessor or the lessees.

DISCUSSION OF THE NET RENT LOSS

The subject property is currently 82% occupied (177 units out of 216 units) and has been averaging a rent-up of approximately 29 units per month for the past six months. We believe this rate of absorption will decrease slightly as more apartments come on the market for rent. The rentals during the past two months have been a little slower than the previous four months even though two months' "free" rent is given on a twelve-month lease. There are 22 apartments left to rent to achieve a 92% stabilized average occupancy of approximately 199 units. However, these units should rent over the next two months. We also anticipate some of the tenants moving, as their leases terminate, because of the "free" rent offered by competing complexes. On the rollover of the leases, it is not anticipated that "free" rent will be granted. It is estimated that approximately 27% of the stabilized net operating income (NOI), which is estimated to be $697,643, will be lost in the first year, a total of $188,364. The NOI is discussed in the income approach section of this report.

LEGAL DESCRIPTION

The subject is legally described as:

> Lot 1, Block 1, County Club Estates Unit 22, Nueces County, Corpus Christi, Texas.

TAXES

Tax information for the subject property has been obtained from the Nueces County Appraisal District. The 1983 assessed value of the land was $378,536. The improvements have not been recorded on the tax roll as of June 1984. An estimate of annual assessed value and taxes has been made based on the assessed value of the Sandcastle I complex located adjacent to the subject property. Both projects are virtually identical in construction, and it is assumed the Appraisal District will be consistent. The total assessed value for Sandcastle I was $3,200,955. The effective tax rate for 1983 was $1.4758 per $100 assessed value. No major tax increases are forecast by the various taxing authorities for 1984. Because Sandcastle II is new, the Appraisal District will probably not estimate any accrued depreciation. The existence of external (economic) obsolescence for a short time period has not been recognized by the taxing agencies as a general rule. After consultation with the tax appraisers, it is believed that an estimate of $23.89 per square foot for 146,506 square feet of building area (see Table II-3) or $3,500,000 is a reasonable estimate of the value for tax purposes. Based on an effective tax ratio of $1.4758 per $100 assessed value, the taxes would be $51,653.

The Nueces County tax assessor has just completed a new assessment of all properties. Under state law all properties are to be taxed at 100% of market value. If the subject were taxed at full market value of $7,200,000 at the current tax rate of $1.4758 per $100.00 of assessed value, the maximum legal taxes would be $106,258 or $0.74 per square foot of building area per year for 146,506 square feet. Although these taxes are not being charged to the ownership of the property at this time (and are not predicted to be in the foreseeable future), a prudent investor would recognize the potential tax burden under the maximum legal tax rate.

Table II-3   SUMMARY OF BUILDING AREAS

Net Rentable Area-Apartments:

48 efficiency units	at	485 SF	23,280 SF
48 1BR/1BA	at	603 SF	28,944 SF
48 1BR/1BA	at	676 SF	32,448 SF
40 1BR/1BA and den	at	726 SF	29,040 SF
32 2BR/2BA	at	917 SF	29,344 SF
216 units with average size of		662 SF	143,056 SF
Office, laundry, and clubhouse areas:			2,500 SF
Storage and mechanical rooms			950 SF
Total gross improvement area:			146,506 SF

Building dimensions and area provided by the owner and developer, Callaway Properties.

Somewhere near here, the appraiser needs to discuss briefly the history of the property, including such items as dates when additions and alterations to the building(s) occurred. It is recommended that a five-year history of prior sales of the appraised property be fully discussed.

DESCRIPTION OF THE IMPROVEMENTS

The Sandcastle II Apartment complex contains 216 units. The complex is located on the northwestern side of Everhart Road, south of Saratoga Road. The development was constructed during 1983 and began renting in January 1984. The current occupancy as of June 1, 1984, is approximately 82%. The entire development is attractively landscaped and maintenance is excellent. The complex features an all adult environment complete with a centrally located swimming pool, clubhouse, laundry facilities, and on-site management. It is conveniently located in a neighborhood composed of condominiums, single-family housing, and other apartment complexes.

Exterior Improvements Description

The Sandcastle II Apartments are constructed of brick veneer and cedar siding. All exterior roofing is composition shingle and all exterior wood siding has been painted or stained. An individual central heating and cooling system is located outside each apartment. The heat pumps have been atttractively landscaped to camouflage their location. The exterior of each apartment building is landscaped with shrubbery, but there is no automatic lawn sprinkler system. The complex has exterior lighting at each unit to provide security and convenience at night.

It may be easier for clients and reviewers to determine the physical features of the building(s) by using the following format:

> INTERIOR WALLS: textured sheetrock walls; grass-cloth wallpaper in
>   dining room; kitchen and bathroom wallpapered.

This format begins with the foundation and proceeds through the exterior and interior walls, roof covering, insulation, and electric service.

Interior Improvements Description

Of the 216 total apartments units, 48 are efficiency units, 48 are small one-bedroom units, 48 are large one-bedroom units, 40 are one-bedroom units with a separate den area, and 32 units have two bedrooms and two baths. A total of 20 of the large one-bedroom, one-bath units and 16 of the two-bedroom, two-bath units have washers and dryers available.

The units with washers and dryers do not have fireplaces.
However market acceptance is currently indicating a
preference for the washer and dryer units over the units
with fireplaces, even though they rent for the same amount.
The construction includes good-quality wall-to-wall
carpeting, textured sheetrock walls, sprayed acoustical
ceilings, single-pane metal-frame windows, and sliding glass
doors. Each unit contains a General Electric range and
frost-free refrigerator and range fan hood. There is a
bathroom ceiling fan vented to the exterior of the unit.
Each apartment has Formica cabinet tops and double stainless
steel sinks. The circuit breaker box for each unit is
located in the kitchen. The fireplaces are metal interior
fixtures with decorative Saltillo tile around the exterior
frame. Each unit has grass-cloth wallpaper in the dining
area, and the kitchen and bathroom are attractively
wallpapered with a wide variety of colors and designs
offered.

The walls are sheetrock with attractive wallpaper, the
Each unit also has a private covered patio and a dead-
bolt lock on the front, exterior door. The apartments are
separately metered for electricity. Water is furnished with
the rental payment, and hot water is provided from the
central boiler room. The units have lined fiberglass
draperies on all windows with mounted traverse rods and
vinyl shades. Overall finish and maintenance is excellent.
Although all 216 units were not inspected, several of each
kind and size were inspected and all improvements were noted
to be in excellent condition. The overall finish of all
interior areas was good and there were no items of deferred
maintenance observed.

The game/party room facility, located adjacent to the
management office, has good-quality wall-to-wall carpeting,
textured sheetrock walls, and sprayed acoustical ceilings
with wallpapered walls in accent areas. The party room
offers vaulted ceilings and a sunken conversation area for
various uses. A fully equipped kitchen is provided in the
party room. The manager's office adjoins the party room and
includes a commode, wall lavatory, and a wet bar with
mirrored shelving.

The laundry rooms provided in the complex contain four
commercial dryers and eight washers. There is a large table
for clothes sorting, and seating is provided for occupants
while laundering. A multipurpose sink is also provided.
The walls are sheetrock with attractive wallpaper, the
ceiling is sprayed acoustical, and the floor is vinyl tile.

Amenities provided in the Sandcastle II Apartment complex include two tennis courts enclosed by a chain link fence, and a large swimming pool with a fountain. The fountain not only provides aeration for pool water, but also provides an attractive setting for the courtyard surrounding the swimming pool. There is a cold-water Jacuzzi leading into the pool area. The pool has a maximum depth of four feet. The area is attractively landscaped with exposed aggregate concrete surrounding the pool and extensive use of shrubbery and flowerbeds for aesthetic appeal. The Sandcastle II Apartment complex provides excellent-quality adult living with many of the major amenities required by the apartment shopper in today's market.

VALUATION PROCEDURES

The cost, market data, and income approaches were all employed in the estimation of the market value of the Sandcastle Apartment complex. In the cost approach to value we have estimated the current cost of labor and materials to construct the improvements new today. After depreciation has been estimated, the value of the site, as if vacant, has been added to the depreciated replacement cost new of the improvements.

Replacement cost new has been utilized in lieu of reproduction cost new; however, our estimate of cost new checks very closely with the historical cost indexed for the time since construction. Replacement cost is the cost of constructing a building, at current prices, having utility equivalent to the subject building, but built with the most modern materials in accordance with current standards, design, and layout. Reproduction cost new is the cost of constructing at current prices an exact duplicate or replica building using the same materials, construction standards, design, layout, and quality workmanship. Because there was no functional obsolescence due to super adequate construction, there was no particular advantage to using replacement cost new versus reproduction cost new, and either would result in the same value conclusions.

In the market data approach we have analyzed transfers of similar apartment building properties located in the City of Corpus Christi. Although many transfers were analyzed, only the most persuasive and recent have been included in this report. Other apartment building sales are available in our file.

In the income approach we have analyzed the apartment rental market, vacancy factors, and operating expenses. The net operating income has been capitalized to produce an indication of capital value by direct capitalization. This particular technique is an economic unit of comparison which is actually more appropriate for use in the market data approach.

Appraisers have utilized cash on cash returns as capitalization rates for either equity or for the entire property as standard tools in income-producing property valuation for many years. Capitalization rates (cash flow rates), as utilized in this report, are the ratio between the next 12 months forecasted net operating income at the prevailing market rate and the sales price or value. Technically, the cash flow cap rate (known as an overall rate for the property (R_o) and equity dividend rate (R_e) for equity) is the investor's desired yield rate minus the change rate adjusted annually for either the property or equity. In practice, the cap rate is derived from market verified comparable sales information. Market-derived cap rates take into account the investors' perceived risk associated with ownership of the property and the investors' anticipated gain or loss upon resale of the property.

Criticize the statement on this page, "Technically, the cash flow rate . . . is the investor's desired yield rate minus the change rate adjusted annually for either the property or equity" (see Chapter 16).

The approaches used, and their net results, have been reconciled into a final indication of value. The valuation procedures, together with the final reconciliation of market value, are discussed in the following sections of this report.

See Chapters 8 and 9 for an explanation of site analysis and valuation considerations.

VALUATION OF THE SANDCASTLE II APARTMENT BUILDING SITE

To assist in estimating the market value of the subject site as if vacant, we have made an investigation to find recent comparable sales which can be compared to the appraised site on the basis of time, location, and physical characteristics.

The subject property has excellent accessibility to major traffic arteries and freeways. Major traffic corridors surrounding the subject site include Everhart Road to the east and Staples Road to the south. The excellent accessibility of the subject site is considered to be one of the primary factors affecting the site value. A plat of the subject site is included on the following page of this report. A summary of the comparable land sales, Table II-4, follows with a discussion of the comparable land sales and a market data map showing the location of the sales. Detailed information on each sale is shown on pages 522 through 535.

The six sales selected for comparison with the subject site are all recent transactions of properties which have been used to develop apartments or townhouses, or purchased with the intent to be used for this purpose. All of the comparable sales utilized in this report reflect cash to the seller. When terms of the transaction are not cash or the equivalent, the sales have been either disregarded or adjusted for "cash equivalency."

It is helpful to a reader to include the adjusted sales price for each comparable sale. Some appraisers use an adjustment grid to reveal the individual adjustments.

Comparable Sale 1 is the June 1984 pending contract of a 5.22-acre tract located on the east side of South Padre Island Drive. The site is zoned B-1 which will permit apartment construction. The purchaser plans to build a retail center on the site. The site is considered to be superior to the subject in location and potential for development and an adjustment downward is indicated when comparing this sale with the subject. This sale tends to indicate the value of the subject site to be $2.60 per square foot of land area.

Comparable Sale 2 is adjacent to comparable sale 1. This tract sold in April 1984 for $3.75 per square foot. The site has frontage on Oso Bay and South Padre Island Drive. The purchaser plans to build a 260-unit apartment complex on the site. This parcel is superior to the subject in

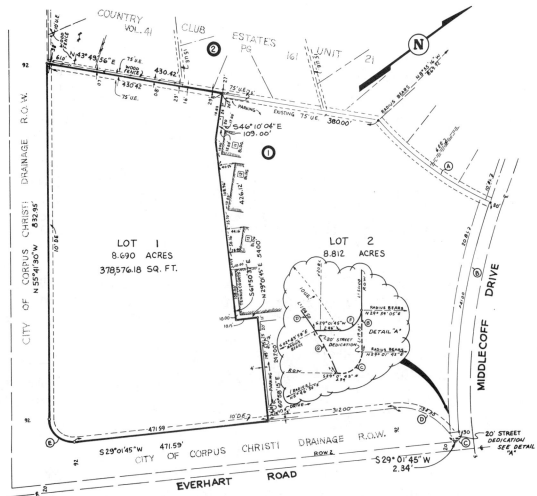

COUNTRY VOL. 41 CLUB ESTATES PG 161 UNIT 21

CITY OF CORPUS CHRISTI DRAINAGE R.O.W.

N 43° 49′ 56″ E   75′ U.E.   430.42

WOOD FENCE

N 55° 41′ 30″ W   832.95′

S 46° 10′ 04″ E   109.00′

EXISTING 75′ U.E.   380.00

RADIUS BEARS N 8 55° 16″ W

LOT 1
8.690 ACRES
378,576.18 SQ. FT.

LOT 2
8.812 ACRES

DETAIL "A"
RADIUS BEARS N 29° 54′ 05″ E
RADIUS BEARS N 29° 01′ 45″ E

S 29° 01′ 45″ W   471.59′
CITY OF CORPUS CHRISTI DRAINAGE R.O.W.

S 29° 01′ 45″ W   2.34′

MIDDLECOFF DRIVE

EVERHART ROAD

GENERAL NOTES
1. 5/8" IRON RODS AT ALL LOT CORNERS
2. TOTAL AREA PLATTED EQUALS 8.690 ACRES
3. ACCESS TO EVERHART FROM LOT 1 WILL BE
   BY BRIDGE (CULVERT CROSSING)

THIS IS TO CERTIFY THAT WE HAVE CONSULTED
THE FLOOD INSURANCE FLOOD HAZARD MAPS AND
FOUND THAT THE PROPERTY DESCRIBED HEREIN IS
NOT LOCATED IN A SPECIAL FLOOD HAZARD AREA.

CURVE INFORMATION

A	B	C	D	E
Δ = 22°39′39″	Δ = 27°01′13″	Δ = 90°00′00″	Δ = 66°40′45″	Δ = 95°16′45″
R = 869.92′	R = 1189.42′	R = 10.00′	R = 152.00′	R = 54.00′
T = 174.31′	T = 285.78′	T = 10.00′	T = 100.12′	T = 59.22′
L = 344.06′	L = 560.93′	L = 15.71′	L = 177.07′	L = 89.80′

F	G
Δ = 89°02′40″	Δ = 8°30′28″
R = 10.00′	R = 152.00′
T = 9.84′	T = 11.31′
L = 15.54′	L = 22.57′ *NOTE Culvert not built as of 3-23-83

100   0   100   200
SCALE IN FEET

WE, URBAN ENGINEERING, HAVE MADE A SURVEY ON THE GROUND
OF THE FOREGOING PROPERTY AND WE HEREBY CERTIFY THAT THIS
MAP AND THE ACCOMPANYING FIELDNOTES ARE TRUE AND CORRECT
ACCORDING TO OUR FINDINGS, AND THAT THERE ARE NO ENCROACHMENTS.

BY: _George M. Pyle_

STATE OF TEXAS
GEORGE M. PYLE
1258
REGISTERED PUBLIC SURVEYOR

Table II-4   SUMMARY OF COMPARABLE LAND SALES

Sale No.	Date of Sale	Location	Zoning	Size Acres/SF	Price per SF
1	06/84	NEC SPID and Southbay	B-4	5.22 AC 227,383 SF	$3.96
2	04/13/84	NS SPID-West of Oso Bay	B-4	5.0 AC 217,800 SF	$3.75
3	12/15/85	1/4 Mile south of Saratoga on Staples	A-2	12.54 AC 546,242 SF	$2.50
4*	09/06/83	NS Saratoga-between Staples and Airline	R-2	9.10 AC 396,396 SF	$1.40
5**	01/30/83	SS Everhart-south of Sandcastle Apts.	A-1	12.38 AC 539,273 SF	$1.70
6***	03/01/83	SPID at Cayo del Oso	A-1	11.33 AC 493,534 SF	$1.96
Subject	03/01/83	6717 Everhard	A-2	8.69 AC 368,576 SF	

*   Mixed zoning containing R-2, Industrial and Commercial.
**   Adjusted for cash equivalency for purposes of analysis to $1.60 per square foot.
*** Adjusted for cash equivalency for purposes of analysis to $1.91 per square foot. This is calculated on the basis of the usable area of 493,534 square feet.

location and an adjustment downward is indicated when comparing this site with the subject. This sale tends to indicate the value of the subject site to be $2.45 per square foot of land area.

Comparable Sale 3 sold on December 15, 1983. It is a parcel containing two 6.27-acre tracts for a total of 12.54 acres. An interview with the realtor involved in the transfer of the property indicated that the property had been under contract for approximately four months. The approximate sales price was $2.50 per square foot. The sale property is

located one-fourth mile south of the intersection of
Saratoga on Staples Drive, about one-quarter mile east of
the subject property. The site is considered to be very
comparable to the subject property on the basis of zoning,
location, access, and highest and best use. This sale tends
to indicate the value of the subject site to be $2.50 per
square foot of land area. There has been very little change
in land prices since the date of this sale.

Comparable Sale 4 is the September 1983 sale of a 9.1-acre
tract which was a portion of a 38-acre parcel. The property
is located on the north side of Saratoga Boulevard between
Staples and Airline Drive. The 9.1-acre tract had an
allocated value of $1.40 per square foot as noted in the
deed records. This property is comparably located to the
subject property. The sale property's zoning is considered
inferior to the subject property due to the fact that it
requires a lower density of apartment dwellings per acre.
An upward adjustment is indicated for zoning. The size of
the two properties is similar. A slight upward adjustment
is considered to be necessary for the increase in land
prices since the date of the sale and an upward adjustment
is also necessary, in our opinion, because this property was
a part of a larger 38-acre transfer. This sale tends to
indicate the value of the subject site to be in the range of
$2.45 to $2.55 per square foot of land area.

Comparable Sale 5 is the January 1983 sale of a 12.38-acre
tract zoned A-1 (Apartment-1). This tract is inferior to
the subject because the zoning requires a lower density of
apartments per acre than the subject. The sale occurred
approximately 18 months ago and an adjustment upward is
indicated for the general increase in land value since the
date of sale and for the interior zoning. This sale tends
to indicate the value of the subject property to be $2.30
per square foot of land area.

Comparable Sale 6 is a March 1983 sale of an 11.33-acre
tract located on South Padre Island Drive at Cayo Del Oso.
The tract is zoned B-4 and would allow commercial as well as
apartment development. The site has a view of and frontage
on Oso Bay. It has been improved since the sale with a 250-
unit apartment complex scheduled to open in approximately
one month. The location is considered to be slightly
superior to the subject. The site is larger than the
subject and larger tracts tend to sell for a lower per unit

value than smaller tracts; thus an upward adjustment is
indicated for the smaller size of the subject and for the
increase in land value since the date of this sale,
approximately 15 months ago.

Conclusion of Land Value:

The comparable sales have a range in prices per square foot
from $1.40 to $3.96, or $2.56. The most recent sale, which
is also the most comparable to the subject property, is Sale
No. 1, which is located immediately east of the subject
property. The other five sales closely support the value of
the subject site indicated by Sale No. 1 after adjustments.
Each of the comparable sales is considered similar to the
subject property on the basis of highest and best use and
ultimate development.
        Based on the sales analyzed, and after making
appropriate adjustments for condition of sale, time,
location, and physical characteristics, the indicated value
of the subject 8.690 acres is estimated to be $2.50 per
square foot, which when multiplied times 378,576 square feet
and rounded, is $946,500.

It generally is advisable to place detailed sales, lease, and construction cost data
in an appendix. The client can study these detailed sections after considering the
summary data in the body of the report.

SALE 1

TYPE OF PROPERTY:
        Vacant Land   SE 278-G   AA01562GSMS

LOCATION:
        Nueces County; NE corner So Padre Island Drive and
        Southbay Dr, Corpus Christie, TX   278G1

GRANTOR:
        Ralph Cook, Pedro Enis

GRANTEE:
        Frank Peerman

TYPE OF INSTRUMENT:
    Under Contract   Status: Sale   Date: 06/00/84
    Volume: Page:

LAND SIZE:
    5.22 acres   227,383 square feet

LEGAL DESCRIPTION:
    Lot 2, Block A, Southbay Annex, Corpus Christi, Nueces
    County, TX

CONSIDERATION AND TERMS:
    $ 3.96 per square foot   Total price: $900,437
                                            GSMS

LAND DESCRIPTION:
    Level tract with frontage on N side of So Padre Island
    Drive zoned B-4

IMPROVEMENTS:
    None

COMMENTS:
    This property is under contract to close. Buyer
    intends to develop the property with a retail center.

SALE 2

TYPE OF PROPERTY:
    Vacant Land   SE 278-G   AA01563GSMS

LOCATION:
    Nueces County; N side So Padre Island Drive, W of Oso
    Bay, Corpus Christi, TX   278G1

GRANTOR:
    William Bonilla

GRANTEE:
    Jackson S. Ryan

TYPE OF INSTRUMENT:
    Warranty Deed Vendors Lien
    Status: Sale   Date: 04/13/84
    Volume: 1913D   Page: 0797

LAND SIZE:
    5.00 acres   217,800 square feet

LEGAL DESCRIPTION:
    Lot 3, Block A, Southbay Annex, Corpus Christi, Nueces
    County, TX

CONSIDERATION AND TERMS:
    $3.75 per square foot   Total price: $816,750
    PN $625,000 @ 12% interest, 10 yr   GSMS

LAND DESCRIPTION:
    Level tract with 432' frontage on N side of So Padre
    Island Drive, bound on N and W sides by Oso Bay; 450'
    deep; zoned B-4

IMPROVEMENTS:
    None

COMMENTS:
    No adjustment is considered to be necessary for cash
    equivalency as the price was not affected by the terms
    of the financing. The buyer intends to construct a
    260-unit garden apartment complex on the site.

                          SALE 3

TYPE OF PROPERTY:
    Vacant Land   SE 278-G   AA00505/

LOCATION:
    Nueces County; 1/4 mile S of Saratoga on Staples,
    Corpus Christie, TX   278G1

GRANTOR:
    Crow Western

GRANTEE:
Joe & Leon Lowe, J Robert & J William House, C House Herman

TYPE OF INSTRUMENT:
Warranty Deed   Status: Sale   Date: 12/15/83
Volume: 1900   Page: 244 +

LAND SIZE:
12.54 acres   546,242 square feet

LEGAL DESCRIPTION:
Flour Bluff and Encinal Farm and Garden Tract #1,
Section 6, Corpus Christi, Nueces County, TX

CONSIDERATION AND TERMS:
$2.50 per square foot   Total price: $1,365,605
Cash-under contract for 4 mos prior to sale

LAND DESCRIPTION:
Level, rectangular tract, no fill required

IMPROVEMENTS:
None

COMMENTS:
Zoned A-2; excellent neighborhood for better quality
apts or garden/condo development.
Also, in Vol. 1900, Pgs. 245-250

SALE 4

TYPE OF PROPERTY:
Vacant Land   SE 278-G   AA00506/

LOCATION:
Nueces County; N side Saratoga Blvd between Staples
and Airline, Corpus Christi, TX   278G1

GRANTOR:
R J Fellows - B R Willford

GRANTEE:
  Smith Tract Assoc (Heuyl, Tucker, Fellows, Olso & Co)

TYPE OF INSTRUMENT:
  Warranty Deed   Status: Sale   Date 09/06/83
  Volume: 1886   Page: 678

LAND SIZE:
  9.10 acres   396,396 square feet

LEGAL DESCRIPTION:
  9.1 AC out of 38-AC parcel, Lot 25, 26, 27, 28, Sec
  12, W 1/2 Lot 30, Lot 31, and 32, Sec 19, Flour Bluff
  and Encinal Farm and Garden Tracts, Corpus Christi,
  Nueces County, TX

CONSIDERATION AND TERMS:
  $1.40 per square foot   Total price: $4,200,000
  Texas Commerce Bank (note in deed) for entire tract
  $554,954

LAND DESCRIPTION:
  Several zonings in overall tract, residential "R-2";
  industrial and commercial. Land is level and is
  located in a rapidly developing area.

IMPROVEMENTS:
  None at time of sale

COMMENTS:
  The tract is zoned for mixed use development. The
  sellers were dissolving their partnership at the time
  of sale. However, this did not influence the sales
  price, in our opinion, to a measurable degree.

  This is a 9.10-acre portion of a 38-acre parcel which
  sold for $4,200,000. The 9.10-acre tract was
  allocated to contribute $1.40 per square foot or
  $554,954. No adjustment is considered necessary for
  cash equivalency as there was third-party financing.

SALE 5

TYPE OF PROPERTY:
  Vacant Land   SE 278-G   AA01610MS

LOCATION:
>   Nueces County; W side Everhart 200 yards S of
>   Sandcastle Apartments, Corpus Christi,
>   TX   278G1

GRANTOR:
>   Roger J Seaman, Jr

GRANTEE:
>   Holly Road, Ltd

TYPE OF INSTRUMENT:
>   Warranty Deed   Status: Sale   Date: 01/30/83
>   Volume: 1865D   Page: 791

LAND SIZE:
>   12.38 acres   539,273 square feet

LEGAL DESCRIPTION:
>   Lot 2 & 5, Section 11, Bohemian Colony, Corpus
>   Christi, Nueces County, TX

CONSIDERATION AND TERMS:
> $1.70 per square foot   Total price: $916,764
>   100% loan; 10.5% int, 30 yr, 12-yr balloon   MS

LAND DESCRIPTION:
>   Vacant, level tract on a major traffic artery. All
>   utilities are available at the site and drainage is
>   adequate. The soil and subsoil conditions are
>   suitable for apartment development.

IMPROVEMENTS:
>   None

COMMENTS:
>   Site of proposed 250-unit apartment complex to be
>   known as Holly Square Apartments. Our investigation
>   indicates that an adjustment for cash equivalency is
>   necessary for the terms of the transaction. If the
>   note was adjusted for the full term of 12 years using
>   a market desired yield rate of 12%, the indicated
>   adjustment is $0.15 per square foot. We believe this
>   adjustment is too severe, as both parties anticipated
>   that the note would not run the full term and

therefore did not affect the price paid by this amount. An adjustment of $0.10 per square foot is believed to be more indicative of the market for this property. The adjusted sales price is $1.60 per square foot.

SALE 6

TYPE OF PROPERTY:
Vacant Land   SE 278-G   AA01611MS

LOCATION:
Nueces County; So Padre Island Dr at Cayo del Oso, Corpus Christi, TX   278G1

GRANTOR:
Cayo del Oso Estate, Ltd

GRANTEE:
Wharf, Ltd

TYPE OF INSTRUMENT:
Warranty Deed   Status: Sale   Date: 03/01/83
Volume: 1869   Page: 984

LAND SIZE:
11.33 acres   754,894 square feet

LEGAL DESCRIPTION:
Lot 1B, Block 1, Newport Marina Estates, Corpus Christi, Nueces County, TX

CONSIDERATION AND TERMS:
$1.96 per square foot   Total price: $967,000
100% loan; 10.5% interest, 30 yr, 10-yr balloon;
$1.96/SF of usable area (493,534 SF)   MS

LAND DESCRIPTION:
5.0 acres are low and are not usable. The site has frontage on Cayo del Oso bay as well as So Padre Island Drive.

IMPROVEMENTS:
None at time of sale

COMMENTS:

Site of a 250-unit apartment complex known as Wharf
Apartments. Our investigation indicates that a small
adjustment for cash equivalency is necessary for the
terms of the transaction. If the note was adjusted
for the full term of 10 years using a market desired
yield rate of 12%, the indicated adjustment is $0.17
per square foot. We believe this adjustment is too
severe, as at the time of the sale there was a good
probability that the note would be paid off prior to
10 years. An adjustment of $0.05 per square foot is
believed to be more indicative of the market for this
property. The adjusted sales price is $1.91 per
square foot based on a usable area of 493,534 square
feet. Zoned A-1.

VALUE INDICATED BY THE COST APPROACH

The first step in the cost approach is to estimate the
reproduction or replacement cost new of the structures
(RCN). The replacement cost new has been estimated for the
Sandcastle II Apartment complex using the Marshall Swift
Cost Service and actual construction costs of similar
projects in the Corpus Christi area. The conclusions are
also supported by the actual construction costs of the
subject property. However, we were not furnished with a
cost breakdown.

The estimated direct costs of the Sandcastle II
Apartment complex are $5,029,950. Indirect costs are added
to this and are estimated to be approximately $1,475,787.
Total estimated replacement cost new is $6,505,737, or
$45.48 per square foot of net rentable area for 143,056
square feet.

The next step in the cost approach is to estimate the
accrued depreciation of the subject property improvements.
Depreciation is defined as a loss in the value of the
improvements (i.e., a deduction from the RCN of the
improvements) from any cause. Depreciation can be
classified into three categories: physical deterioration,
functional obsolescence, and external (economic)
obsolescence. The apartment complex is approximately six
months old and is in excellent condition. This condition
reflects no observed deferred maintenance or significant
physical deterioration.

COMPARABLE LAND SALES

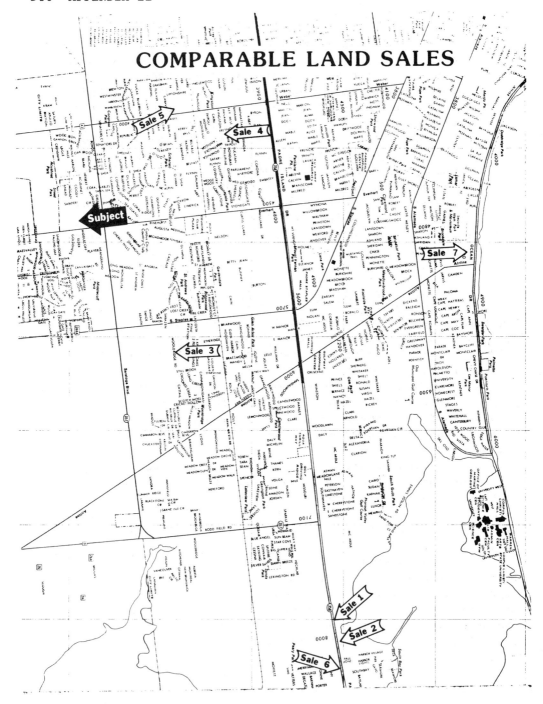

Clients are better able to understand the analysis and conclusions if brief and clear definitions of specialized terms such as "functional obsolescence" are included.

The complex suffers from no functional obsolescence in our opinion. The improvements are well designed and logically situated on the site. The loss of income during the initial lease up period is a form of external obsolescence as it is the result of factors outside the property. This loss in income has been deducted as an undiscounted lump-sum figure. Stabilized occupancy is expected to be reached during the first year of operation and in our opinion, a typical buyer would not discount the rent loss. The resulting depreciated replacement cost new of the improvements is $6,317,373.

The land value has been estimated to be $2.50 per square foot of land area for 378,576 square feet or when rounded, $946,500. When added to the depreciated cost new of the improvements, the indicated market value by the cost approach is $7,264,000. A summary of the calculations of the cost approach follows as Table II-5 of this report.

According to the advantages and disadvantages listed for the depreciated cost approach in Chapter 12, is this valuation approach appropriate for this appraisal assignment?

Table II-5   SUMMARY OF THE COST APPROACH

ESTIMATED REPLACEMENT COST NEW

DIRECT COSTS:	AREA	UNIT COST	TOTAL
Apartment Area	143,056 SF	$34.41	$4,922,557
Office, Laundry, & Clubhouse	2,500 SF	$20.80	52,000
Storage & Mechanical Area	950 SF	$13.33	12,664
Pool & Patio			15,000
Landscaping			18,929
Tennis Court & Fences			8,800
TOTAL DIRECT COSTS			$5,029,950

INDIRECT COSTS:

Interim Construction Interest	352,796	
Permanent Loan Fees	140,960	
Marketing/Legal/ Appraisal	10,000	
Entrepreneurial Profit	972,031	
TOTAL INDIRECT COSTS		1,475,787

TOTAL ESTIMATED REPLACEMENT COST NEW:	$6,505,737

LESS: ACCRUED DEPRECIATION

Physical Deterioration	0	
Functional Obsolescence	0	
External Obsolescence	188,364*	
TOTAL ACCRUED DEPRECIATION		− 188,364

ESTIMATED DEPRECIATED REPLACEMENT COST NEW	$6,317,373
PLUS: ESTIMATED LAND VALUE (378,576 SF @ $2.50)	946,500
INDICATED VALUE BY THE COST APPROACH	$7,263,873

ROUNDED TO $7,264,000

---

*Summary of Present Value of Rent Loss:

	ECONOMIC NET OPERATING INCOME	FORECASTED ANTICIPATED NOI	NOI DIFFERENTIAL
Year 1	$697,643	$509,279	$188,364

CLASS DISCUSSION: What is the purpose of the $188,364 deduction? Should it be made in the capitalized income and market data approaches, as well?

VALUE INDICATED BY THE MARKET DATA APPROACH

The market data approach, which is also known as the direct sales comparison approach, gives consideration to the price paid for comparable properties. An extensive study has been made to find comparable improved sales in the Corpus Christi area. Considered of primary importance are apartment buildings competing with the subject property for tenants. On the following pages of this report, each of the comparable sales utilized are discussed and analyzed. A chart listing all sales in descending order by date is shown on the next page of this report and is identified as Table II-6. This chart summarizes pertinent information concerning these sales, including the number of units, the sales price, the sales price per unit, the indicated sales price per square foot of net rentable area, the gross rent multiplier, the overall capitalization rate, and the average size of the units in each complex. A location map showing the location of each comparable sale in relation to the appraised property is shown on page 522 of this report. Details concerning each sale are listed on page numbers 522 to 535 of this report.

After reviewing Chapter 10, determine if this property was valued on the basis of potential or effective gross income. Discuss the relative merits of each of these appraisal methods.

The comparable sales analyzed indicated occupancy rates from 85% for some of the newer projects to almost 100% in some cases. Most of the apartment investors interviewed were analyzing potential apartment investments in this area using 92% occupancy. For this reason we analyzed the sales using a 8% vacancy factor. Typical operating expenses were also utilized for analysis purposes.

Table II-6   MARKET DATA APARTMENT SALES

Sale No.	Name/Location	Date of Sale	# Units	Sales Price	Price/ Unit	Price/ SF NRA	GRM	OAR	AVG SF/ Unit
1	Sandcastle I 6701 Everhart	1/20/84	216	$ 6,520,000	$30,185	$46.21	7.04	0.098	653
2	Baytree 4645 Ocean Dr.	11/1/83	168	$ 4,600,000	$27,381	$44.62	6.68	0.095	614
3	London House 5757 Woolridge	8/15/83	219	$ 7,660,275	$34,978	$42.61	7.26	0.092	821
4	Barcelona 3926 Panama	5/20/83	154	$ 4,400,000[1]	$28,571	$29.69	5.13	0.107	962
5	Beechtree Weber at Caravelle	4/26/83	782	$18,450,000	$23,593	$44.33	7.02	0.097	532
6	Newport Marina Highway 358	4/21/83	248	$ 6,342,034[2]	$25,573	$34.70	6.30	0.103	737
7	Ocean Palms Ltd. 4325 Ocean Drive	4/15/83	152	$ 4,600,000	$30,263	$35.54	5.65	0.114	852
Subj.	Sandcastle II 6717 Everhart	6/10/84	216						662

[1]Actual sales price was $4,500,000 adjusted for favorable financing; all utilities furnished.
[2]Actual sales price was $6,642,034 adjusted for favorable financing.

COMPARABLE APARTMENT SALES

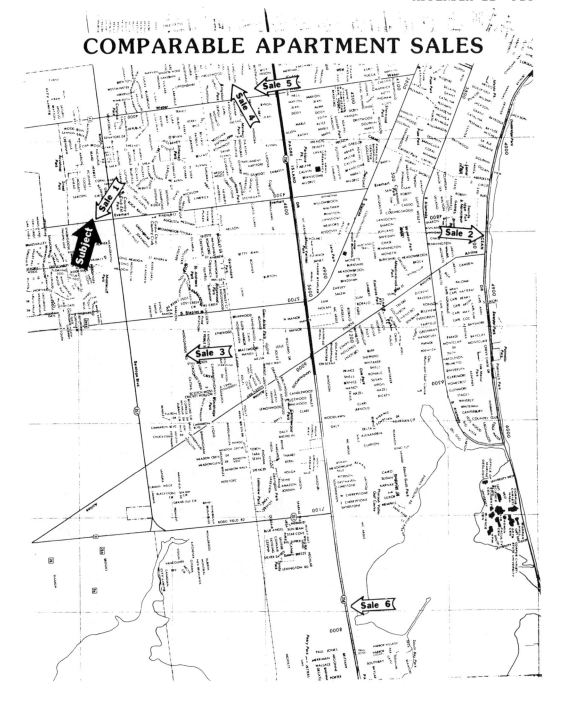

Apartment Sale 1

Name: Sandcastle I

Location: 6717 Everhart, Corpus Christi, Texas

Grantor: Callaway Ltd. Partnership

Grantee: USAA Insurance Co.

Date of Sale: January 20, 1984.

Sales Price: $6,520,000

Terms: Cash.

Volume: D1902, Page 0757.

Comments: No washer and dryer connections; did not include
furniture in finished units. 80% occupied at
time of sale. Currently 98% occupied.

Sandcastle I Financial Analysis
Sale 1, cont.

Gross Potential Income:

No. Units	NRA/SF	Type Unit	Rentable Rate/Mo.	Annual Income
48	485	Efficiency	$295	$169,920
64	603	1BR/1BA	$335-345*	261,120
48	676	1BR/1BA	$355-370*	208,800
24	726	1BR/1BA/Den	$395-410*	115,920
32	917	2BR/2BA	$435-450*	169,920
216	141,088			

Gross Income: $925,680
  Less: Vacancy and Credit Loss @ 8%   - 74,054

Effective Gross Income: $851,626
  Less: Operating Expenses Estimated at
         $1.50/SF NRA @ 141,088 SF   - 211,632

Net Operating Income: $639,994

Indicated Gross Rent Multiplier: (6,520,000/925,680)   7.04

Indicated Effective Gross Income
Multiplier: (6,520,000/851,626)   7.66

Sales price Per Unit: (6,520,000/216) $30,185

Sales Price Per Square Foot NRA: (6,520,000/141,088) $46.21

Indicated Overall Rate: (639,994/6,520,000) = 0.098

---

* With fireplace, higher rate applies.

CLASS DISCUSSION: What other information would you include for improved property sales?

Apartment Sale 2

Name: Bay Tree

Location: 4645 Ocean Drive, Corpus Christi, Texas

Grantor: J. L. Conlee, et al.

Grantee: First Equities Corporation

Date of Sale: November 1, 1983.

Sales Price: $4,600,000

Terms: ±$2,415,000 cash, $2,185,000, 4-year wrap-around
note.

Volume: T1870, Page 817.

Comments: No washer and dryer connections; one swimming
pool; located on 4.71 acres. Totally electric
except for hot water. Tenant pays electric bill.
Approximately 12 years old. 93% occupied at time
of sale.

Baytree Financial Analysis
Sale 2, cont.

Gross Potential Income:

No. Units	NRA/SF	Type Unit	Rentable Rate/Mo.	Annual Income
4	096	Studio	$375	$ 18,000
56	520	Efficiency	$295	198,240
55	650	1BR-1BA	$330	217,800
16	806	1BR-1BA	$360	69,120
32	962	2BR-2BA	$420	161,280
5	Pool-side	1BR-1BA	$400	24,000
168	103,096			

Gross Income:	$688,440
Less: Vacancy and Credit Loss @ 8%	- 55,075
Effective Gross Income:	$633,365
Less: Operating Expenses Estimated at $1.90/SF NRA @ 103,096	- 195,882
Net Operating Income:	$437,483

Indicated Gross Rent Multiplier: (4,600,000/688,440)   6.68

Indicated Effective Gross Income
Multiplier: (4,600,000/633,365)   7.26

Sales Price Per Unit: (4,600,000/168) $27,381

Sales Price Per Square Foot NRA: (4,600,000/103,096) $44.62

Indicated Overall Rate: (437,483/4,600,000) = 0.095

Apartment Sale 3

Name: London House

Location: 5757 Woolridge, Corpus Christi, Texas

Legal Description: Lot 1, Block 1, London House

Grantor: John Sherrod

Grantee: Balcor/American Express

Date of Sale: August 15, 1983.

Sales Price: $7,660,275

Terms: $6,692,500 cash at closing, $600,000 due 2/84,
$357,225 due 2/85, $10,515 due 2/86.

Volume: T1872, Page 1023

Comments: All but one-bedroom units with washer and dryer
connections, cold water furnished; total
electric; Tenant pays own electric bill.
Approximately six months old. 85% occupied at
time of sale.

London House Financial Analysis
Sale 3, cont.

Gross Potential Income:

No. Units	NRA/SF	Type Unit	Rentable Rate/Mo.	Multiplied by 12	Annual Income
80	652	1BR-1BA	$355	$4,260	$340,800
16	817	2BR-1BA	$435	$5,220	83,520
16	817	2BR-1BA*	$450	$5,400	86,400
36	890	2BR-1BA	$450	$5,400	194,400
36	890	2BR-2BA*	$470	$5,640	203,040
11	859	1BR-1.5BA	$410	$4,920	54,120
24	1,165	2BR-2.5BA	$324	$6,300	93,312
219	179,793				

Gross Income: $1,055,592
  Less: Vacancy and Credit Loss @ 8%   − 84,447

Effective Gross Income: $ 971,145
  Less: Operating Expenses Estimated at
    $1.50/SF NRA @ 179,793   − 269,690

Net Operating Income: $ 701,445

Indicated Gross Rent Multiplier: (7,660,275/1,055,592) 7.26

Indicated Effective Gross Income
Multiplier: (6,660,275/971,145)   7.89

Sales Price Per Unit: (7,660,275/219) $34,978

Sales Price Per Square Foot NRA: (7,660,275/179,793) $42.61

Indicated Overall Rate: (701,455/$7,660,275) = 0.092

*Fireplace

CLASS DISCUSSION: Explain and critique why the 8 percent vacancy and credit deduction is used for each comparable sale.

Discuss the pros and cons of the appraiser using net rentable area to develop a unit measure of sales price.

Apartment Sale 4

Name: Barcelona Apartments

Location: 3926 Panama Street, Corpus Christi, Texas

Legal Description: Block A, Carol Place, Corpus Christi, Nueces County, TX.

Grantor: Earl Briggs, et al.

Grantee: Barcelona, Ltd.; Kansas City, MO

Date of Sale: May 20, 1983

Sales Price: $4,500,000 - $100,000 est. for favorable financing = SP of real estate to $4,400,000

Terms: ±$2,800,000 cash, $600,000, 2-year promissory note, at market rate balance $1.1 million, 8-7/8% loan assumption

Volume: T1835, Page 19-21

Comments: Built 1969; all utilities furnished; two pools, no washer and dryer connections. 94% occupied at time of sale. The prevailing rate at the time of the sale was 12% monthly payments with a 7- to 10-year call. In our opinion, the assumption of $1,000,000 at 8-7/8% interest influenced the price paid by approximately $100,000.

Barcelona Apartments Financial Analysis
Sale 4, cont.

Gross Potential Income:

No. Units	NRA/SF	Type Unit	Rentable Rate/Mo.	Multiplied by 12	Annual Income
48	651-701	1BR-1BA	$370-$400	$18,480	$221,760
24	871-923	2BR-1BA	$455	$10,920	131,040
40	1,020-1,125	2BR-2BA	$490	$19,600	235,200
36	1,190-1,216	2BR-2.5BA	$510-$520	$18,540	222,480
6	1,340	3BR-2BA	$665	$ 3,990	47,880
154	148,224				

Gross Income: $858,360
  Less: Vacancy and Credit Loss @ 8%   − 68,669

Effective Gross Income: $789,691
  Less: Operating Expenses Estimated at
         $2.15/SF NRA @ 148,224*   − 318,682

Net Operating Income: $471,009

Indicated Gross Rent Multiplier: (4,400,000/858,360)   5.13

Indicated Effective Gross Income Multiplier:
     (4,400,000/789,691)   5.57

Sales Price Per Unit: (4,400,000/154) $28,751

Sales Price Per Square Foot NRA: (4,400,000/148,224) $29.69

Indicated Overall Rate: (471,009/4,400,000) = 0.107

*All utilities furnished

Apartment Sale 5

Name: Beechtree (formerly The Landing)

Location: 5901 Weber, Corpus Christi, Texas

Legal Description: Portion of Lot 4, Block 3, Carolyn Heights

Grantor: Phase I -Landing I Assoc.
Phase II -Landing II Assoc.
Phase III-Landing III Assoc.
Phase IV -Robert Callaway Co.

Grantee: Hall Beechtree and Assoc.

Date of Sale: April 26, 1983.

Sales Price: $18,450,000

Terms: Assumed an existing note totaling $9,155,000; cash out equity. All notes are assumed to be at market rates.

Volume: 1865, Page 738

Comments: Built in four phases from 1973 to 1979. Only 8 units have washer and dryer connections. All electric; tenant pays electricity. Cold water furnished. 95% occupied at time of sale.

Beechtree Apartments Financial Analysis
Sale 5, cont.

Gross Potential Income:

No. Units	NRA/SF	Type Unit	Rentable Rate/Mo.	Total Rental/Mo.	Annual Income
210	136,691	Phase I	$343 Av	$72,010	$ 864,120
326	112,240	Phase II	$182 Av	59,487	713,844
214	136,598	Phase III	$341 Av	73,080	876,960
32	30,704	Annex	$454 Av	14,520	174,240

782 Total 416,233

Gross Income: $2,629,164
  Less: Vacancy and Credit Loss @ 8%   −   210,333

Effective Gross Income: $2,418,831
  Less: Operating Expenses Estimated at
       $1.50/SF NRA @ 416,233   −   624,335

Net Operating Income: $1,794,496

Indicated Gross Rent Multiplier: (18,450,000/2,629,164) 7.02

Indicated Effective Gross Income Multiplier:
   (18,450,000/2,418,831)   7.63

Sales Price Per Unit: (18,450,000/782) $23,593

Sales Price Per Square Foot NRA: (18,450,000/416,233) $44.33

Indicated Overall Rate: ($1,794,496/$18,450,000) = 0.097

Apartment Sale 6

Name: Newport Marina

Location: Highway 358, Corpus Christi, Texas

Legal Description: Lot 3, Block 1, Turtle Cove #2

Grantor: Newport Marina Associates

Grantee: Roger Seaman Trustee, National Property Investors (NY)

Date of Sale: April 21, 1983

Sales Price: $6,642,034 - $300,000 premium paid for favorable financing = $6,342,034

Terms: $2,703 cash, $3,439,034, 9.63% loan assumption, $500,000, 9%, 2nd PMN

Volume: T1851, Page 382

Comments: Built in 1979. Total electric; tenant pays electricity. Cold water only furnished. Two tennis courts, pool, washer and dryer connections. 92% occupied at time of sale. Terms are estimated to have influenced the price by approximately $300,000.

Newport Marina Financial Analysis
Sale 6, cont.

Gross Potential Income:

No. Units	NRA/SF	Type Unit	Rentable Rate/Mo.	Multiplied by 12	Annual Income
160	663	1BR-1BA	$275-$340	$49,200	$ 590,400
56	856	2BR-1BA	$375	$21,000	252,000
32	899	2BR-2BA	$400-$455	$13,680	164,160
248	182,784				

Gross Income:	$1,006,560
Less: Vacancy and Credit Loss @ 8%	− 80,525
Effective Gross Income	$ 926,035
Less: Operating Expenses Estimated at $1.50/SF NRA @ 182,776	− 271,164
Net Operating Income:	$651,871

Indicated Gross Rent Multiplier: (6,342,034/1,006,560) 6.301

Indicated Effective Gross Income Multiplier:
    (6,342,034/926,035)   6.850

Sales Price Per Unit: (6,342,034/248) $25,573

Sales Price Per Square Foot NRA: (6,342,034/182,776) $34.70

Indicated Overall Rate: ($651,871/$6,342,034) = 0.103

Apartment Sale 7

Name: Ocean Palms

Location: 4325 Ocean Drive, Corpus Christi, Texas

Legal Description: Lot 3, Block 1, Seaside Subdivision,
                    Corpus Christi, Nueces County, Texas.

Grantor: Ocean Palms, Ltd.

Grantee: Joe A. Harter, Trustee

Date of Sale: April 15, 1983

Sales Price: $4,600,000

Terms: Note for $1,350,000 at 14% interest; balloon payment
         due April 15, 1988; interest payable monthly.

Volume: T1821, Page 522-526

Comments: Built in 1975; total electric; two pools, all-
            adult complex, no washer and dryer connections.
            95% occupied at time of sale.

Ocean Palms Financial Analysis
Sale 7, cont.

Gross Potential Income:

No. Units	NRA/SF	Type Unit	Rentable Rate/Mo.	Multiplied by 12	Annual Income
20	650	1BR-1BA	$385	$ 7,700	$ 92,400
60	730	1BR-1BA	$405	$24,300	291,600
54	920	2BR-1.5BA	$475	$25,650	307,800
18	1,275	3BR-2BA	$565	$10,170	122,040
152	129,430				

Gross Income: $813,840
 Less: Vacancy and Credit Loss @ 8%   − 65,107

Effective Gross Income $748,733
 Less: Operating Expenses Estimated at
        $1.50/SF NRA @ 129,430   − 226,503

Net Operating Income: $522,230

Indicated Gross Rent Multiplier: (4,600,000/813,840)   5.65

Sales Price Per Unit: (4,600,000/152) $30,263

Sales Price Per Square Foot NRA: (4,600,000/129,430) $35.54

Indicated Overall Rate: ($522,230/$4,600,000) = 0.114

ANALYSIS OF IMPROVED SALES

The sales analyzed indicated a range in price per unit from
$23,593 to $34,978. The newer and larger apartments
generally command higher prices per unit. The sales
analyzed tend to indicate the proper price per unit for the
subject property to be $33,000. When this is multiplied by
216 units, the indicated value is $7,128,000. See Table
II-7.

The indicated price per square foot of net rentable
area per apartment building has a range of $29.69 to $46.21
per square foot. Once again, the newer apartment buildings
(and the apartments with smaller average sizes) tend to
command a higher price per square foot. Analyzing the sales
most comparable to the subject indicates the price per
square foot for the subject property to be approximately
$50.00. This higher price per square foot is partly
accounted for by the fact that the subject property has
smaller average unit size than all but one of the
comparables. Typically, smaller apartments sell for higher
unit prices per square foot. Also, the sale which is
considered to be most comparable to the subject property is
sale 1, Sandcastle I Apartments. This property sold five
months ago on the basis of $46.21 per square foot of net
rentable area. Making an adjustment upward for the slight
increase in prices since the date of sale indicates an
approximate square foot price of $50.00. Therefore, the
indicated value for the subject property, based on $50.00
per square foot times 143,056 square feet of net rentable
area, is $7,152,800.

The indicated range of the gross rent multipliers
analyzed is from a low of 5.13 to a high of 7.26. Sale 2,
with a gross rent multiplier of 6.68, had lower-than-market
rents at the time of sale. Immediately following the sale,
the new owner raised the rents. Sale 1, most comparable to
the subject, had a gross income multiplier of 7.04. An
analysis of these sales indicates a proper gross rent
multiplier for the subject property to be 7.05, which, when
multiplied by the indicated gross rental income of $991,680,
is $6,991,344.

From each of these value indications must be deducted
the current cost of the rent loss due to a higher-than-
normal vacancy and the free rent being passed on to the
tenants in the subject property at the present time. This
rent loss has been calculated for one year to be 10% of

$697,643 net operating income. Additional income loss, estimated at 17% (which is two months of free rent for a 12-month base period), is added to the vacancy loss. Total net rent loss is estimated to be 27% of the net operating income of $697,643, or $188,364.

The overall rates indicated from an analysis of the comparable sales range from 0.092 to 0.114. The sale most comparable to the subject, sale 1, had an indicated overall rate of 0.098. Other new projects similar to the subject are sale 3, with an overall rate of 0.092, and sale 6, with an overall rate of 0.103. Giving emphasis to the sales most comparable to the subject in relationship to all known apartment sales in Corpus Christi in the past 18 months, the estimated appropriate overall rate for the subject property is concluded to be 0.095.

Table II-7   MARKET APPROACH TO VALUE

Indicated Gross Rent Multiplier

7.05 × $991,680	$6,991,344
Less: Rent Loss for Year 1	− 188,364
Indicated Value of the Appraised Property	(R) $6,803,000

Indicated Price per Square Foot

$50.00 × 143,056 SF NRA	$7,152,800
Less: Rent Loss for Year 1	− 188,364
Indicated Value of the Appraised Property	(R) $6,964,000

Indicated Price per Unit

$33,000 × 216 Units	$7,128,000
Less: Rent Loss for Year 1	− 188,364
Indicated Value of the Appraised Property	(R) $6,940,000

After careful consideration of the value indicated by each of the comparable sales analyzed, it is our opinion that the indicated market value of the Sandcastle apartment building by the market data approach is $6,950,000.

What other acceptable ways are there for accounting for rent losses during the lease-up period for a project?

VALUE INDICATED BY THE INCOME APPROACH

In the income approach to value we have given consideration to the existing rent rate, the types of apartments occupied, the operating expenses, and the current rental structure in the Corpus Christi apartment market. An in-depth rental survey of the Corpus Christi apartments, as of the date of valuation, reveals 43 apartment complexes which are competing with the subject property for tenants. Each apartment complex was analyzed on the basis of number of units, current and past occupancy rate, and the average rental rate per square foot, to assist us in estimating the effective gross income. Comments concerning the current marketing programs in effect, including free rent, free laundry facilities, and amenities such as saunas, security services, and racquetball courts, are also provided. The seven apartment complexes considered most competitive with the subject property are outlined in the following table.

Table II-8   COMPARABLE RENTAL CHART

Property/Address	Total Units	Rent/SF	Occupancy Rate	Comments
Sandcastle I	216	$0.54	98%	No washer/dryer available; one month's free rent with six-month lease.
Walnut Ridge	704	0.54	60%	New complex; free laundry; security patrol; racquetball courts.
London House	219	0.49	93%	Lower rents per square foot than subject; one month's free rent with six-month lease.

Property/Address	Total Units	Rent/SF	Occupancy Rate	Comments
Summer House Condos	136	0.58	65%	$40 rent rebate for six-month lease; garages; ice makers; all have fireplaces. Lease purchase available.
Sugar Tree	250	0.53	96%	New on market; pools; tennis courts. On Oso Bay with excellent view.
The Rafters	250	0.48	52%	Washer and dryer connections; on market two months. No specials. Pool and tennis courts.
Chandler Mill	248	0.55	92%	On market for two months. Pools, tennis courts. No specials.
Sandcastle II	216	0.58	82%	Washer/dryer in 2BR units. One month's free rent with a six-month lease.

The gross potential income, the allowance for vacancy and credit losses, the effective gross income, and the operating expenses, have been estimated for the appraised property. Typical ownership expenses have been estimated to be $1.50 per square foot of net rentable area. We have estimated the value by the income approach by direct capitalization with an overall rate derived from an analysis of the comparable sales. Each analysis reveals that newer, better quality properties have a lower indicated overall rate than older or less desirable properties. The steps to the income approach are outlined in the following pages.

Chapter 15 includes a discussion of reserves for replacements. After having reviewed this discussion, would you have set up reserves for the appraised Property? Explain your decision.

Income and Expense Analysis:

The first step in estimating the Sandcastle Apartments' gross potential income is to compare the subject property with comparable apartment projects. The estimated prevailing market rental for the subject property, as indicated by the comparables, has been noted on the following pages. The gross income provided from the 216 units for unfurnished apartments is based on projected economic rents (without any rent concessions) and is estimated to be $991,680.

The vacancy and collections losses are estimated to be 8% and when subtracted from the gross potential income results in an estimated effective gross income of $912,346.

The operating expenses have been analyzed in two categories: fixed and variable. The fixed expenses include taxes and insurance which do not fluctuate with occupancy. The property taxes are discussed on page number 15 of this report and are estimated to be $51,653. The taxes are based on the experience with Sandcastle Phase I and from inquiry with the tax appraiser. The taxes could double if the property were to be appraised at 100% of market value in accordance with the state law. If the taxes were to be based on a valuation of $7,200,000 at the current tax rate, they would be $106,258 or $54,605 more than projected. The insurance is based on the experience with Sandcastle Phase I. We anticipate that the cost of fire and extended coverage insurance will increase substantially in subsequent years.

The variable expenses change with vacancy levels. The water and sewer costs have been estimated to be approximately 8% higher than the previous year for comparable apartments. This estimate was obtained from the city as the rates have not been set for next year. The

Central Power and Light Company estimates electricity to be approximately 12% higher than last year. Professional management is available in Corpus Christi for 5% of the rent collected. Maintenance and repairs are estimated to be typical for new garden apartments in this area. Advertising expenses are typical for the newer apartments. The operating expenses are estimated to be approximately $1.50 per square foot (143,056 square feet, at $1.50 per square foot) or $214,703 and are subtracted from the effective gross income. The resulting net operating income is $697,643.

Capitalization Analysis:

The overall rates derived from the market sales information indicate a range of from 0.092 to 0.114. This is shown as Figure 5 on page 41 of this report. The overall rates were calculated by dividing the estimated next 12 months net operating income from the sale property by the sales price of the comparable property. This overall capitalization rate reflects the buyers' attitude of the future pattern of the income stream as well as the future value of the property. Sale 1, with an overall rate of 0.098, sale 3, with an overall rate of 0.092, and sale 5, with an overall rate of 0.098, are similar to the subject. After analyzing each of the comparable sales for similarities and dissimilarities when compared to the subject property, an overall rate of 9.5% is considered to be applicable.

When the net operating income is capitalized at an overall rate of 9.5%, the resulting indication of value is $7,343,611 ($697,643/0.095).

From the indicated value of $7,344,000 must be deducted the estimated rent and credit loss for year 1 of $188,364. The value indicated by the income approach after deducting the rent and vacancy loss is $7,156,000 (rounded). The summary of the income approach is shown on the following page as Table II-9.

See Chapter 16 for alternative methods of developing capitalization rates.

Table II-9   INCOME APPROACH SUMMARY

Gross Potential Income for Unfurnished Apartments:

48 efficiency units @ $295/MO × 12 MOS.	$	169,920
48 1BR/1BA @ $350/MO × 12 MOS.		201,600
48 large 1BR/1BA @ $385/MO × 12 MOS.		221,760
40 1BR/1BA/DEN @ $430/MO × 12 MOS.		206,400
32 2BR/2BA @ $500 × 12 MOS.		192,000

Total: 216 units 143,056 SF NRA @ $0.58 SF/MO Av

Total Gross Potential Income for Unfurnished Apartments:	$	991,680
Less: Vacancy and Credit Loss @ 8% (typical)	−	79,334
Effective Gross Income:	$	912,346

Less Operating Expenses:

Fixed Expenses:

Taxes ($0.36/SF NRA)	$51,653
Insurance ($0.05/SF NRA)	7,153

Variable Expenses:

Utilities Water & Sewer ($0.26/SF NRA)	37,195
Gas and Electricity ($0.26/SF NRA)	37,195
Management @ 5% ($0.32/SF NRA)	45,617
Maintenance and Repairs ($0.20/SF NRA)	28,712
Advertising ($0.05/SF NRA)	7,178

Total Operating Expenses (143,056 SF NRA @ $1.50 SF):	214,703
Net Operating Income Capitalized @ 9.5%	$ 697,643
Value Indicated by Direct Capitalization:	$7,343,611
Less: Estimated Rent Loss	− 188,364
Value Indicated by the Income Approach: After Rent and Vacancy Loss	7,155,247
	(R) $7,155,000

> As a check, the operating expense ratio for the appraised property can be compared to a local standard for the same class of property.

RECONCILIATION AND FINAL VALUE ESTIMATE

The value indicated by each of the approaches are as follows:

Value Indicated by the Cost Approach	$7,264,000
Value Indicated by the Market Data Approach	$6,950,000
Value Indicated by the Income Approach	$7,155,000

The three valuation techniques indicate a range of values of approximately 4.5%. Due to the income-producing nature of the property, the greatest weight is given to the income approach. The cost approach is considered to be very persuasive because accurate cost of construction new was available from the Sandpiper Apartments Phase I as well as the appraised property. These figures were also checked with a national cost service and other known construction costs. Also, there were numerous land transfers in the area to assist in estimating the value of the site. There was no physical deterioration apparent and no external or functional obsolescence evident other than the estimated rent loss attributable to the time it will take to achieve stabilized occupancy. The market data approach is considered to be persuasive due to the fact that numerous comparable apartment building sales were available for analysis, one of which was the recent sale of Sandcastle I, a property similar in all respects to the subject property. The income approach has been calculated by direct capitalization with an overall capitalization rate. The Sandcastle II complex offers a modern and convenient garden apartment complex located in one of the fastest-growing and most conveniently located areas of Corpus Christi. This is an optimum location with access to major thoroughfares, and development in the immediate area is of increasing quality and high investor interest. These factors enhance the attractiveness of Sandcastle II to potential investors as well as to potential tenants. The rental market in Corpus Christi continues to expand with the growth of the city, and the demand for quality apartment housing is quite high. Considering these facts, a typical prudent investor would consider the Sandcastle II Apartment complex to be an excellent investment.

See Chapter 24 for a discussion of the purpose of the valuation conclusion or value reconciliation.

As a result of the analysis made and conclusions reached, it is our opinion that the market value of the fee simple title (and leased fee estate) to the Sandcastle II apartment complex, as of June 10, 1984, was:

SEVEN MILLION TWO HUNDRED THOUSAND DOLLARS

($7,200,000)

What, if any, changes would you make in this actual appraisal report after having reviewed Chapter 24?

CERTIFICATE

The undersigned do hereby certify that, except as otherwise noted in this appraisal report:

We have no present or contemplated future interest in the real estate that is the subject of this appraisal report.

We have no personal interest or bias with respect to the subject matter of this appraisal report or the parties involved.

To the best of our knowledge and belief the statements of fact contained in this appraisal report, upon which the analyses, opinions, and conclusions expressed herein are based, are true and correct.

This appraisal report sets forth all of the limiting conditions (imposed by the terms of our assignment or by the undersigned) affecting the analyses, opinions and conclusions contained in this report.

This appraisal report has been made in conformity with and is subject to the requirements of the Code of Professional Ethics and Standards of Professional Conduct of the American Institute of Real Estate Appraisers of the National Association of Realtors.

No one other than the undersigned prepared the analyses, conclusions, and opinions concerning the real estate that are set forth in this appraisal report. All of the undersigned, unless otherwise noted, have inspected the property.

Neither all nor any part of the contents of this report (especially any conclusions as to value, the identity of the appraisers or the firm with which they are connected, or any reference to the American Institute of Real Estate Appraisers or to the M.A.I. or R.M. designation) shall be disseminated to the public through advertising media, public relations media, news media, sales media, or any other public means of communication without the prior written consent and approval of the undersigned.

The American Institute of Real Estate Appraisers conducts a voluntary program of continuing education for its designated members. M.A.I.s and R.M.s who meet the minimum standards of this program are awarded periodic educational certification. Albert Scruggs Love, Jr. is certified under this program through December 31, 1986.

Scruggs Love, Jr   *Mary Jo Stutton Smith*

San Antonio, Texas

Explain how and why you would modify the certificate of value (see Chapter 24).

QUALIFICATIONS OF
ALBERT SCRUGGS LOVE, JR.

Presently, and since 1960, Albert Scruggs Love, Jr., has been engaged in the general real estate consulting and appraisal practice. He is a partner in the firm of Love and Dugger, Real Estate Consultants and Appraisers, 111 Soledad, Suite 890, San Antonio, Texas 78205.

During the time of his employment with the Texas Highway Department in Corpus Christi (1958-1960), his time was divided between reviewing, supervising, and appraising real estate. Since that time, he has been exclusively engaged in the general practice of real estate appraising and property consultation. His practice includes the appraisal of virtually all types of real property.

Generally, the Love and Dugger trade area includes the entire State of Texas, and other appraisals have been made in Arizona, Arkansas, Colorado, Florida, Georgia, Louisiana, New Mexico, Oklahoma, and Tennessee.

His specialized teaching experience, beginning in 1960 up to the present, includes Course II to the Texas Highway Department; Guest Lecturer Course III to the Texas Highway Department; Basic Principles of Real Estate Appraising in the Adult Education Center, San Antonio and at San Antonio College; Course 101 and Course 201, Society of Real Estate Appraisers.

As a faculty member of the American Institute of Real Estate Appraisers, he has instructed Course IA, Real Estate Appraisal Principles, Basic Valuation Procedures, Capitalization Theory and Techniques, and Valuation Analysis and Report Writing.

His educational background includes Texas A&M University, College Station, Texas, from June 1951 through May 1952; Texas A & I University, Kingsville, Texas, BBA Degree, September 1952 through May 1955; and the University of Texas, Graduate School of Commerce, Austin, Texas, with a major in Real Estate, September 1957 through February 1958.

Technical training in Real Estate includes Course I, American Institute of Real Estate Appraisers, 1958, Course II, American Institute of Real Estate Appraisers, 1959; Texas Highway Department, Course III, 1961; Course IV, American Institute of Real Estate Appraisers, 1963; and Course VI, American Institute of Real Estate Appraisers, 1974.

What is the primary purpose of the "Qualifications" section?

Offices of nationally recognized professional appraisal associations include the following:

President, San Antonio Chapter No. 65, Society of Real Estate Appraisers, 1968.

   Secretary, 1967 and 1971;
   Treasurer, 1966;
   Director, 1968-1969;
   Second Vice-President, 1972;
   First Vice-President, 1973;

President, 1974;
Director, 1975, and 1980-1984

Vice Chairman, South Central Regional Committee, American Institute of Real Estate Appraisers, 1979 and 1981.

National Committee Assignments, American Institute of Real Estate Appraisers:

Public Relations Committe, 1979, 1980, and 1981;
Elective Examination Committee, 1977;
Course I-B Sub-Committtee, 1975, 1976, 1977, and 1978;
Vice Chairman, Division of Curriculum, 1979, 1980, and 1981;
Chairman, Division of Curriculum, 1982.

Elected member of the Governing Council, American Institute of Real Estate Appraisers, 1980-1982.

South Central Regional Vice-President, American Institute of Real Estate Appraisers, 1983 and 1984.

Professional Recognition Award, 1976-1982.

Professional Affiliations include the following organizations:

Member, American Institute of Real Estate Appraisers, Cert. No. 3699

Senior Real Property Appraiser, Society of Real Estate Appraisers
Senior Member, American Society of Appraisers
Active Member, San Antonio Board of Realtors
Member, American Right-of-Way Association

QUALIFICATIONS OF
MARY JO HUTTON-SMITH

Presently, and since August 1983, Mary Jo Hutton-Smith has been employed by the firm of Love & Dugger, Real Estate Appraisers and Consultants.

Her educational background includes the University of Tennessee, Knoxville; where she received a Bachelor of Science Degree. She has completed American Institute of Real Estate Courses at the University of Houston, Stanford University, Palo Alto, California, and Texas Real Estate Development Council Workshops on Utility and Pipeline

Appraisals. She is currently completing a Master of Arts in Computer Data Management at Webster University.

Previous appraisal experience includes employment as a staff appraiser with McCrackin-Mundy & Associates of Fairbanks and Anchorage, Alaska, and Seattle, Washington, from 1977 to 1980; and Don R. Ellis & Associates of Del Rio, Texas, from 1980 to 1983.

She holds a Texas Real Estate Sales License and is a member of the American Right-of-Way Association. She was qualified as an expert witness for the Alaska District Court, Fairbanks, Alaska.

Appraisal experience includes a variety of commercial properties, vacant and improved land, agricultural and residential property valuation, lease-hold interest, and special-use properties ranging from federally- and/or state-owned parks to remote recreation lodges.

CONTINGENT AND LIMITING CONDITIONS
(Unless Otherwise Stated in this Report)

The estimate of value for the property analyzed in the attached report is subject to the following limiting conditions:

The legal description furnished the appraiser is assumed to be correct. No responsibility is assumed for matters legal in character, nor is any opinion rendered as to title. All existing liens and encumbrances, if any, have been disregarded, and the property is analyzed as though free and clear and under responsible ownership and competent management.

The boundaries of the land and the dimensions and size thereof as indicated to the appraisers are assumed to be correct, no provision having been made for a special survey of the property. Valuation is reported without regard to questions of encroachments.

The information contained in this report and identified as having been furnished by others is believed to be reliable, but no responsibility is assumed for its accuracy.

No responsibility is assumed, nor is any guarantee made as to the structural soundness of the improvements. The property is assumed to be free of insect infestation and dry rot.

Possession of this report, or a copy thereof, does not carry with it the right of publication, nor may it be used for any other purposes by any but the applicant without the previous written consent of the appraisers.

The appraisers, by reason of this report, are not required to give testimony or attendance in court, or any other hearing with reference to the property in question, unless arrangements therefore have been previously made.

The distribution of the total valuation in this report between the land and the improvements applies only under the existing program of utilization. The separate valuations for land and improvements should not be used in conjunction with any other appraisal and are invalid if so used.

The appraisers have no present or contemplated future interest in the property which is not specifically disclosed in this report. Neither their employment for making this analysis nor the fee to be received therefore are contingent upon the valuation placed on the property.

The value reported is based upon the completion of the proposed improvements substantially in accordance with the plans and specifications provided.

ADDENDUM

Exhibit 1
ARTICLE 9 "A-2" APARTMENT HOUSE DISTRICT REGULATIONS

Section 9-1: The regulations set forth in this article, or set forth elsewhere in this Ordinance when referred to in this article, are the regulations in the A-2 Apartment House District. This, the highest density residential district, is generally located near or within the central part of the city and provides for certain transient residence as well as permanent residence and for certain institutional uses.

Section 9-2 Use Regulations: A building or premises shall be used only for the following purposes:
(1) Any use permitted in the R-1A One-family Dwelling District.
(2) Two-family dwellings other than mobile homes.
(3) Multiple-family dwellings.
(4) Boarding, rooming, and lodging houses.

(5) Private clubs, fraternities, sororities, and
lodges excepting those the chief activity of
which is a service customarily carried on as a
business.

(6) Apartment hotels.

(7) Non-profit, religious, educational, and
philanthropic institutions.

(8) Hospitals, nursing homes, and homes for the aged,
but not including animal hospitals, penal and
mental treatment institutions, office buildings,
or clinics.

(9) Accessory buildings and uses, including for
permitted nonresidential uses and apartment
hotels, one illuminated identification sign which
shall not utilize or incorporate flashing,
moving, or intermittent illumination, shall be
placed flat against the wall of the building,
shall not project more than eighteen (18) inches
from the wall of the building or structure, and
shall not exceed fifteen (15) square feet, and
shall indicate only the name and address of the
building and the management thereof. A building
or group of buildings on a corner lot shall be
permitted one such sign for each fronting street.

Section 9-3 Parking Regulations: The parking regulations
for permitted uses are contained in Article 22.

Section 9-4 Off-street Loading Regulations: The off-street
loading regulations for permitted uses are contained
in Article 23.

Section 9-5 Height, Area, and Bulk Regulations: The height,
area, and bulk requirements shall be as set forth in
the chart of Article 24, and in addition the following
regulations shall apply:

9-5.01 Buildings may exceed sixty (60) feet or four
(4) stories in height provided that forty
percent (40%) of the site is devoted to
nonvehicular open space.

9-5.02 Requirements for floor area per acre shall not
apply to dormitories, fraternities, or
sororities where no cooking facilities are
provided in individual rooms or apartments.

Section 9-6: Supplementary height, area, and bulk
     regulations are contained in Article 27.

PHOTOGRAPHS OF THE APPRAISED PROPERTY

Exhibit A

SUBJECT LOOKING SOUTHWEST
FROM EVERHART ROAD

PHOTOGRAPHS OF THE APPRAISED PROPERTY (cont.)

SUBJECT ENTRY

SUBJECT PATIO AND POOL SHOWING REAR OF CLUBHOUSE

POOL WITH JACUZZI SPA
IN FOREGOUND

GAZEBO AND TENNIS COURTS

APPENDIX III

CASE STUDIES

CASE STUDY 1: LAND DEVELOPMENT APPROACH TO VALUE

A 100-acre tract of land within city limits is to be subdivided into 280 building sites, averaging 75 feet in width.

There is active demand for homes in the $55,000 to $65,000 price bracket. The average price per home is estimated at $60,500. The ratio of land to property value in like subdivisions is 1 to 6 ($1.00 land to $5.00 building investment).

The proposed subdivision is to be improved with all required city utilities, including 60-feet-wide paved roads fitted with concrete curbs and gutters, water, drainage, and sanitary disposal. Telephone and electric service facilities, including street lights, are to be supplied through underground cables laid in steel conduit.

Analysis of development plans indicate total development costs per lot are:

Development costs	$ 3,675
Underground electric utility lines	600
Development fee	2,038
Interest, taxes, legal fees	250
Sales commission (10%)	1,050
Total development costs, excluding overhead and advertising	$ 7,613
First-year average sale price of lots (expected to increase by 8% annually)	$10,500

280 water and sewage distribution connections at $300 per lot.

The developer is to receive a refund of $100 under city regulations at the time each lot is tapped onto the main and becomes active by customer use.

No extra cost for telephone lines or site connections are chargeable to the developer.

Advertising and field overhead costs are estimated at 3.0 percent of gross sales.

Developers currently expect a 10 percent yield on this type of development.

The investment period is scheduled to extend over a four-year period. Lot sales of 70 per year are considered a reasonable certainty.

Based on market analysis and the information, as stated above, supplied by informed sources, derive the land value of the undeveloped tract of land under alternative options as follows:

1. The development for the entire 280-lot subdivision is to be completed and all utilities to be installed during the first year. What price could an investor afford to pay for this land on the basis of the development program above?
2. Suppose that the developer chose to spread out his costs for development, underground electric utility lines, and development fees over *three* years. What effect would this have on the present value of the property? Which development program would you advise him to select?

CASE STUDY 2: APARTMENT HOUSE PROPERTY

Based on field and property data noted below, estimate the following:

1. Value under cost approach.
2. Value under market approach.
3. Value under income approach.
4. Final estimate of value based on correlation of value findings. Give narrative statement supporting judgment weights applied in the derivation of the final estimate of value.

Neighborhood: Location

The subject property is located in a desirable residential area zoned R-3 for high-rise apartments. The neighborhood area is 95 percent developed with a variety of apartment structures ranging in height from three to eight stories. Structures vary in age from two to 20 years. All are in good physical condition.

The area is well located within walking distance of a good grade school, within two blocks of neighborhood shopping, and six blocks from the University campus. A bus stop is one-half block to the north at the intersection of N.W. Beach Boulevard and N.W. 14th Street. The distance to the central city is 3 miles and bus transportation is available at 30-minute intervals from 6 a.m. to 7 p.m. and every hour from 7 p.m. to 2 a.m.

The occupants of the area are mostly college students who in groups of two to four share occupancy. The vacancy ratio reported averages 6 to 8%.

The trend is for continued land use as apartment development. The rental range for unfurnished apartments is $130 to $150 for two-room, kitchen, and bath, and $150 to $200 for three-room, kitchen, and bath apartments. The property is located in the middle of the block on N.W. 14th Street between N.W. Beach Boulevard to the West and N.W. 5th Avenue to the East. The site measures 100 feet on N.W. 14th Street to a depth of 150 feet.

Improvement Data

The subject apartment is a nearly new five-story masonry structure. The exterior walls are brick veneer over concrete blocks. A partial basement contains the manager's apartment, the heater, air conditioning, and elevator equipment and adequate storage facilities for tenants. There are 40 two-room and bath apartments and 20 three-room and bath apartments. Each apartment is equipped with an electric range, dish-washer, and refrigerator.

The building measures 80 feet on N.W. 14th Street to a depth of 90 feet. The overall building height is 56 feet.

The building roof is "built up" and topped with granite chits as protection against heavy rains. Windows are of aluminum sash and of awning-type manufacture.

The floors are carpeted throughout over concrete subfloors. The basement apartment has vinyl tile over concrete slab. The basement utility area is reinforced concrete.

Interior walls are furred out, insulated, and finished with drywall masonry boards. Good-quality paint is used throughout except for feature walls, which are attractively finished with wallpaper. Interior trim is white spruce.

Two-room apartments contain 500 square feet and three-room apartments contain 700 square feet. All bathrooms are fully tiled and fitted with pastel-colored fixtures. Each apartment has extra clothes closets off the entrance foyer and a walk-in closet in the master bedroom. Kitchen floors are covered with grease-proof vinyl tile.

The entire structure is centrally heated and air conditioned with a Carrier Climatrol furnace and condenser. Two standard automatic elevators serve the building. Off-street parking is adequate. The remaining economic life is 50 years. Accrued depreciation is negligible. There is no deferred maintenance. Lobby furniture is valued at $1,500. Land value is well established at $5.00 per square foot.

Assessment and Insurance Data

The subject property is assessed for ad valorem tax purposes at $350,000. Taxes are levied at 13.65 mills by the county and at 8.35 mills by the city.

Comprehensive and fire insurance is based on 80% of building replacement cost new. The insurance rate is 25¢ per $100 per year. Public liability insurance costs $125 per year.

Comparative Sales

	SALE			
	1	2	3	4
Date of sale	Current	6 mo. ago	Current	2 years ago
Sale price	$680,000	$350,000	$710,000	$746,155
Land value	$65,000	$32,000	$70,000	$87,000
No. of apts.	67	40	64	80
No. of rooms	158	94	151	197
Effective gross income	$98,765	$49,735	$102,225	$121,000
Operating ratio	42%	40%	42%	39%
Remaining economic life	45 years	40 years	50 years	48 years
Effective age	5 years	10 years	none	2 years

Time adjustment: 6 months, none; 1 year +5%; 2 years, +10%. Apply the straight-line method of asset recapture in analyzing the market data approach to value. Except for age, apartment structures are comparable in all respects, including location.

Revenue and Expense Data

Rental income:

30—2-room apts at $120
10—2-room apts at $145
15—3-room apts at $155
 5—3-room apts at $185
 1—Basement at $100

Vacancy and collection loss allowance 4%

Note that no revenue is collected from the superintendent who occupies the unfurnished basement apartment. The rental amount is considered part of the superintendent's wages.

Operating expenditures:

Management 5% of effective gross income	
Payroll—superintendent	$ 3,000
Electricity	1,200
Water and sewage charge	1,400
Heating fuel	1,300
Legal and administrative	500
Painting and decorating—every 3 years	
$120 for 2-room apts and $160 for 3-room apts	
Exterior maintenance every 5 years—$4,000	
Supplies	450
Corporate income tax	13,000
Elevator contract	1,000
Amortization	21,750
Repairs and general maintenance	700
Interest on mortgages	31,900

Reserve for replacements:

Ranges—15-year life, cost each	$ 225
Refrigerators—15-year life, cost each	600
Dishwashers—12-year life, cost each	250
Lobby furniture—10-year life	
Equipment—furnace and pumps—15-year life	15,000

Apply the annuity method of capitalization in deriving value via the income approach to value.

The market indicates availability of mortgage funds up to 75% of property value at 10.0% interest. Equity funds are obtainable at an 8% return. Land investors seek an 8.0% return, while apartment investors expect 9.5% return.

Cost Data

Analysis of comparable buildings constructed in recent months as well as information obtained from informed investor–builder supports a replacement cost new of $1.30 per cubic foot exclusive of furniture and kitchen equipment (ranges, refrigerators, and dishwashers). Depreciation is considered negligible. The estimated remaining economic life of the subject property is 50 years.

CASE STUDY 3: RETAIL STORE PROPERTY

Based on field data presented below, analyze the pertinent information and *set up schedules* essential to the derivation of estimates as follows:

1. Value of land.
2. Cost approach to value.
3. Market comparison approach to value.
4. Discount rate applicable to subject property.
5. Income approach to value.
6. Reconciliation and final estimate of value.

In all schedules justify—by explanatory statements—the conclusions reached.

Purpose of Appraisal

To estimate the market value of the subject property for possible sale or long-term lease purposes.

Street Address

925 Broadway, Capital City

Legal Description

The East one half (E½) of the East one half (E½) of Lot 6, Block 42 Old Survey of Capital City, as per public records, Lincoln County, Any State.

Highest and Best Use

The subject property conforms to existing zoning regulations and constitutes the highest and best use of the site.

By highest and best use is meant that legal program of land utilization which will preserve the utility of the property and yield an income which when appropriately capitalized aggregates the highest present value to the land.

National Data

The continued high level of economic activity accounts largely for the firm and steady upward trend in land and realty values throughout the nation. Inflationary tendencies during the past few years have caused real estate values to move upward significantly. The overall increase in property values appears attributable to the following favorable causes:

1. Continued unexpected population increases.
2. Extraordinary family formation—caused by "undoubling" within family units and higher economic standards of living.
3. Increase in marriage rates.
4. Pension and annuity plans.

Politically, too, the U.S. government is taking a positive interest in facilitating the acquisition of realty for home and investment purposes. Activities of HUD and the VA are geared to make ownership of realty possible to any and all who meet the necessary minimum income criteria. All signs point to continued government action to encourage a ready flow of mortgage funds at favorable rates of interest.

In the present and "planned" political and financial climate, investment in real property—when appropriately considered and executed—should prove economically rewarding.

City Data

The community is best known as a trading center for Lincoln County, with a population of 80,000 people. The city is bisected by four important U.S. highways and is well located midway between two large commercial cities 110 miles to the northeast and 90 miles to the southwest.

In proportion to its size the community is one of the leading cities in the state. Its diverse economic activities assure continuous population growth and relative freedom from adverse effects of extreme swings of the business cycle.

Neighborhood Data

The subject property is located in the "hub" of the city and within the old Court House Square. This central business neighborhood encompasses approximately eight blocks bounded by Washington Street on the north, Birch Street on the east, Fort Bliss Avenue on the south, and Coal Street on the west.

The construction of neighborhood shopping centers on Main Street and on Gulf Boulevard during the past eight years have diverted business activity from the subject location. The removal of the old County Court House and its relocation two blocks northwesterly of the business center has also affected adversely the purchasing power of the number of store locations that are vacant and for rent and from the reduction of land value on the west and south side of the square from an estimated $2,000 per front foot in 1975, to $1,500 per front foot in 1985, or 2.5% a year.

There is every indication that property values on the square are about to stabilize. The city has purchased the old hotel property and has announced plans to convert the entire east block of the square into a park and parking lot facility. This form of urban renewal should benefit materially the remaining business properties by eliminating available store competition and further by attracting shoppers from outlying areas to the central city. The store facilities to the south and east of the city square are expected to benefit substantially from the construction of expanded parking lot facilities.

Generally, it is deemed that the neighborhood properties in the "hub" of the city can anticipate a stable and gradually improving financial and value position in the years ahead.

Site Data

The subject property is located on the south side of the city square and in the center of the block bounded by Broadway on the north, Magnolia Street on the west, Main Street on the east, and Ft. King Avenue on the south.

The lot is above street grade and measures 32 feet east and west and 119 feet north and south. The stair area is jointly owned and used, 1.5 feet of space belongs to each of the adjoining properties. The entire stairwell is 3 feet wide. All streets in the area are paved and fitted with sidewalks, curb, and gutters. All public utilities, including storm and sanitary sewage, gas, telephone, electricity, and city water, are available and connected to the site. Fire and police protection are deemed adequate and efficient.

Improvement Data

The improvements consist of a two-story structure built of solid brick, painted white with a stuccoed store front facade. Girders are of wood as are the studs of the interior plastered walls. The roof is "built up" with layers of tar mopped roofing felt. Upstairs windows are of aluminum sash and of awning-type manufacture. Store windows are of standard sheet glass.

The store area is served with two water closets and two lavatories, all in working condition. There are no water closet facilities in the upstairs storeroom areas. Electric wiring has been replaced in the downstairs store area and in the front one-half of the upstairs area. The rear upstairs storage area has old-fashioned open wiring that should be replaced to eliminate a possible fire hazard.

The store finished flooring is of carpeting in the customer display area and of asphalt tile over concrete slab subflooring in the storage and work areas. The upstairs floors are of hard strip pine over rough pine subflooring.

The building is approximately 80 years old and appears structurally in sound condition. The effective age is 45 years. The store front will have to be modernized in three to five years. Complete renovation, including ceiling repairs and redecoration, will be required at the termination of the present lease at an estimated cost of $25,000.

The store area is served with a modern gas-fired heat pump of Arkla Servel Sun Valley manufacture that provides all-year heat and air conditioning.

The remaining economic life under normal maintenance is estimated to be 15 years. Accrued depreciation, not including deferred maintenance, is estimated at $1\frac{1}{2}\%$ a year over the effective building age.

Building Cost

Replacement cost—new is based on comparative building costs and estimated at $25.00 per square foot for the downstairs area of 2,876 square feet, at $21.00 per square foot for the upstairs area (1,900 sq ft) and at $19.50 per square foot for the 263 square foot "lean-to" structure.

The heating and air conditioning system is only three years old and has a present value of $3,500.

Present Occupancy

The subject property is presently leased for $697 per month payable in advance for the downstairs and upstairs areas. The "lean-to" is rented on a month-to-month basis for $48. Properties in this commercial area are rented for periods of 5 to 7 years with options to renew for a like period. Present lease expires at end of current month. Similar properties are experiencing vacancies of 2 percent.

All interior repairs and decorating are the responsibility of the lessee. Lessee pays increases in taxes over those paid at time of lease date. The lessor pays for taxes, which currently amount to $1,250 per year, plus special sewer and water tax of $115 per year. Insurance cost is $435, Management fees are 7 percent and exterior maintenance and repairs average $655. The remaining economic life is 15 years. Recapture of capital is calculated under the straight-line method. The heating and air conditioning system has an estimated life of 15 years.

Market Data

Sale 1: Unimproved site

Date of sale	Six months ago
Sale price	$67,500
Lot size	40′ × 115′
Location	corner
Subject rating	0.95

Sale 2: Unimproved site

Date of sale	Current
Sale price	$75,000
Lot size	44′ × 110′
Location	corner
Subject rating	0.90

Sale 3: Unimproved site

Date of sale	Two years ago
Sale price	$50,000
Lot size	44′ × 110′
Location	interior
Subject rating	1.25

Sale 4: Unimproved site

Sale price	$90,000
Date of sale	Current
Lot size	60′ × 100′
Location	interior
Subject rating	1.00

Sale 5: Store property

Sale price	$73,500
Date of sale	1 year ago
Reported effective gross	$10,800
Estimated operating ratio	35%
Building effective age	30 years
Remaining economic life	20 years
Improvement/property ratio	30%
Building area	7,800 sq ft

Sale 6: Store and loft property

Sale price	$67,500
Date of sale	6 months ago
Reported effective gross	$9,750
Estimated operating ratio	32%
Building effective age	28 years
Remaining economic life	20 years
Improvement/property ratio	35%
Building area	7,750 sq ft

Sale 7: Store Property

Sale price	$84,000
Date of sale	1 year ago
Reported effective gross	$12,450
Estimated operating ratio	38%
Building effective age	35 years
Remaining economic life	20 years
Improvement/property ratio	25%
Building area	7,700 sq ft

Sale 8: Store Property

Sale price	$67,500
Date of sale	1 year ago
Reported effective gross	$9,675
Estimated operating ratio	35%
Building effective age	25 years
Remaining economic life	20 years
Improvement/property ratio	26%
Building area	5,320 sq ft

Market price adjustments are as follows:

Sales 6 months ago	5% up
Sales 1 year ago	10% up
Sales 2 years ago	15% up

Straight-line recapture of building investment is customarily applied to store buildings in the subject area.

CASE STUDY 4: STORE AND OFFICE BUILDING

Analyze the field data and information obtained from reliable sources as set forth below, and prepare schedules to support the following:

1. Cost approach to value.
2. Income approach to value.
3. Market data approach to value.
4. Reconciliation of value estimates and final value conclusion.

Site Data

The subject store and office building is favorably located south of the county court house at the intersection of Pine and Broad Street. The site fronts on Pine Street for a distance of 110 feet to a depth of 120 feet.

The site is level, above street grade and is furnished with all city utilities as well as with natural gas, telephone and TV cable services. Parking is provided across the street on a similar site 100' × 125' which is leased for a period of 10 years with option to renew for an additional five-year lease term at a monthly rental of $1,600.

Improvement Data

The subject property is a four-story steel-reinforced structure faced with natural rock. It was built five years ago and is in excellent physical condition. No deferred maintenance was observed.

The structure contains stores and offices on the ground floor, offices on the second, third and fourth floors, and a fully equipped restaurant on the fourth floor. A single automatic elevator serves the building.

The interior walls are furred out, plastered, and covered with washable wallpaper in the hallways. The interiors of all offices are mahogany paneled. Doors are of solid oak, mahogany stained and fitted with high-grade solid brass door locks and hinges. Floors are of reinforced concrete and covered with wall-to-wall nylon carpet laid over foam rubber. Ceilings are soundproofed with accoustical tile. Picture window construction admits adequate daylight. Artificial lighting is recessed and fluorescent to simulate daylight effect. The structure is fully and thermostatically heated. Air-conditioned cooling capacity is 105 tons output. Each office has outside exposure, providing good lighting throughout.

Building Cost Data

The structure contains 34,400 square feet. Replacement cost new is confirmed by local builders and architects at $41.00 per square foot exclusive of carpets, drapes, and restaurant furnishings and equipment. The replacement cost of furnishings and fixtures is as follows:

Carpets and drapes	$75,000
Restaurant furnishings	$76,000

Income and Expense Data

The subject property has a total net rentable area of 26,000 square feet. The ground floor contains 5,500 square feet and rents at $10.50 per square foot. Upstairs offices occupy 19,500 square feet and rent for $9.50 per square foot. The restaurant is leased for a period of five years at $2,900 per month. All offices and stores are under lease for periods of five to 10 years.

Operating expenses experienced by the subject property appear in line with average office building operating costs as reported by the Research Division of the National Association of Building Owners and Managers. Applicable operating expenditures based on net rentable square foot area is as follows:

Cleaning	99.0¢
Electric	37.0¢
Heat	10.4¢
Air conditioning	31.6¢
Plumbing	4.8¢
Elevator	26.6¢
General expense	27.0¢
General repairs	16.4¢
Alterations	6.8¢
Decorating	9.4¢
Recapture	45.2¢
Management	25.0¢
Mortgage amortization	64.8¢
Taxes and insurance	164.6¢
Estimated life of restaurant furnishings	10 years
Estimated life of carpets and drapes	20 years

Market Indices

Comparative sales indicate a unit value for the land at $20 per square foot. Similar buildings have been acquired at six times the annual gross income.

Investment capital is available as follows:

1st Mortgage 2/3 of value at 12%
2nd Mortgage 1/5 of value at 13%
Equity at 10%

The effective age is 3 years and remaining economic life is 45 years. The annuity method of capitalization is indicated.

CASE STUDY 1: SUGGESTED SOLUTION

	Year 1	Year 2	Year 3	Year 4
Lot sales				
70 × $10,500	$ 735,000			
70 × 11,340		$793,800		
70 × 12,247			$857,290	
70 × 13,227				$925,890
Plus utility refund; 70 × $100	7,000	7,000	7,000	7,000
Total revenue	$ 742,000	$800,800	$864,290	$932,890
Less: Development cost				
(280 × $3,675)	$1,029,000	—		
Underground electric utility lines				
(280 × $600)	168,000	—		
Development fee				
(280 × $2,038)	570,640	—		
Interest, taxes, legal fees				
(70 × $250)	17,500	17,500	17,500	17,500
Sales commission				
(10% × $735,000, etc.)	73,500	79,380	85,729	92,589
Advertising and field overhead costs				
(3% × $735,000, etc.)	22,050	23,814	25,719	27,777
Water and sewer connection fee				
(70 × $300)	21,000	21,000	21,000	21,000
Total expenses	$1,901,690	$141,694	$149,948	$158,866
Net sales revenue	($1,159,690)	$659,106	$714,342	$774,024
Times present worth at 10%	0.909091	0.826446	0.751315	0.683013
	($1,054,264)	$544,716	$536,696	$528,668
Total present worth of 100-acre tract for prescribed subdivision plan		$555,816 or $5,558/acre		

CASE STUDY 1: ALTERNATIVE PLAN SUGGESTED SOLUTION

	Year 1	Year 2	Year 3	Year 4
Total revenue (unchanged)	$742,000	$800,800	$864,290	$932,890
Less:				
Development cost (280 × $3,675)/3	$343,000	$343,000	$343,000	—
Utility lines (280 × $600)/3	56,000	56,000	56,000	—
Development fee (280 × $2,038)/3	190,213	190,213	190,213	—
Interest, taxes, legal fees (70 × $250)	17,500	17,500	17,500	17,500
Sales commission (10% × $735,000, etc.)	73,500	79,380	85,729	92,589
Advertising and field overhead costs (3% × $735,000, etc.)	22,050	23,814	25,719	27,777
Water and sewer connection fee (70 × $300)	21,000	21,000	21,000	21,000
Total expenses	$723,263	$730,907	$739,161	$158,866
Net sales revenue	$ 18,737	$ 69,893	$125,129	$774,024
Times present worth at 10%	0.909091	0.826446	0.751315	0.683013
	$ 17,034	$ 57,763	$ 94,011	$528,668
Total present worth of 100-acre tract under staged development plan	$697,476 or $6,975/acre			

By staging the three categories of development expenses over a three-year period, the present value of the prospective 100-acre subdivision is increased by 25 percent ($6,975 versus $5,558 an acre). Thus the latter method of development is recommended.

CASE STUDY 2: SUGGESTED SOLUTION

1. Cost Approach to Value

Replacement cost new: building cubic
Contents = 80′ × 90′ × 56′ × 403,200
cu ft

403,200 cu ft × $1.30 =	$524,160
Add cost of furniture and equipment:	
60 Ranges at $225 =	13,500
Furniture	1,500
60 Refrigerators at $600 =	36,000
60 Dishwashers at $250 =	15,000
Total cost new	$590,160
Less accrued depreciation	—
Depreciated replacement cost—new	$590,160
Add land value by comparison	
15,000 sq ft × $5.00 =	75,000
Total value—under cost approach	$665,160
Rounded to $665,000	

2. Market Approach to Value

	Sale No.			
	1	*2*	*3*	*4*
Sale price	$680,000	$350,000	$710,000	$746,155
Time adjustment	None	None	None	1.10
Adjusted price	$680,000	350,000	710,000	820,770
Land value	$ 65,000	32,000	70,000	87,000
Building Value	$615,000	318,000	640,000	733,770
Age and condition	1.11[a]	1.25	1.00	1.04
Adjusted for age	$754,800	437,500	710,000	853,600
No. of apartments	67	40	64	80
No. of rooms	158	94	151	197
Price per apartment	$ 11,266	10,938	11,094	10,670
Price per room	$ 4,777	4,654	4,702	4,333
Gross income	$ 98,765	49,735	102,225	112,000
Gross income multiplier	6.9	7.0	6.9	6.9

Market value of subject property
1. 60 Apartments at $11,000 per apartment = $660,000
2. 140 Rooms at $4,700[b] per room = $658,000
3. Gross income $94,122 × 6.9 (multiplier) = $649,442

[a]50 years/45 years = 1.11.
[b]Market indexes based principally on sale 3, because no adjustment for condition and age of building was necessary.

Indicated value via market approach

$655,000

3. Income Approach to Value

Gross revenue		
30 Apts. at $120 × 12 =		$ 43,200
10 Apts. at $145 × 12 =		17,400
15 Apts. at $155 × 12 =		27,900
5 Apts. at $185 × 12 =		11,100
Total revenue		$ 99,600
Less 5.5% vacancy and collection losses		5,478
Effective revenue		$ 94,122
Less operating expenses		
Management 5% =	$4,706	
Real estate taxes		
City $350,000 at 0.01365 =	4,778	
County 350,000 at 0.00835 =	2,923	
Insurance 0.0025 × $590,160 =	1,475	
Liability	125	
Payroll	3,000	
Electricity	1,200	
Water and sewage service	1,400	
Heating fuel	1,300	
Legal, etc.	500	
Painting and decorating	2,667	
Exterior repairs	800	
Supplies	450	
Elevator contract	1,000	
Repairs general	700	
Reserve for replacements		
Ranges $13,500 ÷ 15 =	900	
Refrigerators $36,000 ÷ 15 =	2,400	
Dishwashers $15,000 ÷ 12 =	1,250	
Lobby furnishings $1,500 ÷ 10 =	150	
Equipment $15,000 ÷ 15 =	1,000	
Total operating expense and reserves		$ 32,724
Net operating income		$ 61,398
Interest rate 8.0%		
Income to land		
8.0% × $75,000 =		6,000
Income residual to building		$ 55,378
Building value		
$55,378 × 10.413707		$576,690
(a_n at 9.5%, 50 yr.)		
Add land value of		75,000
Total value—earnings approach		$651,690
Rounded to $652,000		

4. Reconciliation

Analysis of Valuation data discloses the following conclusions:

1. Cost Approach	$665,000
2. Market Approach	655,000
3. Income Approach	652,000

Since only four sales were available for comparison purposes and considerable adjustments were necessary to compensate for time of sale, rate of depreciation, and differences in land value, the market approach in this instance is not wholly reliable as an index of value.

The cost approach set the ceiling of value and proves reliable only if truly comparable replacement costs could be obtained. A change of only 1 percent in the cubic cost of reconstruction would cause a value difference in excess of $5,900 for the subject property. For this reason the cost approach was used only as a check on the reliability of the final estimate of value.

The income approach provides for the subject property a strong indication of value. This is so for two reasons: (1) Value is defined as the present worth of future rights to income, and (2) the value is based on established and competitive income on which investors rely for value comparison with alternative and similar investment properties and/or opportunities.

Based on the considerations detailed above, it is the appraiser's professional and considered opinion that the apartment property warrants a value as of the date of this appraisal in the amount of:

Six Hundred Fifty-Five Thousand Dollars
($655,000)

Certified by
John Doe, M.A.I., S.R.A.
Appraiser

CASE STUDY 3: SUGGESTED SOLUTION

Land Value

	Sale No.			
	1	*2*	*3*	*4*
Price	$67,500	$75,000	$50,000	$90,000
Time adjustment	1.00	1.00	1.05	1.00
Price—adjusted	$67,500	75,000	52,500	90,000
Front feet	40	44	44	60
Area	4,600	4,840	4,840	6,000
Price per front foot	$ 1,688	1,705	1,193	1,500
Price per square foot	$ 14.67	15.50	10.85	15.00
Corner and location adjustment	0.95	0.90	1.25	1.00
Adjusted price (front feet)	$ 1,604	1,534	1,491	1,500
Adjusted price (sq ft)	$ 13.94	13.95	13.56	15.00

Sale 4 required no adjustment and is judged most comparable. Sale 4 also falls well within the limits of comparable value set by sales 1 to 3.

The indicated value of the subject property—based on market comparison—is

32 front feet at $1,500 = $48,000

Cost Approach to Value

	Square Feet	
Main Building Area:		
Downstairs	2,876	
Upstairs	1,900	
Lean-to	263	
Replacement cost new:		
Downstairs 2,876 sq ft at $25.00 =		$ 71,900
Upstairs 1,900 sq ft at $21.00 =		39,900
Lean-to 263 sq ft at $19.50 =		5,128
Total replacement cost new		$116,928
Deferred maintenance:		
Ceiling repairs and redecoration through- out	$25,000	
Wear, tear, and obsolescence based on effective age of 45 years at 1.5% per year = 67.5% of $116,928 =	78,926	
Total accrued depreciation	103,926	
Depreciated building cost		$ 13,002
Add land value—by comparison (32 front feet × $1,500)		48,000
Total value via cost approach		$ 61,002
Rounded to $61,000		

Interest Rate from Market Data

		Sale No.			
		5	6	7	8
A.	Price	$73,500	67,500	84,000	67,500
B.	Building value (%)	30	35	25	26
C.	Building value—amount	$22,050	23,625	21,000	17,550
D.	Effective gross	$10,800	9,750	12,450	9,675
E.	Operating ratio (%)	35	32	38	35
F.	Net operating income	$ 7,020	6,630	7,719	6,289
G.	Recapture rate (%)	5%	5%	5%	5%
H.	Recapture income	$ 1,103	1,181	1,050	878
I.	Net interest income	$ 5,917	5,449	6,669	5,411
J.	Interest rate $I \div A$	8.1	8.1	7.9	8.0

Based on market analysis of comparable properties an interest rate of 8% is indicated.

Market Approach to Value

	Sale No.			
	5	6	7	8
Land value	$51,450	43,875	63,000	49,950
Dep. building value	$22,050	23,625	21,000	17,550
Effective age—adjustment	0.67	0.62	0.78	0.56
Time adjustment	1.10	1.05	1.10	1.10
Adjusted building value	$16,979	15,829	18,480	11,583
Building area (sq ft)	7,800	7,750	7,700	5,320
Building value per square foot	$ 2.18	2.04	2.40	2.18
Gross income multiplier	6.8	6.9	6.7	7.0

A depreciated building value of $2.25 is indicated per square foot. The gross multiplier is 6.9. Based on these indices of value, the market approach yields the following value results:

Building value	5,039 sq ft at $2.25 =	$11,338
Add land value of		48,000
Total value		$59,338
Effective gross income	$8,761 × 6.9 =	$60,451
Rounded to $60,000		

Income Approach to Value

Gross income		$ 8,940
Vacancy and collection loss 2%		179
Effective gross income		$ 8,761
Operating expenses		
R.E. taxes	$1,250	
Special tax	115	
Insurance	435	
Exterior expenses	655	
Management (7%)	613	
Total operating expense		3,068
Net operating income		$ 5,693
Less income to land		
$48,000 at 8% =		3,840
Income to building		$ 1,853
Building value		
$1,853 ÷ 14.67% (0.08 + 0.0667) =		$12,631
Add land value		48,000
Total value		$60,631
Rounded to $60,500		

Value Reconciliation

Value under cost approach	$61,000
Value under market approach	60,000
Value under income approach	60,500

The analysis of market sales and income data support an estimate of $60,000 for the subject property.

CASE STUDY 4: SUGGESTED SOLUTION

1. Cost Approach to Value

Replacement cost new:		
Building: 34,400 sq ft at $41.00 =		$1,410,400
Carpets and drapes		75,000
Restaurant furnishings		76,000
Total replacement cost—new		$1,561,400
Less: accrued depreciation:		
Building—6.7% × $1,410,000		
(3 yr/45 yr)[1] =	$ 94,000	
Carpets and drapes—		
$75,000 at 25% (5 yr/20 yr)[1] =	18,750	
Restaurant furnishings—		
$76,000 at 50% (5 yr/10 yr)[1] =	38,000	150,750
Depreciated replacement cost		$1,410,650
Add: Land value—13,200 sq ft at $20 =		264,000
Value via cost approach		$1,674,650
Rounded to $1,675,000		

[1] Based on straight-line depreciation.

2. Income Approach to Value

Gross income

Ground floor—5,500 sq ft at $10.50 =	$57,750
Upstairs offices—19,500 sq ft at $9.50 =	185,250
Restaurant—$2,900/month × 12 months =	34,800
Total gross income	$277,800
Less: vacancy and collection losses (negligible)[2]	0
Effective gross income	$277,800

Less: operating expenses

Cleaning	$0.990 per square foot
Electric	0.370 per square foot
Heat	0.104 per square foot
Air conditioning	0.316 per square foot
Plumbing	0.048 per square foot
Elevator	0.266 per square foot
General expense	0.270 per square foot
General repairs	0.164 per square foot
Alterations	0.068 per square foot
Decorating	0.094 per square foot
Management	0.250 per square foot
Taxes and insurance	1.646 per square foot
	$4.586 per square foot

Total fixed expenses and maintenance costs	
26,000 sq ft at $4.586 =	$119,236
Replacement of carpets and drapes =	3,750[3]
Replacement of restaurant furnishings =	7,600[4]
Parking lot $1,600/month × 12 =	19,200
Total operating expenses	$149,786
Net operating income	$128,014
Less: income attributable to land	
$264,000 at 7.5%[5]	19,800
Income attributable to building	$108,214

[2]Vacancy and collection losses are assumed to be negligible since the building space is under leases for periods of 5 to 10 years, and in view of the favorable location of the property.

[3]Based on 20-year life, straight-line depreciation.

[4]Based on 10-year life, straight-line depreciation.

[5]The interest rate is calculated by the market data method as follows:

Value of subject site	$20.00 per square foot
Annual rental of similar site across street	
($19,200/12,500 sq ft)	$1.54 per square foot
R_L = $1.54/$20	
= 7.7%	
Rounded to 7.5%	

Capitalized value of building income over
remaining economic life of 45 years at
7.5% interest under the annuity income

method = $108,214 × 12.8186 =	$1,387,155
Add: land value	264,000
Total value	$1,651,155

Rounded to $1,651,000

3. Market Approach to Value

Gross income $277,800 × 6.0 (multiplier) = $1,666,800
Rounded to $1,667,000

4. Reconciliation

The following value estimates were derived from an analysis of the available valuation data:

Cost approach	$1,675,000
Income approach	1,651,000
Market approach	1,667,000

The cost approach is useful as a guide to value since the appraised property is relatively new. Secondary reliance, however, must be attributed to this approach since the improvement is not new, and more reliable estimates are provided by the other approaches to value. Thus the cost approach, yielding an estimate within 1% of the final estimate, was used only as a check on the reliability of the final estimate of value.

Market value may be defined as the estimated price which a property will bring in the open market—given sufficient time and assuming knowledgeable buyer and seller. This definition encompasses both the "barter" and "productivity" aspects of the concept of value since, in effect, the former is based (at least implicitly) on the latter.

The final estimate of value of this property is based primarily on the market comparison approach since no adjustments were required. The income approach—which yields an estimate that is within about 1% of the final estimate—reinforces the reliability of the market approach.

The subject property in the opinion of the appraiser warrants a value as of the date of this appraisal in the amount of:

One Million Six Hundred Seventy Thousand Dollars
($1,670,000)

APPENDIX IV
SUGGESTED SOLUTIONS TO CHAPTER PROBLEMS

CHAPTER 1

1. Everyone has a scale of preference for given goods or services. This preference, or *desire-pull relationship* between an individual and the object or service wanted, is influenced continuously and in varying degrees by personal traits and by cultural, religious, and governmental forces which influence each person as a member of society.
2. It is that price that occurs when the forces of supply and demand are in equilibrium and no artificial or temporary barriers impede either supply or demand.
3. The specific value sought by the appraiser should be clearly stated in the letter of transmittal as well as in the body of the appraisal report, and a definition of value should be fully expressed in order to prevent misinterpretation and error in acting on the basis of a value estimate.
4. The key components of the market value concept are:
   (a) Price a property will bring.
   (b) Buyers and sellers act without compulsion.
   (c) Buyers and sellers are knowledgeable of the property's uses.
   (d) Seller is capable of conveying title.
   (e) Property sells under cash or cash-equivalent terms of sale.
5. A knowledge of value characteristics (utility, scarcity, demand, and transferability) are useful in appraising real property and changes in any of these characteristics allows the appraiser to measure value. Any improvement in any of the value characteristics results in enhanced value of the affected object.
6. The market value concept as currently known has the strengths of being widely accepted and is a normative concept or one that refers to typical behavior, such as usual management, motivations, and expectations of parties in a real estate transaction. On the other hand, weaknesses of the market value concept include the incorrect presumption that ordinary buyers and sellers are bestowed with the patience, resources, and mental prowess to be fully cognizant of all conditions

influencing the present and future uses of the property. It depicts what ought to be in an ideal sense rather than actual conditions that face market participants.

CHAPTER 2

1. Contributions to present-day appraisal practices by the early schools of economic thought are:
    (a) Mercantilism—stressed a "natural" value based on competitive forces in place of "just" value; emphasized production rather than distribution of wealth.
    (b) Physiocrats—did not regard value as intrinsic in things; the concepts of price and value were accepted as interchangeable terms.
    (c) Classical economics—argued that the value of any good or service is equal to the quantity of labor which it allows its owner to purchase; stressed a distinction between "value in use" and "value in exchange"; pointed out difference between "market value" and "market price"; Malthus held that production does not create its own demand; initiated rent theory and began the residual procedure of valuation; "normal" value and market or price were distinguished.
    (d) Austrian school of economics—developed the marginal utility theory of value; began the idea that interest was a measure of time preference for consumption and the present worth theory for discounting future benefits; stressed importance of demand as a value determinant.
    (e) Historical and institutional school—rejected the "economic man" philosophy.
    (f) Neoclassical and equilibrium school of economics—Marshall emphasized a dynamic value theory.
    (g) Early Twentieth Century Value Theory—Mitchell developed business cycle theory and showed how one phase of the economy leads to subsequent stages.
2. Most probable selling price is a prediction rather than a measure of the price that a property will likely bring; similarly, most probable use is market oriented and depicts the use to which the land and building would probably be put instead of representing an idealized value maximization model or abstract set of conditions.
3. Ross's band of investment method of developing a risk rate pioneered use of mortgage terms and equity yields. It was deficient in its failure to provide for equity or debt recapture.
4. Babcock's criticism of the misuse of the cost approach was based on appraisers substituting it for direct market evidence of value.
5. Ellwood substituted the forecast holding period used by investors in place of the much longer and uncertain remaining economic life of a building, held that property appreciated as well as depreciated, and integrated mortgage financing into his development of capitalization rates.
6. The following represent significant contributions to the present appraisal procedures:
    (a) Irving Fisher's linking of interest rate to income and present value.
    (b) Frederick Babcock's emphasis that sales in themselves were not indicative of market value and his criticism of the depreciated cost approach.
    (c) Richard Ratcliff's advocacy of the most probable value concept.
    (d) Thurston Ross's band of investment theory, later refined by Edwin Kazdin as a means for developing capitalization rates.
    (e) Leon Ellwood's preparation of financial tables and emphasis of an appraisal

methodology that more faithfully reflected actual practices of real estate investors.

CHAPTER 3

1. Realty, sometimes called real estate, includes land, building improvements, as well as anything permanently affixed to land or buildings where the reasonable intent—as supported by the method of annexation and the relationship of the parties involved at the time of annexation—causes the article to be classified as a fixture.

2. Police power is the sovereign power of government to restrict the use of realty in order to protect the well-being of its citizens. No compensation is due the affected property owners when this power is invoked. Eminent domain is the right of government to acquire all or part of an owner's land provided that the use is public and just compensation is paid the property owner.

3. An accurate highest and best use analysis is necessary in real property appraising since it provides the basis for the appraised value. If the highest and best use is inaccurate, so will be the amount of the appraised value.

4. The key terms in the highest and best use concept are:

   succession of uses relates to all the short- and long-term uses that allow a property to realize its highest value; *available uses* is important to this concept since only such uses can cause actual value to be realized; *legal uses* mean those uses actually allowed by private and public land use controls and agreements; *physically permitted uses* refers to all those uses permitted by soil conditions, topography, and site shape; and *sufficient demand* simply means that after all the other conditions are met, in order for the property to achieve its full potential, there must be prospective buyers who are able to acquire the property.

5. The marginal productivity concept is applied to the market comparison approach by revealing the value added or loss due to the presence or lack of a particular feature. If, for example, 200-foot depth lots sell for $25,000 and 150-foot sites command a price of $22,000; the 50-foot additional depth beyond 150 feet appears to be worth $3,000. Analysis of such differences in value can be applied to an appraised site.

6. All physical and tangible items which have attributes of, or claims to objects of, value are classified as wealth. Property is a right to control, use, and own wealth. Property as here defined is intangible. The appraiser is concerned with the evaluation of (property) rights in and to wealth. The larger the rights, as a general rule, the greater the future benefits and hence the greater the present value.

7. This statement is true. Where legal requirements cause an increase in construction costs without offsetting benefits resulting from a better housing (and non-housing) product, land values will tend to be lower. Land is "residual" in character under a highest and best use. Legal impediments that lower income inevitably lower the value of land that is subject to adverse controls. This is especially true where communities are competing with each other for population growth and eonomic development.

CHAPTER 4

1. Replacement cost typically is favored over reproduction cost by appraisers since it represents current construction technology and building materials rather than

those used when a building was originally constructed; reproduction cost represents the costs incurred in replicating the building as it was originally built.

2. Before a sale property can be used as an indication of market value, the following conditions must be checked by the appraiser:
   (a) The relationship of the parties.
   (b) The terms of sale and the market conditions.
   (c) The date of sale.
   (d) The effect of changes in the purchasing power of the dollar.

3. The date of sale of a comparable sale property can distort the indicated value of an appraised property by indicating a value when the sale occurred rather than when a property is being appraised. The greatest possibility of distortion comes from an inaccurate adjustment being made in recognition of inflation between the sale date and the appraisal date.

4. In an inflationary market, purchasing power is shifted from the debt position (lender) to the equity position (borrower). Thus the increasing value of the property increases the value of the equity position at the expense of the lender unless there are offsetting provisions in the mortgage contract.

5. A deduction for accrued depreciation is properly made from replacement cost new in the cost approach as a means for deriving the present value of a property. However, this deduction is avoided in the income approach since the tenants and landlords already have adjusted the rent in view of the present state of the property.

6. Activities prevailing during the business cycle include increased or decreased overall employment, wage levels, supply of mortgage funds, interest rates, and personal savings. The building cycle reacts to population changes, family formation, vacancy ratios, and cost of land and housing supply in relation to prevailing and anticipated rental levels. The business cycle operates on the demand side while the building cycle operates on the supply side.

7. (a) *Value* is the present worth of future rights to income—or in terms of barter, the power of a good or service to command other goods or services in exchange. (b) *Price* is the monetary measure of dollar value given in exchange for a good or service. Price may be more or less than value. It is only when the price paid is *warranted* that price and value are in equilibrium. (c) *Cost* is a monetary measure of past sacrifices of the factors of production or expenditure for a good or service. Costs may further be identified as historical, original, replacement, or reproduction, depending on the meaning of the term. (d) *Warranted cost* occurs when the agents of production equal value. Costs which are not justified cannot equal value because no informed buyer will pay more for a good or service than is warranted under existing economic conditions.

8. By use of the cost approach only, Mr. Baker could commit a serious error in value. A hotel in the desert costs as much if not more to construct than a hotel in a large city when built in conformity with the concept of highest and best land use. The value of the desert hotel no doubt is zero. To establish value for loan purposes, Mr. Baker should check the findings derived under the cost approach with value results obtained under the market and income approaches to value.

CHAPTER 5

1. Breaking down racial and sex barriers has greatly broadened employment and housing opportunities for racial minorities and women. The results have been to expand the market for real estate and to qualify both groups for more ex-

pensive housing. Thus housing demand has risen along with values due to these improved employment and housing opportunities.

2. Generally, the sequence of events associated with municipal housing rent control laws has been (a) the quality of housing suffers and the quantity is reduced, (b) the private ownership sector withdraws, and (c) the government (using tax dollars) attempts to provide replacement housing.

3. The average household size in this country has decreased from 4.93 in 1890 to 2.76 in 1980. The effect of these smaller households has been to stimulate demand for housing.

4. The rate of savings influences a nation's well-being. If this rate is too low, then insufficient capital is available to maintain modern industry, causing that nation to be noncompetitive in a worldwide economy, with a resulting rising level of unemployment. An unusually high rate of savings could prove harmful to the economy by reducing the level of consumption.

5. Probable advantages of deregulation of the savings and loan industry for housing are to allow S&Ls to pay competitive interest rates, thus reducing disintermediation; another alleged advantage is to reduce the irregular nature of their capital flows. However, if the interest rates paid to investors are too high, the corresponding interest rates on mortgages may become so high as to adversely affect homeownership.

6. In recent years there has been a leveling off in the rate of homeownership in this country. Such a "steady-state" condition is neither unusual nor unexpected since many people today prefer a more mobile and less burdensome life-style that is provided by apartment living. It can be conjectured that homeownership causes a greater sense of social responsibility and interest in society and the well-being of neighborhoods and communities. A shift toward apartment residency has fostered growth of the ministorage industry. Any abatement in homeownership would probably retard suburban nonresidential growth, which traditionally provides residential supporting services.

7. No, zoning regulations cannot prevent value decline. Zoning regulations, however, must be complemented by demand, appropriate acccess, and transportation as well as suitable site conditions.

CHAPTER 6

1. Earlier causes of urbanization—such as government, commerce, culture, religion, courts, and mutual protection—can be applied to present regional analysis. An understanding of the motivation for earlier people agglomerating aids us in analyzing contemporary regions since many of these basic motivations persist today.

2. The names and basic features of each of the urban growth theories follow:
   (a) *Concentric ring growth theory* by Ernest Burgess divided a city into a series of fixed rings extending from the center (central business district) outward through the successive zones of transition, low-income housing, middle- to high-income housing, to the commuter's zone.
   (b) *Axial growth theory* by Richard Hurd depicted city growth along transportation routes, with the resulting land use patterns resembling the spokes of a star.
   (c) *Sector growth theory* by Homer Hoyt focused on residential neighborhoods. He found that high-grade residential areas progressed along lines of travel

        toward flood-free areas, open country, and toward the homes of community leaders.

    (d) *Multiple nuclei growth theory* by Chauncey Harris and Edward Ullman revealed discrete forms of land use activity with certain similar activities grouped together because they benefited from close proximity and certain activities located away from other dissimilar activities, such as homes and factories.

3. There are different interpretations of this question by each student. Nevertheless, a person analyzing a region would benefit from a knowledge of the different land uses in different parts of a region, the natural and fabricated forces that shape urban growth, and a more informed view of metropolitan growth and decline that these static growth models can cause.

4. Economic base analysis assists in the understanding of regional economy by showing how a region "earns its living." It breaks a community down into the export and service industries, and then strives to forecast any change in employment for these two components of the local economy.

5. The main purposes of regional economic and population analysis are to determine demographic trends, diversity and strength of employment opportunities, proposed directions and nature of future growth, and the comparative supply and demand for real estate.

6. In addition to the 10 economic measures listed in the chapter, other possibilities are rental levels and vacancy levels for different categories of realty, changes in mortgage terms and interest rates, average number of days required to sell a home, developed but unsold residential sites, capital improvement budgets for each local jurisdiction, and changes in vehicular traffic on specified roads.

CHAPTER 7

1. The two major misconceptions in neighborhood analysis in the past have been to approach it from (a) an idealized notion of what a neighborhood should be rather than what it actually is, and (b) that the introduction of racial minorities automatically caused property values to decline.

2. Linkages are defined as external economies or centripetal forces. Linkages are the periodic interaction between people or establishments that hold them together. Examples of linkages are where machine work is subcontracted by one business for other nearby businesses or where close proximity to legal or advertising services makes a particular location attractive for a small business unable to afford such specialized in-house staff.

3. A neighborhood's popularity and property values in it rise and fall in a cyclical manner. The appraiser must know which phase of its life cycle a neighborhood is in when an appraisal is made of a property in the neighborhood so that he or she can accurately estimate the effect of neighborhood age and obsolescence on amenities of ownership or income from its use over the remaining economic life of the subject property.

4. Neighborhoods can be delineated in the following ways: physical boundaries, legal and governmental factors, and price levels of residences.

5. The answer to this question is based on each person's experiences.

6. Ten residential neighborhood characteristics that should be investigated by the appraiser include nature of terrain, drainage facilities, proximity to schools, stores and recreational facilities, freedom from hazards and adverse influences, income and education of residents, age grouping and size of families, extent of development, percentage of homes that are owner occupied, and zoning and deed restrictions.

7. The earlier practice of "redlining" was intended to indicate neighborhoods that had septic system failures. Later it was used by mortgage lenders to avoid making loans in high-risk neighborhoods. By failing to infuse mortgage capital into these neighborhoods, owners lacked funds for selling and repairing their homes, which accelerated the decline of the neighborhood and in turn the value of properties in such urban areas.

8. Traffic analysis is important in all types of neighborhoods. Neighborhood traffic conditions play a crucial role in the succcess of retail districts and especially, shopping centers. These centers are largely dependent on a sizable unimpeded flow of vehicular traffic. For industrial neighborhoods it is important that there be adequate access to markets, to sources of materials, subcontractors, and a skilled work force; adequate circulation and parking for trucks are also needed. Residential neighborhoods are enhanced when public transit is readily available at reasonable costs.

CHAPTER 8

1. Ten square chains (10 × 66 ft × 66 ft) equals 1 acre.
2. A square acre has 43,560 sq ft (= 208.71 feet on each side).
3. Three major concerns in conducting a site analysis are:
   (a) Determining highest and best use.
   (b) Measuring the marginal productivity of the site.
   (c) Determining optimum size and depth of the site.
4. One advantage of the monument method of site description is that it is based on a physical survey of the property, using physical landmarks. A disadvantage of this method is that the physical landmarks or monuments may be moved or disappear over time.
5. A knowledge of soil conditions is important to a proper site analysis because such conditions affect the potential use and value of a site.
6. The inherent weakness of depth tables is that they are inflexible and may bear little relationship to local value patterns.

CHAPTER 9

1. Five purposes for separate site appraisals include:
   (a) Local real estate tax assessments.
   (b) Separation of land and improvements for federal taxes.
   (c) To ascertain a property's highest and best use.
   (d) Insurance.
   (e) Site leases
2. The stated consideration (price) may be inaccurate in a deed for any of the following four reasons:
   (a) The buyer may want to give the appearance of having paid a higher price than was actually paid.
   (b) The seller may try to save money by paying a lower amount of revenue stamps than is justified by the actual sales price.
   (c) In some states, only the cash portion of transactions need be considered; whereas in others, state revenue stamps represent the full consideration of the sale.

(d) In the case of property exchanges, the interested parties may understate or overstate the transaction price for tax or other purposes which prove mutually advantageous.

3. An appraiser should thoroughly understand the conditions that existed when a property sold in order to accurately measure the current value of the appraised property. For example, a site may have sold as an unfinished parcel, lacking its present zoning and curbs and gutters. Also it may have sold in a "buyers' market" while at the date of appraisal the market had reversed to become a "sellers' market."

4. The four basic categories of adjustments made for comparable sales are date of sale, conditions of sale, location, and physical features. These adjustments may be in some combination of percentage, dollar, plus or minus, or by multiplication. The appraiser should never adjust for features not considered by market participants.

5. The sales comparison approach is preferable over the land residual method whenever there are a sufficient number of recent sales of similar properties. It is an easily understood method that is based on actual transactions. On the other hand, the land residual method provides a useful method for judging the highest and best use of a site. Further, it has its place when there is a dearth of comparable land sales and the value of the improvements can be accurately judged.

6. The land developmental method is an acceptable alternative to the sales comparison method when the tract of land is capable (physically and economically) of being subdivided. Accompanying its use should be an accurate highest and best use analysis, an accurate accounting of all the expenditures necessary to produce the forecast income, accurate depiction of the income each year of the marketing period, and careful selection and use of the discount rate.

7. (a) No, the buildings have identical values. The extra cost of blasting rock is a charge ascribable to land. (b) After blasting, yes—before blasting, no. The value of lot B before blasting was only $5,000. (c) The nature of blasting expenditures is a land development cost chargeable to land to bring it up to its highest and best use.

CHAPTER 10

1. See Chapter 17 for calculator keystroke sequence or use financial tables.

$$\text{Installment to amortize 1 for 12\%, 25 yr.} \quad \frac{0.010532}{0.011716} = 0.898960$$

Installment to amortize 1 for 13%, 20 yr.

Cash equivalent = ($125,000)(0.80)(0.898960) = $89,896

+ Down payment (0.20 × $125,000)   25,000

                                                                   $114,896

2. A comparatively small net adjustment may not represent the most comparable sale because of several offsetting positive and negative adjustments. For example, a net adjustment of $500 could result from five positive adjustments of $25,000 and six negative adjustments equal to $24,500.

3. Adjustments initially should be made for time and conditions of sale prior to considering differences in physical and locational features in order to reveal the price that the sale property would have brought in the current market.

4. Use of the assessed value–sales price appraisal technique might have the weak-

nesses of only being a check on the accuracy of the market sales approach, the assessment ratio for a particular property may be off considerably, and, finally, it is appraising on the basis of someone else's estimate.

5. A problem that can occur when applying a market-derived GIM to an appraised property's effective gross income is that some property owners simply will not furnish the needed effective gross income information. Also, there is the potential problem of the appraiser obtaining a GIM based on potential gross income and applying it to the effective gross income of the appraised property.

6. The advantages of the GIM as a means of estimating market value are:
   (a) It is readily understood by clients.
   (b) It is based exclusively on market events.
   Disadvantages of the GIM appraisal technique include:
   (a) Its being based on a property's gross income which might be similar to an appraised property's gross income, but the net operating income of the comparable property may differ sharply from that of the appraised property.
   (b) It fails to account for the remaining economic life of either the sale or subject property.
   (c) Adjustments in the gross income or sales price tend to distort the GIM since property features already have been considered and "adjusted" by the buyer and seller.

CHAPTER 11

1. The higher the rise of a roof, the more lasting the roof shingle coverage, because of lessened wear and tear from rain, hail, snow, or tornadic winds. A rise that is too slight permits rain and wind to drive under the shingles, weakening the shingle fastenings and the undercover roof seal.

2. "R value" measures the insulating quality of the material. The higher the R value, the better the insulation.

3. Elevations show the exterior sides of a building as it appears after all structural work has been completed. As a rule, each building side is viewed by an elevation and, for identification, marked as north, south, east, and west or by structural designation as front, rear, left, and right side elevation.

4. Six attributes of good floor planning include:
   (a) Orientation of rooms to capture prevailing breezes, sunshine, and beauty of area views surrounding the property.
   (b) Proper placing of picture window and large window areas to assure adequate light and fenestration for all rooms.
   (c) Provision for entrance hall or foyer (with guest closet space) to shield living room from direct view and drafts.
   (d) Grouping of bed and bedroom areas to assure maximum of privacy. A separate entrance to the bedroom wing or access without a view from or crossing of living room area is considered a must.
   (e) Proper functional layout of kitchen area to conserve steps in housekeeping.
   (f) Location of kitchen near entrance and side doors to minimize traffic flow.

5. Written specifications supplement the plans, elevations, and related drawings and sketches. In fact, written instructions are deemed of greater importance than graphic illustrations, and where these two are in conflict, it is the written word that is guiding and legally binding. Specifications historically have served as a contract document between builder and owner and are intended to avoid

disputes or misunderstandings concerning details of construction. They permit accurate estimating of required labor, quality of materials, and costing of contractors' and subcontractors' services in accordance with plan requirements. Specifications also safeguard against expensive omissions when construction costs are estimated and minimize construction delays due to misunderstanding of building plans.

6. Five matters of structural design that affect revenue, maintenance, management and, possibly, the remaining economic life of the building are:
   (a) Good lighting and adequate, concealed telephone and electric wiring to serve anticipated maximum service loads.
   (b) Sufficiency of central heating under individual unit or zone controls.
   (c) Capacity and readiness to supply air conditioning where competitively necessary.
   (d) High ratio of net rentable area as percentage of total building square foot area.
   (e) Necessary off-street parking.

CHAPTER 12

1. Determination of a site's highest and best use establishes a "yardstick" against which accrued depreciation of the improvements is measured. That is, accrued depreciation is the difference between cost new and market value. Market value in turn is a function of a site's highest and best use.

2. (a) The most important advantage of the depreciated cost approach is that it can be used to estimate the financial feasibility of a proposed property. That is, if the value indicated by the sales and income approaches exceeds the current reproduction cost, the property is feasible. The major disadvantage of the depreciated cost approach is that it requires great diligence in maintaining current data as well as in carefully recognizing differences in cost due to different sizes and quality of materials. (Other answers may be selected by the reader.)
   (b) *Advantage*: Any time the value of a property exceeds its reproduction cost, the developer is justified to proceed with the venture, assuming that a sufficient profit margin is realized.

      Disadvantage: Often, and especially for old properties, it is much too time consuming and expensive for an appraiser to use the depreciated cost approach. Additionally, the accrued depreciation estimate for such properties may be so large as to be questionable.

3. Accrued depreciation may be defined as the difference between cost new of a building(s) and current market value.

4. The principal difference between direct and indirect construction costs is that direct costs include labor and materials, while indirect costs are all other costs, including such charges as property management fees and professional service fees.

5. The comparative advantages of the replacement cost method are that it is based on modern materials, methods, and technology which are comparatively easy to obtain. Functional obsolescence is already excluded from this cost. On the other hand, the reproduction cost offers the advantage of showing the current cost of recreating the appraised building exactly as it was built and of the original materials.

6. (a) Builders' Detailed Inventory Method

   Advantage: It provides a detailed and accurate cost estimate for each major labor and material construction item when applied with care.

   Disadvantage: It is time consuming and costly; the typical appraiser is not technically trained or qualified to undertake such minute and detailed cost studies.

   (b) Quantity Survey Method

   Advantage: It is simpler than the builders' detailed inventory method and is preferred by architects in the costing of residences.

   Disadvantage: It is too time consuming for most appraisal assignments and is best used by trained cost estimators.

   (c) Unit-in-Place Construction Method

   Advantage: It is useful for estimating construction additions or deletions from given plans and specifications.

   Disadvantage: Because of the difficulty of accurately reducing carpentry and finishing work to a unit basis, this method of cost estimating is only infrequently used by builders and developers and is not recommended as a valuation tool for real estate appraisers.

   (d) Segregated or Trade Breakdown Method

   Advantage: It generally represents how most residential and small commercial property builders prepare their cost bids; it is fairly well understood by clients.

   Disadvantage: It is unreliable unless the appraiser inspects the building and judiciously compares the nature and quality of the building to the benchmark building in a cost manual or to figures provided by a local contractor.

   (e) Comparative Market Method

   Advantage: This method provides speedy cost estimates by the appraiser and is sufficiently accurate for standardized and relatively new buildings.

   Disadvantage: Generally, no two buildings are exactly alike in kind and quality of construction; and unless adjustments are made to reflect these differences, the margin of possible error may prove too great to make the estimate reliable as a guide to building costs.

CHAPTER 13

1. Accrued depreciation is similar to amortization in that both measure loss in value. However, these two concepts differ in that accrued depreciation measures actual or estimated loss in value, as expressed by the difference between current cost new and market value of the building(s) while amortization provides for future recapture of an asset via reserve provisions. Amortization is also known as "book depreciation" and is an accounting rather than an economic concept.

2. The causes of accrued depreciation for each of the three forms of accrued depreciation are:

   (a) *Physical deterioration*: caused by (1) wear and tear through use, (2) action of the elements such as termites, and (3) structural impairment through neglect, fire, water, explosion, and vandalism.

   (b) *Functional obsolescence*: caused by (1) faulty design, (2) inadequacy of structural facilities, (3) superadequacy of structural facilities, and (4) outmoded equipment.

(c) *External obsolescence*: caused by (1) neighborhood hazards and nuisances, (2) change in zoning and highest and best land use classification, (3) over- or underimprovement of land, and (4) decreasing demand.

A prospective owner or tenant would probably account for each of these deficiencies by paying a lower price or rental for such adversely affected property.

3. Economic life is more important than physical life for investment purposes because at the end of a building's productive or economic life the investor probably will need to raze or rehabilitate the building even though the structure may be structurally adequate and capable of surviving for many more years.

4. Building value = replacement cost minus accrued depreciation.

Replacement cost =	$120,000
− Accrued depreciation	
($120,000)[15/(15 + 45)]	30,000
Depreciated building cost	$ 90,000
+ Lot value	15,000
Total property value	$105,000

5. The principal criteria used to determine if a building suffers from curable or incurable physical deterioration is (a) the necessity to cure defects to provide for efficient (economical) operation, and (b) the cost to cure relative to value added or the increase in net operating income for the property as a whole.

6. Functional obsolescence–curable is defined as modernization and improvements which are essential and economically justified and which would be found in a new and comparable building. Five examples of this form of obsolescence are modernization of bathroom and kitchen, upgrading insulation, modernizing the heating system, adding needed closets, and replacing outdated fixtures.

7. The steps involved in estimating market value via the engineering breakdown method are:
   (a) Estimate physical deterioration–curable.
   (b) Estimate physical deterioration–incurable by breaking the structure into its major parts and via the age-life method, estimate the deterioration per structural part.
   (c) Estimate functional obsolescence–curable.
   (d) Estimate functional obsolescence–incurable.
   (e) Estimate external obsolescence–as related to improvements.
   The total of these deductions is the total acccrued depreciation. Care must be taken to avoid duplicating depreciation charges.

8.
Current reproduction cost	$135,000
Present value of dwelling	
($125,000 − $28,000)	97,000
Depreciated cost of dwelling	$ 38,000
Annual rate of depreciation	2%
($38,000/$135,000) ÷ 14 years	

9. Office building:

Sale price $175,000 at 125% of cost
Cost = $175,000 ÷ 1.25 = $140,000
Gain = $175,000 − $140,000 = $35,000

Apartment building:

Sale price: $175,000 at 75% of cost
Cost = $175,000 ÷ .75 = $233,333
Loss = $233,333 − $175,000 = $58,333
    Net loss = $58,333 − $35,000 = $23,333

CHAPTER 14

1. Market rent is defined as the amount of rent the appraised property probably would command at the date of appraisal. Contract rent is the rental income earned by the property as a result of contractual commitments which bind owners and tenants for a stipulated future time. These two rents may be equal when the contract rent matches the prevailing rent for similar properties.

2. Annual income declines $(I) = \dfrac{R \times D}{R + D}$

$$= \frac{0.10 \times 0.025}{0.10 + 0.025}$$

$$= \frac{0.0025}{0.1250}$$

$$= 0.02$$

3. At that future time when an improved property's building income is surpassed by the land earnings, it is likely that the site has become too valuable to be encumbered by the existing improvements. At this time, the building has reached the end of its economic life and may need to either be renovated or demolished.

4. The following five items should be considered by an appraiser in deriving the market rent for an apartment property: (1) building size, (2) quality of construction, (3) neighborhood, (4) location and site characteristics, and (5) amount and quality of furnishings and fixtures.

5. The appraiser must account for unusually high vacancy levels during the "rent-up" period even though vacancies may stabilize at lower levels later because to use the unrealized higher occupancy (lower vacancy) level overstates the income and in turn present value of the appraised property.

6. Unless the appraiser accurately accounts for the actual leased area for comparable rental properties, the income applied to the appraised property probably will either be under- or overstated.

7. For short-term leases, the lessor generally pays all operating costs, whereas the lessee tends to bear these expenses under long-term leases.

8. The accuracy of an appraisal report can be improved by the appraiser understanding such future payment provisions in leases as how much space and under what terms the space is being leased. The demised premises are measured differently, the netness of leases varies, and a variety of future payment provisions exist. The appraiser must know more than simply the square foot rental per month or year for the comparable and appraised properties.

9. Yes—assuming all other things remain equal—the passage of time has affected the value of this property. The building is 10 years older and thus nearer the end of its economic life. Value is based on the present worth of future rights to income, and these inevitably are reduced as the structure ages, even though annual income does not diminish.

10. To the extent that past managerial practices influence future income favorably or unfavorably, value is affected. Past managerial practices are of interest to an appraiser because exceptional management over past years may reduce future operating costs and produce a flow of income in excess of that which ordinarily can be anticipated under "typical" operations. Conversely, poor management over past years may cause excessive operational outlays in future years in order to bring the property up to the income performance expected under "typical" management and operation.

11. Past and present income serve as benchmarks for forecasting the anticipated future flow of income. Value should always be based on future rights to income and not on established past or present income.

Chapter 15

1. The following three items in an owner's income–expense statement should be disallowed for appraisal purposes: (1) mortgage debt service, (2) capital improvements shown as operating expenses, and (3) building depreciation.

2. Fixed expenses are those expenses that must be paid regardless of the occupancy level. Variable expenses tend to vary with the occupancy level and include the property management fee, repairs, and utility charges.

3. An argument for including replacement reserves in the operating expenses is that unless these future expenses are recognized on an annualized basis, the net operating income will be overstated for the appraised property. Conversely, if expense data compiled for comparable properties omit this charge and the comparable sales' overall capitalization rate is computed accordingly, then to include it for the subject property will distort the appraised value.

4. Assume:

Net operating income, excluding
   real estate taxes = $72,000
Market derived capitalization rate =   10%
Tax rate =   2%

Market value = $72,000 ÷ 0.12
            = $600,000

5. An inaccurate operating expense ratio can distort an estimated net operating income for an appraised property in the following three ways:
   (a) Different building designs can cause different expense ratios.
   (b) Buildings of different ages or in different locations can experience different income levels but the same square foot expenses.
   (c) The netness of leases can alter the share of expenses by the lessor and in turn affect the operating expense ratio.

6. Replacement reserves can be set up in the following three ways:
   (a) Identify the short-lived items that must be replaced during the remaining economic life of the building; determine how many times the item will need to be replaced; estimate its cost; determine the total cost; and finally, determine the annualized average replacement cost.
   (b) Estimate the replacement cost of the short-lived item for its initial replacement. Multiply this cost by the appropriate sinking fund factor, using the number of years the replacement item is expected to last.

(c) Forecast replacement reserves over the expected holding period for the investment. The annual dollar requirements for these replacement costs are then computed by multiplying the replacement costs by a sinking fund factor for the remaining period.

Each student should express his or her own reasons for choosing one of the foregoing methods.

7. Property B has the greater value because of its favorable operating ratio compared with property A. The income from B is less risky than income from property A; hence income from B will be capitalized at a lower rate of interest. A 20 percent drop in revenue wipes out the net operating income for A but lowers the net operating income for B by only $8,000, or 40 percent.

8. Gross revenue ($275 × 12 × 40) $132,000
   Collection and vacancy losses 5%[a] 6,600

   Effective gross revenue $125,400

Operating Expenses	As Reported	As Adjusted
Taxes on land and building	$14,400	$14,400
Power and light	1,200	1,200
Depreciation provision[b]	9,600	
Repairs	4,800	4,800
Renovating and painting	7,200	7,200
Janitor expense	1,200	1,200
Extermination	360	360
Replacements:		
40 ranges[c]		
(8-year life)	18,000	2,250
40 refrigerators[c]		
(12-year life)	36,000	3,000
New roof[d]	6,600	330
Legal fees	720	720
Corporation tax[e]	1,800	
Income tax[e]	2,100	
Mortgage interest[f]	7,200	
Mortgage amortization[f]	6,000	

[a]It is good business practice to provide for collection and vacancy losses. Observation reveals that losses and vacancies currently average 5 percent of gross revenues for similar properties.

[b]In appraising, depreciation provision should not be treated as an operating expense. The capitalization process already provides for a return of the building's capital value. If depreciation is to be treated as an expense item then the remaining net income must be capitalized as a perpetuity. It is customary to capitalize over the life of the building, or an even shorter period. Depreciation, thus, is automatically cared for through amortization in the capitalization process.

[c]Since the equipment has 8- and 12-year service lives, the expenses per annum should only include the proportionate share of such expenses, in this case as follows:

Ranges $18,000 ÷ 8 = $2,250 per annum
Refrigerators $36,000 ÷ 12 = $3,000 per annum

[d]Expenditure for a new roof based on 20-year life.

[e]Corporation taxes and income taxes are not operating expenses but rather income expenses. Personal or corporate taxes are not considered in the appraising of real property.

[f]Mortgage payments or amortization are not considered unless the problem calls for valuation of the equity. Property is appraised on a cash sale basis; adjustments may then be made for the nature of the sale terms.

Operating Expenses	As Reported	As Adjusted	
Management fees[9]	7,200	6,270	
Water	2,700	2,700	
Fire insurance (three-year policy)	3,600	1,200	
Paving assessment	2,400		
Promotion and advertising	1,500	1,500	
Adjusted operating expenses			$ 47,130
Net operating income			$ 78,270
Income attributable to land: 10% of $120,000 =			12,000
Income attributable to building			$ 66,270
Building value (present worth of an annuity of $66,270 at 10%) $66,270 × 9.779051 =			$648,058
Add land value (via market approach)			120,000
Total value of apartment property			$768,058

[9]Management fees generally range from 5 to 7 percent of effective gross revenue; 5 percent is used here.

9. If the loss in dollars due to depreciation could be estimated with reasonable accuracy, the depreciation amount could be treated as an operating cost and the net income *after depreciation* capitalized by the rate of interest in the same manner that income to land is capitalized. In practice, however, depreciation is estimated as a "rate" per annum and this rate of amortization or rate of future depreciation is added to the prevailing interest rate to form a rate of capitalization. In this case depreciation as an amount must not be deducted as an operating expense. To do so would penalize the property twice and lower the value accordingly—and erroneously.

10. (a)

Net income after taxes		$ 1,600,000
Taxes as billed		615,000
Net income before interest and amortization		$ 2,215,000
Land rate of capitalization:		
Interest rate	0.09	
Tax rate	0.03	
Total rate	0.12	
Land income: $I = V \times R$ $5,000,000 \times 0.12 =$		600,000
Income residual to building		$ 1,615,000
Building value:		
Interest rate	0.090	
Recapture rate	0.025	
Tax rate	0.030	
Total rate	0.145	

Value: $V = I/R$

$\$1,615,000 \div 0.145 =$	$\$11,137,931$

Property value:

Building	$\$11,140,000$ (rounded)
Land	$\underline{5,000,000}$
Total	$\$16,140,000$

(b) Property taxes:

$\$16,140,000 \times 0.03 =$	$\$\ \ \ \ 484,200$

(c) Net income after taxes:

$\$2,215,000 - \$484,200 = \$1,730,800$

Chapter 16

1. An amortization rate provides for the periodic recapture of an investment at a designated interest rate and is part of a mortgage rate. A mortgage rate consists of both an amortization rate and an interest rate.
2. A capitalization rate generally is applied to an appraised property's net operating income, whereas a factor such as a gross income multiplier is applied to either the potential gross income or the effective gross income of a property. Income is divided by a capitalization rate and multiplied by a factor to derive value.
3. Beginning with $V = I/R$, it can be changed as follows to find R and I: $R = I/V$ and $I = R \times V$.
4. The basic difference between an equity dividend and an equity yield rate is that the former considers the relationship of cash flow to the investor's equity investment; the latter rate is based on this relationship plus any forecast future change in value that might occur upon sale of the property.
5. $R_M = 0.1449$; $R_E = 0.07$; $R_O = ?$

$$0.75 \times 0.1449 = 0.1087$$
$$0.25 \times 0.07 \ \ \ = \underline{0.0175}$$
$$R_O \ \ \ \ \ \ \ \ \ \ \ \ = 0.1262$$

The above-computed capitalization rate is applied to the NOI even though the equity dividend rate is based on before-tax cash flow. This may prove to be an interesting subject for class discussion.

6. $V_M = \$36,800/0.1449$

   $= \$253,968$

   $V_P = \$253,968/0.75$

   $= \$338,624$

   $R_O = \$46,000/\$338,624$

   $= 0.1358$

7.

Potential gross income	$\$25,000$
less vacancy and collection losses (6%)	$\underline{1,500}$
Effective gross income	$\$23,500$
less operating expenses (40% EG1)	$\underline{9,400}$
Net operating income	$\$14,100$

$R_O = \$14,100/\$117,500$

$= 0.1200$

8. $R_O = Y_O - \Delta a$
   $= 0.11 - (-0.20/10)$
   $= 0.11 + 0.02$
   $= 0.11$

9. $R_O = \$77,000/\$550,000$
   $= 0.1400$
   $R_L = \$12,000/\$100,000$
   $= 0.1200$

$$
\begin{array}{rclcl}
1.00 & \times & 0.14 & = & 0.1400 \\
-0.15 & \times & 0.12 & = & \underline{0.0180} \\
\hline
0.85 & & R_B & & 0.1220 \\
\end{array}
$$

$R_B = 0.1220/0.85$
$\quad = 0.1435$

10. All other things remaining equal, a decline in income because of the imposition of added taxes lowers the value of the affected property.
    (a) The value of the land prior to the imposition of the tax was
       $V = I/R$ or $\$2,000 \div 0.10$ \$20,000
    (b) The value of the land after the tax levy is
       $V = I/R$ or $\$1,800 \div 0.10$ $\underline{18,000}$

       Capital levy   \$ 2,000
    (c) Levy at 8% $= V = I/R = \$200 \div 0.08$
       $\$ 2,500$

11. (a) *Overall rates of capitalization ratio* are derived by dividing net income before interest and amortization by total value (land and improvements) of the property.
    (b) *Fractional rates* are ratios derive by dividing income attributable to a fraction of the property by the value of the part. Thus mortgage rates, equity rates, land rates, and building rates are fractional rates.

12. Property A $0.25 \times 6\%$ $=$ 1.5%
                  $0.75 \times 8\%$ $=$ $\underline{6.0}$

                  Total $=$ 7.5%
        Property B $0.50 \times 6\%$ $=$ 3.0%
                  $0.50 \times 9\%$ $=$ $\underline{4.5}$

                  Total $=$ 7.5%
        Property C $0.75 \times 7\%$ $=$ 5.25%
                  $0.25 \times 9\%$ $=$ $\underline{2.25}$

                  Total $=$ 7.5%

13. Income of $\$25,000 \div 2.5 = \$10,000$ maximum interest
    $\$10,000$ interest $\div 0.10$ (mortgage rate) $= \$100,000$ mortgage
    $\$100,000$ mortgage $\div 0.60$ (loan to value ratio) $=$
    $\quad \$166,667$ or value of property
    $\$25,000$ income $\div \$166,667$ (value) $= 15\%$ overall capitalization rate

14. Overall capitalization rate (R_0) is equal to property yield rate (Y_0) when no future change in value is expected. R_0 accounts only for current income and value while Y_0 includes the current relationship in addition to all future changes in income and value.

Chapter 17

1. Compound amount of 1 for 10%, 22 years $= 8.140275$

$$\text{Future worth of 1 per period } (S_n) = \frac{S^n - 1}{i}$$
$$= \frac{8.140275 - 1}{0.10}$$
$$= \frac{7.140275}{0.10}$$
$$= 71.402750$$
$$\text{Sinking fund factor} = (1/S_n) = \frac{1}{71.402750}$$
$$= 0.014005$$

2. To make the calculations, it first is necessary to find either the compound amount of 1 or the present worth of 1 factors.

3. Use the 10 percent sinking fund factor for 12 years:

$$0.046763 \times \$10,000 = \$467.63$$

4. Use the 10 percent compound amount of 1 factor for 16 years:

$$4.594973 \times \$5,000 = \$22,975$$

Note: This problem assumes annual installments.

5. First find the R_M for 25 years and then the R_M for 17 years $(25 - 8)$. R_M (25 years) $= 0.110168$; R_M (17 years) $= 0.124664$

$$\text{Mortgage balance} = (0.110168/0.124664)(\$75,000)$$
$$= \$66,279$$
$$\text{Equity buildup} = \$75,000 - \$66,279$$
$$= \$8,721$$

Thus the client will not accumulate via amortization the desired $10,000.

6. If Table 17.1 is used, it must be extended to 65 years by multipying some combination of factors equal to 65 years.

$$\text{PW} = (0.008519)(0.239392)(\$600,000)$$
$$= \$1,224$$

7. PW of income receivable at beginning of period requires that the EOY factor be adjusted to a BOY factor as follows:

$$\text{PW} = (7.606080)(1.10)(\$4,000)$$
$$= \$33,467$$

8. Years 1–3 $2.486852 \times \$10,000 = \$24,869$
     4–6 $(4.355261 - 2.486852) \times \$12,000 = 22,421$
     7–9 $(5.759024 - 4.355251) \times \$13,500 = \underline{18,951}$

Total present worth $\$66,241$

9. Original investment of $3,000 at 6 percent compound interest
   over 10 years should grow to $3,000 × 1.79 or $5,370

   Annuity of $100 at 6 percent compound interest
   over 10 years should grow to $100 × 13.18 or   <u>1,318</u>

   Total investment at end of tenth year $6,688

10. (a) The present value of an annuity is the total discounted present worth of each annuity payment. (b) Present value of an annuity of $1.00 at 10 percent interest over a period of three years is $2.49. (See persent worth of annuity table in this chapter.)

11. (a) $500 × 7.606080 (PW of annuity at 10 percent) = $3,803
   (b) $500 × 9.992700[1] (PW of annuity at 10 percent) = $4,996
   (c) $500 × 10 or $500 ÷ 0.10 = $5,000

12. The 10 percent sinking fund table shows a rate per dollar of 0.017460. Multiplying this by $1,000 gives the answer of $17.46. If $17.46 is placed in a sinking fund annually at 10 percent compound interest over a period of 20 years, the fund will accumulate to $1,000 over this period of time.

13. Table of amortization for a $10,000 mortgage over eight years at 8 percent interest per annum:

Year	Month	Periodic Payment	2/3 Percent Interest	Amortization	Remaining Value
0	0	—	—	—	$10,000.00
0	1	$141.37	66.67	74.70	9,925.30
0	2	141.37	66.17	75.20	9,850.10

14.

	1st Year	2nd Year[2]	3rd to 40th Years
Net income	$47,500.00	$60,000.00	$70,000.00
Building life—40 years			
Property rate—10%			
Present value factor 10%	00.909091	0.826446	8.043514
Present value of property returns	$ 43,182	$ 49,587	$ 563,046
Property value = $43,182 + $49,587 + $563,046 = $655,815			

CHAPTER 18

1. PW via Ring factor capitalization:

PW = 7.14286 × $10,000
= $71,429

[1](0.008519)^2 = 0.000073; inserted the present worth of 1 per period equation

$$[a_n = \frac{1 - V^n}{i} = \frac{1 - 0.000073}{0.10} = 9.992700,$$

which is the present worth of 1 factor at 10% annually for 100 years]

[2]Present value factor for year 2 is the difference between the year 2 and year 1 factors; similarly, the factor for the years 3 through 40 is computed by subtracting the year 2 factor from the year 40 factor.

2. $V = I/R$; $R = 0.10$ (interest) $+ 0.020952$ (sinking fund factor)
$\quad\quad = 0.120952$
$\quad V = \$10,000/0.120952$
$\quad\quad = \$82,677$

3. $V = I/R$ $\quad\quad$ or $\quad V = I \times R$
$\quad\quad = \$10,000/0.110168$ $\quad\quad\quad = \$10,000 \times 9.077040$
$\quad\quad = \$90,770$ $\quad\quad\quad\quad\quad\quad = \$90,770$

4. The annuity method of capitalization is similar to the sinking fund method except that no fund is established in which the annual amortization provisions are to accumulate. Instead, the periodic payments for amortization of investment capital are made available to the property user or owner for immediate reinvestment in other property. The rates of earning for both the property as a whole and for portions of the investment returned each year through amortization provision—and which are available for reinvestment—are considered as one and the same.

5. $V = I \times R$
$\quad\quad = \$10,000 \times 9.077040$
$\quad\quad = \$90,770$

6. Both NPV and IRR are discounted cash flow techniques where future income is discounted to produce a present value. NPV is based on a specified discount rate, and if the discounted inflows and outflows produce a positive value, the proposition under study is judged to be feasible. IRR goes a step further to indicate the exact yield rate for the investment.

7. (a) $350,000 ($200,000 land plus $150,000 cost of remodeling)

   (b)

$200,000 at 9% =	$18,000
150,000 at 11.5% (9% + 2.5%) =	17,250
Taxes	14,500
Total net rental	$49,750

   (c)

$200,000 at 9% =	$18,000
250,000 at 13% (9% + 4%) =	32,500
Taxes	14,500
Total net rental	$65,000

   (d) As shown in (c), above, the prudent buyer wants a return on the investment at the going rate, plus amortization requirements to depreciate the investment over the estimated remaining life of the improvements, plus property taxes due.

CHAPTER 19

1. The relative merits of each of the three physical residual techniques are:
   (a) *Land residual technique:* applies when the appraised buildings are new and their values are known or can be estimated with reasonable accuracy.
   (b) *Building residual technique:* useful when the site value can readily be estimated by the comparable sales approach and the building is old and substantially depreciated.
   (c) *Property residual technique:* applicable when it is difficult to allocate total property income between the site and building(s), or when the building is old or there is a lack of comparable site sales.

2. NOI $25,000
   Less income to building (I_B)
   ($150,000)(0.10 + 0.05) 22,500

   Income available to land (I_L) $ 2,500
   Land value ($2,500/0.10) = $ 25,000
   + Building value 150,000

   Property value $175,000

3. Value of income stream
   (7.606080 × $50,000) $380,304
   + Value of reversion
   (0.239392 × $300,000) 71,818

   Present worth of property $452,122

4. Use linear change equation $R = Y - \Delta 1/n$.
   NOI $75,000
   − Building income ($100,000)(0.10 − 0.10/10) 9,000

   = Land income $66,000
   Capitalized at land rate (0.10 − 0.80/10)
   = Land value $3,300,000
   + Building value 100,000

   = Property value $3,400,000

5. NOI $90,000
   − Land income
   ($200,000)(0.10 − 0.025) 15,000

   = Building income $75,000
   Capitalized at building rate (0.10 − 0.0032)
   = Building value (rounded) $775,000
   + Land value 200,000

   = Property value $975,000

$$CR_L = \frac{\Delta I \times Y}{\Delta I + Y} = \frac{(0.30/9)(0.10)}{0.30/9 + 0.10} = \frac{(0.0333)(0.10)}{0.0333 + 0.10} = 0.0250$$

$$CR_B = \frac{(0.03/9)(0.10)}{0.03/9 + 0.10} = \frac{0.0003}{0.1033} = 0.0032$$

6. NOI $ 50,000
   Capitalized by R_O
   (0.10 − $2,500/$50,000 = 0.05
   Property value $1,000,000

7. (a) Whenever land value is known with accuracy, the appraiser should use the building residual method of capitalization.
   (b) Net operating income $12,000
   Income to land $20,000 × 0.08 = − 1,600
   Income to furnishings $11,000 × 0.20 = − 2,200

   Net income residual to building $ 8,200
   Building value = $8,200 ÷ 0.12 = $68,333

8. Total value $150,000
   Land value − 25,000

   Building value 125,000

Total income		$14,000
Land income $25,000 × 0.06		−1,500
Building income		$12,500

(a) Building rate $12,500 ÷ $125,000 = 0.10 or 10%

(b) Building rate	0.10	
Recapture rate (straight line)	−0.05	
Interest rate	0.05	or 5%

(c) Building rate—Inwood factor
(factor = value ÷ income) 10.0000

7.5% Inwood factor	10.194
8.0% Inwood factor	9.818
0.5% differential factor	0.376
7.5% Inwood factor	10.194
X% Inwood factor	10.000
X differential	0.194

$$\frac{X}{0.5} = \frac{0.194}{0.376}, \text{ hence } X = 0.258$$

Interest rate that corresponds with Inwood factor of 10.00 =
7.5% + 0.258% = 7.758%

CHAPTER 20

1. It is desirable to calculate the value of the unencumbered fee interest prior to estimating the value of the leased fee or the leasehold interests so that the entire unencumbered value can serve as a benchmark against which the reasonableness of the value of the parts can be judged.
2. Under the terms of a lease, a landlord is entitled to:
   (a) Receive the contract rent agreed on under terms of the lease for the duration of the lease period.
   (b) Repossession of the property upon termination of the lease.
3. Present value of market rent

$14,000 × 6.144567	$ 86,024
Present worth of excess rent	
$1,000 × 5.426243	5,426
	$91,450
Reversionary property value	
$100,000 × 0.385543	$ 38,554
Total value of leased fee	$130,004

4.

Year 1	$1,000 × 0.909091	$ 909
2	1,200 × 0.826446	992
3–5	1,500 (3.790787 − 1.735537)	3,083
6–10	2,200 (6.144567 − 3.790787)	5,178
		$10,162
		×1.10
		11,178
PW of income stream		
+ Reversionary value of property		
($200,000 × 0.385543)		77,109
Total present value of property		$87,271

5. (a) Economic rent $10,000
      − Contract rent   8,000

      Leasehold income $ 2,000
      Value of leasehold estate
        ($2,000 × 3.790787) $7,582
    (b) Leasehold value $ 7,582
      + Leased fee value   90,293

    Total property value $97,875

6. (a) A sandwich leasehold occurs when a leasehold interest is subleased to a third
    party; the original lessee becomes a sublandlord and both legally and eco-
    nomically is sandwiched between the fee owner and the subtenant.
    (b) (1) Leased fee interest at 10%, 7 years:
          $2,000 × 4.868419 = $ 9,737
        + PW of land reversion
          $100,000 × 0.513158   51,316

        Total PW of leased fee $61,053
      (2) Sandwich leasehold:
        Subtenant annual rental $ 3,000
        Market annual rental   2,000

        Sandwich leasehold rental $ 1,000
        Discounted at 12%, 7 years   × 4.563757

        PW of sandwich leasehold $ 4,564
      (3) Sublessee's interest:
        PW of property $70,000
        − Value of leased fee $ 61,053
        − Value of sandwich leasehold   4,564   65,617

        Value of sublessee's interest $ 4,383

7. An annuity of $600 invested at compound interest of 7 percent over five years
will grow to $600 × 5.75 or $3,450. This amount represents the full cost of the
leasehold to date.

8. (a) The lessor's interest:
      $10,000 (for 5 years) × 4.2124 = $ 42,124
      $12,000 (for next 35 years) × 10.8339
          (15.0463 − 4.2124) =   130,007
      Land reversion = $240,000 × 0.0972 =   23,328
      Total lessor's interest $195,459
    (b) The lessee's interest:
      1. Land income $240,000 × 0.06 = $ 14,400
          Less contract rent for 5 years   10,000

          Net to lessee $ 4,400
      2. Land income next 35 years $ 14,400
          Less contract rent   12,000

          Net to lessee $ 2,400
      Value: $4,400 × 4.2124 = $ 18,535
          $2,400 × 10.8339 (15.0463 − 4.2124)   26,001

      Total value in land $ 44,536
      Value of building as appraised   160,000

      Total value, lessee $204,536

Summary:

Lessor's interest		$195,459
Lessee's interest		204,536
Total		$399,995
Say		$400,000

9. (a) Mrs. A's interest:

Income of $3,000 × 9.644159 (Inwood)	$ 28,932
Land reversion $75,000 × 0.035584	2,669
Total	$ 31,601

(b) Mr. B's interest at 10%:

Income of $8,000 − $3,000 = $5,000 × 9.644159 = $48,221

(c) Mr. C's interest at 10%:

Income of $12,000 − $8,000 = $4,000 × 9.644159 = $38,577

In practice the interests of B and C would be capitalized at a higher rate—perhaps 12 and 14 percent, respectively.

CHAPTER 21

1. Equity yield rate differs from equity dividend rate by accounting for future value changes in addition to the "cash on cash" return recognized by the equity dividend rate.
2. The steps in computing equity dividend rate are:
   1   Compute potential gross income
   2 − vacancy and collection losses
   3 = effective gross income
   4 − operating expenses
   5 = net operating income
   6 − annual mortgage debt service
   7 = cash flow (before taxes)

             Equity dividend rate = step 7 divided by owner's equity

3.

NOI		$ 50,000
− Mortgage debt service		
($200,000 × 0.75)(0.110168)		16,525
Annual cash flow		$ 33,475
PW of 1/period for 10 years		× 6.144567
PW of equity position		$205,689
Sale price of property	$300,000	
− Mortgage balance in 10 years		
($150,000)(0.110168/0.131474*)	125,692	
Equity value 10 years hence	$174,308	
Reversionary value factor	× 0.385543	

Present value of equity reversion	$ 67,203
+ Mortgage value at date of appraisal	150,000
Total value of property	$422,892

*R_M for remaining loan term of 15 years.

4. Loan balance after 6 years

($90,000)(0.106079/0.111300*) =	$ 85,778

Thus, equity buildup

($90,000 − $85,778) =	$ 4,222

*R_M for remainder of loan term of 24 years.

5. Interest paid during fifteenth year:

Annual mortgage payment	
($90,000 × 0.106079)	$ 9,547

Find loan balance at beginning and end of year 15.

Loan balance at beginning of year 15	
0.0106079/0.127817	0.829929
Less loan balance at end of year 15	
0.106079/0.131474	0.806844
Loan amortization in year 15	0.023085
times original loan	× $ 90,000
Equity accumulation	$ 2,078
Annual loan payment	$ 9,547
− Equity accumulation	2,078
= Interest paid in year 15	$ 7,469

6. Property A equity yield = 11.85%

Property B equity yield = 8.90%

7. R = $Y − MC^*$ + dep. or − app. $1/S_{\overline{n}|}$

 = 0.14 = (0.80)(0.039224) − 0.10 × 0.151284

 = 0.14 − 0.031379 − 0.015128

 = 0.093493

PW = $48,000/0.093493

 = $513,408

$^*C$ = $Y + (P × 1/S_{\overline{n}|}) − f$

 = 0.14 + (1 − 0.110168/0.117460)(0.151284) − 0.110168

 = 0.14 + (0.062081)(0.151284) − 0.110168

 = 0.14 + 0.009392 − 0.110168

 = 0.039224

8. (a) *Effective gross revenue* is the amount of realizable revenue anticipated after deduction of vacancy and collection losses. (b) *Occupancy ratio* is a ratio or percent of rentable space occupied to total available rental space in a building. (c) *Collection losses* are uncollectible rent. (d) *Net operating income* is income after deduction of operating costs from effective gross revenue. It is capitalizable income before interest charges on the investment and amortization charges to recapture the investment over the estimated economic life of the property. (e) *Operating ratio* is a percent relationship of operating expenses to effective gross revenue. (f) *Fixed charges* are expenditures such as taxes, fuel costs, and insurance which do not vary significantly with occupancy or operation of the property. (g) *Equity*

income is income left after deduction for costs (interest and amortization) of borrowed mortgage funds. (h) *Trading on the equity* is the practice of borrowing funds at a rate less than that earned by the property as a whole. Trading on the equity increases the rate of earnings on the equity capital. (i) *Yield on equity investment* is a percentage ratio of equity income to equity capital.

9. 8 years = 96 months
8% interest per annum = $\frac{2}{3}$% interest per month
$I = V \times R = \$10,000 \times 0.014137 = \$141.37$

10.

Property income	\$ 60,000
Mortgage—debt service payments	37,920
Equity—cash flow	\$ 22,080

(a) Present worth of cash flow—10 years at 10% =
    \$22,080 × 6.144567   \$135,672
    Present worth of cash reversion on date of sale:
      \$500,000 − \$263,400

(b) Add present worth of reversionary equity =
    \$236,600 × 0.385543 (10%) =   91,219

(c) Total present worth of equity   \$226,891

(d) Add present value of mortgage   300,000

(e) Purchase price to yield 10% rate of equity return   \$526,891
        Rounded to \$527,000

11. Solution:

Purchase price	\$400,000
Mortgage loan	280,000
Cash-equity investment	120,000

Selling price \$400,000 × 0.925 =		\$370,000
Mortgage balance—15 years remaining—\$2,702 monthly payment × 93.057439[1] (180-month factor at 10%) =		251,441
(a) Reversion to equity		\$118,559
Revenue	\$ 45,000	
Debt service	32,424	
(b) Cash flow	\$ 12,576	

Trial interest yield rate of 10%:
    Present worth of \$12,576 for 5 years =
      \$12,576 × 3.790787   \$ 47,673
    Present worth of reversion of
      \$118,559 × 0.620921   73,616
    Total present value of equity at 10%   \$121,289

Trial interest yield rate of 11%:
    Present worth of \$12,576 for 5 years
      \$12,576 × 3.695897[1] =   \$46,480
    Present worth of reversion of
      \$118,559 × 0.593451   70,359
    Total present value of equity at 11%   \$116,839

[1]See the calculator keystroke sequence in Chapter 17.

Interpolation for accurate yield rate:

1. Equity value at 10% = $121,289
   Equity value at 11% = 116,839

   Differences for 1% = $ 4,450
2. Equity value at 10% 121,289
   Equity value at X% 120,000

   Difference $ 1,289

Rate to be added to 8%:

$$\frac{\$1,289}{\$4,450} = 0.29\% + 10\% = \underline{10.29\%}$$

12. $P = \dfrac{R_M - I}{R_{MP} - I} = \dfrac{0.110168 - 0.10}{0.131474 - 0.10} = \dfrac{0.010168}{0.031474} = 0.323060$

CHAPTER 22

1. Public bodies have been given the power of eminent domain since the strength of private ownership is derived from the strength and power of a sovereign government formed to enforce and protect such rights as are vested in the individual under constitutional guardianship. It is fundamental, therefore, that rights essential to the maintenance and welfare of society must be paramount to those claimed by individuals in the pursuit of their separate interests.
2. The following six legal requirements generally must be followed by government to protect private rights when the power of eminent domain is used:
   (a) Authority and necessity of taking.
   (b) Indication of public use for which land is condemmed.
   (c) Survey of land and description.
   (d) Complaint and summons of owners.
   (e) Interest to be acquired.
   (f) Necessary parties defendant.
3. Just compensation is defined as payment for the value of the property physically taken and to offset a loss in value, if any, to the remaining parcel on account of severance of a part from the unity of the whole property. Excluded are losses incurred by the exercise of the police power of the government.
4. The conventional definition of market value is inapplicable to eminent domain cases because the "willing buyer–willing seller" concept is seldom fulfilled. In fact, the seller generally is unwilling to sell his or her property to the condemnor.
5. Economic unity is established by the following court-proved rules:
   (a) *Contiguity of location:* The affected property must be a continuous, unbroken tract.
   (b) *Unity of ownership:* The condemned property must be under the same ownership.
   (c) *Unity of use as evidenced by economic unity (utility) rather than physical unity:* This means that the entire property must be placed to the same type of use so that if agricultural land is acquired its damages do not carry over to the remaining land.
6. The before-and-after rule for appraising land for eminent domain projects

involves estimating the value of the whole property before the taking and again after the taking. The difference in value is judged to be the just compensation due the property owner.

7. Consequential damages relate to just compensation for a property owner in that in practice it denotes damage suffered by owners as a result of proposed public improvements where no real property is physically taken.

CHAPTER 23

1. Unit valuation is defined as an appraisal of an integrated property as a whole without any reference to the value of its component parts.

2. Cost no longer provides an accurate measure of the value of railroads and public utilities because of the passage of time, technological changes, economic obsolescence, and overregulation. Costs that serve as a basis for rate making purposes at best set a ceiling of value.

3. The steps involved in measuring railroad obsolescence via the blue chip method are:
   (a) Selection of the "blue chip" railroads.
   (b) Selection of a number of recognized quality and efficiency factors in a railroad transportation system.
   (c) Comparison of each of the quality or efficiency factors for the railroad being appraised with the same factor for the standard or "blue chip."

4. Embedded interest costs are criticized for ad valorem tax purposes because under the stock and debt approach to value, the low-interest-bearing bonds are evaluated at discount market prices that in effect convert embedded capital costs to a yield that reflects current costs. Thus the appraiser takes away under the income approach what he or she grants under the market approach.

5. Five possible causes of deviations in appraisal estimates of railroad and public utility property area:
   (a) The cause and measurement of external obsolescence.
   (b) Means and ways of estimating capitalizable income.
   (c) Development of capitalization rates and influence on same from embedded capital debt.
   (d) Use of straight-line versus sinking fund method of capital recapture.
   (e) Treatment of rental payments for leased property.

6. Use of sinking fund or annuity method of capitalization is preferable to the straight-line method of capital recapture only where the anticipated income stream from existing property is either contractually guaranteed or not subject to decline because of use, wear, or other causes of depreciation.

CHAPTER 24

1. (a) Appraisal process is defined as an orderly plan of action used to produce a professional appraisal report.
   (b) An understanding of this process benefits the appraiser by aiding him or her to reach a sound conclusion or estimate of value.

2. Appraisers ordinarily make the following four assumptions regarding appraisals:
   (a) That the title is held in fee simple and that no legal claims, easements, restrictions, or other rights affect the title or use of the property except those stated to the appraiser by the applicant.

    (b) That the title and his or her valuation are subject to corrections which an accurate survey of the property may reveal.

    (c) That the sale of property will be on a cash or cash equivalent basis.

    (d) That no responsibility can be taken by the appraiser for matters legal in nature.

3. An appraiser should define the appraised value in his or her report in order to avoid serious misunderstanding and possibly disciplinary action under the code of ethics to which all professional appraisers, as members of their respective appraisal societies, subscribe.

4. The reconciliation process allows the appraiser to correlate each of the approaches to value to produce a final value conclusion. Care must be taken in weighing the results on the basis of accuracy and completeness of data and in the light of market conditions that prevail on the date of the appraisal.

5. Steps in the "Analyses and Conclusions" section of an appraisal are:

    (a) Explanation of the appraisal process and the methods used to reach the value conclusions.

    (b) Separate analysis via the depreciated cost, market sales comparison, and capitalized income approaches.

    (c) Reconciliation of the values indicated by each of the approaches used.

    (d) Inclusion of a statement of limiting conditions, certificate of value, and a statement of the appraiser's professional qualifications.

6. Characteristics of a well-written appraisal report include: being logical and orderly; being clear, direct, yet comprehensive; being readable; avoiding use of the first person; and using appropriate words, summaries, and illustrations.

7. Professional appraisers discourage use of the letter report because it does not include the steps leading to the appraiser's value conclusion and they often are unusable for loan or sale purposes.

8. Certification is where the appraiser warrants his or her findings and disclaims any personal interest in the property that could influence his or her value findings. Limiting conditions is where the appraiser sets forth the areas—in the fields of surveying, engineering, or law—in which he or she disclaims liability.

9. Education is important to professionals so that they keep abreast of modern developments in theory and practice. This education may be obtained in a formal setting or informally through experience, intensive reading, attendance at seminars, workshops, and through related organizational and professional activities.

10. The real estate appraiser is responsible to the public by estimating value objectively and independent of the client's cause or the compensation paid for services rendered. The appraiser should charge a fee that relates to the quantity and character of the service; commissions should always be avoided. As a rule, competitive bidding should be avoided since it fails to recognize differences in appraisers' experience, skill, integrity, and education.

11. An appraiser should never speak disparagingly of another appraiser because it leaves bitter feelings. One cannot rise above competition by trying to pull others down. Such success comes from hard work, preparation, and maintenance of high professional standards.

12. A confidential relationship should be maintained between the appraiser and his or her clients because to do otherwise undermines strength of character and may have serious repercussions for practitioners as well as for the person and the profession.

13. To accept the results of another's work without analysis and explanation weakens the basis for the appraiser's valuation findings. Alternatively, for an appraiser to reject a feasibility study of a presumably qualified analyst, he or she should show why his or her opinion has greater merit.

APPENDIX V

TABLES

Present Worth of an Annuity of $1 Table for Selected Interest Rates Based on Straight-Line Theory of Depreciation Under the Direct-Ring Method of Capitalization[a]

Period	10%	Period	10%
1	0.90909	26	7.22230
2	1.66667	27	7.29714
3	2.30771	28	7.36844
4	2.85714	29	7.43594
5	3.33333	30	7.50019
6	3.74995	31	7.56098
7	4.11765	32	7.61905
8	4.44444	33	7.69231
9	4.73687	34	7.72732
10	5.00000	35	7.77780
11	5.23809	36	7.82607
12	5.45464	37	7.87234
13	5.65227	38	7.92823
14	5.83328	39	7.95919
15	5.99999	40	8.00000
16	6.15385	41	8.03923
17	6.29644	42	8.07696
18	6.42855	43	8.11326
19	6.55308	44	8.14817
20	6.66667	45	8.18197
21	6.77415	46	8.21429
22	6.87500	47	8.24565
23	6.96966	48	8.27588
24	7.05882	49	8.30510
25	7.14286	50	8.33333

[a]What $1 payable periodically for the remaining economic life of an investment and with annual interest paid on the entire investment is worth today.
Formula:

$$\text{Ring factor} = \frac{1}{\text{str.-line rate}} \text{ or } \frac{1}{\text{int. rate} + \text{depre. rate}}$$

Example: Factor for 20 years is

$$\frac{1}{0.10 + 1/20} = \frac{1}{0.10 + 0.05} = \frac{1}{0.15} = 6.66667$$

Amortization Schedule for a $50,000 Investment Providing for Annual Amortization and Interest at 10 Percent over a 30-Year Period[a]

Year	Annual Payment	Interest on Investment at 10%	Amortization Annual	Amortization Cumulative	Remaining Investment
1	$5,303.96	$5,000.00	$ 303.96	$ 303.96	$49,696.04
2	5,303.96	4,969.60	334.36	638.32	49,361.68
3	5,303.96	4,936.17	367.79	1,006.11	48,993.89
4	5,303.96	4,899.39	404.57	1,410.68	48,589.32
5	5,303.96	4,858.93	445.03	1,855.71	48,144.29
6	5,303.96	4,814.43	489.53	2,345.24	47,654.76
7	5,303.96	4,765.48	538.48	2,883.72	47,116.28
8	5,303.96	4,711.63	592.33	3,476.05	46,523.95
9	5,303.96	4,652.40	651.56	4,127.61	45,872.39
10	5,303.96	4,587.24	716.72	4,844.33	45,155.67
11	5,303.96	4,515.57	788.39	5,632.72	44,367.28
12	5,303.96	4,436.73	867.23	6,499.95	43,500.05
13	5,303.96	4,350.01	953.95	7,453.90	42,546.10
14	5,303.96	4,254.61	1,049.35	8,503.25	41,496.75
15	5,303.96	4,149.68	1,154.28	9,657.53	40,342.47
16	5,303.96	4,034.25	1,269.71	10,927.24	39,072.76
17	5,303.96	3,907.28	1,396.68	12,323.92	37,676.08
18	5,303.96	3,767.61	1,536.35	13,860.27	36,139.73
19	5,303.96	3,613.97	1,689.99	15,550.26	34,449.74
20	5,303.96	3,444.97	1,858.99	17,409.25	32,590.75
21	5,303.96	3,259.08	2,044.88	19,454.13	30,545.87
22	5,303.96	3,054.59	2,249.37	21,703.50	28,296.50
23[b]	5,303.96	2,829.65	2,474.31	24,177.81	25,822.19
24	5,303.96	2,582.22	2,721.74	26,899.55	23,100.45
25	5,303.96	2,310.05	2,993.91	29,893.46	20,106.54
26	5,303.96	2,010.65	3,293.31	33,186.77	16,813.23
27	5,303.96	1,681.32	3,622.64	36,809.41	13,190.59
28	5,303.96	1,319.06	3,984.90	40,794.31	9,205.69
29	5,303.96	920.57	4,383.39	45,177.70	4,822.30
30	5,303.96	482.23	4,821.73	50,000.00	0.00

[a]Assumes end-of-year payments.
[b]After the loan is approximately 75% expired, the original principal has been only 50% amortized.

Land Measurement Table

Acreage

		1 Acre Equals Rectangle:	
Acres	Square Feet	Width	Length
1	43,560		
2	87,120	16.5	2,640.0
3	130,680	33.0	1,320.0
4	174,240	50.0	871.2
5	217,800	66.0	660.0
6	261,360	75.0	580.8
7	304,920	100.0	435.6
8	348,480	132.0	330.0
9	392,040	150.0	290.4
10	435,600	208.71	208.71

Linear Measure

12 inches (in.)	make 1 foot	(ft)
3 feet	make 1 yard	(yd)
5½ yards or 16½ feet	make 1 rod	(rd)
40 rods	make 1 furlong	(fur)
8 furlongs, 320 rods, or 5,280 feet	make 1 statute mile	(mi)

Square Measure[a]

144 square inches (sq. in.)	make 1 square foot	(sq ft)
9 square feet	make 1 square yard	(sq yd)
30¼ square yards	make 1 square rod	(sq rd)
40 square rods	make 1 rood	(R)
4 rods or 43,560 square feet	make 1 acre	(A)
640 acres	make 1 square mile	(sq mi)

Surveyor's Linear Measure

7.92 inches (in.)	make 1 link	(l)
25 links	make 1 rod	(rd)
4 rods or 66 feet	make 1 chain	(ch)
80 chains	make 1 mile	(mi)

Surveyor's Square Measure

625 square links (sq l.)	make 1 pole	(P)
16 poles	make 1 square chain	(sq ch)
10 square chains	make 1 acre	(A)
640 acres	make 1 square mile	(sq mi)
36 square miles (6 mi. square)	make 1 township	(Tp)

Metric Conversions

1 meter = { 39.37 inches / 3.28083 feet / 1.0936 yards	1 kilometer = 0.062137 mile
	1 foot = 0.3048 meter
1 centimeter = 0.3937 inch	1 inch = { 2.54 centimeters / 25.4 millimeters
1 millimeter = { 0.03937 inch, or / approximately / 1/25 in.	1 yard = 0.9144 meter
	1 rod = 5.029 meters
	1 mile = 1.6093 kilometers

[a]1 acre in square form equals 208.71 feet on each side.

APPENDIX VI

SEGREGATED OR TRADE BREAKDOWN METHOD FOR AN OFFICE BUILDING

BANKS, OFFICES, AND PUBLIC BUILDINGS
(CALCULATOR METHOD)

FLOOR AREA - PERIMETER MULTIPLIERS

AVG FLOOR AREA Sq. M	Sq. Ft	46 / 150	53 / 175	61 / 200	76 / 250	91 / 300	122 / 400	152 / 500	183 / 600	213 / 700	244 / 800	305 / 1000	366 / 1200	427 / 1400	488 / 1600	549 / 1800	610 / 2000
93	1,000	1.221	1.266														
139	1,500	1.105	1.146	1.191													
186	2,000	1.040	1.072	1.105	1.168												
232	2,500	1.000	1.027	1.052	1.105	1.155											
279	3,000	.975	.997	1.018	1.061	1.105	1.191										
372	4,000		.958	.975	1.007	1.040	1.105	1.168									
465	5,000		.936	.949	.975	1.000	1.052	1.105	1.155								
557	6,000			.932	.958	.975	1.018	1.061	1.105	1.146							
743	8,000				.926	.942	.975	1.007	1.040	1.105	1.105						
929	10,000				.910	.923	.949	.975	1.000	1.040	1.052	1.105					
1,115	12,000					.910	.932	.952	.975	1.000	1.018	1.061	1.105				
1,301	14,000					.900	.920	.938	.956	.975	.993	1.030	1.067	1.105			
1,486	16,000						.910	.926	.942	.958	.975	1.007	1.040	1.075	1.105		
1,672	18,000						.903	.918	.932	.946	.960	.990	1.018	1.046	1.076	1.105	
1,858	20,000							.910	.923	.936	.949	.975	1.000	1.027	1.052	1.078	1.105
2,323	25,000							.897	.910	.918	.936	.962	.969	.990	1.011	1.032	1.052
2,787	30,000								.897	.906	.928	.948	.949	.965	.983	1.000	1.018
3,252	35,000									.897	.915	.932	.934	.949	.963	.978	.993
3,716	40,000									.890	.904	.919	.923	.936	.949	.962	.975
4,645	50,000										.897	.910	.908	.918	.928	.938	.948
6,968	75,000											.879	.885	.892	.900	.908	.915
9,290	100,000											.871	.876	.881	.887	.892	.897

Header: left two columns = AVERAGE FLOOR AREA (Sq. M / Sq. Ft). Remaining columns = AVERAGE PERIMETER (M. / FT.).

STORY HEIGHT MULTIPLIERS

Multiply base cost by following multipliers for any variation in average story height from the 12 foot (3.66 M.) base.

AVERAGE WALL HT. (M.)	(FT.)	SQUARE FOOT OR SQUARE METER MULTIPLIER	CUBIC FOOT MULTIPLIER		AVERAGE WALL HT. (M.)	(FT.)	SQUARE FOOT OR SQUARE METER MULTIPLIER	CUBIC FOOT MULTIPLIER
2.44	8	.900	1.350		4.57	15	1.069	.855
2.74	9	.928	1.237		4.88	16	1.092	.819
3.05	10	.953	1.144		5.49	18	1.138	.758
3.35	11	.977	1.066		6.10	20	1.184	.710
3.66	12	1.000	1.000		7.31	24	1.276	.638
3.96	13	1.023	.944		8.53	28	1.367	.586
4.27	14	1.046	.897		9.75	32	1.459	.547

TYPICAL BUILDING LIVES

OCCUPANCY	CLASS A	B	C	D	S
Good and excellent offices, banks, libraries	60	60	55	50	50
Average offices, banks, and libraries	55	55	50	45	45
Low cost offices, banks, and libraries	50	50	45	40	40
Good and excellent medical offices	50	50	45	40	40
Average and low cost medical offices	45	45	40	35	35
Good and excellent governmental buildings	60	60	55	50	40
Average and low cost governmental buildings	55	55	50	45	40
Good and excellent general hospitals	50	50	45	40	40
Average and low cost general hospitals	45	45	45	40	35
Good and excellent convalescent hospitals	50	50	45	40	40
Average and low cost convalescent hospitals	45	45	40	35	35
Average and good dispensaries	40	35	35	30	30
Good jails	55	55	50	45	---
Average and low cost jails	50	50	45	40	40
Good and excellent fire stations	50	50	45	40	35
Average and low cost fire stations	45	45	40	35	35
Average and good veterinary hospitals	45	45	40	40	35
Low cost veterinary hospitals	---	---	35	30	30

Courtesy of Marshall and Swift, Los Angeles, California.

CURRENT COST MULTIPLIERS

These multipliers bring costs from preceding pages up to date. Also apply Local Multipliers, Pages 99-5 thru 8.

CALCULATOR SECTIONS

		11	12	13	14	15	16	17
EASTERN	S	1.15	1.11	1.08	1.06	1.00	1.23	1.21
	D	1.14	1.10	1.07	1.05	1.00	1.26	1.24
	C	1.15	1.11	1.08	1.05	1.00	1.26	1.24
	B	1.16	1.11	1.08	1.06	1.00	1.27	1.24
	A	1.16	1.11	1.08	1.06	1.00	1.27	1.24
CENTRAL	S	1.12	1.09	1.07	1.05	1.00	1.21	1.19
	D	1.11	1.08	1.07	1.05	1.00	1.23	1.21
	C	1.12	1.09	1.07	1.05	1.00	1.23	1.21
	B	1.12	1.09	1.07	1.05	1.00	1.24	1.22
	A	1.13	1.09	1.07	1.05	1.00	1.25	1.22
WESTERN	S	1.14	1.09	1.07	1.06	1.00	1.23	1.21
	D	1.13	1.09	1.07	1.06	1.00	1.26	1.24
	C	1.15	1.10	1.08	1.06	1.00	1.27	1.25
	B	1.15	1.10	1.08	1.06	1.00	1.27	1.25
	A	1.15	1.10	1.08	1.06	1.00	1.27	1.25

SEGREGATED COST SECTIONS

		41	42	43	44	45	46	47
EASTERN	S	1.19	1.12	1.09	1.07	1.03		
	D	1.17	1.11	1.08	1.07	1.02	1.24	1.22
	C	1.19	1.12	1.09	1.07	1.02	1.27	1.25
	B	1.19	1.12	1.09	1.07	1.02	1.28	1.26
	A	1.19	1.12	1.09	1.07	1.03	1.29	1.26
CENTRAL	S	1.17	1.10	1.08	1.06	1.02		
	D	1.15	1.09	1.08	1.06	1.02	1.22	1.20
	C	1.16	1.10	1.08	1.06	1.02	1.25	1.22
	B	1.17	1.10	1.08	1.06	1.02	1.26	1.23
	A	1.17	1.10	1.08	1.06	1.02	1.27	1.24
WESTERN	S	1.20	1.10	1.08	1.07	1.02		
	D	1.17	1.10	1.08	1.07	1.02	1.25	1.22
	C	1.20	1.11	1.09	1.07	1.02	1.28	1.25
	B	1.20	1.11	1.09	1.07	1.03	1.29	1.26
	A	1.20	1.11	1.09	1.07	1.03	1.29	1.26

UNIT-IN-PLACE COSTS (SECTIONS 51 – 67)

Sec. Page		Eastern	Central	Western
51 - 2	Concrete Foundations	1.07	1.06	1.08
51 - 3	Piling	1.07	1.06	1.07
51 - 6	Steel and Concrete Frame	1.07	1.06	1.08
51 - 6	Wood Frame	1.07	1.06	1.07
52 - 4	Interior Construction	1.07	1.06	1.07
52 - 4	Bank Vaults and Vault Doors	1.07	1.06	1.07
53 - 1 - 5	Heating, Cooling & Ventilating	1.05	1.04	1.05
53 - 6 - 9	Plumbing, Fire Protection, etc.	1.05	1.05	1.05
53 - 10, 11	Electrical	1.05	1.05	1.05
54 - 1 - 6	Roofs	1.06	1.05	1.07
55 - 4 - 6	Wall Costs	1.03	1.03	1.03
56 - 1, 2	Stained Glass	1.02	1.02	1.02
56 - 6	Store Fronts	1.02	1.02	1.02
56 - 7, 8	Stonework	1.02	1.01	1.02
58 - 1 - 3	Cold Storage	1.02	1.02	1.02
58 - 2 - 6	Elevators	1.02	1.02	1.02
61 - 1 - 6	Tanks	1.03	1.03	1.03

Sec. Page		Eastern	Central	Western
62 - 1	Pipelines	1.02	1.02	1.02
62 - 1	Railroad Spurs	1.02	1.01	1.02
62 - 2	Steel Stacks, Metal Waste Chutes	1.02	1.02	1.02
62 - 2	Masonry & Concrete Chimneys	1.02	1.01	1.02
62 - 3	Incinerators, Compactors	1.02	1.02	1.02
62 - 4	Grain Elevators	1.02	1.02	1.02
62 - 5 - 7	Prefabricated Metal Buildings	1.02	1.02	1.02
62 - 5 - 7	Service Stations	1.02	1.02	1.02
63 - 1 - 4	Trailer and Mfg. Housing Parks	1.02	1.02	1.02
63 - 5 - 7	Manufactured Housing	1.02	1.02	1.02
64 - 1	Industrial Pumps and Boilers	1.01	1.01	1.02
64 - 2	Electric Motors	1.01	1.01	1.02
65 - 1 - 6	Equipment Costs	1.01	1.01	1.01
66 - 1	Subdivision Costs	1.02	1.02	1.08
66 - 2 - 4	Yard Improvements	1.07	1.06	1.07
67 - 1, 2	Recreational Facilities	1.07	1.06	1.08
67 - 3, 4	Recreational Facilities	1.07	1.06	1.08

Courtesy of Marshall and Swift, Los Angeles, California.

OFFICES, PUBLIC BUILDINGS AND SCHOOLS

(SEGREGATED COST METHOD)

Office buildings, public buildings, and schools comprise a wide range of buildings from the small neighborhood office and bungalow classroom to the multistory sky-scrapers and huge courthouses. Within each group, certain segregated costs may have a great variance.

Interior construction in most of these buildings usually can be priced very well on the square foot basis, however, in buildings such as offices with large open areas, it may be advisable to check by the built-up cost method in Section 52.

Plumbing costs are given on the basis of floor area, however, it may be better in many cases to make an actual count of fixtures and to price them from Section 53. Mixed occupancies should be appraised by separating the areas and pricing each occupancy on its individual basis.

Miscellaneous interior additives include special items found in some buildings which are not usually included in the general contract for the building, but are a necessary part of the occupancy.

SEGREGATED COSTS

(For explanation of the rating numbers which head the cost columns, see Section 40.)

EXCAVATION AND SITE PREPARATION	1	2	3	4
Excavation (per cu. ft.)	$ .10	$ .14	$ .20	$ .28
Fill (per cu. ft. of compacted earth)	.12	.15	.18	.22
Site preparation (per sq. ft. of site)	.08	.10	.13	.17

FOUNDATION — Apply to total floor area including basements, but excluding mezzanines.

	1	2	3	4
Class A	$ .94	$1.22	$1.59	$2.06
Class B	.98	1.37	1.64	2.12
Class C bearing wall	.89	1.17	1.53	2.00
Class C non-bearing wall	.82	1.05	1.43	1.88
Class D masonry veneer	.81	1.04	1.35	1.74
Class D siding or stucco	.78	1.00	1.28	1.64
Class S	.76	.99	1.28	1.66

For one story buildings with foundations and footings formed and poured monolithically with floor slabs, use 70% of the above costs, for that floor only.
Add 2% for each foot over 12' average story height.
Deduct 2% for each foot under 12' average story height.
Deduct .8% for each story over one, above ground, for multistory buildings.
Add for pilings from Section 51.

FRAME — Apply to total floor area including basements.

	1	2	3	4
Bearing walls, wood or steel floor supports only	$ .60	$ .69	$ .79	$ .91
Steel, fireproofed, Class A	5.32	6.59	8.16	10.10
Concrete, reinforced, Class B	4.75	5.84	7.19	8.85
Steel, Class C and D	2.24	2.78	3.44	4.26
Steel, Class S	1.84	2.25	2.75	3.36

	1	2	3	4
FRAME — (Continued)				
Wood, mill type construction	$2.09	$2.48	$2.93	$3.48
Wood, post and beam construction	1.62	1.87	2.15	2.48

Add 3% for each foot of average story height over the 12' base height.
Deduct 3% for each foot under the 12' base.

For multistory buildings, add 2% for each story over one, above ground to apply against the total floor area.

FLOOR STRUCTURE — Apply to area of described floor.

	1	2	3	4
Concrete: on ground	$1.50	$1.77	$2.08	$2.45
pan or waffle slab and joists	4.46	4.97	5.55	6.16
elevated flat slab and joists	4.76	5.38	6.07	6.86
precast joists and deck	4.01	4.55	5.16	5.85
cored plank on bearing walls	3.41	3.88	4.42	5.04
Steel joists: flat slab	5.22	6.01	6.92	7.96
corrugated deck and concrete	4.79	5.51	6.33	7.28
cellular deck and concrete	---	6.42	7.48	8.71
precast deck	4.43	5.09	5.85	6.72
wood sheathing	3.43	3.88	4.39	4.96
Wood joists and sheathing	2.92	3.34	3.81	4.36
Wood joists and bridging only	2.41	2.75	3.15	3.60
Add for each inch of sheathing over 1"	.47	.53	.60	.68
Add for vapor barrier	.19	.27	.38	.53
Add for insulation	.26	.33	.42	.54
Add for 1-1/2" - 2" foamed concrete surfacing	.35	.41	.49	.58

Courtesy of Marshall and Swift, Los Angeles, California.

OFFICES, PUBLIC BUILDINGS AND SCHOOLS
(SEGREGATED COST METHOD)

FLOOR COVER — Apply to area of described floor.

	1	2	3	4
Asphalt tile	$.70	$.79	$.89	$1.00
Brick pavers, in concrete	3.75	4.20	4.70	5.25
Carpet and pad	1.30	1.80	2.50	3.50
Computer floor, on stanchions	8.25	9.50	11.00	12.75
Cork	1.60	1.85	2.15	2.50
Diato, magnesite, etc.	2.05	2.40	2.80	3.25
Epoxy, urethane, neoprene, 1/32" - 1/16"	1.45	1.75	2.10	2.50
1/8" - 3/8"	2.10	2.80	3.70	4.90
Add for colored chips or glitter	.60	.75	.95	1.20
Hardener and sealer, concrete	.30	.37	.46	.58
Hardwood	3.00	3.45	4.00	4.60
Linoleum	1.30	1.50	1.75	2.05
Rubber tile or sheet	1.40	1.65	1.95	2.30
Softwood	2.00	2.30	2.60	3.00
Terrazzo (exclusive of base slab)	3.00	3.85	4.99	6.25
Tile, ceramic or quarry	4.00	4.70	5.55	6.50
Wood over concrete:				
Hardwood	3.45	4.00	4.70	5.45
Parquet blocks in mastic	3.00	3.45	3.95	4.50
Vinyl asbestos tile	.82	.90	.98	1.07
Vinyl sheet	1.25	1.60	2.00	2.55
Vinyl tile	1.35	1.65	2.00	2.40
Add 15% for conductive floor coverings.				

CEILING — Apply to area of described ceiling.

	1	2	3	4
Acoustical ceilings:				
Metal panels, including pads and suspension system	$2.90	$3.35	$3.85	$4.45
Mineral fiber, fiberglass	.94	1.09	1.27	1.48
Wood or cane fiber	.80	.88	.96	1.05
Gypsum board, taped and painted	.75	.83	.98	1.02
Paint only, bottom of roof or floor	.23	.32	.42	.56
Plaster on lath:				
Acoustical	1.14	1.30	1.49	1.70
Spray-on, thin-coat w/texture on lath or drywall	.70	.77	.84	.92
Standard, add 10% for Keene's	.98	1.13	1.31	1.52
Add for metal lath	.09	.11	.14	.18
Plaster on masonry soffit:				
Acoustical	1.02	1.17	1.35	1.55
Spray-on, thin-coat w/texture	.60	.66	.72	.79
Standard, add 10% for Keene's	.88	1.01	1.15	1.32
Plastic panels, with suspension system, but excluding lighting, (in electrical cost)	2.65	3.15	3.75	4.50
Plywood or hardboard panels	1.55	1.95	2.40	3.00

CEILING EXTRAS — Add to ceiling costs.

	1	2	3	4
Wood furring	$.37	$.46	$.57	$.70
Metal furring	.54	.66	.81	1.00
If ceiling structure is required which is not part of the roof or floor structure, add	.60	.72	.87	1.05
Suspended ceiling, add	.64	.75	.89	1.05
Ceiling insulation, add	.27	.32	.39	.46

INTERIOR CONSTRUCTION — Apply to total floor area. See Section 52 if detailed costs are desired. Hospital interiors include Group I equipment.

Add or deduct 5% for each foot of variation from 12' average story height.

FRAME INTERIOR PARTITIONS

	1	2	3	4
Banks (excluding vaults) Class A & B	$13.80	$16.25	$19.10	$22.45
Class C, D, & S	12.00	14.20	16.75	19.80
Convalescent hospitals, Class A & B	12.75	14.65	16.83	19.40
Class C, D, & S	9.15	11.00	13.25	15.95
Dispensaries	5.45	6.60	8.00	9.70
Fire stations	7.31	9.43	12.17	15.71
Governmental buildings, Class A & B	11.75	15.15	19.55	25.20
Class C, D, & S	9.80	12.90	16.95	22.30
Hospitals, Class A & B	17.80	20.05	22.55	25.40
Class C, D, & S	13.80	15.65	17.75	20.15
Jails (excluding jail hardware)	6.40	7.25	8.21	9.30
Libraries, Class A & B	9.91	11.70	13.85	16.35
Class C, D, & S	8.05	9.76	11.84	14.36
Medical office buildings, Class A & B	13.00	15.50	18.50	22.10
Class C, D, & S	10.55	12.15	14.05	16.20
Office buildings, Class A & B	9.05	11.63	14.05	19.20
Class C, D, & S	6.81	8.74	11.22	14.40
Veterinary hospitals	6.12	8.07	10.64	14.02
Schools, elementary and secondary:				
entire school	10.40	12.10	14.05	16.34
classrooms	8.26	9.64	11.24	13.12
gyms	5.15	6.16	7.37	8.82
manual arts	6.02	6.98	8.09	9.38
multi-purpose	8.62	10.03	11.66	13.56
Schools, college level:				
entire school	10.93	12.25	13.73	15.38
arts and crafts	8.84	9.82	10.90	12.10
classrooms	11.31	12.68	14.20	15.91
commons	10.08	11.31	12.69	14.24
lecture halls (excluding fixed seating)	8.24	10.16	12.53	15.45
physical education (excluding pools)	5.91	7.32	9.08	11.25
science buildings (excluding equipment)	8.64	10.35	12.40	14.86
Add for fixed seating from Section 65.				

OFFICES, PUBLIC BUILDINGS AND SCHOOLS

(SEGREGATED COST METHOD)

MASONRY INTERIOR PARTITIONS

	1	2	3	4
Banks (excluding vaults) Class A & B	$15.10	$17.70	$20.70	$24.25
Class C, D, & S	13.25	15.55	18.25	21.40
Convalescent hospitals, Class A & B	13.90	15.95	18.30	21.00
Class C, D, & S	9.80	11.55	13.65	16.10
Dispensaries	6.01	7.22	8.68	10.44
Fire stations	8.01	10.27	13.18	16.90
Governmental buildings, Class A & B	12.85	16.50	21.20	27.20
Class C, D, & S	10.80	14.10	18.40	24.00
Hospitals, Class A & B	19.50	21.85	24.50	27.50
Class C, D, & S	15.10	17.05	19.25	21.70
Jails (excluding jail hardware)	7.10	7.99	8.98	10.10
Libraries, Class A & B	10.85	12.75	15.00	17.65
Class C, D, & S	8.80	10.65	12.85	15.55
Medical office buildings, Class A & B	14.25	16.90	20.10	23.85
Class C, D, & S	11.55	13.26	15.24	17.50
Office buildings, Class A & B	9.95	12.70	(16.26)	20.75
Class C, D, & S	7.50	9.56	(12.18)	15.52
Veterinary hospitals	6.72	8.81	11.53	15.14
Schools, elementary and secondary:				
entire school	11.40	13.20	15.25	17.65
classrooms	9.04	10.50	12.20	14.17
gyms	5.65	6.71	7.98	9.48
manual arts	6.62	7.64	8.81	10.16
multi-purpose	9.44	10.93	12.66	14.66
Schools, college level:				
entire school	12.02	13.39	14.91	16.60
arts and crafts	9.74	10.75	11.86	13.08
classrooms	12.45	13.86	15.43	17.18
commons	11.08	12.35	13.78	15.36
lecture halls (excluding fixed seating)	9.05	11.12	13.66	16.79
physical education (excluding pools)	6.50	8.00	9.86	12.15
science buildings (excluding equipment)	9.50	11.31	13.47	16.04

Add for fixed seating from Section 65.

MISCELLANEOUS — Apply to total square feet of building area, if required. These costs vary greatly and the following typical cost ranges should be used with caution. Built-in equipment which is normally included under the general contract is included in the interior construction costs.

	1	2	3	4
Bank equipment (counters, vault doors, etc.)	$ 9.50	$14.15	$21.05	$31.30
Jail equipment (cell blocks, locking devices, etc.)	9.75	12.65	16.40	21.25
Hospital equipment (Groups II and III)	10.50	13.00	16.15	20.00
Hospital pneumatic conveyor system	1.25	1.45	1.74	2.05
College commons kitchen equip.	2.75	3.25	3.90	4.65
Science, fixed laboratory equipment	6.00	7.05	8.30	9.75

BANK VAULTS — Per square foot of vault area. Add or deduct 2% for each foot of height variation from 12' standard.

	1	2	3	4
Money	$63.00	$75.00	$89.00	$106.00
Record storage	20.00	24.00	29.00	35.00

PLUMBING — Apply to total floor area or use Section 53 for cost per fixture. The following costs represent typical ranges only.

	1	2	3	4
Banks	$ 1.80	$ 2.83	$ 4.38	$ 6.68
Convalescent hospitals	3.50	4.78	6.52	8.90
Dispensaries	2.76	3.58	4.65	6.04
Fire stations	2.19	3.52	5.50	8.47
Governmental buildings	1.85	3.05	4.84	7.50
Hospitals	5.01	6.96	9.67	13.43
Jails	4.08	6.06	9.01	13.39
Libraries	1.48	2.28	3.47	5.23
Medical office buildings & clinics	2.56	3.72	5.97	9.03
Office buildings	1.17	(2.04)	3.33	5.26
Veterinary hospitals	2.44	3.55	5.17	7.50
Schools, elementary	1.96	2.86	4.19	6.12
secondary	1.97	2.90	4.26	6.27
Schools, college level:				
entire school	2.01	3.04	4.60	6.97
arts and crafts	1.82	2.65	3.85	5.60
classrooms	2.03	2.98	4.37	6.42
commons	2.23	3.14	4.42	6.22
lecture halls	1.93	2.78	3.99	5.74
physical education	2.38	3.22	4.35	5.89
science buildings	2.57	3.68	5.28	7.56

SPRINKLERS — Apply to sprinklered area. Costs include all piping and connections to main, but do not include tanks.

	1	2	3	4
5,000 square feet	$ 1.29	$ 1.53	$ 1.82	$ 2.16
10,000	1.17	1.39	1.64	1.95
15,000	1.11	1.31	1.55	1.84
20,000	1.06	1.25	1.49	1.76
30,000	1.00	1.18	1.40	1.66
40,000	.97	1.14	1.34	1.59
50,000	.93	1.10	1.30	1.54
75,000	.89	1.06	1.24	1.45
100,000	.85	1.00	1.18	1.39
125,000	.82	.97	1.14	1.35
150,000	.80	.94	1.11	1.31
200,000	.77	.91	1.07	1.26
250,000	.75	.88	1.04	1.22
300,000	.73	.86	1.01	1.19
400,000	.71	.83	.98	1.15

Courtesy of Marshall and Swift, Los Angeles, California.

OFFICES, PUBLIC BUILDINGS AND SCHOOLS

(SEGREGATED COST METHOD)

HEATING, COOLING, AND VENTILATING — Apply to total floor area.

✓ Add or deduct 3% for each foot of variation in average story height from 12' base.

Costs are given for gas-fired heating surfaces. Add or deduct as follows for other fuels.

Coal stoker for hot air	+ 7%	Coal, hand-fired	– 2%
Coal stoker for boiler	+ 7%	Oil-fired	+ 7%

For General Hospitals use costs in Section 15.

	1	2	3	4
Electric cable or baseboard	$ 1.45	$ 1.96	$ 2.65	$ 3.59
Electric wall heaters	.66	.82	1.02	1.27
Forced air	1.51	2.16	3.07	4.37
Furnace, floor or wall	.65	.82	1.03	1.30
Hot water, baseboard or radiators	2.73	3.84	5.39	7.57
Space heaters, with fan	.44	.63	.90	1.29
Steam radiator, with boiler	2.37	3.34	4.71	6.64
without boiler	1.95	2.83	4.10	5.94
Zoned A.C., hot & chilled water	5.78	7.89	10.77	14.70
warm & cooled air	3.28	4.02	7.43	11.17
Package heating & cooling, short ducts	2.68	(3.69)	(5.09)	7.03
Heat pump	3.10	4.48	6.34	9.06
Evaporative coolers	1.18	1.44	1.76	2.15
Refrigerated air conditioning	1.70	2.51	3.71	5.49
Ventilation only, with ducts & blowers	.44	.60	.83	1.14

ELECTRICAL AND LIGHTING — Apply to total floor area. Hospitals are listed by occupancy but are not included in the general tables.

Few Outlets	1	2	3	4
Non-metallic	$ 1.85	$ 2.35	$ 2.98	$ 3.78
Armored cable (BX)	2.22	2.82	3.57	4.53
Flexible conduit	2.65	3.37	4.28	5.43
Rigid conduit	3.18	4.04	5.12	6.50

Average Number of Outlets	1	2	3	4
Non-metallic	$ 2.26	$ 2.95	$ 3.86	$ 5.04
Armored cable (BX)	2.81	3.67	4.79	6.25
Flexible conduit	3.50	4.56	5.94	7.74
Rigid conduit	4.36	5.67	7.38	9.60

Many Outlets	1	2	3	4
Non-metallic	$ 3.02	$ 3.94	$ 5.15	$ 6.72
Armored cable (BX)	3.94	5.11	6.64	8.62
Flexible conduit	5.15	6.64	8.57	11.06
Rigid conduit	6.72	8.62	11.06	14.18

Unfinished Areas	1	2	3	4
Non-metallic	$ .62	$ .75	$ .90	$ 1.08
Armored cable (BX)	.73	.87	1.04	1.24
Flexible conduit	.88	1.05	1.26	1.51
Rigid conduit	1.08	1.29	1.53	1.82

ELECTRICAL AND LIGHTING (continued)

Typical costs for some occupancies.	1	2	3	4
Banks, Class A & B	$ 5.11	$ 7.37	$10.64	$15.36
Class C, D, & S	4.13	6.40	9.91	13.86
Convalescent hospitals	2.99	5.22	7.53	10.78
Dispensaries	2.96	3.85	5.00	6.50
Fire stations	2.72	4.27	6.55	9.60
Governmental buildings, Class A & B	3.89	5.67	8.26	12.03
Class C, D, & S	3.72	5.33	7.64	10.95
Hospitals, Class A & B	6.80	9.47	13.19	18.36
Class C, D, & S	5.16	7.26	10.22	14.38
Jails	4.11	6.11	9.10	13.53
Libraries, Class A & B	4.84	6.48	8.67	11.61
Class C, D, & S	3.04	4.49	6.64	9.82
Medical offices, Class A & B	3.68	5.31	7.66	11.06
Class C, D, & S	2.96	4.43	6.63	9.92
Office buildings, Class A & B	2.70	4.29	6.68	10.26
Class C, D, & S	1.96	3.51	(5.81)	9.25
Schools, elementary	2.70	3.82	5.69	7.62
secondary	2.86	4.03	5.67	7.98
colleges and universities	3.49	5.02	7.20	10.34
Veterinary hospitals	2.54	3.71	5.42	7.91

EXTERIOR WALL — Apply to total wall area.

Concrete or Masonry Walls	1	2	3	4
Block, concrete, 6"	$ 7.74	$ 8.54	$ 9.41	$10.38
8"	8.25	9.13	10.10	11.18
12"	9.28	10.36	11.56	12.90
16"	10.30	11.57	13.00	14.60
Brick, block back-up, 8"	9.04	10.06	11.18	12.44
12"	10.06	11.28	12.65	14.18
16"	11.14	12.54	14.11	15.88
Brick, common, 8"	10.28	11.43	12.70	14.12
12"	11.35	12.77	14.38	16.18
16"	12.41	14.12	16.05	18.26
Brick, grouted or cavity, 9" - 10" reinforced	11.28	12.52	(13.90)	15.44
block back-up, 9" - 10"	10.18	11.32	(12.59)	14.00
block back-up, 12" - 14"	11.26	12.52	13.92	15.48
Brick, 6" SCR modular	7.64	8.51	(9.48)	10.56
*Add for face brick	1.15	1.30	(1.50)	1.70
Concrete, reinforced, poured in place, tilt-up, panels, 4"	6.63	7.69	8.93	10.36
6"	7.53	8.67	9.98	11.49
8"	8.68	9.85	11.18	12.68
12"	10.58	11.70	12.95	14.32

Courtesy of Marshall and Swift, Los Angeles, California.

OFFICES, PUBLIC BUILDINGS AND SCHOOLS
(SEGREGATED COST METHOD)

EXTERIOR WALL (continued)

	1	2	3	4
Local stone veneer, block back-up, 12"	$11.75	$13.40	$15.30	$17.50
For each 4" variation in thickness	.85	.90	1.00	1.05
Stone: ashlar veneer, block back-up, 12"	14.75	16.60	18.65	21.00
For each 4" variation in thickness	.85	.90	1.00	1.05
Tile, structural clay, 6"	7.72	8.68	9.75	10.96
10"	9.18	10.18	11.29	12.52
Add for glazed block or tile, each side	1.05	1.20	1.35	1.55
Add for pilasters	.47	.56	.67	.80
Add for bond beams	.52	.61	.71	.83
Add for insulation	.31	.40	.52	.68

√ **Note** - The additional cost for face brick is the difference between the cost of face brick and common brick in place as part of a wall. For cost of face brick veneer, see Wall Ornamentation.

Curtain Walls

	1	2	3	4
Concrete and glass panels, precast	$12.25	$14.25	$16.50	$19.00
Metal and glass panels (ordinary)	13.50	15.00	18.00	21.50
Stainless steel or bronze and glass	20.00	23.25	26.75	31.00
Stone or marble panels, block back-up	16.00	19.00	22.50	27.00
Steel studs and stucco	7.00	8.00	9.15	10.50
Add for insulation, insulated area only	.39	.49	.61	.76

Pre-Engineered Walls - Class S

	1	2	3	4
Sandwich panels, steel or aluminum, both sides	$ 7.50	$ 8.60	$ 9.85	$11.30
glass exterior, metal interior	8.50	9.80	11.30	13.00
asbestos cement, two sides	6.50	7.50	8.65	10.00
steel exterior, gypsum board interior	7.00	8.05	9.25	10.60

Wood Framed Walls — Class D

	1	2	3	4
Aluminum siding	$ 6.15	$ 6.85	$ 7.62	$ 8.48
Asbestos siding	5.56	6.11	6.72	7.39
Asphalt siding	5.22	5.71	6.25	6.84
Hardboard sheet, embossed	5.81	6.39	7.02	7.72
Hardboard siding, horizontal	6.11	6.82	7.62	8.51
Plywood, textured	5.56	6.26	7.09	8.02
Shingles or shakes, wood	6.02	6.76	7.60	8.54
Stucco	5.92	6.74	7.66	8.72
Wood siding	6.24	7.13	8.15	9.31
Veneer, common brick	7.60	8.65	9.85	11.20
face brick	8.80	10.00	11.40	12.95
stone	10.40	11.85	13.50	15.40
Add for sheathing	.34	.41	.50	.60
Add for insulation	.26	.31	.38	.46

EXTERIOR AND BASEMENT STAIRS — Per Riser.

	1	2	3	4
Concrete	$ 68.	$ 82.	$ 99.	$ 120.
Steel pans or prefab. concrete on steel structure	70.	82.	96.	113.
Steel or aluminum grating	85.	98.	113.	130.
Wood	23.	32.	44.	60.
Fire escapes: see Section 55.				

BASEMENT WALLS — Apply to basement wall area.

	1	2	3	4
Brick masonry	$ 7.15	$ 7.95	$ 8.90	$ 9.90
Concrete block, reinforced, 8"	4.85	5.40	6.00	6.65
12"	5.65	6.25	6.90	7.60
Concrete, reinforced, 8"	5.80	6.45	7.20	8.00
12"	6.80	7.55	8.40	9.35
16"	7.90	8.75	9.75	10.80
Waterproofing	.42	.52	.65	.80

WALL ORNAMENTATION — Apply to ornamented area.

	1	2	3	4
Brick, face, Roman or Norman	$ 3.90	$ 4.55	$ 5.35	$ 6.25
face, standard size	4.55	5.25	6.10	7.05
select common	4.20	4.80	5.55	6.35
used	4.60	5.20	5.90	6.70
Concrete, ornamental cast stone	9.10	10.75	12.70	15.00
Concrete block, imitation flagstone	3.50	4.15	4.90	5.80
solar screen	3.70	4.30	5.00	5.80
split face, fluted, or slumpstone	4.00	4.60	5.25	6.00
glazed one side, add	1.60	1.75	1.90	2.05
Granite, ashlar or panel	17.00	20.25	24.25	29.00
Limestone, ashlar veneer	11.75	14.00	16.75	20.00
Marble, panels	14.50	17.00	19.75	23.00
Metal panels, screens, louvers	9.10	9.00	11.50	14.75
Sandstone, ashlar veneer	11.50	13.35	15.50	18.00
Slate, panels	13.50	15.50	17.50	20.00
Stone veneer, local	8.50	9.75	11.25	13.00
Stucco on masonry	1.10	1.30	1.50	1.75
Terra cotta	10.75	12.50	14.50	17.00
Tile, ceramic	5.25	6.00	6.75	7.75
mosaics	7.75	9.25	11.25	13.50
Vitrolite (structural glass)	9.00	10.25	11.75	13.50
For wood ornamentation, see Section 55.				

OFFICES, PUBLIC BUILDINGS AND SCHOOLS

(SEGREGATED COST METHOD)

ROOF STRUCTURE — Apply to ground floor area.

	1	2	3	4
Concrete joists, slab	$ 4.32	$ 4.91	$ 5.57	$ 6.33
precast joists and deck	3.68	4.14	4.68	5.27
thin shell	6.25	7.65	9.40	11.50
cored plank on bearing walls	3.12	3.50	3.95	4.42
Steel joists, concrete slab	4.82	5.52	6.32	7.23
gypsum on formboard	3.54	3.90	4.29	4.72
precast deck	4.12	4.62	5.19	5.82
steel deck	3.72	4.40	5.20	6.14
steel deck, gypsum or concrete	4.34	5.13	6.07	7.18
wood or composition deck	3.21	3.57	3.97	4.42
Steel space frame and sheathing (three dimensional)	8.00	10.25	(13.25)	17.00
Wood joists, wood or composition deck	2.68	3.03	3.42	3.86

ROOF COVER — Apply to roof area.

	1	2	3	4
Aluminum, corrugated or crimped	$ 1.20	$ 1.45	$ 1.75	$ 2.10
Aluminum shingles	1.80	2.05	2.30	2.60
Asbestos shingles	1.55	1.75	2.00	2.30
Built-up composition	.69	.88	(1.12)	1.43
Composition, roll, mineral surface	.36	.41	.47	.54
Composition shingles, to 235#	.65	.72	.80	.89
over 235#	.80	.94	1.10	1.29
Copper, flatlock	4.40	5.00	5.70	6.50
standing seam	4.30	4.80	5.35	6.00
batten seam	4.60	5.25	6.00	6.85
Elastomeric, Hypalon-Neoprene, Silicone	1.90	2.25	2.70	3.20
Shakes, wood	1.45	1.65	1.85	2.10
wood, fire-resistant	1.65	1.90	2.15	2.45
Shingles, wood	1.30	1.50	1.75	2.00
Slate	2.70	3.20	3.75	4.45
Steel, galvanized	1.25	1.45	1.70	2.00
porcelain enamel shingles	2.75	3.20	3.70	4.30
Terne, flat or standing seam	2.30	2.70	3.20	3.80
batten seam	2.90	3.35	3.90	4.50
Tile, clay	2.40	2.80	3.30	3.85
concrete	1.95	2.20	2.45	2.75
plastic	1.80	2.05	2.30	2.60
Add for roof insulation	.37	.52	.72	1.00

TRUSSES AND GIRDERS — Apply to area supported.

	1	2	3	4
Steel trusses or longspan girders	$ 1.00	$ 1.24	$ 1.53	$ 1.90
Timber trusses	1.10	1.37	1.70	2.12
Glued, laminated trusses or girders	1.07	1.28	1.54	1.84

ELEVATORS — Apply against area served if detailed costs from Section 58 are not used.

	1	2	3	4
Office and medical office buildings				
Class A & B	$ 1.28	$ 1.95	$ 2.97	$ 4.52
Class C, D, & S	.66	.97	1.41	2.06
Governmental buildings, Class A & B	1.70	2.37	3.30	4.58
Class C, D, & S	.49	.73	1.09	1.64
Hospitals (including dumb waiters)	1.51	2.27	3.40	5.11
Schools and libraries	.45	.79	1.40	2.49

NUMBER OF STORIES MULTIPLIER

To allow for the cost of hoisting materials, increased labor costs, and miscellaneous costs due to high rise construction, multiply the total Segregated Cost of above-ground portions of the building by 100% plus .3% for each story over three.

Examples:

Six story building: Multiplier = 1.009
Twenty-three story building: Multiplier = 1.060

COMPLETION OF BUILDING VALUATION

Contractor's overhead and profit, sales taxes, permit fees, and insurance during construction are included in the above costs. Interest on interim construction financing is also included, but not financing costs, real estate taxes, or brokers' commissions.

Architect's fees are not included and should be added from Section 99, Page 2.

Depreciation suggestions are given in Section 97.

Fire insurance exclusion suggestions based on percentages of the total cost are listed in Section 96. The portion to be excluded may be deducted directly from the segregated cost components, or omitted, instead of using a percentage of the total cost, if appropriate.

Current Cost Multipliers and Local Multipliers which bring the basic costs up to date for each locality are found in the Green Supplement, Section 99.

Courtesy of Marshall and Swift, Los Angeles, California.

ARCHITECT'S FEES

EXPLANATION

The tables of architect's fees are based on composite curves derived from many actual fees charged, recommendations of several architectural committees in various states, and architectural time studies. In cases where superior quality and detail are required, the fee may be higher than the average, while very low quality and standardized buildings may call for a fee which is lower.

The fee schedules contain approximately 30% for contract administration and supervision. In many cases, this function may be performed by the contractor, an employee of the owner, or an outside consultant. In any case, this is a proper charge against the building and the total fee should be added to building costs computed from the Unit-in-Place or the Segregated Costs.

PROJECT COST Up To		I	II	III	IV	V	VI
TABLE							
$	50,000	10.7	9.7	8.7	7.9	7.1	6.4
	100,000	10.3	9.3	8.4	7.6	6.9	6.2
	200,000	10.0	9.1	8.2	7.4	6.7	6.1
	500,000	9.5	8.6	7.8	7.1	6.4	5.8
	1,000,000	9.2	8.4	7.6	6.9	6.3	5.7
	2,000,000	8.8	8.0	7.3	6.6	6.0	5.5
	3,000,000	8.7	7.9	7.2	6.5	5.9	5.4
	5,000,000	8.4	7.7	7.0	6.4	5.8	5.3
	10,000,000	8.1	7.4	6.8	6.2	5.7	5.2
	20,000,000	7.8	7.1	6.5	6.0	5.5	5.0
	50,000,000	7.5	6.9	6.3	5.7	5.2	4.8
	and up	7.3	6.7	6.1	5.6	5.1	4.7

EXCLUSION OF ARCHITECT'S FEE

The exclusion of the architect's fee from the replacement cost for insurance purposes is a matter of underwriting and not of valuation. Plans and specifications can sometimes be re-used in case of total loss but this is not common practice and when used, they usually are greatly modified and a second fee may be imposed.

TABLE I

Furnishings and Interiors
Special Lighting

Luxury Residences
Mausoleums and Memorials

TABLE II

Airport Terminals
Cathedrals
Specialized College Buildings
Convention Centers
Governmental Buildings
Hospitals and Mental Institutions

Laboratories
Libraries
Medical Schools
Museums and Galleries
Penal Institutions
Store Fronts

TABLE III

Banks and Financial Institutions
Churches
Communications and Broadcasting
Convalescent Hospitals
Country Clubs and Marinas
Detention Buildings
Fire and Police Stations
Fraternal Buildings
Hotels and City Clubs

Medical Office Buildings
Major Post Office Buildings
Public Health Centers
Resort Lodges
Secondary Schools and Colleges
Specialty Shops
Stadiums and Sports Facilities
Theaters and Auditoriums
Veterinary Hospitals

TABLE IV

Apartments and Dormitories
Bus Stations
Clubhouses and Gymnasiums
Cold Storage Buildings
Convents and Rectories
Department Stores and Shopping Centers
Elementary Schools
Eng. & Research Industrial Buildings
Fraternity and Sorority Houses

Homes for the Elderly
Laundries and Cleaners
Maintenance Hangars
Mortuaries
Motels
Office Buildings
Public Recreation Facilities
Residences, Individual
Restaurants and Clubs

TABLE V

Armories and Bowling Alleys
Automotive Centers and Showrooms
Branch Post Offices
Creameries
Dairies or Milking Barns
Discount Stores
Dispensaries

Distribution Warehouses
Docks and Wharfs
Loft Buildings
Manufacturing Industrial Buildings
Markets and Retail Stores
Multiples and Row Houses
Storage Hangars

TABLE VI

Farm Structures
Garages and Parking Structures
Service Stations

Shipping Docks & Transfer Points
Storage Warehouses
Utility Buildings

Courtesy of Marshall and Swift, Los Angeles, California.

ELEVATORS

SELECTIVE-COLLECTIVE PASSENGER ELEVATORS
(passenger-operated geared electric elevators)

TYPE OF CONTROL	SPEED (Feet per minute)	CAPACITY (Pounds)	COST PER SHAFT			PLUS COST PER STOP
			POWER-OPERATED DOORS		MANUAL DOORS	
			Car and shaft	Shaft only		
A. C. Rheostatic	50	1,200	$18,750	$17,250	$16,000	$2,500
		2,000	22,750	20,500	18,750	2,600
A. C. Rheostatic	100	1,200	24,000	22,275	19,750	2,500
		2,000	27,000	24,650	22,750	2,600
A. C. Rheostatic	150	1,200	26,000	24,000	22,250	2,500
		2,000	29,000	26,500	25,000	2,600
Variable Voltage	150	1,500	39,500	37,000	35,000	2,600
		2,000	43,000	40,400	38,250	2,650
		2,500	47,000	44,300	42,000	2,675
		3,000	51,250	48,500	46,000	2,700
		4,000	61,000	58,000	55,000	2,750
		5,000	72,750	69,500	66,000	2,850
Variable Voltage	200	1,500	40,500	37,600	36,500	2,600
		2,000	44,250	41,250	40,000	2,650
		2,500	48,500	45,400	43,750	2,675
		3,000	52,750	49,500	48,000	2,700
		4,000	63,000	59,600	57,750	2,750
		5,000	75,500	71,850	69,500	2,850
Variable Voltage	250	1,500	44,000	40,700	39,000	2,600
		2,000	47,750	44,300	42,500	2,650
		2,500	51,750	48,200	46,500	2,675
		3,000	56,000	52,300	50,750	2,700
		4,000	66,000	62,100	60,500	2,750
		5,000	77,500	73,350	72,000	2,850
Variable Voltage	300	1,500	46,750	42,900	42,000	2,600
		2,000	50,750	46,750	45,750	2,650
		2,500	55,000	50,900	50,000	2,675
		3,000	60,000	55,800	54,500	2,700
		4,000	70,500	66,100	65,000	2,750
		5,000	83,250	78,600	77,250	2,850
Variable Voltage	350	1,500	52,000	47,500	46,750	2,600
		2,000	56,000	51,400	50,500	2,650
		2,500	60,500	55,800	54,750	2,675
		3,000	65,250	60,500	59,250	2,700
		4,000	76,000	71,000	69,500	2,750
		5,000	88,500	83,250	81,500	2,850

HYDRAULIC ELEVATORS: Use 70% of the cost per shaft of a comparable A.C. rheostatic elevator plus 175% of the cost per stop.

SMALL ELEVATORS: Small office and apartment elevators with simple call system and push button control, four passenger cab, and two or three stops, cost $20,000 to $27,000.

PENTHOUSE ELEVATORS: For elevators operating between upper floors only, add $825 for each building floor to bottom of shaft.

Courtesy of Marshall and Swift, Los Angeles, California.

APPENDIX VII

VALUATION SYMBOLS AND EQUATIONS

Symbols

a	Annual annualizer
app	appreciation, expressed as a percent of initial value or income
ATCF	After-tax cash flow (post-income taxes)
BOP	Beginning of period, converted for EOP by $(1 + i)$ (EOP factor)
BTCF	Before tax cash flow
C	Mortgage coefficient
CF	Cash flow, generally considered the same as BTCF
CR	Compound rate
DCR	Debt coverage ratio
Δ	Change, especially total change in value or income over a specified period
dep	depreciation, expressed as a percent of initial value or income
DS	Debt service, the dollar amount required to repay a mortgage, usually expressed on an annual basis
EGI	Effective gross income, sometimes called collectible rent
EGIM	Effective gross income multiplier
EOP	End of period
F	Reciprocal of capitalization rate
f	Mortgage rate, same as R_M
GI	Gross income, also called potential or forecast gross income

GIM	Gross income multiplier
I	Income
i	Effective interest rate; nominal annual interest rate divided by number of installments per year
I_B	Building income
I_E	Equity income
I_P	Property income
IRR	Internal rate of return
M	Loan-to-value ratio (L/V)
n	Number of compounding periods, sometimes called projection period
NIR	Net income ratio
NOI	Net operating income
NPV	Net present value
OE	Operating expenses
OER	Operating expense ratio
$1/x$	Reciprocal; 1 divided by a quantity
P	Percent of loan amortized for projection period
PW	Present worth, or present value
R_B	Building capitalization rate
R_E	Equity dividend rate
R_L	Land capitalization rate
R_M	Mortgage rate, including principal amortization and effective interest rate; sometimes called annual mortgage constant rate
R_O	Overall capitalization rate
Σ	Sigma, or sum of
V	Value
V_B	Value of building
V_E	Value of equity
V_L	Value of land (site)
V_M	Value of mortgage
V_P	Value of entire property
Y_E	Equity yield rate
Y_0	Property yield rate

Present and Future Functions of One

Present

V^n	Present worth of 1, the reversion factor	$1/S^n$
$a_{\overline{n}\|}$	Present worth of one per period, sometimes called Inwood factor	$\dfrac{1 - V^n}{i}$
$1/a_{\overline{n}\|}$	Installment to amortize	$\dfrac{i}{1 - V^n}$

Future

| S^n | Compound amount of one | $(1 + i)^n$ |
| $S_{\overline{n}\|}$ | Future worth of one per period | $\dfrac{S^n - 1}{i}$ |

$1/S_{\overline{n}|}$ Sinking fund factor, sometimes called amortization rate $\quad \dfrac{i}{S^n - 1}$

MB Mortgage balance, sometimes called balloon

EQUATIONS

$a = 1/S_{\overline{n}|}$ for level income stream and changing value; $a = 1/n$ for straight-line income and value change; $a =$ annual compound rate for exponential change in income and value

$C = Y + (P \times 1/S_{\overline{n}|}) - f$

$CR = \dfrac{\Delta I \times Y}{\Delta I + Y}$

$DCR = NOI/DS$

$\Delta I = \dfrac{R \times D}{R + D}$ with $R =$ interest rate and $D =$ recapture rate

$> =$ greater than

$I = V/R$

$IRR = CF_0 + \dfrac{CF_1}{1 + IRR} + \dfrac{CF_2}{(1 + IRR)^2} + \dfrac{CF_3}{(1 + IRR)^3}$
$$+ \cdots + \dfrac{CF_n}{(1 + IRR)^n} = 0$$

$< =$ less than

$MB = \dfrac{a_{\overline{n}|} \text{ for full loan term}}{a_{\overline{n}|} \text{ for remaining loan term}}$

$NIR = 1 - OE/EGI$

$NPV = CF_0 = \dfrac{CF_1}{1 + i} = \dfrac{CF_2}{(1 + i)^2} + \dfrac{CF_3}{(1 + i)^3} + \cdots + \dfrac{CF_n}{(1 + i)^n}$

$OER = OE/EGI$

$P = \dfrac{R_M - I}{R_{MP} - I}$

with R_M being the mortgage rate for the full loan term; I being the nominal interest rate, and R_{MP} being the mortgage rate for the projection period

$R = I/V$

$R = Y - MC + \text{dep.} \; 1/S_{\overline{n}|}$

$R = Y - MC - \text{app.} \; 1/S_{\overline{n}|}$

$R = Y$, when there is no forecast change in value

$R > Y$, when property expected to depreciate

$R < Y$, when property expected to appreciate

$$R_B = \frac{(I_P) - (V_L \times R_L)}{V_B}$$ a similar procedure is used to compute R_L and R_E

$R_M = 1/S_{\overline{n}|} + i$

$R_O = Y_O - \Delta a$

$R_O = (M)(R_M)(\text{DCR})$

$R_O = 1 - \text{OER/EGIM}$

$V = \text{GI} \times \text{GIM}$

$V = I/R$

$Y_O = R_O + \Delta a$

INDEX